W9-CNF-468

A Literary History of the English People

From the Origins to the End of the Middle Ages

MEDIÆVAL LONDON

From manuscript 16 F.II in the British Museum

A Literary History of
The English People

From the Origins to the
End of the Middle Ages

By

J. J. Jusserand

Third Edition

GORDIAN PRESS
NEW YORK
1969

Originally Published 1926
Reprinted 1969

Library of Congress Catalog Card Number 68-29336

Published by
Gordian Press

PREFACE.

MANY histories have preceded this one ; many others will come after. Such is the charm of the subject, that volunteers will never be lacking to undertake this journey so hard, so delightful too.

As years go on, the journey lengthens : wider grows the field, further advance the seekers, and from the top of unexplored headlands, through morning mists, they descry the outlines of countries till then unknown. They must be followed to realms beyond the grave, to the silent domains of the dead, across barren moors and frozen fens, among chill rushes and briars that never blossom, till those Edens of poetry are reached, the echoes of which, by a gift of the fairies or the muses, still vibrate to the melody of voices long since hushed.

More has been done during the last eighty years to shed light on the origins, than in all the rest of modern times. Deciphering, annotating, printing, have gone on at an extraordinary pace and without interruption ; the empire of letters has thus been enlarged, according to the chances of the explorators' discoveries, by gardens and deserts, cloudy immensities, and boundless forests ; its limits have receded into space : at least so it seems to us. We laugh at the simplicity of honest Robertson, who in 1769 was dismayed at the superabundance of historical documents accessible in his time : the day is not far distant when we shall be laughed at in the same way for our own simplicity.

The field of literary history widens in another manner yet, and that affects us more nearly. The years glide on so rapidly that the traveller who started to explore the lands of former times, absorbed by his task, oblivious of days and months, is surprised on his return at beholding how the domain of the past has increased. To the past belongs Tennyson, the laureate ; to the past belongs Browning, and that ruddy smiling face, manly and kind, which the traveller to realms beyond intended to describe from nature on his coming back among living men, has faded away, and the grey slab of Westminster covers it. A thing of the past, too, the master who first in France showed the way, daring in his researches, straightforward in his judgments, unmindful of consequences, mindful of Truth alone ; whose life was a model no less than his work. The work subsists, but who shall tell what the life has been and what there was beneficent in that patriarchal voice with its clear, soft, and dignified tones ? The life of Taine is a work which his other works have not sufficiently made known.

The task is an immense one ; its charm can scarcely be expressed. No one can understand, who has not been there himself, the delight found in those far-off retreats, sanctuaries beyond the reach of worldly troubles. In the case of English literature the delight is the greater from the fact that those distant realms are not the realms of permanent death ; daylight is perceived in the distance ; the continuity of life is felt. The dead of Westminster have left behind them a posterity, youthful in its turn, and life-giving. The descendants move around us ; under our eyes the inheritors of what has been prepare what shall be. In that lies one of the great attractions of this literature, and of the French one, too. Like the French it has remote origins ; it is ample, beautiful, measureless ; no one will go the round of it ; it is impossible to write a thoroughly complete history thereof. An attempt has been made in this line for French literature ; the work undertaken over two centuries ago by the Benedictines, continued by the Institute of France, is still in progress ; it consists at this day in thirty-five volumes in quarto, and only the XIVth century has been reached. And with all that immense past and those far-distant origins, those two literatures have a splendid present betokening a splendid future. Both are alive to-day and vigorous. Ready to baffle the predictions of miscreants, they show no sign of decay. They are ever ready for transformations, not for death. Side by side or face to face, in peace or war, both literatures as both peoples have been in touch for centuries, and in spite of hatreds and jealousies they have more than once vivified each other. These actions and reactions began long ago, in Norman times and even before ; when Taillefer sang of Roland, and when Alcuin taught Charlemagne.

The duty of the traveller visiting already visited countries is to not limit himself to general descriptions but to make with particular care the kind of observations for which circumstances have fitted him best. If he has the eye of the painter, he will trace and colour with careful accuracy hues and outlines ; if he has the mind of the scientist, he will study the formation of the ground and classify the flora and fauna. If he has no other advantage but the fact that circumstances have caused him to live in the country, at various times, for a number of years, in contact with the people, in calm days and stormy days, he will perhaps make himself useful, if, while diminishing somewhat in his book the part usually allowed to technicalities and æsthetic problems, he increases the part allotted to the people and to the nation : a difficult task assuredly ; but whatever may be his too legitimate

misgivings, he must attempt it, having no other
chance, when so much has been done already, to be
of any use. The work in such a case will not be,
properly speaking, a " History of English Literature," but rather a " Literary History of the
English People."

Not only will the part allotted to the nation itself
be greater in such a book than habitually happens,
but several manifestations of its genius, generally
passed over in silence, will have to be studied. The
ages during which the national thought expressed
itself in languages other than the national one, will
not be allowed to remain blank, as though, for complete periods, the inhabitants of the island had
ceased to think at all. The growing into shape of
the people's genius will have to be studied with
particular attention. The Chapter House of Westminster will be entered, and there shall be seen how
the nation, such as it was then represented, became
conscious, even under the Plantagenets, of its existence, rights, and power. Philosophers and reformers must be questioned concerning the theories
which they spread : and not without some purely
literary advantage. Bacon, Hobbes, and Locke
are the ancestors of many poets who have never
read their works, but who have breathed an air
impregnated with their thought. Dreamers will
be followed, singers, tale-tellers, and preachers,
wherever it pleases them to lead us : to the
Walhalla of the north, to the green dales of Erin, to

the Saxon church of Bradford-on-Avon, to Blackheath, to the " Tabard " and the " Mermaid,"
to the " Globe," to " Will's " coffee house, among
ruined fortresses, to cloud-reaching steeples, or
along the furrow sown to good intent by Piers the
honest Plowman.

The work, the first part of which is included in
the present volume, will be divided into various
instalments ; but as " surface as small as possible
must be offered to the shafts of Fortune," each
instalment will make a complete whole in itself,
the first telling the literary story of the English
up to the Renaissance, the rest as fate will allow.

No attempt has been made to say everything,
Benedictine fashion.   Many notes will, however,
allow the curious to go themselves to the sources,
to verify, to see with their own eyes and, if they
find cause (*absit omen !*), to disagree.

The need for a new edition has allowed the
author to make some changes and emendations
necessitated by the passing of time, by new discoveries, and by the placing of better texts at the
disposal of an ever-growing multitude of truth-
loving, beauty-loving students.

PARIS, *July* 26, 1925.

TABLE OF CONTENTS.

xi

CHAPTER III.

THE NATIONAL POETRY OF THE ANGLO-SAXONS.

CHAPTER IV.

CHRISTIAN LITERATURE AND PROSE LITERATURE OF THE ANGLO-SAXONS.

BOOK II.

THE FRENCH INVASION.

CHAPTER I.

BATTLE.

CHAPTER II.

LITERATURE IN THE FRENCH LANGUAGE UNDER THE NORMAN AND ANGEVIN KINGS.

BOOK III.

ENGLAND TO THE ENGLISH.

CHAPTER I.

THE NEW NATION.

CHAPTER II.

CHAUCER.

CHAPTER III.

THE GROUP OF POETS.

CHAPTER IV.

WILLIAM LANGLAND AND HIS VISIONS.

CHAPTER V.

PROSE IN THE FOURTEENTH CENTURY.

CHAPTER VI.

THE THEATRE.

CHAPTER VII.

THE END OF THE MIDDLE AGES.

BOOK I.

THE ORIGINS.

CHAPTER I.

BRITANNIA.

I.

THE people that now occupies England was formed, like the French people, by the fusion of several superimposed races. In both countries the same chief races mingled at about the same period, but in different proportions and under dissimilar social conditions. Hence the striking resemblances and sharply defined contrasts that exist in the genius of the two nations, and the contradictory sentiments which mutually animated them from century to century, those combinations and recurrences of esteem that rose to admiration, and jealousy that swelled to hate. Hence, again, the unparalleled degree of interest they offer, one for the other. The two people are so dissimilar that in borrowing reciprocally they run no risk of losing their national characteristics and becoming another's image ; and yet, so much alike are they, it is impossible that what they borrowed should remain barren and unproductive. These loans act like leaven : the products of English thought during the Augustan age of British literature were mixed with French leaven, and the products of French thought during the romantic period of the nineteenth century were penetrated with English yeast.

Ancient writers have left us little information concerning the remotest times and the oldest inhabitants of the

British archipelago ; works which would be invaluable to us exist only in meagre fragments. Important gaps have fortunately been filled, owing to modern Science and to her manifold researches. She has inherited the wand of the departed wizards, and has touched with her talisman the gate of sepulchres ; the tombs have opened and the dead have spoken. What countries did thy war-ship visit ? she inquired of the Scandinavian viking. And in answer the dead man, asleep for centuries among the rocks of the Isle of Skye, showed golden coins of the caliphs in his skeleton hand. These coins are not a figure of speech ; they are real, and may be seen at the Edinburgh Museum. The wand has touched old undeciphered manuscripts, and broken the charm that kept them dumb. From them rose songs, music, love-ditties, and war-cries : phrases so full of life that the living hearts of to-day have been stirred ; words with so much colour in them that the landscape familiar to the eyes of Celts and Germans has risen before us such as it was two thousand years ago.

Much remains undiscovered, and the dead hold secrets they may yet reveal. In the unexplored tombs of the Nile valley will be found one day, among the papyri stripped from Ptolemaic mummies, the account of a journey made to the British Isles about 330 B.C., by a Greek of Marseilles named Pytheas, a contemporary of Aristotle and Alexander the Great, of which a few sentences only have been preserved.[1] But even now the darkness which enveloped the origin has been partly cleared away.

To the primitive population, the least known of all, that reared the stones of Carnac in France, and in England the gigantic circles of Stonehenge and Avebury, succeeded in

---

[1] On Pytheas, see *e.g.* Elton, "Origins of English History," London, 1890, 8vo (2nd ed.), pp. 12 and following. He visited the coasts of Spain, Gaul, Britain, and returned by the Shetlands. The passages of his journal preserved for us by the ancients are given on pp. 400 and 401.

both countries, many centuries before Christ, the Celtic race.

The Celts (κελταί) were thus called by the Greeks from the name of one of their principal tribes, in the same way as the French, English, Scottish, and German nations derive theirs from that of one of their principal tribes. They occupied, in the third century before our era, the greater part of Central Europe, of the France of to-day, of Spain, and of the British Isles. They were neighbours of the Greeks and Latins ; the centre of their possessions was in Bavaria. From there, and not from Gaul, set out the expeditions by which Rome was taken, Delphi plundered, and a Phrygian province rebaptized Galatia. Celtic cemeteries abound throughout that region; the most remarkable of them was discovered, not in France, but at Hallstadt, near Salzburg, in Austria.[1]

The language of the Celts was much nearer the Latin tongue than the Germanic idioms ; it comprised several dialects, and amongst them the Gaulish, long spoken in Gaul, the Gaelic, the Welsh, and the Irish, still used in Scotland, Wales, and Ireland. The most important of the Celtic tribes, settled in the main island beyond the Channel, gave itself the name of Britons. Hence the name of Britain borne by the country, and indirectly that also of Great Britain, now the official appellation of England. The Britons appear to have emigrated from Gaul and established themselves among the other Celtic tribes already settled in the island, about the third century before Christ.

During several hundred years, from the time of Pytheas to that of the Roman conquerors, the Mediterranean world remained ignorant of what took place among insular

[1] See, on this subject, A. Bertrand, " La Gaule avant les Gaulois," Paris, 1891, 8vo (2nd ed.), pp. 7 and 13 ; D'Arbois de Jubainville, " Revue Historique," January–February, 1886 ; by the same, " Les Celtes," Paris, 1904.

Britons, and we are scarcely better informed than they were. The centre of human civilisation had been moved from country to country round the great inland sea, having now reached Rome, without anything being known save that north of Gaul existed a vast country, surrounded by water, rich in tin mines, covered by forests, prairies, and morasses, from which dense mists arose.

Three centuries elapse ; the Romans are settled in Gaul. Cæsar, at the head of his legions, has avenged the city for the insults of the Celtic invaders, but the strife still continues; Vercingetorix has not yet appeared. Actuated by that sense of kinship so deeply rooted in the Celts, the effects of which are still to be seen from one shore of the Atlantic to the other, the Britons had joined forces with their compatriots of the Continent against the Roman. Cæsar resolved to lead his troops to the other side of the Channel, but he knew nothing of the country, and wished first to obtain information. He questioned the traders ; they told him little, being, as they said, acquainted only with the coasts, and that slightly. Cæsar embarked in the night of August 24th–25th, the year 55 before our era ; it took him somewhat more time to cross the strait than is now needed to go from Paris to London. His expedition was a real voyage of discovery ; and he was careful, during his two sojourns in the island, to examine as many people as possible, and note all he could observe concerning the customs of the natives. The picture he draws of the former inhabitants of England strikes us to-day as very strange. " The greater part of the people of the interior," he writes, " do not sow ; they live on milk and flesh, and clothe themselves in skins. All Britons stain themselves dark blue with woad, which gives them a terrible aspect in battle. They wear their hair long, and shave all their body except their hair and moustaches."

Did we forget the original is in Latin, we might think

the passage was extracted from the travels of Captain Cook; and this is so true that, in the account of his first journey around the world, the great navigator, on arriving at the island of Savu, notices himself the similitude.

With the exception of a few details, the Celtic tribes of future England were similar to those of future France.[1] Brave like them, with an undisciplined impetuosity that often brought them to grief (the impetuosity of Poictiers and Nicopolis), curious, quick-tempered, prompt to quarrel, they fought after the same fashion as the Gauls, with the same arms; and in the Witham and Thames have been found bronze shields similar in shape and carving to those graven on the triumphal arch at Orange, the image of which has now recalled for eighteen centuries Roman triumph and Celtic defeat. Horace's saying concerning the Gaulish ancestors applies equally well to Britons: never "feared they funerals."[2] The grave was for them without terrors; their faith in the immortality of the soul absolute; death for them was not the goal, but the link between two existences; the new life was as complete and desirable as the old, and bore no likeness to that subterranean survival, believed in by the ancients, partly localised in the sepulchre, with nothing sweeter in it than those sad things, rest and oblivion. According to Celtic belief, the dead lived again under the light of heaven; they did not descend, as they did with the Latins, to the land of shades. No Briton, Gaul, or Irish could have under-

---

[1] "Proximi Gallis, et similes sunt . . . Sermo haud multum diversus : in deposcendis periculis eadem audacia . . . plus tamen ferociæ Britanni præferunt, ut quos nondum longa pax emollierit . . . manent quales Galli fuerunt." Tacitus, "Agricola," xi. "Ædificia fere Gallicis consimilia," Cæsar "De Bello Gallico," v. The south was occupied by Gauls who had come from the Continent at a recent period. The Iceni were a Gallic tribe ; the Trinobantes were Gallo-Belgæ.

[2] " Te non paventis funera Galliæ
Duraque tellus audit Hiberiæ."
("Ad Augustum," Odes, iv. 14.)

stood the melancholy words of Achilles: "Seek not, glorious
Ulysses, to comfort me for death ; rather would I till the
ground for wages on some poor man's small estate than reign
over all the dead." [1]   The race was an optimistic one.   It
made the best of life, and even of death.

These beliefs were carefully fostered by the druids,
priests and philosophers, whose part has been the same in
Gaul, Ireland, and Britain.   Their teaching was a cause of
surprise and admiration to the Latins.   "And you, druids,"
exclaims Lucan, "dwelling afar under the broad trees of
the sacred groves, according to you, the departed visit not
the silent Erebus, nor the dark realm of pallid Pluto ; the
same spirit animates a body in a different world.   Death,
if what you say is true, is but the middle of a long life.
Happy the error of those that live under Arcturus ; the
worst of fears is to them unknown—the fear of death !" [2]

The inhabitants of Britain possessed, again in common
with those of Gaul, a singular aptitude to understand
and learn quickly.   A short time after the Roman Conquest it becomes hard to distinguish Celtic from Roman
workmanship among the objects discovered in tombs.
Cæsar is astonished to see how his adversaries improve
under his eyes.   They were simple enough at first ;
now they understand and foresee, and baffle his military
stratagems.   To this intelligence and curiosity is due, with
all its advantages and drawbacks, the faculty of assimila-

----

[1] "Odyssey," xi. ll. 488 ff.

[2] "Et vos . . . Druidæ . . .

    . . . nemora alta remotis
    Incolitis lucis, vobis auctoribus, umbræ
    Non tacitas Erebi sedes, Ditisque profundi
    Pallida regna petunt ; regit idem spiritus artus
    Orbe alio : longæ (canitis si cognita) vitæ
    Mors media est.   Certe populi quos despicit Arctos,
    Felices errore suo, quos ille timorum
    Maximus, haud urget leti metus."

                    ("Pharsalia," book i.)

tion possessed by this race, and manifested to the same extent by no other in Europe.

The Latin authors also admired another characteristic gift in the men of this race: a readiness of speech, an eloquence, a promptness of repartee that distinguished them from their Germanic neighbours. The people of Gaul, said Cato, have two passions: to fight well and talk cleverly (*argute loqui*).[1] This is memorable evidence, since it reveals to us a quality of a literary order : we can easily verify its truth, for we know now in what kind of compositions, and with what talent the men of Celtic blood exercised their gift of speech.

II.

That the Celtic tribes on both sides of the Channel closely resembled each other in manners, tastes, language, and turn of mind cannot be doubted. " Their language differs little," says Tacitus ; "their buildings are almost similar,"[2] says Cæsar. The similitude of their literary genius is equally certain, for Cato's saying relates to continental Celts and can be checked by means of Irish poems and tales. Welsh stories of a later date afford us evidence fully as conclusive. If we change the epoch, the result will be the same ; the main elements of the Celtic genius have under-

---

[1] " Pleraque Gallia duas res industriosissime persequitur, rem militarem et argute loqui." " Origins," quoted by the grammarian Charisius. In Cato's time (third–second centuries B.C.) the word Gallia had not the restricted sense it had after Cæsar, but designed the whole of the Celtic countries of the Continent. The ingenuity of the Celts manifested itself also in their laws: " From an intellectual point of view, the laws of the Welsh are their greatest title to glory. The eminent German jurist, F. Walter, points out that, in this respect, the Welsh are far in advance of the other nations of the Middle Ages. They give proof of a singular precision and subtlety of mind, and a great aptitude for philosophic speculation." " Les Mabinogion," by J. Loth, Paris, 1889, 2 vols. 8vo, vol. i. p. 7, 2nd ed. 1913.

[2] See *supra*, p. 7, note 1.

gone no modification ; Armoricans, Britons, Welsh, Irish, and Scotch, are all inexhaustible tale-tellers, skilful in dialogue, prompt at repartee, and never to be taken unawares. Gerald de Barry, the Welshman, gives us a description of his countrymen in the twelfth century, which seems a paraphrase of what Cato had said of the Gaulish Celts fourteen hundred years before.[1]

Ireland has preserved for us the most ancient monuments of Celtic thought. Nothing has reached us of those "quantities of verses" that, according to Cæsar, the druids taught their pupils in Gaul, with the command that they should never be written.[2] Only too well was the injunction obeyed. Nothing, again, has been transmitted to us of the improvisations of the Gallic or British bards (βάρδοι), whose fame was known to, and mentioned by, the ancients. In Ireland, however, Celtic literature had a longer period of development. The country was not affected by the Roman Conquest ; the barbarian invasions did not bring about the total ruin they caused in England and on the Continent. The clerks of Ireland in the seventh and eighth centuries committed to writing the ancient epic tales of their land. Notwithstanding the advent of Christianity, the pagan origins constantly reappear in these narratives, and we are thus taken back to the epoch when

---

[1] "De curia vero et familia viri, ut et circumstantibus risum moveant sibique loquendo laudem comparent, facetiam in sermone plurimam observant ; dum vel sales, vel lædoria, nunc levi nunc mordaci, sub æquivocationis vel amphibolæ nebula, relatione diversa, transpositione verborum et trajectione, subtiles et dicaces emittunt." And he cites examples of their witticisms. "Descriptio Kambriæ," chap. xiv., De verborum facetia et urbanitate. "Opera," Brewer, 1861–91, 8 vols., vol. vi., Rolls.

[2] He says, in reference to the pupils of the Druids, "De Bello Gallico," book vi. : "Magnum ibi numerum versuum ediscere dicuntur, itaque nonnulli annos vicenos in disciplina permanent ; neque fas esse existimant ea litteris mandare." One of the reasons of this interdiction was to guard against the scholars ceasing to cultivate their memory, a faculty considered by the Celts as of the highest importance.

they were primarily composed, and even to the time when the events related are supposed to have occurred. That time is precisely the epoch of Cæsar and of the Christian era. Important works have, in our day, thrown a light on this literature [1]; but all is not yet accomplished, and it has been computed that the entire publication of the ancient Irish manuscripts would fill about a thousand octavo volumes. It cannot be said that the people who produced these works were men of scanty speech; and here again we recognise the immoderate love of tales and the curiosity that Cæsar had noticed in the Celts of the Continent.[2]

Most of those Irish stories are part of the epic cycle of Conchobar and Cuchulaïnn, and concern the wars of Ulster and Connaught. They are in prose, interspersed with verse. Long before being written, they existed in the shape of well-established texts, repeated word for word by men whose avocation it was to know and remember, and who spent their lives in exercising their memory. The corporation of the *File*, or seers, was divided into ten classes, from the *Oblar*, who knew only seven stories, to the *Ollam*, who knew three hundred and fifty.[3] Unlike the bards, the File never invented, they remembered; they were obliged to know, not any stories whatsoever, but certain particular tales; lists of them have been found, and not a few of the stories entered in these catalogues have come down to us.

[1] Those *e.g.* of Whitley Stokes, Rhys, J. G. Evans, d'Arbois de Jubainville, J. Loth, Dottin, Windisch, Zimmer, Kuno-Meyer, Thurneysen; *c.f.* "Rev. Celtique," "Bibliography of Irish Philology," Dublin, Stationery Office, 1913.

[2] "Est autem hoc Galliæ consuetudinis; ut et viatores etiam invitos consistere cogant: et quod quisque eorum de quaque re audierit aut cognoverit quærant, et mercatores in oppidis vulgus circumsistat: quibus ex regionibus veniant, quasque res ibi cognoverint pronunciare cogant." Book iv.

[3] To wit, 250 long and 100 short ones. D'Arbois de Jubainville, "Introduction à l'étude de la Littérature Celtique," 1883, pp. 322-333; being vol. 1 of the "Cours de Littérature Celtique." Cf. Dottin, "Les Littératures Celtiques," 1924.

If we look through the collections that have been made of
them, we can see that the Celtic authors of that period are
already remarkable for qualities that have since shone with
extreme brilliancy among various nations belonging to the
same race: the sense of form and beauty, the dramatic
gift, the fertility of invention.[1] This is all the more noticeable as the epoch was a barbarous one, and a multitude
of passages recall the wild savageness of the people. We
find in these legends as many scenes of slaughter and
ferocious deeds as in the oldest Germanic poems: *Pro-
vincia ferox*, said Tacitus of Britain. The time is still
distant when woman shall become a deity; the murder of
a man is compensated by twenty-one head of cattle, and
the murder of a woman by three head only.[2] The warlike
valour of the heroes is carried as far as human nature
and imagination allow; not even Roland or Ragnar Lodbrok die more heroically than Cuchulaïnn, who, mortally
wounded, dies standing:

" He fixed his eye on this hostile group. Then he leaned
himself against the high stone in the plain, and, by means

---

[1] See, with reference to this, the "Navigation of Mael-Duin," a christianised
narrative, probably composed in the tenth century, under the form in which
we now possess it, but " the theme of which is fundamentally pagan." Here
are the titles of some of the chapters: "The isle of enormous ants.—The
island of large birds.—The monstrous horse.—The demon's race.—The house
of the salmon.—The marvellous fruits.—Wonderful feats of the beast of the
island.—The horse-fights.—The fire beasts and the golden apples.—The castle
guarded by the cat.—The frightful mill.—The island of black weepers."
Translation by Lot in " L'Épopée Celtique," of D'Arbois de Jubainville,
Paris, 1892, 8vo, pp. 449 ff. See also Joyce, " Old Celtic Romances,"
1879 ; on the excellence of the memory of Irish narrators, even at the present
day, see Joyce's Introduction.

[2] D'Arbois de Jubainville, " L'Épopée Celtique," pp. xxviii and following.
"Celtic marriage is a sale. . . . Physical paternity has not the same importance as with us " ; people are not averse to having children from their
passing guest. " The question as to whether one is physically their father offers
a certain sentimental interest ; but for a practical man this question presents
only a secondary interest, or even none at all." *Ibid.*, pp. xxvii–xxix.

of his belt, he fastened his body to the high stone. Neither sitting nor lying would he die ; but he would die standing. Then his enemies gathered round him. They remained about him, not daring to approach ; he seemed to be still alive." [1]

At the same time, things of beauty have their place in these tales. There are birds and flowers; women are described with loving admiration ; their cheeks are purple " as the fox-glove," their locks wave in the light.

Above all, such a dramatic gift is displayed as to stand unparalleled in any European literature at its dawn.[2] Celtic poets excel in the art of giving a lifelike representation of deeds and events, of graduating their effects, and making their characters talk ; they are matchless for speeches and quick repartees. Compositions have come down to us that are all cut out into dialogues, so that the narrative becomes a drama. In such tales as the " Murder of the Sons of Usnech," or " Cuchulaïnn's Sickness," in which love finds a place, these remarkable traits are to be seen at their best. The story of " Mac Datho's Pig " is as powerfully dramatic and savage as the most cruel Germanic or Scandinavian songs ; but it is at the same time infinitely more varied in tone and artistic in shape. Pictures of everyday life, familiar fireside discussions abound, together with the scenes of blood loved by all nations in the season of their early manhood.

" There was," we read, "a famous king of Leinster, called Mac Datho. This king owned a dog, Ailbe by name, who defended the whole province and filled Erin with his fame." [3] Ailill, king of Connaught, and Conchobar, king

---

[1] The Murder of Cuchulaïnn, " L'Épopée Celtique en Irlande," p. 346.

[2] The same quality is found in the literature of Brittany ; the major part of its monuments (of a more recent epoch) consists of religious dramas cr mysteries. These dramas, mostly unpublished, are exceedingly numerous.

[3] " L'Épopée Celtique," pp. 66 and following.

of Ulster, claim the dog; and Mac Datho, much per-
plexed, consults his wife, who suggests that he should promise Ailbe to both. On the appointed day, the warriors
of the two countries come to fetch the dog of renown, and
a grand banquet is served them by Mac Datho, the principal dish of which is a rare kind of pig—"three hundred
cows had fed him for seven years." Scarcely are the guests
seated, when the dialogues begin :

"That pig looks good," says Conchobar.

"Truly, yes," replies Ailill ; "but, Conchobar, how shall
he be carved ? "

"What more simple in this hall, where sit the glorious
heroes of Erin ?" cried, from his couch, Bricriu, son of
Carbad. "To each his share, according to his fights
and deeds. But ere the shares are distributed, more
than one rap on the nose will have been given and
received."

"So be it," said Ailill.

"'Tis fair," said Conchobar. "We have with us the
warriors who defended our frontiers."

Then each one rises in turn and claims the honour
of carving: I did this.—I did still more.—I slew thy
father.—I slew thy eldest son.—I gave thee that wound
that still aches.

The warrior Cet had just told his awful exploits when
Conall of Ulster rises against him and says:

"Since the day I first bore a spear, not often have I
lacked the head of a man of Connaught to pillow mine
upon. Not a single day or night has passed in which I
slew not an enemy."

"I confess it," said Cet, "thou art a greater warrior
than I ; but were Anluan in this castle, he at least could
compete with thee ; 'tis a pity he is not present."

"He is here !" cried Conall, and drawing from his belt
Anluan's head, he flung it on the table.

In the " Murder of the Sons of Usnech,"[1] woman plays the principal part. The mainspring of the story is love, and by it the heroes are led to death, a thing not to be found elsewhere in the European literature of the period. Still, those same heroes are not slight, fragile dreamers ; if we set aside their love, and only consider their ferocity, they are worthy of the Walhalla of Woden. By the following example we may see how the insular Celts could love and die.

The child of Fedelmid's wife utters a cry in its mother's womb. They question Cathba the chief druid, who answers : " That which has clamoured within thee is a fair-haired daughter, with fair locks, a majestic glance, blue eyes, and cheeks purple as the fox-glove " ; and he foretells the woes she will cause among men. This girl is Derdriu ; she is brought up secretly and apart, in order to evade the prediction. One day, " she beheld a raven drink blood on the snow." She said to Leborcham :

" The only man I could love would be one who united those three colours : hair as black as the raven, cheeks red as blood, body as white as snow."

" Thou art lucky," answered Leborcham, "the man thou desirest is not far to seek, he is near thee, in this very castle ; it is Noïsé, son of Usnech."

" I shall not be happy," returned Derdriu, " until I have seen him."

Noïsé justifies the young girl's expectations ; he and his two brothers are incomparably valiant in war, and so swift are they that they outrun wild animals in the chase. Their songs are delightfully sweet. Noïsé is aware of the druid's prophecy, and at first spurns Derdriu, but she conquers him by force. They love each other. Pursued by their enemies the three brothers and Derdriu emigrate to Scotland, and take refuge with the king of Albion. One day

" L'Epopée Celtique en Irlande," pp. 217 and following.

the king's steward " sees Noïsé and his wife sleeping side
by side. He went at once and awoke the king.

"'Till now,' he said, 'never had we found a woman
worthy of thee ; but the one who lies in the arms of Noïsé
is the one for thee, king of the West ! Cause Noïsé to be
put to death, and marry his wife.'

"'No,' answered the king ; 'but bid her come to me
daily in secret.'

" The steward obeyed the king's commands, but in vain ;
what he told Derdriu by day she repeated to her husband
the following night."

The sons of Usnech perish in an ambush. Conchobar
seizes on Derdriu, but she continues to love the dead.
" Derdriu passed a year with Conchobar ; during that time
never was a smile seen on her lips ; she ate not, slept not,
raised not her head from off her knees. When the musicians and jugglers tried to cheer her grief by their play,
she told . . ." she told her sorrow, and all that had made
the delight of her life " in a time that was no more."

" I sleep not, I dye no more my nails with purple ; lifeless is my soul, for the sons of Usnech will return no more.
I sleep not half the night on my couch. My spirit travels
around the multitudes. But I eat not, neither do I
smile."

Conchobar out of revenge delivers her over for a year
to the man she most hates, the murderer of Noïsé, who
bears her off on a chariot ; and Conchobar, watching this
revolting sight, mocks her misery. She remains silent.
" There in front of her rose a huge rock, she threw herself
against it, her head struck and was shattered, and so she
died."

An inexhaustible fertility of invention was displayed by
the Celtic makers. They created the cycle of Conchobar,
and afterwards that of Ossian, to which Macpherson's
" adaptations " gave such world-wide renown that in the last

century they directed Lamartine's early steps towards the
realms of poetry. Later still they created the cycle of
Arthur, most brilliant and varied of all, a perennial source
of poetry, from whence the great French poet of the twelfth
century sought his inspiration, and whence the famous
laureate of Victorian days found his. They collect in
Wales the marvellous tales of the "Mabinogion"[1]; in
them we find enchanters and fairies, women with golden
hair, silken raiment, and tender hearts. They hunt, and a
white boar starts out of the bushes; following him they
arrive at a castle there, "where never had they seen trace
of a building before." Pryderi ventures to penetrate into
the precincts : "He entered and perceived neither man, nor
beast ; no boar, no dogs, no house, no place of habitation.
On the ground towards the middle there was a fountain
surrounded by marble, and on the rim of the fountain, rest-
ing on a marble slab, was a golden cup, fastened by golden
chains tending upwards, the ends of which he could not
see. He was enraptured by the glitter of the gold, and the
workmanship of the cup. He drew near and grasped it.
At the same instant his hands clove to the cup, and his
feet to the marble slab on which it rested. He lost his
voice, and was unable to utter a word." The castle fades
away ; the land becomes a desert once more ; the heroes
are changed into mice ; the whole looks like a fragment
drawn out of Ariosto, by Perrault, and told by him in his
own way to children.

No wonder if the descendants of these indefatigable
inventors are men with rich literatures, not meagre literatures of which it is possible to write a history without

[1] From "Mabinog" apprentice-bard, ed. Rhys and Gwenogvryn, 1887,
prose narratives, of divers origin, in Welsh. They "appear to have been
composed at the end of the XIIth century"; the MS. we possess is of the
XIVth ; some pagan elements carry us back "to the most distant past of the
history of the Celts." "Les Mabinogion," trans. by J. Loth, Paris, 2nd
ed. 1913. English transl. by Lady Charlotte Guest, ed. Nutt 1902.

omitting anything, but deep and inexhaustible ones. The ends of their golden chains are not to be seen. And if a copious mixture of Celtic blood flows, though in different proportions, in the veins of the French and of the English, it will be no wonder if they happen some day to produce the greater number of the plays that are acted, and of the novels that are read, all over the civilised world.

III.

After a second journey, during which he passed the Thames, Cæsar departed with hostages, this time never to return. The real conquest took place under the emperors, beginning from the reign of Claudius, and for three centuries and a half Britain was occupied and ruled by the Romans. They built a network of roads, of which the remains still subsist; they marked the distances by milestones, sixty of which have been found, and one, at Chesterholm, is still standing; they raised, from one sea to the other, against the people of Scotland, two great walls; one of them in stone, flanked by towers, and protected by moats and earth-works.[1] Fortified after the Roman fashion, defended by garrisons, the groups of British huts became cities; and villas, similar to those the remains of which are met with under the ashes of Pompeii and in the sands of Africa, rose in York, Bath, London, Lincoln, Cirencester, Aldborough, Woodchester, Bignor, Chedworth, and other places where they have since been found. Beneath the shade of the druidical oaks, the Roman glazier blew his light variegated flasks; the mosaic maker seated

---

[1] In several places have been found the quarries from which the stone of Hadrian's wall was taken, and inscriptions bearing the name of the legion or of the officer charged with extracting it: " Petra Flavi[i] Carantini," in the quarry of Fallowfield. " The Roman Wall," by the Rev. J. C. Bruce, 1867, 4to (3rd ed.), pp. 141, 144, 185. *Cf. e.g.* F. Sagot, " La Bretagne Romaine," 1911 ; Haverfield, " The Roman occupation of Britain," ed. G. Macdonald, 1924.

Orpheus on his panther, with his fingers on the Thracian lyre. Altars were built to the Roman deities ; later to the God of Bethlehem, and one at least of the churches of that period still subsists, St. Martin of Canterbury.[1] Statues were raised for the emperors ; coins were cast ; weights were cut ; ore was extracted from the mines ; the potter moulded his clay vases, and, pending the time when they should be exhibited behind the glass panes of the British Museum, the legionaries used them to hold the ashes of their dead.

However far he went, the Roman carried Rome with him ; he required his statues, his tessellated pavements, his frescoes, his baths, all the comforts and delights of the Latin cities. Theatres, temples, towers, palaces rose in many of the towns of Great Britain, and some years ago a bathing room was discovered at Bath[2] a hundred and eleven feet long. Several centuries later Gerald de Barry passing through Caerleon noticed with admiration " many remains of former grandeur, immense palaces . . . a gigantic tower, magnificent baths, and ruined temples."[3] The emperors could well come to Britain ; they found themselves at home. Claudius, Vespasian, Titus, Hadrian, Antoninus Pius came there, either to win the title of " the Britannic " or to enjoy the charms of peace. Severus died at York in 211, and Caracalla there began his reign. Constantius Chlorus came to live in that town, and died

---

[1] C. F. Routledge, " History of St. Martin's Church, Canterbury." The ruins of a tiny Christian basilica, of the time of the Romans, were discovered at Silchester, in May, 1892.

[2] Quantities of statuettes, pottery, glass cups and vases, arms, utensils of all kinds, sandals, styles for writing, fragments of colossal statues, mosaics, &c., have been found in England, and are preserved in the British Museum and in the Guildhall of London, in the museums of Oxford and of York, in the cloisters at Lincoln, &c. The great room at Bath was discovered in 1880 ; the piscina is in a perfect state of preservation, part of the leaden pipes being still *in situ.*

[3] "Itinerarium Cambriæ," b. i. chap. v.

there; and the prince destined to sanction the Romans' change of religion, Constantine the Great, was proclaimed emperor in the same city. Celtic Britain, the England that was to be, had become Roman and Christian, a country of land tillers who more or less spoke Latin.[1]

But the time of transformation was drawing nigh, and an enemy was already visible, against whom neither Hadrian's wall nor Antoninus' ramparts could prevail; for he came not from the Scottish mountains, but, as he himself said in his war-songs, "by the way of the whales." A new race of men had appeared on the shores of the island. After relating the campaigns of his father-in-law, Agricola, whose fleet had sailed around Britain and touched at the Orkneys, the attention of Tacitus had been drawn to Germany, a wild mysterious land. He had described it to his countrymen; he had enumerated its principal tribes, and among many others he had mentioned one which he calls *Angli*. He gives the name, and says no more, little suspecting the part these men were to play in history. The first act that was to make them famous throughout the world was to overthrow the political order, and to sweep away the civilisation, which the conquests of Agricola had established amongst the Britons.

---

[1] "Ut qui modo linguam abnuebant, eloquentiam concupiscerent: inde etiam habitus nostri honor, et frequens toga; paullatimque discessum ad delenimenta vitiorum, porticus et balnea, et conviviorum elegantiam." Tacitus, "Agricolæ Vita," xxi.

CHAPTER II.

THE GERMANIC INVASION.

"To say nothing of the perils of a stormy and unknown sea, who would leave Asia, Africa, or Italy for the dismal land of the Germans, their bitter sky, their soil the culture and aspect of which sadden the eye, unless it be one's mother country?" Such is the picture Tacitus draws of Germany, and he concludes from the fact of her being so dismal, and yet inhabited, that she must always have been inhabited by the same people. What others would have immigrated there of their own free will? For the natives, however, this land of clouds and morasses is their home; they love it, and they remain there.

The great historian's book shows how little of impenetrable Germany was known to the Romans. All sorts of legends were current respecting this wild land, supposed to be bounded on the north-east by a slumbering sea, "the girdle and limit of the world," a place so near to the spot where Phœbus rises "that the sound he makes in emerging from the waters can be heard, and the forms of his steeds are visible." This is the popular belief, adds Tacitus; "the truth is that nature ends there." [1]

In this mysterious land, between the forests that sheltered them from the Romans and the grey sea washing with long waves the flat shores, tribes had settled and multiplied

[1] "De Moribus Germanorum," b. ii. chap. xlv.

which, contrary to the surmise of Tacitus, had probably
left the mild climate of Asia for this barren country ; and,
though they had at last made it their home, many of them
whose names alone figure in the Roman's book had not
adopted it for ever ; their migrations were about to begin
again.

This group of Teutonic peoples, with ramifications extending far towards the pole, was divided into two principal
branches: the Germanic branch, properly so called, which
comprised the Goths, Angles, Saxons, the upper and lower
Germans, the Dutch, the Frisians, the Lombards, the
Franks, the Vandals, &c. ; and the Scandinavian branch,
settled farther north and composed of the Danes, Nor-
wegians, and Swedes. The same region which Tacitus
describes as bordering on the place ".where nature ends,"
held thus in his day tribes that would later have for their
capitals, towns founded long before by the Celts : London,
Vienna, Paris, and Milan.

Many hundred years before settling there, these men
had already found themselves in contact with the Celts,
and, at the time the latter were powerful in Europe,
terrible wars had arisen between the two races. But all
the north-east, from the Elbe to the Vistula, continued
impenetrable ; the Germanic tribes remained there intact,
they united with no others, and alone might have told if
the sun's chariot was really to be seen rising from the
ocean, and splashing the sky with salt sea foam. From
this region were about to start the wild host destined to
conquer the isle of Britain, to change its name and
rebaptize it in blood.

Twice, during the first ten centuries of our era, the
Teutonic race hurled upon the civilised world its savage
hordes of warriors, streams of molten lava. The first
invasion was vehement, especially in the fifth century,
and was principally composed of Germanic tribes, Angles,

Franks, Saxons, Burgundians, Vandals; the second exercised its greatest ravages in the ninth century, at the time of Charlemagne's successors, and proceeded mostly from the Scandinavian tribes, called Danish or Norman by contemporary chroniclers.

From the third century after Christ, fermentation begins among the former of these two groups. No longer are the Germanic tribes content with fighting for their land, retreating step by step before the Latin invader; alarming symptoms of retaliation manifest themselves, like the rumblings that herald the great cataclysms of nature.

The Roman, in the meanwhile, wrapped in his glory, continued to rule the world and mould it to his image; he skilfully enervated the conquered nations, instructed them in the arts, inoculated them with his vices, and weakened in them the spring of their formerly strong will. They called civilisation, *humanitas*, Tacitus said of the Britons, what was actually "servitude." [1] The frontiers of the empire were now so far distant that the roar of the advancing tide scarcely reached Rome. What was overheard of it acted as a stimulus to pleasure, added point to the rhetorician's speeches, excitement to the circus games, and a halo to the beauty of red-haired courtesans. The Romans had reached that point in tottering empires, at which the threat of calamities no longer arouses dormant energy, but only whets and renews the appetite for enjoyment.

Meanwhile, far away towards the north, the Germanic tribes, continually at strife with their neighbours, and warring against each other, without riches or culture, ignorant and savage, preserved their strength and kept their ferocity. They hated peace, despised the arts, and had no literature but drinking- and war-songs. They take an interest only in hunting and war, said Cæsar; from their

[1] " Agricola," xxi.

earliest infancy they endeavour to harden themselves physically.[1] They were not inventive; they learned with more difficulty than the Celts; they were violent and irrepressible. The little that is known of their customs and character points to fiery souls that may rise to great rapturous joys but have an underlayer of gloom, a gloom sombre as the impenetrable forest, sad as the grey sea. For them the woods are haunted, the shades of night are peopled with evil spirits, in their morasses half-divine monsters lie coiled. "They worship demons," wrote the Christian chroniclers of them with a sort of terror.[2] These men will enjoy lyric songs, but not charming tales; they are capable of mirth but not of gaiety; powerful but incomplete natures that will need to develop fully without having to wait for the slow procedure of centuries, an admixture of new blood and new ideas. They were to find in Britain this double graft, and an admirable literary development was to be the consequence. They set out then to accomplish their work and follow their destiny, having doubtless much to learn, but having also something to teach the enervated nations, the meaning of a word unknown till their coming, the word "war" (*guerre, guerra*). After the time of the invasions "bellicose," "belliqueux," and such words lost their strength and realism, and were left for songsters to play with if they liked; a tiny phenomenon, the sign of terrible transformations.

The invaders bore various names. The boundaries of their tribes, as regards population and territory, were vague, and in nowise resembled those of the kingdoms traced on our maps. Their groups united and dissolved continually. The most powerful among them absorb their

---

[1] "Vita omnis in venationibus atque in studiis rei militaris constitit; ab parvulis labori ac duritiei student." "De Bello Gallico," book vi.

[2] "Saxones, sicut omnes fere Germaniam incolentes nationes, et natura feroces, et cultui dæmonum dediti." Eginhard, "Vita Karoli," vii.

neighbours and cause them to be forgotten for a time, their names frequently recur in histories ; then other tribes grow up ; other names appear, others die out. Several of them, however, have survived : Angles, Franks, Saxons, Burgundians, Lombards, Suevi, and Alemanni, which became the names of great provinces or mighty nations. The more important of these groups were rather an agglomeration of tribes than nations properly so called ; thus under the name of Franks were comprised, in the third century, the Sicambers, the Chatti, the Chamavi ; while the Suevi united, in the time of Tacitus, the Lombards, Semnones, Angles, and others. But all were bound by the tie of a common origin ; their passions, customs, and tastes, their arms and costumes were similar.[1]

This human multitude once put in motion, nothing was able to stop it, neither the military tactics of the legions nor the defeats which it suffered ; neither rivers nor mountains, nor the dangers of unknown seas. The Franks, before settling in Gaul, traversed it once from end to end, crossed the Pyrenees, ravaged Spain, and disappeared in Mauritania. Transported once in great numbers to the shores of the Euxine Sea, and imprudently entrusted by the Romans with the defence of their frontiers, they embark, pillage the towns of Asia and Northern Africa, and return to the mouth of the Rhine. Their expeditions intercross each other ; we find them everywhere at once ; Franks are seen at London, and Saxons at Angers. In 406, Gaul is overrun with barbarians, Vandals, Saxons, Burgundians, Alemanni ; every point of the territory is in

---

[1] The arms of the Franks and those of the Anglo-Saxons, the former preserved in the Museum of St. Germain, and the latter in the British Museum, are similar, and differ widely from those of the Celts. The shields, a part of the equipment, which among all nations are found highly ornamented, were equally plain with the Franks and Angles ; the *umbo* or boss in the centre was, in those of both nations, of iron, and shaped like a rude dish-cover, which has often caused them to be catalogued as helmets or military head-pieces.

flames; the noise of a falling empire reaches St. Jerome, in his cell at Bethlehem, and in an eloquent letter he deplores the disaster of Christendom : " Who could ever have believed the day would come when Rome should see war at her very gates, and fight, not for glory but for safety ? Fight, say I ? Nay, redeem her life with treasure." [1]

Treasure did not suffice ; the town was taken and re- taken. Alaric sacked the capital in 410, and Genseric in 455. During several centuries all who emerge from this human tide, and are able to rule the tempest, are either barbarians or crowned peasants. In the fifth and sixth centuries a Frank reigns at Paris, Clovis ; an Ostrogoth at Ravenna, Theodoric ; a peasant at Byzantium, Justinian ; Attila's conqueror, Aëtius, is a barbarian ; Stilicho is a Vandal in the service of the Empire. A Frank king- dom has grown up in the heart of Gaul ; a Visigoth kingdom has Toulouse for its capital ; Genseric and his Vandals are settled in Carthage ; the Lombards, in the sixth century, cross the mountains, establish themselves in ancient Cisalpine Gaul, and drive away the inhabitants towards the lagoons where Venice is to rise. The isle of Britain has likewise ceased to be Roman, and Germanic kingdoms have been founded there.

Mounted on their ships, sixty to eighty feet long, by ten or fifteen broad, of which a specimen can be seen at the museum of Kiel,[2] the dwellers on the shores of the Baltic

---

[1] " Innumerabiles et ferocissimæ nationes universas Gallias occuparunt. . . . Quis hoc crederet ? . . . Romam in gremio suo non pro gloria, sed pro salute pugnare ? Imo ne pugnare quidem, sed auro et cuncta supellectile vitam redimere." Epistola cxxiii. ad Ageruchiam, in the " Patrologia " of Migne, vol. xxii., col. 1057–8.

[2] This ship was discovered in 1863 in a peat bog of Sleswig, that is in the very country of the Angles ; judging by the coins found at the same time, it must belong to the third century. It measures 22 metres, 67 centimetres in length, 3 metres, 33 centim. in breadth, and 1 metre 19 centim. in height. Specimens of Scandinavian ships have also been discovered. When a chief died his ship was buried with him, as his chariot or horse was in other countries. A de-

and North Sea had at first organised plundering expeditions against the great island. They came periodically and laid waste the coasts ; and on account of them the inhabitants gave to this part of the land the name of *Littus Saxonicum*. Each time the pirates met with less resistance, and found the country more disorganised. In the course of the fifth century they saw they had no need to return annually to their morasses, and that they could without trouble remain within reach of plunder. They settled first in the islands, then on the coasts, and by degrees in the interior. Among them were Jutes of Denmark (Jutland), Frisians, Franks, Angles from Sleswig, and Saxons from the vast lands between the Elbe and Rhine.

These last two, especially, came in great numbers, occupied wide territories, and founded lasting kingdoms. The Angles, whose name was to remain affixed to the whole nation, occupied Northumberland, a part of the centre, and the north-east coast, from Scotland to the present county of Essex ; the Saxons settled further south, in the regions which were called from them Essex, Sussex, Middlesex, and Wessex : Saxons of the east, south, centre, and west. It was in these two groups of tribes,

scription of a Scandinavian funeral (the chief placed on his boat, with his arms, and burnt, together with a woman and some animals killed for the occasion) has been handed down to us in the narrative of the Arab Ahmed Ibn Fozlan, sent by the caliph Al Moktader, in the tenth century, as ambassador to a Scandinavian king established on the banks of the Volga (*Journal Asiatique*, 1825, vol. vi. pp. 16 ff.). In some cases there was an interment but no incineration, and thus it is that Norse ships have been found. Two of these precious relics are preserved in the museum of Christiania. One of them, discovered in 1880, constructed out of oaken planks held together by iron nails, still retained several of its oars ; they were about seven yards long, and must have been thirty-two, sixteen on each side. This measurement seems to have been normal, for the "Anglo-Saxon Chronicle" says that Alfred had ships built twice the size of ordinary ships, and gave them "sixty oars or more" (*sub anno* 897). A ship constructed on the exact model of the Scandinavian barks went by its own means from Bergen to New York at the time of the Chicago Exposition, 1893. It was found to be perfectly seaworthy, even in rough weather.

or kingdoms, that literature reached the greatest development, and it was principally between them also that the
struggle for supremacy set in, after the conquest. Hence
the name of Anglo-Saxons generally given to the inhabitants of the soil, in respect of the period during which
purely Germanic dialects were spoken in England. This
composite word, recently the cause of many quarrels,
has the advantage of being clear; long habit is in its
favour; and its very form suits an epoch when the country
was not unified, but belonged to two principal agglomera-
tions of tribes, that of the Angles and that of the Saxons.[1]

In the same way as in Gaul, the invaders found themselves in the presence of a people infinitely more civilised
than themselves, skilled in the arts, excellent agriculturists,
rich traders, on whose soil arose those large towns that
the Romans had fortified, and connected by roads. Never

[1] It may be added in favour of this same word that it is difficult to replace
it by another as clear and convenient. Some have proposed "Old English,"
as having the advantage of better representing the continuity of the national
history, and marking less conspicuously the break occasioned by the Norman
Conquest. "Anglo-Saxon" before the Conquest, "English" after, implies a
radical change, a sort of renovation in the people of England. It is added, too,
that this people already bore in the days of King Alfred the name of English.
But why conceal that this break and this renovation are historical facts? In
language, for example, the changes have been such that, as it has been justly
observed, classical English resembles Anglo-Saxon less than the Italian of
to-day resembles Latin. Still it would not be considered wise on the part of
the Italians to give the name of "Old Italians" to their Roman ancestors,
though they spoke a similar language, were of the same blood and lived in the
same land. As for Alfred, he calls himself sometimes king of the Saxons "rex
Saxonum," sometimes king of the Angles, sometimes king of the Anglo-Saxons:
"Ægo Aelfredus, gratia Dei, Angol Saxonum rex." Asser calls him "Angul-
Saxonum rex." Æthelstan calls himself "rex Angul-Saxonum" (Kemble,
"Codex" ii. p. 124; Grein, "Anglia," i. p. 1; de Gray Birch, "Cartularium
Saxonicum," 1885, ii. p. 333). They never call themselves, as may be believed,
"Old English." The word, besides, is not of an easy use. In one of his
works the great historian, Freeman, speaks of people who were "men of old
English birth." Another describes Alfred as deciding to translate a Latin text
"into Old English," which he certainly never did. Abbot, later Cardinal,
Gasquet, writes a book on the "Old English Bible," dealing, some will think,
with A.S. versions; they will be wrong.

had they beheld anything like it, nor had they names for
such things. They had in consequence to make additions
to their vocabulary. Not knowing how to designate these
unfamiliar objects, they left them the names they bore
in the language of the inhabitants: *castrum, strata, colonia;*
which became in their language *chester, street,* or *strat,* as
in Stratford, and *coln* as in Lincoln.

The Britons who had taken to the toga—"frequens
toga," says Tacitus—and who were no longer protected
by the legions, made a vain resistance ; the advancing tide
of barbarians swept over them, they ceased to exist as
a nation. Contributions were levied on the cities, the
country was laid waste, villas were razed to the ground,
and on all the points where the natives endeavoured to
face the enemy, fearful hecatombs were slaughtered by
the worshippers of Woden.

They could not, however, destroy all ; and here comes
in the important question of Celtic survival. Some
admirers of the conquerors credit them with superhuman
massacres. According to them no Celt survived, and the
race was either driven forth into Wales or destroyed, so
that the whole land had to be repopulated, and that a
new and wholly Germanic nation, as pure in blood as the
tribes by the Elbe were supposed to be, grew up on
British soil. But if facts are examined it will be found
that this title to "glory" cannot be claimed for the
invaders. The deed was an impossible one ; let that be
their excuse. To destroy a whole nation by the sword
exceeds human power, and there is no example of it.
We know, besides, that in this case the task would have
been an especially hard one, for the population of Britain,
even at the time of Cæsar, was dense: *hominum infinita
multitudo,* he says in his Commentaries. The invaders,
on the other hand, found themselves in presence of an
intelligent, laborious, assimilable race, trained by the

Romans to usefulness. The first of these facts precludes the hypothesis of a general massacre ; and the second the hypothesis of a total expulsion, or of such extinction as threatens the inassimilable native of Australia.

In reality, all the documents which have come down to us, and all the verifications made on the ground, contradict the theory of an annihilation of the Celtic race. To begin with, we can imagine no systematic destruction after the introduction of Christianity among the Anglo-Saxons, which took place at the end of the sixth century. Then, the chroniclers speak of a general massacre of the inhabitants, in connection with two places only : Chester and Anderida.[1] We can ascertain even to-day that in one of these cases the destruction certainly was complete, since this last town was never rebuilt, and only its site is known. That the chroniclers should make a special mention of the two massacres proves these cases were exceptional. To argue from the destruction of Anderida to the slaughter of the entire race would be as little reasonable as to imagine that the whole of the Gallo-Romans were annihilated because the ruins of a Gallo-Roman city, with a theatre seating seven thousand people have been discovered in a spot uninhabited to-day, near Sanxay in Poictou. Excavations recently made in England have shown, in a great number of cemeteries, even in the region termed *Littus Saxonicum,* where the Germanic population was densest, Britons and Saxons sleeping side by side, and nothing could better point to their having lived also side by side. Had a wholesale massacre taken place, the victims would have had no sepulchres, or at all events they would not have had them amongst those of the slayers.

In addition to this, it is only by the preservation of the

---

[1] "Anglo-Saxon Chronicle," Rolls, *sub anno* 491.

pre-established race that the change in manners and customs, and the rapid development of the Anglo-Saxons can be explained. These roving pirates lose their taste for maritime adventure ; they build no more ships ; their intestine quarrels are food sufficient for what is left of their warlike appetites. Whence comes it that the instincts of this impetuous race are to such a degree moderated ? Doubtless from the quantity and fertility of the land they had conquered, and from the facility they found on the spot for turning that land to account. These facilities consisted in the labour of others. The taste for agriculture did not belong to the race. Tacitus represents the Germans as cultivating only what was strictly necessary.[1] The Anglo-Saxons found in Britain wide tracts of country tilled by romanised husbandmen ; after the time of the first ravages they recalled them to their toil, but assigned its fruits to themselves. Well, therefore, might the same word be used by the conquerors to designate the native Celt and the slave. They established themselves in the fields, and superintended their cultivation after their fashion ; their encampments became boroughs: Nottingham, Buckingham, Glastonbury, which have to the present day retained the names of Germanic families or tribes. The towns of more ancient importance, on the contrary, have retained Celtic or Latin names: London, York, Lincoln, Winchester, Dover, Cirencester, Manchester, &c.[2] The Anglo-Saxons did not destroy them, since they are still extant, and only mingled

---

[1] " De Moribus Germanorum," xv., xxvi.

[2] Names of villages recalling German clans or families are very numerous on the eastern and southern coasts. "They diminish rapidly as we move inland, and they die away altogether as we approach the purely Celtic west." Fourteen hundred such names have been counted, of which 48 occur in Northumberland, 127 in Yorkshire, 76 in Lincolnshire, 153 in Norfolk and Suffolk, 48 in Essex, 60 in Kent, 86 in Sussex and Surrey, only 2 are found in Cornwall, 6 in Cumberland, 24 in Devon, 13 in Worcester, 2 in Westmoreland, and none in Monmouth." Grant Allen, "Anglo-Saxon Britain " (S.P.C.K.), p. 43.

in a feeble proportion with their population, having, like all
Germans, a horror of sojourning in cities. "They avoided
them, regarding them as tombs," they thought that to
live in towns was like burying oneself alive.[1]   The preservation in England of several branches of Roman industry
is one proof more of the continuance of city life in the
island ; had the British artisans not survived the invasion,
there would never have been found in the tombs of the
conquerors those glass cups of elaborate ornamentation,
hardly distinguishable from the products of the Roman
glass-works, and which the clumsy hands of the Saxon
were certainly incapable of fusing and adorning.[2]

The Britons, then, subsist in large numbers, even in the
eastern and southern counties, where the Germanic settle-
ment was most dense, but they subsist as a conquered race ;
they till the ground in the country, and in the cities occupy
themselves with manual labour.   Wales and Cornwall
alone, in the isle of Britain, were still places of refuge for
independent Celts. The idiom and traditions of the ancient
inhabitants were there preserved. In these distant retreats,
at the foot of Snowdon, in the valley of St. David's, beneath
the trees of Caerleon, popular singers accompany on their
harps the old national poems ; perhaps they even begin to
chaunt those tales telling of the exploits of a hero destined
to the highest renown in literature, King Arthur.

[1] Ammianus Marcellinus: " Ipsa oppida, ut circumdata retiis busta decli-
nant "; in reference to the Franks and Alemanni, " Rerum Gestarum," lib.
xvi., cap. ii. Tacitus says the same thing for the whole of the Germans :
"Nullas Germanorum populis urbes habitari, satis notum est. . . . Colunt
discreti ac diversi, ut fons, ut campus, ut nemus placuit. Vicos locant, non in
nostrum morem, connexis et cohærentibus ædificiis : suam quisque domum
spatio circumdat." " De Moribus Germanorum," xvi.

[2] It seems impossible to admit, as has been suggested, that these frail objects
should have been saved from the plunder and burning of the villas and preserved by the Anglo-Saxons as *curiosities*. Glasses with knobs, "*à larmes*,"
abound in the Anglo-Saxon tombs, and similar ones have been found in the
Roman tombs of an earlier epoch, notably at Lépine, in the department of the
Marne.

But in the heart of the country the national tongue had been for a long time constantly losing ground ; the Britons had learnt Latin, many of them ; they now forget it by degrees, as they had previously forgotten Celtic, and learn instead the language of their new masters. It was one of their national gifts, a precious and fatal one ; they were swift to learn.

In France the result of the Germanic conquest was totally different ; the Celtic language reappeared there no more than in England. It has only survived in the extreme west.[1] But in France the Germanic idiom did not overpower the Latin ; the latter persisted, so much so that the French tongue has remained a Romance language. This is owing to two great causes. Firstly, the Germans came to France in much smaller numbers than to England, and those that remained had been long in contact with the Romans ; secondly, the romanising of Gaul had been more complete. Of all the provinces of the Empire, Gaul, the birthplace of Cornelius Gallus, Trogus Pompeius, Domitius Afer, Petronius, Ausonius, Sidonius Apollinaris, prided itself on speaking the purest Latin, and on producing the best poets. Whether we take material monuments or literary ones, the difference is the same in the two countries. In England theatres, towers, temples, all marks of Latin civilisation, had been erected, but not so numerous, massive, or strong that the invaders were unable to destroy them. At the present time only shapeless remnants exist above ground. In France, the barbarians came, plundered, burnt, razed to the ground all they possibly could ; but the work of destruction was too great, the multitude of temples and palaces was more than their strength was equal to, and the torch fell from their tired hands. Whereas in England

[1] Where the Celtic element was reinforced, at the commencement of the sixth century, by a considerable immigration of Britons driven from England. Hence the name of Bretagne, given then for the first time to Armorica.

4

excavations are made in order to discover the remains of ancient Latin civilisation, in France we need only raise our eyes to behold them. Could the grave give up a Roman of the time of the Cæsars, he would still at this day be able to worship his divine emperors in the temples of Nîmes and Vienne ; pass, when entering Reims, Orange, or Saintes under triumphal arches erected by his ancestors ; he might recognise their tombs at the "Aliscamps" of Arles ; could see *Antigone* played at Orange, and seated on the gradines of the amphitheatre, facing the blue horizon of Provence, still behold blood flowing in the arena.

Gaul was not, like Britain, disorganised and deprived of its legions when the Germanic hordes appeared ; the victor had to reckon with the vanquished ; the latter became not a slave but an ally, and this advantage, added to that of superior numbers and civilisation, allowed the Gallo-Roman to reconquer the invader. Latin tradition was so powerful that it was accepted by Clovis himself. That long-haired chieftain donned the toga and chlamys ; he became a *patrice ;* although he knew by experience that he derived his power from his sword, it pleased him to ascribe it to the emperor. He had an instinct of what Rome was. The prestige of the emperor was worth an army to him, and assisted him to rule his latinised subjects. Conquered, pillaged, sacked, and ruined, the Eternal City still remained fruitful within her crumbling walls. Under the ruins subsisted living seeds, one, amongst others, most important of all, containing the great Roman idea, the notion of the State. The Celts hardly grasped it, the Germans only at a late period. Clovis, barbarian though he was, became imbued with it. He endeavoured to mould his subjects, Franks, Gallo-Romans, and Visigoths, so as to form a State, and in spite of the disasters that followed, his efforts were not without some durable results.

In France the vanquished taught the victors their language; the grandsons of Clovis wrote Latin verses; and it is owing to poems written in a Romance idiom that Karl the Frank became the " Charlemagne " of legend and history; so that at last the new empire founded in Gaul had nothing Germanic save the name. The name, however, has survived, and is the name of France.

Thus, and not by an impossible massacre, can be explained the different results of the invasions in France and England. In both countries, but less abundantly in the latter, the Celtic race has been perpetuated, and the veil which covers it to-day, a Latin or Germanic tissue, is neither so close nor so thick that we cannot distinguish through its folds the forms of British or Gaulish genius ; a very special and easily recognisable genius, very different from that of the ancients, and differing still more from that of the Teutonic invaders.

CHAPTER III.

THE NATIONAL POETRY OF THE ANGLO-SAXONS.

I.

TOWARDS the close of the fifth century, the greater part of England was conquered ; the rulers of the land were no longer Celts or Romans, but men of Germanic origin, who worshipped Thor and Woden instead of Christ, and whose language, customs, and religion differed entirely from those of the people they had settled amongst and subjugated.

The force of circumstances produced a fusion of the two races, but during many centuries no literary fusion took place. The mind of the invader was not actuated by curiosity ; he intrenched himself in his tastes, content with his own literature. " Each one," wrote Tacitus of the Germans, "leaves an open space around his dwelling." The Anglo-Saxons remained in literature a people of isolated dwellings. They did not allow the traditions of the vanquished Celts to blend with theirs, and, in spite of their early conversion to Christianity, they preserved, almost without change, the main characteristics of the race from which they were descended.

Their vocabulary, save for the introduction of a few words, taken from the Church Latin, their grammar, their prosody, all remain Germanic. In their verse the cadence is marked, not by an equal number of syllables, but by about the same number of accents; they have not the recurring sounds of rime, but they have, like the Germans and Scandinavians, *alliteration*, that is, the repetition of the same letters at the beginning of certain syllables. "Each long verse has four accented syllables, while the number of unaccented syllables is indifferent, and is divided by the cæsura into two short verses, bound together by alliteration: two accented syllables in the first short line and one in the second, beginning with any vowel or the same consonant"[1] (or consonants giving about the same sound):

*F*lod under *f*oldan · nis thät *f*eor heonon.

"The water sinks underground; it is not far from here." (*Beowulf.*) The rules of this prosody, not very difficult in themselves, are made still easier by a number of licenses and exceptions. The taste for alliteration was destined to survive; it has never completely disappeared in England. We find this ornamentation even in the Latin of poets posterior to the Norman Conquest, like Joseph of Exeter in the twelfth century:

*A*ʊdit et *a*ʊdet
Dux *f*alli : *f*atisque *f*avet quum *f*ata recuset.[2]

The famous Visions of Langland, in the fourteenth century, are in alliterative verse; under Elizabeth alliteration became one of the peculiarities of the florid prose

---

[1] H. Sweet, "Sketch of the History of Anglo-Saxon poetry," in Hazlitt's Warton, ii. p. 3.

[2] "De Bello Trojano," iii., line 108. Rime, however, commenced to appear in a few rare Christian poems of the end of the Anglo-Saxon period. On the use, rather rare, of alliteration in old French, which nevertheless has been preserved in several current expressions, such as "gros et gras," "bel et bon," &c., see Paul Meyer, "Romania," vol. xi. p. 572 : "De l'allitération en Roman de France."

called Euphuism.   Nearer to our own time, Byron makes
a frequent use of alliteration :

> Our bay
> Receives that prow which proudly spurns the spray ;
> How gloriously her gallant course she goes :
> Her white wings flying—never from her foes.   (*Corsair.*)

The purely Germanic period of the literary history of
England lasted six hundred years, that is, for about the
same length of time as divides us from the reign of Henry
III.   Rarely has a literature been more consistent with
itself than the literature of the Anglo-Saxons.   They were
not as the Celts, quick to learn; they had not the curiosity,
loquacity, taste for art which were found in the subjugated
race.   They developed slowly.   Those steady qualities
which were to save the Anglo-Saxon genius from the
absolute destruction which threatened it at the time of
the Norman Conquest resulted in the production of
literary works evincing, one and all, such a similitude
in tastes, tendencies, and feelings that it is extremely
difficult to date and localise them.   At the furthest end
of the period, the Anglo-Saxons continued to enjoy,
Christian though they were, and in more and more intimate
contact with latinised races, legends and traditions going
back to the pagan days, nay, to the days of their continental life by the shores of the Baltic.   Late manuscripts
have preserved for us their oldest conceptions, by which
is shown the continuity of taste for them.   The early
pagan character of the poetry in " Widsith," in the
" Lament of Deor," in part of " Beowulf," is undoubted ; still
those poems continued to be copied up to the last century
of the Anglo-Saxon rule ; it is, in fact, only in manuscripts
of that date that we have them.   An immense amount of
labour, ingenuity, and knowledge has been spent on questions of date and place, but the difficulty is such, and that
literature forms such a compact whole, that the best and

highest authorities have come on all points to contrary conclusions. The very greatness of their effort and amplitude of their science happens thus to be the best proof of the singular cohesion between the various produce of the Anglo-Saxon mind. Of all the poets of the period, the one who had the strongest individuality, as well as the greatest genius, one whom we know by name, Cynewulf, the only one whose works are authentic, being signed, who thus offered the best chance to critics, has caused as many disagreements among them as any stray leaf of parchment in the whole collection of Anglo-Saxon poetry. According to Ten Brink he was born between 720 and 730 ; according to Earle he more probably lived in the eleventh century, at the other end of the period.[1] One authority sees in his works the characteristics of the poetry of Northumbria, another inclines towards Mercia. All possible dates have been assigned to the beautiful poem of " Judith," from the seventh to the tenth century. "Beowulf" was written in Northumbria according to Stopford Brooke, in Mercia according to Earle, in Wessex according to Ten Brink. The attribution of " Andreas " to Cynewulf has been renewed by Gollancz, and denied by Fritzsche. " Dream of the Rood " follows similar fluctuations. The truth is that while there were doubtless movement and development in Anglo-Saxon poetry, as in all human things, they were very slow and difficult to measure. When material facts and landmarks are discovered, still it will remain true that till then authorities, judging poems on their own merits, could not agree as to their classification, so little apparent was the movement they represent. Anglo-Saxon poetry is like the river Saone ; one doubts which way it flows.

[1] " His date has been variously estimated from the 8th to the 11th century. The latter is the more probable." Earle, " Anglo-Saxon Literature," 1884, p. 228. *Cf.* A. S. Cook, " The Christ of Cynewulf," Boston, 1900, p. lxviii.

Let us therefore t ke this literature as a whole, and confess that the division here adopted, of national and worldly and of religious literature, is arbitrary, and is merely used for the sake of convenience. Religious and worldly, northern and southern literature overlap ; but they most decidedly belong to the same Anglo-Saxon whole.

This whole has strong characteristics of its own, a force, a passion, a grandeur, unexampled at that day. Contrary to what is found in Celtic literature, there is no place in the monuments of Anglo-Saxon thought for either light gaiety, or those shades of feeling which the Celts could already express at that remote period. The new settlers are strong, but not agile. Of the two master passions attributed by Cato to the inhabitants of Gaul, one alone, the love of war, *rem militarem*, is shared by the dwellers on the shores of the northern ocean ; the other, *argute loqui*, is unknown to them.

Members of the same family of nations established by the shores of the North Sea, as the classic nations were on the Mediterranean coasts in the time of the emperors, the Anglo-Saxon, the German, and the Scandinavian tribes spoke dialects of the same tongue, preserved common traditions and the memory of an identical origin. Grein has collected in his "Anglo-Saxon Library" all that remains of the ancient literature of England ; Powell and Vigfusson have comprised in their "Corpus Poeticum Boreale" all we possess in the way of poems in the Scandinavian tongue, formerly composed in Denmark, Norway, the Orkneys, Iceland, and even Greenland, within the Arctic circle.[1] The resemblances between the two

[1] Grein. "Bibliothek der Angelsæchsischen Poesie," ed. Wülker ; Cassel, 1883 ff. (and the separate texts in the "Library of A.S. Poetry" and the "Albion Series," both Boston, in progress) ; "Corpus Poeticum Boreale, from the earliest to the XIIIth Century," ed. and transl. by G. Vigfusson and F. York Powell, Oxford, 1883, 2 vols. Other important monuments of Scandinavian lit. are found in "Edda Snorri," ed. Sigurdsson, Copenhagen, 1848,

collections are striking, the differences are few. In both
series it seems as if the same people were revealing its
origins, and leading its heroes to Walhalla.[1] The Anglo-
Saxon tale of Beowulf and the Scandinavian saga of
Gretti, the Anglo-Saxon story of Waldhere and the
Scandinavian and Germanic tale of the Niblungs and
Volsungs,[2] turn on the same incidents or are dedicated
to the same heroes, represent a similar ideal of life,
similar manners, the same race. They are all of them
part of the literary patrimony common to the men of
the North.

As happened with the Celts, the greater number of the
monuments of ancient Germanic and Scandinavian literature has been preserved in the remotest of the countries
where the race established itself ; distance having better
sheltered it from wars, the songs and manuscripts were

2 vols. ; " Norroen Fornkvædi," ed. S. Bugge, Christiania, 1867 (contains the
collection usually called Edda Sæmundi) ; " Icelandic Sagas," ed. Vigfusson,
London, 1887, 2 vols. (collection of the " Master of the Rolls " ; contains, vol.
i., " Orkneinga Saga " and " Magnus Saga " ; vol. ii., " Hakonar Saga ") ;
" Sturlunga Saga," including the " Islendiga Saga of Lawman Thordsson, and
other works," ed. Vigfusson, Oxford, 1878, 2 vols. ; " Heimskringla Saga, or
the Sagas of the Norse Kings, from the Icelandic of Snorre Sturlason," ed.
S. Laing and R. B. Anderson, London, 1889, 4 vols. 8vo. ; " Origines Islan-
dicæ," by Vigfusson and Powell, Oxford, 1905, 2 vols. See also the " Northern
Library " (London, Nutt), and the " Saga Library," founded in 1890 by
W. Morris and Eirikr Magnusson (Quaritch, London). The prose Edda is a
collection of narratives of the twelfth century, retouched by Snorri in the
thirteenth ; the Edda in verse (trans. Bellows, N.Y., 1923) is a collection of
poems of various dates that go back in part to the eighth and ninth centuries.
On the meaning of the word Edda, see " Corp. Poetic," I. xxvi. *Saga*
means a narrative ; the Sagas are narratives in prose of an epic character ;
they flourished especially in the twelfth and thirteenth centuries. A complete bibliography is at the end of Vol. I. of the Cambridge " History of
English Literature."

[1] The Anglo-Saxon and the Scandinavian collections both contain the same
kind of poems, and especially epic poems, elegies and laments, moral poems,
war songs, aphorisms, riddles, some of which continue to puzzle our wisest.

[2] The oldest fragments of this epic are found in the *Edda* in verse ; a complete version exists in Icelandic prose ("Volsunga Saga") XIIth century ;
the German version (" Nibelungenlied ") is of the end of the same century.

more easily saved from destruction. Most of the Celtic tales extant at this day have been preserved in Ireland ; and most of the pieces collected in the " Corpus Poeticum Boreale " have been taken from Icelandic documents.

Manners and beliefs of the northern people are abundantly illustrated by the poems included in this collection. We find ourselves amid giants and dwarfs, monsters, dragons, unconquerable heroes, bloody battles, gloomy omens, magic spells, and enchanted treasures. The poet leads us through halls with ornamented seats, on which warriors spend long hours in drinking ; to pits full of serpents into which the vanquished are thrown ; in the midst of dismal landscapes where gibbeted corpses swing in the wind ; to mysterious islands where whirlwinds of flame shoot from the tombs, and where the heroine arrives on her ships, her " ocean steeds," to evoke the paternal shade, behold once more the beloved being in the midst of infernal fires, and receive from his hands the enchanted and avenging sword. Armed Valkyrias cross the sky ; ravens comment on the actions of men ; the tone is sad and doleful, sometimes so curt and abrupt that, in order to follow the poet's fantastic imaginations, a marginal commentary would be necessary, as for the " Ancient Mariner " of Coleridge, in whom lives again something of the spirit of this literature.

Scenes of slaughter and torture abound of course, as they do with all primitive nations ; the victims laugh in the midst of their sufferings ; they sing their death-song. Sigfried roasts the heart of his adversary, Fafni, the man-serpent, and eats it. Eormunrek's feet and hands are cut off and thrown into the fire before his eyes. Skirni, in order to win Gerda's love for his master, heaps curses upon her, threatens to cut off her head, and by these means succeeds in his embassy.[1] Gunnar, wanting to keep for

[1] " Lay of Skirni."—" Corpus Poeticum," i. p. 114.

himself the secret of the Niblungen treasure, asks for the heart of his own brother, Hogni :

" Hogni's bleeding heart must be laid in my hand, carved with the keen-cutting knife out of the breast of the good knight.

" They carved the heart of Hialli (the thrall) from out his breast, and laid it bleeding on a charger, and bore it to Gunnar.

" Then spake Gunnar, king of men : ' Here I have the heart of Hialli the coward, unlike the heart of Hogni the brave. It quakes greatly as it lies on the charger, but it quaked twice as much when it lay in his breast.'

" Hogni laughed when they cut out the quick heart of that crested hero ; he had little thought of whimpering. They laid it bleeding on the charger and bore it before Gunnar.

" Then spake Gunnar, the Hniflungs' hero : 'Here I have the heart of Hogni the brave, unlike the heart of Hialli the coward ; it quakes very little as it lies on the charger, but it quaked much less when it lay in his breast.' "

Justice being thus done to his brother, and feeling no regret, Gunnar's joy breaks forth ; he alone now possesses the secret of the Niblungen (Hniflungs') treasure, and "the great rings shall gleam in the rolling waters rather than they shall shine on the hands of the sons of the Huns." [1]

From this example, and from others which it would be easy to add, it can be inferred that *nuances* and refined sentiments escape the comprehension of such heroes ; they waste no time in describing things of beauty ; they care not if earth brings forth flowers, or if women have cheeks " purple as the fox-glove." Neither have these men any aptitude for light repartee ; they do not play, they kill ; their jests fell the adversary to the ground. " Thou hast

---

[1] "Alta-Kvida."—"Corpus Poeticum," i. p. 48. This is one of the most ancient poems in the collection.

eaten the fresh-bleeding hearts of thy sons, mixed with honey, thou giver of swords," says Queen Gudrun to Attila, the historic king of the Huns, who, in this literature, has become the typical foreign hero ; " now thou shalt digest the gory flesh of man, thou stern king, having eaten of it as a dainty morsel, and sent it as a mess to thy friends." Such is the kind of jokes they enjoy ; the poet describes the speech of the Queen as " a word of mockery." [1] The exchange of mocking words between Loki and the gods is of the same order as Gudrun's speech. Cowards! cries Loki to the gods; Prostitutes! cries he to the goddesses ; Drunkard! is the reply of both. There is no question here of *argute loqui.*

Violent in their speech, cruel in their actions,[2] they love all that is fantastic, prodigious, colossal ; and this tendency appears even in the writings where they wish to amuse ; it is still more marked there than in the ancient Celtic tales. Thor and the giant go a-fishing, the giant puts two hooks on his line and catches two whales at once. Thor baits his hook with an ox's head and draws out the great serpent which encircles the earth.[3]

Their violence and energy spend their force, and then the man, quite another man it would seem, veers round ; the once dauntless hero is now daunted by shadows, by thoughts, by nothing. Those strong beings, who laugh when their hearts are cut out alive, are the prey of vague thoughts. Already in that far-off time their world, which appears to us so young, seemed old to them.

---

[1] " Alta-Kvida."—" Corpus Poeticum," i. p. 51.

[2] A single example will be as good as many : " One of the Viking leaders got the nickname of Börn (Child) because he had been so tender-hearted as to try and stop the sport of his followers, who were tossing young children in the air and catching them upon their spears. No doubt his men laughed not unkindly at this fancy of his, and gave him the nickname above mentioned." C. F. Keary, "The Vikings in Western Christendom," 789-888, London, 1891, 8vo, p. 145.

[3] " Hymis-Kvida."—" Corpus Poeticum," i. p. 222.

They were acquainted with causeless regrets, vain sorrows, and disgust of life. No literature has produced a greater number of disconsolate poems. Mournful songs abound in the " Corpus Poeticum " of the North.

II.

With beliefs, traditions, and ideas of the same sort, the Anglo-Saxons had landed in Britain and settled there.[1]

[1] The most valuable monuments of Anglo-Saxon literature and art are contained in the following MSS. :

I. *Poetry.*—MS. of " Beowulf," preserved in the British Museum, Cotton. Vitell., A. xv., written towards the end of the tenth or beginning of the eleventh century. It contains also, *e.g.* the fine poem of "Judith."

A fragment of a poem on Waldhere, preserved in the Copenhagen Library.

The Exeter MS., "Codex Exoniensis," written in the tenth or eleventh century and given by Leofric, first bishop of Exeter (d. 1072), to the cathedral library of this town, where it is still preserved. It contains a variety of poetic pieces : Christ, St. Guthlac, Phenix, Wanderer, Seafarer, Widsith, (important ed. Chambers, 1912), Panther, Whale, Deor, Ruin, Riddles, &c.

The "Codex Vercellensis," MS. CXVII in the *Archivio* of the cathedral, Vercelli in Lombardy, containing : Andreas, The Departed Soul's Addiess to the Body, Dream of the Holy Rood, Elene, &c., written XIth century (*infra*, p. 70) ; inscribed on the back : " Homiliarum liber ignoti idiomatis."

The Bodleian MS., Junius xi., containing a poetical version of part of the Bible, some of which is attributed to Cædmon, written in the tenth century.

The Paris Anglo-Saxon Psalter (Bibliothèque Nationale, Lat. 8824), written XIth century, composed IXth–Xth, 50 psalms in prose, 100 in verse.

II. *Prose.*—The Epinal MS. containing an Anglo-Saxon glossary (eighth century according to Mr. Sweet, ninth according to Sir E. Maunde Thompson). Gregory's " Regula Pastoralis " (the copy of Werferth, bishop of Worcester).

The MS. of the " Anglo-Saxon Chronicle," the Winchester text, in the library of Corpus Christi College, Cambridge, MS. lxxiii.

The MSS. of the homilies of Ælfric and Wulfstan, Junius xxii. and Junius xcix., in the Bodleian, the MS. of the Blickling homilies (Blickling Hall, Norfolk), and the " Codex Vercellensis " (part of its contents being prose).

III. *Miniatures.*—The splendid Lindisfarne Gospels, MS. Cotton. Nero, D. iv., in the British Museum, eighth-ninth century, in Latin with Anglo-Saxon glosses, date from Anglo-Saxon times, but are due to Irish hands ; ed. Miilar, 1923, fol. See J. O. Westwood, "Facsimiles of the Miniatures and Ornaments of Anglo-Saxon and Irish MSS." London, Quaritch, 1868, fol., " Palæographia Sacro Pictoria," London, 1844, fol., also the fine pen-and-ink drawings in the above mentioned MS. Junius xi., in the Bodleian Library.

Established in their "isolated dwellings," if they leave
them it is for action ; if they re-enter them it is for solitary
reverie, or sometimes for orgies. The main part of their
original literature, like that of their brothers and cousins
on the Continent, consists of triumphal songs and heartrending laments.   It is contemplative and warlike.[1]

They have to fight against their neighbours, or against
their kin from over the sea, who in their turn wish to seize
upon the island.   The war-song remains persistently in
favour with them, and preserves, almost intact, its
characteristics of haughty pride and ferocity.   Its cruel
accents recur even in the pious poems written after the
conversion, and in the middle of the monotonous tale told
by the national annalist.   The Anglo-Saxon monk who
draws up in his cell the chronicle of the events of the year,
feels his heart beat at the thought of a great victory, and
in the midst of the placid prose which serves to register
eclipses of the moon and murders of kings, he suddenly
inserts the bounding verse of an enthusiastic war-song :

" This year, King Æthelstan, lord of earls, ring-giver of
warriors, and his brother eke Edmund Ætheling, life-long
glory in battle won at Brunanburh. . . . The foes lay low,
the Scots people and the shipman death-doomed fell.
The field streamed with warriors' blood what time the sun
up, at morning-tide, the glorious star, glided o'er grounds,
God's candle bright the eternal Lord's, until the noble
creature sank to its setting."

The poet describes the enemy's defeat and flight, the
slaughter that ensues, and with cries of joy calls upon

---

[1] *Cf.* Tacitus, who says of the Germans : " Celebrant carminibus antiquis
(quod unum apud illos memoriæ et annalium genus est). . . ." " De Moribus," i.
Eginhard in the ninth century notices the same sort of songs among the
Franks established in Gaul : " Item barbara et antiquissima carmina, quibus
veterum regum actus et bella canebantur. . . ." " Vita Karoli," cap. xxix.
(ed. Ideler, " Leben und Wandel Karl des Grossen," Hamburg and Gotha,
1839, 2 vols. 8vo, vol. i. p. 89).

the flocks of wild birds, the "swart raven with horned neb," and "him of goodly coat, the eagle," and the "greedy war hawk," to come and share the carcases. Never was so splendid a slaughter seen, "from what books tell us, old chroniclers, since hither from the east Angles and Saxons ('Engle and Seaxe'), came to land, o'er the broad seas, Britain ('Brytene') sought, proud war-smiths, the Welsh ('Wealas') o'ercame, men for glory eager, the country gain'd."[1]

The writer's heart swells with delight at the thought of so many corpses, of so great a carnage and so much gore; he is happy and triumphant, he dwells complacently on the sight, as poets of another day and country would dwell on the thought of paths "where the wind swept roses" (où le vent balaya des roses).

These strong men lend themselves willingly, as do their kin over the sea, to the ebb and flow of powerful contrary feelings, and rush body and soul from the extreme of joy to the acme of sorrow. The mild *sérénité*, enjoyed by men with classical tendencies was to them unknown, and the word was one which no Norman Conquest, no Angevin rule, could, for a long time, force into the language; it was unwanted, for the thing was unknown. But they listen with unabated pleasure, late in the period, to the story of heroic deeds performed on the Continent by men

---

[1] "Anglo-Saxon Chronicle" (Rolls), i. p. 200; ii. p. 86; year 937. The song on the battle of Brunanburh, won by the Anglo-Saxons over the Scotch and Danes, has been translated by Tennyson. Other war songs, a few out of a great many, have come down to us, some inserted in the Anglo-Saxon Chronicle, some in separate fragments (like the song on the death of Byrhtnoth, defeated and killed by the Danes after a hard fight, at the battle of Maldon, 991, ed. Sedgefield, Boston, 1904). Among the more remarkable is the very old fragment on the "Battle of Finnsburg," discovered, like the Waldhere fragment, in the binding of a book. This battle is alluded to in "Beowulf." The fragment has been printed by Grein in his "Bibliothek," vol. i., and is to be found in the chief recent editions of "Beowulf."

of their own race, whose mind was shaped like theirs, and who felt the same feelings. The same blood and soul sympathy which animates them towards their own King Æthelstan, lord of earls, ring-giver of warriors—not a myth that one, not a fable his deeds—warms the songs they devote to King Waldhere of Aquitaine, to the Scandinavian warrior Beowulf, and to others, probably, who belonged to the same Germanic stock. Not a word of England or the Angles is said in those poems ; still they were popular in England. The Waldhere song, of which some sixty lines have been preserved, on two vellum leaves discovered in the binding of an old book, told the story of the hero's flight from Attila's Court with his bride Hildgund and a treasure (treasures play a great part in those epics), and of his successive fights with Gunther and Hagen while crossing the Vosges. These warriors, after this one appearance, vanish altogether from English literature, but their literary life was continued on the Continent ; their fate was told in Latin in the tenth century by a monk of St. Gall, and again they had a part to play in the German " Nibelungenlied." Beowulf, on the contrary, Scandinavian as he was, is known only through the Anglo-Saxon poet. In " Beowulf," as in " Waldhere," feelings, speeches, manners, ideal of life are the same as with the heroes of the " Corpus Poeticum Boreale." The whole obviously belongs to the same group of nations.[1]

The strange poem of " Beowulf,"[2] the most important

---

[1] G. Stephens, " Two leaves of King Waldere's lay," Copenhagen and London, 1860, 8vo ; R. Peiper, " Ekkehardi primi Waltharius," Berlin, 1873.

[2] " Autotypes of the unique Cotton MS. Vitellius, A. xv. in the British Museum," with transliteration and notes, by J. Zupitza, E.E.T.S., 1882 ; " Beowulf" (Heyne's text), ed. Harrison and Sharp, Boston, several ed. " Beowulf," ed. Holthausen, Heidelberg, 1905, ed. Wyatt and Chambers, Cambridge, 1914, ed. Klaeber, Boston, 1924. English translations by T. Arnold, J. M. Garnett, J. Earle, J. R. Clark Hall, Tinker. See Tinker, " The Translations of Beowulf," N.Y., 1903 ; a bibliography of the whole,

monument of Anglo-Saxon literature, was discovered at
the end of the eighteenth century, in a manuscript written
about the year 1000,[1] and is now preserved in the British
Museum. Few works have been more discussed ; it has
been the cause of literary wars, in which the learned men
of England, Denmark, Sweden, Germany, France, and
America have taken part ; and peace is not yet signed.

This poem, like the old Celtic tales, is a medley of pagan
legends, which did not originally concern Beowulf in particular,[2] and of historical facts; the various parts, after a separate literary life, having been put together, perhaps in the
eighth century, perhaps later, by an Anglo-Saxon Christian, who added new discrepancies in trying to adapt the
old tale to the faith of his day. No need to expatiate on
the incoherence of a poem formed of such elements. Its
heroes are at once pagan and Christian ; they believe in
Christ and in Weland ; they fight against the monsters of
Scandinavian mythology, and see in them the descendants
of Cain ; historical facts, such as a battle of the sixth
century, mentioned by Gregory of Tours, where the victory
remained to the Frankish ancestor,[3] are mixed up with
tales of fantastic duels below the waves.

subject is in the important "Beowulf, an Introduction to the Poem," by
R. K. Chambers, Cambridge, 1921. *Cf.* Lawrence, Publications Mod. Lang.
Assn. of Ama., xxvii, 208, xxxiii, 547. The poem consists of 3,183 long
lines of alliterative verse, divided into 41 sections ; it is not quite equal in
length to a third of the Æneid.

[1] H. L. D. Ward, "Catalogue of Romances," vol. ii., London, 1893, p. 1.

[2] This explains how we find them used in Scandinavian literature as part of
the life of totally different heroes ; the Icelandic saga of Gretti tells how Glam,
another Grendel, is destroyed by Gretti, another Beowulf. On these resemblances, see Excursus iii. in the "Corpus Poeticum Boreale," ii. 501 ; and
II. Gering, "Der Beówulf und die Islaendische Grettisaga," in "Anglia,"
iii. 74.

[3] In Gregory of Tours, book iii. chap. 3 ("Historia Ecclesiastica Francorum," Société de l'histoire de France, vol. i. p. 270) ; in "Beowulf" ll.
1202 *et seq.* :—

Gehwearf thá in Francna fæthm feorh cynninges ;—

According to a legend partly reproduced in the poem, the Danes had no chief. They beheld one day a small ship on the sea, and in it a child, and with him one of those ever-recurring treasures. They saw in this mysterious gift a sign from above, and took the child for their ruler; "and he was a good king." When that king, Scyld, died, they placed him once more on a bark with treasures, and the waters bore him away, no one ever knew whither.

One of his successors, Hrothgar,[1] who held his court, like the Danish kings of to-day, in the isle of Seeland, built in his old age a splendid hall, Heorot, wherein to feast his warriors and distribute rings among them. They drank merrily there, while the singer sang "from far-off ages the origin of men." But there was a monster named Grendel, who lived in the darkness of lonely morasses. He "bore impatiently for a season to hear each day joyous revelry loud-sounding in the hall, where was the music of the harp, and the clear piercing song" of the "scôp." When night came, the fiend "went to visit the grand house, to see how the Ring-Danes after the beer-drinking had settled themselves in it. Then found he therein a crowd of nobles (æthelinga) asleep after the feast; they knew no care."[2] Grendel removed thirty of them to his lair, and they were killed by "that dark pest

"The life of the king [Higelac] became the prey of the Franks." Grundtvig was the first to identify Higelac with the Chlochilaicus of Gregory of Tours. The battle took place about 525; the Scandinavians led by "Chlochilaicus" were plundering lands belonging to Thierry, king of Austrasia (511–534), eldest son of Clovis, when he sent against them his son Theodebert, famous since, who was to die on his way to Constantinople in an expedition against the Emperor Justinian. Theodebert entirely routed the enemy, and took back their plunder, killing their chief, the Chlochilaicus of Gregory, the Huiglaucus "qui imperavit Getis, et a Francis occisus est" of an old "Liber monstrorum," the Higelac of our poem. See H. L. D. Ward, "Catalogue of Romances in the British Museum," vol. ii. 1893, pp. 6 ff.

[1] According to the poem, the line of succession was: Scyld, Beowulf (not our hero), Healfdene, Heorogar, Hrothgar.

[2] "Beowulf," 1876, T. Arnold's translation.

of men, that mischief-working being, grim and greedy, savage and fierce." Grendel came again and "wrought a yet worse deed of murder." The thanes ceased to care much for the music and glee of Heorot. " He that escaped from that enemy kept himself ever afterwards far off in greater watchfulness."

Higelac, king of the Geatas (who the Geatas were is doubtful; perhaps Goths of Gothland in Sweden, perhaps Jutes of Jutland [1]), had a nephew, Beowulf, son of Ecgtheow, of the royal Swedish blood, who heard of the scourge. Beowulf went with his companions on board a ship; "the foamy-necked cruiser, hurried on by the wind, flew over the sea, most like to a bird," and followed "the path of the swans." For the North Sea is the path of the swans as well as of the whales, and the wild swan abounds to this day on the coasts of Norway.[2] Beowulf landed and proposed to Hrothgar to rid him of the monster.

Hrothgar does not conceal from his guests the terrible danger they are running: " Often have boasted the sons of battle, drunken with beer, over their cups of ale, that they would await in the beer-hall, with their deadly sharp-edged swords, the onset of Grendel. Then in the morning, when the daylight came, this mead-hall, this lordly chamber, was stained with gore, all the bench-floor drenched in blood, the hall in carnage. . . ." The Geatas persist in their undertaking, and they are feasted by their host: "Then was a bench cleared for the sons of the Geatas, to sit close together in the beer-hall; there the stout-hearted ones went and sat, exulting clamorously. A thane attended to their wants, who carried in his

---

[1] This last opinion has been defended by Fahlbeck, accepted by Vigfusson, and rejected by Chambers. Heorot, according to the latter, is Leire, near Roskilde, an opinion contested after new excavations (1924) by Dr. Herben of Princeton.

[2] They are numerous especially in the province of Finmarken; they are to be found farther south in winter.

hands a chased ale-flagon, and poured the pure bright liquor."

Night falls ; the Geat and his companions remain in the hall and " bow themselves to repose." Grendel the " night walker came prowling in the gloom of night . . . from his eyes there issued a hideous light, most like to fire. In the hall he saw many warriors, a kindred band, sleeping all together, a group of clansmen. Then he laughed in his heart." He did not tarry, but seized one of the sleepers, " tore him irresistibly, bit his flesh, drank the blood from his veins, swallowed him by large morsels ; soon had he devoured all the corpse but the feet and hands." He then finds himself confronted by Beowulf. The fight begins under the sounding roof, the gilded seats are overthrown, and it was a wonder the hall itself did not fall in ; but it was " made fast with iron bands." At last Grendel's arm is wrenched off, and he flees towards his morasses to die.

While Beowulf, loaded with treasure, returns to his own country, another scourge appears. The mother of Grendel wishes to avenge him, and, during the night, seizes and eats Hrothgar's favourite warrior. Beowulf comes back and reaches the cave of the fiends under the waters ; the fight is an awful one, and the hero was about to succumb, when he caught sight of an enormous sword forged by the giants. With it he slays the foe ; and also cuts off the head of Grendel, whose body lay there lifeless. At the contact of this poisonous blood the blade melts entirely, " just like ice, when the Father looseneth the bonds of frost, unwindeth the ropes that bind the waves."

Later, after having taken part in the historic battle fought against the Franks, in which his uncle Higelac was killed, Beowulf becomes king, and reigns fifty years. In his old age, he has to fight once more a monster, " a fierce Fire-drake," that held the usual treasure. He is victorious ; but sits down wounded on a stone, feeling that he is about

to die. " Now go thou quickly, dear Wiglaf," he says to
the only one of his companions who had come to his
rescue, "to spy out the hoard under the hoar rock ; . . .
make haste now that I may examine the ancient wealth,
the golden store, may closely survey the brilliant cunningly-
wrought gems, that so I may the more tranquilly, after
seeing the treasured wealth, quit my life, and my country,
which I have governed long." Bowls and dishes, a sword
"shot with brass," a standard "all gilded, . . . locked
by strong spells," from which issued "a ray of light,"
are brought to him. He enjoys the sight ; and here,
out of love for his hero, the Christian compiler of the
story, after having allowed him to satisfy so much of
his heathen tastes, prepares him for heaven, and makes
him utter words of gratitude to "the Lord of all, the King
of glory, the eternal Lord" ; which done, Beowulf, a
heathen again, is permitted to order for himself such a
funeral as the Geatas of old were accustomed to : " Rear
a mound, conspicuous after the burning, at the headland
which juts into the sea. That shall, to keep my people
in mind, tower up on Hrones-ness, that seafaring men
may afterwards call it Beowulf's Mound, they who drive
from far their roaring vessels over the mists of the floods."
Wiglaf vainly tries to revive him with water ; and
addressing his unworthy companions, who then only dare
to come out of the wood, expresses gloomy forebodings
as to the future of his country: "Now may the people
expect a time of strife, as soon as the king's fall shall
become widely known to the Franks and Frisians. . .
To us never after [the quarrel in which Higelac died] was
granted the favour of the Merovingians (*Mere- Wioinga*).
Nor do I expect at all any peace or faith from the Swedish
people. . . ." The serpent is thrown "over the wall-cliff;
they let the waves take, the flood close upon, the keeper
of the treasures." A mound is built on the hill, "widely

visible to seafaring men. . . . They placed on the barrow
rings and jewels, . . . they let the earth hold the treasure
of earls, the gold in the sand where it now yet re-
maineth, as useless to men as it [formerly] was." [1]   They
ride about the mound, recounting in their chants the
deeds of the dead : " So mourned the people of the
Geatas, his hearth-companions, for their lord's fall ; said
that he was among world-kings the mildest and the
kindest of men, most gracious to his people and most
desirous of praise."

The ideal of a happy life has somewhat changed since
the days of Beowulf. Then, as we see, happiness consisted in the satisfaction of very simple and primitive
tastes, in fighting well, and after the fight eating and
drinking heartily, and listening to songs and music, and
after the music enjoying a sound sleep. The possession
of many rings, handsome weapons and treasure, was also
indispensable to make up complete happiness ; so much
so that, out of respect towards the chief, some of his rings
and jewels were buried with him, " useless to men," as
the author of " Beowulf " says, not without a touch of
regret. Such was the existence led by those companions
of Hrothgar, who are described as enjoying the happiest
of lives before the appearance of Grendel, and who " knew
no care." All that is tender, and would most arouse the
sensibility of the sensitive men of to-day, is considered
childish, and awakes no echo : " Better it is for every one
that he should avenge his friend than that he should
mourn exceedingly," says Beowulf ; very different from
Roland, the hero of France, he too of Germanic origin,
but living in a different *milieu*, where his soul has been
refined. " When Earl Roland saw that his peers lay

---

[1] According to the account of a Scandinavian burial left by Ahmed Ibn
Fozlan (tenth century, see above, p. 27), the custom was to bury with the dead
ornaments and gold embroideries to the value of a third part of what he left.

dead, and Oliver too, whom he so dearly loved, his heart melted ; he began to weep ; colour left his face."

> Li cons Rodlanz, quant il veit morz ses pers
> Ed Olivier qu'il tant podeit amer,
> Tendror en out, commencet à plorer,
> En son visage fut molt descolorez.[1]

Beowulf crushes all he touches ; in his fights he upsets monsters, in his talks he tumbles his interlocutors headlong. His retorts have nothing winged about them ; he does not use the feathered arrow, but the iron hammer. Hunferth taunts him with not having had the best in a swimming match. Beowulf replies by a strong speech, which can be summed up in few words : liar, drunkard, coward, murderer! It seems an echo from the banqueting hall of the Scandinavian gods ; in the same manner Loki and the goddesses played with words. For the assembled warriors of Hrothgar's court Beowulf goes in nowise beyond bounds ; they are not indignant, they would rather laugh. So did the gods.

Landscape painting in the Anglo-Saxon poems is adapted to men of this stamp. Their souls delight in the bleak boreal climes, the north wind, frost, hail, ice, howling tempest and raging seas, recur as often in this literature as blue waves and sunlit blossoms in the writings of men to whom these exquisite marvels are familiar. Their descriptions are all short, save when they refer to ice or snow, or the surge of the sea. The Anglo-Saxon poets dwell on such sights complacently ; their tongue then is loosened. In " Beowulf," the longest and truest description is that of the abode of the monsters : " They inhabit the dark land, wolf-haunted slopes, windy head-

---

[1] "Chanson de Roland," line 2804.

lands, the rough fen-way, where the mountain stream, under the dark shade of the headlands, runneth down, water under land. It is not far from hence, a mile by measure, that the mere lies ; over it hang groves of [rimy] trees, a wood fast-rooted, [and] bend shelteringly over the water ; there every night may [one] see a dire portent, fire on the flood. No one of the sons of men is so experienced as to know those lake-depths. Though the heath-ranging hart, with strong horns, pressed hard by the hounds, seek that wooded holt, hunted from far, he will sooner give up his life, his last breath on the bank, before he will [hide] his head therein. It is not a holy place. Thence the turbid wave riseth up dark-hued to the clouds, when the wind stirreth up foul weather, until the air grows gloomy, the heavens weep."

The same unchanging genius manifests itself in the national epic, in the shorter songs, and even in the prose chronicles of the Anglo-Saxons. To their excessive enthusiasms succeed periods of complete depression ; their orgies are followed by despair ; they sacrifice their life in battle without a frown, and yet, when the hour for thought has come, they are harassed by the idea of death. Their national religion foresaw the end of the world and of all things, and of the gods even. Listen, once more, to the well-known words of one of them :

" Human life reminds me of the gatherings thou holdest with thy companions in winter, around the fire lighted in the middle of the hall. It is warm in the hall, and outside howls the tempest with its whirlwinds of rain and snow. Let a sparrow enter by one door, and, crossing the hall, escape by another. While he passes through, he is sheltered from the wintry storm ; but this moment of peace is brief. Emerging from the cold, in an instant he disappears from sight, and returns to the cold again. Such is the life of man ; we behold it for a short time, but

what has preceded and what is to follow, we know
not. . . ." [1]

Would not Hamlet have spoken thus, or Claudio?

> Ay, to die and go we know not where;
> To lie in cold obstruction. . . .

Thus spoke, nine centuries before them, an Anglo-Saxon
chief who had arisen in the council of King Eadwine and
advised him, according to Bede, to adopt the religion of
the monks from Rome, because it solved the fearful
problem. In spite of years and change, this anxiety did
not die out; it was felt by the Puritans, and Bunyan, and
Dr. Johnson, and the poet Cowper.

Another view of the problem was held by races imbued
with classical ideas, the French and others; classical equanimity influenced them. Let us not poison our lives by the
idea of death, they used to think, at least before our period;
there is a time for all things, and it will be enough to remember death when its hour strikes. "Mademoiselle," said La
Mousse to the future Madame de Grignan, too careful of
her beautiful hands, "all that will decay." "Yes, but it is
not decayed yet," answered Mademoiselle de Sévigné,
summing up in a single word the philosophy of many
French lives. We will sorrow to-morrow, if need be, and
even then, if possible, without darkening our neighbours'

---

[1] "Talis mihi videtur, vita hominum præsens in terris ad comparationem
ejus, quod nobis incertum est, temporis, quale cum te residente ad cœnam
cum ducibus ac ministris tuis tempore brumali, accenso quidem foco in medio
et calido effecto cœnaculo, furentibus autem foris per omnia turbinibus hiema-
lium pluviarum vel nivium, adveniensque unus passerum, citissime pervolaverit;
qui cum per unum ostium ingrediens, mox per aliud exierit. Ipso quidem
tempore quo intus est, hiemis tempestati non tangitur, sed tamen parvissimo
spatio serenitatis ac momentum excurso, mox de hieme in hiemem regrediens,
tuis oculis elabitur. Ita hæc vita hominum ad modicum apparet; quid autem
sequatur, quidve præcesserit, prorsus ignoramus. Unde si hæc nova doctrina
certius aliquid attulit merito esse sequenda videtur." Bede, "Historia Ecclesiastica gentis Anglorum," Book II. cap. 13, year 627; *infra*, p. 67.

day with any grief of ours. Let us retire from life, as from a drawing-room, discreetly, "as from a banquet," said La Fontaine.[1] And this good grace, which is not indifference, but which little resembles the anguish and enthusiasms of the North, is also in its way the mark of strong minds. For they were not made of insignificant beings, those generations who went to battle and left the world without a sneer or a tear; with ribbons on the shoulder and a smile on the lips.[2]

Examples of Anglo-Saxon poems, either dreamy or warlike, could easily be multiplied. We have the lamentations of the man without a country, of the friendless wanderer, of the forlorn wife, of the patronless singer, of the wave-tossed mariner; and these laments are always associated with the grand Northern landscapes of which little had been made in ancient literatures :

" That the man knows not, to whom on land all falls out most joyfully, how I, miserable and sad on the ice-cold sea, a winter pass'd, with exile traces . . . of dear kindred bereft, hung o'er with icicles, the hail in showers flew; where I heard nought save the sea roaring, the ice-cold wave. At times the swan's song I made to me for pastime . . . night's shadow darken'd, from the north it snow'd, frost bound the land, hail fell on the earth, coldest of grain.

[1] Je voudrais qu'à cet âge,
On sortît de la vie ainsi que d'un banquet,
Remerciant son hôte. (viii. 1.)

[2] Ragnar Lodbrok, thrown among serpents in a pit, defies his enemies, and bids them beware of the revenge of Woden (" Corpus Poeticum Boreale," vol. ii. pp. 341 ff.). In the prisons, at the time of the Terreur, the guillotine was a subject for *chansons*. The mail steamer *la France* caught fire, part of the cargo being gunpowder ; the ship is about to be blown up ; a foreign witness writes thus : " Tous jusqu'aux petits marmitons rivalisaient d'élan, de bravoure et de cette gaieté gauloise dans le péril qui forme un des beaux traits du caractère national." Baron de Hübner, " Incendie du paquebot la France," Paris, 1887. This account was written, according to what the author told me, on the day after the fire was unexpectedly mastered.

. . ." Or, in another song : " Then wakes again the friend-less mortal, sees before him fallow ways, ocean fowls bathing, spreading their wings, rime and snow descending with hail mingled ; then are the heavier his wounds of heart." [1]

There are descriptions of dawn in new and unexpected terms : " The guest slept within until the black raven, blithe-hearted, gave warning of the coming of the heaven's joy, the bright sun, and of robbers fleeing away." [2] Never did the palaces of Rome, the peristyles of Athens, the balconies of Verona, the terraces of Versailles, see morn-ings dawn like unto these, to the raven's merry shriek. The sea of the Anglo-Saxons is not the Mediterranean, washing with its blue waves the marble walls of villas ; it is the North Sea, with its grey billows, bordered by barren shores and chalky cliffs.

---

[1] "Codex Exoniensis," ed. Thorpe, 1842, "Seafarer," p. 306, "Wanderer," p. 291 (new ed. by Gollancz, E. E. T. S., 1895 ff.). See also " Deor the Scald's Complaint," one of the oldest poems in "Codex Exoniensis," the "Wife's Complaint," the "Ruin," also in "Codex Exoniensis " ; the subject of this last poem has been shown by Earle to be probably the town of Bath.

[2] T. Arnold's "Beowulf," p. 118, l. 1800.

CHAPTER IV.

THE CHRISTIAN LITERATURE AND PROSE LITERATURE OF THE ANGLO-SAXONS.

I.

AUGUSTINE, prior of St. Martin of Rome, sent by Gregory the Great, arrived in 597. To the Germanic pirates established in the isle of Britain, he brought a strange teaching. The ideas he tried to spread have become so familiar to us, we can hardly realise the amazement they must have caused. To these fearless warriors who won kingdoms at the point of their spears, and by means of their spears too won their way into Walhalla, who counted on dying one day, not in their beds, but in battle, so that the Valkyrias, "choosers of the slain," might carry them to heaven on their white steeds, to these men came a foreign monk, and said: Be kind ; worship the God of the weak, who, unlike Woden, will reward thee not for thy valour, but for thy mercy.

Such was the seed that Rome, ever life-giving, now endeavoured to sow among triumphant sea-rovers. The notion of the State and the notion of the Church both rose out of the ruins of the Eternal City ; ideas equally powerful, but almost contradictory, which were only to be reconciled after centuries of confusion, and alternate periods of violence and depression. The princes able to foresee the necessary fusion of these two ideas, and who made attempts, however rude, to bring it about were rare, and have remained for ever famous : Charlemagne in France and Alfred the Great in England.

The miracle of conversion was accomplished in the isle, as it had been on the Continent. Augustine baptized King Æthelberht in 597, and celebrated mass in the Roman church of St. Martin, Canterbury. The religion founded by the Child of Bethlehem conquered the savage Saxons, as it had conquered the debauched Romans ; the difficulty and the success were equal in both cases. In the Germanic as in the Latin country, the new religion had to stem the stream ; the Romans of the decadence and the men of the North differed in their passions, but resembled each other in the impetuosity with which they followed the lead of their instincts. To both, the apostle came and whispered : Curb thy passions, be hard upon thyself and merciful to others ; blessed are the simple, blessed are the poor ; as thou forgivest so shalt thou be forgiven ; thou shalt not despise the weak, thou shalt *love* him ! And this unexpected teaching was heard each day, like a counsel and a threat, in the words of the morning prayer, in the sound of the bells, in the music of pious chants.

The conversion was at first superficial and limited to outward practices ; the warrior bent the knee, but his heart remained the same. The spirit of the new religion could not as yet penetrate his soul ; he remained doubtful between old manners and new beliefs, and after fits of repentance and relapses into savagery, the converted chieftain finally left this world better prepared for Walhalla than for Paradise. Those who witnessed his death realised it themselves. When Theodoric the Great died in his palace at Ravenna, piously and surrounded by priests, Woden was seen, actually seen, bearing away the prince's soul to Walhalla.

The new converts of Great Britain understood the religion of Christ much as they had understood that of

Thor. Only a short distance divided man from godhood in heathen times ; the god had his passions and his adventures, he was intrepid, and fought even better than his people. For a long time, as will happen with neophytes, the new Christians continued to seek around them the human god who had disappeared in immensity ; they addressed themselves to him as they had formerly done to the deified heroes, who, having shared their troubles, must needs sympathise with their sorrows. For a long time, contradictory faiths were held side by side. Christ was believed in, but Woden was still feared, and secretly appeased by sacrifices. Kings are obliged to publish edicts, forbidding their subjects to believe in the ancient divinities, whom they now term "demons"; but that does not prevent the monks who compile the "Anglo-Saxon Chronicle" from tracing back the descent of their princes to Woden: if it is not deifying, it is at least ennobling them.[1]

Be your obedience qualified by reason, St. Paul had said. That of the Anglo-Saxons was not so qualified. On the contrary, they believed out of obedience, militarily. Following the prince's lead, all his subjects are converted ; the prince goes back to heathendom ; all his people become heathens again. From year to year, however, the new re-

---

[1] "Hengest and Horsa . . . were the sons of Wihtgils; Wihtgils was the son of Witta, Witta of Wecta, Wecta of Woden. From Woden sprang all our royal kin" (year 449, "Anglo-Saxon Chronicle," Peterborough text). "Penda was the son of Pybba, Pybba of Cryda . . . Wærmund of Wihtlæg, Wihtlæg of Woden" (*Ibid.* : year 626). Asser names Geata "a pagan God" among Alfred's ancestors. Orderic Vital, born in England, and writing in Normandy, in the twelfth century, continues to trace back the descent of the kings of England to Woden : "a quo Angli feriam [iv]^{am} Wodenis diem nuncupant" ("Hist. Eccl.," ed. Le Prevost, vol. iii. p. 161). "Wodenis dies" has become Wednesday ; in the same fashion, and even more characteristically, the feast of the northern goddess Eostra has become "Easter": "Eostur-monath, qui nunc paschalis mensis interpretatur, quondam a dea eorum quæ Eostre vocabatur . . . nomen habuit," Bede, "De Temporum Ratione" in Migne's "Patrologia," xc., col. 357. Similar genealogies occur in Matthew Paris, thirteenth century, "Chronica Majora," vol. i. pp. 188-9, 422 (Rolls).

ligion progresses, while the old is waning; this phenomenon
is brought about, in the south, by the influence of Augustine and the monks from Rome ; and in the north, owing
mainly to Celtic monks from the monastery of Iona,
founded in the sixth century by St. Columba, on the model
of the convents of Ireland. About the middle of the seventh
century the work is nearly accomplished ; the old churches
abandoned by the Romans have been restored ; many
others are built ; one of them still exists at Bradford-on-
Avon in very good state of preservation [1] ; monasteries are
founded, centres of culture and learning.   Some of the rude
princes who reign in the country set great, examples of
devotion to Christ and submission to the Roman pontiff.
They date their charters from the "reign of our Lord Jesus
Christ, reigning for ever." [2]   The Princess Hilda founds, in
the seventh century, the monastery of Streoneshalch, and
becomes its abbess ; Ceadwalla dies at Rome in 689, and is
buried in St. Peter's, under the *Porticus Pontificum,* opposite the tomb of St. Gregory the Great.[3] Æthelwulf, king
of the West Saxons, goes also on a pilgrimage to Rome
"in great state, and remains twelve months, after which he
returns home ; and then Charles, king of the Franks, gave
him his daughter in marriage." [4] He sends his son Alfred
to the Eternal City ; and the Pope takes a liking to the
young prince, who was to be Alfred the Great.

The notion of moderation and measure is unknown to
these enthusiasts, who easily fall into despair.   In the fol-

[1] This unique monument seems to be of the eighth century. *Cf.* "Pre-Con-
quest Churches of Northumbria," an article by C. Hodges in the "Reliquary,"
July, 1893. *Cf.* G. B. Brown, "Arts in Early England," II, 2d ed. 1925.

[2] For example, charter of Offa, dated 793, "Matthæi Parisiensis . . .
Chronica Majora," ed. Luard (Rolls), vol. vi., "Additamenta," pp. 1, 25,
&c. : "Regnante Domino nostro Jesu Christo in perpetuum."

[3] "King Ceadwalla's tomb in the ancient basilica of St. Peter," by Mr.
D. Tesoroni, Rome, 1891, 8vo.

[4] Anglo-Saxon Chronicle, year 855.   The princess was Judith, daughter of
Charles the Bald.   Hincmar, archbishop of Reims, blessed the marriage.

lowing period, after the Norman Conquest, when manners and customs were beginning to change, the chronicler, William of Malmesbury, trying to draw a correct picture of the ancient owners of the land, is struck by the exaggerations of the Saxons' temperament. Great numbers of them are drunkards, they lead dissolute lives, and reign as ferocious tyrants ; great numbers of them, too, are pious, devout, faithful even unto martyrdom : " What shall I say of so many bishops, hermits, and abbots ? The island is rendered famous by the relics of native saints, so numerous that it is impossible to visit a borough of any importance without hearing the name of a new saint. Yet the memory of many has vanished, for lack of writers to preserve it ! " [1]

The taste for proselytism, of which the race has since given so many proofs, is early manifested. Once converted, the Anglo-Saxons produce missionaries, who in their turn carry the glad tidings to their pagan brothers on the Continent, and become saints of the Roman Church. St. Wilfrith leaves Northumberland about 680, and goes to preach the Gospel to the Frisians ; St. Willibrord starts from England about 690, and settles among the Frisians and Danes [2] ; Winfrith, otherwise called St. Boniface (an approximate translation of his name), sojourns in Thuringia and Bavaria, " sowing," as he says, " the evangelical seed among the rude and ignorant tribes of Germany." [3] He reorganises the Church of the Franks, and dies martyrised

---

[1] " Quid dicam de tot episcopis . . . "&c. " Willelmi Malmesbiriensis. . . . Gesta regum Anglorum," ed. Hardy, London, 1840, 2 vols. 8vo, vol. ii. p. 417.

[2] See his will and various documents concerning him in Migne's " Patrologia," vol. lxxxix., col. 535 *et seq.*

[3] " Fraternitatis vestræ pietatem intimis obsecramus precibus ut nos inter feras et ignaras gentes Germaniæ laborantes, vestris sacrosanctis orationibus adjuvemur." Boniface to Cuthberht and others, year 735, in Migne's " Patrologia," vol. lxxxix., col. 735.

by the Frisians in 755. Scarcely is the hive formed when it begins to swarm. The same thing happened with all the sects created later in the English land.

II.

With religion had come Latin letters. Those same Anglo-Saxons, whose literature at the time of their invasion consisted in the songs mentioned by Tacitus, " carmina antiqua," which they trusted to memory alone, who compiled no books and who for written monuments had Runic inscriptions graven on utensils or on commemorative stones, now have, in their turn, monks who compose chronicles, and kings who know Latin. Libraries are formed in the monasteries ; schools are attached to them : manuscripts are there copied and illuminated in beautiful caligraphy and splendid colours. The volutes and knots with which the worshippers of Woden ornamented their fibulæ, their arms, the prows of their ships, are reproduced in purple and azure, in the initials of the Gospels. The use made of them is different, the taste remains the same.

The Anglo-Saxon missionaries and learned men correspond with each other in the language of Rome. Boniface, in the wilds of Germany, remains in constant communication with the prelates and monks of England ; he begs for books, asks for and gives advice ; his letters have come down to us, and are in Latin. Ealhwine or Alcuin, of York, called by Charlemagne to his court, freely bestows, in Latin letters, good advice on his countrymen. He organises around the great Emperor a literary academy, where each bears an assumed name ; Charlemagne has taken that of David, his chamberlain has chosen that of Tyrcis, and Alcuin that of Horatius Flaccus. In this " hôtel de Rambouillet " of the Karlings, the affected style was as much relished as at the fair Arthénice's, and Alcuin, in his barbarous Latin, has a studied elegance that might vie with the conceits of Voiture.[1]

Aldhelm (or Ealdhelm, d. 709) writes a treatise on Latin prosody, and, adding example to precept, composes riddles and a Eulogy of Virgins in Latin verse.[2] Æddi (Eddius Stephanus) writes a life, also in Latin, of his friend St. Wilfrith.[3]

The history of the nation had never been written. On the Continent, and for a time in the island, rough war-songs were the only annals of the Anglo-Saxons. Now they have Latin chronicles, a Latin which Tacitus might have smiled at, but which he would have understood. Above all, they have the work of the Venerable Bede (Bæda), the most important Latin monument of all the Anglo-Saxon period.

Bede was born in Northumbria, about 673, the time when the final conversion of England was being accomplished. He early entered the Benedictine monastery of Jarrow, and remained there till his death. It was a recently founded convent, established by Benedict Biscop, who had enriched it with books brought back from his journeys to Rome. In this retreat, on the threshold of which worldly sounds expired, screened from sorrows, surrounded by disciples who called him " dear master, beloved father,"

---

[1] " Ide) hæc Vestræ Excellentiæ dico . . . ut aliquos ex pueris nostris remittam, qui excipiant nobis necessaria quæque, et revehant in Franciam flores Britanniæ: ut non sit tantummodo in Eborica hortus conclusus, sed in Turonica emissiones Paradisi cum pomorum fructibus, ut veniens Auster perflare hortos Ligeris fluminis et fluant aromata illius . . ." Migne's "Patrologia," vol. c., col. 208. Many among Alcuin's letters are directed to Anglo-Saxon kings whom he does not forbear to castigate, threatening them, if need be, with the displeasure of the mighty emperor : " Ad Offam regem Merciorum ; " " Ad Cœnulvum regem Merciorum," year 796, col. 213, 232.

[2] Works in Migne's "Patrologia," vol. lxxxix. col. 87 *et seq.* They include, besides his poetry ("De laude Virginum," &c.), a prose treatise : " De Laudibus Virginitatis," and other works in prose. He uses alliteration in his Latin poems.

[3] " Vita Sancti Wilfridi episcopi Eboracensis, auctore Eddio Stephano," in Gale's "Historiæ Britannicæ, Saxonicæ, Anglo-Danicæ Scriptores x." Oxford, 1691, 2 vols. fol., vol. i. pp. 50 ff.

Bede allowed the years of his life to glide on, his sole ambition being to learn, write and teach.

The peaceful calm of this sheltered existence, which came to an end before the time of the Danish invasions, is reflected in the writings of Bede. He left a great number of works: interpretations of the Gospels, homilies, letters, lives of saints, works on astronomy, a "De Natura Rerum" where he treats of the elements, of comets, of winds, of the Nile, of the Red Sea, of Etna; a "De Temporibus," devoted to bissextiles, to months, to the week, to the solstice; a "De Temporum Ratione" on the months of the Greeks, Romans, and Angles, the moon and its power, the epact, Easter, &c. He wrote hymns in Latin verse, and a life of St. Cuthberht; lastly, and above all, he compiled in Latin prose, a "Historia ecclesiastica gentis Anglorum,"[1] which has remained the basis of all the histories composed after his. In it Bede shows himself as he was: honest, sincere, sedate, and conscientious. He quotes his authorities which are, for the description of the island and for the most ancient period of his history, Pliny, Solinus, Eutropius, Orosius, Gildas. From the advent of Augustine his work becomes his own; he collects documents, memoranda, testimonies, frequently legends, and publishes the whole without any criticism, but without falsifications. He lacks art, but not honesty.

Latinist though he was, he did not despise the national literature in spite of its ruggedness. He realised it was truly a literature; he made translations in Anglo-Saxon, but they are lost; he was versed in the national poetry, "doctus in nostris carminibus," writes his pupil Cuthberht,[2]

---

[1] Ed. G. H. Moberly, Oxford, 1881; C. Plummer, Oxford, 1896, 2 vols Complete works, Giles, 1843, and in Migne's "Patrologia," vol. xc. ff. *Cf.* Roger, "L'Enseignement des Lettres d'Ausone à Alcuin," Paris, 1905, ch. viii. ff. ; Sandys, "Classical Scholarship," Cambridge, 1903, ch. xxiv.

[2] Letter of Cuthberht, later abbot of Wearmouth and Jarrow, to his friend

who pictures him on his deathbed, muttering Anglo-Saxon verses. He felt the charm of the poetic genius of his nation, and for that reason has preserved and naïvely related the episodes of Cædmon in his stable,[1] and of the Saxon chief comparing human life to the sparrow flying across the banquet hall.

Bede died on the 27th of May, 735, leaving behind him such a renown for sanctity that his bones were the occasion for one of those pious thefts common in the Middle Ages. In the XIth century a priest of Durham removed them to the cathedral of that town, where they remained until the Reformation, when they were scattered. St. Boniface, on receiving the news of this death, far away in Germany, begged his friends in England to send him the works of his compatriot ; the homilies of Bede would assist him, he said, in composing his own, and his commentaries on the Scriptures would be "a consolation in his sorrows."[2]

III.

Anglo-Saxon monks now speak Latin ; some, since the coming of Theodore of Tarsus,[3] even know a little Greek ;

Cuthwine, on the death of Bede, printed with the "Historia Ecclesiastica." Bede is represented, on his death-bed, "in nostra lingua, ut erat doctus in nostris carminibus, dicens de terribili exitu animarum e corpore :

Fore the nei-faerae naenig uuiurthit
Thonc snottura. . . ."

"Ere that forced journey, no one may be more prudent. . . ." "Historia Ecclesiastica," ed. Plummer, I, pp. clx, lxxiv.

Bede had translated the Gospel of St. John, but this work is lost.

[1] See below, p. 70.

[2] Letter of the year 735, "Cuthberto et aliis" ; letter of 736 to Ecgberht, Archbishop of York. He received the books, and expressed his delight at them ; he sent in exchange pieces of cloth to Ecgberht ; letter of the year 742 ; "Patrologia," vol. lxxxix.

[3] Archbishop of Canterbury, seventh century.

an Anglo-Saxon king sleeps at Rome, under the arches of
St. Peter's ; Woden has left heaven ; on the soil convulsed
by so many wars, the leading of peaceful, sheltered lives,
entirely dedicated to study, has become possible : and such
was the case with Bede. Has the nation really changed
and do we find ourselves already in the presence of men
with a partly latinised genius, such men as the English
were hereafter to be? Not yet. The heart and mind
remain the same ; the surface alone is modified, and that
slightly. The full infusion of the Latin element, which is
to transform the Anglo-Saxons into English, will take
place several centuries hence, and will be the result of a
last invasion. The genius of the Teutonic invaders continues nearly intact, and nothing proves this more clearly
than the Christian poetry composed in the native tongue,
and produced in Britain after the conversion. The same
impetuosity, passion, and lyricism, the same magnificent
apostrophes which gave its character to the old pagan
poetry are found again in Christian songs, as well as the
same recurring alternatives of deep melancholy and noisy
exultation.

The Anglo-Saxon poets describe the saints of the
Gospel, and it seems as though the companions of Beowulf
stood again before us : " So, we have learned, in days
of yore, of twelve beneath the stars, heroes gloriously
blessed." These " heroes," these " warriors," are the twelve
apostles. One of them, St. Andrew, arrives in an uninhabited country ; not a desert in Asia, nor a solitude in
Greece ; it might be the abode of Grendel : " Then was
the saint in the shadow of darkness, warrior hard of
courage, the whole night long with various thoughts beset ;
snow bound the earth with winter-casts ; cold grew the
storms, with hard hail-showers ; and rime and frost, the
hoary warriors, locked up the dwellings of men, the settlements of the people ; frozen were the lands with cold

icicles, shrunk the water's might ; over the river streams,
the ice made a bridge, a pale water road." [1]

They have accepted the religion of Rome ; they believe
in the God of Mercy ; they have faith in the apostles
preaching the doctrine of love to the world : peace on
earth to men of good will ! But that warlike race would
think it a want of respect to see in the apostles mere
pacifici, and in the Anglo-Saxon poems they are constantly
termed " warriors."

At several different times these new Christians translated
parts of the Bible into verse, and the Bible became Anglo-
Saxon, not only in language, but in tone and feeling as
well. The first attempt of this kind was made by that
herdsman of the seventh century, named Cædmon, whose
history has been told by Bede. He was so little gifted by
nature that when he sat, on feast days, at one of those
meals " where the custom is that each should sing in turn,
he would leave the table when he saw the harp approaching
and return to his dwelling," unable to find verses to sing
like the others. One night, when the harp had thus put
him to flight, he had, in the stable where he was keeping
the cattle, a vision. " Sing me something," was the command of a mysterious being. " I cannot," he answered,
" and the reason why I left the hall and retired here is that
I cannot sing." " But sing thou must." " What shall I
sing, then ? " " Sing the origin of things." Then came at
once into his mind " excellent verses " ; Bede translates a
few of them, which are very flat, but he generously lays the
fault on his own translation, saying : " Verses, even the
very best, cannot be turned word for word from one
language into another without losing much of their beauty

---

[1] Kemble, " Codex Vercellensis," Ælfric Soc. 1847–56 ; Part I., ll. 1 ff.,
2507 ff. On " Andreas," see Skeat, " Furnivall Miscellany," 408 ; Krapp,
" Andreas and the Fates of the Apostles," Boston, 1906, Introd. The
Vercelli MS. (see Krapp, p. x) has been phototyped by R. Wülker, Leipzig,
1894. *Cf.* above p. 45. A use of acid has defaced a few places.

and dignity," [1] a remark which has stood true these many centuries. Taken to the abbess Hilda, of Streoneshalch, Cædmon roused the admiration of all, became a monk, and died like a saint, "and no one since, in the English race, has ever been able to compose pious poems equal to his, for he was inspired by God, and had learnt nothing of men." Some tried, however.

An incomplete translation of the Bible in Anglo-Saxon verses has come down to us, the work apparently of several authors of different epochs.[2] Cædmon may be one of them : the question has been the cause of immense discussions, and remains doubtful.

The tone is haughty and peremptory in the impassioned parts; abrupt appositions keep the attention fixed upon the main quality of the characters, the one by which they are meant to live in memory ; triumphant accents accompany the tales of war ; the dismal landscapes are described with care, not to say with loving delight. Ethereal personages

[1] "Neque enim possunt carmina, quamvis optime composita ex alia in aliam linguam ad verbum sine detrimento sui decoris ac dignitatis transferri." "Historia Ecclesiastica," book iv. chap. xxiv., ed. Plummer, I, 260.

[2] "Cædmon's metrical paraphrase of parts of the Holy Scripture . . . with translation," by B. Thorpe, Soc. of Antiquaries, 1832. An ed. by Junius (Francis Dujon, born at Heidelberg, d. at Windsor, 1678) had been published at Amsterdam in 1655, and may have been known to Milton (cf. "Cædmon und Milton," by R. Wülker, in "Anglia," vol. iv. p. 401). Junius was the first to attribute this anonymous poem, or rather collection of poems ("Genesis," "Exodus," "Daniel," "Christ and Satan ") to Cædmon. "Genesis" is made up of two different versions of different dates, clumsily put together. German critics, and especially Prof. Ed. Sievers ("Der Heliand," Halle, 1875), have conclusively shown that lines 1 to 234, and 852 to the end, belong to the same and older version ; lines 235 to 851, inserted without much care, as they retell part of the story to be found also in the older version, are of a more recent date, and show a strong resemblance to the old Germanic poem "Heliand" (Healer, Saviour) in alliterative verse, of the ninth century Cf Bradley, "The Cædmonian Genesis," in "Essays by Members of the Engl. Assn.," VI.

Another biblical story was paraphrased in Anglo-Saxon verse, and was the subject of the beautiful poem of "Judith," preserved in the same MS. as "Beowulf." Grein's "Bibliothek," i., and ed. A. S. Cook, Boston, 1903.

become in this popular Bible tangible realities. The fiend approaches Paradise with the rude wiles of a peasant. Before starting he takes a helmet, and fastens it tightly on his head. He presents himself to Adam as coming from God : " The all-powerful above will not have trouble himself, that on this journey he should come, the Lord of men, but he his vassal sendeth." [1]

Hell, the deluge, the corruption of the grave, the last judgment, the cataclysms of nature, are favourite subjects with these poets. Inward sorrows, gnawing thoughts that " besiege " men, doubts, remorse, gloomy landscapes, all afford them abundant inspiration. Satan in his hell has fits of anguish and hatred, and the description of his tortures seems a rude draft of Milton's awful picture.

Cynewulf,[2] one of the few poets of the Anglo-Saxon period known by name, and the greatest of all, feels the pangs of despair ; and then rises to ecstasies, moved by religious love ; he speaks of his return to Christ with a passionate fervour, foreshadowing the great conversions of the Puritan epoch. He ponders over his thoughts " in the narrowness of night. . . . I was stained with my deeds,

---

[1] " Metrical Paraphrase," pp. 29 ff.

[2] Four poems have come down to us signed by means of an acrostic on the Runic letters of his name : " Elene " (on the finding of the cross), " Fates of the Apostles " (both in " Codex Vercellensis "), "Juliana " and " Christ " (in " Codex Exoniensis "; " Christ," ed. Gollancz, London, 1892, or A. S. Cook, Boston, 1900). Many other poems, and even the whole of " Codex Vercellensis," have been attributed to him. The eighty-nine riddles of " Codex Exoniensis," some of which continue to puzzle the readers of our day, are also considered by some as his : one of the riddles is said to contain a charade on his name, but there are doubts ; ample discussions have taken place, and authorities disagree : " The eighty-sixth riddle, which concerns a wolf and a sheep, was related," said Dietrich, "to Cynewulf;" but Professor Morley considers that this same riddle " means the overcoming of the Devil by the hand of God." Stopford Brooke, " Early English Literature," chap. xxii. Many of those riddles were adapted from the Latin of Aldhelm and others. This sort of poetry enjoyed great favour, as the Scandinavian " Corpus Poeticum " also testifies. What is " Men's damager, words' hinderer, and yet words' arouser?" —" Ale." " Corpus Poeticum," i. p. 87.

bound by my sins, buffeted with sorrows, bitterly bound, with misery encompassed. . . ." Then the cross appears to him in the depths of heaven, surrounded by angels, sparkling with jewels, flowing with blood. A sound breaks through the silence of the firmament; life has been given to "the best of trees," and it speaks: "It was long ago, yet I remember it, that I was cut down, at the end of a wood, stirred from my sleep." The cross is carried on the top of a mountain: "Then the young hero made ready, that was Almighty God. . . . I trembled when the champion embraced me." [1]

The poem in which St. Andrew figures as a "warrior bold in war," attributed also to the same Cynewulf, is filled by the sound of the sea; all the sonorities of the ocean are heard, with the cadence and the variety of the ancient Scandinavian sagas; a multitude of picturesque and living expressions designate a ship: "Foamy-necked it fareth, likest unto a bird it glideth over ocean;" it follows the path of the swans, and of the whales, borne by the ocean stream "to the rolling of the waters . . . the clashing of the sea-streams . . . the clash of the waves." The sea of these poets, contrary to what Tacitus thought, was not a slumbering sea; it quivers, it foams, it sings.

St. Andrew decides to punish by a miracle the wild

[1] "Elene," in "Codex Vercellensis," II. 73 (or ed. Kent, Boston, 1889), and "Holy Rood" (this last of doubtful authorship), *ibid.* 84 ff., or ed. Cook, Oxford, 1905. Lines resembling some of the verses in "Holy Rood" have been found engraved in Runic letters on the cross at Ruthwell, Scotland; "Vetusta Monumenta," iv. 54; see G. Stephens, "The Old Northern Runic Monuments of Scandinavia and England," London, 1866–8, i. 405 ff., J. K. Hewison, "Runic Roods," Glasgow, 1914. Resemblances have also been pointed out, showing the frequence of such poetical figures, with the Anglo-Saxon inscription of a reliquary preserved at Brussels: "Rood is my name, I once bore the rich king, I was wet with dripping blood." The reliquary contains a piece of the true cross, which is supposed to speak these words. The date is believed to be about 1100. H. Logeman, "l'Inscription Anglo-Saxonne du reliquaire de la vraie croix au trésor de l'église des SS. Michel et Gudule," Gand, Paris and London, 1891, 8vo (with facsimile), pp. 7 and 11.

inhabitants of the land of Mermedonia. We behold, as in the Northern sagas, an impressive scene, and a fantastic landscape : " He saw by the wall, wondrous fast upon the plain, mighty pillars, columns standing driven by the storm, the antique works of giants. . . .

" Hear thou, marble stone ! by the command of God, before whose face all creatures shall tremble, . . . now let from thy foundation streams bubble out . . . a rushing stream of water, for the destruction of men, a gushing ocean ! . . .

" The stone split open, the stream bubbled forth ; it flowed over the ground, the foaming billows at break of day covered the earth. . . ."

The sleeping warriors are awakened by this "bitter service of beer." They attempt to "fly from the yellow stream, they would save their lives in mountain caverns " ; but an angel " spread abroad over the town pale fire, hot warlike floods," and barred them the way ; " the waves waxed, the torrents roared, fire-sparks flew aloft, the flood boiled with its waves ; " on all sides were heard groans and the " death-song." [1] Let us stop ; but the poet continues ; he is enraptured at the sight ; no other description is so minutely drawn. Ariosto did not find a keener delight in describing with leisurely pen the bower of Alcina.

The religious poets of the Anglo-Saxons open the graves ; the idea of death haunts them as much as it did their pagan ancestors ; they look intently at the " black creatures, grasping and greedy," and follow the process of decay to the end. They address the impious dead : " It would have been better for thee very much . . . that thou hadst been created a bird, or a fish in the sea, or

---

[1] " Codex Vercellensis," part i. pp. 29, 86 ff. " Andreas " is imitated from a Greek story of St. Andrew, of which some Latin version was probably known to the Anglo-Saxon poet. It was called " Πράξεις 'Ανδρέου καὶ Ματθαίου ; " a copy of it is preserved in the National Library, Paris, Greek MS. 881, fol. 348.

like an ox upon the earth hadst found thy nurture going in the field, a brute without understanding ; or in the desert of wild beasts the worst, yea, though thou hadst been of serpents the fiercest, then as God willed it, than thou ever on earth shouldst become a man, or ever baptism should receive." [1]

> . . . This soul should fly from me,
> And I be changed into some brutish beast.
> All beasts are happy, for when they die
> Their souls are soon dissolved in elements. . . .
> O soul ! be changed into small water-drops,
> And fall into the ocean ; ne'er be found.

So will, unknown to him, the very same thoughts be expressed by an English poet of a later day. [2]

Dialogues are not rare in these poems; but they generally differ very much from the familiar dialogue of the Celts. They are mostly epic in character, lyric in tone ; with abrupt apostrophes causing the listener to start, like the sudden sound of a trumpet. When the idea is more fully developed the dialogue becomes a succession of discourses, full of eloquence and power sometimes, but still discourses. We are equally far in both cases from the conversational style so frequent in the Irish stories. [3]

---

[1] "Departed Soul's Address to the Body," " Codex Vercellensis," II. 104.

[2] Marlowe's " Dr. Faustus." See also, " Be Domes Dæge," a poem on the terrors of judgment (ed. Lumby, Early English Text Society, 1876). *Cf.* the long and eloquent description of St. Guthlac's death, "Cod. Exon." II.

[3] See examples of such dialogues and speeches in "Andreas " ; " The Holy Rood" (in "Cod. Vercell."); in Cynewulf's "Christ" ("Cod. Exoniensis"), &c. In this last poem occurs one of the few examples we have of familiar dialogue in Anglo-Saxon (a dialogue between Mary and Joseph, the tone of which recalls the Mysteries of a later date) ; but it seems to be "derived from an undiscovered hymn arranged for recital by half choirs." Gollancz, "Christ," Introd., p. xxi. Another example consists in the scene of the temptation in *Genesis* (*Cf.* "S. Aviti . . . Viennensis Opera," Paris, 1643 p. 230). See also the prose "Dialogue of Salomon and Saturnus " (Kemble, Ælfric Society, 1848, 8vo), an adaptation of a work of eastern origin, popular on the Continent, and the fame of which lasted all through the Middle

The devotional poetry of the Anglo-Saxons includes translations of the Psalms,[1] lives of saints, maxims, moral poems, and symbolic ones, where the supposed habits of animals are used to illustrate the duties of Christians. One of this latter sort has for its subject the whale "full of guile," another the panther [2]; a third (incomplete) the partridge; a fourth, by a different hand, and evincing a very different sort of poetical taste, the phenix. This poem is the only one in the whole range of Anglo-Saxon literature in which the warmth and hues of the south are preserved and sympathetically described. It is a great change to find a piece of some length with scarcely any frost in it, no stormy waves and north wind. The poet is himself struck by the difference, and notices that it is not at all there "as here with us," for there "nor hail nor rime on the land descend, nor windy cloud." In the land of the phenix there is neither rain, nor cold, nor too great heat, nor steep mountains, nor wild dales; there are no cares, and no

Ages and the Renaissance; it was well known to Rabelais: "Qui ne s'adventure n'a cheval ni mule, ce dict Salomon.—Qui trop s'adventure perd cheval 'et mule respondit Malcon." "Vie de Gargantua." Saturnus plays the part of the Malcon or Marcol of the French version; the Anglo-Saxon text is a didactic treatise, cut into questions and answers : " Tell me the substance of which Adam the first man was made.—I tell thee of eight pounds by weight.—Tell me what they are called.—I tell thee the first was a pound of earth," &c. (p. 181).

[1] MS. Lat. 8824 in the Paris Nation. Libr., Lat. and A.-S., part in prose; some pen-and-ink drawings ;—"Ce livre est au duc de Berry—Jehan." It has been published by Thorpe: "Libri Psalmorum, cum paraphrasi Anglo-Saxonica," London, 1835; the prose part alone by J. W. Bright and others, "West Saxon Psalms," Boston, 1907. See also "Eadwine's Canterbury psalter" (Latin and Anglo-Saxon), ed. F Harsley, E.E T.S., 1889 ff., 8vo.

[2] In "Codex Exoniensis." Series of writings of this kind enjoyed at an early date a wide popularity ; they were called " Physiologi "; there are some in nearly all the languages of Europe, also in Syriac, Arabic, Ethiopian, &c. The original seems to have been composed in Greek, at Alexandria, in the second century of our era (F. Lauchert, "Geschichte des Physiologus," Strasbourg, 1889, 8vo). To the " Physiologi" succeeded in the Middle Ages "Bestiaries," works of the same sort, also very numerous and very popular. A number of commonplace sayings or beliefs, which have survived up to our day (the faithfulness of the dove, the fatherly love of the pelican), are derived from "Bestiaries."

sorrows. But there the plains are evergreen, the trees always bear fruit, the plants are covered with flowers. It is the home of the peerless bird. His eyes turn to the sun when it rises in the east, and at night he " looks earnestly when shall come up gliding from the east over the spacious sea, heaven's beam." He sings, and men never heard anything so exquisite. His note is more beautiful than the sound of the human voice, than that of trumpets and horns, than that of the harp, than " any of those sounds that the Lord has created for delight to men in this sad world."

When he grows old, he flies to a desert place in Syria. Then, "when the wind is still, the weather is fair, clear heaven's gem holy shines, the clouds are dispelled, the bodies of waters stand still, when every storm is lull'd under heaven, from the south shines nature's candle warm," the bird begins to build itself a nest in the branches, with forest leaves and sweet-smelling herbs. As the heat of the sun increases " at summer's tide," the perfumed vapour of the plants rises, and the nest and bird are consumed. There remains something resembling a fruit, out of which comes a worm, that develops into a bird with gorgeous wings. Thus man, in harvest-time, heaps grains in his dwelling, before " frost and snow, with their predominance earth deck, with winter weeds." From these seeds in springtime, as out of the ashes of the phenix, will come forth living things, stalks bearing fruits, "earth's treasures." Thus man, at the hour of death, renews his life, and receives at God's hands youth and endless joy.[1]

[1] " Codex Exoniensis," pp. 197 ff. This poem is a paraphrase of a " Carmen de Phœnice" attributed to Lactantius, filled with conceits in the worst taste:

> Mors illi venus est ; sola est in morte voluptas :
> Ut possit nasci hæc appetit ante mori.
> Ipsa sibi proles, suus est pater et suus hæres.
> Nutrix ipsa sui, semper alumna sibi ;
> Ipsa quidem, sed non eadem, quæ est ipsa nec ipsa est. . . .

"Incerti auctoris Phœnix, Lactantio tributus," in Migne's " Patrologia," vol. vii. col. 277. A. S. Cook, "Elene, Phœnix, Physiologus," 1919.

There are, doubtless, rays of light in Anglo-Saxon literature, which appear all the more brilliant for being surrounded by shadow; but this example of a poem sunny throughout is unique. To find others, we must wait till Anglo-Saxon has become English literature.

IV.

Besides their Latin writings and their devotional poems, the converted Anglo-Saxons produced many prose works in their national tongue. Germanic England greatly differed in this from Germanic France. In the latter country the language of the Franks does not become acclimatised; they see it themselves, and feel the impossibility of resisting; Latin, is in general use, they have their national law written in Latin, *Lex Salica.* The popular speech, which will later become the French language, is nothing but a Latin *patois*, and is not admitted to the honour of being written. Notwithstanding all the care with which archives have been searched, no specimens of French prose have been discovered for the whole time corresponding to the Anglo-Saxon period save one or two short fragments.[1] With the Anglo-Saxons, laws,[2] chronicles, and sermons for the common people were written in the national tongue; and, as Latin

[1] The most important of which is the famous Strasbourg pledge, February 19, 842, preserved by the contemporary historian Nithard. See "Les plus anciens monuments de la langue française," by Gaston Paris, Société des anciens Textes, 1875, fol.

[2] Thorpe, "Ancient Laws and Institutes of England," London, 1840, 1 vol. fol.; laws of Ina, king of Wessex, 688–726, of Alfred (with an important Introd. by him), Æthelstan, &c. We have also quantities of deeds and charters, in Latin and in Anglo-Saxon. See J. M. Kemble, "Codex Diplomaticus Ævi Saxonici," English Historical Society, 1839–40, 6 vols.; De Gray Birch, "Cartularium Saxonicum, or a Collection of Charters relating to Anglo-Saxon History," London, 1885 ff., 4to; Earle, "A Handbook to the Land Charters, and other Saxonic Documents," Oxford, 1888.

was only understood by few, to these monuments was added a series of translations.[1] The English country can thus pride itself upon a literature which for antiquity is unparalleled in Europe.

The chief promoter of the art of prose was that Alfred (or Aelfred) whom Pope Leo IV. had adopted as a spiritual son, and who reigned over the West Saxons from 871 to 901. Between the death of Bede and the accession of Alfred, a great change had occurred in the island; towards the end of the eighth century a new foe had appeared, the Scandinavian invader. Stormy days have returned, the flood-gates have reopened; human torrents sweep the land, and each year spread further and destroy more. In vain the Anglo-Saxon kings, and in France the successors of Charlemagne, annually purchase their departure, thus following the example of falling Rome. The northern hordes come again in greater numbers, allured by the ransoms, and they carry home such quantities of English coins that "at this day larger hoards of Æthelred the Second's coins have been found in the Scandinavian countries than in our own, . . . and the national museum at Stockholm is richer in this series than our own national collection."[2] These men, termed Danes, Northmen, or Normans, by the Anglo-Saxon and French chroniclers, reap-

---

[1] Translations of scientific treatises such as the "De Natura Rerum" of Bede, made in the tenth century (Wright's "Popular Treatises on Science," 1841, 8vo); various treatises published by Cockayne, "Leechdoms, Wortcunnings and Starcraft . . . being a Collection of Documents . . . illustrating the History of Science . . . before the Norman Conquest," 1864, 3 vols. 8vo (Rolls).—"Three Old English Prose Texts," among which a version of the famous "Epistola Alexandri ad Aristotelem," ed. S. Rypins, E.E.T.S., 1924; transl. of the history of "Apollonius of Tyre" (Thorpe, London, 1834, 12mo). —Translations by King Alfred and his bishops, see below pp. 81 ff. The monuments of Anglo-Saxon prose have been collected by Grein, "Bibliothek der Angelsächsischen Prosa," ed. Wülker, Cassel, 1872 ff.

[2] Grueber and Keary, "A Catalogue of English Coins in the British Museum," Anglo-Saxon series, vol. ii. 1893, 8vo, p. lxxxi.

peared each year; then, like the Germanic pirates of the fifth century, spared themselves the trouble of useless journeys, and remained in the proximity of plunder, settling first on the coasts, then in the interior. We find them established in France about the middle of the ninth century; in England they winter in Thanet for the first time in 851, and after that do not leave the country. The small Anglo-Saxon kingdoms, alive only to local interests, and unable to unite in a common resistance, are for them an easy prey. The Scandinavians move about at their ease, sacking London and the other towns. They renew their ravages at regular intervals, as men would go fishing at the proper season.[1] They are designated throughout the land by a terribly significant word: "the Army." When the Anglo-Saxon chronicles make mention of "the Army" the northern vikings are always meant, not the defenders of the country. Monasteries are burnt by the invaders with no more remorse than if they were peasants' huts; the vikings do not believe in Christ. Once more, and for the last time, Woden has worshippers in Britain.

Harassed by the Danes, having had to flee and disappear and hide himself, Alfred, after a long period of reverses, resumed the contest with a better chance, and succeeded in setting limits to the Scandinavian incursions. England was divided in two parts, the north belonging to the Danes, and the south to Alfred, with Winchester for his capital.[2]

In the tumult caused by these new wars, what the

---

[1] According to evidence derived from place-names, the Danish invaders have left their strongest mark in Yorkshire and Lincolnshire, and after that in "Leicestershire, Rutland, Nottingham, and East Anglia." Keary, "Vikings in Western Christendom," 1891, p. 353. *Cf.* Allen Mawrer, "Place-names of Northumberland and Durham," Cambridge, 1921.

[2] Peace of Wedmore, sworn by Alfred and Guthrum the Dane, 878. The text has been preserved and figures among the laws of Alfred.

Saxons had received of Roman culture had nearly all been swept away. Books had been burnt, clerks had forgotten their Latin ; the people were relapsing by degrees into barbarism. Formerly, said Alfred, recalling to mind the time of Bede and Alcuin, " foreigners came to this land in search of wisdom and instruction, and we should now have to get them from abroad if we wanted to have them." He does not believe there existed south of the Thames, at the time of his accession, a single Englishman " able to translate a letter from Latin into English. When I considered all this, I remembered also how I saw, before it had been all ravaged and burnt, how the churches throughout the whole of England stood filled with treasures and books, and there was also a great multitude of God's servants, but they had very little knowledge of the books, for they could not understand anything of them, because they were not written in their own language." It is a great wonder that men of the preceding generation, " good and wise men who were formerly all over England," wrote no translation. There can be but one explanation : " They did not think that men would ever be so careless, and that learning would so decay." Still the case is not absolutely hopeless, for there are many left who " can read English writing." Remembering which, " I began, among other various and manifold troubles of this kingdom, to translate into English the book which is called in Latin Pastoralis, and in English Shepherd's Book (' Hirdeboc '), sometimes word for word, and sometimes according to the sense, as I had learnt it from Plegmund my archbishop, and Asser my bishop, and Grimbold my mass-priest, and John my mass-priest." [1] These learned men, and especially the Welsh-

---

[1] H. Sweet, " King Alfred's West-Saxon version of Gregory's Pastoral Care," E.E.T.S., 1871–72, 8vo, pp. 2 *et seq.* Plegmund was an Anglo-Saxon, Asser a Welshman (author of " De Rebus gestis Ælfredi," ed. Stevenson, 1904), Grimbold a Frank, John a Saxon from continental Saxony.

man Asser, who was to Alfred what Alcuin was to Charlemagne, helped him to spread learning by means of translations and by founding schools. They explained to him the hard passages, to the best of their understanding, which it is true was not always perfect.

Belonging to the Germanic race by his blood, and to the Latin realm by his culture, keeping as much as he could the Roman ideal before his eyes, Alfred evinced during all his life that composite genius, at once practical and passionate, which was to be, after the Norman Conquest, the genius of the English people. He was thus an exceptional man, and showed himself a real Englishman before the time. Forsaken by all, his destruction being, as it seemed, a question of days, he does not yield ; he bides his time, and begins the fight again when the day has come. His soul is at once noble and positive ; he does not busy himself with learning out of vanity or curiosity or for want of a pastime ; he wishes to gather from books substantial benefits for his nation and himself. In his wars he remembers the ancients, works upon their plans, and finds that they answer well. He chooses, in order to translate them, books likely to fill up the greatest gaps in the minds of his countrymen, "some books which are most needful for all men to know,"[1] the book of Orosius, which will be for them as a handbook of universal history ; the Ecclesiastical History of Bede, that will instruct them concerning their own past. He teaches laymen their duties with the "Consolation" of Boethius, and ecclesiastics with the Pastoral Rule of St. Gregory.[2]

[1] Preface of Gregory's "Pastoral Care."

[2] King Alfred's "Orosius," ed. H. Sweet, E.E.T.S., 1883. Orosius, a Spaniard, wrote at the beginning of the fifth century. "King Alfred's . . . version of Boethius," ed. Fox, 1864, or Sedgefield, Oxford, 1899-1900. "King Alfred's West-Saxon vers. of Gregory's Pastoral Care," ed. Sweet, E.E.T.S., 1871-2. This last is the most faithful of Alfred's translations ; he attached great importance to the work, and sent a copy of it to all his bishops.

His sole aim being to instruct, he does not hesitate to curtail his authors when their discourses are useless or too long, to comment upon them when obscure, to add passages when his own knowledge allows him. In his translation of Bede, he sometimes contents himself with the titles of the chapters, suppressing the rest; in his Orosius he supplements the description of the world by details he has collected himself concerning those regions of the North which had a national interest for his compatriots. He notes down, as accurately as he can, the words of a Scandinavian whom he had seen, and who had undertaken a voyage of discovery, the first journey towards the pole of which an account has come down to us :

"Ohthere told his lord, king Alfred, that he dwelt north-most of all Northmen. He said that he dwelt in the land to the northward, along the west sea.[1] He said, however, that that land is very long north from thence, but it is all waste, except in a few places where the Fins here and there dwell, for hunting in the winter, and in the summer for fishing in that sea. He said that he was desirous to try, once on a time, how far that country extended due north; or whether any one lived to the north of the waste. He then went due north, along the country, leaving all the way, the waste land on the right, and the wide sea on the left, for three days: he was as far north as the whale-hunters go at the farthest. Then he proceeded in his course due north as far as he could sail within another three days. Then the land there inclined due east, or the sea into the land, he knew not which; but he knew that he there waited for a west wind, or a little north, and sailed thence eastward along that land, as far as he could

The copy of Werferth, bishop of Worcester, is preserved in the Bodleian Library. "The O.E. version of Bede's Ecclesiast. Hist, of the Engl. People," ed. Miller, E.E.T.S., 1890. "K. Alfred's version of St. Augustine's Soliloquies," ed. Hargrove, New York, 1902. The authenticity of the two last is doubtful.

[1] The sea to the west of Norway, that is the German Ocean.

sail in four days." He arrived at a place where the land
turned to the south, evidently surrounding the White Sea,
and he found a broad river, doubtless the Dwina, that he
dared not cross on account of the hostility of the inhabitants.
This was the first tribe he had come across since his departure ; he had only seen here and there some Fins,
hunters and fishers. " He went thither chiefly, in addition
to seeing the country, on account of the walruses, because
they have very good bone in their teeth ; some of those
teeth they brought to the king ; and their hides are very
good for ship ropes." Ohthere, adds Alfred, was very rich ;
he had six hundred tame reindeer ; he said the province
he dwelt in was called Helgoland, and that no one lived
north of him.[1] The traveller gave also some account of
lands more to the south, and even more interesting for his
royal listener, namely Jutland, Seeland, and Sleswig, that
is, as Alfred is careful to notice, the old mother country :
" In these lands the Angles dwelt, before they came hither
to this land."

When he has to deal with a Latin author, Alfred uses as
much liberty. He takes the book that the adviser of
Theodoric the Great, Boethius, had composed while in
prison, and in which we see a personified abstraction,
Wisdom, bringing consolation to the unfortunate man
threatened with death. No work was more famous in the
Middle Ages ; it helped to spread the taste for abstract
personages, owing to which so many shadows, men-virtues
and men-vices, were to tread the boards of the mediæval
stage, and the strange plays called *Moralities* were to enjoy
a long-lived popularity. The first in date of the numerous
translations made of Boethius is that of Alfred.

---

[1] To-day Helgeland, in the northern part of Norway. Alfred's " Orosius,"
Thorpe's translation, printed with the " Life of Alfred the Great," by Pauli,
in Bohn's Antiquarian Library, pp. 249 ff. ; Anglo-Saxon text in Sweet,
"King Alfred's Orosius," 1883, p, 17. Alfred adds the account of yet
another journey, undertaken by Wulfstan.

Under his pen, the vague Christianity of Boethius[1] becomes a naïve and superabundant faith; each episode is moralised; the affected elegance of the model disappears, and gives place to an almost childlike and yet captivating sincerity. The story of the misfortunes of Orpheus, written by Boethius in a very pretentious style, has in Alfred's translation a charm of its own, the charm of the wild flower.

Among the innumerable versions of this tale, the king's is certainly the one in which art has the least share, and in which emotion is most communicative: "It happened formerly that there was a harper in the country called Thrace, which was in Greece. The harper was inconceivably good. His name was Orpheus. He had a very excellent wife who was called Eurydice. Then began men to say concerning the harper that he could harp so that the woods moved, and the stones stirred themselves at the sound, and the wild beasts would run thereto, and stand as if they were tame; so still that though men or hounds pursued them, they shunned them not. Then said they that the harper's wife should die, and her soul should be led to hell. Then should the harper become so sorrowful that he could not remain among other men, but frequented the wood, and sat on the mountain both day and night, weeping and harping, so that the woods shook, and the rivers stood still, and no hart shunned any lion, nor hare any hound; nor did cattle know any hatred, or any fear of others, for the pleasure of the sound. Then it seemed to the harper that nothing in this world pleased him. Then thought he that he would seek the gods of hell and endeavour to allure them with his harp, and pray that they would give him back his wife."

---

[1] The researches of Usener have placed beyond a doubt that Boethius (d. 525) was a Christian: but Christianity is scarcely visible in the "Consolatio," which is entirely "inspirée d'Aristote et de Platon." Gaston Paris, *Journal des Savants*, 1884, p. 576.

He goes down to the nether region ; at the sweetness of his harping, Cerberus " began to wag his tail." Cerberus was " the dog of hell; he had three heads." " A very horrible gatekeeper," Charon by name, " had also three heads," according to the calculation of Alfred, whose mythology is not very safe. Charon welcomes the harper, " because he was desirous of the unaccustomed sound " ; all sufferings cease at the melody of the harp ; the wheel of Ixion ceases to turn ; the hunger of Tantalus is appeased ; the vulture ceases to torment King Tityus ; and the prayer of Orpheus is granted.

" But men can with difficulty, if at all, restrain love ! " Orpheus retraces his steps, and, contrary to his promise, looks behind and stretches his hand towards the beloved shadow, and the shadow fades away. Moral—for with Alfred everything has a moral—when going to Christ, never look behind, for fear of being beguiled by the tempter : a practical conclusion not to be found in Boethius.[1]

Following the king's example, the bishops and monks set to work again. Werferth, bishop of Worcester, translates the famous dialogues of St. Gregory, filled with miracles and marvellous tales.[2] In the monasteries the old national Chronicles, written in the Anglo-Saxon tongue, are copied, corrected, and continued. These Chronicles existed before Alfred, but they were instilled with a new life owing to his influence. Seven of them have come down to us.[3] It is

[1] S. Fox, " King Alfred's Boethius," chap. xxxv. (*Cf.* Sedgefield, II. 116.)

[2] " Bischofs Wærferth Ubersetzung der Dialoge Gregors des Grossen," ed. Hecht, 1900–7, 2 vols. In Earle, a detailed account of it with Alfred's preface, " Anglo-Saxon Literature," 1884, pp. 193 ff.

[3] These seven Chronicles, more or less complete, and differing more or less from one another, are the chronicles of Winchester, St. Augustine of Canterbury, Abingdon, Worcester, Peterborough, the bilingual chronicle of Canterbury, and the Canterbury edition of the Winchester chronicle. They begin at various dates, the birth of Christ, the crossing of Cæsar to Britain, &c., and usually come down to the eleventh century. The Peterborough text alone continues

not yet history; events are registered in succession, usually without comment; kings ascend the throne and they are killed; bishops are driven from their seats, a storm destroys the crops; the monk notes all these things, and does not add a word showing what he thinks of them.[1] He writes as a recorder, chary of words. The reader's feelings will be moved by the deeds registered, not by the words used. Of kings the chronicler will often say, "he was killed," without any observation: "And king Osric was killed. . . . And king Selred was killed. . . ." Why say more? it was an everyday occurrence; there was nothing curious about it. But a comet is not seen every day; a comet is worth describing: "678.—In this year, the star [called] comet appeared in August, and shone for three months every morning like sunbeam. And bishop Wilfrith was driven from his bishopric by king Ecgferth." We are far from the art of Gibbon or Carlyle. Few monuments, however, are more precious than those old annals.; for no people in Europe can pride itself on having chronicles so ancient written in its national language.

"Every craft and every power," said Alfred once, speaking then his own mind, "soon becomes old and is passed over in silence, if it be without wisdom. . . . This is now especially to be said, that I wished to live honourably whilst I lived, and, after my life, to leave to the men who

as late as the year 1154. The Peterborough and Winchester versions are the most important; both have been published by Plummer and Earle, "Two of the Saxon Chronicles," Oxford, 1892 ff. The seven texts have been printed by Thorpe, with a translation, "The Anglo-Saxon Chronicle," 1861, 2 vols 8vo (Rolls). The Winchester chronicle contains the poems on the battle of Brunanburh (*supra*, p. 46), the accession of Edgar, &c.; the MS. is preserved in the library of Corpus Christi, Cambridge; the Peterborough MS. is in the Bodleian Library (Laud, 636). New transl. by E. E. C. Gomme, 1909.

[1] Except in some very rare cases. For example, year 897: "Thanks be to God, the Army had not utterly broken up the Angle race." Comments are more frequent in the latter portions of the Chronicles, especially at the time of and after the Norman invasion.

were after me my memory in good works." [1]   It happened
as he had wished.   Long after his death, his influence was
still felt ; he was the ideal his successors strove to attain
to ; even after the Norman Conquest he continued to be :
" Englene herde, Englene derling." [2]

V.

Alfred disappears ; disturbances begin again ; then, in
the course of the tenth century, comes a fresh period of
comparative calm.   Edgar is on the throne, and the archbishop St. Dunstan rules under his name.[3]

Helped by Bishop Æthelwold, Dunstan resumed the
never-ending and ever-threatened task of teaching the
people and clergy ; he endowed monasteries, and like
Alfred created new schools and encouraged the translation
of pious works.   Under his influence collections of sermons
in the vulgar tongue were formed.[4]   Several of these
collections have come down to us : one of them, the
Blickling Homilies (from Blickling Hall, Norfolk, where
the manuscript was found), was compiled before 971 [5] ;
others are due to the celebrated monk Ælfric, who became
abbot of Eynsham in 1005, and wrote most of his works

---

[1] S. Fox, " King Alfred's Boethius," London, 1864, 8vo, chap. xvii. p. 61.
This chapter corresponds only to the first lines of chap. vii. book ii. of the
original.   Most of it is added by Alfred, who gives in it his opinion of the
" craft " of a king, and of the " tools " necessary for the same.

[2] In the " Proverbs of Alfred," an apocryphal compilation made after the
Norman Conquest ; with Kemble's " Dialogue of Salomon," 1848.

[3] King from 959 to 975 ; St. Dunstan, archbishop of Canterbury, died in
988.   See Stubbs, " Memorials of St. Dunstan " (Rolls Series).

[4] Connected with this movement are the translations of the Gospels : Skeat,
"The Gospels in Anglo-Saxon," Cambridge, 1871-87, 4 vols. ; "The Gospels
in West Saxon," ed. J. W. Bright, Boston, 1904-6 ; "The Gospel of Nico-
demus," ed. Hulne, "Publ. Mod. Lang. Assn. of America," xiii, 457.

[5] See "Blickling homilies," XI., ed. R. Morris, 1874 ff., E.E.T.S.   *Cf.*
the sermons, and the prose " Guthlac," in " Codex Vercellensis."

about this time [1] ; another collection includes the sermons of Wulfstan, bishop of York from 1002 to 1023.[2]

These sermons, most of which are translated from the Latin, "sometimes word for word and sometimes sense for sense," according to the example set by Alfred, were destined for "the edification of the ignorant, who knew no language" except the national one.[3]

The congregation being made up mostly of rude, uneducated people, must be interested in order that it may listen to the sermons ; the homilies are therefore filled with legendary information concerning the Holy Land, with minute pictures of the devil and apostles, with edifying tales full of miracles. In the homilies of Blickling, the church of the Holy Sepulchre is described in detail, with its sculptured portals, its stained-glass and its lamps, that threefold holy temple, existing far away at the other extremity of the world, in the distant East.[4] This church

---

[1] "The Sermones Catholici, of Homilies or Ælfric," ed. Thorpe, Ælfric Society, 1844-6, 2 vols. ; "Ælfric's Lives of Saints, being a set of Sermons," &c., ed. W. W. Skeat, E.E.T.S., 1881 ff. Ælfric translated part of the Bible : "The O.E. version of the Heptateuch, Ælfric's Treatise on the O. and N. Testament," ed. Crawford 1922. He wrote also important works on astronomy and grammar, a "Colloquium" in Latin and Anglo-Saxon : "Ælfric's Grammatik und Glossar," ed. J. Zupitza, 1880, 8vo, &c.

[2] The homilies of Wulfstan were published by Arthur Napier : "Wulfstan, Sammlung der ihm zugeschriebenen Homilien nebst Untersuchungen über ihre Echtheit," Berlin, 1883 (62 pieces, some only of undoubted authenticity ; *Cf.* Kinard, "A Study of Wulfstan's Homilies," Baltimore, 1897).

[3] "Transtulimus hunc codicem ex libris latinorum . . . ob ædificationem simplicium . . . ideoque nec obscura posuimus verba, sed simplicem Anglicam, quo facilius possit ad cor pervenire legentium vel audientium, ad utilitatem animarum suarum quia alia lingua nesciunt erudiri quam in qua nati sunt. Nec ubique transtulimus verbum ex verbo, sed sensum ex sensu. . . . Hos namque auctores in hac explanatione sumus sequuti, videlicet Augustinum Hipponensem, Hieronimum, Bedam, Gregorium, Smaragdum et aliquando Haymonem." Ælfric's preface for his "Sermones Catholici." In the preface of his sermons on the lives of Saints, Ælfric states that he intends not to translate any more, "ne forte despectui habeantur margarite Christi."

[4] "The Blickling Homilies," Sermon XI.

has no roof, so that the sky into which Christ's body ascended can be always seen; but, by God's grace, rain water never falls there. The preacher is positive about his facts; he has them from travellers who have seen with their own eyes this cathedral of Christendom.

Ælfric also keeps alive the interest of the listeners by propounding difficult questions to them which he answers himself at once. "Now many a man will think and inquire whence the devil came? . . . Now some man will inquire whence came his [own] soul, whether from the father or the mother? We say from neither of them; but the same God who created Adam with his hands . . . that same giveth a soul and life to children." [1] Why are there no more miracles? "These wonders were needful at the beginning of Christianity, for by these signs was the heathen folk inclined to faith. The man who plants trees or herbs waters them so long until they have taken root; when they are growing he ceases from watering. Also, the Almighty God so long showed his miracles to the heathen folk until they were believing: when faith had sprung up over all the world, then miracles ceased." [2]

The lives of the saints told by Ælfric recall at times tales in the Arabian Nights. There are transformations, disparitions, enchantments, emperors who become hermits, statues that burst, and out of which comes the devil. "Go," cries the apostle to the fiend, "go to the waste where no bird flies, nor husbandman ploughs, nor voice of man sounds." The "accursed spirit" obeys, and he appears all black, "with sharp visage and ample beard. His locks hung to his ankles, his eyes were scattering fiery sparks, sulphureous flame stood in his mouth, he was fright-

---

[1] " Sermones Catholici," pp. 12–13.

[2] *Ibid.* pp. 304–5. See also, in the sermon on St. John the Baptist, a curious satire on wicked talkative women, pp. 476–7.

fully feather-clad." [1] This is already the devil of the
Mysteries, the one described by Rabelais, almost in the
same words. We can imagine the effect of so minute a
picture on the Saxon herdsmen assembled on Sunday in
their little mysterious churches, almost windowless, like
that of Bradford-on-Avon.

One peculiarity makes these sermons remarkable ; in
them can be discerned a certain effort to attain to literary
dignity. The preacher tries his best to speak well. He
takes all the more pains because he is slightly ashamed,
being himself learned, to write in view of such an illiterate
public. He does not know any longer Alfred's doubts,
who, being uncertain as to which words best expressed the
meaning of his model, put down all those his memory or
glossary supply : the reader would choose. The authors
of these homilies purposely write prose which comes near
the tone and forms of poetry. Such are almost always
the beginnings of literary prose. They go as far as to
introduce a rude cadence in their writings, and adapt
thereto the special ornament of Germanic verse, alliteration. Wulfstan and Ælfric frequently afford their audience
the pleasure of those repeated sonorities, so much so that
it has been possible to publish a whole collection of
sermons by the latter in the form of poems.[2] Moreover,
the subject itself is often poetic, and the priest adorns his
discourse with images and metaphors. Many passages of
the " Blickling Homilies," read in a translation, might easily
be taken for poetical extracts. Such are the descriptions
of contemporaneous evils, and of the signs that will herald
the end of the world, that world that " fleeth from us

---

[1] Sermon for the 25th of August, on the martyrdom of St. Bartholomew,
pp. 454 ff. The portrait of the saint is as minutely drawn : " he has fair and
curling locks, is white of body, and has deep eyes and moderate nose," &c.

[2] Skeat, " Ælfric's Lives of Saints," 1881.

with great bitterness, and we follow it as it flies from us, and love it although it is passing away." [1]

Such are also the descriptions of landscapes, where even now, in this final period of the Anglo-Saxon epoch, northern nature, snow and ice are visibly described, as in "Beowulf," with delight, by connoisseurs : "As St. Paul was looking towards the northern region of the earth, from whence all waters pass down, he saw above the water a hoary stone, and north of the stone had grown woods, very rimy. And there were dark mists ; and under the stone was the dwelling-place of monsters and execrable creatures." [2]

Thus Anglo-Saxon literature, in spite of the efforts of Cynewulf, Alfred, Dunstan, and Ælfric goes on repeating itself. Poems, histories, and sermons are conspicuous, now for their grandeur, now for the emotion that is in them ; but their main qualities and main defects are very much alike ; they give an impression of monotony. The same notes, not very numerous, are incessantly repeated. The Angles, Saxons, and other conquerors who came from Germany have remained, from a literary point of view, nearly intact in the midst of the subjugated race. Their literature is almost stationary ; it does not perceptibly move and develop. A graft is wanted ; Rome tried to insert one, but a few branches only were vivified, not the whole tree ; and the fruit is the same each year, wild and sometimes poor.

The political state of the country leaves on the mind a similar impression. The men of Germanic blood established in England remain, or nearly so, grouped together in tribes ; their hamlet is the mother country for them. They are unable to unite against the foreign foe. Their

---

[1] "The Blickling Homilies," Sermons X. and XI.
[2] *Ibid.*, Sermon XVII.

subdivisions undergo constant change, much as they did, centuries before, on the Continent. A swarm of petty kings, ignored by history, are known to have lived and reigned, owing to their name having been found appended to charters ; there were kings of the Angles of the South, kings of half Kent, kings with fewer people to rule than a village mayor of to-day. They are killed, and, as we have seen, the thing is of no importance.

The Danes come again ; at one time they own the whole of England, which is thus subject to the same king as Scandinavia. Periods of unification are merely temporary, and due to the power or the genius of a prince : Alfred, Æthelstan, Cnut the Dane; but the people of Great Britain keep their tendency to break up into small kingdoms, into earldoms, as they were called in the eleventh century, about the end of the period ; into tribes, in reality, as when they inhabited the Germanic land. Out of this chaos how can a nation arise ? a nation that may give birth to Shakespeare, crush the Armada, people the American continent ? No less than a miracle is needed. The miracle took place : it was the battle of Hastings.

BOOK II.

THE FRENCH INVASION.

CHAPTER I.

BATTLE.

I.

GERMANIC England gave itself a king for the last time at the death of Edward the Confessor. Harold, son of Godwin, was elected to succeed him. A momentous crisis, the greatest in English history, was drawing near.

An awful problem had to be solved. Divided, helpless, uncertain, England could no longer remain what she had been for six hundred years. She stood vacillating, drawn by contrary attractions to opposite centres, half-way between the North, that had last invaded the land, and the South, that had taught and christianised the nation. On both sides fresh invaders threaten her ; which will be the winner? Should the North triumph, England will be bound for centuries to the Germanic nations, whose growth will be tardy, and whose literary development will be slow, so slow indeed that men still alive as this book was being written could have seen with their own eyes the great poet of the race, Goethe, who died in 1832. ´Should the South carry the day, the growth will be speedy and the preparation rapid. Like France, Italy, and Spain, England will have at the Renaissance a complete literature of her own, and be able to produce a Shakespeare, as Italy produced an Ariosto, Spain a Cervantes, and France a Montaigne, a Ronsard and a Rabelais.

The problem was solved in the autumn of 1066. On the morrow of Harold's election, the armies of the North and South assembled, and the last of the invasions began.

The Scandinavians took the sea again. They were led by Harold Hardrada, son of Sigurd, a true romance hero, who had fought in many wars, and once defended by his sword the throne of the eastern emperors.[1] To the South another fleet collected, commanded by William of Normandy; he, too, an extraordinary man, bastard of that Robert, known in legend as Robert the Devil who had long since started on a pilgrimage to Jerusalem from which he never returned. The Normans of Scandinavia and the Normans of France were about to play a match of which England was the stake.

The Scandinavians were the first to land. Hardrada entered York, and for a moment it seemed as if victory would belong to the people of the North. But Harold of England rushed to meet them, and crushed them at Stamford-bridge; his brother, the rebel Tosti, fell on the field of battle, and Hardrada died of an arrow-wound in the throat. All was over with Scandinavia; there remained the Normans of France.

Who were these Normans? Very different from those of the other army, they no longer had anything Scandinavian or Germanic about them; and thus they stood a chance of furnishing the Anglo-Saxons with the graft they needed. Had it not been for this, their invasion would have carried no more important result than that of the Danes in the ninth century; but the consequences were

---

[1] Schlumberger, "Epopée Byzantine," last vol., 1905, p. 288. The romantic events in the life of Harold Hardrada Sigurdson are the subject of an Icelandic saga in prose, by Snorre Sturlason (born at Hvam in Iceland, 1178): "The Heimskringla Saga, or the Sagas of the norse kings," ed. Laing and R. B. Anderson, London, 1889, vols. iii. and iv. A detailed account of the battle at "Stanforda-Bryggiur" (Stamford-bridge), will be found in chaps. 89 ff.; the battle of "Helsingja port" (Hastings), is told in chap. 100.

to be very different. The fusion between Rollo's pirates, and the already dense population of the rich province called after them Normandy, had been long accomplished. It was less a fusion than an absorption, for the natives were much more numerous than the settlers. From the time of the second duke, French had again become the language of the mass of the inhabitants. They were Christians; they had French manners, chivalrous tastes, castles, convents, and schools; and the blood that flowed in their veins was mostly French. Thus it was that they could set forth in the eleventh century for the conquest of England as representatives of the South, of Latin civilisation, of Romance letters, and of the religion of Rome. William came blessed by the Pope, with a banner borne before him, the gift of Alexander II., wearing a hair of St. Peter's in a ring, having secured by a vow the favour of one of France's patrons, that same St. Martin of Tours, whose church Clovis had enriched, and whose cape Hugues Capet had worn: whence his surname.

No Beowulf, no northern hero is sung of in William's army; but there resound verses on the most popular of French fighters. According to the poet Wace, who took great trouble in gathering information (quoting once his own father), the minstrel Taillefer rode before the soldiers, singing "of Charlemagne, and of Roland, and Oliver, and the vassals who fell at Roncevaux."[1]

> [1] Taillefer ki mult bien chantout,
> Sor un cheval ki tost alout,
> Devant le duc alout chantant
> De Karlemaigne et de Rolant
> E d'Oliver et des vassals
> Qui morurent en Rencevals.

"Maistre Wace's Roman de Rou," ed. Andresen, Heilbronn, 1877, 2 vols. 8vo, p. 349, a statement reproduced or corroborated by several chroniclers:

The army, moreover, was not exclusively composed of men from Normandy.[1] It was divided into three parts ; to the left the Bretons and Poictevins ; the Normans in the centre ; and to the right the French, properly so called. No doubt was possible ; William's army was a French army ; all contemporary writers describe it as such, and both parties give it that name. In the " Domesday Book," written by order of William, his people are termed "Franci"; on the Bayeux tapestry, embroidered soon after the Conquest, the inscription at the place where the battle is represented runs : " Hic Franci pugnant" (Here fight the French). Crowned king of England, William continues to call his followers " Frenchmen."[2] The Anglo-Saxon Chronicles, on the other side, describe the invaders sometimes as Normans, and sometimes as Frenchmen, " Frenciscan." " And the French had possession of the place of carnage," says the Worcester annalist, after giving an account of the battle of Hastings ; and he bestows the appellation of Normans upon the men of Harold Hardrada. A similar view is taken farther north. Formerly, we read in a saga, the same tongue was spoken in England and Norway, but

---

" Tunc cantilena Rollandi inchoata. . . ." William of Malmesbury, early XIIth cent. " Gesta Regum Anglorum," ed. Hardy, 1840, III , 415.

[1] William of Poictiers, a Norman by birth (he derived his name from having studied at Poictiers) and a chaplain of the Conqueror, says that his army consisted of " Mancels, French, Bretons, Aquitains, and Normans " ; his statement is reproduced by Orderic Vital : " Insisterunt eis Cenomannici, Franci, Britanni, Aquitani et miserabiliter pereuntes cadebant Angli." " Hist. ecclesiastica," in Migne, clxxxviii. col. 298. Vital was born nine years only after the Conquest, and he spent most of his life among Normans in the monastery of St. Evroult. Gaimar, in " Lestorie des Engles " (written before 1147), calls the victors " des Frenceis."

[2] Charter of William to the city of London : " Will'm kyng gret . . . ealle tha burhwaru binnan Londone, Frenicisce and Englisce, freondlice " (greets all the burghers within London, French and English, friendly). At a later date, again, Richard Cœur-de-Lion, in a charter for Lincoln, sends his greetings to his subjects "tam Francis quam Anglis," A.D. 1194. Stubbs, " Select Charters," Oxford, 1876, pp. 82 and 266.

not after the coming of William of Normandy, "because
he was French." [1]

As to Duke William, he led his army of Frenchmen in
French fashion, that is to say gaily. His state of mind
is characterised not by any overflow of warlike joy or fury,
but by good humour. Like the heroes of the Celtic poems,
like the inhabitants of Gaul in all ages, he is prompt at
repartee (*argute loqui*). He stumbles in stepping off the
ship, which is considered by all as a bad omen : " It is
a most fatal omen," we read in an ancient Scandinavian poem, " if thou stumble on thy feet when march-
ing to battle, for evil fairies stand on either side of thee,
wishing to see thee wounded." [2] It means nothing, said
the duke to his followers, save that I take possession of
the land. At the moment of battle he puts his hauberk
on the wrong way : another bad omen. Not at all, he
declares, it is a sign I shall turn out different ; " King
I shall be, who duke was ":

> Le nom qui ert de duchée
> Verreiz de duc en rei torné ;
> Reis serai qui duc ai esté. [3]

He challenges Harold to single combat, as the Gauls
did their adversaries, according to Diodorus Siculus ; and
as Francis I. will do later when at feud with Charles V. He
was to die in an expedition undertaken out of revenge
for an epigram of the king of France, and to make good
his retort.

---

[1] "Gunnlangs Saga," in "Three northern Love Stories and other Tales,"
edited by Erikr Magnusson, and William Morris, London, 1875, 12mo.

[2] "The old play of the Wolsungs," in "Corpus Poeticum Boreale," i.
p. 34.

[3] "Maistre Wace's Roman de Rou," ed. Andresen, line 7749. The same
story is reproduced by William of Malmesbury (twelfth century) : "Arma
poposcit, moxque ministrorum tumultu loricam inversam indutus, casum risu
correxit, vertetur, inquiens, fortitudo comitatus mei in regnum." "Gesta
Regum Anglorum," 1840, English Historical Society, book iii. p. 415.

The evening of the 14th of October, 1066, saw the fate of England decided. The issue of the battle was doubtful. William, by a series of ingenious ideas, secured the victory. His foes were the victims of his cleverness; they were "ingenio circumventi, ingenio victi." [1] He ordered his soldiers to simulate a flight; he made his archers shoot upwards, and the arrows falling among the entrenched Saxons wrought great havoc. One of them put out Harold's eye; the English chief fell by his standard, and soon after the battle was over, one of the most memorable ever won by an army of Frenchmen.

The duke had vowed to erect on the field of the fight an abbey to St. Martin of Tours. He kept his word, but the building never bore among men the name of the saint; it received and has retained to this day the appellation of "Battle." Its ruins, preserved with pious care, overlook the dales where the host of the Conqueror gathered for the attack. Far off through the hills, then covered by the yellowing leaves of the forest of Anderida, glistens, between earth and sky, the grey sea that brought over the Norman fleet eighteen centuries ago. Heaps of stones, overgrown with ivy, mark the place where Harold fell, the last king of English blood who ever sat upon the throne of Great Britain. It is a secluded spot; large cedars, alders, and a tree with white foliage form a curtain, and shut off from the outer world the scene of the terrible tragedy. A solemn silence reigns; nothing is visible through the branches, save the square tower of the church of Battle, and the only sound that floats upwards is that of the old clock striking the hours. Ivy and climbing roses cling to the grey stones and fall in light clusters along the low walls of the crypt; the roses shed their leaves, and the soft autumn breeze scatters the white

---

[1] William of Malmesbury, *Ibid.*

petals on the grass, amidst fragments to which is attached
one of the greatest memories in the history of humanity.

The consequences of " the Battle " were indeed immense,
far more important than those of Agincourt or Austerlitz:
a whole nation was transformed and became a new one.
The vanquished Anglo-Saxons no more knew how to
defend themselves and unite against the French than
they had formerly known how to unite against the Danes.
To the momentary enthusiasm that had gathered around
Harold many energetic supporters succeeded a gloomy
dejection. Real life exhibited the same contrasts as
literature. Stirred by sudden impulses, the natives vainly
struggled to free themselves, incapable even in this pressing danger of combined and vigorous action ; then they
mournfully submitted to fate. The only contemporary
interpreter of their feelings known to us, the Anglo-Saxon
chronicler, bewails the Conquest, but is more struck by
the ravages it occasions than by the change of domination it brings about. " And Bishop Odo and Earl William
[Fitz-Osbern]," he says, " remained here and wrought
castles widely throughout the nation, and oppressed the
poor people, and ever after that it greatly grew in evil. May
the end be good when God will." So much for the
material disaster, now for the coming of the foreigner :
" And then came to meet him Archbishop Ealdred [of
York], and Eadgar child and Earl Eadwine, and Earl
Morkere, and all the best men of London, and then, from
necessity, submitted when the greatest harm had been
done, and it was very imprudent that it was not done
earlier, as God would not better it for our sins." [1]

People with a mind so full of elegiac sentiments fall an

---

[1] "Anglo-Saxon Chronicle" (Rolls), year 1066, Worcester text (Tib. B. IV.).
Same statement in William of Malmesbury, who says of his compatriots that
" uno prælio et ipso perfacili se patriamque pessundederint." " Gesta Regum
Anglorum," English Historical Society, p. 418.

easy prey to men who know how to *will*. Before dying William had taken everything, even a part of Wales; he was king of England, and had so completely changed the fortunes of his new country that its inhabitants, so used to invasions, were never again to see rise, from that day to this, the smoke of an enemy's camp.

II.

From the outset William seems to have desired and foreseen it. Practical, clear-minded, of firm will, imbued with the notion of State, he possessed in the highest degree the qualities his new subjects most lacked. He knew neither doubts nor vain hesitations; he was an optimist, always sure of success: not with the certitude of the blind who walk confidently to the river, but with the assurance of clear-sighted people, who leave the goddess Fortune so little to do, it were a miracle if she did less for them. His lucid and persistent will is never at fault. In the most critical moment of the battle a fatal report is circulated that the duke has been killed; he instantly tears off his helmet and shows himself with uncovered face, crying: "I am alive! here I stand, and by God I shall conquer!" [1]

All his life, he conforms his actions to his theories; having come as the heir of the Anglo-Saxon princes, he behaves as such. He visits his estate, rectifies its boundaries, protects its approaches, and, in spite of the immensity of the work, takes a minute inventory of it. [2]

---

[1] So says William of Poictiers, and Orderic Vital after him: ". . . Nudato insuper capite, detractaque galea exclamans: me inquit conspicite; vivo et vincam, opitulante Deo." "Orderici Vitalis Angligenæ . . . Historiæ Ecclesiasticæ, Libri XIII.," in Migne's "Patrologia," vol. clxxxviii. col. 297.

[2] The inventory is carried down to details; answers are required to a number of questions: ". . . Deinde quomodo vocatur mansio, quis tenuit eam tempore Regis Eadwardi; quis modo tenet; quot hidæ; quot carrucæ in dominio; quot hominum; quot villani; quot cotarii; quot servi; quot liberi

This inventory is the Domesday, a unique monument; such that no nation in Europe possesses the like. On the coins, he so exactly imitates the type adopted by his predecessors that it is hard to distinguish the pennies of William from those of Edward. Before the end of his reign, he was the master or conqueror of all, and had made his authority felt and accepted by all, even by his brother Bishop Odo, whom he arrested with his own hands, and caused to be imprisoned " as Earl of Kent," he said, with his usual readiness of word, to avoid a quarrel with the Church.

And so it was that, in spite of their terrible sufferings, the vanquished were unable to repress a certain sentiment which predisposed them to a fusion with the victor, namely admiration. Never had they seen energy, power, or knowledge like unto that. The judgment of the Anglo-Saxon chronicler on William may be considered as being the judgment of the nation itself concerning its new masters : " That King William about whom we speak was a very wise man, and very powerful, more dignified and strong than any of his predecessors were. He was mild to the good men who loved God, and over all measure severe to the men who gainsayed his will. . . . So also was he a very rigid and cruel man, so that no one durst do anything against his will. . . . He spared not his own brother named Odo. . . . Among other things is not to be forgotten the good peace that he made in this land, so that a man who had any confidence in himself might go over his realm with his bosom full of gold unhurt." The land of the Britons, " Brytland " or Wales, was in his

homines ; quot sochemani ; quantum silvæ ; quantum prati; quot pascuorum ; quot molendina ; quot piscinæ," &c., &c. "Domesday for Ely "; Stubbs, " Select Charters," Oxford, 1876, p. 86. The Domesday has been published in facsimile by the Record Commission: " Domesday Book, or the great survey of England, of William the Conqueror, 1086," edited by Sir Henry James, London and Southampton, 1861–3, 2 vols. 4to.

power, Scotland likewise; he would have had Ireland
besides had he reigned two years longer.   It is true he
greatly oppressed the people, built castles, and made
terrible game-laws : " As greatly did he love the tall
deer as if he were their father.   He also ordained concerning the hares that they should go free." [1]   Even in
the manner of presenting grievances we detect that
special kind of popularity which attaches itself to the
tyranny of great men.   The England of the Anglo-
Saxons had been defeated, but brilliant destinies were
in store for the country ; the master was hated but
not despised.

These great destinies were realised.   The qualities of
which William gave the example were rare in England
but common in France ; they were those of his people and
country, those of his lieutenants ; they naturally reappear
in many of his successors.   These are, as a rule, energetic
and headstrong men, who never hesitate, who believe in
themselves, are always ready to run all hazards, and to
attempt the impossible, with the firm conviction that they
will succeed ; they are never weary of fighting and taking ;
the moment never comes when they can enjoy their conquests in peace ; in good as in evil they never stop half-
way ; those who incline to tyranny become, like Stephen,
the most atrocious tyrants [2] ; those who incline to the
manners and customs of chivalry carry them, like Richard
Cœur-de-Lion, so far as to plainly forget that they have
a kingdom to rule.   The most intelligent become, like
Henry II., incomparable statesmen ; those who have a
taste for art give themselves up to it with such passion

---

[1] Peterborough text of the " Anglo-Saxon Chronicle," year 1086.

[2] To the extent that England resembled then Jerusalem besieged by Titus :
" Quid multa ?   In diebus eis multiplicata sunt mala in terra, ut si quis ea
summatim recenseat, historiam Josephi possint excedere."   John of Salisbury,
"Policraticus," book vi. chap. xviii.

that they jeopardise, like Henry III., even their crown, and care for nothing but their masons and painters. They are equally ready for sword and word fights, and they offer both to all comers. They constantly risk their lives; out of twelve Norman or Angevin princes six die a violent death.

All their enterprises are conceived on a gigantic scale. They carry war into Scotland, into Ireland, into Wales, into France, into Gascony, later on into the Holy Land and into Spain. The Conqueror was on his way to Paris when he received, by accident, being at Mantes, fifteen leagues from the capital, a wound of which he died. These qualities are in the blood. A Frenchman, Henry of Burgundy, seizes on the county of "Porto" in 1095, out of which his successors make the kingdom of "Portugal"; a Norman, Robert Guiscard, conquers Sicily, takes Naples, forces his alliance upon the Pope, overawes Venice, and the same year beats the two emperors; his son Bohemond establishes himself as reigning prince in Antioch in 1099, and fighting with great composure and equanimity against Turk and Christian, establishes out of hand a little kingdom which lasted two centuries. They find in England miserable churches; they erect new ones, "of a style unknown till then," writes William of Malmesbury,[1] which count among the grandest ever built. The splendid naves of St. Albans, Westminster, Canterbury, Winchester, York, Salisbury, rise heaven-wards; the towers of Ely reach to the skies; the west front of Lincoln, adorned with marvellous carvings, rears itself on the hill above the town; Peterborough opens its

---

[1] "Videas ubique in villis ecclesias, in vicis et urbibus monasteria, novo ædificandi genere consurgere." The buildings of the Anglo-Saxons, according to the testimony of the same, who may have seen many as he lived in the twelfth century, were very poor; they were pleased with "pravis et abjectis domibus." "Gesta Regum Anglorum," ed. Hardy, 1840, book iii. p. 418.

wide bays, deep as the portals of French churches; Durham, a heavy and massive pile built by knight-bishops, overlooks the valley of the Wear, and seems a divine fortress, a castle erected for God. The donjons of the conquerors, Rochester, London, Norwich, Lincoln, Newcastle-on-Tyne, are enormous, square and thick, so high and so solid that the idea of taking these giant structures could never occur to the native dreamers, who wait "till the end shall be good when God pleases"!

The masters of the land are ever ready for everything, and find time for everything: if their religious edifices are considered, it seems as though they had cared for nothing else; if we read the accounts of their wars, it appears as if they were ever on their way to military expeditions, and never left the field of battle. Open the innumerable manuscripts which contain the monuments of their literature: these works can be meant, it seems, but for men of leisure, who have interminable days to spend in leisurely pastimes; they make their Benoits de Sainte-More give them an account of their origins in chronicles of 43,000 lines. This literature is ample, superabundant, with numberless branches and endless ramifications; they have not even one literature only; they have three: a French, a Latin, and later an English one.

Their matchless strength and their indomitable will further one particular cause: the infusion of French and Latin ideas in the Anglo-Saxon people, and the connection of England with the civilisations of the South. The task was arduous: Augustine, Alfred, Dunstan, kings and saints, had attempted it and failed; the Normans tried and succeeded. It was their custom to be successful.

Powerful means were at their disposal, and they knew how to make the best of them. Firstly, the chiefs of the nation are French; their wives are mostly French too: Stephen, Henry II., John, Henry III., Edward I., Edward

II., Richard II., all marry Frenchwomen. The Bohuns (from whom came the Herefords, Essexes, Northamptons), the Beauchamps (Warwick), the Mowbrays (Nottingham Norfolk), the Bigods (Norfolk), the Nevilles (Westmoreland, Warwick), the Montgomerys (Shrewsbury, Pembroke, Arundel), the Beaumonts and the Montforts (Leicester), are Frenchmen. People of less importance married to English women — "matrimonia quoque cum subditis jungunt" [1]—rear families which for many years remain French.

During a long period, the centre of the thoughts and interests of the kings of England, French by origin, education, manners, and language, is in France. William the Conqueror bequeaths Normandy to his eldest son, and England to his younger. Not one among them is buried at Westminster before 1272 ; they sleep their last sleep most of them at Caen or Fontevrault [2]; out of the thirty-five years of his reign, Henry II. spends more than twenty-one in France, and less than fourteen in England.[3] Before his accession Richard Cœur-de-Lion only came to England twice in twenty years. They successively make war on France, not from hatred or scorn, not because they wish to destroy her, but because they wish to be kings of France themselves. They admire and wish to possess her ; their ideal, whether moral, literary, administrative, or religious, is above all a French ideal. They are knights, and introduce into England the fashion of tournaments, "conflictus gallici," says Matthew Paris. They wish to have a University, and they

---

[1] William of Malmesbury, *ut supra*, p. 420.

[2] The Conqueror was buried at Caen ; Henry II. and Richard Cœur-de-Lion at Fontevrault in Anjou. Henry III. was buried at Westminster, but his heart was sent to Fontevrault, and the chapter of Westminster still possesses the deed drawn at the moment when it was placed in the hands of the Angevin abbess, 20 Ed. I. (exhibited in the chapter house).

[3] "Henry II.," by Mrs. J. R. Green, 1888, p. 22 ("Twelve English Statesmen").

copy for Oxford the regulations of Paris. Henry III.
quarrels with his barons, and whom does he select for an
arbiter but his former enemy, Louis IX., king of France,
the victor of Taillebourg? They organise in England a
religious hierarchy, so similar to that of France that the
prelates of one country receive constantly and without
difficulty promotion in the other. John of Poictiers, born
in Kent, treasurer of York, becomes bishop of Poictiers
and archbishop of Lyons, while still retaining the living
of Eynesford in Kent; John of Salisbury, secretary of the
archbishop of Canterbury, becomes bishop of Chartres;
Ralph de Sarr, born in Thanet, becomes dean of Reims[1];
others are appointed bishops of Palermo, Messina, and
Syracuse.

Impetuous as are these princes, ready at every instant
to run all risks and play fast and loose, even when, like
William I., old and ill, one precious quality of their temper
diminishes the danger of their rashness. They undertake,
as though for a wager, superhuman tasks, but once undertaken they proceed to the fulfilling of them with a lucid
and practical mind. It is this practical bent of their mind,
combined with their venturesome disposition, that has
made of them so remarkable a race, and enabled them to
transform the one over which they had now extended
their rule.

Be the question a question of ideas or a question of facts,
they behave in the same manner. They perceive the
importance both of ideas and of those who wield them, and
act accordingly; they negotiate with the Pope in Rome,
with St. Martin in heaven, even with God; they promise
nothing for nothing; however exalted the power with
which they treat, what they agree to must be bargains,
Norman bargains.

The so-called bull "Laudabiliter," of the English Pope

[1] Stubbs, "Seventeen Lectures," 1886, p. 131.

Nicholas Breakspeare (Adrian IV.) concerning Ireland
is of disputed authenticity ; but Henry II.'s bargaining
with Rome before starting on his expedition is authentic.
His dealings closely resembled William the Conqueror's
own before the invasion of England. If technically maybe
Henry's negotiation failed, practically it succeeded, and as
the event showed, he could act unhampered as he pleased.[1]
But the most remarkable view suggested to these men by
this particular turn of their mind consisted in the value
they chose to set, even at that distant time, on "public
opinion," if we may use the expression, and on literature
as a means of action.

This was a stroke of genius ; William endeavoured, and
his successors imitated him, to do for the past what he was
doing for the present : to unify. For this, the new dynasty
wanted the assistance of poets, and it called upon them.
William had persistently given himself out to be not only
the successor, but the rightful heir of Edward the Confessor,
and of the native kings. During several centuries the poets
who wrote in the French tongue, the Latin chroniclers, the
English rimers, as though obedient to a word of command,
blended all the origins together in their book ; French,
Danes, Saxons, Britons, Trojans even, according to them,

[1] Pope Adrian was very fond of Henry ("Sicut mater unicum amat filium,
ita vos diligebat," wrote John of Salisbury to the King, "Epistolæ," in
"Opera Omnia," Giles, 1848, i. 46) ; yet he would not grant Ireland to him
as an absolute possession, but only as a fief to be held from the Holy See. "Ad
preces meas," writes John of Salisbury, the Pope's great friend (*infra*, p. 188),
"illustri regi Anglorum, Henrico secundo, concessit et dedit Hiberniam. . . .
Annulum quoque per me transmisit aureum, smaragdo optimo decoratum, quo
fieret investitura juris in gerenda Hibernia." "Metalogicus," *ibid.*, v. 205.
But Henry wanted absolute possession ; he continued to negociate with Rome,
and when at length he invaded Ireland, having no regular agreement with
the Holy See, he managed to enjoy, in fact, the help of Alexander III., who
wrote to the local princes recommending fidelity to Henry, Sept. 20, 1172.
See O. J. Thatcher, "Studies on Adrian IV.," in "Decennial Publications of
the University of Chicago," 1903. Miss Norgate's art. in "Engl. Historic. Rev.,"
vol. viii., and Orpen, "Ireland under the Normans," Oxford, 4 vols., 1911 ff.

formed one sole race ; all these men had found in England a common country, and their united glories were the general heritage of posterity. With a persistency which lasted from century to century, they displaced the national point of view, and ended by establishing, with every one's assent, the theory that the constitution and unity of a nation are a question not of blood but of place ; consanguinity matters little ; the important point is to be compatriots. All the inhabitants of the same country are one people: the Saxons of England and the French of England are nothing but Englishmen.

All the heroes who shone in the British Isle are now indiscriminately sung by the poets, who celebrate Brutus, Arthur, Hengist, Horsa, Cnut, Edward, and William in impartial strains. They venerate in the same manner all saints of whatever blood who have won heaven by the practice of virtue on English ground. Here again the king, continuing the wise policy of his ancestors, sets the example. On Easter Day, 1158, Henry II. and his wife Aliénor of Aquitaine enter the cathedral of Worcester, wearing their crowns, and present themselves before the tomb of the holy protector of the town. They remove their crowns, place them on his tomb, and swear never to wear them again. The saint was not a French one, but Wulfstan, the last Anglo-Saxon bishop, one who held the see at the time of the Conquest.[1]

The hint has been given ; the clerks have taken it. Here is a poem of the thirteenth century, on Edward the Confessor ; it is composed in the French tongue by a Norman monk of Westminster Abbey, and dedicated to Aliénor of Provence, wife of Henry III. In it we read:

[1] As little French as could be, for he did not even know the language of the conquerors, and was on that account near being removed from his see : "quasi homo idiota, qui linguam gallicam non noverat nec regiis consiliis interesse poterat." Matthew Paris, "Chronica Majora," year 1095.

" In this world there is, we dare to say, country, kingdom, nor empire where so many good kings and saints have lived as in the isle of the English . . . holy martyrs and confessors, many of whom died for God ; others were very strong and brave as Arthur, Edmund, and Cnut."

This is a characteristic example of these new tendencies. The poem is dedicated to a Frenchwoman by a Norman of England, and begins with the praise of a Briton, a Saxon, and a Dane.[1]

In the compiling of chronicles, clerks proceed in the same manner, and this is still more significant, for it clearly proves that the pressing of literature into the service of political ideas is the result of a decided will, and of a pre-conceived plan, and not of chance. The chroniclers do, indeed, write by command, and by express desire of the kings their masters. One of them begins his history of England with the siege of Troy, and relates the adventures of the Trojans and Britons, as willingly as those of the Saxons or Normans ; another writes two separate books, the first in honour of the Britons, and the second in honour of the Normans ; a third, who goes back to the time when " the world was established," does not get down to the dukes of Normandy without having narrated first the story of Antenor the Trojan, an ancestor of the Normans, as he

---

[1] En mund ne est (ben vus l'os dire),
   Pais, reaume, ne empire
   U tant unt esté bons rois
   E seinz, cum en isle d'Englois,
   Ki après règne terestre
   Or règnent reis en célestre,
   Seinz, martirs, e cunfessurs,
   Ki pur Deu mururent plursurs ;
   Li autre, forz e hardiz mutz,
   Cum fu Arthurs, Aedmunz e Knudz.

"Lives of Edward the Confessor," ed. Luard (Rolls), 1858, " Estoire de Seint Aedward le Rei." *Cf.* Tennyson, " Saxon and Norman and Dane are we." " Welcome to Alexandra," March 7, 1863.

believes.[1]   The origin of the inhabitants of the land must
no longer be sought for under Scandinavian skies, but on
Trojan fields.   From the smoking ruins of Pergamus came
Francus, father of the French, and Æneas, father of Brutus
and of the Britons of England.   Thus the nations on both
sides of the Channel have a common and classic ancestry.
There is Trojan blood in their veins, the blood of Priam
and of the princes who defended Ilion.[2]

[1] These three poets, all of them subjects of the English kings, lived in the
twelfth century ; the oldest of the three was Gaimar, who wrote, between 1147
and 1151 (P. Meyer, "Romania," vol. xviii. p. 314), his "Estorie des
Engles" (ed. Hardy and Martin, Rolls, 1888, 2 vols., 8vo), and, about
1145, a translation in French verse of the "Historia Britonum" of Geoffrey
of Monmouth (see below, p. 132).—Wace, born at Jersey (1100 ?-1175,
G. Paris), translated also Geoffrey into French verse ("Roman de Brut," ed.
Leroux de Lincy, Rouen, 1836, 2 vols. 8vo), and wrote between 1160 and
1174 his "Geste des Normands" or "Roman de Rou" (ed. Andresen,
Heilbronn, 1877, 2 vols. 8vo).   He wrote also metrical lives of saints, &c.—
Benoit de Sainte-More, besides his metrical romances (see below, p. 129), wrote,
by command of Henry II., a great "Chronique des ducs de Normandie" (ed.
Francisque Michel, "Documents inédits," Paris, 1836, 3 vols. 4to).

[2] Even under the Roman empire, non-latin nations had attributed to
themselves a Trojan origin.   Lucan states that the men of Auvergne were
conceited enough to consider themselves allied to the Trojan race.   Ammianus
Marcellinus, fourth century, states that similar traditions were current in Gaul
in his time : "Aiunt quidam paucos post excidium Trojæ fugientes Græcos
ubique dispersos, loca hæc occupasse tunc vacua."   "Rerum Gestarum," lib.
xv. cap. ix.   During the Middle Ages a Roman ancestry was attributed to the
French, Britons, Lombards, Normans, Scotch, etc.   The history of Brutus,
father of the Britons, is in the "Historia Britonum" which has come down
to us under the name of Nennius, VIIIth or IXth century, the author stating
that he drew his information from "annalibus Romanorum" (ed. Stevenson,
Engl. Hist. Soc., 1838, p. 7 ; cf. Newell in "Publ. Mod. Lang. Assn. of
Ama.," xx., 622).   The English historians after him, up to modern times,
accepted the same legend ; it is reproduced by Matthew Paris in the thirteenth
century, by Ralph Higden in the fourteenth, by Holinshed in Shakesperean
times : "This Brutus . . . was the sonne of Silvius, the sonne of Ascanius,
the sonne of Æneas the Troian, begotten of his wife Creusa, and borne in
Troie, before the citie was destroied."   Chronicles, 1807, 6 vols. fol. book ii.
chap. 1.   In France at the Renaissance, Ronsard chose for his hero Francus
the Trojan, "because," as he says, "he had an extreme desire to honour
the house of France," and Ariosto in Italy did not fail to bestow Trojan
ancestors on the house of Este.   In vain had Erasmus derided these very
"follies" in his "Praise of Folly."

From theory these ideas passed into practice, and thus received a lasting consecration ; another bond of fraternity was established between the various races living on the soil of Great Britain : that which results from the memory of wars fought together. William and his successors, when at least it is of their interest to do so, do not distinguish between their subjects. All are English, and they are all led together to battle against their foes of the Continent. So that this collection of scattered tribes, on an island which a resolute invader had formerly found it so easy to conquer, now gains victories in its turn, and takes an unexpected rank among nations. David Bruce is made prisoner at Neville's Cross ; Charles de Blois at Roche Derien ; King John at Poictiers ; Du Guesclin at Nava-rette. Hastings has made the defeat of the Armada possible ; William of Normandy stamped on the ground, and a nation came forth.

CHAPTER II.

*LITERATURE IN THE FRENCH LANGUAGE
UNDER THE NORMAN AND ANGEVIN KINGS.*

I.

WHAT previous invaders of the island had been unable to accomplish, the French of William of Normandy were finally to realise. By the rapidity and thoroughness of their conquest, by securing to themselves the assistance of those who knew how to use a pen, by their continental wars, they were to bring about the fusion of all the races into one, and teach them, whether they intended it or not, what a mother country was.

They taught them something else besides, and the results of the Conquest were not less remarkable from a literary than from a political point of view. A new language and new ideas were introduced by them into England, and a strange phenomenon occurred, one almost unique in history. For about two or three hundred years, the French language remained superimposed upon the English; the upper layer slowly infiltrated the lower, was absorbed, and disappeared in transforming it. But this was the work of centuries. "And then comes, lo!" writes an English chronicler more than two hundred years after Hastings, "England into Normandy's hand; and the Normans could speak no language but their own, and they spoke French here as they did at home, and taught it to their children : so that the high men of this land, who are come of their race, keep all to that speech which they have taken from them." People of a lower sort, " low men," stick to their English ; all those who do not know French are men of no account. " I ween that in all the world there is no country that holds not to her own speech, save England alone." [1]

The diffusion of the French tongue was such that it seemed at one time as if a disappearance of English were possible. All over the great island people were found speaking French, and they were always the most powerful, the strongest, richest, or most knowing in the land, whose favour it was well to gain, and whose example it was well to imitate. Men who spoke only English remained all their lives, as Robert of Gloucester tells us, men of " little," of nothing. In order to become something the first condition was to learn French. This condition remained so long a necessary one, it was even impossible to foresee that it should ever cease to exist; and the wisest, during that period, were of opinion that only works written in French were assured of longevity. Gerald de Barry, who had written in Latin, regretted at the end of his life that he had not employed the French language, " gallicum," which would have secured to his works, he thought, a greater and more lasting fame.[2]

---

[1] Thus com lo Engelond · in to Normandies hond ;
  And the Normans ne couthe speke tho · bot hor owe speche,
  And speke French as hii dude atom · and hor children dude also teche,
  So that heiemen of this lond · that of hor blod come
  Holdeth alle thulke speche · that hii of hom nome ;
  Vor bote a man conne Frenss · me telth of him lute,
  Ac lowe men holdeth to engliss · and to hor owe speche yute.
  Ich wene ther ne beth in al the world · contreyes none
  That ne holdeth to hor owe speche · bote Engelonde one.

W. A. Wright, " Metrical Chronicle of Robert of Gloucester " (Rolls), 1887, vol. ii. p. 543. Concerning Robert, see below, p. 122.

[2] Letter of the year 1209, by which Gerald sends to King John the second edition of his "Expugnatio Hiberniæ "; in " Giraldi Cambrensis Opera" (Rolls), vol. v. p. 410. Further on he speaks of French as of " communi idiomate."

Besides the force lent to it by the Conquest, the diffusion of the French tongue was also facilitated by the marvellous renown it then enjoyed throughout Europe. Never had it a greater ; men of various races wrote it, and the Italian Brunetto Latini, who used it, gave among other reasons for so doing, "that this speech is more delightful and more common to all people."[1] Such being the case, it spread quickly in England, where it was, for a long time, the language used in laws and deeds, in the courts of justice, in Parliamentary debates,[2] the language used by the most refined poets of the period.

And thus it happened that next to authors, French by race and language, subjects of the kings of England, were found others employing the same idiom, though of English blood. They strove, to the best of their ability, to imitate the style in favour with the rulers of the land, they wrote chronicles in French, as did, in the twelfth and fourteenth centuries, Jordan Fantosme[3] and Peter de Langtoft ; religious poems, as Robert of Greteham, Robert Grosseteste, William of Wadington did in the thirteenth ; romances in verse, like those of Hue of Rotelande (twelfth century) ; moralised tales in prose, like those of Nicole Bozon ; lyric poems,[4] or *fabliaux,*[5] like those composed

---

[1] "La parleure est plus delitable et plus commune à toutes gens." "Li livres dou Trésor," thirteenth century (a sort of philosophical, historical, scientific, &c., cyclopædia), ed. Chabaille, Paris, "Documents inédits," 1863, 4to. Dante cherished "the dear and sweet fatherly image " of his master, Brunetto, who recommended to the poet his " Trésor," for, he said, "in this book I still live." "Inferno," canto xv.

[2] For the laws, see the "Statutes of the Realm," 1819–28, Record Commission, 11 vols. fol. ; for the accounts of the sittings of Parliament, "Rotuli Parliamentorum," London, 1767–77, 6 vols. fol. ; for the accounts of lawsuits, the "Year Books," ed. Horwood, Rolls, 1863 ff.

[3] Author of a "Chronique de la guerre entre les Anglois et les Escossois," 1173–74, in French verse, ed. R. Howlett: "Chronicles of the reigns of Stephen, Henry II., and Richard I." (Rolls), 1884 ff., vol. iii. p. 203.

[4] See below, pp. 122, 123, 130, 214.

[5] Example ; "Romanz de un chivaler e de sa dame e de un clerk," written

by various anonymous writers; didactic poems and ballads such as those we owe, quite at the end of the period, in the second half of the fourteenth century, to Chaucer's friend, John Gower.

At this distance from the Conquest, French still played an important, though greatly diminished, part; it remained, as will be seen, the language of the Court; the accounts of the sittings of Parliament continued to be written in French; a London citizen registered in French on his note-book all that he knew concerning the history of his town.[1] As Robert of Gloucester had said, the case was an unparalleled one. This French literature, the work of Englishmen, consisted, of course, mainly in imitations of French models, and need not detain us long; still, its existence must be remembered, for no other fact shows so well how thorough and powerful the French invasion had been.

What, then, were the models copied by these imitators, and what the literature and ideas that, thanks to the Conquest, French-speaking poets acclimatised in lately-Germanic England? What sort of works pleased the rulers of the country; what writings were composed for them; what manuscripts did they order to be copied for their libraries? For it must not be forgotten, when studying the important problem of the diffusion of French ideas among men of English race, that it matters little whether the works most liked in England were composed by French subjects of the king of France, or by French subjects of the king of England; it matters little whether these ideas went across the Channel, carried over by poets, or by

in French by an Englishman in the thirteenth century, ed. Paul Meyer, "Romania," vol. i. p. 70. It is an adaptation of the well-known *fabliau* of the " Bourgeoise d'Orléans " (in Montaiglon and Raynaud, " Recueil général des Fabliaux," 1872, vol. i. p. 117). See below, p. 225.

[1] " Croniques de London . . . jusqu'à l'an 17Ed.III.," ed. Aungier, Camden Society, 1844, 4to.

manuscripts. What *is* important is to see and ascertain that works of a new style, with new aims in them, and belonging to a new school of art, enjoyed in England a wide popularity after the Conquest, with the result that deep and lasting transformations affected the æsthetic ideal and even the way of thinking of the inhabitants. What, then, were these ideas, and what was this literature?

II.

This literature little resembled that liked by the late masters of the country. It was as varied, superabundant, and many-coloured as the other was grand, monotonous, and melancholy. The writings produced or simply admired by the conquerors were, like themselves, at once practical and romantic. They had, together with a multitude of useful works, a number of charming songs and tales, the authors of which had no aim but to please.

The useful works are those so-called scientific treatises in which everything is taught that can be learned, including virtue : "Image du Monde," "Petite Philosophie," "Lumière des laïques," "Secret des Secrets," &c.[1]; or those chronicles which so efficaciously served the political views of the

---

[1] "Image du Monde," thirteenth century, a poem, very popular both in France and in England, of which "about sixty MSS. are known," "Romania," vol. xv. p. 314; some of the MSS. were written in England.—"Petite Philosophie," also in verse, being an "abrégé de cosmographie et de géographie," "Romania," xv. p. 255.—"Lumière des laïques," a poem, written in the thirteenth century, by the Anglo-Norman Pierre de Peckham or d'Abernun, *ibid.* p. 287.—"Secret des Secrets," an adaptation, in French prose, of the "Secretum Secretorum," wrongly attributed to Aristotle, this adaptation being the work of an Irishman, Geoffrey de Waterford, who translated also Dares and Eutrope, thirteenth century (see "Histoire Littéraire de la France," vol. xxi. p. 216).—To these may be added translations in French of various Latin works, books on the properties of things, law books, such as the "Institutes" of Justinian, turned into French verse by the Norman Richard d'Annebaut, and the "Coutume de Normandie," turned also into verse, by Guillaume Chapu, also a Norman, both living in the thirteenth century.

rulers of the land ; or else pious works that showed men the way to heaven.

The principal historical works are, as we have seen, those rimed in the twelfth century by Gaimar, Wace, and Benoit de Sainte-More, lengthy stories, each being more flowery than its predecessor, and more thickly studded with digressions of all sorts, and descriptions in all colours, written in short and clear verse, with bell-like tinklings. The style is limpid, simple, transparent : it flows like those wide rivers without dykes, which cover immense spaces with still and shallow water.[1]

In the following century the most remarkable work is the biography in verse of William le Maréchal, earl of Pembroke, one of those knights of proud mien who still appear to breathe as they lie on their tombs in Temple Church. This Life is the best of its kind and period ; the anonymous author who wrote it to order has the gift, unknown to his predecessors, of condensing his subject, of grouping his characters, of making them move and talk. As in Temple Church, on the monument he erects to them, they seem to be living.[2]

[1] See above, p. 113. The wealth of this historical literature in the French tongue is greater at first than that of the literature produced by the subjects of the French kings. Besides the great chronicles, many other works might be quoted, such as lives of saints, which are sometimes historical biographies (St. Edward, St. Thomas Becket, &c.); the "Histoire de la Guerre Sainte," an account of the third crusade, by Ambrose, a companion of King Richard Cœur-de-Lion, edited by Gaston Paris ("Documents inédits," 1897) ; the "Estoire le roi Dermot," on the troubles in Ireland, written in the thirteenth century ("Song of Dermot and the Earl," ed. Orpen, Oxford, 1892, 8vo ; *cf.* P. Meyer, "Romania," vol. xxi. p. 444), &c.

[2] This Life was written in the thirteenth century, by order of Earl William, son of the hero of the story. Its historical accuracy is remarkable. The MS. was discovered by M. Paul Meyer, and published by him : "Histoire de Guillaume le Maréchal," 3 vols., Paris, 1892 ff., Société de l'histoire de France. On the value of this Life, see an article by the same, "Romania," vol. xi. The slab in the Temple Church is in an excellent state of preservation ; the image of the earl seems to be a portrait ; the face is that of an old man with many wrinkles ; the sword is out of the scabbard, and held in the right hand ; its point is driven through the head of an animal at the feet of the earl.

Another century passes, the fashion of writing history in French verse still subsists, but will soon die out. Peter de Langtoft, a true Englishman as his language sufficiently proves, yet versifies in French, in the fourteenth century, a history of England from the creation of the world to the death of Edward I. But the times are changing, and Peter, last representative of an art that is over,[1] is a contemporary of that other Englishman, Robert of Gloucester, first representative of an art that begins, a distant ancestor of Gibbon and Macaulay. In sedate and manly, but somewhat monotonous strains, Robert tells in his turn the history of his country; differing in this respect from the others, he uses the English tongue; he is by no means cosmopolitan, but only and solely English. In the very first lines he makes this characteristic declaration: "England is a very good land; I ween the best of any. . . . The sea goes all about it; it stands as in an isle; it has the less to fear from foes. . . . Plenty of all goods may be found in England." [2]

The way to heaven is taught, after the Conquest, in innumerable French works, in verse and prose, paraphrases of the psalms and gospels, lives of the saints, manuals of

---

[1] Jean de Waurin, who wrote in French prose in the fifteenth century his "Chroniques et anchiennes istoires de la Grant-Bretaigne" (ed. Hardy, Rolls, 1864 ff.) was a Frenchman of France, who had fought at Agincourt on the French side. The chronicle of Peter de Langtoft, canon of Bridlington, Yorkshire, who lived under Edward I. and Edward II., was printed by Thomas Wright, 1866 (Rolls), 2 vols. 8vo.

[2] Engelond his a wel god lond · ich wene ech londe best . . .
The see geth him al aboute · he stond as in an yle,
Of fon hii dorre the lasse doute · bote hit be thorgh gyle . . .
Plente me may in Engelond · of alle gode ise.

W. A. Wright, "Metrical Chronicle of Robert of Gloucester," 1887 (Rolls), vol. i. pp. 1, 2. Robert's surname, "of Gloucester," is not certain; see Mr. Wright's preface, and his letter to the *Athenæum*, May 19, 1888. He is very hard (too hard it seems) on Robert, of whose work he says: "As literature it is as worthless as twelve thousand lines of verse without one spark of poetry can be."

penitence, miracles of Our Lady, moralised tales, bestiaries, and sermons.[1] The number of the French-speaking population had so increased in the kingdom that it was not

[1] Among writings of this sort, composed in French either by Frenchmen or by Englishmen, and popular in England, may be quoted : Penitential Psalms, a French version very popular in England, in a MS. preserved at the University Library, Cambridge, thirteenth century ("Romania," vol. xv. p. 305).—Explanation of the Gospels : the "Miroir," by Robert de Greteham, in 20,000 French verses (*Ibid.*).—Lives of Saints : life of Becket in "Materials for the history of Thomas Becket," ed. Robertson, 1875 ff., 7 vols., and "Fragments d'une vie de St. Thomas" (with very curious designs), edited by Paul Meyer, 1885, 4to, Société des Anciens Textes ; life of St. Catherine, by Sister Clemence de Barking, twelfth century (G. Paris, "Romania," xiii. p. 400) ; life of St. Josaphaz and life of the Seven Sleepers, by Chardry, thirteenth century ("Chardry's Josaphaz," &c., ed. Koch, Heilbronn, 1879, 8vo) ; life of St. Gregory the Great, by Augier, of St. Frideswide's, Oxford, thirteenth century (text and commentary in "Romania," xii. pp. 145 ff.) ; lives of St. Edward (ed. Luard, Rolls, 1858) ; mention of many other lives in French (others in English) will be found in Hardy's "Descriptive Catalogue," Rolls, 1862 ff.—Manuals and treatises : by Robert Grosseteste, William de Wadington and others (see below, p. 214).— Works concerning Our Lady : "Adgars Marien Legenden," ed. Carl Neuhaus, Heilbronn, 1886, 8vo (stories in French verse of miracles of the Virgin, by Adgar, an Anglo-Norman of the twelfth century ; some take place in England) ; "Joies de Notre Dame," "Plaintes de Notre Dame," French poems written in England, thirteenth century (see "Romania," vol. xv. pp. 307 ff.).— Moralised tales and Bestiaries : "Bestiaire" of Philippe de Thaon, a Norman priest of the twelfth century, in French verse (includes a "Lapidaire" and a "Volucraire," on the virtues of stones and birds), text in T. Wright, "Popular Treatises on Science," London 1841, Historical Society, 8vo ; see also P. Meyer, "Recueil d'anciens textes," Paris, 1877, 8vo, p. 286), the same wrote also an ecclesiastical "Comput" in verse (ed. Mall, Strasbourg, 1873, 8vo) ; "Bestiaire divin," by Guillaume le Clerc, also a Norman, thirteenth century (ed. Hippeau, Caen, 1852, 8vo), to be compared to the worldly "Bestiaire d'Amour," of Richard de Fournival, thirteenth century (ed. Hippeau, Paris, 1840, 8vo) ; translation in French prose, probably by a Norman, of the Latin fables (thirteenth century) of Odo de Cheriton, "Romania," vol. xiv. p. 388, and Hervieux, "Fabulistes Latins," vol. ii. ; "Contes moralisés de Nicole Bozon," ed. P. Meyer and Lucy Toulmin Smith, Paris, 1889, 8vo, Société des Anciens Textes, in French prose, fourteenth century.—Sermons : "Reimpredigt," ed. Suchier, Halle, 1879, 8vo, in French verse, by an Anglo-Norman ; on sermons in French and in Latin, see Lecoy de la Marche, "La Chaire française an moyen âge," Paris, 1886, 8vo, 2nd ed. ; at p. 282, sermon on the Passion by Geoffrey de Waterford in French verse, Anglo-Norman dialect.

absurd to preach in French, and some of the clergy inclined all the more willingly to so doing that many of
the higher prelates in the land were Frenchmen. "To
the simple folk," says, in French, an Anglo-Norman
preacher, "have I simply made a simple sermon. I did
not make it for the learned, as they have enough writings
and discourses. For these young people who are not
scholars I made it in the Romance tongue, for better will
they understand the language they have been accustomed
to since childhood."

> A la simple gent
> Ai fait simplement
> Un simple sarmun.
> Nel fis as letrez
> Car il unt assez
> Escriz e raisun.
>
> Por icels enfanz
> Le fis en romanz
> Qui ne sunt letré
> Car miel entendrunt
> La langue dunt sunt
> Dès enfance usé.[1]

Religious works, as well as the chronicles, are mainly
written in a clear, thin, transparent style ; the world can
be seen through the light religious veil ; the reader's attention wanders. In truth the real religious poems we owe
to the Normans are those poems in stone, erected by their
architects at Ely, Canterbury, York, Lincoln, Durham.
Much more conspicuous was the literature of the
imagination composed for them, a radiant literature made
of numberless romaunts, songs, and love-tales. They had

---

[1] "Reimpredigt," ed. Suchier, Halle, 1879, p. 64. There were also sermons
in English (see next chapter) ; Jocelin de Brakelonde says in his chronicle
that sermons were delivered in churches, "gallice vel potius anglice, ut
morum fieret edificatio, non literaturæ ostensio," year 1200 ; Camden
Society, 1840, p. 95 (also in "Memorials of St. Edmund's Abbey," Rolls,
1890, vol. i.).

no taste for the doleful tunes of the Anglo-Saxon poet;
his sadness was repellent to them, his despairs they
abhorred; they turned the page and shut the book with
alacrity. They were happy men; everything went well
with them; they wanted a literature meant for happy men.

III.

First of all they have epic tales; but how different from
"Beowulf"! The Song of Roland, whose high deeds were
held the glorious heirloom of the Normans as well as of
all Frenchmen, is the most warlike poem in the literature
of mediæval France, the one that best recalls the Germanic
origins of the race; yet a wide interval already separates
these origins from the new nation; the change is striking.[1]
Massacres, it is true, still occupy the principal place,
and a scent of blood pervades the entire poem; hauberks
torn open, bodies hewn in two, brains scattered on
the grass, the steam rising from the battle, fill the
poet's heart with rapture, and his soul is roused to
enthusiasm. But a place is also kept for tender sentiments, and another for winged speeches. Woman is
not yet the object of this tenderness; Charlemagne's
peers do not remember Aude while they fight; they
expire without giving her a sigh. But their eyes are
dim with tears at the recollection of fair France; they
weep to see their companions lie prostrate on the grass;

[1] "La Chanson de Roland, texte critique, traduction et commentaire," by
Léon Gautier, 1872, many ed. ; others with translation *e.g.* by Clédat, 1886-7,
by Bédier, 1922 ; with a photographic reprod. of the Oxford MS. by Stengel,
1878. On the Charlemagne romances composed in England, see G. Paris,
"Histoire poétique de Charlemagne, 1865, pp. 155 ff. (ed. P. Meyer, 1905).
The unique MS. of the "Chanson," written about 1170, is at Oxford, where
it was found in the XIXth century, first printed, 1837. See Gaston Paris's
"Littérature française au moyen âge," 1905, pp. 55 ff. ; Steelmann, "Biblio-
graphie des Rolandsliedes," 1889; Bédier, "Les Légendes épiques," 4 vols.,
1914-21, vol. iii.

the real mistress of Roland, the one to whom his last thought reverts, is not Aude but Durandal, his sword. This is his love, the friend of his life, whose fate, after he shall be no more, preoccupies him.   Just as this sword has a name, it has a life of its own ; Roland wishes it to die with him ; he would like to kill it, as a lover kills his mistress to prevent her falling into the hands of miscreants. " The steel grates, but neither breaks nor notches.   And the earl cries: Holy Mary, help me ! . . . Ah ! Durandal, so dearly beloved, how white and clear thou art! how thou shinest and flashest in the sunlight. . . . Ah ! Durandal, fair and holy art thou !" [1]   In truth, this is his love. Little, however, does it matter to ascertain with what or whom Roland is in love; the thing to be remembered is that he has a heart which can be touched and moved, and can indeed feel, suffer, and love.

At Roncevaux, as well as at Hastings, French readiness of wit appears even in the middle of the battle.   Archbishop Turpin, so imposing when he bestows the last benediction on the row of corpses, keeps all through the fight a good-humour similar to that of the Conqueror. " This Saracen seems to me something of a heretic," [2] he says, espying an enemy; and he fells him to earth.   Oliver, too, in a passage which shows that if woman has no active part assigned to her in the poem she had begun to play an important one in real life, slays the caliph and says : Thou at least shalt not go boasting of our defeat, " either to thy wife or to any lady in thy land." [3]

[1] Croist li aciers, ne fraint ne s'esgruignet ;
    Et dist li cuens : " Sainte Marie, aiude ! . . .
    E ! Durendal, com iés et clére et blanche !
    Contre soleil si reluis et reflambes ! . . .
    E ! Durendal, com iés bèle et saintisme ! "

[2] Cil Sarrazins me semblet mult herites.

[3] Ne a muillier n'a dame qu'as veüt
    N'en vanteras el' regne dunt tu fus.

It will finally be noticed that the subject of this epic, the oldest in France, is a defeat, thus showing, even in that far-distant age, what the heroic ideal of the nation was to be, that is, not so much to triumph as to die well. She will never lay down her arms merely because she is beaten; but only when enough of her sons have won glory by their death. Even when victory is impossible, the nation, though resigned to the inevitable, still fights for honour. Such as we see her in the Song of Roland, such she appears in Froissart, and such she has ever shown herself: "For never was the realm of France so broken, but that some one to fight against could be found there." [1]

The conquerors of England are complete men; they are not only valiant, they are learned; they not only want information about the immediate past of their own race, but are also interested in the distant past of other civilized nations; they make their poets tell them of the heroes of Greece and Rome, and immense metrical works are devoted to these personages, which will beguile the time and drive ennui away from castle-halls. These poems form a whole cycle; Alexander is the centre of it, as Charlemagne is of the cycle of France, and Arthur of the cycle of Britain.

The poets who write about these famous warriors endeavour to satisfy at once the contradictory tastes of their patrons for marvels and for truth. Their works are a collection of attested prodigies. They are unanimous in putting aside Homer's story, which does not contain enough miracles to please them, and, being in consequence little disposed to leniency, they reject the whole of it as apocryphal. I confess, says one of them, that Homer was a "marvellous clerk," but his tales must not be believed: "For well we know, past any doubt, that he

---

[1] "Car le Royaume de France ne fut oncques si desconfis que on n'y trouvast bien tousjours à qui combattre." Prologue of the Chronicles, Luce's edition, vol. i. p. 212.

was born more than a hundred years after the great host was gathered together." [1]

But the worst forger of Alexandria obtains the confidence of our poets ; they read with admiration in old manuscripts a journal of the siege of Troy, and the old manuscripts declare the author of this valuable document to be Dares the Phrygian. The work has its counterpart executed in the Grecian camp by Dictys of Crete. No doubt crosses their mind ; here is authenticity and truth, here are documents to be trusted ; and how interesting they are, how curious ! the very journal of an eye-witness ; truth and wonder made into one.

For Alexander they have a no less precious text : the Pseudo-Callisthenes, composed in Greek at Alexandria, of which a Latin version of the fourth century still exists. They are all the better disposed towards it that it is a long tissue of marvels and fabulous adventures. [2] For the history of Thebes they are obliged to content themselves with Statius, and for that of Rome with Virgil, that same Virgil who became by degrees, in mediæval legends, an enchanter, the Merlin of the cycle of Rome. He had, they believed, some weird connection with the powers of darkness ; for he had visited them and described in his " Æneid " their place of abode : no one was surprised at seeing Dante take him for a guide.

What these poets wished for was a certificate of authenticity at starting. Once they had it, they took no further

---

[1] Car bien scavons sanz nul espoir
   Q'il ne fu pius de c ans née
   Q'li grans ost fu assemblée.

MS. fr. 60 in the National Library, Paris, fol. 42 ; contains : "Li Roumans de Tiebes qui fu racine de Troie la grant.—Item toute l'histoire de Troie la grant," the latter by Benoit de Sainte-More, *infra*, p. 130.

[2] "Alexandre le Grand, dans la littérature française du moyen âge," by P. Meyer, Paris, 1886, 2 vols, 8vo (vol. i. texts, vol. ii. history of the legend) ; vol. ii. p. 182.

trouble ; it was their passport ; and with a well-worded
passport one can go a long way. After having blamed
Homer and appealed to Dares, they felt themselves above
suspicion, laid hands on all they could, and invented in
their turn. Here is, for example, an episode in the
romance of Alexander, a story of maidens in a forest,
who sink underground in winter and reappear in spring
in the shape of flowers : it will be vainly sought for in
Callisthenes ; it is of Eastern origin, and is found in
Edrisi. For want of better, and to avoid the trouble of
naming names, the authors will sometimes refer their
public to " Latin books," and such was the renown of
Rome that the reader asked nothing more.

No need to add that manners and dresses were scarcely
better observed than probability. Everything in these
poems was really *translated ;* not only the language of the
ancients, but their raiment, their civilisation, their ideas.
Venus becomes a princess ; the heroes are knights, and
their costumes are so much in the fashion of the day that
they serve us to date the poems. The miniatures conform
to the tale ; tonsured monks bear Achilles to the grave ;
they carry tapers in their hands. Queen Penthesilea,
" doughty and bold, and beautiful and virtuous," rides
astride, her heels armed with huge red spurs.[1] Œdipus
is dubbed a knight ; Æneas takes counsel of his " barons."
This manner of representing antiquity lasted till the
Renaissance ; and till much later, on the stage. Under
Louis XIV., Augustus wore a perruque " in-folio " ; and
in the eighteenth century Mrs. Hartley played Cleopatra in
paniers on the English stage.

In accordance with these ideas were written in French,
for the benefit of the conquerors of England, such tales as
the immense " Roman de Troie," by Benoit de Sainte-

[1] MS. fr. 782 at the National Library, Paris, containing poems by Benoit de
Sainte-More, fol. 151, 155, 158.

More, in which is related, for the first time in any modern
language, the story of Troilus and Cressida ; the anonymous
" Roman de Thèbes," ab. 1150 ; that of " Eneas," composed
during the same period ; the History of Alexander, or
the " Roman de toute Chevalerie," a vast compilation, one
of the longest and dullest that be, written in the beginning
of the thirteenth century by Eustace or Thomas of Kent ;
the Romance of " Ipomedon," and the Romance of " Pro-
thesilaus," by Hue of Rotelande, composed before 1191 ;
and many others besides [1]: all romances destined to
people of leisure, delighting in long descriptions, in prodigious adventures, in enchantments, in transformations,
in marvels. Alexander converses with trees who foretell
the future to him ; he drinks from the fountain of youth ;
he gets into a glass barrel lighted by lamps, and is let
down to the bottom of the sea, where he watches the
gambols of marine monsters ; his army is attacked by
wild beasts that, unaffrighted by flames, squat in the midst
of the fires intended to scare them away. He places the
corpse of the admiral who commanded at Babylon in an
iron coffin, that four loadstones hold to the vault. The
authors give their imagination full scope ; their romances
are operas ; at every page we behold a marvel and a

---

[1] Benoit de Sainte-More, a poet of the court of Henry II., wrote his " Roman
de Troie " about 1160 (G. Paris) ; ed. Joly, Paris, 1870 ; ed. Constans, Paris,
1904, ff.—" Le Roman de Thèbes," ed. L. Constans, Paris, 1890, 2 vols.
8vo, wrongly attributed to Benoit de Sainte-More, indirectly imitated from the
" Thebaid " of Statius.—" Eneas," a critical text, ed. J. Salverda de Grave,
Halle, Bibliotheca Normannica, 1891, 8vo, also attributed, but wrongly it
seems, to Benoit ; the work of a Norman, twelfth century ; imitated from the
" Æneid."—The immense poem of Eustache or Thomas de Kent is still unpublished ; the author imitates the romance in " alexandrines " of Lambert le
Tort and Alexandre de Paris, twelfth century, ed. Michelant, Stuttgart,
1846.—The romances of Hue de Rotelande (Rhuddlan in Flintshire ?) are also
in French verse, and were composed between 1176-7 and 1190-1 (see Ward,
"Catalogue of Romances," 1883, vol. i. pp. 728 ff.); his "Ipomedon" has
been edited by Kölbing and Koschwitz, Breslau, 1889, 8vo ; his " Prothe-
silaus " by F. Kluckow, Halle, 1925.

change of scene ; here we have the clouds of heaven, there
the depths of the sea. I write of these more than I believe,
" equidem plura transcribo quam credo," Quintus Curtius
had already said.[1]

Just as they had curiously inspected their new domains,
appropriating to themselves as much land as possible, so
the conquerors inspected the literatures of their new compatriots. If, as will be seen, they drew little from the
Saxon, it is not because they were absolutely ignorant of
it, but because they never could well understand its genius.
Amongst the different races with which they now found
themselves in contact, they were at once attracted by
intellectual sympathy to the Celtic, whose mind resembled
their own. Alexander had been an amusement, Arthur
became a passion. To the Anglo-Norman singers are
due the most ancient and beautiful poems of the Briton
cycle that have come down to us.

In the " matter " of France, the heroic valour of the
defenders of the country forms the principal interest of
the stories ; in the matter of Rome, the " mirabilia " ; and,
in the matter of Britain, love. We are farther and farther
removed from Beowulf.

At the time of the Conquest a quantity of legends and
tales were current concerning the Celtic heroes of Britain,
some of whom were quite independent of Arthur ; nevertheless all ended by being grouped about him, for he was
the natural centre of all this literature : " The Welsh have
never ceased to rave about him up to our day," wrote the
grave William of Malmesbury in the century after the
Conquest ; he was a true hero, and deserved something
better than the " vain fancies of dreamers." William
obviously was not under the spell of Arthurian legends.[2]

[1] Lib. IX. cap. ii.
[2] " Hic est Arthur de quo Britonum nugæ hodieque delirant, dignus plane
quod non fallaces somniarent fabulæ, sed veraces prædicarent historiæ." " De

Wales, Brittany, and Cornwall were the centres where these legends had developed ; the Briton harpists had, by the beauty of their tales, and the sweetness of their music, early acquired a great reputation. It was a recommendation for a minstrel to be able to state that he was a Briton, and some usurped this title, as does Renard the fox, in the " Roman de Renart." [1]

One thing, however, was lacking for a time to the complete success of the Arthurian epic : the stamp of authenticity, the Latin starting-point. An Anglo-Norman clerk furnished it, and bestowed upon this literature the Dares it needed. Professional historians were silent, or nearly so, respecting Arthur ; Gildas, in the sixth century, never mentions him ; " Nennius," in the eighth or ninth, briefly praises him as an invincible fighter.[2] Geoffrey of Monmouth makes up for this deficiency.[3]

His predecessors knew nothing, he knows everything ;

Gestis," ed. Stubbs, Rolls, vol. i. p. 11. Henry of Huntingdon, on the other hand, unable to identify the places of Arthur's battles, descants upon the vanity of fame and glory, " popularis auræ, laudis adulatoriæ, famæ transitoriæ. . . ." " Historia Anglorum," Rolls, p. 49.

    [1] Says the Wolf ("Roman de Renart," ed. Martin, vol. i. pp. 66, 67) :

> Dont estes vos ? de quel païs ?
> Vos n'estes mie nes de France . . .
> —Nai, mi seignor, mais de Bretaing . . .
> —Et savez vos neisun mestier ?
> —Ya, ge fot molt bon jogler . . .
> Ge fot savoir bon lai Breton.

Cf. F. Lot, " Etudes sur la provenance du cycle Arthurien," " Romania," xxiv.

    [2] Gildas, " De Excidio Britanniæ," ed. J. Stevenson, English Historical Society, 1838, 8vo ; Nennius, " Historia Britonum," same editor, place, and date, p. 47 ; cf. above, p. 14.

    [3] His " Historia" was edited by Giles, London, 1844, 8vo, and by San Marte, " Gottfried von Monmouth Historia regum Britanniæ," Halle, 1854, 8vo.   Geoffrey of Monmouth, or rather Geoffrey Arthur, a name which had been borne by his father before him (Galffrai or Gruffyd in Welsh), first translated from Welsh into Latin the prophecies of Merlin, included afterwards in his " Historia " ; bishop of St. Asaph, 1152 ; died at Llandaff, 1154. See Ward, " Catalogue of Romances," vol. i. pp. 203 ff.

his British genealogies are precise, his narratives are detailed, his enumerations complete. The mist had lifted, and the series of these kings about whom so many charming legends were afloat now appeared as clear as the succession of the Roman emperors. In their turn they present themselves with the authority conferred at that time in the world by great Latin books. They ceased to be the unacknowledged children of anybody's fancy ; they had, to own them, not some stray minstrel, but a personage of importance, known to the king of the land, who was to become bishop of St. Asaph, and be a witness at the peace of 1153, between Stephen of Blois and the future Henry II. In 1139, the "Historia Regum Britanniæ" had appeared, and copies began to circulate. Henry of Huntingdon, stopping at the Abbey of Bec, in Normandy, in the month of January of that year, finds one, and is filled with astonishment. "Never," writes he to one of his friends, "had I been able to obtain any information, oral or written, on the kings from Brutus to Cæsar. . . . But to my amazement I have just discovered—stupens inveni—a narrative of these times."[1] It was Geoffrey's book.

The better to establish his authority, Geoffrey himself had been careful to appeal to a mysterious source, a certain book of which no trace has ever been found, and which he pretends was given him by his friend Walter, Archdeacon of Oxford. Armed with this proof of authenticity, which no one could contest, he ends his history by a half-serious, half-joking challenge to the professional chroniclers of his time. "I forbid William of Malmesbury and Henry of Huntingdon to speak of the British kings, seeing that they have never had in their hands the book Walter, Archdeacon of Oxford, brought me from Brittany." Cervantes never spoke with more gravity of Cid Hamet-ben-Engeli.

[1] Ward, "Catalogue of Romances," vol. i. p. 210.

Such a work could not fail of success; it had a prodigious fame. Some historians lodged protests; they
might as well have protested against Dares. Gerald de
Barry cried out it was an imposture; and William of
Newbury inveighed against the impudence of "a writer
called Geoffrey," who had made "Arthur's little finger
bigger than Alexander's back."[1] In vain; copies of the
"Historia Regum" multiplied to such an extent that the
British Museum alone now possesses thirty-four of them.
The appointed chronicler of the Angevin kings, Wace,
translated it into French about 1155, with the addition of
several legends omitted by Geoffrey, that of the Round
Table among others.[2] It was turned into Latin verse,
into French alexandrines, into Welsh prose; no honour
was denied it. From this time dates the literary fortune
of Arthur, Merlin, Morgan the fairy, Perceval, Tristan
and Iseult, Lancelot and Guinevere, whose deeds and loves
have been sung from century to century, down to the day
of Shakespeare, of Swinburne, and Tennyson.

The finest poems the Middle Ages devoted to them
were written in French on English ground, and especially
the most charming of all, dedicated to that Tristan,[3] whom

[1] " Quidam nostris temporibus, pro expiandis his Britonum maculis, scriptor
emersit, ridicula de eisdem figmenta contexens, . . . Gaufridus hic dictus est . . .
Profecto minimum digitum sui Arturi grossiorem facit dorso Alexandri magni."
"Guilielmi Neubrigensis Historia," ed. Hearne, Oxford, 1719, 3 vols. 8vo,
" Proemium "; end of the twelfth century.

[2] " Le Roman de Brut," ed. Le Roux de Lincy, Rouen, 1836–38, 2 vols.
8vo. *Cf.* P. Meyer, "De quelques chroniques anglo-normandes qui ont
porté le nom de Brut," Paris, 1878, "Bulletin de la Société des Anciens Textes
français."

[3] The oldest poems we have in which the early songs on Tristan were
gathered into one whole are: 1st, the "Tristan" of Thomas, an Anglo-
Norman who wrote in French between 1155 and 1170; 2nd, the "Tristan"
of Béroul and an anonym, a quite different version written in Normandy
shortly after 1191 (same origin as the coeval German poem of Eilhart von
Oberge, ed. Lichtenstein, Strasbourg, 1877). A third was the work of the
famous Chrestien de Troyes, same century. We have only fragments of the

Dante places by Helen of Troy in the group of lovers. " I beheld Helen, who caused such years of woe, and I saw great Achilles . . . Paris and Tristan." ¹

Tristan's youth was spent in a castle of Léonois, by the sea. One day a Norwegian vessel, laden with stuffs and with hunting-birds, brings to before the walls. Tristan comes to buy falcons ; he lingers to play chess with the merchants ; the anchor is weighed, and Tristan is borne off in the ship. A storm drives the vessel on the coast of Cornwall, and the youth is conducted before King Marc. Harpers were playing ; Tristan remembers Briton lays ; he takes the harp, and so sweet is his music that "many a courtier remains there, forgetting his very name."²
Marc (who turns out to be his uncle) takes a fancy to him, and dubs him knight. " Should any one," says the author of one of the versions of Tristan, " inquire of me concerning the dress of the knights, I will tell him in a few words ; it was composed of four stuffs : courage, richness, skill, and courtesy."

Morolt, the giant, comes to claim a tribute of sixty youths and maidens, in the name of the king of Ireland.

---

two first ; the last is entirely lost. It has been, however, possible to recon-stitute the poem of Thomas mainly " by means of three versions : a German one (by Gottfried of Strasbourg, incomplete), a Norwegian one (in prose, ab. 1225, faithful but compressed), and an English one (XIVth century, a greatly impaired text)." G. Paris, " Litt. française au moyen âge," 1905, p. 101. J. Loth, "Contributions à l'étude des Romans de la Table Ronde," 1912.

Texts : " Le Roman de Tristan par Béroul et un anonyme," ed. E. Muret, 1903 ; " Le Roman de Tristan par Thomas," ed. Bédier, 1902-5 (both Soc. des Anc. Textes Français) ; adaptation in mod. Fr. prose, by Bédier, Paris [1900].—" Die Nordische und die Englische Version der Tristan-Sage," ed. Kölbing, Heilbronn, 1878-83, 2 vols. 8vo ; vol. i., " Tristrams Saga ok Isoudar" (Norwegian prose) ; vol. ii., " Sir Tristram " (English verse).— "Gottfried von Strassburg Tristan," ed. Reinhold Bechstein, Leipzig, 3rd ed., 1890 (German verse).

¹ " Inferno," canto v.

² The following analysis is mainly made after " Tristan et Iseult, poème de Gotfrit de Strasbourg, comparé à d'autres poèmes sur le même sujet," by A. Bossert, Paris, 1865, 8vo. Gottfried wrote at the beginning of XIIIth cent.

They were proceeding to select these victims, when Tristan challenges the giant and kills him ; but he is wounded by a poisoned weapon, and, day by day, death draws nearer. No one can cure this poison except the queen of Ireland, sister of the dead man. Tristan, disguised as a poor harper, has himself put on a bark and arrives in Dublin, where the queen heals him. The queen had a daughter, Iseult, with fair hair ; she begs the harper to instruct the young girl. Iseult becomes perfect : " She can both read and write, she composes epistles and songs ; above all, she knows many [Briton] lays. She is sought after for her musical talent, no less than for her beauty, a silent and still sweeter music that through the eyes insinuated itself into the heart." All her life she remembered the teaching of Tristan, and in her sorrows had recourse to the consoling power of music. When sitting alone and sad, she would sing "a touching song of love," on the misfortunes of Guiron, killed for the sake of his lady. This lay "she sings sweetly, the voice accords with the harp, the hands are beautiful, the lay is fine, sweet the voice and low the tone." [1]

Tristan's task being accomplished, he returns to Cornwall. One day a swallow drops at the feet of King Marc a golden hair, so soft and brilliant, so lovable, that the king swears to marry no other woman but her of the golden hair.[2] Tristan starts in quest of the woman. The

---

[1]   En sa chambre se set un jur,
       E fait un lai pitus d'amur :
       Coment dan Guirun fu surpris,
       Pur l'amur de sa dam ocis. . . .
       La dame chante dulcement,
       La voiz acorde à l'estrument ;
       Les mainz sunt bels, li lais bons
       Dulce la voiz e bas li tons.
" Roman de Tristan," ed. Bédier, i. p. 295.

[2] On this incident, the earliest version of which is as old as the fourteenth century B.C., having been found in an Egyptian papyrus of that date, see Gaston Paris, " Poèmes et Légendes du Moyen-Age," Paris, 1900, p. 135.

woman is Iseult ; he brings her to Cornwall. While at
sea the two young people swallow by mistake an enchanted draught, a " boivre" destined for Marc and his
betrothed, which had the virtue of producing a passion
that only death could end. The poison slowly takes
effect ; their sentiments alter. " All that I know troubles
me, and all I see pains me," says Iseult. " The sky,
the sea, my own self oppress me. She bent forward,
and leant her arm on Tristan's shoulder : it was her
first caress. Her eyes filled with repressed tears ; her
bosom heaved, her lips quivered, and her head remained
bent."

The marriage takes place. Marc adores the queen,
but she thinks only of Tristan. Marc is warned, and
exiles Tristan, who, in the course of his adventures,
receives a present of a wonderful dog. This dog wore a
bell on his neck, the sound of which, so sweet it was,
caused all sorrow to be forgotten. He sends the dog to
Iseult, who, listening to the bell, finds that her grief fades
from her memory ; and she removes the collar, unwilling
to hear and to forget.

Iseult is at last repudiated, and Tristan bears her off by
lonely paths, through forest depths, until they reach a
grotto of green marble carved by giants in ages past. An
aperture at the top let in the light, lindens shaded the
entrance, a rill trickled over the grass, flowers scented
the air, birds sang in the branches. Here nothing more
existed for them save love. " Nor till the might of
August "—thought the old poet, and said a more recent
one—

> Nor till the might of August overhead
> Weighed on the world, was yet one roseleaf shed
> Of all their joys warm coronal, nor aught
> Touched them in passing ever with a thought
> That ever this might end on any day,
> Or any night not love them where they lay ;

But like a babbling tale of barren breath
Seemed all report and rumour held of death,
And a false bruit the legend tear impearled
That such a thing as change was in the world.[1]

King Marc's hunt passes by the grotto; through an opening at the top he chances to perceive her who had been "the springtide of his life, fairer than ever at this moment . . . her mouth, her brow, every feature was so full of charm that Marc was fascinated, and, seized with longing, would fain on that face have pressed a kiss. . . . A wreath of clover was woven in her unbound locks. . . . When he saw that the sun overhead let fall through the crevice a ray of light on Iseult's face, he feared lest her hue should suffer. He took grass and flowers and foliage with which he closed the aperture, then blessing the lady, he commended her to God, and departed weeping." [2]

Once more the lovers are separated, this time for ever. Years pass; Tristan has made himself famous by his exploits. He is without news of his love, doubtless forgotten. He marries another Iseult, and lives with her near Penmarch in Brittany. Wounded to death in a fight, he might be cured by the queen of Cornwall, and in spite of his marriage, and the time that has elapsed, he sends her word to leave all and join him. If Iseult comes, the ship is to have a white sail; if she refuses, a black one. Iseult still loves. At the first word she puts to sea; but storms arise, then follows a dead calm; Tristan feels life ebb from him with hope. At last the vessel appears, and Tristan's wife sees it from the shore with its white sail. She had overheard Tristan's message; she returns, lies, and announces the arrival of a black sail. Tristan tears the bandage from his wound and dies. When the true Iseult lands, the knell is tolling from the steeples of Brittany;

[1] Swinburne, "Tristram of Lyonesse and other poems."
[2] Bosert, pp. 62, 68, 72, 82.

she rushes in, finds her lover's corpse already cold, and
expires beside him.   They were buried in the same church
at Carhaix, one at each end ; out of one of the tombs
grew a vine, and out of the other grew a rose tree, and
the branches, creeping along the pillars, interlaced under the
vaulted roof.   The magic draught thus proved stronger
than death.

In the ancient epic poems, love was nothing, here it is
everything ; and woman, who had no part, now plays the
first ; warlike feats are henceforth only a means to win her
heart.   Grass has grown over the bloody vale of Roncevaux,
which is now enamelled with flowers ; Roland's love,
Durandal, has ascended to heaven, and will return no
more.   The new poets are the exact antithesis of the
former ones.   Religion, virtue, country, now count for
nothing ; love defies, nay more, replaces them.   Marc's
friends, who warn him, are traitors and felons, vowed to
scorn and hate, as were formerly Gannelons, who betrayed
fair France.   To be in love is to be worthy of heaven,
is to be a saint, and to practise virtue.   This theory, put
forward in the twelfth century by the singers of the British
cycle, has survived, and will be found again in d'Urfé's
" Astrée," in Byron, and in Musset.

These tales multiply, and their worldly, courteous,
amorous character becomes more and more predominant.
Woman already plays the part that she plays in the novels
of yesterday.   A glance opens Paradise to Arthur's
knights ; they find in a smile all the magic which it
pleases us, the living of to-day, to discover there.   A trite
word of farewell from the woman they cherish is transformed by their imagination, and they keep it in their
hearts as a talisman.   Who has not cherished similar
talismans ?   Lancelot recalls the past to queen Guinevere :
" And you said, God be with you, fair, gentle friend !
Never since have these words left my heart.   It is these

words that shall make me a *preux*, if ever I am one; for never since was I in such great peril but that I remembered these words. They have comforted me in all my sorrows; these words have kept and guarded me from all danger; these words have fed me when hungry and made me wealthy when poor."

"By my troth," said the queen, "those words were happily spoken, and blessed be God who caused me to speak them. But I did not put into them as much as you saw, and to many a knight have I spoken the same without thinking they were more than words."

After being a saint, the beloved object becomes a goddess; her wishes are decrees, her mysterious caprices are laws which must not even be questioned; harder rules of love are from year to year imposed on the heroes; they are expected to turn pale at the sight of their mistress; Amadas, seeing Ydoine, turns pale and faints;[2] Lancelot espying a hair of Guinevere well-nigh faints; they observe the thirty-one regulations laid down by André le Chapelain, to guide the perfect lover.[3] After having been

----

[1] "Et vous deistes, ales a Dieu, beau doulx amis. Ne oncques puis du cueur ne me pot issir; ce fut li moz qui preudomme me fera si je jamais le suis; car oncques puis ne fus à si grant meschief qui de ce mot ne me souvenist; cilz moz me conforte en tous mes anuys; cilz moz m'a tousjours garanti et gardé de tous périlz; cilz moz m'a saoulé en toutes mes faims; cilz moz me fait riche en toutes mes pouretés. Par foi fait la royne cilz moz fut de bonne heure dit, et benois soit dieux qui dire le me fist. Mais je ne le pris pas si acertes comme vous feistes. A maint chevalier l'ay je dit là où oncques je n'y pensay fors du dire seulement." MS. fr. 118 in the Nat. Libr., Paris, fol. 219; XIVth cent. The history of Lancelot was told in verse and prose in almost all the languages of Europe from the XIIth cent. One of the oldest versions was the work of an Anglo-Norman. Most famous of those poems, the "Conte de la Charrette," by Chrestien de Troyes, written between 1164 and 1172 (G. Paris, "Romania," xii. 463). See Miss Weston, "Legend of Sir Lancelot," 1901, Lot in "Bibl. Ecole des Hautes Etudes," 1918, No. 226.

[2] French verse, written in England, XIIth cent., G. Paris, "Furnivall Miscellany," 1901, p. 392.

[3] "Omnis consuevit amans in coamantis aspectu pallescere," &c. Rules supposed to have been discovered by a knight at the court of Arthur, and

first an accessory, then an irresistible passion, love, that the poets think to magnify, will soon be nothing but a ceremonial. From the time of Lancelot we border on folly ; military honour no longer counts for the hero; Guinevere out of caprice orders Lancelot to behave "his worst"; without hesitating or comprehending he obeys, and covers himself with shame. Each successive romance writer goes a step farther, and makes new additions ; we come to immense compositions, to strings of adventures without any visible link ; to heroes so uniformly wonderful that they cease to inspire interest and to cause wonder. Tristan's rose-bush twined itself around the pillars, the pillars are lacking now, and the clusters of flowers trail on the ground. Tristan was a harbinger of Musset; Guinevere gives us a desire for a Cervantes.

Meanwhile, the minstrels of the twelfth and thirteenth centuries enjoy their success and their fame; their number increases ; they are welcomed in the castles, hearkened to in the towns ; their tales are copied in manuscripts, more and more magnificently painted. They celebrate, in England as in France, Gauvain, " le chevalier aux demoiselles," Ivain, " le chevalier au lion," Merlin, Joseph of Arimathea, Perceval and the quest of the mysterious Graal, and all the rest of the Round Table heroes.[1]

IV.

They have also shorter narratives in prose and verse, the subject of which is generally love, drawn from French,

transcribed in the " Flos Amoris," or " De Arte honeste amandi," of André le Chapelain, thirteenth century ; " Romania," vol. xii. p. 532.

[1] The three last (partly lost), by Rob. de Boron, a Frenchman from Franche-Comté, early XIIIth cent. " Perceval " had been begun by Chrestien de Troyes (" Samm. Werke," ed. Förster, Halle, 1896 ff.). See G. Paris, " Hist. littéraire de la France," vol. xxx., " Litt. au Moyen Age," pp. 92 ff. ; Ward, " Catalogue of MS. Romances," 1883 (on Merlin, pp. 278 ff. ; on other prophecies, and especially those by Thomas of Erceldoune, p. 328 ; these last ed. by Alois Brandl, " Thomas of Erceldoune," Berlin, 1880, " Sammlung Englischer Denkmäler," and by the E.E.T.S., 1875).

Latin, Greek, and even Hindu legends,[1] stories like those
of Amis and Amile, of Floire and Blanchefleur, lays like
those of Marie de France.[2]   Marie was Norman, and lived
in the time of Henry II., to whom she dedicated her
poems.   They are mostly graceful love-tales, sweetly
told, without affectation or effort, and derived from Celtic
originals, some being of Armorican and some of Welsh
descent.   Several are devoted to Tristan and other
Arthurian knights.   In the lay of the Ash, Marie tells
a story of female virtue, the main incidents of which will
be found again later in the tale of Griselda.   Her lay of
the Two Lovers would have delighted Musset:

"Truth is that in Neustria, which we call Normandy,"
lived once a nobleman who had a beautiful daughter;
every one asked her in marriage, but he always refused,
so as not to part from her.   At last he declared he would
give his daughter to the man who could carry her to the
top of the mountain.   All tried, but all failed.

A young count falls in love with her, and is loved again.
She sends him to an old aunt of hers, who lives at Salerno,

---

[1] On legends of Hindu origin and for a long time wrongly attributed to the
Arabs, see Gaston Paris, "le Lai de l'Oiselet," Paris, 1884, 8vo.   See also the
important work of M. Bédier, "les Fabliaux," Paris, 1893, 8vo, in which the
evidence concerning the Eastern origin of tales is carefully sifted and restricted
within the narrowest limits: very few come from the East, not the bulk of
them, as was generally admitted.

[2] For Amis, very popular in England, see Kölbing, "Amis and Amiloun,"
Heilbronn, 1884 (*cf.* below, p. 229), and "Nouvelles françoises en prose du
treizième siècle" (several are of the twelfth), ed. by Moland and d'Héricault,
Paris, 1856, 16mo; these "Nouvelles" include: "l'Empereur Constant,"
"les Amitiés de Ami et Amile," "le roi Flore et la belle Jehanne," "la
Comtesse de Ponthieu," "Aucassin et Nicolette."—The French text of "Floire
et Blanceflor" is to be found in Edelstand du Meril, "Poèmes du treizième
siècle," Paris, 1856, 16mo.—For Marie, see H. Suchier, "Die Lais der Marie
de France," Halle, Bibliotheca Normannica, 1885, Hoepffner, "Marie de
France, les Lais," 1921; her fables are in vol. ii. of "Poésies de Marie de
France," ed. Roquefort, Paris, 1819, 2 vols. 8vo.   See also Bédier's article in
the *Revue des Deux Mondes*, Oct. 15, 1891, the chapter on Marie in Hervieux, "Fabulistes Latins," 1883-4, 2nd part, chap. i., and *infra*, p. 229.

and will give him certain potions to increase his strength.
He does all she bids him. On the day appointed, provided
with a draught to swallow during the trial, he takes the
fair maiden in his arms. She had fasted for many days so
as to weigh less, and had put on an exceedingly light garment : " Except her shift, no other stuff she wore " ;

N'ot drap vestu fors la chemise.

He climbs half-way, then begins to flag ; but he wishes
to owe everything to his energy, and, without drinking,
slowly continues to ascend. He reaches the top and falls
dead. The young girl flings away the now useless flask,
which breaks ; and since then the mountain herbs
moistened by the potion have wonderful healing powers.
She looks at her lover and dies, like the Simonne of
Boccaccio and of Musset. They were buried on the
mountain, where has since been built "the priory of the
Two Lovers."

The rulers of England delight in still shorter poems, but
again on the same theme : love. Like the rest of the
French, they have an innate fondness for a kind of
literature unknown to their new compatriots : namely,
chansons. They composed a great number of them, and
listened to many more of all sorts. The subjects of the
kings of England became familiar with every variety of
the kind ; for the Angevin princes now possessed such wide
domains that the sources of French poetry, poetry of the
North, poetry of the South, lyrical poetry of Poictou and of
Maine, gushed forth in the very heart of their empire.[1]

Their English subjects got acquainted with these poems
in two ways : firstly, because many of those songs were
sung in the island ; secondly, because many English-

[1] On this subject, see Gaston Paris's criticism of the "Origines de la poésie
lyrique en France " of Jeanroy, in the " Journal des Savants," 1892.

men, soldiers, clerks, minstrels, messengers, followed the
king and stayed with him in the parts where the main
wells and fountains of the French *chanson* happened to be.[1]
They became thus familiarised with the "reverdies," May
songs, which celebrate springtime, flowers, and free loves ;
"carols," or dancing songs ; "pastourelles," the wise or
foolish heroines of which are shepherdesses ; "disputoisons"
or debates, to which kind belongs the well-known song of
"transformations" introduced by Mistral in his "Mireio,"
and set to music by Gounod ; "aube" songs, telling the
complaint of lovers, parted by dawn, and in which, long
before Shakespeare, the Juliets of the time of Henry II.
said to their Romeos :

> It is not yet near day ;
> It was the nightingale and not the lark.

> Il n'est mie jors, saverouze au cors gent,
> Si m'aït amors, l'aloete nos ment.[2]

"It is not yet near day, my sweet one ; love be my help,
the lark lies." In these songs, the women are slight and

[1] One fact among many shows how constant was the intercourse on the
Continent between Frenchmen of France and Englishmen living or travelling
there, namely, the knowledge of the English language shown in the twelfth
and thirteenth centuries by the authors of several branches of the " Roman de
Renart," and the caricatures they drew of English people, which would have
amused nobody if the originals of the pictures had not been familiar to all.
(See Branches I[b] and XIV. in Martin's edition.)

[2] Jeanroy, " Origines de la poésie lyrique en France, au moyen âge," 2nd
ed. 1904, p. 68. An allusion in a crusade song of the twelfth century shows
that this *motif* was already popular then. It is found also in much older poetry
and more remote countries, for Jeanroy quotes a Chinese poem, written before
the seventh century of our era, where, it is true, a mere cock and mere flies
play the part of the Verona lark and nightingale : " It was not the cock, it was
the hum of flies," or in the Latin translation of Father Lacharme : " Fallor,
non cantavit gallus, sed muscarum fuit strepitus," *ibid.*, p. 70.

On *chansons* written in French by Anglo-Normans, see " Mélanges de poésie
anglo-normande," by P. Meyer, in " Romania," vol. iv. p. 370, and " Les
Manuscrits Francais de Cambridge," by the same, *ibid.*, vol. xv.

lithe; they are more gentle than doves; their faces are all
pink and white: "If the flowers of the hawthorn were
united to the rose, not more delicate would be their colour
than that on my lady's clear face."

> Si les flurs d[el] albespine
> Fuissent à roses assis,
> N'en ferunt colur plus fine
> Ke n'ad ma dame au cler vis.[1]

With these songs, Love ventures out of castles; we find
him "in cellars, or in lofts under the hay."[2] He steals
even into churches, and a sermon that has come down to
us, preached in England in the thirteenth century, has for
text, instead of a verse of Scripture, a verse of a French
song: "Fair Alice rose at morn, clothed and adorned her
body; an orchard she went in, five flowers there she found,
a wreath she made with them of blooming roses; for God's
sake, get you gone, you who do not love!" and with meek
gravity the preacher goes on: Belle Alice is or might be
the Virgin Mary; "what are those flowers," if not "faith,
hope, charity, virginity, humility?"[3] The idea of turning
worldly songs and music to religious ends is not, as we see,
one of yesterday.

[1] Anglo-Norman song, written in England, in the thirteenth century,
"Romania," vol. xv. p. 254.

[2] "La Plainte d'amour," from a MS. in the University Library, Cambridge,
GG I. 1, "Romania," *ibid.*

> [3] Bele Aliz matin leva,
> Sun cors vesti e para,
> Enz un verger s'entra,
> Cink flurettes y truva,
> Un chapelet fet en a
> De rose flurie;
> Pur Deu, trahez vus en là
> Vus ki ne amez mie.

The text of the sermon, as we have it is in Latin; it has long but wrongly
been attributed to Stephen Langton; printed by T. Wright in his "Biographia
Britannica, Anglo-Norman period," 1846, p. 446.

Tristan has led us very far from Beowulf, and fair Alice
leads us still farther from the mariner and exile of Anglo-
Saxon literature. To sum up in a word which will show
the difference between the first and second period : on the
lips of the conquerors of Hastings, odes have become
chansons.

V.

Nothing comes so near ridicule as extreme sentiments,
and no men had the sense of the ridiculous to a higher
degree than the new rulers of the English country. At
the same time with their chivalrous literature, they had a
mocking one. They did not wait for Cervantes to begin
laughing ; these variable and many-sided beings sneered
at high-flown sentiments and experienced them too.
They sang the Song of Roland, and read with delight
a romance in which the great emperor is represented
strutting about before his barons, his crown on his head
and his sword in his hand, asking the queen if he is not the
most admirable prince in the world.[1] To his surprise, the
queen says no, there is a better, there is King Hugon,
emperor of Greece and of Constantinople. Charlemagne
wishes to verify on the spot, and pledges his word that he
will cut the queen's head off if she has not spoken truth.
He mounts a donkey ; the twelve peers follow his example,
and in this fashion the flower of French chivalry takes its
way to the East.

At Constantinople, the city of marvels, which had not
yet become the city of mosques, but was still enriched by
the spoils of Athens and Rome, where St. Sophia shone
with all the glory of its mosaics intact, where the palace of
the emperors dazzled the sight with its gold and its statues,

---

[1] "Le Pélerinage de Charlemagne," eleventh century.   Only one MS. has
been preserved, written in England, in the thirteenth century ; it has been
edited by Koschwitz, "Karls des Grossen Reise nach Jerusalem und Kon-
stantinopel," Heilbronn, 1880, 8vo.   *Cf.* "Romania," vol. ix.

the French princes could scarcely believe their eyes. At every step they were startled by some fresh wonder; here bronze children blowing horns; there a revolving hall set in motion by the sea-breeze; elsewhere a carbuncle which illuminated apartments at night. The queen might possibly have spoken truth. Evening draws on, they drink deep, and, excited by their potations, indulge in *gabs*, or boasts, that are overheard by a spy, and carefully noted. Ogier the Dane will uproot the pillar which supports the whole palace; Aïmer will make himself invisible and knock the emperor's head on the table; Roland will sound his horn so loudly that the gates of the town will be forced open. Threatened and insulted by his guests, Hugon declares they shall either accomplish their *gabs* or pay for their lies with their heads.

This is too much, and the author changes his tone. Will God permit the confusion of the emperor of the Franks, however well deserved it be? "Vivat qui Francos diligit Christus!" was already written in the Salic law: Christ continues to love the Franks. He takes their cause into His own hands, not because of their deserts but because they are Franks. By a miracle, one after another, the *gabs* are realised; Hugon acknowledges the superiority of Charles, who returns to France, enriches St. Denis with incomparable relics, and forgives the queen. This poem is exactly contemporaneous with the Song of Roland.

But there is better still, and the comedy is much more general in the famous "Roman de Renart."[1] This

---

[1] "Le Roman de Renart," ed. E. Martin, Strasbourg, 1882-7, 4 vols. 8vo; contains: vol. i., the old series of branches; vol. ii., the additional branches; vol. iii., variants; vol. iv., notes and tables. Most of the branches were composed in Normandy, Ile-de-France, Picardy; the twelfth is the work of Richard de Lison, a Norman, end of the twelfth century; several, for example the fourteenth, evince on the part of their author a knowledge of the English tongue and manners. See Sudre, "Les Sources du Roman de Renart," Paris, 1892; L. Foulet, "Le Roman de Renard," Paris, 1914.

romance, of which the branches are of various epochs and by various authors, was composed partly in the continental estates of the kings of England, partly in the France of French kings. It was built up, section after section, during several centuries, beginning with the twelfth : built like a cathedral, each author adding a wing, a tower, a belfry, a steeple ; without caring, most of the time, to make known his name; so that the poem has come down to us, like the poems in stone of the architects, anonymous, or nearly so, the work of every one, an expression and outcome of the popular mind.

For many Frenchmen of ancient France, a *chanson* was a sufficient revenge, or at least served as a temporary one. So much pleasure was taken in it, that by such means the tyranny of the ruler was forgotten. On more than one occasion where in other countries a riot would have been unavoidable, in France a song has sufficed ; discontent, thus attenuated, no longer rose to fury. More than one jacquerie has possibly been delayed, if not averted, by the "Roman de Renart."

In this ample comedy everybody has a part to perform ; everybody and everything is in turn laughed at : the king, the nobles, the citizens, the Pope, the pilgrims, the monks, every belief and every custom,[1] religion, and justice, the powerful, the rich, the hypocrites, the simple-minded ; and, so that nothing shall be wanting, the author scoffs at himself and his caste ; he knows its failings, points them out and laughs at them. The tone is heroi-comical : for the jest to take effect, the contrast must be clearly visible, and we should keep in view the importance of principles and the majesty of kings :

[1] Caricature of a funeral ceremony :—

> Brun li ors, prenez vostre estole . . .
> Sire Tardis li limaçons
> Lut par lui sol les trois leçons
> Et Roenel chanta les vers. (Vol. i. p. 12.)

" Lordings, you have heard many a tale, related by many a tale-teller, how Paris ravished Helen, the trouble it brought him, and the sorrow! . . . also gests and fabliaux; but never did you hear of the war—such a hard one it was, and of such great import — between Renard and Ysengrin." [1]

The personages are animals; their sentiments are human; king lion swears like a man [2]; but the way in which they sit, or stand, or move, is that of their species. Every motion of theirs is observed with that correctness of eye which is always found in early times among animal painters, long before painters of the human figure rise to the same excellence. There are perfect descriptions of Ysengrin, who feels very foolish after a rebuke of the king's, and "sits with his tail between his legs"; of the cock, monarch of the barn-yard; of Tybert the cat; of Tardif the slug; of Espinar the hedgehog; of Bruin the bear; of Roonel the mastiff; of Couard the hare; of Noble the lion. The arrival of a procession of hens at Court is an excellent scene of comedy.

" Sir Chanteclair, the cock, and Pinte, who lays the big eggs, and Noire, and Blanche, and la Roussette, were dragging a cart with drawn curtains. A hen lay in it prostrate. . . . Renard had so maltreated her, and so

---

[1] Seigneurs, oï avez maint conte
Que maint conterre vous raconte,
Conment Paris ravi Eleine,
Le mal qu'il en ot et la paine . . .
Et fabliaus, chansons de geste . . .
Mais onques n'oïstes la guerre,
Qui tant fu dure et de grant fin
Entre Renart et Ysengrin.
(Prologue of Branch II.)

[2] " Or dont," dit Nobles, " au deable !
Por le cuer be, sire Ysengrin,
Prendra ja vostre gerre fin?" (Vol. i. p. 8.)

pulled her about with his teeth, that her thigh was broken, and a wing torn off her side." [1]

Pinte, moved to tears and ready to faint, like Esther before Ahasuerus, tells the king her woes. She had five brothers, Renard has devoured every one; she had five sisters, but "only one has Renard spared; all the rest have passed through his jaws. And you, who lie there on your bier, my sweet sister, my dear friend, how plump and tender you were! What will become of your poor unfortunate sister?" [2] She is very near adding in Racine's words: "Mes filles, soutenez votre reine éperdue!" Anyhow, she faints.

"The unfortunate Pinte thereupon fainted and fell on the pavement; and so did the others, all at once. To assist the four ladies all jumped from their stools, dog and wolf and other beasts, and threw water on their brows." [3]

[1] . . . Sire Chanticler li cos,
　　Et Pinte qui pont les ues gros
　　Et Noire et Blanche et la Rossete
　　Amenoient une charete
　　Qui envouxe ert d'une cortine.
　　Dedenz gisoit une geline
　　Que l'en amenoit en litère
　　Fete autresi con une bère.
　　Renart l'avoit si maumenée
　　Et as denz si desordenée
　　Que la cuisse li avoit frete
　　Et une ele hors del cors trete.　(Vol. i. p. 9.)

[2] . . . Renart ne l'en laissa
　　De totes cinc que une soule:
　　Totes passèrent par sa goule.
　　Et vos qui là gisez en bère,
　　Ma douce suer m'amie chère,
　　Con vos estieez tendre et crasse!
　　Que fera vostre suer la lasse?　(Vol. i. p. 10.)

[3] Pinte la lasse à ces paroles
　　Chaï, pamée el pavement
　　Et les autres tot ensement.
　　Por relever les quatre dames,
　　Se levèrent de leurs escames

The king is quite upset by so moving a sight: "His head out of anger he shakes; never was so bold a beast, a bear be it or a boar, who does not fear when their lord sighs and howls. So much afraid was Couard the hare that for two days he had the fever; all the Court shakes together, the boldest for dread tremble. He, in his wrath, raises his tail, and is moved with such pangs that the roar fills the house; and then this was his speech: 'Lady Pinte,' the emperor said, 'upon my father's soul'"[1] . . .

Hereupon follows a solemn promise, couched in the most impressive words, that the traitor shall be punished; which will make all the more noticeable the utter defeat which verbose royalty soon afterward suffers. Renard worsts the king's messengers; Bruin the bear has his nose torn off; Tybert the cat loses half his tail; Renard jeers at them, at the king, and at the Court. And all through the story he triumphs over Ysengrin, as Panurge over Dindenault, Scapin over Géronte, and Figaro over Bridoison. Renard is the first of the family; he is such a natural and spontaneous creation of the French mind that we see him reappear from century to century, the same character under different names.

> Et chen et lou et autres bestes,
> Eve lor getent sor les testes.

> [2] Par mautalant drece la teste,
> Onc n'i ot si hardie beste,
> Or ne sangler, que poor n'et
> Quant lor sire sospire et bret.
> Tel poor ot Coars li lèvres
> Que il en ot deus jors les fèvres.
> Totc la cort fremist ensemble,
> Li plus hardis de peor tremble.
> Par mautalent sa coue drece,
> Si se débat par tel destrece
> Que tot en sone la meson,
> Et puis fu tele sa reson.
> Dame Pinte, fet l'emperere,
> Foi que doi à l'ame mon père. . . •

One last point to be noted is the impression of open air given by nearly all the branches of this romance, in spite of the brevity of the descriptions. We are in the fields, by the hedges, following the roads and the footpaths ; the moors are covered with heather ; the rocks are crowned by oaken copse, the roads are lined with hawthorn, cabbages display in the gardens the heavy mass of their clustering leaves. We see with regret the moment when " the sweet time of summer declines." Winter draws near, a north wind blows over the paths leading to the sea. Renard "dedenz sa tour" of Maupertuis lights a great wood fire, and, while his little ones jump for joy, grills slices of eels on the embers.

Renard was popular throughout Europe. In England parts of the romance were translated or imitated ; superb manuscripts were illuminated for the libraries of the nobles; the incidents of this epic were represented in tapestry, sculptured on church stalls, painted on the margins of English missals. At the Renaissance Caxton, with his Westminster presses, printed a Renard in prose.[1]

Above, below, around these greater works, swarms the innumerable legion of satirical fabliaux and laughable tales. They, too, cross the sea, slight, imperceptible, wandering,

---

[1] Examples of sculptures in the stalls of the cathedrals at Gloucester, St. David's, &c. ; of miniatures, MS. 10 E iv. in the British Museum (English drawings of the beginning of the fourteenth century, one of them reproduced in " English Wayfaring Life," p. 309) ; of manuscripts : MS. fr. 12,583 in the National Library, Paris, " Cest livre est à Humfrey duc de Gloucester, liber lupi et vulpis " ; of a translation in English of part of the romance : " Of the Vox and the Wolf" (time of Edward I., in Wright's " Selection of Latin Stories," Percy Society ; see below, pp. 228 ff.). Caxton issued in 1481 " Thystorye of Reynard the Foxe," reprinted by Thoms, Percy Society, 1844, 8vo. The MS. in the National Library, mainly followed by Martin in his edition, offers "a sort of mixture of the Norman and Picard dialects. The vowels generally present Norman if not Anglo-Norman characteristics." " Roman de Renart," vol. i. p. 2. *Cf.* below, vol. ii. p. 103.

thus continuing those migrations so difficult to trace, the laws of which learned men of all nations have vainly sought to discover. They follow all roads; nothing stops them. Pass the mountains and you will find them; cross the sea and they have preceded you; they spring from the earth; they fall from heaven; the breeze bears them along like pollen, and they go to bloom on other stems in unknown lands, producing thorny or poisonous or perfumed flowers, and flowers of every hue. All those varieties of flowers are sometimes found clustered in unexpected places, on wild mountain sides, along lonely paths, on the moors of Brittany or Scotland, in royal parks and in convent gardens. At the beginning of the seventh century the great Pope St. Gregory introduces into his works a number of " Exempla," saying: " Some are more incited to the love of the celestial country by stories—exempla—than by sermons ;" [1] and in the gardens of monasteries, after his day, more and more miscellaneous grow the blossoms. They are gathered and preserved as though in herbals, collections are made of them, from which preachers borrow ; tales of miracles are mixed with others of a less edifying nature.

Stop before the house of this anchoress, secluded from the world, and absorbed in pious meditations, a holy and quiet place. An old woman sits under the window; the anchoress appears above and a conversation begins. Let us listen; it is a long time since both women have been listened to. What is the subject of their talk? The old woman brings news of the outer world, relates stories, curious incidents of married and unmarried life, tales of wicked wives and wronged husbands. The recluse laughs: " os in risus cachinnosque dissolvitur "; in a word, the old

---

[1] In Migne's " Patrologia," vol. lxxvii. col. 153. " Dialogorum Liber I."; Prologue,

woman amuses the anchoress with fabliaux in an embryonic state. This is a most remarkable though little known example, for we can here observe fabliaux in a rudimentary stage, and going about in one more, and that a rather unexpected way. Is the case of this anchoress a unique one? Not at all; there was scarcely any recluse at that day, "vix aliquam inclusarum hujus temporis," without a friendly old woman to sit before her window and tell her such tales: of which testifies, in the twelfth century, Aelred, abbot of Rievaulx.[1]

From the thirteenth century, another medium of diffusion, a conspicuous and well-known one, is added to the others: not only minstrels, but wandering friars now carry tales to all countries; it is one of the ways they count on for securing a welcome. Their sermons raise a laugh, the success of their fables encourages their rivals to imitate them; the Councils vainly interfere, and reiterate, until after the Renaissance, the prohibition "to provoke shouts of laughter, after the fashion of shameless buffoons, by ridiculous stories and old wives' tales."[2] Dante had also protested, and Wyclif likewise, without more success than the Councils. "Thus," said Dante, "the ignorant sheep come home from pasture, wind-fed. . . . Jests and buffooneries are preached. . . . St. Anthony's swine fattens by these means, and others, worse than swine, fatten too."[3] But collections succeeded to collections, and room was found in them for many a scandalous tale, for that of the Weeping Bitch, for example, one of the most travelled of

[1] "De vita eremitica," in Migne's "Patrologia," vol. xxxii. col. 1451, text below, p. 213.

[2] Council of Sens, 1528, in "The Exempla, or illustrative Stories from the Sermones Vulgares of Jacques de Vitry," ed. T. F. Crane, London, 1890, 8vo, p. lxix. This collection of sermons with *exempla*, compiled by Jacques de Vitry (born ab. 1180, d. ab. 1239), was one of the most popular, and is one of the most curious of its kind. *Cf.* below, p. 183.

[3] Si che le pecorelle, che non sanno,
　　Tornan dal pasco pasciute di vento . . .

all, as it came from India, and is found everywhere, in Italy, France, and England, among fabliaux, in sermons, and even on the stage.[1]

The French who were now living in England in large numbers, introduced there the taste for merry tales of trickery and funny adventures, stories of curious mishaps of all kinds; of jealous husbands, duped, beaten, and withal perfectly content, and of fit wives for such husbands. It already pleased their teasing, mocking minds, fond of generalisations, to make themselves out a vicious race, without faith, truth, or honour: it ever was a *gab* of theirs. The more one protests, the more they insist; they adduce proofs and instances; they are convinced and finally convince others. In our age of systems, this magnifying of the abject side of things has been termed "realism"; for so-called "realism" is nothing more. True it is that if the home of tales is "not where they are born, but where they are comfortable," [2] France was a home for them. They reached there the height of their prosperity; the turn of mind of which they are the outcome has by no means disappeared; even to-day it is everywhere found, in the public squares, in the streets, in the newspapers, theatres, and novels. And it serves, as it did formerly, to make

> Ora si va con motti, e con iscede
> A predicare. . . .
>
> Di questo ingrassa il porco Sant' Antonio,
> Ed altri assai, che son peggio che porci,
> Pagando di moneta senza conio.
>
> ("Paradiso," canto xxix.)

[1] To be found, *e.g.*, in Jacques de Vitry, *ibid.* p. 105: "Audivi de quadam vetula que non poterat inducere quandam matronam ut juveni consentiret," &c. See below, pp. 225, and 447.

[2] Bédier, "Les Fabliaux," Paris, 1893, 8vo, p. 241; Bédier's definition of the same is as follows: "Les fabliaux sont des contes à rire, en vers." p. 6. The principal French collections are: Barbazan and Méon, "Fabliaux et contes des poètes français," Paris, 1808, 4 vols. 8vo; Montaiglon and Raynaud, "Recueil général et complet des Fabliaux," Paris, 1872–90, 6 vols. 8vo.

wholesale condemnations easy, very easy to judges who
may be dazzled by this jugglery of the French mind, who
look only at the goods exhibited before their eyes, and
who scruple the less to pass a sentence as they have to
deal with a culprit who confesses. But judge and culprit
both forget that, next to the realism of the fabliaux, there
is the realism of the Song of Roland, not less real, perhaps
more so ; for France has *lived* by her Song of Roland
much more than by her merry tales, that song which was
sung in many ways and for many centuries. Du Guesclin
and Corneille both sang it, each after his fashion ; its
echoes were heard since on the Marne and at Verdun.

On the same table may be found " La Terre," and
"Grandeur et Servitude." In the same hall, the same
minstrel, representing in his own person the whole library
of the castle, used formerly to relate the shameful tale of
Gombert and the two clerks, juggle with knives, and sing
of Roland. " I know tales," says one, " I know fabliaux,
I can tell fine new *dits*. . . . I know the fabliau of the
'Denier' . . . and that of Gombert and dame Erme. . . .
I know how to play with knives, and with the cord and
with the sling, and every fine game in the world. I can
sing at will of King Pepin of St. Denis . . . of Charlemagne
and of Roland, and of Oliver, who fought so well ; I know
of Ogier and of Aymon." [1]

All this literature went over the Channel with the
conquerors. Roland came to England, so did Renard,
so did Gombert. They contributed to transform the
mind of the vanquished race, and the vanquished race
contributed to transform the descendants of the victors.

---

[1] Ge sai contes, ge sai fableax,
   Ge sai conter beax diz noveax, &c.

"Des deux bordeors ribauz," in Montaiglon and Raynaud, "Recueil général,"
vol. i. p. 11.

CHAPTER III.

LATIN.

I.

THE ties with France were close ones; those with Rome were no less so. William had come to England, politically as the heir of the Anglo-Saxon kings, and with regard to ecclesiastical affairs as the Pope's chosen, blessed by the head of Christianity. In both respects, notwithstanding storms and struggles, the tradition thus started was continued under his successors.

At no period of the history of England was the union with Rome closer, and at no time, not even in the Augustan Age of English literature was there a larger infusion of Latin ideas. The final consequence of Henry II.'s quarrel with Thomas Becket was a still more complete submission of this prince to the Roman See. John Lackland's fruitless attempts to reach absolute power resulted in the gift of his domains to St. Peter and the oath of fealty sworn by him as vassal of the Pope: "We, John, by the grace of God, king of England, lord of Ireland, duke of Normandy, earl of Anjou, . . . Wishing to humiliate ourselves for Him who humiliated Himself for us even unto death . . . freely offer and concede to God and to our lord Pope Innocent and his Catholic successors, all the kingdom of

England and all the kingdom of Ireland for the remission of our sins,"[1] May 15, 1213.

From the day after Hastings the Church is seen establishing herself on firm basis in the country; she receives as many, and even more domains than the companions of the Conqueror. In the county of Dorset, for instance, it appears from Domesday that "the Church with her vassals and dependents enjoyed more than a third of the whole county, and that her patrimony was greater than that of all the Barons and greater feudalists combined."[2]

The religious foundations are innumerable, especially at the beginning; they decrease as the time of the Renaissance draws nearer. Four hundred and eighteen are counted from William Rufus to John, a period of one hundred years; one hundred and thirty-nine during the three following reigns: a hundred and eight years; twenty-three in the fourteenth century, and only three in the fifteenth.[3]

This number of monasteries necessitated considerable intercourse with Rome; many of the monks, often the abbots, were Italian or French; they had suits in the court of Rome, they laid before the Pope at Rome, and later at Avignon, their spiritual and temporal difficulties; the most important abbeys were "exempt," that is to say, under the direct jurisdiction of the Pope without passing

---

[1] "Volentes nos ipsos humiliare pro Illo Qui Se pro nobis humiliavit usque ad mortem . . . offerimus et libere concedimus Deo et . . . domino nostro papæ Innocentio ejusque catholicis successoribus, totum regnum Angliæ et totum regnum Hiberniæ, cum omni jure et pertinentiis suis, pro remissione peccatorum nostrorum." Hereupon follows the pledge to pay for ever to the Holy See "mille marcas sterlingorum," and then the oath of fealty to the Pope as suzerain of England. Stubbs, "Select Charters," Oxford, 1876, 3rd ed., pp. 284 ff.

[2] R. W. Eyton, "A key to Domesday, snowing the Method and Exactitude of its Mensuration . . . exemplified by . . . the Dorset Survey," London, 1878, 4to, p. 156.

[3] "Historical maps of England during the first thirteen centuries," by C. H. Pearson, London, 1870, fol. p. 61.

through the local episcopal authority. This was the
case with St. Augustine of Canterbury, St. Albans, St.
Edmund's, Waltham, Evesham, Westminster, &c. The
clergy of England had its eyes constantly turned Rome-
wards.

This clergy was very numerous; in the thirteenth
century its ranks were swelled by the arrival of the mendicant friars: Franciscans and Dominicans, the latter representing more especially doctrine, and the former practice.
The Dominicans expound dogmas, fight heresy, and
furnish the papacy with its Grand Inquisitors [1]; the
Franciscans do charitable works, nurse lepers and wretches
in the suburbs of the towns. All science that does not
tend to the practice of charity is forbidden them : " Charles
the Emperor," said St. Francis, " Roland and Oliver, all
the paladins and men mighty in battle, have pursued the
infidels to death, and won their memorable victories at the
cost of much toil and labour. The holy martyrs died
fighting for the faith of Christ. But there are in our time,
people who by the mere telling of their deeds, seek honour
and glory among men. There are also some among you
who like better to preach on the virtues of the saints than
to imitate their labours. . . . When thou shalt have a
psalter so shalt thou wish for a breviary, and when thou
shalt have a breviary, thou shalt sit in a chair like a great
prelate, and say to thy brother : ' Brother, fetch me my
breviary.' " [2]

[1] Concerning their power and the part they played, see for example the con-
firmation by Philip VI. of France, in November, 1329, of the regulations submitted to him by that " religious and honest person, friar Henri de Charnay,
of the order of Preachers, inquisitor on the crime of heresy, sent in that
capacity to our kingdom and residing in Carcassonne." Sentences attain not
only men, but even houses ; the king orders : " *Premièrement*, quod domus,
plateæ et loca in quibus hæreses fautæ fuerunt, diruantur et nunquam postea
reedificentur, sed perpetuo subjaceant in sterquilineæ vilitati," &c. Isambert's
" Recueil des anciennes Lois," vol. iv. p. 364.

[2] " Speculum vitæ B. Francisci et sociorum ejus," opera Fratris G. Spoel-
berch, Antwerp, 1620, 8vo, part i. chap. iv.

Thirty-two years after their first coming there were in England twelve hundred and forty-two Franciscans, with forty-nine convents, divided into seven custodies: London, York, Cambridge, Bristol, Oxford, Newcastle, Worcester.[1] "Your Holiness must know," writes Robert Grosseteste, bishop of Lincoln, to Pope Gregory IX., " that the friars illuminate the whole country by the light of their preaching and teaching. Intercourse with these holy men propagates voluntary poverty and scorn of the world. . . . Oh! could your Holiness see how piously and humbly the people hasten to hear from them the word of life, to confess their sins, and learn the rules of good conduct! . . . "[2] Such was the beginning; what followed was far from resembling it. The point to be remembered is another tie with Rome, represented by these new Orders: even the troubles that their faults gave rise to later, their quarrels with the secular clergy, the monks and the University, the constant appeals to the Pope that were a result of these disputes, the obstinacy with which they endeavoured to form a Church within the Church, all tended to increase and multiply the relations between Rome and England.

The English clergy was not only numerous and largely endowed ; it was also very influential, and played a considerable part in the policy of the State. When the Parliament was constituted the clergy occupied many seats, the king's ministers were usually churchmen; the high Chancellor was a prelate.

The action of the Latin Church made itself also felt on the nation by means of ecclesiastical tribunals, the powers of which were considerable ; all that concerned clerks, or related to faith and beliefs, to tithes, to deeds and contracts having a moral character, wills for instance, came within

[1] Brewer and Howlett, " Monumenta Franciscana," Rolls, 1858–82, 8vo, vol. i. p. 10.

[2] Letter of the year 1238 or thereabout ; " Roberti Grosseteste Epistolæ," ed. Luard, Rolls, 1861, p. 179.

the jurisdiction of the religious magistrate. This justice
interfered in the private life of the citizens ; it had an in-
quisitorial character ; it wanted to know if good order
reigned in households, if the husband was faithful and the
wife virtuous ; it cited adulterers to its bar and chastised
them. Summoners (Chaucer's somnours) played the part
of spies and public accusers ; they kept themselves well
informed on these different matters, were constantly on the
watch, pried into houses, collected and were supposed to
verify evil reports, and summoned before the ecclesiastical court those whom Jane's or Gilote's beauty had
turned from the path of conjugal fidelity. It may be
readily imagined that such an institution afforded full
scope for abuses ; it could hardly have been otherwise
unless all the summoners had been saints, which they were
not ; some among them were known to compound with
the guilty for money and call the innocent before the
judge in order to gratify personal spite.[1] Their misdeeds
were well known but not easy to prove ; so that Chaucer's
satires did more to ruin the institution than all the petitions
to Parliament. These summoners were also in their own
way, mean as that was, representatives of the Latin country,
of the spiritual power of Rome ; they knew it, and made
the best of the stray Latin words that had lodged in their
memory ; they used them as their shibboleth.

---

[1] A bettre felaw sholde men noght finde,
He wolde suffre, for a quart of wyn,
A good felawe to have his concubyn
A twelf-month and excuse him atte fulle.

Prologue of the " Canterbury Tales." The name of summoner was held in
little esteem, and no wonder:

" Artow thanne a bailly?"—" Ye," quod he ;
He dorste nat for verray filthe and shame
Seye that he was a somnour for the name.

("Freres Tale," l. 94.)

Bishops kept seigneurial retinues, built fortresses[1] and lived in them, had their archers and their dogs, hunted, laid siege to towns, made war, and only had recourse to excommunication when all other means of prevailing over their foes had failed. Others among them became saints: both in heaven and on earth they held the first rank. Like the sovereign, they knew, even then, the worth of public opinion; they bought the goodwill of wandering poets, as that of the press was bought in the day of Defoe. The itinerant minstrels were the newspapers of the period; they retailed the news and distributed praise or blame; they acquired over the common people the same influence that "printed matter" has had in more recent times. Hugh de Nunant, bishop of Coventry, accuses William de Long-champ, bishop of Ely, and Chancellor of England, in a letter still extant, of having inspired the laudatory verses —one might almost say the articles—that minstrels come from France, and paid by him, told in public places, "in plateis," not without effect, "for already, according to public opinion, no one in the universe was comparable to him."[2]

Nothing gives so vivid an impression of the time that has elapsed, and the transformation in manners that has

----

[1] They built a good many. Alexander, bishop of Lincoln, after having been a parish priest at Caen, first tried his hand as a builder, in erecting castles; he built some at Newark, Sleaford, and Banbury. He then busied himself with holier work and endowed Lincoln Cathedral with its stone nave. This splendid church had been begun on a spot easy to defend by another French bishop, Remi, formerly monk at Fécamp: "Mercatis igitur prædiis, in ipso vertice urbis juxta castellum turribus fortissimis eminens, in loco forti fortem, pulchro pulchrum, virgini virgineam construxit ecclesiam; quæ et grata esset Deo servientibus et, ut pro tempore oportebat, invincibilis hostibus." Henry of Huntingdon, "Historia Anglorum," Rolls, p. 212.

[2] "Epistola Hugonis . . . de dejectione Willelmi Eliensis episcopi Regis cancellarii," in Hoveden, "Chronica," ed. Stubbs, Rolls, vol. iii. p. 141, year 1191: "Hic ad augmentum et famam sui nominis, emendicata carmina et rhythmos adulatorios comparabat, et de regno Francorum cantores et joculatores muneribus allexerat, ut de illo canerent in plateis: et jam dicebatur ubique, quod non erat talis in orbe." See below, pp. 222, 345.

occurred, as the sight of that religious and warlike tourna-
ment of which England was the field under Richard Cœur-
de-Lion, and of which the heroes were all prelates, to wit :
these same William de Longchamp, bishop of Ely, and
Hugh de Nunant, bishop of Coventry ; then Hugh de
Puiset, bishop of Durham, Geoffrey Plantagenet, archbishop
of York, and some others.

Hugh de Puiset, a scion of the de Puisets, viscounts
of Chartres, grandson of the Conqueror, cousin to King
Richard, bishop palatine of Durham, wears the coat of
mail, fortifies his castles, storms those of his enemies,
builds ships, adds a beautiful "Lady chapel" to his
cathedral, and spends the rest of his time in hunting.

William de Longchamp, his great rival, grandson of a
Norman peasant, bishop of Ely, Chancellor of England,
seizes on Lincoln by force, lives like a prince, has an escort
of a thousand horsemen, adds to the fortifications of the
Tower of London and stands a siege in it. He is obliged
to give himself up to Hugh de Nunant, another bishop ; he
escapes disguised as a woman ; he is recognised, imprisoned
in a cellar, and exiled ; he then excommunicates his
enemies. Fortune smiles on him once more and he is
reinstated in his functions.

Geoffrey Plantagenet, a natural son of Henry II., the
only child who remained always faithful to the old king,
had once thought he would reach the crown, but was
obliged to content himself with becoming archbishop of
York. As such, he scorned to ally himself either with
Longchamp or with Puiset, and made war on both
impartially. Longchamp forbids him to leave France ;
nevertheless Geoffrey lands at Dover, the castle of which
was held by Richenda, sister of the Chancellor. He
mounts his horse and gallops towards the priory of
St. Martin ; Richenda sends after him, and one of the
lady's men was putting his hand on the horse's bridle,

when our lord the archbishop, shod with iron, gave a
violent kick to the enemy's steed, and tore his belly open;
the beast reared, and the prelate, freeing himself, reached
the priory.   There he is under watch for four days, after
which he is dragged from the very altar, and taken to the
castle of Dover.   At last he is liberated, and installed in
York; he immediately commences to fight with his own
clergy; he enters the cathedral when vespers are half
over; he interrupts the service, and begins it over again;
the indignant treasurer has the tapers put out, and the
archbishop continues his psalm-singing in the dark.   He
excommunicates his neighbour Hugh de Puiset, who is
little concerned by it; he causes the chalices used by the
bishop of Durham to be destroyed as profaned.

Hugh de Puiset, who was still riding about, though
attacked by the disease that was finally to carry him off,
dies full of years in 1195, after a *reign* of forty-three years.
He had had several children by different women: one of
them, Henri de Puiset, joined the Crusade; another,
Hugh, remained French, and became Chancellor to King
Louis VII.[1]

These warlike habits are only attenuated by degrees.
In 1323 Edward II. writes to Louis de Beaumont, bishop
of Durham, reproaching a noble like him for not defending
his bishopric any better against the Scotch than if he were
a mutterer of prayers like his predecessor.   Command is
laid upon bishop Louis to take arms and go and camp on
the frontier.   In the second half of the same century,
Henry le Despencer, bishop of Norwich, hacks the
peasants to pieces, during the great rising, and makes
war in Flanders for the benefit of one of the two popes.

Side by side with these warriors shine administrators,
men of learning, saints, all important and influential

---

[1] See Stubbs, Introductions to the "Chronica Magistri Rogeri de Hove-
dene," Rolls, 1868, 4 vols. 8vo, especially vols. iii. and iv.

personages in their way. Such are, for example, Lanfranc, of Pavia, late abbot of St. Stephen at Caen, who, as archbishop of Canterbury, reorganised the Church of England; Anselm of Aosta, late abbot of Bec, also an archbishop, canonised at the Renaissance, the discoverer of the famous "ontological" proof of the existence of God, a paradoxical proof the inanity of which it was reserved for St. Thomas Aquinas to demonstrate; Gilbert Foliot, a Frenchman, bishop of London, celebrated for his science, a strong supporter of Henry II.; Thomas Becket, of Norman parentage, archbishop and saint, whose quarrel with Henry II. divided England, and almost divided Christendom too; Hugh, bishop of Lincoln under the same king, of French origin, and who was also canonised; Stephen Langton, archbishop of Canterbury, who contributed as much as any of the barons to the granting of the Great Charter, and presided over the Council of London, in 1218, where it was solemnly confirmed [1]; Robert Grosseteste,[2] famous for his learning and holiness, his theological treatises, his sermons, his commentaries on Boethius and Aristotle, his taste for the divine art of music, which according to him "drives away devils." Warriors or saints, all these leaders of men keep, in their difficulties, their eyes turned towards Rome, and towards the head of the Latin Church.

[1] Lanfranc, 1005?-1089, archbishop in 1070; "Opera quæ supersunt," ed. Giles, Oxford, 1843, 2 vols. 8vo.—St. Anselm, 1033-1109, archbishop of Canterbury in 1093; works ("Monologion," "Proslogion," "Cur Deus homo," &c.) in Migne's "Patrologia," vol. clviii. and clix.—Stephen Langton, born ab. 1150, of a Yorkshire family, archbishop in 1208, d. 1228.

[2] A declared supporter of the Franciscans, and an energetic censor of the papal court, bishop of Lincoln 1235-53, has left a vast number of writings, and enjoyed considerable reputation for his learning and sanctity. His letters have been edited by Luard, "Roberti Grosseteste . . . Epistolæ," London, 1861, Rolls. See below, p. 213; *Cf.* Stevenson, "Grosseteste," 1899. Roger Bacon praised highly his learned works, adding, however: "quia Græcum et Hebræum non scivit sufficienter ut per se transferret, sed habuit multos adjutores." "Rogeri Bacon Opera . . . inedita," ed. Brewer, 1859, Rolls, p. 472.

II.

At the same time as the monasteries, and under the shadow of their walls, schools and libraries multiplied. The Latin education of the nation is resumed with an energy and perseverance hitherto unknown, and this time there will be no relapse into ignorance; protected by the French conquest, the Latin conquest is now definitive.

Not only are religious books in Latin, psalters, missals and decretals copied and collected in monasteries, but also the ancient classics. They are liked, they are known by heart, quoted in writings, and even in conversation. An English chronicler of the twelfth century declares he would blush to compile annals after the fashion of the Anglo-Saxons; this barbarous manner is to be avoided; he will use Roman salt as a condiment: "et exarata barbarice romano sale condire."[1] Another, of the same period, has the classic ideal so much before his eyes that he makes William deliver, on the day of Hastings, a speech beginning: "O mortalium validissimi!"[2]

A prelate who had been the tutor of the heir to the throne, and died bishop palatine of Durham, Richard de Bury,[3] collects books with a passion equal to that which

---

[1] "Gesta Regum Anglorum," by William of Malmesbury, ed. Hardy, 1840, "Prologus." He knew well the "Anglo-Saxon Chronicle" and used it : "Sunt sane quædam vetustatis indicia chronico more et patrio sermone, per annos Domini ordinata," p. 2.

[2] "Heᴠʳici archidiaconi Huntendunensis Historia Anglorum," Rolls, 1879, p. 201.

[3] He derived his name from Bury St. Edmund's, near which he was born on January 24, 1287. He was the son of Sir Richard Aungerville, Knight, whose ancestors had come to England with the Conqueror. He became the king's receiver in Gascony, fulfilled missions at Avignon in 1330 when he met Petrarch ("vir ardentis ingenii," says Petrarch of him), and in 1333. He became in this year bishop of Durham, against the will of the chapter, who had elected Robert de Graystanes, the historian. He was lord Treasurer, then high Chancellor in 1334-5, discharged new missions on the Continent, followed Edward III. on his expedition of 1338, and died in 1345.

will be later displayed at the court of the Medici. He has emissaries who travel all over England, France, and Italy to secure manuscripts for him ; with a book one can obtain anything from him ; the abbot of St. Albans, as a pro-pitiatory offering sends him a Terence, a Virgil, and a Quinctilian. His bedchamber is so encumbered with books that one can hardly move in it.[1] Towards the end of his life, never having had but one passion, he undertook to describe it, and, retired in his manor of Auckland, he wrote in Latin prose his " Philobiblon."[2] In this short treatise he defends books, Greek and Roman antiquity, poetry, too, with touching emotion ; he is seized with indignation when he thinks of the crimes of high treason against manuscripts, daily committed by pupils who in spring dry flowers in their books ; and of the ingratitude of wicked clerks, who admit into the library dogs, or falcons, or worse still, a two-legged animal, "bestia bipedalis," more dangerous "than the basilisk, or aspic," who, discovering the volumes "insufficiently concealed by the protecting web of a dead spider," condemns them to be sold, and converted for her own use into silken hoods and furred gowns.[3] Eve's descendants continue, thinks the bishop, to wrongfully meddle with the tree of know-ledge.

[1] " Registrum Palatinum Dunelmense," Rolls, iii. p. cxlvi. *Cf.* " R. d'Aungerville, Fragments of his Register," Surtees Soc. 1910.

[2] The best edition is that given by E. C. Thomas, "The Philobiblon of Richard de Bury," London, new ed. 1903, Latin text with an English transla-tion. The Introduction contains a biography in which some current errors have been corrected, and notes on the various MSS. According to seven MSS. the "Philobiblon" would be the work of Robert Holkot, and not of Richard de Bury, but this appears to be a mistaken attribution.

[3] "Occupant etenim,' the books are represented to say, "loca nostra, nunc canes, nunc aves, nunc bestia bipedalis, cujus cohabitatio cum clericis vetabatur antiquitus, a qua semper, super aspidem et basilicum alumnos nostros docuimus esse fugiendum. . . Ista nos conspectos in angulo, jam defunctæ araneæ de sola tela protectos . . . mox in capitogia pretiosa . . . vestes et varias furra-turas . . . nos consulit commutandos " (chap. iv. p. 32).

What painful commiseration did he not experience on penetrating into an ill-kept convent library! "Then we ordered the book-presses, chests, and bags of the noble monasteries to be opened ; and, astonished at beholding again the light of day, the volumes came out of their sepulchres and their prolonged sleep. . . Some of them, which had ranked among the daintiest, lay for ever spoilt, in all the horror of decay, covered by filth left by the rats ; they who had once been robed in purple and fine linen now lay on ashes, covered with a cilice." [1] The worthy bishop looks upon letters with a religious veneration, worthy of the ancients themselves ; his enthusiasm recalls that of Cicero ; no one at the Renaissance, not even the illustrious Bessarion, has praised old manuscripts with a more touching fervour, or more nearly attained to the eloquence of the great Latin orator when he speaks of books in his "Pro Archia" : "Thanks to books," says the English prelate, "the dead appear to me as though they still lived. . . . Everything decays and falls into dust, by the force of Time ; Saturn is never weary of devouring his children, and the glory of the world would be buried in oblivion, had not God as a remedy conferred on mortal man the benefit of books. . . . Books are the masters that instruct us without rods or ferulas, without reprimands or anger, without the solemnity of the gown or the expense of lessons. Go to them, you will not find them asleep ; question them, they will not refuse to answer ; if you err, no scoldings on their part ; if you are ignorant, no mocking laughter." [2]

These teachings and these examples bore fruit ; in renovated England, Latin-speaking clerks swarmed. It is often difficult while reading their works to discover whether they are of native or of foreign extraction ; national hates with them are less strong than with the rest of their

[1] Chap. viii. p. 66.   [2] Chap. i. pp. 11, 13.

compatriots ; most of them have studied not only in England but in Paris ; science has made of them cosmopolitans ; they belong, above all, to the Latin country, and the Latin country has not suffered.

The Latin country had two capitals, a religious capital which was Rome, and a literary capital which was Paris. " In the same manner as the city of Athens shone in former days as the mother of liberal arts and the nurse of philosophers, . . . so in our times Paris has raised the standard of learning and civilisation, not only in France but in all the rest of Europe, and, as the mother of wisdom, she welcomes guests from all parts of the world, supplies all their wants, and submits them all to her pacific rule." [1] So said Bartholomew the Englishman in the thirteenth century. " What a flood of joy swept over my heart," wrote in the following century another Englishman, that same Richard de Bury, " every time I was able to visit that paradise of the world, Paris ! My stay there always seemed brief to me, so great was my passion. There were libraries of perfume more delicious than caskets of spices, orchards of science ever green . . ." [2] Paris held without contest the first rank; it counted among its students, kings, saints, popes, statesmen, poets, learned men come from all countries, Italians like Dante, Englishmen like Stephen Langton, who all could say, like Duns Scot : " Gallia me docuit."

Its lustre dates from the twelfth century. At that time

---

[1] " Sicut quondam Athenarum civitas mater liberalium artium et literarum, philosophorum nutrix et fons omnium scientiarum Græciam decoravit, sic Parisiæ nostris temporibus, non solum Franciam imo totius Europæ partem residuam in scientia et in moribus sublimarunt. Nam velut sapientiæ mater, de omnibus mundi partibus advenientes recolligunt, omnibus in necessariis subveniunt, pacifice omnes regunt . . ." " Bartholomæi Anglici De . . . Rerum . . . Proprietatibus Libri xviii.," ed. Pontanus, Francfort, 1609, 8vo. Book XV. chap. 57, " De Francia," p. 653.

[2] " Philobiblon," chap. viii. p. 69. In his " De Naturis Rerum " (Rolls, 1863, p. 311) Neckham had declared that Paris carried the palm for theology and liberal arts. *Cf.* Rashdall, " The Universities of Europe," Oxford, 1895.

a fusion took place between the theological school of Notre-Dame, where shone, towards the beginning of the century, Guillaume de Champeaux, and the schools of logic that Abélard's teaching gave birth to on St. Geneviève's Mount. This state of things was not created, but consecrated by Pope Innocent III., a former student at Paris, who by his bulls of 1208 and 1209 formed the masters and students into one association, *Universitas.*[1]

According to a mediæval custom, which has been perpetuated in the East, and is still found for instance at the great University of El Azhar at Cairo, the students were divided into nations : France, Normandy, Picardy, England. It was a division by races, and not by countries ; the idea of mother countries politically divided being excluded, in theory at least, from the Latin realm. Thus the Italians were included in the French nation, and the Germans in the English one. Of all these foreigners the English were the most numerous ; they had in Paris six colleges for theology alone.

The faculties were four in number : theology, law, medicine, arts. The latter, though least in rank, was the most important from the number of its pupils, and was a preparation for the others. The student of arts was about fifteen years of age ; he passed a first degree called "déterminance" or bachelorship ; then a second one, the licence, after which, in a solemn ceremony termed *inceptio*, commencement, the corporation of masters invested him with the cap, the badge of mastership. He was pledged to then dispute for forty successive days with every comer ; then, still very youthful, and frequently beardless, he himself began to teach. A master who taught was called a Regent, *Magister regens.*

[1] On the old University of Paris, see Ch. Thurot's excellent essay : "De l'organisation de l'enseignement dans l'Université de Paris au moyen âge,' Paris, 1850, 8vo. The four nations, p. 16 ; the English nation, p. 32 ; its colleges, p. 28 ; the degrees in the faculty of arts, pp. 43 ff.

The principal schools were situated in the "rue du Fouarre" (straw, litter), "vico degli Strami," says Dante, a street that still exists under the same name, but the ancient houses of which are gradually disappearing. In this formerly dark and narrow street, surrounded by lanes with names carrying us far back into the past ("rue de la Parcheminerie," &c.), the most illustrious masters taught, and the most singular disorders arose. The students, come from the four corners of Europe without a farthing, having, in consequence, nothing to lose, and to whom ample privileges had been granted, did not shine by their discipline. Neither was the population of the quarter an exemplary one.[1] We gather from the royal ordinances that the rue du Fouarre, "vicus ultra parvum pontem, vocatus gallice la rue du Feurre," had to be closed at night by barriers and chains, because of individuals who had the wicked habit of establishing themselves at night, with their *ribaudes*, "mulieres immundæ!" in the lecture-rooms, and leaving, on their departure, by way of a joke, the professor's chair covered with "horrible" filth. Far from feeling any awe, these evil-doers found, on the contrary, a special amusement in the idea of perpetrating their jokes in the *sanctum* of philosophers, who, says the ordinance of the wise king Charles V., "should be clean and honest, and inhabit clean, decent, and honest places."[2]

Teaching, the principal object of which was logic, consisted in the reading and interpreting of such books as were considered authorities. "The method in expounding is always the same. The commentator discusses in a

---

[1] Their servants were of course much worse in every way; they lived upon thefts, and had even formed on this account an association with a captain at their head: "Cum essem Parisius audivi quod garciones servientes scholarium, qui omnes fere latrunculi solent esse, habebant quendam magistrum qui princeps erat hujus modi latrocinii." Th. Wright, "Latin stories from MSS. of the XIIIth and XIVth Centuries," London, 1842, tale No. cxxv.

[2] May, 1358, in Isambert's "Recueil des anciennes Lois," vol. v. p. 26.

prologue some general questions relating to the work he is about to lecture upon, and he usually treats of its material, formal, final, and efficient causes. He points out the principal divisions, takes the first member of the division, subdivides it, divides the first member of this subdivision, and thus by a series of divisions, each being successively cleft into two, he reaches a division which only comprises the first chapter. He applies to each part of the work the same process as to its whole. He continues these divisions until he comes to having before him only one phrase including one single complete idea."

Another not less important part of the instruction given consisted in oratorical jousts ; the masters disputed among themselves, and the pupils did likewise. In a time when paper was scarce and parchment precious, disputes replaced our written exercises. The weapons employed in these jousts were blunt ones ; but as in real tournaments where "armes courtoises" were used, disputants were sometimes carried away by passion, and the result was a true battle: "They scream themselves hoarse, they lavish unmannerly expressions, abuse, threats, upon each other. They even take to cuffing, kicking, and biting." [1]

Under this training, rudimentary though it was, superior minds became sharpened, they got accustomed to think, to weigh the pros and cons, to investigate freely ; a taste for intellectual things was kept up in them. The greatest geniuses who had come to study Aristotle on St. Geneviève's Mount were always proud to call themselves pupils of Paris. But narrow minds grew there more narrow; they remained, as Rabelais will say later, foolish and silly, dreaming, stultified things, "tout niais, tout rêveux et rassotés." John of Salisbury, a brilliant scholar of Paris in the twelfth century, had the curiosity to come, after a long absence, and see his old companions "that dialectics still

[1] Thurot, *ut supra,* pp. 73, 89.

detained on St. Geneviève's Mount." "I found them," he tells us, "just as I had left them, and at the same point; they had not advanced one step in the art of solving our ancient questions, nor added to their science the smallest proposition. . . . I then clearly saw, what it is easy to discover, that the study of dialectics, fruitful if employed as a means to reach the sciences, remain inert and barren if taken as being itself the object of study." [1]

During this time were developing, on the borders of the Isis and the Cam, the Universities, so famous since, of Oxford and Cambridge; but their celebrity was chiefly local, and they never reached the international reputation of the one at Paris. Both towns had flourishing schools in the twelfth century; in the thirteenth, these schools were constituted into a University, on the model of Paris; they were granted privileges, and the Pope, who would not let slip this opportunity of intervening, confirmed them.[2]

The rules of discipline, the teaching, and the degrees are the same as at Paris. The turbulence is just as great; there are incessant battles; battles between the students of the North and those of the South, "boreales et australes," between the English and Irish, between the clerks and the laity. In 1214 some clerks are hung by the citizens of the town; the Pope's legate instantly makes the power of Rome felt, and avenges the insult sustained by privileged persons belonging to the Latin country. During ten years the inhabitants of Oxford shall remit the students half their rent; they shall pay down fifty-two shillings each year on

---

[1] In his "Metalogicus," "Opera Omnia," ed. Giles, Oxford, 1848, 5 vols. 8vo, vol. v. p. 81. *Cf.* Neckham, "De Naturis Rerum," Rolls, p. 311.

[2] Innocent IV. confirms (ab. 1254) all the "immunitates et laudabiles, antiquas, rationabiles consuetudines" of Oxford: "Nulli ergo hominum liceat hanc paginam nostræ protectionis infringere vel ausu temerario contraire." "Munimenta Academica, or documents illustrative of academical life and studies at Oxford," ed. Anstey, 1868, Rolls, 2 vols. 8vo, vol. i. p. 26. *Cf.* W. E. Gladstone, "An Academic Sketch," Oxford, 1892.

St. Nicholas' day, in favour of indigent students ; and they shall give a banquet to a hundred poor students. Even the bill of fare is settled by the Roman authority : bread, ale, soup, a dish of fish or of meat ; and this for ever. The perpetrators of the hanging shall come barefooted, without girdle, cloak or hat, to remove their victims from their temporary resting-place, and, followed by all the citizens, bury them with their own hands in the place assigned to them in consecrated ground.

In 1252 the Irish and "Northerners" begin to fight in St. Mary's Church. They are obliged by authority to appoint twelve delegates, who negotiate a treaty of peace. In 1313 a prohibition is proclaimed against bearing names of nations, these distinctions being a constant source of quarrels. In 1334 such numbers of "Surrois" and "Norrois" clerks are imprisoned in Oxford Castle after a battle, that the sheriff declares escapes are sure to occur.[1] In 1354 a student, seated in a tavern, "in taberna vini," pours a jug of wine over the tavern-keeper's head, and breaks the jug upon it. Unfortunately the head is broken as well ; the "laity" take the part of the victim, pursue the clerks, kill twenty of them, and fling their bodies " in latrinas " ; they even betake themselves to the books of the students, and "slice them with knives and hatchets." During that term, "oh! woe! no degrees in Logic were taken at the University of Oxford." [2] In 1364 war breaks out again between the citizens and students, "commissum fuit bellum," and lasts four days.

Regulations, frequently renewed, show the nature of the principal abuses. These laws pronounce: excommunication against the belligerents ; exclusion from the University against those students who harboured "little

[1] " Rolls of Parliament," 8 Ed. III. vol. ii. p. 76.
[2] Robert of Avesbury (a contemporary, he died ab. 1357), "Historia Edvardi tertii," ed. Hearne, Oxford, 1720, 8vo, p. 197.

women" (*mulierculas*) in their lodgings, major excommunication and imprisonment against those who amuse themselves by celebrating bacchanals in churches, masked, disguised, and crowned "with leaves or flowers"; all this about 1250. The statutes of University Hall, 1292, prohibit the fellows from fighting, from holding immodest conversations together, from telling each other love tales, "fubulas de amasiis," and from singing improper songs.[1]

The lectures bore on Aristotle, Boethius, Priscian, and Donatus; Latin and French were studied; the fellows were bound to converse together in Latin; a regulation also prescribed that the scholars should be taught Latin prosody, and accustomed to write epistles "in decent language, without emphasis or hyperbole, . . . and as much as possible full of sense."[2] Objectionable passages are to be avoided; Ovid's "Art of Love" and the book of love by Pamphilus are prohibited.

From the thirteenth century foundations increase in number, both at Oxford and Cambridge. Now "chests" are created, a kind of pawnbroking institution for the benefit of scholars; now a college is created like University College, the most ancient of all, founded by William of Durham, who died in 1249, or New College, established by the illustrious Chancellor of Edward III. William of Wykeham. Sometimes books are bequeathed, as by Richard de Bury and Thomas de Cobham in the fourteenth century,

---

[1] "Vivant omnes honeste, ut clerici, prout decet sanctos, non pugnantes, non scurrilia vel turpia loquentes, non cantilenas sive fabulas de amasiis vel luxuriosis, aut ad libidinem sonantibus narrantes, cantantes aut libenter audientes." "Munimenta Academica," i. p. 60.

[2] Regulation of uncertain date belonging to the thirteenth (or more probably to the fourteenth) century, concerning pupils in grammar schools; they will be taught prosody, and will write verses and epistles : " Literas compositas verbis decentibus, non ampullosis aut sesquipedalibus et quantum possint sententia refertis." They will learn Latin, English, and French "in gallico ne lingua illa penitus sit omissa." "Munimenta Academica," i. p. 437. *Cf.* Leach, " The Schools in medieval England," 1914.

or by Humphrey of Gloucester, in the fifteenth.[1]   The
journey to Paris continues a title to respect, but it is no
longer indispensable.

III.

With these resources at hand, and encouraged by the
example of rulers such as Henry "Beauclerc" and Henry
II., the subjects of the kings of England latinised themselves in great numbers, and produced some of the Latin
writings which enjoyed the widest reputation throughout
civilised Europe. They handle the language with such
facility in the twelfth century, one might believe it to be
their mother-tongue ; the chief monuments of English
thought at this time are Latin writings. Latin tales,
chronicles, satires, sermons, scientific and medical works,
treatises on style, prose romances, and epics in verse, all
kinds of composition are produced by Englishmen in
considerable numbers.

One of them writes a poem in hexameters on the Trojan
war, which doubtless bears traces of barbarism, but more
resembles antique models than any other imitation made
in Europe at the time. It was attributed to Cornelius
Nepos, so late even as the Renaissance, though the author,
Joseph of Exeter,[2] who composed it between 1178 and

---

[1] Another sign of the times consists in the number of episcopal letters
authorizing ecclesiastics to leave their diocese and go to the University. Thus,
for example, Richard de Kellawe, bishop of Durham, 1310-16, writes to
Robert de Eyrum : " Quum per viros literatos Dei consuevit Ecclesia venustari,
cupientibus in agro studii laborare et acquirere scientiæ margaritam . . .
favorem libenter et gratiam impertimus . . . ut in loco ubi generale viget
studium, a data præsentium usque in biennium revolutum morari valeas."
" Registrum Palatinum Dunelmense," ed. Hardy, Rolls, 1873, 4 vols. 8vo,
vol. i. p. 288 (many other similar letters).

[2] Josephus Exoniensis, or Iscanus, followed Archbishop Baldwin to the
crusade in favour of which this prelate had delivered the sermons, and undertaken the journey in Wales described by Gerald de Barry. Joseph sang the
expedition in a Latin poem, " Antiocheis," of which a few lines only have

1183, had dedicated his work to Baldwin, archbishop of
Canterbury, and mentioned in it Arthur, "flos regum
Arthurus," whose return was still expected by the Britons,
"Britonum ridenda fides." Joseph is acquainted with the
classics; he has read Virgil, and follows to the best of his
ability the precepts of Horace.[1] Differing in this from
Benoit de Sainte-More and his contemporaries, he depicts
heroes that are not knights, and who at their death are
not buried in Gothic churches by monks chanting psalms.
This may be accounted a small merit; at that time, however, it was anything but a common one, and, in truth,
Joseph of Exeter alone possessed it.

In a variety of less ambitious Latin poems, much
ingenuity, observation, sometimes wit, but occasionally
only commonplace wisdom, were expended by Godfrey of
Winchester, who composed epigrams about the commencement of the twelfth century; by Henry of Huntingdon,
the historian, who wrote some also; by Alexander Neckham, author of a "Novus Æsopus" and of several metrical
treatises; Alain de l'Isle and John de Hauteville, who
both, long before Jean de Meun, made Nature discourse,
"de omni re scibili"[2]; Walter the Englishman, and Odo

been preserved. In his Trojan poem he follows, as a matter of course, Dares;
the work was several times printed in the Renaissance and since : "Josephi
Iscani . . . De Bello Trojano libri . . . auctori restituti . . . a Samuele
Dresemio," Francfort, 1620. I have shown that the MS. lat. 15015 in the
National Library, Paris, contains a series of explanatory notes written in the
thirteenth century, concerning this poem (I printed the first book of them).

[1] For example, in his opening lines, where he adheres to the simplicity
recommended by the Latin master:
Iliadum lacrymas concessaque Pergama fatis,
Prælia bina ducum, bis adactam cladibus urbem,
In cineres querimur.

[2] "Anglo-Latin satirical poets of the XIIth Century," ed. Th. Wright, 1872,
Rolls, 2 vols.; contains, *e.g.* : "Godfredi prioris Epigrammata" (one in praise
of the Conqueror, ii. 149); "Henrici archidiaconi historiæ liber undecimus"
(that is H. of Huntingdon; fine epigram "in seipsum," ii. 163); "A.
Neckham De Vita Monachorum" (the same, 1157–1217, wrote prose treatises

13

of Cheriton, authors in the twelfth and thirteenth centuries of Latin fables, John of Salisbury, Walter Map,[1] and above all, by Nigel Wireker, who wrote in flowing verse the comical story of Burnellus, the ass whose tail was too short.[2]

Burnellus, type of the ambitious monk, escapes from his stable, and wishes to rise in the world. He consults Galen, who laughs at him, and sends him to Salerno.[3] At Salerno he is again made a fool of, and provided with elixirs, warranted to make his tail grow to a beautiful length. But in passing through Lyons on his return, he quarrels with the dogs of a wicked monk called Fromond; while kicking right and left he kicks off his vials, which break, while Grimbald, the dog, cuts off half his too short tail. A sad case! He revenges himself on Fromond, however, by drowning him in the Rhone, and, lifting up his voice, he makes then the valley ring with a "canticle" celebrating his triumph.[4]

What can he do next? It is useless for him to think of attaining perfection of form ; he will shine by his science ; he will go to the University of Paris, that centre of all

on theological, scientific, and grammatical subjects ; *e.g.*, a "De Naturis Rerum," with a metrical "De laudibus divinæ Sapientiæ," Rolls, 1863) ; "Alani Liber de Planctu Naturæ" (in "Opera," Antwerp, 1654, the nationality of Alain, 12th cent., is doubtful) ; "Joannis de Altavilla Architrenius" (that is the arch-weeper ; lamentations of a young man on his past, his faults, the faults of others ; Nature comforts him and he marries Moderation ; the author, a Norman, wrote ab. 1184).

[1] For the Latin fables of Walter the Englishman, Odo de Cheriton, Neckham, &c., see Hervieux, les "Fabulistes latins, Paris, 1883–99, 5 vols. (text, commentary, imitations). On J. of Salisbury and Map, *infra*, pp. 188, 190.

[2] "Speculum Stultorum," in Wright, "Anglo-Latin satirical poets"; *ut supra.* Nigel (twelfth century) had for his patron William de Longchamp, bishop of Ely (see above, p. 163), and fulfilled ecclesiastical functions in Canterbury.

[3] In titulo caudæ Francorum rex Ludovicus
Non tibi præcellit pontificesve sui.   (Vol. i. p. 17.)

[4] Cantemus, socii ! festum celebremus aselli !
Vocibus et votis organa nostra sonent.
Exultent asini, læti modulentur aselli,
Laude sonent celebri tympana, sistra, chori !   (p. 48.)

light; he will become "Magister," and be appointed bishop. The people will bow down to him as he passes; it is a dream of bliss, La Fontaine's story of the "Pot au Lait."

He reaches Paris, matriculates among the English nation, and falls to studying; at the end of a year he has been taught many things, but is only able to say "ya" (semper ya repetit). He continues to work, scourges himself, follows the lectures for many years, but still knows nothing but "ya," and remains an ass.[1] What then? He will found an abbey, the rule of which shall combine the delights of all the others: it will be possible to gossip there as at Grandmont, to leave fasting alone as at Cluny, to dress warmly as among the Premonstrants and to have a female friend like the secular canons; it will be a Thélème even before Rabelais.

But suddenly an unexpected personage appears on the scene, the donkey's master, Bernard the peasant, who had long been on the look-out for him, and by means of a stick the magister, bishop, mitred abbot, is led back to his stall.

Not satisfied with the writing of Latin poems, the subjects of the English kings would construct theories and establish the rules of the art. It was carrying boldness very far; they did not realise that theories can only be laid down with safety in periods of maturity, and that in formulating them too early there is risk of propagating nothing but the rules of bad taste. This was the case with Geoffrey de Vinesauf, at the beginning of the thirteenth century. Geoffrey is sure of himself; he learnedly joins

[1] Jam pertransierat Burnellus tempora multa
Et prope completus septimus annus erat,
Cum nihil ex toto quodcunque docente magistro
Aut socio potuit discere præter ya.
Quod natura dedit, quod secum detulit illuc,
Hoc habet, hoc illo nemo tulisse potest . . .
Semper ya repetit. (p. 64.)

example to precept, he juggles with words ; he soars on high, far above men of good sense. It was with great reason his work was called the New art of poetry, "Nova Poetria,"[1] for it has nothing in common with the old one, with Horace's. It is dedicated to the Pope, and begins by puns on the name of Innocent[2] ; it closes with a comparison between the Pope and God : "Thou art neither God nor man, but an intermediary being whom God has taken into partnership. . . . Not wishing to keep all for himself, he has taken heaven and given thee earth ; what could he do better ? "[3]

Precepts and examples are in the same style. Geoffrey teaches how to praise, blame, and ridicule ; he gives models of good prosopopœias ; prosopopœias for times of happiness : an apostrophe to England governed by Richard Cœur-de-Lion (we know how well he governed) ; prosopopœia for times of sorrow : an apostrophe to England, whose sovereign (this same Richard) has been killed on a certain Friday :

"England, of his death thou thyself diest ! . . . O lamentable day of Venus ! O cruel planet ! this day has been thy night, this Venus thy venom ; by her wert thou

<hr/>

[1] "Galfridi de Vinosalvo Ars Poetica," ed. Leyser, Helmstadt, 1724. He wrote other works ; an "Itinerarium regis Anglorum Richardi I." (in "Rerum Anglicarum Scriptores" of Gale, 1684 ff., fol., vol. ii.) has been doubtfully attributed to him ; see Hauréau, "Notices et Extraits des Manuscrits," xxiv. 321 ff. According to Stubbs ("Itinerarium . . . Regis Ricardi," 1864, Rolls), the real author is Richard, canon of the Holy Trinity, London. Cf. Faral, "Arts Poétiques du xiie et du xiiie siécle," Paris, 1923.

[2] Papa stupor mundi, si dixero Papa *Nocenti :*
Acephalum nomen tribuam tibi ; si caput addam,
Hostis erit metri, &c.

[3] Nec Deus es nec homo, quasi neuter es inter utrumque,
Quem Deus elegit socium. Socialiter egit
Tecum, partitus mundum. Sed noluit unus
Omnia. Sed voluit tibi terras et sibi cœlum.
Quid potuit melius ? quid majus ? cui meliori ? (p. 95.)

vulnerable! . . . O woe and more than woe! O death! O truculent death! O death, I wish thou wert dead! It pleased thee to remove the sun and to obscure the soil with obscurity!"[1]

Then follow counsels as to the manner of treating ridiculous people[2]: they come in good time, and we shall not have far to go to find an occasion for using them. Geoffrey's style makes us understand the wisdom of the Oxford regulations prescribing simplicity and prohibiting emphasis; the more so if we consider that Geoffrey did not innovate, but merely turned into rules the tastes of many. Before him men of comparatively sound judgment, like Joseph of Exeter, had forgotten themselves so far as to apostrophize in these terms the night in which Troy was taken: "O night, cruel night! night truly noxious! troublous, sorrowful, traitorous, sanguinary night!"[3] &c.

IV.

The series of Latin prose authors of that epoch, grave or facetious, philosophers, moralists, satirists, historians, men of science, romance and tale writers, is still more remarkable in England than that of the poets. Had they only

---

[1] Tota peris ex morte sua. Mors non fuit ejus,
  Sed tua. Non una, sed publica, mortis origo.
  O Veneris lacrimosa dies! o sydus amarum!
  Illa dies tua nox fuit et Venus illa venenum;
  Illa dedit vulnus . . .
  O dolor! o plus quam dolor! o mors! o truculenta
  Mors! Esses utinam mors mortua! quid meministi
  Ausa nefas tantum? Placuit tibi tollere solem
  Et tenebris tenebrare solum. (p. 18.)

[2] Contra ridiculos si vis insurgere plene
  Surge sub hac forma. Lauda, sed ridiculose.
  Argue, sed lepide, &c. (p. 21.)

[3] Nox, fera nox, vere nox noxia, turbida, tristis.
  Insidiosa, ferox, &c. (" De Bello Trojano," book vi. l. 760.)

suspected the importance of the native language and left Latin, several of them would have held a very high rank in the national literature.

Romance is represented by Geoffrey of Monmouth, who in the twelfth century wrote his famous " Historia Regum Britanniæ," the influence of which in England and on the Continent has already been seen. Prose tales were written in astonishing quantities, in the twelfth and thirteenth centuries, by those pious authors who, under pretext of edifying and amusing their readers at the same time, began by amusing, and frequently forgot to edify. They put into their collections all they knew in the way of legends, jokes, and facetious stories. England produced several such collections ; their authors usually add a moral to their tales, but sometimes omit it, or else they simply say: " Moralise as thou wilt ! "

In these innumerable well-told tales, full of sprightly dialogue, can be already detected something of the art of the *conteur* which will appear in Chaucer, and something almost of the art of the novelist, destined five hundred years later to reach such a high development in England. The curiosity of the Celt, reawakened by the Norman, is perpetuated in Great Britain ; stories are doted on there. " It is the custom," says an English author of the thirteenth century, " in rich families, to spend the winter evenings around the fire, telling tales of former times. . . ."[1]

Subjects for tales were not lacking. The last researches have about made it certain that the immense "Gesta Romanorum," so popular in the Middle Ages, were compiled

---

[1] " Cum in hyemis intemperie post cenam noctu familia divitis ad focum, ut potentibus moris est, recensendis antiquis gestis operam daret. . . ." "Gesta Romanorum," version compiled in England, ed. Hermann Oesterley, Berlin, 1872, 8vo, chap. clv.

in England about the end of the thirteenth century.[1] The collection of the English Dominican John of Bromyard, composed in the following century, is still more voluminous. Some idea can be formed of it from the fact that the printed copy preserved at the National Library of Paris weighs fifteen pounds.[2]

Everything is found in these collections, from mere jokes and happy retorts to real novels. There are coarse fabliaux in their embryonic stage, objectionable tales where the frail wife derides the injured husband, graceful stories, miracles of the Virgin. We recognise in passing some fable that La Fontaine has since made famous, episodes out of the "Roman de Renart," anecdotes drawn from Roman history, adventures that, transformed and remodelled, have at length found their definitive rendering in Shakespeare's plays.

All is grist that comes to the mill of these authors; their stories are of French, Latin, English, Hindu origin. It is plain, however, that they write for Englishmen, as many of their stories are localised in England, and quotations in English are here and there inserted into the tale.[3]

[1] Such is the conclusion come to by Oesterley. The original version, according to him, was written in England; on the Continent, where it was received with great favour, it underwent considerable alterations, and many stories were added. The "Gesta" have been wrongly attributed to Pierre Bercheur. Translations into English prose were made in the fifteenth century: "The early English version of the Gesta Romanorum," ed. S. J. H. Herrtage, Early English Text Society, 1879, 8vo.

[2] Seven kilos, 200 gr. "Doctissimi viri fratris Johannis de Bromyard . . . Summ[a] prædicantium," Nurenberg, 1485, fol. The subjects are arranged in alphabetical order: Ebrietas, Luxuria, Maria, &c. *Cf.* "An Alphabet of Tales," translated into English, XVth cent. (some much more comical than edifying). E.E.T.S. 1904, ff.

[3] Such is the case in several of the stories collected by Th. Wright: "A Selection of Latin Stories from MSS. of the XIIIth and XIVth Centuries, a contribution to the History of Fiction," London, Percy Society, 1842, 8vo. In No. XXII., "De Muliere et Sortilega," the incantations are in English verse; in No. XXXIV. occurs a praise of England, "terra pacis et justitiæ"; in No. XCVII. the hermit who got drunk repents and says "anglice":

Whil that I was sobre sinne ne dede I nowht,
But in drunkeschipe I dede ye werste that mihten be thowte,

In turning the pages of these voluminous works, glimpses
will be caught of the Wolf, the Fox, and Tybert the cat ;
the Miller, his son and the Ass ; the Women and the Secret
(instead of eggs, it is here a question of " exceedingly black
crows ") ; the Rats who wish to hang a bell about the Cat's
neck.   Many tales, fabliaux, and short stories will be recognised that have become popular under their French,
English, or Italian shape, such as the lay of the " Oiselet," [1]
the " Chienne qui pleure," or the Weeping Bitch, the lay
of Aristotle, the Geese of Friar Philip, the Pear Tree, the
Hermit who got drunk.   Some of them are very indecent,
but they were not left out of the collections on that account,
any more than miniaturists were forbidden to paint on the
margins of holy, or almost holy books, scenes that were far
from being so.   A manuscript of the decretals, for example,
painted in England at the beginning of the fourteenth
century, exhibits a series of drawings illustrating some of
these stories, and meant to fit an obviously unexpurgated
text.[2]

The Virgin plays her usual part of an indulgent protec-
tress ; the story-tellers strangely deviate from the sacred
type set before them in the Scriptures.   They represent
her as the Merciful One whose patience no crime can
exhaust, and whose goodwill is enlisted by the slightest
act of homage.   She is transformed and becomes in their

---

[1] That one in verse, with a mixture of English words. Ha! says the peasant:

Ha thu mi swete bird, ego te comedam.

" Early Mysteries and other Latin poems of the XIIth and XIIIth Centuries,"
ed. Th. Wright, London, 1838, 8vo, p. 97.   Cf. G. Paris, " Lai de l'Oiselet,"
Paris, 1884.

[2] These series of drawings in the margins are like tales without words ;
several among the most celebrated of the fabliaux are thus represented ; among
others : the Sacristan and the wife of the Knight ; the Hermit who got drunk ;
a story recalling the adventures of Lazarillo de Tormes (unnoticed by the historians of Spanish fiction), &c.   Some drawings of this sort from MS. 10 E iv.
in the British Museum are reproduced in " English Wayfaring Life," pp.
21, 28, 405, &c.

hands an intermediate being between a saint, a goddess,
and a fairy. The sacristan-nun of a convent, beautiful as
may be believed, falls in love with a clerk, doubtless a
charming one, and, unable to live without him, "throws
her keys on the altar, and roves with her friend for five
years outside the monastery." Passing by the place at the
end of that time, she is impelled by curiosity to go to the
convent and inquire concerning herself, the sacristan-nun
of former years. To her great surprise she hears that the
sister continues there, and edifies the whole community by
her piety. At night, while she sleeps, the Virgin appears
to her in a vision, saying : " Return, unfortunate one, to thy
convent! It is I who, assuming thy shape, have fulfilled
thy duties until now." [1] A conversion of course follows. A
professional thief, who robbed and did nothing besides,
" always invoked the Virgin with great devotion, even when
he set out to steal." [2] He is caught and hanged ; but the
Virgin herself upholds him, and keeps him alive ; he is
taken down, and becomes a monk.

Another tale, of a romantic turn, is at once charming,
absurd, immoral, edifying, and touching : " Celestinus
reigned in the City of Rome. He was exceedingly
prudent, and had a pretty daughter." [3] A knight fell in
love with her, but, being also very prudent after a fashion,
he argued thus: " Never will the emperor consent to give
me his daughter to wife, I am not worthy ; but if I could
in some manner obtain the love of the maiden, I should
ask for no more." He went often to see the princess, and

[1] " Redi, misera, ad monasterium, quia ego, sub tua specie usque modo
officium tuum adimplevi." Wright's " Latin Stories," p. 95. Same story
in Barbazan and Méon, " Nouveau Recueil," vol. ii. p. 154: " De la Segre-
taine qui devint fole au monde."

[2] " Latin Stories," p. 97 ; French text in Barbazan and Méon, vol. ii. p.
443: " Du larron qui se commandoit à Nostre Dame toutes les fois qu'il aloit
embler."

[3] " Latin Stories," p. 114, from the version of the " Gesta Romanorum,"
compiled in England : " De milite conventionem faciente cum mercatore."

tried to find favour in her eyes, but she said to him : " Thy trouble is thrown away ; thinkest thou I know not what all these fine speeches mean ? "

He then offers money : " It will be a hundred marks," says the emperor's daughter. But when evening comes the knight falls into such a deep sleep that he only awakes on the following morning. The knight ruins himself in order to obtain the same favour a second time, and succeeds no better than at first. He has spent all he had, and, more in love than ever, he journeys afar to seek a lender. He arrives " in a town where were many merchants, and a variety of philosophers, among them master Virgil." A merchant, a man of singular humour, agrees to lend the money ; he refuses to take the lands of the young man as a security ; " but thou shalt sign with thy blood the bond, and if thou dost not return the entire sum on the appointed day, I shall have the right to remove with a well-sharpened knife all the flesh off thy body."

The knight signs in haste, for he is possessed by his passion, and he goes to consult Virgil. " My good master," he says, using the same expression as Dante, " I need your advice ; " and Virgil then reveals to him the existence of a talisman, sole cause of his irresistible desire to sleep. The knight returns with speed to the strange palace inhabited by the still stranger daughter of this so " prudent " emperor ; he removes the talisman, and is no longer overpowered by sleep.

To many tears succeeds a mutual affection, so true, so strong, accompanied by so much happiness, that both forget the fatal date. However, start he must. " Go," says the maiden, and offer him double, or treble the sum ; offer him all the gold he wishes ; I will procure it for thee." He arrives, he offers, but the merchant refuses : " Thou speakest in vain ! Wert thou to offer me all the wealth of the city, nothing would I accept but what has been signed, sealed, and settled between us." They go before the judge ; a condemnation is sure to ensue.

The maiden, however, kept herself well informed of all that went on, and, seeing the turn affairs were taking, " she cut her hair, donned a rich suit of men's clothes, mounted a palfrey, and set out for the palace where her lover was about to hear his sentence." She asks to be allowed to defend the knight. " But nothing can be done," says the judge. She offers money to the merchant, which he refuses ; she then exclaims : " Let it be done as he desires ; let him have the flesh, and nothing but the flesh ; the bond says nothing of the blood." Hearing this, the merchant replies : " Give me my money and I hold you clear of the rest." " Not so," said the maiden. The merchant is confounded, the knight released ; the maiden returns home hurriedly, puts on her female attire, and hastens out to meet her lover, eager to hear all that has passed.

" O my dear mistress, that I love above all things, I nearly lost my life this day ; but as I was about to be condemned, suddenly appeared a knight of an admirable presence, so handsome that I never saw his like." How could she, at these words, prevent her sparkling eyes from betraying her ? " He saved me by his wisdom, and nought had I even to pay.

" *The Maiden.*—Thou might'st have been more generous, and brought home to supper the knight who had saved thy life.

" *The Knight.*—He appeared and disappeared so suddenly I could not.

" *The Maiden.*—Would'st thou recognise him again if he returned ?

" *The Knight.*—I should, assuredly." [1]

---

[1] " Ait miles, ' o carissima domina, mihi præ omnibus prædilecta hodie fere vitam amisi; sed cum ad mortem judicari debuissem, intravit subito quidam

She then puts on again her male attire, and it is easy to imagine with what transports the knight beheld his saviour in his friend. The end of this first outline of a "Merchant of Venice" is not less naïve, picturesque, and desultory than the rest: "Thereupon he immediately married the maiden," and they led saintly lives. We are not told what the prudent emperor Celestinus thought of this "immediately."

Next to these compilers whose works became celebrated, but whose names for the most part remained concealed, stood professional authors, who were and wanted to be known, and who enjoyed a great personal fame. Foremost among them were John of Salisbury and Walter Map, men of thought, wit, and learning.

John of Salisbury,[1] a former pupil of Abélard, a friend of St. Bernard, Thomas Becket, and the English Pope Adrian IV., often sent to the court of Rome, which he visited ten times in twelve years, writes in Latin his "Policratic," or "De nugis Curialium," his "Metalogic,"[2] his "Enthetic,"[3] and his eulogy on Becket, his remarkable

---

miles formosus valde, bene militem tam formosum nunquam antea vidi, et me per prudentiam suam non tantum a morte salvavit, sed etiam me ab omni solutione pecuniæ liberavit.' Ait puella : ' Ergo ingratus fuisti quod militem ad prandium, quia vitam tuam taliter salvavit, non invitasti.' Ait miles : Subito intravit et subito exivit.' Ait puella : ' Si cum jam videres, haberes notitiam ejus?' At ille 'Etiam optime.'" *Ibid.*

[1] Born ab. 1120. Pope Adrian IV. (Nicholas Breakspear) had great friendship for him : " Fatebatur etiam," John wrote somewhat conceitedly, "publice et secreto quod me præ omnibus mortalibus diligebat. . . . Et quum Romanus pontifex esset, me in propria mensa gaudebat habere convivum, et eundem scyphum et discum sibi et mihi volebat, et faciebat, me renitente, esse communem " ("Metalogicus," in "Opera Omnia," ed. Giles, v. 205). John of Salisbury died in 1180, being then bishop of Chartres, a dignity to which he had been raised, he said, " divina dignatione et meritis Sancti Thomæ " (Demimuid, "Jean de Salisbury," 1873, p. 275).

[2] Both in prose. "Policraticus, from πόλις and χρατεῖν. Ed. Webb, Oxford, 1909, 2 vols. Th. Becket's copy is in Corpus Christi College, Cambridge.

[3] "Entheticus, a collection of short poems, some on philosophical subjects, some on contemporary men and matter.

series of letters.[1] John is only too well versed in the classics, and he quotes them to an extent that does more credit to his erudition than to his taste ; but he has the gift of observation, and his remarks on the follies of his time have a great historical value. In his "Policratic" is found a satire on a sort of personage who was then beginning to play his part again, after an interruption of several centuries, namely, the *curialis*, or courtier ; a criticism on histrions who, with their indecent farces, made a rough prelude to modern dramatic art ; a caricature of those fashionable singers who disgraced the religious ceremonies in the newly erected cathedrals by their songs resembling those "of women . . . of sirens . . . of nightingales and parrots."[2] He ridicules hunting-monks, and also those chiromancers for whom Becket himself had a weakness. "Above all," says John, by way of conclusion and apology, "let not the men of the Court upbraid me for the follies I lend them ; maybe I did not mean them at all, but I satirised myself and those like me, and it would be hard indeed if I were forbidden to castigate both myself and my friends."[3] In his "Metalogic," he scoffs at the vain dialectics of silly logicians, Cornificians, as he calls them, an appellation that stuck to them all through the Middle Ages, and at their long

---

[1] "Joannis Saresberiensis . . . Opera omnia," ed. Giles, Oxford, 1848, 5 vols. On his having Aristotle copied " at any cost," see I. p. 54, year 1167.

[2] "Ipsum quoque cultum religionis incestat, quod ante conspectum Domini, in ipsis penetralibus sanctuarii, lascivientis vocis luxu, quadam ostentatione sui, muliebribus modis notularum articulorumque cæsuris stupentes animulas emollire nituntur. Quum præcinentium et succinentium, canentium et decinentium, præmolles modulationes audieris, Sirenarum concentus credas esse, non hominum, et de vocum facilitate miraberis quibus philomena vel psitaccus, aut si quid sonorius est, modos suos nequeunt coæquare." "Opera," vol. iii. p. 38. *Cf.* below, p. 440.

[3] "Quæ autem de curialibus nugis dicta sunt, in nullo eorum, sed forte in me aut mei similibus deprehendi ; et plane nimis arcta lege constringor, si meipsum et amicos castigare et emendare non licet." "Opera," vol. iv. p. 379 (Maupassant used to put forth in private conversation exactly the same plea as an apology for " Bel-Ami ").

phrases interlarded with so many negative particles that, in order to find out whether yes or no was meant, it became necessary to examine if the number of noes was an odd or even one.

Bold ideas abound with John of Salisbury; he praises Brutus; he is of opinion that the murder of tyrants is not only justifiable, but an honest and commendable deed: "Non modo licitum est, sed æquum et justum." Whatever may be the apparent prosperity of the great, the State will go to ruin if the common people suffer: "When the people suffer, it is as though the sovereign had the gout"[1]; he must not imagine he is in health; let him try to walk, and down he falls.

Characteristics of the same sort are found, with much more sparkling wit, in the Latin works of Walter Map.[2] This Welshman has the vivacity of the Celts his compatriots; he was celebrated at the court of Henry II., and throughout England for his repartees and witticisms, so celebrated indeed that he himself came to agree to others' opinion, and thought them worth collecting. He thus formed a very bizarre book, without beginning or end, in which he noted, day by day,[3] all the curious things he had heard— "ego verbum audivi"—and with greater abundance those he had said, including a great many puns. Thus it happens that certain chapters of his " De Nugis Curialium," a title that the work owes to the success of John of Salis-

---

[1] " Afflictus namque populus, quasi principis podagram arguit et convicit. Tunc autem totius reipublicæ salus incolumis præclaraque erit, si superiora membra si impendant inferioribus et inferiora superioribus pari jure respondeant." "Policraticus"; "Opera," vol. iv. p. 52.

[2] Born probably in Herefordshire, studied at Paris, fulfilled various diplomatic missions, was justice in eyre 1173, canon of St. Paul's 1176, archdeacon of Oxford, 1197. He spent his last years in his living of Westbury on the Severn, and died about 1210. J. Bardoux, " De Waltero Mappio," 1900.

[3] " Hunc in curia regis Henrici libellum raptim annotavi schedulis." " De Nugis Curialium," ed. M. R. James, Oxford, 1914, Dist. iv., Epilogus; Engl. translation by Tupper and Ogle, 1924.

bury's, are real novels, and have the smartness of such;
others are real fabliaux, with all their coarseness; others
are scenes of comedy, with dialogues, and indications of the
characters as in a play [1]; others again are anecdotes of the
East, " quoddam mirabile," told on their return by pilgrims
or crusaders.

Like John of Salisbury, Map had studied in Paris, fulfilled missions to Rome, and known Becket; but he shared
neither his sympathy for France, nor his affection for St.
Bernard. In the quarrel which sprung up between the
saint and Abélard, he took the part of the latter. Though
he belonged to the Church, he is never weary of sneering
at the monks, and especially at the Cistercians; he imputes
to St. Bernard abortive miracles. " Placed," says Map, " in
the presence of a corpse, Bernard exclaimed : ' Walter,
come forth! '—But Walter, as he did not hear the voice of
Jesus, so did he not listen with the ears of Lazarus, and
came not." [2] Women also are for Map the subject of
constant satires; he was the author of that famous " Dis-
suasio Valerii ad Rufinum de ducenda uxore," [3] well known
to the Wife of Bath and which the Middle Ages persistently
attributed to St. Jerome. Map had asserted his authorship
and stated that he had written the dissertation " changing
only our names," assuming for himself the name of Valerius
" me qui Walterus sum," and calling his uxorious friend
Rufinus because he was red-haired. But it was of no avail,
and St. Jerome continued to be the author, in the same
way as Cornelius Nepos was credited with having written
Joseph of Exeter's " Trojan War," dedicated though it was
to the archbishop of Canterbury. Map is very strong in
his advice to his red-haired friend, who " was bent upon

[1] For example, *ibid.* iii. 2, " De Societate Sadii et Galonis," Dialogue
between three women, Regina, Lais, and Ero, III. ch. 2.

[2] " Galtere, veni foras !—Galterus autem, quia non audivit vocem Jhesus,
non habuit aures Lazari et non venit." " De Nugis," I. ch. 24.

[3] " De Nugis," Dist. iv.

being married, not loved, and aspired to the fate of Vulcan, not of Mars."

As a compensation many poems in Latin and French were attributed to Map, of doubtful authenticity. That he wrote verses and was famous as a poet there is no question, but what poems were his we do not know for certain. To him was ascribed most of the "Goliardic" poetry current in the Middle Ages, so called on account of the principal personage who figures in it, Golias, the type of the gluttonous and debauched prelate. Some of those poems were merry songs full of humour and *entrain*, perfectly consistent with what we know of Map's fantasy : " My supreme wish is to die in the tavern ! May my dying lips be wet with wine ! So that on their coming the choirs of angels will exclaim : ' God be merciful to this tippler ! ' " [1] Doubts exist also as to what his French poems were ; most of his jokes and repartees were delivered in French, as we know from the testimony of Gerald de Barry,[2] but what he wrote in that language is uncertain. The " Lancelot " is assigned to him in many manuscripts and is perhaps his work.[3]

[1] Th. Wright, "The Latin poems commonly attributed to Walter Mapes," London, Camden Society, 1841, 4to (*cf.* "Romania," vol vii. p. 94) :

> Meum est propositum in taberna mori ;
> Vinum sit appositum morientis ori,
> Ut dicant cum venerint angelorum chori :
> Deus sit propitius huic potatori.
>
> ("Confessio Goliæ.")

On "Goliardois" clerks, see Bédier, "les Fabliaux," Paris, 1893, 8vo, pp. 348 ff. *Cf.* Breul, "The Cambridge Songs," Cambridge, 1916.

[2] In his prefatory letter to king John, Gerald says that "vir ille eloquio clarus, W. Mapus, Oxoniensis archidiaconus," used to tell him that he had derived some fame and benefits from his witticisms and sayings, "dicta," which were in the common idiom, that is in French, "communi quippe idiomate prolata." "Opera," Rolls, vol. v. p. 410.

[3] Map, however, never claimed the authorship of this work. The probability of his being the author rests mainly on the allusion discovered by Ward in the works of Hue de Rotelande, a compatriot and contemporary of Map, who seems to point him out as having written the "Lancelot." "Catalogue of Romances," 1883, vol. i. pp. 734 ff.

V.

The subjects of the Angevin kings also took part in the scientific movement. In the ranks of their literary men using the Latin language are jurists, physicians, savants, historians, theologians, and, among the latter, some of the most famous doctors of the Middle Ages: men like Adelard of Bath and Michael Scot, translators of Greek and Arabic scientific treatises;[1] Alexander of Hales, the "irrefragable doctor"[2]; Roger Bacon, the "admirable doctor"; Duns Scot, the "subtle doctor"; Adam de Marisco, friend and adviser of Simon de Montfort, the "illustrious doctor"; Ockham, the "invincible doctor": Bradwardine, the "profound doctor," and yet others.

Great Roger Bacon endeavours to clear up the chaos of the sciences; he forestalls his illustrious namesake, and classifies the causes of human errors.[3]

Bartholomew the Englishman,[4] another savant, also universal and widely celebrated, writes one of the oldest

[1] Respectively XIIth and XIIIth cent., on whom, Haskins, "Studies in the History of Mediæval Science," Cambridge, Mass. 1924, chap. II, XIII.

[2] Alexander, of Hales, Gloucestershire, lectured at Paris, d. 1245; wrote a "Summa" at the request of Innocent II.: "Alexandri Alensis Angli, Doctoris irrefragabilis . . . universæ theologiæ Summa," Cologne, 1622, 4 vols. fol. He dea's in many of his "Quæstiones" with subjects, usual then in theological books, but which seem to the modern reader very strange indeed. Many sermons and pious treatises were also written in Latin during this period, by Aelred of Rievaulx and by others; see Migne's "Patrologia," vol. cxcv.

[3] Born in Somersetshire, studied at Oxford and Paris, d. 1292. See *e.g.*, "Opus Majus," ed. Bridges, 3 vols. 1900; parts of "Opus Minus" and "Opus Tertium," in "Opera inedita," Brewer, 1859; "Opera hactenus inedita," ed. Steele; "Roger Bacon Essays" (with bibliography) ed. Little, 1914. Many curious inventions are alluded to by Bacon: diving bells, "Opera inedita," p. 533; gunpowder, 536; oarless and very swift boats; carriages without horses running at an extraordinary speed: "Item currus possunt fieri ut sine animali moveantur impetu inæstimabili," p. 553. On the causes of errors, that is authority, habit, &c., see "Opus majus," I.

[4] Concerning Bartholomæus Anglicus, sometimes but wrongly called de Glanville, see the notice by Mr. Delisle ("Histoire Littéraire de la France," vol. xxx. pp. 334 ff.), who has demonstrated that he lived in the thirteenth

encyclopedias. His Latin book, translated into several languages, and of which there are many very beautiful manuscripts,[1] comprises everything, from God and the angels down to beasts. Bartholomew teaches theology, philosophy, geography, and history, the natural sciences, medicine, worldly civility, and the art of waiting on table. Nothing is too high, or too low, or too obscure for him ; he is acquainted with the nature of angels, as well as with that of fleas : " Fleas bite more sharply when it is going to rain." He knows about diamonds, " stones of love and reconciliation " ; and about man's dreams " that vary according to the variation of the fumes that enter into the little chamber of his phantasy " ; and about headaches that arise from " hot choleric vapours, full of ventosity " ; and about the moon, that " engenders dew " ; and about everything in fact.

Duns Scot discusses the greatest problems of soul and matter, and amid many contradictions, and much obscurity, arrives at this conclusion, that matter is one : " Socrates and the brazen sphere are identical in nature." He almost reaches this further conclusion, that " being is one."[2] His

and not in the fourteenth century. It is difficult to admit with M. Delisle that Bartholomew was not English. As we know that he studied and lived on the Continent the most probable explanation of his surname is that he was born in England. See also his praise of England, xv–14. His " De Proprietatibus " (Francfort, 1609, many ed.) was translated into English by Trevisa, in 1398, in French by Jean Corbichon, at the request of the wise king Charles V., in Spanish and in Dutch. To the same category belongs Gervase of Tilbury in Essex, who wrote, also on the Continent, between 1208 and 1214, his " Otia imperialia," where he gives an account of chaos, the creation, the wonders of the world, &c. ; in Leibnitz " Scriptores Rerum Brunsvicensium," Hanover, 1707, p. 881 ; extracts by Stevenson in his " Radulphi de Coggeshall Chronicon," 1875, Rolls, p. 419, and F. Liebrecht, Hanover, 1856.

[1] There are eighteen in the National Library, Paris. One of the finest is the MS. 15 E ii. and iii. in the British Museum (French text); *in fine :* " Escript par moy Jo Duries et finy à Bruges le XXVᵉ jour de May, anno 1482."

[2] Studied at Oxford, then at Paris, where he taught with great success, d. at Cologne in 1308. " Opera Omnia," ed. Luc Wadding, 1639, 12 vols. fol. See, on him, " Histoire littéraire de la France," vol. xxiv. p. 404.

reputation is immense during the Middle Ages; it diminishes at the Renaissance, and Rabelais, drawing up a list of some remarkable books in the St. Victor library, inscribes on it, between the " Maschefaim des Advocats " and the "Ratepenade des Cardinaux," the works of the subtle doctor under the irreverent title of " Barbouillamenta Scoti."

Ockham, in the pay of Philippe-le-Bel—for England, that formerly had to send for Lanfranc and Anselm, can now furnish the Continent with doctors—makes war on Boniface VIII., and, drawing his arguments from both St. Paul and Aristotle, attacks the temporal power of the popes.[1] Archbishop Bradwardine,[2] who died in the great plague of 1349, restricts himself to theology, and in a book famous during the Middle Ages, defends the "Cause of God" against all sceptics, heretics, infidels, and miscreants, confuting them all, and even Aristotle himself.[3]

No longer is Salerno alone to produce illustrious physicians, or Bologna illustrious jurists. A " Rosa Anglica," the work of John of Gaddesden, court physician under Edward II., has the greatest success in learned Europe, and teaches how the stone can be cured by rubbing the invalid with a paste composed of crickets and beetles pounded together, "but taking care to first remove the heads and wings."[4] A multitude of prescriptions, of the same stamp most of them, are set

[1] The works of Ockham (fourteenth century) have not been collected. See, *e.g.*, his "Summa totius logicæ," ed. Walker, 1675, 8vo, his " Compendium errorum Johannis papæ," Lyons, 1495, fol.

[2] Born at Chichester ab. 1290, taught at Oxford, became chaplain to Edward III. and Archbishop of Canterbury. " De Causa Dei contra Pelagium et de virtute causarum ad suos Mertonenses, Libri III.," London, 1618, fol.

[3] " Contra Aristotelem, astruentem mundum non habuisse principium temporale et non fuisse creatum, nec præsentem generationem hominum terminandam, neque mundum nec statum mundi ullo tempore finiendum." I, i.

[4] " Joannis Anglici praxis medica Rosa Anglica dicta," Augsb., 1595, i. 496. See G. Dock, " Printed editions of Gaddesden," in "Janus," XII, viii.

down in this book, which was still printed and considered as an authority at the Renaissance.

The jurists are numerous ; through them again the action of Rome upon England is fortified. Even those among them who are most bent upon maintaining the local laws and traditions, have constantly to refer to the ancient law-makers and commentators ; Roman law is for them a sort of primordial and common treasure, open to all, and wherewith to fill the gaps of the native legislation. The first lessons had been given after the Conquest by foreigners : the Italian Vacarius, brought by Theobald, Archbishop of Canterbury, had professed law at Oxford in 1149.[1] Then Anglo-Normans and English begin to codify and interpret their laws ; they write general treatises ; they collect precedents ; and so well do they understand the utility of precedents that these continue to have in legal matters, up to this day, an importance which no other nation has credited them with. Ralph Glanville, Chief Justice under Henry II., writes or inspires a "Treatise of the laws and customs of England "[2] ; Richard, bishop of London, compiles a "Dialogue of the Exchequer,"[3] full of wisdom, life, and even a sort of humour ; Henry of Bracton,[4] the most renowned of all, logician, observer, and

[1] On Vacarius, see "Magister Vacarius primus juris Romani in Anglia professor ex annalium monumentis et opere accurate descripto illustratus," by C. F. C. Wenck, Leipzig, 1820, 8vo.

[2] "Tractatus de Legibus et Consuetudinibus Angliæ," finished about 1187 (ed. Wilmot and Rayner, London, 1780, 8vo) ; was perhaps the work of his nephew, Hubert Walter, but written under his inspiraton.

[3] "Dialogus de Scaccario," written 23 Henry II., text in Stubbs, "Select Charters," Oxford, 1876, p. 168.

[4] "Henrici de Bracton de Legibus et Consuetudinibus Angliæ, Libri V.," ed. Travers Twiss, Rolls, 1878 ff., 6 vols ; ed. Woodbine, Yale University Press, 1915, ff. Bracton adopts some of the best known among the definitions and maxims of Roman Law : "Filius hæres legittimus est quando nuptiæ demonstrant," vol. ii. p. 18 ; a treasure is "quædam vetus depositio pecuniæ vel alterius metalli cujus non extat modo memoria," vol. ii. p. 230. On "Bracton and his relation to Roman law," see C. Güterbock, translated with notes by Brinton Coxe, Philadelphia, 1866, 8vo.

thinker, composes in the thirteenth century an ample treatise, of which several abridgments[1] were afterwards made for the convenience of the judges, and which is still consulted.

In the monasteries, the great literary occupation consists in the compiling of chronicles. Historians of Latin tongue abounded in mediæval England, nearly every abbey had its own. A register was prepared, with a loose leaf at the end, "scedula," on which the daily events were inscribed in pencil, "cum plumbo." At the end of the year the appointed chronicler, "non quicumque voluerit, sed cui injunctum fuerit," shaped these notes into a continued narrative, adding his remarks and comments, and insertiug the entire text of the official documents sent by authority for the monastery to keep, according to the custom of the time.[2]   In other cases, of rarer occurrence, a chronicle was compiled by some monk who, finding the life in cloister very dull, the offices very long, and the prayers somewhat monotonous, used writing as a means of resisting temptations and ridding himself of vain thoughts and the remembrance of a former worldly life.[3]   Thus there exists

---

[1] By Gilbert de Thornton, ab. 1292 ; by the author of "Fleta seu Commentarius juris Anglicani," ab. the same date.

[2] The loose leaf was then removed, and a new one placed instead, in view of the year to come : "In fine vero anni non quicumque voluerit sed cui injunctum fuerit, quod verius et melius censuerit ad posteritatis notitiam transmittendum, in corpore libri succincta brevitate describat ; et tunc veteri scedula subtracta nova imponatur." "Annales Monastici," ed. Luard, Rolls, 1864-9, 5 vols. 8vo, vol. iv. p. 355 ; Annals of the Priory of Worcester ; preface. Concerning the "Scriptoria" in monasteries and in particular the "Scriptorium" of St. Albans, see Hardy, "Descriptive Catalogue," 1871, Rolls, vol. iii. pp. xi. ff.

[3] "Sedens igitur in claustro, pluries fatigatus, sensu habetato, virtutibus frustratus, pessimis cogitationibus sæpe sauciatus, tum propter lectionum longitudinem ac orationum lassitudinem, propter vanas jactantias et opera pessima in sæculo præhabita . . ." He has recourse, as a cure, to historical studies, "ad rogationem superiorum meorum." "Eulogium historiarum ab orbe condito usque ad A.D. 1366," by a monk of Malmesbury, ed. Haydon, Rolls, 1858, 2 vols. 8vo, vol. i. p. 2.

an almost uninterrupted series of English chronicles, written in Latin, from the Conquest to the Renaissance. The most remarkable of these series is that of the great abbey of St. Albans, founded by Offa, a contemporary of Charlemagne, and rebuilt by Paul, a monk of Caen, who was abbot in 1077.

Most of these chronicles are singularly impartial; the authors freely judge the English and the French, the king and the people, the Pope, Harold and William. They belong to that Latin country and that religious world which had no frontiers. The cleverest among them are remarkable for their knowledge of the ancients, for the high idea they conceive, from the twelfth century on, of the historical art, and for the pains they take to describe manners and customs, to draw portraits and to preserve the memory of curious incidents. Thus shone, in the twelfth century, Orderic Vital, author of an "Ecclesiastical History" of England [1]; Eadmer, St. Anselm's biographer [2]; sharp-witted Richard of Devizes [3]; Gerald De Barry, otherwise Geraldus Cambrensis, a fiery, bragging Welshman, who exhibited both in his life and works the temperament of a Gascon [4]; Jocelin de Brake-

[1] "Orderici Vitalis Angligenæ Historiæ ecclesiasticæ Libri XIII.," ed. Le Prevost, Paris, 1838-55, 5 vols. 8vo. Vital was born in England, but lived and wrote in the monastery of St. Evroult in Normandy, where he had been sent "as in exile," and where, "as did St. Joseph in Egypt, he heard spoken a language to him unknown."

[2] D. ab. 1144. "Eadmeri Historia novorum in Anglia," ed. Martin Rule, Rolls, 1884; in the same volume: "De vita et conversatione Anselmi."

[3] "De Rebus Gestis Ricardi I." in "Chronicles of . . . Ric. I.," ed. Howlett, Rolls, 1886.

[4] "Giraldi Cambrensis Opera," ed. Brewer (and others), 1861-91, 8 vols. 8vo, Rolls. Gerald was born in the castle of Manorbeer, near Pembroke, of which ruins subsist. He was the son of William de Barry, of the great and warlike family that was to play an important part in Ireland. His mother was Angareth, grand-daughter of Rhys ap Theodor, a Welsh prince. He studied at Paris, became chaplain to Henry II., sojourned in Ireland, helped Archbishop Baldwin to preach the crusade in Wales, and made considerable but fruitless efforts to be appointed bishop of St. Davids. At length he settled in peace

londe, the lively chronicler of Bury St. Edmunds,[1] William
of Malmesbury,[2] Henry of Huntingdon,[3] &c.

These two last have a sort of passion for their art,
and a deep veneration for the antique models. William
of Malmesbury is especially worthy of remembrance and
respect. Before beginning to write, he had collected a
multitude of books and testimonies ; after writing he looks
over and revises his text ; he never considers, with famous
Abbé Vertot, that "son siège est fait," that it is too late
to mend. He is alive to the interest offered for the
historian by the customs of the people, and by these
characteristic traits, scarcely perceptible sometimes, which
are nevertheless landmarks in the journey of mankind
towards civilisation. His judgments are appreciative and
thoughtful ; he does something to keep awake the reader's
attention, and notes down, with this view, many anecdotes,
some of which are excellent prose tales. Seven hundred
years before Mérimée, he tells in his own way the story of
the "Vénus d'Ille."[4] He does not reach the supreme
heights of art, but he walks in the right way ; he does not
know how to blend his hues, as others have done since, so
as to delight the eye with many-coloured sights ; but he

and died there, ab. 1216 ; his tomb, greatly injured, is still to be seen in
the church. Principal works, all in Latin (see above, p. 117) ; "De Rebus a
se gestis ; " "Gemma Ecclesiastica ; " "De Invectionibus ; " "Speculum
Ecclesiæ ; " "Topographia Hibernica ; " "Expugnatio Hibernica ; " "Itinerarium Kambriæ ; " "Descriptio Kambriæ ; " "De Principis Instructione."

[1] In "Memorials of St. Edmund's Abbey," Rolls, 1890, vol. I.

[2] "Willelmi Malmesbiriensis Monachi, Gesta Regum Anglorum atque
Historia Novella," ed. T. D. Hardy, London, English Historical Society, 1840,
2 vols. 8vo ; or the Stubbs edition, Rolls, 1887 ff. ; "De Gestis Pontificum
Anglorum," ed. Hamilton, Rolls, 1870. William seems to have written
between 1114 and 1123 and to have died ab. 1142, or shortly after.

[3] "Henrici Archidiaconi Huntendunensis Historia Anglorum" (A.C. 55 to
A.D. 1154), ed. T. Arnold, Rolls, 1879. Henry writes much more as a
dilettante than William of Malmesbury ; he seems to do it mainly to please
himself ; clever at verse writing (see above, p. 177), he introduces in his Chronicle
Latin poems of his own composition. His chronology is vague and faulty.

[4] "De Annulo statuæ commendato," vol. i. p. 354.

already paints in colours. To please his reader, he suddenly and naïvely says : " Now, I will tell you a story. Once upon a time. . . ." But if he has not been able to skilfully practice latter-day methods, it is something to have tried, and so early recognised the excellence of them.

In the thirteenth century rose above all others Matthew Paris,[1] an English monk of the Abbey of St. Albans, who in his sincerity and conscientiousness, and in his love for the historical art, resembles William of Malmesbury. He, too, wants to interest ; a skilful draughtsman, " pictor peroptimus,"[2] he illustrates his own manuscripts ; he depicts scenes of religious life, a Gothic shrine carried by monks, which paralytics endeavour to touch, an architect receiving the king's orders, an antique gem of the treasury of St. Albans which, curiously enough, the convent lent pregnant women in order to assist them in child-birth ; a strange animal, little known in England : " a certain elephant,"[3] drawn from nature, with a replica of his trunk in another position, " the first, he says, that had been seen in the

---

[1] " Matthæi Parisiensis . . . Chronica Majora," ed. H. R. Luard, Rolls, 1872 ff., 7 vols. ; " Historia Anglorum, sive ut vulgo dicitur Historia Minor," ed. Madden, Rolls, 1866 ff., 3 vols. Matthew was English ; his surname of " Paris " or " the Parisian " meant, perhaps, that he had studied at Paris, or perhaps that he belonged to one of the families of Paris which existed then in England (Jessopp, "Studies by a Recluse," London, 1893, p. 46). He was received into St. Albans' monastery in 1217, and was sent on a mission to King Hacon in Norway in 1248-9. Henry III., a weak king but an artist born, valued him greatly. He died in 1259. The oldest part of Matthew's chronicle is founded upon the work of Roger de Wendover, another monk of St. Albans, who died in 1236, leaving " Flores Historiarum " (ed. Hewlett, Rolls).

[2] So says Walsingham ; see Madden's preface to the " Historia Anglorum," vol. iii. p. xlviii.

[3] MS. Nero D i. in the British Museum, fol. 22, 23, 146, 169. The attribution of these drawings to Matthew has been contested : their authenticity seems, however, probable. See, *contra*, Hardy, vol. iii. of his " Descriptive Catalogue." See also the MS. Royal 14 C vii., with maps and itineraries ; a great Virgin on a throne, with a monk at her feet : " Fret' Mathias Parisiensis," fol. 6 ; fine draperies with many folds, recalling those in the album of Villard de Honecourt.

country." [1] The animal came from Egypt, and was a gift from Louis IX. of France to Henry III. Matthew notes characteristic details showing what manners were; he gives great attention to foreign affairs, and also collects anecdotes, for instance, of the wandering Jew, who still lived in his time, a fact attested in his presence by an Archbishop of Armenia, who came to St. Albans in 1228. The porter of the prætorium had struck Jesus saying: "Go on faster, go on; why tarriest thou?" Jesus, turning, had looked at him with a stern countenance and replied: "I go on, but thou shalt tarry till I come." Since then Cartaphilus tarries, and his life begins again with each successive century. Matthew profits by the same occasion to find out about Noah's ark, and informs us that it was still to be seen, according to the testimony of this prelate, in Armenia.[2]

In the fourteenth century the most illustrious chroniclers were Ralph Higden, whose Universal History became a sort of standard work, was translated into English, printed at the Renaissance, and constantly copied and quoted[3]; Walter of Hemingburgh, Robert of Avesbury, Thomas Walsingham,[4] not to mention many anonymous authors. Several among the historians of that date, and Walsingham in particular, would, on account of the dramatic vigour of their pictures, have held a conspicuous place

---

[1] Year 1255 : "Missus est in Angliam quidam elephas quem rex Francorum pro magno munere dedit regi Angliæ. . . . Nec credimus alium unquam visum fuisse in Anglia." "Abbreviatio Chronicorum," following the "Historia Anglorum" in Madden's edition, vol. iii. p. 344.

[2] "Chronica Majora," vol. iii. pp. 162 ff. The story of Cartaphilus was already in Roger de Wendover, who was also present in the monastery when the Armenian bishop came. The details on the ark are added by Matthew.

[3] "Polychronicon Ranulphi Higden, monachi Cestrensis . . . with the English translation of John Trevisa," ed. Babington and Lumby, Rolls, 1865 ff., 8 vols. Higden died about 1363. See below, p. 406.

[4] See below, pp. 405, 412 ff.

in the literature of mediæval England had they not written in Latin, like their predecessors.[1]

From these facts, and from this ample, many-coloured literary growth, may be gathered how complete the transformation was, and how strong the intellectual ties with Rome and Paris had become; also how greatly the inhabitants of England now differed from those Anglo-Saxons, that the victors of Hastings had found " agrestes et pene illiteratos," according to the testimony of Orderic Vital. Times are changed: " The admirable Minerva visits human nations in turn. . . . she has abandoned Athens, she has quitted Rome, she withdraws from Paris; she has now come to this island of Britain, the most remarkable in the world; nay more, itself an epitome of the world." [2] Thus could speak concerning his country, about the middle of the fourteenth century, when the

---

[1] A great many other English chroniclers wrote in Latin, and among their number: Florence of Worcester, Simeon of Durham, Fitzstephen, the pseudo Benedict of Peterborough, William of Newburgh, Roger de Hoveden (d. ab. 1201) in the twelfth century; Gervase of Canterbury, Radulph de Diceto, Roger de Wendover, Radulph de Coggeshall, John of Oxenede, Bartholomew de Cotton, in the thirteenth; William Rishanger, John de Trokelowe, Nicolas Trivet, Richard of Cirencester, Knighton, in the fourteenth. A large number of chronicles are anonymous. Most of those works have been published by the English Historical Society, the Society of Antiquaries, and especially by the Master of the Rolls in the great collection : " The Chronicles and Memorials of Great Britain and Ireland . . . published under the direction of the Master of the Rolls," London, 1857 ff., in progress. See also the "Descriptive Catalogue of materials relating to the History of Great Britain and Ireland, to the end of the reign of Henry VII." by Sir T. D. Hardy, Rolls, 1862- 6. 3 vols. 8vo.

[2] The contrast between the time when Richard writes and the days of his youth, when he studied at Paris, is easy to explain. The Hundred Years' War had begun, and well could the bishop speak of the decay of studies in the capital, "ubi tepuit, immo fere friguit zelus scholæ tam nobilis, cujus olim radii lucem dabant universis angulis orbis terræ . . . Minerva mirabilis nationes hominum circuire videtur. . . . Jam Athenas deseruit, jam a Roma recessit, jam Parisius præterivit, jam ad Britanniam, insularum insignissimam, quin potius microcosmum accessit feliciter." " Philobiblon," chap. ix. p. 89, In the same words nearly, but with a contrary intent, Count Cominges, ambas-

results of the attempted experiment were certain and manifest, that great lover of books, a late student at Paris, who had been a fervent admirer of the French capital, Richard de Bury, Bishop of Durham.

sador to England, assured King Louis XIV. that " the arts and sciences some-times leave a country to go and honour another with their presence. Now they have gone to France, and scarcely any vestiges of them have been left here," April 2, 1663. " A French Ambassador at the Court of Charles II.," 1892, p. 205.

CHAPTER IV.

LITERATURE IN THE ENGLISH LANGUAGE.

I.

ENGLISH in the meanwhile had survived, but it had been also transformed, owing to the Conquest. To the disaster of Hastings succeeded, for the native race, a period of stupor and silence, and this was not without some happy results. The first duty of a master is to impose silence on his pupils; and this the conquerors did not fail to do. There was silence for a hundred years.

The clerks were the only exception; men of English speech remained mute. They barely recopied the manuscripts of their ancient authors, the list of whose names was left closed; they listened without comprehending to the songs the foreigner had acclimatised in their island. The manner of speech and the subjects of the discourses were equally unfamiliar; and they stood silent amidst the merriment that burst out like a note of defiance in the literature of the victors.

Necessity caused them to take up the pen once more. After as before the Conquest the rational object of life continued to be the gaining of heaven, and it would have been a waste of time to use Latin in demonstrating this truth to the common people of England. French served for the new masters, and for their group of adherents; Latin for the clerks; but for the mass of " lowe men," who are always the most numerous, it was indispensable to talk

English. "All people cannot," had said Bishop Grosseteste in his French "Château d'Amour," "know Hebrew, Greek, and Latin"—"nor French," adds his English translator some fifty years later; for which cause :

> On Englisch I-chul mi resun schowen
> Ffor him that con not i-knowen
> Nouther Ffrench ne Latyn.[1]

The first works written in English, after the Conquest, were sermons and pious treatises, some imitated from Bede, Ælfric, and the ancient Saxon models, others translated from the French. No originality or invention; the time is one of depression and humiliation ; the victor sings, the vanquished prays.

The twelfth century, so fertile in Latin and French works, only counts, as far as English works are concerned, devotional books in prose and verse. The verses are uncouth and ill-shaped ; the ancient rules, half-forgotten, are blended with new ones only half understood. Many authors employ at the same time alliteration and rime, and sin against both. The sermons are usually familiar in their style and kind in their tone; they are meant for the poor and miserable to whom tenderness and sympathy must be shown.[2] The listeners want to be consoled ; they are also interested, as formerly, by stories of miracles, and scared into virtue by descriptions of hell ; confidence again is given them by instances of Divine mercy.[3]

---

[1] "Castel of Love," "made in the latter half of the XIIIth century," in Horstmann and Furnivall, "Minor Poems of the Vernon MS.," E.E.T.S., 1892. Part I. p. 356, see below, p. 213. Grosseteste had said : all cannot

> Saver le langage en fin
> D'Ebreu, de griu ne de latin. (*Ibid.* p. 355.)

[2] On the MSS. and editions of the works of the period, see J. E. Wells, "Manual of . . . Middle English," 1916, ff.

[3] Among the collections of English sermons from the twelfth to the fourteenth century, see "An Old English Miscellany," ed. Morris, Early English Text Society, 1872, 8vo ; pp. 26 ff., a translation in English prose of the thirteenth

Like the ancient churches the collections of sermons bring before the eye the last judgment and the region of hell, with its monstrous torments, its wells of flames, its ocean with seven bitter waves : ice, fire, blood . . . a rudimentary rendering of legends interpreted in their turn by Dante in his poem, and Giotto in his fresco.[1] The thought of Giotto especially, when reading those sermons, recurs to the memory, of Giotto with his awkward and audacious attempts, Giotto so remote and yet so modern, childish and noble at the same time, who represents devils roasting the damned on spits, and on the same wall tries to paint

century of some of the sermons of Maurice de Sully ; p. 187, "a lutel soth sermon " in verse, with good advice to lovers overfond of "Malekyn " or "Janekyn."—" Old English homilies and homiletic treatises . . . of the XIIth and XIIIth centuries," ed. Morris, E.E.T.S., 1867-73, 2 vols. 8vo ; prose and verse (specimens of music in the second series) ; several of those pieces are mere transcripts of Anglo-Saxon works anterior to the Conquest ; p. 159, the famous " Moral Ode," twelfth century, on the transitoriness of this life : " Ich em nu alder thene ich wes," &c., in rimed verse (*cf.* " Old English Miscellany," p. 58, and " Anglia," i. p. 6).—" The Ormulum, with the notes and glossary of Dr. R. M. White," ed. R. Holt, Oxford, 1878, 2 vols. 8vo, an immense compilation in verse, of which a part only has been preserved, the work of Ormin, an Augustinian canon, early XIIIth century ; contains a paraphrase of the gospel of the day followed by an explanatory sermon ; *cf.* Napier, " Notes on Ormulum " in " History of the Holy Rood Tree," E.E.T.S., 1894. S. Holm, " Corrections . . . in the Ormulum MS." Upsala, 1922.—" Hali Meidenhad . . . an alliterative Homily of the XIIIth century," ed. Cockayne and Furnivall, E.E.T.S. in prose.—" Engl. metrical Homilies," ed. J. Small, Edinburgh, 1862, 8vo, homilies interspersed with *exempla*, compiled ab. 1330.— " Religious pieces in prose and verse," ed. G. G. Perry, E.E.T.S., 1867 ; statement in a sermon by John Gaytrige, fourteenth century, that " oure ffadire the byschope " has prescribed to each member of his clergy " opynly, one ynglysche apone sonnondayes, preche and teche thaym that they hase cure off " (p. 2).

[1] Sermon IV. on Sunday (imitated from the French) in Morris's " Old English Homilies," 1867. St. Paul, led by St. Michael, at the sight of so many sufferings, weeps, and God consents that on Sundays the condemned souls shall cease to suffer. This legend was one of the most popular in the Middle Ages ; it was told in verse or prose in Greek, Latin, French, English, &c. See Ward, " Catalogue of MS. Romances," vol. ii. 1893, pp. 397 ff. : " Two versions of this vision existed in Greek in the fourth century." An English metrical version has been ed. by Horstmann and Furnivall, " Minor Poems of the Vernon MS.," E.E.T.S., 1892, p. 251.

the Unseen and disclose to view the Unknown, Giotto with his search after the impossible, an almost painful search, the opposite of antique wisdom, and the sublime folly of the then nascent modern age. Not far from Padua, beside Venice, in the great Byzantine mosaic of Torcello, can be seen a last reflection of antique equanimity. Here the main character of the judgment-scene is its grand solemnity; and from this comes the impression of awe left on the beholder ; the idea of rule and law predominates, a fatal law against which nothing can prevail ; fate seems to preside, as it did in the antique tragedies.

In the English sermons of the period it is not the art of Torcello that continues, but the art of Giotto that begins. From time to time among the ungainly phrases of an author whose language is yet unformed, amidst mild and kind counsels, bursts forth a resounding apostrophe which causes the whole soul to vibrate, and has something sublime in its force and brevity: " He who bestows alms with ill-gotten goods shall not obtain the grace of Christ, any more than he who having slain thy child brings thee its head as a gift! " [1]

The Psalter,[2] portions of the Bible,[3] lives of the

---

[1] " Old English homilies and homiletic treatises . . . of the XIIth and XIIIth Centuries," ed. with translation, by R. Morris, London, E.E.T.S., 1867, 8vo, vol. i. p. 39.

[2] The Psalter was translated into English, in verse, in the second half of the thirteenth century : " Anglo-Saxon and Early English Psalter," Surtees Society, 1843-7, 8vo ; then in prose with a full commentary by Richard Rolle, of Hampole (on whom see below, p. 216) : " The Psalter or the Psalms of David," ed. Bramley, Oxford, 1884, 8vo ; again in prose, towards 1327, by an anonym, who has been wrongly believed to be William de Shoreham, a monk of Leeds priory : " The earliest English prose Psalter, together with eleven Canticles," ed. Bülbring, E.E.T.S., 1891. The seven penitential psalms were translated in verse in the second half of the fourteenth century by Richard of Maidstone ; one is in Horstmann and Furnivall : " Minor Poems of the Vernon MS.," p. 12.

[3] " The Story of Genesis and Exodus," ab. 1250 (ed. Morris, E.E.T.S.) ; shortly before the whole Bible had been translated into French ; see Berger, " La Bible française au Moyen Age," 1884.

saints,[1] were put into verse.   Metrical lives of saints fill
manuscripts of prodigious size.   A complete cycle of them,
the work of several authors, in which are mixed together
old and novel, English and foreign, materials, was written in
English verse in the thirteenth century : " The collection
in its complete state is a ' Liber Festivalis,' containing
sermons or materials for sermons, for the festivals of the
year in the order of the calendar, and comprehends not
only saints' lives for saints' days but also a ' Temporale '
for the festivals of Christ," &c.[2]   The earliest complete
manuscript was written about 1300, an older but incomplete one belongs to the years 1280-90, or thereabout.[3]   In these collections a large place, as might be
expected, is allowed to English saints :

> Wolle ye nouthe i-heore this englische tale · that is here i-write ?

It is the story of St. Thomas Becket : "Of Londone is
fader was."   St. Edward was " in Engeland oure kyng " ;
St. Kenelm,

> Kyng he was in Engelond · of the march of Walis ;

***

[1] See, e.g., " The early South-English Legendary or lives of Saints ; I.,
MS. Laud, 108, in the Bodleian Library," ed. C. Horstmann, E.E.T.S., 1887,
8vo.—Furnivall, " Early English Poems and Lives of Saints," Berlin, Philological Soc., 1862, 8vo.—" Materials for the history of Thomas Becket," ed.
Robertson, Rolls, 1875 ff., 7 vols.—" St. Erkenwald," ed. Gollancz, Oxf.
1923.—Several separate Lives of Saints have been published by the E.E.T.S.

[2] Horstmann, " The early South-English Legendary," p. vii.   The same
intends to publish other texts, and to clear the main problems connected with
them ; "but it will," he says, "require more brains, the brains of several
generations to come, before every question relative to this collection can be
cleared."   Ibid.

[3] The latter is the MS. Laud 108 in the Bodleian, edited by Horstmann ;
the other is the Harleian MS. 2277 in the British Museum ; specimens of its
contents have been given by Furnivall in his " Early English poems " (ut
supra).

St. Edmund the Confessor "that lith at Ponteneye,"

> Ibore he was in Engelond · in the toun of Abyndone.

St. Swithin " was her of Engelonde ; " St. Wulfstan, bishop
of Worcester,

> Was here of Engelonde . . .
> The while he was a yong child · clene lif he ladde i-nough;
> Whenne other children ornen to pleye · toward churche he drough.
> Seint Edward was kyng tho · that nouthe in heovene is.

St. Cuthbert was born in England ; St. Dunstan was an
Englishman.   Of the latter a number of humorous legends
were current among the people, and were preserved by
religious poets ; he and the devil played on each other
numberless tricks in which, as behoves, the devil had the
worst ; these adventures made the subject of amusing
pictures in many manuscripts.   A woman, of beautiful
face and figure, calls upon the saint, who is clear-sighted
enough to recognise under this alluring shape the arch-
foe ; he dissembles.   Being, like St. Eloi, a blacksmith, as
well as a saint and a State minister, he heats his tongs
red-hot, and turning suddenly round, while the other was
watching confidently the effect of his good looks, catches
him by the nose.   There was a smell of burnt flesh, and
awful yells were heard many miles round, for the " tonge
was al afure " : it will teach him to stay at home and blow
his own nose :

> As god the schrewe hadde ibeo · atom ysnyt his nose.[1]

With this we have graceful legends, like that of St.
Brandan, adapted from a French original, being the

---

[1] From MS. Harl. 2277, in Furnivall's " Early English poems," 1862,
p. 34.

story of that Irish monk who, in a leather bark, sailed in search of Paradise,[1] and visited marvellous islands where ewes govern themselves, and where the birds are angels transformed. The optimistic ideal of the Celts reappears in this poem, the subject of which is borrowed from them. " All there is beautiful, pure, and innocent; never was so kind a glance bestowed on the world, not a cruel idea, not a trace of weakness or regret." [2]

The mirth of St. Dunstan's story, the serenity of the legend of St. Brandan, are examples rarely met with in this literature. Under the light ornamentation copied from the Celts and Normans, is usually seen at that date the sombre and dreamy background of the Anglo-Saxon mind. Hell and its torments, remorse for irreparable crimes, dread of the hereafter, terror of the judgments of God, the brevity of life, are, as they were before the Conquest, favourite subjects with the national poets. They recur to them again and again; French poems describing the same are those they imitate the more willingly; the tollings of the funeral bell are heard each day in their compositions. Why cling to this perishable world ? it will pass as "the schadewe that glyt away;" man will fade as a leaf, "so lef on bouh." Where are Paris, and Helen,

---

[1] In the faireste lond huy weren · that evere mighte beo.
   So cler and so light it was · that joye thare was i-nogh ;
   Treon thare weren fulle of fruyt · wel thicke ever-ech bough . . .
   Hit was evere-more day : heom thoughte, and never-more nyght.

Life of St. Brendan who " was here of oure londe," in Horstmann's " South-English Legendary," p. 220. See also " St. Brandan, a mediæval Legend of the Sea," ed. T. Wright, Percy Society, 1844 ; Francisque Michel, " Les Voyages Merveilleux de St. Brandan à la recherche du Paradis terrestre, légende en vers du XIIe. Siècle," Paris, 1878 ; *cf.* " Navigation de la barque de Mael Duin," in d'Arbois de Jubainville's " L'Epopée Celtique en Irlande," 1892, pp. 449 ff. (above p. 12).

[2] Renan, " Essais de morale et de critique," Paris, 1867, 3rd edition, p. 446.

and Tristan, and Iseult, and Cæsar? They have fled out
of this world as the shaft from the bowstring :

> Heo beoth iglyden ut of the reyne,
> So the scheft is of the cleo.[1]

Treatises of various kinds, and pious poems, abound
from the thirteenth century ; all adapted to English life
and taste, but imitated from the French. The " Ancren
Riwle," or rule for Recluse women, written in prose in the
thirteenth century is perhaps an exception : it would be in
that case the first in date of the original treatises written
in English after the Conquest.[2] This Rule is a manual of
piety for the use of women who wish to dedicate themselves to God, a sort of " Introduction à la Vie dévote," as
mild in tone as that of St. Francis de Sales, but far more
rigorous in its precepts. The author addresses himself
specially to three young women of good family, who had
resolved to live apart from the world without taking any
vows. He teaches them to deprive themselves of all that
makes life attractive ; to take no pleasure either through
the eye, or through the ear, or in any other way. He

[1] By Thomas de Hales, " Incipit quidam cantus quem composuit frater
Thomas de Hales." He was a friend of Adam de Marisco and lived in the
XIIIth century. " Old Engl. Miscellany," ed. Morris, E.E.T.S., 1872, p. 94.

[2] The " Ancren Riwle," edited and translated by J. Morton, Camden Soc.,
1853. Seven MSS. in English have been preserved, two in Latin, abbreviated
from the English. According to Bramlette, the original was in Latin,
(" Anglia," xv.) ; to G. C. Macaulay, French (" Mod. Lang. Notes," ix.) ; to
Miss Dymes, English (" English Assoc. Essays," ix.). A MS. in French :
" La Reule des femmes religieuses et recluses," greatly suffered in the fire of
the Cottonian Library. The ladies for whom this book was written lived at
Tarrant Kaines, in Dorset, where a convent for monks had been founded by
Ralph de Kaines, son of one of the companions of the Conqueror. It is not
impossible that the original text was the French one ; French fragments
subsist in the English version. The anonymous author had taken much trouble
about this work. " God knows," he says, " it would be more agreeable to
me to start on a journey to Rome than begin to do it again." A journey to
Rome was not then a pleasure trip.

gives rules for getting up, for going to bed, for eating and for dressing. His doctrine may be summed up in a word : he teaches self-renunciation. But he does it in so kindly and affectionate a tone that the life he wishes his penitents to submit to does not seem too bitter ; his voice is so sweet that the existence he describes seems almost sweet. Yet all that could brighten it must be avoided ; the least thing may have serious consequences : " of little waxeth mickle."

Not a glance must be bestowed on the world ; the young recluses must even deny themselves the pleasure of looking out of the parlour windows. They must bear in mind the example of Eve: " When thou lookest upon a man thou art in Eve's case ; thou lookest upon the apple. If any one had said to Eve when she cast her eye upon it : ' Ah ! Eve, turn thee away ; thou castest thine eyes upon thy death,' what would she have answered ?— ' My dear master, thou art in the wrong, why dost thou find fault with me ? The apple which I look upon is for-bidden me to eat, not to look at.'—Thus would Eve quickly enough have answered. O my dear sisters, truly Eve hath many daughters who imitate their mother, who answer in this manner. But ' thinkest thou,' saith one, ' that I shall leap upon him though I look at him ? '—God knows, dear sisters, that a greater wonder has happened. Eve, thy mother leaped after her eyes to the apple ; from the apple in Paradise down to the earth ; from the earth to hell, where she lay in prison four thousand years and more, she and her lord both, and taught all her offspring to leap after her to death without end. The beginning and root of this woful calamity was a light look. Thus often, as is said, ' of little waxeth mickle.' " [1]

[1] P. 53, Morton's translation. The beginning of the quotation runs thus in the original : " Hwoso hevede iseid to Eve theo heo werp hire eien therone, A ! wend te awei ! thu worpest eien o thi death ! Hwat heved heo i-onswered ? Me leove sire, ther havest wouh. Hwarof kalenges tu me ? The eppel that ich loke on is forbode me to etene, and nout forto biholden."

The temptation to look and talk out of the window was one of the greatest with the poor anchoresses ; not a few found it impossible to resist it. Cut off from the changeable world, they could not help feeling an interest in it, so captivating precisely because, unlike the cellular life, it was ever changing. The authors of rules for recluses insisted therefore very much upon this danger, and denounced such abuses as Aelred, abbot of Rievaulx, reveals, as we have seen, so early as the twelfth century : old women, talkative ones and newsbringers, sitting before the window of the recluse, "and telling her tales, and feeding her with vain news and scandal, and telling her how this monk or that clerk or any other man looks and behaves." [1]

Most of the religious treatises in English that have come down to us are of a more recent epoch, and belong to the first half of the fourteenth century. In the thirteenth, as has been noticed, many Englishmen considered French to be, together with Latin, the literary language of the country ; they endeavoured to handle it, but not always with great success. Robert Grosseteste, who, however, recommended his clergy to preach in English, had composed in French a " Château d'Amour," an allegorical poem, with keeps, castles, and turrets, " les quatre tureles en haut," which are the four cardinal virtues, a sort of pious Romaunt of the Rose. William of Wadington had likewise written in French his " Manuel des Pechiez," not without an inkling

---

[1] "Vix aliquam inclusarum hujus temporis solam invenies, ante cujus fenestram non anus garrula vel nugigerula mulier sedeat quæ eam fabulis occupet, rumoribus aut detractionibus pascat, illius vel illius monachi vel clerici, vel alterius cujuslibet ordinis viri formam, vultum, moresque describat. Illecebrosa quoque interserat, puellarum lasciviam, viduarum, quibus libet quid-quid libet, libertatem, conjugum in viris fallendis explendisque voluptatibus astutiam depingat. Os interea in risus cachinnosque dissolvitur, et venenum cum suavitate bibitum per viscera membraque diffunditur." "De vita eremetica Liber," cap. iii., Reclusarun cum externis mulieribus confabulationes ; in Migne's "Patrologia," vol. xxxii. col. 1451. See above, p. 153. Aelred wrote this treatise at the request of a sister of his, a sister " carne et spiritu."

that his grammar and prosody might give cause for laughter. He excused himself in advance: "For my French and my rimes no one must blame me, for in England was I born, and there bred and brought up and educated."[1]

These attempts become rare as we approach the fourteenth century, and English translations and imitations, on the contrary, multiply. We find, for example, translations in English verse of the "Château"[2] and the "Manuel"[3]; a prose translation of that famous "Somme des Vices et des Vertus," composed by Friar Lorens in 1279, for Philip III. of France, a copy of which, chained to a pillar of the church of the Innocents, remained open for the convenience of the faithful[4]; a bestiary (in verse, XIIIth

---

[1] De le franceis, ne del rimer
Ne me dait nuls hom blamer,
Kar en Engleterre fu né
E norri ordiné et alevé.

Furnivall, "Roberd of Brunne's Handlyng Synne," &c., Roxb. Club, 1862, p. 413.

[2] French text of the "Château" in Cooke, "Carmina Anglo-Normannica," 1852, Caxton Society; English versions in Horstmann and Furnivall, "The minor Poems of the Vernon MS.," Early English Text Society, 1892, pp. 355, 407; Weymouth: "Castell off Love . . . an early English translation of an old French poem by Robert Grosseteste," Philological Society, 1864, 4to; Halliwell, "Castle of Love," Brixton Hill, 1849, 4to. See above, p. 205.

[3] The "Manuel des Pechiez," by William de Wadington, as well as the English metrical translation (a very free one) written in 1303 by Robert Mannyng, of Brunne, Lincolnshire (1260?–1340?), have been edited by Furnivall: "Handlyng Synne," London, Roxburghe Club, 1862, 4to, contains a number of *exempla* and curious stories. The same Mannyng wrote, after Peter de Langtoft, an Englishman who had written in French (see above, p. 122), and after Wace, a metrical chronicle, from the time of Noah down to Edward I.: "The Story of England . . . A.D. 1338," ed. Furnivall, Rolls, 1887, 2 vols. 8vo. He is possibly the author of a metrical meditation on the Last Supper imitated from his contemporary St. Bonaventure: "Meditacyuns on the Soper of our Lorde," ed. Cowper, E.E.T.S., 1875, 8vo.

[4] "The Ayenbite of Inwyt or Remorse of Conscience, in the Kentish Dialect, 1340 A.D., edited from the autograph MS.," by R. Morris, E.T.T.S. The "Ayenbite" is the work of Dan Michel, of Northgate, Kent, who belonged

century), writings on the Virgin, legends of the Cross, stories of the Passion, visions of heaven and hell [1]; a Courier of the world, "Cursor Mundi," in verse,[2] containing the history of the Old and New Testaments. A mass of legends are found in the "Cursor," that of the Cross for instance, made out of three trees, a cypress, a cedar, and a pine, symbols of the Trinity. These trees had sprung from three pips given to Seth by the guardian angel of Paradise, and placed under Adam's tongue at his death ; their miraculous existence is continued on the mountains, and they play a part in all the great epochs of Jewish history, in the time of Moses, Solomon, &c.

to "the bochouse of Saynt Austines of Canterberi." The work deals with the Ten Commandments, the seven deadly sins, informs us that "the sothe noblesse comth of the gentyl herte . . . Ase to the bodye : alle we byeth children of one moder, thet is of erthe" (p. 87). Some of the chapters of Lorens's "Somme" were adapted by Chaucer in his Parson's tale. See Wallenberg, "The Vocabulary of Dan Michel," Upsala, 1923.

[1] See in particular: "Legends of the Holy Rood, symbols of the Passion and Cross Poems, in old English of the XIth, XIVth, and XVth centuries," ed. Morris, E.E.T.S., 1871.—"An Old English Miscellany containing a Bestiary, Kentish sermons, Proverbs of Alfred and religious poems of the XIIIth century," ed. Morris, E.E.T.S., 1872.—"The religious poems of William de Shoreham," first half of the fourteenth century. ed. T. Wright, Percy Society, 1849, on sacraments, commandments, deadly sins, &c. ; "Poems," ed. Konrath, E.E.T.S. 1902.—"The Minor Poems of the Vernon MS.," ed. Horstmann and Furnivall, E.E.T.S., 1892 ; contains a variety of poems in the honour of the Virgin, pious tales, "a dispitison bitweene a good man and the devel," p. 329, meditations, laments, vision of St. Paul, &c., of various authors and dates, mostly of the thirteenth and fourteenth centuries.—"The Northern Passion," ed. Miss Foster, E.E.T.S., 1913-6.—On visions of heaven and hell (vision of St. Paul, of Tundal, of St. Patrick, of Thurkill), and on the Latin, French, and English texts of several of them, see Ward, "Catalogue of Romances," 1893, vol. ii. pp. 397 ff.

[2] "Cursor Mundi, the cursur of the world," ed. R. Morris, E.E.T.S., 1874-93, 7 parts, compiled ab. 1300 from the "Historia Ecclesiastica" of Peter Comestor, the "Fête de la Conception" of Wace, the "Château d'Amour" of Grosseteste, &c. (Haenisch "Inquiry into the sources of the Cursor Mundi," *ibid.* part vii.). The work has been wrongly attributed to John of Lindbergh. See Morris's preface, p. xviii. *Cf.* Napier, "History of the Holy Rood Tree," E.E.T.S., 1894, Eng., Lat. and Fr. prose texts of the Cross legend. It is represented in the frescoes of Piero della Francesca, Arezzo.

Similar legends adorn most of these books : what good could they accomplish if no one read them ? And to be read it was necessary to please. This is why verse was used to charm the ear, and romantic stories were inserted to delight the mind, for, says Robert Mannyng in his version of the " Manuel des Pechiez," " Many people are so made that it pleases them to hear stories and verses, in their games, in their feasts, and over their ale." [1]

Somewhat above this group of translators and adaptators rises a more original writer, Richard Rolle of Hampole, noticeable for his English and Latin compositions, in prose and verse, and still more so by his character.[2] He is the first on the list of those lay preachers, of whom England has produced a number, whom an inward crisis brought back to God, and who roamed about the country as volunteer apostles, converting the simple, edifying the wise, and, alas ! affording cause for laughter to the wicked. They are taken by good folks for saints, and for madmen by sceptics : such was the fate of Richard Rolle, of George Fox, of Bunyan, and of Wesley ; the same man lives on

[1] For lewde men y undyrtoke,
On Englyssh tunge to make thys boke :
For many ben of swyche manere
That talys and rymys wyl blethly here
Yn gamys and festys and at the ale.

" Roberd of Brunne's Handlyng Synne, A.D. 1303 with Le Manuel des Pechiez by W. of Wadington," ed. Furnivall, Roxburghe Club, 1862, p. 2.

[2] There exist Latin and English texts of his works, the latter being generally considered as translations made by himself. Chief writing, his dull but very popular moral poem : " The Pricke of Conscience," ed. Morris, Philol. Soc., 1863 (authenticity contested by Miss H. E. Allen). He wrote also a prose translation of " The Psalter," with a commentary (mainly from Peter Lombard, see Paues, " A 14th cent. Engl. Biblical version," 1902, p. xxxvii), ed. Bramley, Oxford, 1884, " English Prose Treatises," ed. G. G. Perry, E.E.T.S.. 1866, " Minor Works " ed. Miss Hodgson, 1924. See also " D. Richardi Pampolitani Psalterium Davidicum atque alia . . . Monumenta," Cologne, 1536, fol. Horstmann, " Rich. Rolle of Hampole," London, 1895 ff. ; " Incendium Amoris," ed. Miss Deanesly ; Wells, " Manual of Middle English," 1916, pp. 444, 837.

through the ages, and the same humanity heaps on him at once blessings and ridicule.

Richard was of the world, and never took orders. He had studied at Oxford. One day he left his father's house, desiring to give himself up to a contemplative life. From that time he mortifies himself, he fasts, he prays, he is tempted ; the devil appears to him under the form of a beautiful young woman, whom he had known formerly and who, he tells us with less humility than we are accustomed to from him, " loved me not a little with good love." [1] But though the wicked one shows himself in this case even more wicked than with St. Dunstan, and Rolle has no red-hot tongs to frighten him away, still the devil is again worsted, and the adventure ends as it should.

Rolle has ecstasies, he sighs and groans ; people come to visit him in his solitude ; he is found writing much, "scribentem multum velociter." He is requested to stop writing, and speak to his visitors ; he talks to them, but continues writing, " and what he wrote differed entirely from what he said." This duplication of the personality lasted two hours.

He leaves his retreat and goes all over the country, preaching abnegation and a return to Christ. He finally settled at Hampole, where he wrote his principal works, and died in 1349. Having no doubt that he would one day be canonised, the nuns of a neighbouring convent caused the office of his feast-day to be written ; and this office, which was never sung, as Rolle never received the hoped-fcr dignity, is the main source of our information concerning him.[2]

[1] " When I had takene my syngulere purpos and lefte the seculere habyte, and I be-ganne mare to serve God than mane, it fell one a nyghte als I lay in my reste, in the begynnynge of my conversyone, thare appered to me a full faire yonge womane, the whilke I had sene be-fore, and the whilke luffed me noght lyttil in gude lufe." " English Prose Treatises," p. 5.

[2] "Officium de Sancto Ricardo eremita." The office contains hymns in the

His style and ideas correspond well to such a life. His thoughts are sombre, Germanic anxieties and doubts reappear in his writings, the idea of death and the image of the grave cause him anguish that all his piety cannot allay. His style, like his life, is uneven and full of change; to calm passages, to beautiful and edifying tales succeed bursts of passion ; his phrases then become short and breathless ; interjections and apostrophes abound. " Ihesu es thy name. A! A! that wondyrfull name! A! that delittabyll name! This es the name that es abowve all names. . . . I yede (went) abowte be Covaytyse of riches and I fande noghte Ihesu. I rane be Wantonnes of flesche and I fand noghte Ihesu. I satt in companyes of Worldly myrthe and I fand noghte Ihesu. . . . Tharefore I turnede by anothire waye, and I rane a-bowte be Poverte, and I fande Ihesu pure, borne in the worlde, laid in a crybe and lappid in clathis."¹ Rolle of Hampole is, if we except the doubtful case of the " Ancren Riwle," the first English prose writer after the Conquest who can pretend to the title of original author. To find him we have had to come far into the fourteenth century. When he died, in 1349, Chaucer was about ten years of age and Wyclif thirty.

honour of the saint : " Rejoice, mother country of the English ! . . ."

> Letetur felix Anglorum patria . . .
> Pange lingua graciosi Ricardi preconium,
> Pii, puri, preciosi, fugientis vicium.

" English Prose Treatises," pp. xv and xvi.

¹ " English Prose Treatises," pp. 1, 4, 5. *Cf.* Rolle's Latin text, " Nominis Iesu encomion ": " O bonum nomen, o dulce nomen," &c., in " Richardi Pampolitani, . . . Monumenta," Cologne, 1536, fol. cxliii. At the same page, the story of the young woman.

II.

We are getting further and further away from the Conquest, the wounds inflicted by it begin to heal, and an audience is slowly forming among the English race, ready for something else besides sermons.

The greater part of the nobles had early accepted the new order of things, and had either retained or recovered their estates. Having rallied to the cause of the conquerors, they now endeavoured to imitate them, and had also their castles, their minstrels, and their romances. They had, it is true, learnt French, but English remained their natural language. A literature was composed that resembled them, English in language, as French as possible in dress and manners. About the end of the twelfth century or beginning of the thirteenth, the translation of the French romances began. First came war stories, then love tales.

Thus was written by Layamon, about 1205, the first metrical chronicle or romance, after "Beowulf," in English literature.[1] The vocabulary of the "Brut" is Anglo-Saxon; there are but eighty-seven words of French origin in the whole of this lengthy poem, and yet on each page it is easy to recognise the ideas and the chivalrous tastes introduced by the French. The strong will with

---

[1] "Layamon's Brut or Chronicle of Britain, a poetical Semi-Saxon paraphrase of the Brut of Wace," ed. by Sir Fred. Madden, London, Society of Antiquaries, 1847, 3 vols. 8vo.—*Cf.* Ward, "Catalogue of Romances," vol. i. 1883: "Many important additions are made to Wace, but they seem to be mostly derived from Welsh traditions," p. 269. Wace's "Geste des Bretons," or "Roman de Brut," written in 1155, was ed. by Leroux de Lincy, Rouen, 1836, 2 vols. 8vo. *Cf.* P. Meyer, "De quelques Chroniques Anglo-Normandes qui ont porté le nom de Brut," Bulletin de la Société des Anciens Textes français, 1878. Layamon, son of Leovenath, lived at Ernley, now Lower Arley, on the Severn; he uses sometimes alliteration and sometimes rime in his verse. The MS. Cott. Otho C. xiii contains a "somewhat modernised" version of Layamon's "Brut," late thirteenth or early fourteenth century (Ward, *ibid.*). On Layamon and his work, see "Anglia," i. p. 197, and ii. p. 153; Wells, "Manual of Middle English," pp. 32, 191, 792.

which they blended the traditions of the country has borne its fruits. Layamon considers that the glories of the Britons are English glories, and he celebrates their triumphs with an exulting heart, as if British victories were not Saxon defeats. Bede, the Anglo-Saxon, and Wace, the Norman, "a Frenchis clerc" as he calls him, are, in his eyes, authorities of the same sort and same value, equally worthy of filial respect and belief. "It came to him in mind," says Layamon, speaking of himself, "and in his chief thought that he would of the English tell the noble deeds. . . . Layamon began to journey wide over this land and procured the noble books which he took for pattern. He took the English book that St. Bede made," and a Latin book by " St. Albin "; a third book he took "and laid in the midst, that a French clerk made, who was named Wace, who well could write. . . . These books he turned over the leaves, lovingly he beheld them . . . pen he took with fingers and wrote on book skin." [1] He follows mainly Wace's poem, but paraphrases it ; he introduces legends that were unknown to Wace, and adds speeches to the already numerous speeches of his model. These discourses consist mostly of warlike invectives ; before slaying, the warriors hurl defiance at each other ; after killing his foe, the victor allows himself the pleasure of jeering at the corpse, and his mirth resembles very much the mirth in Scandinavian sagas. "Then laughed Arthur, the noble king, and gan to speak with gameful words : 'Lie now there, Colgrim. . . . Thou climbed on this hill wondrously high, as if thou wouldst ascend to heaven, now thou shalt to hell. There thou mayest know much of your kindred ; and greet thou there Hengest . . . and Ossa, Octa and more of thy kin, and bid them there dwell winter and summer, and we shall in

---

[1] Madden, *ut supra*, vol. i. p. 1.

land live in bliss.'" [1] This is an example of a speech added to Wace, who simply concludes his account of the battle by:

> Mors fu Balduf, mors fu Colgrin
> Et Cheldric s'en ala fuiant. [2]

In such taunts is recognised the ferocity of the primitive epics, those of the Greeks as well as those of the northern nations. Thus spoke Patroclus to Cebrion when he fell headlong from his chariot, " with the resolute air of a diver who seeks oysters under the sea."

After Layamon, translations and adaptations soon become very plentiful, metrical chronicles, like the one composed towards the end of the thirteenth century by Robert of Gloucester,[3] are compiled on the pattern of the French ones, for the use and delight of the English people ; chivalrous romances are also written in English. The love of extraordinary adventures, and of the books that tell of them, had crept little by little into the hearts of these islanders, now reconciled to their masters, and led by them all over the world. The minstrels or wandering poets of English tongue are many in number ; no feast is complete without their music and their songs ; they are welcomed in the castle halls ; they can now, with as bold a voice as

---

[1] Madden, *ut supra*, vol. ii. p. 476. The original text (printed in short lines by Madden and here in long ones) runs thus :

> Tha loh Arthur · the althele king,
> And thus yeddien agon · mid gommenfulle worden:
> Lien nu there Colgrim · thu were iclumben haghe . . .
> Thu clumbe a thissen hulle · wunder ane hæghe,
> Swulc thu woldest to hævene · nu thu scalt to hælle ;
> Ther thu miht kenne · muche of thine cunne,
> And gret thu ther Hengest · the cnihten wes fayerest,
> Ebissa and Ossa · Octa and of thine cunne ma,
> And bide heom ther wunie · wintres and sumeres,
> And we .·ullen on londe · libben in blisse.

[2] " Roman de Brut," vol. ii. p. 57.

[3] On Robert, see above, pp. 117, 122. On his sources, see Ellmer, " Anglia," x. pp. 1. ff., 291 ff. ; Wells, " Manual of Middle English," p. 196.

their French brethren, bespeak a cup of ale, sure not to be refused :

> At the beginning of ure tale,
> Fil me a cuppe of ful god ale,
> And y wile drinken er y spelle (tell forth),
> That Crist us shilde alle fro helle ! [1]

They stop also on the public places, where the common people flock to hear of Charlemagne and Roland [2] ; they even get into the cloister. In the thirteenth and fourteenth centuries, nearly all the stories of the heroes of Troy, Rome, France, and Britain are put into English verse:

> For hem that knowe no Frensche · ne never underston.[3]

" Men like," writes shortly after 1300, the author of the " Cursor Mundi " :

> Men lykyn jestis for to here
> And romans rede in divers manere
> Of Alexandre the conqueroure,
> Of Julius Cesar the emperoure,
> Of Grece and Troy the strong stryf
> There many a man lost his lyf,
> Of Brute that baron bold of hond,
> The first conqueroure of Englond,
> Of Kyng Artour. . . .
> How Kyng Charlis and Rowlond fawght
> With Sarzyns aold they be cawght,
> Of Trystrem and Isoude the swete,
> How they with love first gan mete . . .
> Stories of diverce thynggis,
> Of pryncis, prelatis and of kynggis,
> Many songgis of divers ryme,
> As English Frensh and Latyne.[4]

---

[1] " Lay of Havelok," ed. Skeat, Oxford, 1915, end of XIIIth century, p. 1.

[2] On wandering minstrels, " Engl. Wayfaring Life," 1920, pp. 194 ff.

[3] " William of Palerne, translated from the French at the command of Sir Humphrey de Bohun, ab. 1350," ed. Skeat, E.E.T.S., 1867, l. 5533.

[4] "Cursor Mundi," ed. Morris, Part V. p. 1651. A large number of English mediæval romances will be found among the publications of the Early English Text Society (*e.g.* : Ferumbras, Otuel, Huon of Burdeux, Charles the Grete, Four Sons of Aymon, Sir Bevis of Hamton, King Horn, Havelok the Dane, Guy of Warwick, William of Palerne, Generides, Morte Arthure, Love-

Some Germanic or Saxon traditions, such as the story of Havelok, a Dane who ended by reigning in England, or that of Horn and Rymenhild,[1] his betrothed, had been adopted by the French poets. They were taken from them again by the English minstrels, who, however, left these old heroes their French dress. Had they not followed the fashion, few would have cared for their work. Goldborough or Argentille, the heroine of the romance of Havelok, was originally a Valkyria ; now, under her French disguise, she is scarcely recognisable, but she is liked as she is.[2] Valkyrias were no more.

Some English heroes of a more recent period also find

---

lich's History of the Holy Grail, Joseph of Arimathie, Sir Gawaine and the Green Knight, &c.), the Camden and the Percy Societies, the Roxburghe and the Bannatyne Clubs. Some also have been published by Kölbing in his "Altenglische Bibliothek," Heilbronn ; by H. W. Weber : " Metrical Romances of the XIIIth, XIVth, and XVth centuries," Edinburgh, 1810, 3 vols., &c. See also H. L. D. Ward, " Catalogue of MS. Romances in the British Museum," 1883 ff. Best classified account of this literature, with analyses of main works, in Schofield " Engl. Lit. fr. the Conquest to Chaucer," 1906, ch. v.

[1] Principal versions : " Horn et Rymenhild," in French verse, by Thomas (not the same as the Thomas of " Tristan " ; see Söderhjelm, " Romania," xv. 575), ab. 1170, ed. R. Brede and E. Stengel, " Das Anglonormanische Lied vom wackern Ritter Horn," Marburg, 1883 ; " King Horn," in English verse, XIIIth cent. (short and pregnant), and "Horn Childe," à debased Engl. version of the XIVth cent., both ed. by Jos. Hall, Oxford, 1901. *Cf.*, *e.g.* : Ward, " Catal. of Romances," i. p. 447 ; Wissmann, " Anglia," iv. p. 342 ; Schofield (according to whom the original version must have been a Norse saga, and Horn's realm, Sudene, was the Isle of Man), in " Publications of the Mod. Language Association of America," xviii. 1.

[2] A sign however of a Scandinavian origin consists in the flame that comes out of the mouth of Havelok at night, and betrays his royal blood. The events take place at Lincoln, Grimsby, and in Denmark ; the seal of Grimsby engraved in the thirteenth century represents, besides " Habloc " and " Goldeburgh," " Gryem," the founder of the town, and supposed father of the hero. Gaimar, the chronicler, wrote in French verse the story of Havelok ; see " Lestorie des Engles," ed. Hardy and Martin, Rolls, 1888. *Ibid.*, another French version, also of the XIIth cent. : " Le Lai d'Haveloc." The English text, " Havelok the Dane," ed. Skeat, Oxford, 1902, was probably written between 1296 and 1300 (see the letter of J. W. Hales to the *Athenæum*, Feb. 23, 1889), *cf.* Ward's " Catalogue," i. p. 423. On Warner's adaptation, *infra* ii. 339.

a place in this poetic pantheon, thanks again to French poets, who make them fashionable by versifying about them.   In this manner were written, in French, then in English, the adventures of Waltheof, and of Sir Guy of Warwick who marries the beautiful Felice, goes to Palestine, kills the giant Colbrant on his return, and dies piously in a hermitage.[1]   Thus are likewise told the deeds of famous outlaws, as Fulke Fitz-Warin, a proto-type of Robin Hood, who lived in forests with the fair Mahaud,[2] as Robin Hood will do later with Maid Marian.[3] Several of these heroes, Guy of Warwick in particular, enjoyed such lasting popularity that it has scarcely died out to this day.   Their histories were reprinted at the Renaissance ; they were read under Elizabeth, and plays were drawn from them ; and when, with Defoe, Richard-son, and Fielding, novels of another kind took their place in the drawing-room, their life continued still in the lower

[1] "Guy of Warwick," ed. Zupitza, E.E.T.S., 1875–91 (*cf.* Ward's "Cata-logue of Romances," i. p. 471).   "All the Middle English versions of the Romances of Guy of Warwick are translations from the French. . . . The French romance was done into English several times.   We possess the whole or considerable fragments of, at least, four different Middle English versions" (Zupitza's Preface).

[2] Part of the adventures of Fulke belongs to history ; his rebellion actually took place in 1201.   His story was told in a French poem, written before 1314 and turned into prose before 1320 (the text, though in French, is remarkable for its strong English bias) ; an English poem on the same subject is lost. (Ward, "Catalogue of Romances," i. pp. 501 ff.)   The version in French prose has been edited by J. Stephenson, with his Ralph de Coggeshall, Rolls, 1875, p. 277, and by Moland and d'Héricault in their " Nouvelles en prose du quatorzième Siècle," Paris, 1858.   See also the life of the outlaw Hereward, in Latin, twelfth century : "De Gestis Herewardi Saxonis," in the "Chroniques Anglo-Normandes," of F. Michel, Rouen, 1836–40, vol. ii.

[3] It is possible that Robin Hood existed, in which case it seems probable he lived under Edward II.   "The stories that are told about him, however, had almost all been previously told, connected with the names of other outlaws such as Hereward and Fulke Fitz-Warin." Ward, "Catalogue of Romances," i. pp. 517 ff.   He was the hero of many songs, from the fourteenth century ; most of those we have belong, however, to the sixteenth.

sphere to which they had been consigned. They supplied the matter for those popular *chap books*[1] that have been reprinted even in our time, the authors of which wrote, as did the rimers of the Middle Ages, " for the love of the English people, of the people of merry England." *Englis lede of meri Ingeland.*[2]

" Merry England " became acquainted with every form of French mirth ; she imitated French chansons, and gave a place in her literature to French fabliaux. Nothing could be less congenial to the Anglo-Saxon race than the spirit of the fabliaux. This spirit, however, was acclimatised in England ; and, like several other products of the French mind, was grafted on the original stock. The tree thus bore fruit which would never have ripened as it did, without the Conquest. Such are, in the period we are reaching, the works of Chaucer. The most comic and *risqué* stories, those same stories meant to raise a laugh which we have seen old women tell at parlour windows, in order to cheer recluse anchoresses, were put into English verse, from the thirteenth to the fifteenth century. Thus we find under an English form such stories as the tale of " La Chienne qui pleure,"[3] "Le lai du

[1] On the transformations of Guy of Warwick and representations of him in chap books, see " English Novel in the Time of Shakespeare," pp. 64, 350.

[2] " Cursor Mundi," i. p. 21. *Cf.* Bartholomew the Englishman, in his " De Proprietatibus Rerum," book xv., chap. xiv., thus translated by Trevisa: "Englonde is fulle of myrthe and of game and men oft tymes able to myrth and game, free men of harte and with tongue, but the honde is more better and more free than the tongue."—"Cest acteur monstre bien en ce chapitre qu'il fut Anglois," observes with some spite Corbichon, the French translator of Bartholomew, writing, it is true, during the Hundred Years' War.

[3] English text : "Dame Siriz" in Th. Wright, "Anecdota Literaria," London, 1844, 8vo, p. 1 ; and in Goldbeck and Mätzner, "Altenglische Sprachproben," Berlin, 1867, p. 103. French text in the " Castoiement d'un père à son fils," Barbazan and Méon, "Fabliaux," vol. ii. The English text belongs to the end of the thirteenth century, and the story is localised in England ; mention is made of "Botolfston," otherwise, St. Botolph or Boston. See above, p. 154 ; on a dramatisation of the story, see below, pp. 446 ff.

Cor,"[1] " La Bourse pleine de sens," [2] the praise of the land of " Coquaigne,"[3] &c. :

> Thogh paradis be miri and bright
> Cokaygn is of fairir sight.
> What is ther in paradis
> Bot grasse and flure and grene ris (branches) ?
> Thogh ther be joi and grete dute (pleasure)
> Ther nis mete bote frute . . .
> Bot watir manis thurste to quenche ;
> Beth ther no man but two,
> Hely and Enok also

And it cannot be very pleasant to live without more company ; one must feel " elinglich." But in " Cokaygne " there is no cause to be " elinglich " ; all is meat and drink there ; all is day, there is no night :

> Al is dai, nis ther no nighte,
> Ther nis baret (quarrel) nother strif . . .
> Ther nis man no womman wroth,
> Ther nis serpent, wolf no fox ;

---

[1] Story of a drinking horn from which husbands with faithless wives cannot drink without spilling the contents. Arthur invites his knights to try the experiment, and is not a little surprised to find that it turns against himself. French text : " Le lai du Cor, restitution critique," by F. Wulff, Lund, 1888, 8vo, written by Robert Biquet in the twelfth century ; only one MS. (copied in England) has been preserved. English text : " The Cokwolds Daunce," from a MS. of the fifteenth century, in Hazlitt's " Remains of the early popular poetry of England," London, 1864, 4 vols. 8vo, vol. i. p. 35. *Cf.* Le " Mantel Mautaillé," in Montaiglon and Raynaud, " Recueil Général," vol. iii., and " La Coupe Enchantée," by La Fontaine.

[2] French text : " De pleine Bourse de Sens," by Jean le Galois, in Montaiglon and Raynaud, " Recueil Général," vol. iii. p. 88. English text : " How a Merchande dyd his wyfe betray," in Hazlitt's " Remains " (*ut supra*), vol. i. p. 196. Of the same sort are " Sir Cleges " (Weber, " Metrical Romances," 1810, vol. i.), the " Tale of the Basyn " (in Hartshorne, " Ancient Metrical Tales," London, 1829, p. 202), a fabliau, probably derived from a French original, etc.

[3] English text : " The Land of Cokaygne " (end of the fourteenth century, seems to have been originally composed in the thirteenth), in Goldbeck and Mätzner, " Altengische Sprachproben," Berlin, 1867, part i., p. 147 ; also in Furnivall, " Early English Poems," Berlin, 1862, p. 156. French text in Barbazan and Méon, " Fabliaux," vol. iii. p. 175 : " C'est li Fabliaus de Coquaigne."

no storm, no rain, no wind, no flea, no fly; there is no Enoch nor any Elias to be sure ; but there are women with nothing pedantic about them, who are as loving as they are lovable.

Nothing less Saxon than such poems, with their semi-impiety, which would be absolute impiety if the author seriously meant what he said. It is the impiety of Aucassin, who refuses (before it is offered him) to enter Paradise : " In Paradise what have I to win? Therein I seek not to enter, but only to have Nicolete, my sweet lady that I love so well. . . . But into Hell would I fain go; for into Hell fare the goodly clerks, and goodly knights that fall in harness and great wars, and stout men-at-arms, and all men noble. . . . With those would I gladly go, let me but have with me Nicolete, my sweetest lady."[1] We must not take Aucassin at his word; there was ever froth on French wine.

Other English poems scoff at chivalrous manners, which are ridiculed in verse, in paintings, and sculptures[2]; or at the elegancies of the bad parson who puts in his bag a

[1] "Aucassin and Nicolete," Andrew Lang's translation, London, 1887, p. 12. The French original in verse and prose, a *cante-fable*, belongs to the twelfth century. Text in Moland and d'Héricault, "Nouvelles françoises en prose," Paris, 1856, H. Suchier, Paderborn, 1899, Mario Roques, Paris, 1925. *Cf.* "Romania," April, 1900.

[2] Knights are represented in many MSS. of English make, fighting against butterflies or snails, and undergoing the most ridiculous experiences ; for example, in MS. 10 E iv. and 2 B vii. in the British Museum, early fourteenth century ; the caricaturists derive their ideas from French tales written in derision of knighthood. Poems with the same object were composed in English ; one of a later date has been preserved : " The Turnament of Totenham " (Hazlitt's "Remains," iii. p. 82, *cf.* below, II. p. 116); the champions of the tourney are English artisans :

> Ther hoppyd Hawkyn
> Ther dawnsid Dawkyn
> Ther trumpyd Tymkyn
> And all were true drynkers.

comb and " a shewer " (mirror).[1]   Other poems are adaptations of the " Roman de Renart." [2]   The new spirit has
penetrated so well into English minds that the adaptation
is sometimes worthy of the original.

> A vox gon out of the wode go,
> Afingret (hungered) so that him wes wo ;
> He nes (ne was) nevere in none wise
> Afingret erour (before) half so swithe.
> He ne hoeld nouther wey ne strete,
> For him wes loth men to mete ;
> Him were levere meten one hen,
> Than half an oundred wimmen.

But not a hen does he come across ; they are suspicious,
and roost out of reach.   At last, half dead, he desires to
drink, and sees a well with two pails on the chain ; he
descends in one of the pails, and finds it impossible to
scramble out : he weeps for rage.   The wolf, as a matter of
course, comes that way, and they begin to talk.   Though
wanting very much to go, hungrier than ever, and determined to make the wolf take his place, Renard would not
have been Renard had he played off this trick on his
gossip plainly and without a word.   He adds many words,
all sparkling with the wit of France, the wit that is to be

---

[1] He putteth in hys pawtener
A kerchyf and a comb,
A shewer and a coyf
To bynd with his loks,
And ratyl on the rowbyble
And in non other boks
Ne mo ;
Mawgrey have the bysshop
That lat hyt so goo.

"A Poem on the times of Edward II.," ed. Hardwick, Percy Society, 1849,
p. 8.
[2] "The Vox and Wolf," time of Edward I., in Mätzner, "Altenglische
Sprachproben," Berlin, 1867, part i. p. 130; also in Th. Wright, "Latin
Stories," 1842, p. xvi.   This story of the adventure in the well forms Branch
IV. of the French text, Martin, "Roman de Renart," Strasbourg, 1882,
vol. i. p. 146.

inherited by Scapin and by Figaro. The wolf, for his
part, replies word for word by a verse of Molière's Orgon.
Renard will only allow him to descend into the Paradise
whither he pretends to have retired, after he has confessed,
forgiven all his enemies—Renard being one—and is ready
to lead a holy life. Ysengrin agrees, confesses, and forgives ; he feels his mind quite at rest, and exclaims in his
own way :

> Et je verrais mourir frère, enfants, mère et femme,
> Que je m'en soucierais autant que de cela. [1]

> Nou ich am in clene live,
> Ne recche ich of childe ne of wive.

The wolf goes down, Renard goes up ; as the pails
meet, the rogue wickedly observes :

> Ac ich am therof glad and blithe
> That thou art nomen in clene live,
> Thi soul-cnul (knell) ich wile do ringe,
> And masse for thine soule singe.

But he considers it enough for his purpose to warn the
monks that the devil is at the bottom of their well. With
great difficulty the monks draw up the devil, which done
they beat him, and set the dogs on him.

Some graceful love tales, popular in France, were translated and enjoyed no less popularity in England, where
there was now a public for literature of this sort. Such
was the case for Amis and Amile, Floire and Blanchefleur,
and many others.[2] As for *chansons*, there were imitations

---

[1] Tartufe, i. 6.

[2] "Amis and Amiloun," ed. Kölbing, Heilbronn, 1884, 8vo, French and
English texts, in verse. French text in prose, in Moland and d'Héricault,
"Nouvelles . . . du XIIIᵉ. Siècle," 1856, 16mo.—French text of "Floire" in
Edelstand du Méril, "Poèmes du XIIIᵉ. Siècle," Paris, 1856. English text :
"Floris and Blaunchefllur," ed. Hausknecht, Berlin, 1885, 8vo; see also
Lumby, "Horn . . . with fragments of Floriz," E.E.T.S., 1886; *cf.* Krappe,
"Mod. Lang. Rev." Ap. 1923. The popularity of this tale is shown by the
fact that four or five different versions of it in English have come down to
us.—Lays by Marie de France were also translated into English : "Le Lay le

of May songs, "disputoisons," [1] and carols ; love, roses, and birds were sung in sweet words to soft music [2] ; so was spring, the season of lilies, when the flowers give more perfume, and the moon more light, and women are more beautiful :

Wymmen waxeth wonder proude.[3]

Their beauties and merits are celebrated one by one, as in a litany ; for, said one of those poets, an Englishman who wrote in French :

Beauté de femme passe rose.[4]

Freine," "The Ash," in verse, beginning of XIVth century ; Engl. text in "Anglia," iii. 415 ; "Sir Launfal," by Thomas Chestre, XVth or late XIVth century, in "Ritson's Metrical Romances," ed. Goldsmid, Edinb., 1884.

[1] Examples of "estrifs," debates or "disputoisons": "The Thrush and the Nightingale," on the merits of women, time of Edward I. (with a title in French : "Si comence le cuntent par entre le mauvis et la russinole"); "The Debate of the Carpenter's Tools" (both in Hazlitt's "Remains," i. 50, 79); "The Debate of the Body and the Soul" in Mätzner's "Altenglische Sprachproben," i. 90), same subject in French verse, thirteenth century, "Monumenta Franciscana," i. 587 ; "The Owl and the Nightingale," XIIIth cent., ed. Atkins, 1922, the most remarkable of all ; the birds forcefully vaunt their merits on the allegorical meaning of which critics, however, disagree ; resourceful but rabid, they almost come to blows. "Winnere and Wastoure," on social questions, ab. 1352, ed. Gollancz, 1920, continues the series which I recently saw renewed in America when, for their amusement, members of Congress playfully disputed in a theatre under the presidency of the Speaker whether it is more honourable to be lean or to be fat.

[2] Litanies of love :

Love is wele, love is wo, love is geddede,
Love is lif, love is deth, &c.

Th. Wright, "Anecdota Literaria," London, 1844, p. 96, time of Ed. I., imitated from the "Chastoiement des Dames," in Barbazon and Meon, ii.

[3] Th. Wright, "Specimens of Lyric Poetry," time of Ed. I., Percy Soc., 1842, p. 43. Cf. Jeanroy, "Origines de la poésie lyrique Française," 2nd ed. 1904.

[4] They wrote in French, Latin, and English, using sometimes the three languages in the same song, sometimes only two of them (Wright, ibid., p. 64):

Scripsi hæc carmina in tabulis !
Mon ostel est en mi la vile de Paris :
May y sugge namore, so wel me is ;
Yef hi deye for love of hire, duel hit ys.

In honour of them were composed stanzas spangled with admiring epithets, glittering.like a golden shower; innumerable songs were dedicated to their ideal model, the Queen of Angels; others to each one of their physical charms, their "vair eyes"[1] and their eyes "gray y-noh": those being the colours preferred; their skin white as milk, "soft ase sylk"; those scarlet lips that served them to read romances, for romances were read aloud, and not only with the eyes[2]; their voice more melodious than a bird's song. In short, from the time of Edward II. that mixture of mysticism and sensuality appears which was to become one of the characteristics of the fourteenth century.

The poets who made these songs, charming as they were, rarely succeeded however in perfectly imitating the light pace of the cheerful French muse. In reading a great number of the songs of both countries, one is struck by the difference. The English spring is mixed with winter, and the French with summer; England sings of May, remembering April, France sings of May looking forward to June.

> Blow northerne wynd,
> Sent thou me my suetyng,
> Blow, northerne wynd, blou, blou, blou ![3]

says the English poet. Contact with the new-comers had modified the gravity of the Anglo-Saxons, but without sweeping it away wholly and for ever: the possibility of

---

[1] Femmes portent les oyls veyrs
    E regardent come faucoun.

T. Wright, "Specimens," p. 4.

[2] Heo hath a mury mouth to mele,
    With lefly rede lippes lele
    Romaunz for te rede.

Ibid., p. 34.   [3] Ibid., p. 51.

recurring gloom is felt even in the midst of the joy of "Merry England."

But the hour draws near when for the first time, and in spite of all doleful notes, the joy of "Merry England" will bloom forth freely. Edward III. is on the throne, Chaucer is just born, and soon the future Black Prince will win his spurs at Crécy.

BOOK III.

ENGLAND TO THE ENGLISH.

CHAPTER I.

THE NEW NATION.

I.

In the course of the fourteenth century, under Edward III. and Richard II., a double fusion, which had been slowly preparing during the preceding reigns, is completed and sealed for ever; the races established on English ground are fused into one, and the languages they spoke become one also. The French are no longer superposed on the natives; henceforth there are only English in the English island.

Until the fourteenth year of Edward III.'s reign, whenever a murder was committed and the authors of it remained unknown, the victim was *primâ facie* assumed to be French, " Francigena," and the whole county was fined. But the county was allowed to prove, if it could, that the dead man was only an Englishman, and in that case there was nothing to pay. Bracton, in the thirteenth century, is very positive; an inquest was necessary, " ut sciri possit utrum interfectus *Anglicus* fuerit, vel *Francigena*." [1] The *Anglicus* and the *Francigena* therefore still subsisted, and were not equal before the law. The rule had not fallen into disuse, since a formal statute was needed to repeal it, the statute of

[1] "De Legibus et Consuetudinibus Angliæ," book iii. treatise ii. chap. xv. (Rolls, vol. ii. p. 385.) No fine if the defunct is English : " Pro Anglico vero et de quo constari possit quod Anglicus sit, non dabitur murdrum."

1340, which abolishes the " presentement d'Englescherie," [1] thus sweeping away one of the most conspicuous marks left behind by the Conquest.

About the same time the fusion of idioms took place, and the English language was definitively constituted. At the beginning of the fourteenth century, towards 1311, the text of the king's oath was to be found in Latin among the State documents, and a note was added declaring that " if the king was illiterate," he was to swear in French [2]; it was in the latter tongue that Edward II. took his oath in 1307 ; the idea that it could be sworn in English did not occur. But when the century was closing, in 1399, an exactly opposite phenomenon happened. Henry of Lancaster usurped the throne and, in the Parliament assembled at Westminster, pronounced in English the solemn words by which he claimed the crown : " In the name of Fadir, Son and Holy Gost, I, Henry of Lancastre, chalenge yis Rewme of Yngland." [3]

During this interval, the union of the two languages had taken place. The work of aggregation can be followed in its various phases, and almost from year to year. In the first half of the century, the " lowe men," the " rustics," *rurales homines*, are still keen to learn French, *satagunt omni nisu ;* they wish to frenchify, *francigenare*,[4] themselves, in order to imitate the nobles, and be more thought of. Their efforts had a remarkable result, precisely for the

[1] But it lingered later : Gross, "Select cases fr. the Coroners' Rolls,"Selden Soc.

[2] " Si rex fuerit litteratus, talis est. . . . Forma juramenti si Rex non fuerit litteratus : Sire, voilez vous graunter et garder . . . les leys et les custumes . . &c." " Statutes of the Realm," *sub anno* 1311, vol. i. p. 168.

[3] " Rotuli Parliamentorum," vol. iii. p. 422 ; see below, p. 421.

[4] Ralph Higden, " Polychronicon " (Rolls), vol. ii. p. 158. " Hæc quidem nativæ linguæ corruptio provenit hodie multum ex duobus quod videlicet pueri in scolis contra morem cæterarum nationum, a primo Normannorum adventu derelicto proprio vulgari, construere gallice compelluntur ; item quod filii nobilium ab ipsis cunabulorum crepundiis ad gallicum idióma informantur. Quibus profecto rurales homines assimilari volentes ut per hoc spectabiliores videantur, francigenare satagunt omni nisu."

reason that they never succeeded in speaking pure French, and that in their ill-cleared brains the two languages were never kept distinctly apart. The nobles, cleverer men, could speak both idioms without confounding them, but so could not these *rurales*, who lisped the master's tongue with difficulty, mixing together the two vocabularies and the two grammars, mistaking the genders, assigning, for want of better knowledge, the neuter to all the words that did not designate beings with a sex, in other words, strange as it may seem, creating the new language. It was on the lips of "lowe men" that the fusion first began; they are the real founders of modern English ; the "French of Stratford-at-Bow" had not less to do with it than the "French of Paris."

Even the nobles had not been able to completely escape the consequences of a perpetual contact with the *rurales*. Had these latter been utterly ignorant of French, the language of the master would have been kept purer, but they spoke the French idiom after a fashion, and their manner of speaking it had a contagious influence on that of the great. In the best families, the children being in constant communication with native servants and young peasants, spoke the idiom of France less and less correctly. From the end of the thirteenth century and the beginning of the fourteenth, they confuse French words that bear a resemblance to each other, and then also commences for them that annoyance to which so many English children have been subjected, from generation to generation down to our time : the difficulty of knowing when to say *mon* and *ma*— "kaunt dewunt dire moun et ma "—that is how to distinguish the genders. They have to be taught by manuals, and the popularity of one written by Walter de Biblesworth,[1] in the fourteenth century, shows how greatly such

----

[1] "A volume of Vocabularies, from the Xth to the XVth Century," ed. Thomas Wright, London, 1857, 4to, pp. 143 ff. See also P. Meyer, "Romania," vol. xiii. p. 502.

treatises were needed.   " Dear sister," writes Walter to the
Lady Dionyse de Montchensy, "I have composed this work
so that your children can know the properties of the things
they see, and also when to say *mon* and *ma*, *son* and *sa*, *le* and
la, *moi* and *je*."   And he goes on showing at the same time
the maze and the way out of it: "You have *la lèvre* and *le
lièvre ;* and *la livre* and *le livre*.   The *lèvre* closes the teeth
in ; *le lièvre* the woods inhabits ; *la livre* is used in trade ;
le livre is used at church." [1]

Inextricable difficulties!   And all the harder to unravel
that Anglo-Saxon too had genders, equally arbitrary, which
did not agree with the French ones.   It is easy to conceive
that among the various compromises effected between the
two idioms, from which English was finally to emerge, the
principal should be the suppression of this cumbersome
distinction of genders.

What happened in the manor happened also in the
courts of justice.   There French was likewise spoken, it
being the rule, and the trials were apparently not lacking
in liveliness, witness this judge whom we see para-
phrasing the usual formula : " Allez à Dieu," or " Adieu,"
and wishing the defendant, none other than the bishop
of Chester, to "go to the great devil "—" Allez au grant
déable." [2]—("'What,' said Ponocrates, 'brother John, do
you swear?' 'It is only,' said the monk, 'to adorn my
speech.   These are colours of Ciceronian rhetoric.'")—

[1] Vus avet la levere et le levere
   E la livere et le livere.
   La levere si enclost les dens ;
   Le levre en boys se tent dedens,
   La livere sert en marchaundye,
   Le livere sert en seynt eglise.

[2] Apostrophe of judge John de Moubray, Easter session, 44Ed.III.,
" Year-books of Edward I.," ed. Horwood (Rolls), 1863 ff., vol. i. p. xxxi.
Judge Hengham interrupts a counsel, saying: " Do not interpret the statute in
your own way ; we know it better than you, for we made it "—" Ne glosez
point le statut ; nous le savoms meuz de vous, qar nous le feimes." *Ibid.*

But from most of the speeches registered in French in the "Year-books," it is easily gathered that advocates, *serjeants* as they were called, did not express themselves without difficulty, and that they delivered in French what they had thought in English.

Their trouble goes on increasing. In 1300 a regulation in force at Oxford allowed people who had to speak in a suit to express themselves in " *any* language generally understood." [1] In the second half of the century, the difficulties have reached such a pitch that a reform becomes indispensable ; counsel and clients no longer understand each other. In 1362, a statute ordains that henceforward all pleas shall be conducted in English, and they shall be enrolled in Latin ; and that in the English law courts " the French language, which is too unknown in the said realm," [2] shall be discontinued.

This ignorance is now notorious. Froissart remarks on it ; the English, he says, do not observe treaties faithfully, " and to this they are inclined by their not understanding very well all the terms of the language of France ; and one does not know how to force a thing into their

[1] "Grosso modo et idiomate quocunque communiter intelligibili factum proponant." "Munimenta Academica " (Rolls), p. 77.

[2] " Pur ce qe monstré est souventefoitz au Roi par prélatz, ducs, counts, barons et toute la commune, les grantz meschiefs qe sont advenuz as plusours du realme de ce qe les leyes, custumes et estatutz du dit realme ne sont pas conuz communément en mesme le realme, par cause q'ils sont pledez, monstrez et juggez en lange Franceis q'est trop desconue en dit realme, issint qe les gentz qi pledent ou sont empledez en les courtz le Roi et les courtz d'autres n'ont entendement ne conissance de ce q'est dit por eulx ne contre eulx par lour sergeantz et autres pledours . . ." that henceforth all plaids "soient pledetz, monstretz, defenduz, responduz, debatuz et juggez en la lange engleise ; et q'ils soient entreez et enroullez en latin." 36 Ed. III., stat. i. chap. 15, "Statutes of the Realm." In spite of these arrangements, the accounts of the pleas continued to be transcribed in French into the " Year-books," of which several have been published in the collection of the Master of the Rolls. Writing about the year 1300, the author of the Mirror of Justice had still made choice of French as being the "language best understood by you and the common people."

head unless it be all to their advantage." [1]   Trevisa, about
the same time, translating into English the chronicle of
Ralph Higden, reaches the passage where it is said that all
the country people endeavour to learn French, and inserts
a note to rectify the statement.   This manner, he writes, is
since the great pestilence (1349) " sumdel i-chaunged," and
to-day, in the year 1385, " in alle the gramere scoles of
Engelond, children leveth Frensche and construeth and
lerneth an Englische."   This allows them to make rapid
progress ; but now they " conneth na more Frensche than
can hir (their) lift heele, and that is harme for hem, and
(if) they schulle passe the see and travaille in straunge
landes and in many other places.   Also gentil men haveth
now moche i-left for to teche here children Frensche." [2]

The English themselves laugh at their French ; they are
conscious of speaking, like Chaucer's Prioress, the French
of Stratford-at-Bow, or, like Avarice in the " Visions " of
Langland, that " of the ferthest end of Norfolke." [3]

There will shortly be found in the kingdom personages
of importance, exceptions it is true, with whom it will be
impossible to negotiate in French.   This is the case with
the ambassadors sent by Henry IV., that same Henry of
Lancaster who had claimed the crown by an English
speech, to Flanders and France in 1404.   They beseech
the " Paternitates ac Magnificentias " of the Grand Council
of France to answer them in Latin, French being " like

[1]   " Chroniques," ed. Luce, vol. i. p. 306.
[2]   " Polychronicon " (Rolls), ii. 159 (Higden's Latin and Trevisa's version).
[3]   And I can no Frenche in feith · but of the ferthest ende of Norfolke.
" Visions," ed. Skeat, B, v. 239.   *Cf.* " Testament of Love," ab. 1387:
" But certes there ben some that speken their poysye mater in Frenche, of
whiche speche the Frenche men have as good a fantasye as we have in hering
of Frenche mennes English."   Supplt. to " Works of Chaucer," Skeat, vii. 1.
The MS. DD 12.23 of the University Library, Cambridge, contains " a treatise
on French conjugations ; " it " can only serve to show how great was the corruption of current French in England in the fourteenth century."   P. Meyer,
" Romania," xv. 262.

Hebrew" to them; but the Magnificents of the Grand Council, conforming to a tradition which has remained unbroken down to our day, refuse to employ for the negotiation any language but their own.[1] Was it not still, as in the time of Brunetto Latini, the modern tongue most prized in Europe? In England even, men were found who agreed to this, while rendering to Latin the tribute due to it; and the author of one of the numerous treatises composed in this country for the benefit of those who wished to keep up their knowledge of French said: "Sweet French is the finest and most graceful tongue, the noblest speech in the world after school Latin, and the one most esteemed and beloved by all people. . . . And it can be well compared to the speech of the angels of heaven for its great sweetness and beauty."[2]

In spite of these praises, the end of French, as the language "most esteemed and beloved," was near at hand in

[1] The ambassadors are: "Thomas Swynford, miles, custos castri villæ Calisii et Nicholaus de Rysshetoun, utriusque juris professor." They admit that French is the language of treaties; but Latin was used by St. Jerome. They write to the duchess of Burgundy: "Et quamvis treugæ generales inter Angliam et Franciam per Dominos et Principes temporales, videlicet duces Lancastriæ et Eboraci necnon Buturiæ ac Burgundiæ, bonæ memoriæ, qui perfecte non intellexerunt latinum sicut Gallicum, de consensu eorumdem expresso, in Gallico fuerunt captæ et firmatæ, litteræ tamen missivæ ultro citroque transmissæ . . . continue citra in Latino, tanquam idiomate communi et vulgari extiterunt formatæ; quæ omnia habemus parata ostendere, exemplo Beati Ieronimi . . ." In no wise touched by this example, the French reply in their own language, and the ambassadors, vexed, acknowledge the receipt of the letter in somewhat undiplomatic terms: "Vestras litteras scriptas in Gallico, nobis indoctis tanquam in idiomate Hebraico . . . recipimus Calisii." "Royal and Historical Letters," ed. Hingeston, 1860 (Rolls), i. 357, 397. A discussion of the same kind takes place, with the same result, under Louis XIV. See "A French Ambassador at the Court of Charles II.," p. 140.

[2] "Doulz françois qu'est la plus bel et la plus gracious language et plus noble parler, après latin d'escole, qui soit ou monde, et de tous gens mieulx prisée et amée que nul autre. . . . Il peut bien comparer au parler des angels du ciel, pour la grant doulceur et biaultée d'icel." "La manière de Langage," composed in 1396, at Bury St. Edmund's, ed. Paul Meyer, "Revue Critique," vol. x. p. 382.

England.   Poets like Gower still use it in the fourteenth century for some of their works, and prose writers like the author of the "Croniques de London"[1]; but these are exceptions.   It remains the idiom of the Court and the great; the Black Prince selects French verses to be graven on his tomb : these are nothing but curious cases.   Better instructed than the lawyers and suitors in the courts of justice, the members of Parliament continue to use it ; but English makes its appearance even among them, and in 1363 the Chancellor has opened the session by a speech in English, the first ever heard in Westminster.

The survival of French was at last nothing but an elegance; it was still learnt, but only as Madame de Sévigné studied Italian, " pour entretenir noblesse." Among the upper class the knowledge of French was a traditional accomplishment, and it has continued to be one to our day.   At the beginning of the sixteenth century the laws were still, according to habit, written in French; but complaints on this score were made to Henry VIII., and his subjects pointed out to him that this token of the ancient subjection of England to the Normans of France should be removed.   This mark has disappeared, not however without leaving some trace behind, as laws continue to be assented to by the sovereign in French : " Le Roi le veut."   They are vetoed in the same manner : " Le Roi s'avisera "; though this last manner is less frequently resorted to than in the time of the Plantagenets.

French disappears.   It does not disappear so much because it is forgotten as because it is gradually absorbed. It disappears, and so does the Anglo-Saxon; a new language is forming, an offspring of the two others, but distinct from them, with a new grammar, versification, and

[1] Middle of the fourteenth century, ed. Aungier, Camden Society, 1884, 4to.

vocabulary. It less resembles the Anglo-Saxon of Alfred's time than the Italian of Dante resembles Latin.

The vocabulary is deeply modified. It numbered before the Conquest a few words of Latin origin, but not many ; they were words recalling the great works of the Romans, such as *street* and *chester*, from *strata* and *castrum*, or else words borrowed from the language of the clerks, and concerning mainly religion, such as *mynster, tempel, bisceop*, derived from *monasterium, templum, episcopus*, &c. The Conquest was productive of a great change, but not all at once ; the languages, as has been seen, remained at first distinctly separate ; then in the thirteenth, and especially in the fourteenth century, they permeated each other, and were blended into one. In 1205, only fifty words of Latin origin were found in the sixteen thousand long lines of Layamon's " Brut "; a hundred can be counted in the first five hundred lines of Robert of Gloucester about 1298, and a hundred and seventy in the first five hundred lines of Robert Mannyng of Brunne, in 1303.[1]

As we advance further into the fourteenth century, the change is still more rapid. Numerous families of words are naturalised in England, and little by little is constituted that language the vocabulary of which contains to-day twice as many words drawn from French or Latin as from Germanic sources. At the end of Skeat's " Etymological Dictionary," [2] there is a table of the words of the language classified according to their derivation ; the words borrowed from Germanic or Scandinavian idioms fill seven columns and a half ; those taken from the French, and the Romance or classic tongues, sixteen columns.

It is true the proportion of words used in a page of

---

[1] As an example of a composition showing the parallelism of the two vocabularies in their crude state, one may take the treatise on Dreams (time of Edward II.), published by Wright and Halliwell, which begins with the characteristic words ; " Her comensez a bok of Swevenyng." " Reliquiæ Antiquæ." [2] London, 1882, several ed.

ordinary English does not correspond to these figures. With some authors in fact it is simply reversed ; with Shakespeare, for instance, or with Tennyson, who exhibit a marked predilection for Anglo-Saxon words. It is nevertheless to be observed : first, that the constitution of the vocabulary with its majority of Franco-Latin words is an actual fact ; then that in a page of ordinary English the proportion of words having a Germanic origin is increased by the number of Anglo-Saxon articles, conjunctions, and pronouns, words that are merely the servants of the others, and are, as they should be, more numerous than their masters. A much nearer approach to the numbers supplied by the lists of Skeat will be made if real words only are counted, those which are free and independent citizens of the language, and not the shadow nor the train-bearer of any other.

The contributive part of French in the new vocabulary corresponds to the branches of activity reserved to the new-comers. From their maternal idiom have been borrowed the words that composed the language of war, of commerce, of jurisprudence, of science, of art, of metaphysics, of pure thought, and also the language of games, of pastimes, of tourneys, and of chivalry. In some cases no compromise took place, neither the French nor the Anglo-Saxon word would give way and die, and they have both come down to us, alive and irreducible : *act* and *deed; captive* and *thrall; chief* and *head*, &c.[1] It is a trace of the Conquest, like the formula : " Le Roi le veut."

Chaucer, in whose time these double survivals were naturally far more numerous than they are to-day, often

---

[1] See a list of such words in Earle, " Philology of the English Tongue," 5th edition, Oxford, 1892, 8vo, p. 84. On the disappearance of Anglo-Saxon proper names, and the substitution of Norman-French names, " William, Henry, Roger, Walter, Ralph, Richard, Gilbert, Robert," see Grant Allen, " Anglo-Saxon Britain," ch. xix., Anglo-Saxon Nomenclature.

uses both words at once, sure of being thus intelligible to all:

> They callen love a woodnes or a folye.[1]

Versification is transformed in the same fashion; here again the two prosodies arrive at a compromise. Native verse had two ornaments: the number of accents and alliteration; French verse in the fourteenth century had also two ornaments, the number of syllables and rime. The French gave up their strict number of syllables, and consented to note the number of accents; the natives discarded alliteration and accepted rime in its stead. Thus was English verse created, its cadence being Germanic and its rime French, and such was the prosody of Chaucer, who wrote his "Canterbury Tales" in rimed English verse, with five accents, but with syllables varying in number from nine to eleven.

The fusion of the two versifications was as gradual as that of the two vocabularies had been. Layamon in the thirteenth century mingled both prosodies in his "Brut," sometimes using alliteration, sometimes rime, and occasionally both at once. The fourteenth century is the last in which alliterative verse really flourished, though it survived even beyond the Renaissance. In the sixteenth century a new form was tried; rime was suppressed mainly in imitation of the Italians and the ancients, and blank verse was created, which Shakespeare and Milton used in their masterpieces[2]; but alliteration never found place again in the normal prosody of England.

Grammar was affected in the same way. In the Anglo-Saxon grammar, nouns and adjectives had declensions as in German; and not very simple ones. "Not only had our old adjectives a declension in three genders, but more than this, it had a double set of trigeneric inflexions,

---

[1] "Troilus," iii. stanza 191.   [2] *Infra*, II. pp. 145 ff.

Definite and Indefinite, Strong and Weak, just like that
which makes the beginner's despair in German."[1]   Verbs
were conjugated without auxiliaries ; and as there was no
particular inflection to indicate the future, the present was
used instead, a very indifferent substitute, which did not
contribute much to the clearness of the phrase.   Degrees
of comparison in the adjectives were marked, not by
adverbs, as in French, but by differences in the termina-
tions.   In short, the relations of words to each other, as
well as the particular part they had to play in the phrase,
were not indicated by other special words, prepositions,
adverbs or auxiliaries, those useful menials, but by varia-
tions in the endings of the terms themselves, that is, by
inflections.   The necessity for a compromise with French,
which had lost its primitive declensions and inflections,
hastened an already begun transformation and resulted in
the new language's possessing in the fourteenth century a
grammar remarkably simple, brief and clear.   Auxiliaries
were introduced, and they allowed every shade of action,
action that has been, or is, or will be, or would be, to be
clearly defined.   The gender of nouns used to present
all the troublesome singularities which persist in German
or French ; *mona*, moon, was masculine as in German ;
sunne, sun, was feminine; *wif*, wife, was not feminine
but neuter ; as was also *mæden*, maiden.   "A German
gentleman," as " Philologus " has so well observed,
" writes a masculine letter of feminine love to a neuter
young lady with a feminine pen and feminine ink on
masculine sheets of neuter paper, and encloses it in a
masculine envelope with a feminine address to his darling,
though neuter, Gretchen.   He has a masculine head, a
feminine hand, and a neuter heart."[2]   Anglo-Saxon
gentlemen were in about the same predicament, before

[1] Earle's "Philology of the English Tongue," 5th ed., Oxford, 1892,
p. 379.   [2] *Ibid.* p. 377.

William the Conqueror came in his own way to their help and rescued them from this maze. In the transaction which took place, the Anglo-Saxon and the French both gave up the arbitrariness of their genders ; nouns denoting male beings became masculine, those denoting female beings became feminine ; all the others became neuter ; *wife* and *maiden* resumed their sex, while *nation, sun* and *moon* were neuter. Nouns and adjectives lost their declensions ; adjectives ceased to vary in their endings according to the nouns they were attached to, and yet the clearness of the phrase was not in the least obscured.

In the same way as with the prosody and vocabulary, these changes were effected by degrees. Great confusion prevailed in the thirteenth century ; the authors of the "Brut" and the "Ancren Riwle" have visibly no fixed ideas on the use of inflections, or on the distinctions of the genders. Only under Edward III. and Richard II. were the main principles established upon which English grammar rests. As happened also for the vocabulary, in certain exceptional cases the French and the Saxon uses have been both preserved. The possessive case, for instance, can be expressed either by means of a proposition, in French fashion : "The works of Shakespeare," or by means of the ancient genitive : "Shakespeare's works."

Thus was formed the new language out of a combination of the two others. In our time, moved by a patriotic but rather preposterous feeling, some have tried to react against the consequences of the Conquest, and undo the work of eight centuries. They have endeavoured to exclude from their writings words of Franco-Latin origin, in order to use only those derived from the Anglo-Saxon spring. A vain undertaking : the progress of a ship cannot be stopped by putting one's shoulder to the bulkheads ; a singular misapprehension of history besides. The English people is the offspring of two nations ; it has a father and a mother, whose union has been fruitful if stormy ; and the parent disowned by some to-day, under cover of filial tenderness toward the other, is perhaps not the one who devoted the least care in forming and instructing the common posterity of both.

II.

The race and the language are transformed ; the nation also, considered as a political body, undergoes change. Until the fourteenth century, the centre of thought, of desire, and of ambition was, according to the vocation of each, Rome, Paris, or that movable, ever-shifting centre, the Court of the king. Light and power, advancement in the world, all proceeded from these various centres. In the fourteenth century, what took place for the race and language takes place also for the nation. It coalesces and condenses; it becomes conscious of its own limits ; it discerns and maintains them. The action of Rome is circumscribed ; appeals to the pontifical Court are prohibited,[1] and, though they still continue to be made, the oft-expressed wish of the nation is that the king should be judge, not the pope ; it is the beginning of the religious supremacy of the English sovereigns. Oxford has grown ;

---

[1] See the series of the statutes of *Provisors* and *Præmunire*, and the renewals of the same (against presentations to benefices by the Pope and appeals to the Court of Rome), 25 Ed. III. st. 6; 27 Ed. III. st. 2 ; 3 Rich. II. chap. 3; 12 Rich. II. chap. 15; 13 Rich. II. st. 2, chap. 2; 16 Rich. II. chap. 5. All have for their object to restrict the action of the Holy See in England, conformably to the desire of the Commons, who protest against these appeals to the Roman Court, the consequences of which are "to undo and adnul the laws of the realm" (25 Ed. III. 1350–1), and who also protest against "the Court of Rome which ought to be the fountain-head, root, and source of holiness," and which from coveteousness has assumed the right of presenting to numberless benefices in England, so much so that the taxes collected for the Pope on this account "amount to five times as much as what the king gets from all his kingdom each year." Good Parliament of 1376, "Rotuli Parliamentorum," vol. ii. p. 337 ; see below, p. 419.

it is .no longer indispensable to go to Paris in order to learn. Limits are established : the wars with France are royal and not national ones. Edward III., having assumed the title of king of France, his subjects compel him to declare that their allegiance is only owned to him as king of England, and not as king of France.[1] No longer is the nation Anglo-French, Norman, Angevin, or Gascon ; it is English ; the nebula condenses into a star.

The first consequences of the Conquest had been to bind England to the civilisations of the south. The experiment had proved a successful one, the results obtained were definitive ; there was no need to go further, the ties could now without harm slacken or break. Owing to that evolutionary movement ever at play in human affairs, this first experiment having been perfected after a lapse of three hundred years, a counter-experiment now begins. A new centre, unknown till then, gradually draws to itself every one's attention ; it will soon attract the eyes of the English in preference to Rome, Paris, or even the king's Court. This new centre is Westminster. There, an institution derived from French and Saxonic sources, but destined to be then abortive in France, is developed to an extent unparalleled in any other country. Parliament, which was, at the end of the thirteenth century, in an embryonic state, is found at the end of the fourteenth completely constituted, endowed with all its actual elements, with power, prerogatives, and an influence in the State that it has rarely surpassed at any time.

Not in vain have the Normans, Angevins, and Gascons given to the men of the land the example of their clever and shrewd practice. Not in vain have they blended the two races into one : their peculiar characteristics have been infused into their new compatriots so much so that from the first day Parliament begins to feel

[1] Year 1340, 14 Ed. III., " Rotuli Parliamentorum," vol. ii. p. 104.

conscious of its strength, it displays bias most astonishing to behold : it thinks and acts and behaves as an assembly of Normans. The once violent and vacillating Anglo-Saxons, easily roused to enthusiasm and brought down to despair, now calculate, consider, deliberate, do nothing in haste, act with diplomatic subtlety, *bargain.* All dealings between the Court and Parliament, in the fourteenth century, are a series of bargains ; Parliament pays on condition that the king reforms ; nothing for nothing : and the fulfilling of the bargain is minutely watched. It comes to this at last, that Parliament proves more Norman than the Court ; it manœuvres with more skill, and remains master of the situation ; "à Normand, Normand et demi." The Plantagenets behold with astonishment the rise of a power they are now unable to control ; their offspring is hardy, and strong, and beats its nurse.

After the attempts of Simon de Montfort, Edward I. had convened, in 1295, the first real Parliament. He had reasserted the fundamental principle of all liberties, by appropriating to himself the old maxim from Justinian's code, according to which "what touches the interests of all must be approved by all."[1] He forms the habit of appealing to the people ; he wants them to know the truth, and decide according to truth which is in the right, whether the king or his turbulent barons[2] ; he behaves on occasion as if he felt that *over* him was the nation. And this strange sight is seen : the descendant of the Norman autocrats

---

[1] "Sicut lex justissima, provida circumspectione sacrorum principum stabilita, hortatur et statuit ut quod omnes tangit ab omnibus approbetur. . . ." Rymer, "Fœdera," 1705, vol. ii. p. 689. This Roman maxim was known and appealed to, but not acted upon in France. See Commines, "Mémoires," book v. chap. xix.

[2] "For some folks," says he, "might say and make the people believe things that were not true." By some folks, "acuns gentz," he means Bohun and Bigod. Proclamation of 1297, in Rymer, "Fœdera," 1705, vol. ii. p. 783.

modestly explains his plans for war in Flanders and in France, excuses himself for the aid he is obliged to ask of his subjects, and even condescends to solicit the spiritual benefit of their prayers : " He the king, on this and on the state of himself and of his realm, and how the business of his realm has come to naught, makes it known and wants that all know the truth, which is as follows . . . He can neither defend himself nor his realm without the help of his good people. And it grieves him sorely to have them, on this account, so heavily charged. . . . And he prays them to take as an excuse for what he has done, that that he did not do in order to buy lands and tenements, or castles and towns, but to defend himself, and them, and the whole kingdom. . . . And as he has great faith that the good prayers of his good people will help him very much in bringing this business to a good end, he begs that they will intently pray for him and those that with him go." [1]

At first, Parliament is astonished : such excess of honour alarms it ; then it understands the chance that offers, and guesses that in the proffered bargain it may very well be the winner. This once understood, progress is rapid, and from year to year can be observed the growth of its definitive privileges. The Commons have their Speaker, " M. Thomas de Hungerford, knight, who had the words for the Commons of England " [2] ; they want deputies to be elected by " due election," and they protest against all interference of the Government ; against official candidacies, and against the election of royal functionaries. On difficult questions, the members request to be allowed to return to their counties and consult with their constituents before

---

[1] Rymer, " Fœdera," 1705, vol. ii. p. 783, year 1297 ; original in French.

[2] " Monsieur Thomas de Hungerford, chivaler, qui avoit les paroles pour les Communes d'Engleterre en cest Parlement." Parliament of 1376-7, 51 Ed. III. " Rotuli," vol. ii. p. 374.

voting.[1]   In spite of all the aristocratic ideas with which
they are still imbued, many of those audacious members
who clamour for reforms and oppose the king are very
inconsiderable people, and such men are seen taking their
seats at Westminster as "Walterus l'espicer," "Paganus le
tailour," "Radulphus le teynturer," "Ricardus orfèvre." [2]

Great is the power of this mixed gathering.   No new
taxes can be levied without its consent ; every individual,
every personage, every authority having a petition to present, or a complaint to make, sends it to the assembly of
Westminster.   The king consults it on peace or war :   "So,"
says the Chamberlain to the Commons in 1354, "you are
willing to assent to a permanent treaty of peace, if one can
be obtained?   And the said Commons answered entirely
and unanimously : Yes, yes ! (Oïl ! Oïl !)" [3]

Nothing is too great or too small for Parliament to
attend to ; the sovereign appeals to it, and the clergy too,
and beggars also.   In 1330, the poor, the "poverail," of
Greenwich, complain that alms are no longer bestowed on
them as formerly, to the great detriment, say they, of the
souls of the benefactors of the place "who are in Purga-
tory." [4]   Convents claim privileges that time has effaced ;

[1] Examples : that the deputies of the counties "soient esluz par commune
élection de les meillours gentz des dity countées et nemye certifiez par le viscont
(sheriff) soul, saunz due élection."   Good Parliament of 1376.—Petition that
the sheriffs shall not be able to stand for the counties while they continue in
office, 1372, 46 Ed. III., "Rotuli Parliamentorum," vol. ii. p. 310; that no
representative "ne soit viscont ou autre ministre," 13 Ed. III., year 1339.—
Petition of the members of Parliament to be allowed to return and consult their
constituents : "Ils n'oseront assentir tant qu'ils eussent conseillez et avysez
les communes de lour pais."   1339, "Rot. Parl.," vol. ii. p. 104; see below,
p. 418.

[2] "Return of the names of every member returned to serve in each Parliament," London, 1878, fol. (a Blue Book).—There is no doubt in several cases
that by such descriptions was meant the *actual* profession of the member.   Ex. :
"Johannes Kent, mercer," p. 217.   [3] "Rot. Parl.," vol. ii. p. 262.

[4] Petition of the "poverail" of Greenwich and Lewisham on whom alms
are no longer bestowed (one *maille* a week to every beggar that came) to the
"grant damage des poores entour, et des almes les fondours que sont en Purgatorie."   4 Ed. III. "Rotuli Parliamentorum," vol. ii. p. 49.

servants ask for their wages; the barber of Edward II.
solicits the maintenance of favours granted by a prince he
had bled and shaved for twenty-six years.[1]

And before the same gathering of men, far different
quarrels are brought forth. The king's ministers, Latymer
and Neville, are impeached; his mistress Alice Perrers
hears sentence[2]; his household, personal attendants and
expenses are reformed; and from then can be foreseen a time
when, owing to the tread of centuries, the king will reign
but no longer govern. Such is almost the case even in the
fourteenth century. Parliament deposes Richard II., who
fancied himself king by right divine, and claimed, long
before the Stuarts, to hold his crown, "del doun de Dieu,"
as a "gift of God."[3] In the list of grievances drawn up by
the assembly to justify the deposition, figures the assertion
attributed to the king "that the laws proceeded from his lips
or from his heart, and that he alone could make or alter the
laws of his kingdom."[4] In 1399 such language was already
held to be criminal in England. In 1527 Claude Gaillard,
prime President of the Parliament of Paris, says in his
remonstrance to Francis I., king of France: "We do not
wish, Sire, to doubt or question your power; it would be a
kind of sacrilege, and we well know you are above all law,

[1] 4 Ed. III., "Rotuli Parliamentorum," vol. ii. p. 33.

[2] Good Parliament of 1376.

[3] The Commons had been bold enough to complain of the expenses of the
king and of the too great number of prelates and ladies he supported : "de la
multitude d'Evesques qui ont seigneuries et sont avancez par le Roy et leur
meignée ; et aussi de pluseurs dames et leur meignée qui demuront en l'ostel
du Roy et sont à ses costages." Richard replies in an angry manner that he
"voet avoir sa régalie et la libertée roiale de sa corone," as heir to the throne
of England "del doun de Dieu." 1397, "Rotuli Parliamentorum," vol. iii. p.
339. The Commons say nothing more, but they mark the words, to remember
them in due time.

[4] "Dixit expresse, velut austero et protervo, quod leges sue erant in ore suo
et aliquotiens in pectore suo. Et quod ipse solus posset mutare et condere
leges regni sui." "Rotuli Parliamentorum," vol. iii. p. 419.

and that statutes and ordinances cannot touch you. . . ." [1]
The ideas on political "sacrilege" differed widely in the
two countries.

From the end of the fourteenth century, an Englishman
could already say as he does to-day: My business is not
the business of the State, but the business of the State is
my business. The whole of the English constitution, from
the vote on the taxes to the *habeas corpus*, is comprised in
this formula. In France the nation, practical, lucid, and
logical in so many things, but easily amused, and too fond
of chansons, neglected the opportunities that offered ; the
clect failed to attend the sittings ; the bargains struck were
not kept to. The Westminster Parliament voted sub-
sidies on condition that reforms would be instituted ;
the people paid and the king reformed. In France, on
the contrary, during the Middle Ages, the people tried not
to pay, and the king tried not to reform. Thus the levying
of the subsidy voted by the States-General of 1356-7, was
the cause of bloody riots in France ; the people, un-
enlightened as to their own interests, did their best to
destroy their defenders : the agents of the States-General
were massacred at Rouen and Arras ; King John "the
Good " published a decree forbidding the orders of the
States to be fulfilled, and acquired instant popularity by
this the most tyrannic measure of all his reign.

These differences between the two political bodies had
important consequences with regard to the development

---

[1] Chéruel, "Dictionnaire des Institutions de la France," at the word
Parlement. As early as the thirteenth century, Bracton, in England, declared
that "laws bound the legislator," and that the king ought to obey them ; his
theory, however, is less bold than the one according to which the Commons act
in the fourteenth century : "Dicitur enim rex," Bracton observes, "a bene
regendo et non a regnando, quia rex est dum bene regit, tyrannus dum populum
sibi creditum violenter opprimit dominatione. Temperet igitur potentiam suam
per legem quæ frenum est potentiæ, quod secundum leges vivat, quod hoc
sanxit lex humana quod leges suum ligent latorem." "De Legibus," 3rd part
chap. ix.

of thought in the two countries; they also excited the wonder and sometimes the admiration of the French. "The king of England must obey his subjects," says Froissart, "and do all they want him to."[1] "To my mind," writes Commines, "of all the communities I know in the world, the one where public business is best attended to, where the people are least exposed to violence, where there are no buildings ruined and pulled down on account of wars, that one is England."[2] "The English are the masters of their king," writes Ambassador Courtin in 1665, in almost the same words as Froissart, "their king can do nothing, unless what he wants is what they will."[3]

III.

Now are the vanquished and the victors of Hastings blended into one nation, and they are endowed with a Parliament as a safeguard for their liberties. "This is," Montesquieu said later, "the nation in the world that has best known how to avail itself at the same time of those three great things: religion, trade, and liberty."[4] Four hundred years before Montesquieu it already availed itself of these three great things; under Edward III. and Richard II., England was what it has ever been since, a "merchant island."[5]

Its mines are worked, even those of "sea-coal," as it was then called, "carboun de meer."[6] It has a numerous

[1] "Chroniques," ed. S. Luce, i. p. 337

[2] "Mémoires," ed. Dupont, Société de l'histoire de France, 1840 ff., vol. ii. p. 142, *sub anno*, 1477.

[3] Unpublished letter to Hugues de Lionne, from London, July 6, 1665, Archives des Affaires Etrangères, vol. lxxxvi.

[4] "Esprit des Lois," vol. xx. chap. vii., "Esprit de l'Angleterre sur le Commerce."

[5] A. Sorel, "l'Europe et la Révolution Française," vol. i. p. 337.

[6] Parliament reverts at different times to these mines in the fourteenth century : "Come en diverses parties deinz le Roialme d'Engleterre sont diverses miners des carbons, dont les Communes du dit partie ont lour sustenantz en grande partie . . ." 51 Ed. III., "Rotuli Parliamentorum."

mercantile navy which carries to the Baltic, to Iceland, to Flanders, to Guyenne, and to Spain, wool, skins, cloth, wheat, butter and cheese, " buyre et furmage." Each year the galleys of Venice come laden with cotton, silks from Damascus, sugar, spices, perfumes, ivory, and glass. The great commercial houses, and the merchant corporations are powers in the State; Edward III. grants to the London gilds the right of electing members to Parliament, and they preserved this right until the Reform Bill of 1832. The wealthy merchants lent money to the king ; they were called to his councils ; they behaved as great citizens. Anthony Blache lends Edward III. 11,720 pounds ; the Blankets of Bristol gather enormous wealth; John Blanket dies in 1405, bequeathing a third of his fortune to his wife, a third to his children, and a third to the poor ; John Philpot, a grocer of London, embarks on his ships and fights for the kingdom ; Richard Whittington, he of the legendary cat, is famed in history for his wealth and liberality, and was mayor of London in 1398, 1406, and 1419. These merchants are ennobled, and from their stock spring earls and dukes ; the De la Poles, wool-merchants of Hull, mortgage their property for the king. William de la Pole rescues Edward III., detained in Flanders by want of money, and is made a knight-banneret ; his son Michael is created earl of Suffolk ; one of his grandsons is killed at Agincourt ; another besieges Orléans, which is delivered by Joan of Arc ; he becomes duke of Suffolk, is impeached in 1450 for high treason and beheaded ; no honour is lacking to the house.

From the time of the Edwards, the Commons are very touchy upon the subject of the maritime power and glory of their country ; they already consider the ocean as their appointed realm. Do they observe, or fancy they observe, any diminution in the strength of England ? They complain to the king in remonstrances more than once heard

again, word for word, within the halls of Westminster:
"Twenty years ago, and always before, the shipping of the
Realm was in all the ports and good towns upon the sea
or rivers, so noble and plenteous that all the countries held
and called our said sovereign, the King of the Sea."[1]
At this time, 1372, the country is, without possibility of
doubt, the England of the English. ✓

From that period the English are found either singly
or in small bands on all the seas and on all the highways.[2]
Their nature has been modified; the island no longer
suffices them as it sufficed the Anglo-Saxons. "Il ne
sait rien, qui ne va hors"—he knows nothing who stirs not
out—think they with Des Champs; they are keen to see
what goes on elsewhere, and like practical folks to profit
by it. When the opportunity is good they seize it, whatsoever its nature; encountering Saracens they slay them:
so much towards Paradise; moving about in Italy they
are not long in discovering the advantages offered by a
condottiere's existence. They adopt and even perfect it,
and after their death are magnificently buried in the
cathedral of Florence, and Paolo Uccello paints their portrait on the wall.[3] On every occasion they behave like
Normans; in the halls of Westminster, in their City count-

---

[1] 46 Ed. III., "Rotuli Parliamentorum," vol. ii. p. 311. The king returns
a vague answer. See below, pp. 515, 517.

[2] "They travaile in every londe," says Gower of them, in his "Confessio
Amantis," ed. Pauli, vol. iii. p. 109.

[3] "Joannes Acutus, eques Britannicus (John Hawkwood) . . . rei militaris
peritissimus . . . Pauli Vccelli opus," inscription on the "grisaille," painted
by Uccello, in the fifteenth century, in memory of Hawkwood, who died in the
pay of Florence, in 1394. He was the son of a tanner, and was born in Essex;
the Corporation of Tailors claimed that he had started in life among them;
popular tales were written about him: "The honour of the Taylors, or the
famous and renowned history of Sir John Hawkwood, knight, containing his
. . . adventures . . . relating to love and arms," London, 1687, 4to. The
painting by Uccello has been removed from the choir, transferred on canvas
and placed against the wall at the entrance of the cathedral at Florence.

ing houses, on the highroads of Italy and on the ocean they everywhere resemble the rulers whose spirit has passed into them, and prove themselves to be at once adventurous and practical. " They are good walkers and good horsemen," said Ralph Higden of them in the fourteenth century, adding: " They are curious, and like to tell the wonders they have seen and observed." How many books of travel we owe to this propensity ! " They roam over all lands," he continues, " and succeed still better in other countries than in their own. . . . They spread over the earth ; every land they inhabit becomes as their own country." [1] They are themselves, and no longer seek to be any one else ; they cease by degrees to *francigenare*. This combination of boldness and obstinacy that is theirs, is the blend of qualities by which distant settlements can be established and kept ; to these qualities must be traced the founding of the English colonial empire, and the power which allowed the Plantagenet kings to aspire, as early as the fourteenth century, to be the " Rois de la Mier."

Trade brings luxury, comfort, and the love of art in its train. The same happened in London as in Venice, Florence, and Bruges ; these merchants and nobles were fond of beautiful things. It is an era of prosperity for imagers, miniaturists, painters, and sculptors.[2] The wealthy

---

[1] " Polychronicon," ed. Babington, Rolls, vol. ii. pp. 166, 168.

[2] The most brilliant specimens of the paintings of the time were, in England, those to be seen in St. Stephen's chapel in the palace of Westminster. It was finished about 1348, and painted afterwards. The chief architect was Thomas of Canterbury, master mason ; the principal painters (judging by the highest salaries) were Hugh of St. Albans and John Cotton (" Fœdera," 1705, vol. v. p. 670; vi. 417). This chapel was burnt in the nineteenth century with the rest of the Houses of Parliament ; nothing remains but the crypt ; fragments of the paintings have been saved, and are preserved in the British Museum. They represent the story of Job. The smiling aspect of the personages should be noted, especially that of the women, with the look of happiness about them.

order to be chiselled for themselves ivory Virgins whose
tender, half-mundane smile, is not less charming for the
doubt it leaves whether it is of earth or of heaven ; devotional tablets in painted ivory, in gold, or translucid enamels;
golden goblets with figures, silver cups "enamelled with
children's games," salt-cellars in the shape of lions or dogs,
"golden images of St. John the Baptist, in the wilderness," [1]
all those precious articles with which our museums are filled.
Edward II. sends to the Pope in 1317, among other gifts,
a golden ewer and basin, studded with translucid enamels,
supplied by Roger de Frowyk, a London goldsmith, for the
price of one hundred and forty-seven pounds. Humphrey
de Bohun, who died in 1361, said his prayers to beads of
gold ; Edward III. played chess on a board of jasper
and crystal, silver mounted. The miniaturists represent
Paradise on the margin of missals, or set forth in colours
some graceful legend or fantastic tale, with knights, flowers,
and butterflies.[2] In spite of foreign wars, local insurrections,
the plague that returns periodically, 1349, 1362, 1369, 1375,
the great uprising of the peasantry, 1381, the troubles and
massacres which followed, art prospers in the fourteenth
century, and what chiefly characterises it is that it is all
a-smile.

That such things were coeval is not so astonishing as

See the jewels and other valuables enumerated in the English wills of the
fourteenth century : "A collection of . . . wills," London, Nichols, 1780,
4to, pp. 37, 50, 112, 113, and in "The ancient Kalendars and Inventories
of the Treasury," ed. Palgrave, London, 1836, 3 vols. 8vo, Chess-table of
Edward III., vol. iii. p. 173. *Cf.* for France, "Inventaire du mobilier
de Charles V.," ed. Labarte ("Documents inédits"), 1879, 4to.

[2] Edward III. buys of Isabella of Lancaster, a nun of Aumbresbury, a
manuscript romance that he keeps always in his room, for the price of 66
pounds, 13 shillings, and 4 pence (at that time the price of an ox was about
twelve shillings). For the young Richard were bought two volumes, one containing the Romaunt of the Rose, the other the Romances of Perceval and
Gawain ; the price paid for them, and for a Bible besides, being 28 pounds
(9 Ed. III. and 3 Ric. II., "Issues of the Exchequer," ed. Devon, 1837,
pp. 144 and 213). *Cf.* "Hist. Littéraire de la France," xxxi. 281.

it may seem. Life was still at that time so fragile
and so often threatened, that the notion of its being
suddenly cut off was a familiar one even from childhood.
Wars, plagues, and massacres never took one unawares ;
they were a matter of course, and were expected ; the
prospect of such misfortunes saddened the minds less
than it does now that they have become less frequent.
People were then always ready to fight, to kill, and to be
killed.   Games resembled battles, and battles games : the
favourite exercises were tournaments ; life was risked for
nothing, as an amusement.   Innumerable decrees [1] forbade
those pastimes on account of the deaths they caused,
and the troubles they occasioned ; but the amusement was
the best available, and the decrees were left unobserved.
Edward starts on his war to France, and his knights, following his example, take their falconers and their hounds
along with them, as though they were going to a hunt.[2]
Never was felt to a greater degree what Rabelais terms
"the scorn of fortuitous things."   Times have changed, and
until we go back to a similar state of affairs, which is not
impossible, we come into the world with ideas of peace and
order, and of a life likely to be a long one.   We are indignant if it is threatened, very sad when the end draws near ;
with more lasting happinesses we smile less often.   Froissart paints in radiant colours, and the subject of his pictures
is the France of the Hundred Years' War.   The "merry
England" of the "Cursor Mundi" and after is the England
of the great plagues, and of the rising of the peasants,
which had two kings assassinated out of four.   It is also
the England whose Madonnas smile.

---

[1] More than forty for the reign of Edward II. are to be found in the
"Fœdera."

[2] " Et si y avoit pluiseurs des seigneurs et des riches hommes qui avoient
leurs chiens et leurs oizins ossi bien comme li rois leurs sirs."   Campaign of
1360, Froissart, ed. Luce, book i. chap. 83.

In architecture the English favour the development of
that kind of special Gothic of which they are the inventors,
the Perpendicular, a rich and well-ordered style, terrestrial,
practical, pleasant to look upon. No one did more to
secure it a lasting fame than the Chancellor of Edward
III. and of Richard II., William of Wykeham, bishop of
Winchester, the restorer of Windsor, founder of New
College at Oxford, the greatest builder of the century.[1]
The walls and vaulted roofs of chapels are thick inlaid
with ornaments ; broad windows let in multi-coloured
light through their stained-glass panes ; golden-haired
angels start from the cornices ; architecture smiles too,
and its smile, like that of the Madonnas, is half religious
and half mundane.

Less care is taken to raise strong houses than formerly ;
among the numerous castles with which the land bristles
may be seen, in the distant valley where the ancient
town of St. David's lies screened, a bishop's palace
that would have suited neither William de Longchamp
nor Hugh de Puiset, a magnificent dwelling, without
towers of defence, or moats, or drawbridges, an exceptional
dwelling, built as though the inhabitants were already
secure of the morrow.[2]

The outside is less rude, and the inside is adorned and
enriched ; life becomes more private than it used to be ;

[1] Born at Wykeham, Hampshire, 1324, of an obscure family (whence his
famous motto, " Manners makyth man," that is to say, moral qualities
alone make a man of worth), clerk of the king's works in 1356, present at the
peace of Brétigny, bishop of Winchester 1366, Chancellor in 1367, and again
under Richard II. He died aged eighty-four, under Henry IV. The list
of his benefices (Oct., 1366) fills more than four pages in Lowth (" Life
of W. of Wykeham," Oxford, 1777, pp. 28 ff.). Froissart notes the immense
influence which " Wican " had in the State.

[2] Built almost entirely by Bishop Gower, 1328–47, the " Wykeham of Saint
David's." " History and Antiquities of St. David's," by Jones and Freeman,
London, 1856, 4to, pp. 189 ff. There now remain only ruins, but they are
among the most beautiful that can be seen.

existence less patriarchal and more refined; those who still cling to old customs complain that the rich man dines in a chamber with a chimney, and leaves the large hall which was made for men to take their meals in together.[1] The walls of these chambers with chimneys are painted or covered with hangings; tapestries represent, as do those of Edward II., the king surrounded by his nobles,[2] or, like those of the Black Prince, the "Pas de Saladin," or "sea-sirens," with a border of "swans with ladies' heads," "and ostrich feathers"; or, again, like those of Sir John Falstofe, in the following century, the adoration of the shepherds, a hawking scene, the siege of Falaise (taken in 1417), a woman playing the harp near a castle, "a giant piercing a boar with a spear": all of which are the more noticeable as they are nothing but literature put into colours or embroidery.[3]

[1] Now hath uche riche a reule · to eten by hym-selve
In a pryve parloure · for pore mennes sake,
Or in a chambre with a chymneye · and leve the chief halle,
That was made for meles · men te eten inne.

"Visions Concerning Piers Plowman" (ed. Skeat), text B, passus x. line 96.

[2] For this tapestry the king paid thirty pounds to Thomas de Hebenhith, mercer of London. ("Wardrobe accounts of Edward II."—"Archæologia," vol. xxvi. p. 344.)

[3] Will of the Black Prince, in Nichols, "A Collection of Wills," London. 1780, 4to; inventory of the books of Falstofe (who died under Henry VI.), "Archæologia," vol. xxi. p. 232; in one single castle belonging to him, that of Caister near Yarmouth, were found after his death 13,400 ounces of silver. Already in the thirteenth century, Henry III., who had a passion for art, had caused to be painted in his chamber in the Tower the history of Antioch (3rd crusade), and in his palace of Clarendon that "Pas de Saladin" which was the subject of one of the Black Prince's tapestries; he had a painting of Jesse on the mantelpiece of his chimney at Westminster. (Hardy, "A description of the close rolls in the Tower," London, 1833, 8vo, p. 179, and Devon, "Issues of the Exchequer," 1837, p. 64.) He was so fond of the painting executed for him at Clarendon, that he ordered it to be covered with a linen cloth in his absence, so that it would not get injured. In the fourteenth century the walls were hung instead of being painted, as in the thirteenth; rich people had "salles"—that is to say, suits of hangings for a room. Common ones were made at Norwich; the finest came from Flanders.

The conveniences and elegancies of the table are now attended to ; cooks write out their recipes in English ; stewards draw up in the same language protocols concerning precedence, and the rules which a well-trained servant should observe. Such a one does not scratch his head, and avoids sneezing in the dish ; he abstains from wiping the plates with his tongue, and in carving takes the meat in his left hand and the knife in his right, forks being then unknown ; he gives each one his proper place, and remembers "that the Pope hath no peere." When the master dresses, he must be seated on a chair by the fire, a " kercheff" is spread over his shoulders, and he is " curteisly" combed with an ivory comb ; he is rinsed " with rose-watur warme " ; when he takes a bath the air is scented with herbs hanging from the ceiling. When he goes to bed the cats and dogs which happen to be in his room should be driven away, or else a little cloth provided for them.

The food is rich and combines extraordinary mixtures. Hens and rabbits are eaten chopped up with pounded almonds, raisins, sugar, ginger, herbs dipped in grease, onions and salt ; if the mixture is not thick enough, rice flour is added, and the whole coloured with saffron. Cranes, herons, and peacocks are cooked with ginger. Great attention is paid to outward appearance and to colour ; the dishes must be yellow or green, or adorned with leaves of gold and silver, a fashion still preserved in the East. Elaborate cakes, " subtleties " as they were then termed, are also served ; they represent :

> Maydon Mary that holy virgyne
> And Gabrielle gretynge hur with an Ave.[1]

---

[1] These recipes and counsels are found in : " The forme of Cury, a roll of ancient English cookery compiled about A.D. 1390, by the master-cook of King Richard II.," ed. Pegge, London, 1780, 8vo (found too in the " Antiquitates Culinariæ," of Warner, 1791, 4to). The prologue informs us

People adorn their bodies as well as their houses ; luxury in dress is carried to such an excess that Parliament finds it necessary to interfere, and forbids women of the lower classes to wear any furs except cat and rabbit.[1] Edward III. buys of master Paul de Monteflor gowns for the queen, in " stuffs from over the sea," to the enormous amount of 1,330 pounds. He himself wears a velvet waistcoat, on which he has caused golden pelicans to be embroidered by William Courtenay, a London embroiderer. He gives his mistress Alice Perrers 21,868 large pearls, and thirty ounces of smaller ones. His daughter Margaret receives from him two thousand pearls as a wedding present ; he buys his sister Aliénor a gilded carriage, tapestried and embroidered, with cushions and curtains of silk, for which he pays one thousand pounds.[2] At that time one might for the same sum have bought a herd of sixteen hundred oxen.

The sense of beauty, together with a reverence for and a worship of it, was spreading among the nation whose thoughts shortly before used to run in quite different lines. Attention is paid to physical beauty, such as it had never received before. Men and women wear tight garments, showing the shape of the figure. In the verses he selected for his tomb at Canterbury, the Black Prince

that this master-cook of Richard's had been guided by principle, and that the book " was compiled by assent and avysement of maisters [of] phisik and of philosophie that dwellid in his court."—" The boke of Nurture folowyng Englondis gise by me John Russell," ed. Furnivall, Early English Text Society, 1868, 8vo. Russell was marshal of the hall to Humphrey, duke of Gloucester ; he wrote when he was old, in the first part of the fifteenth century ; as he claims to teach the traditions and good manners of former times, it must be supposed the customs he describes date from the reign of Richard II. See below, p. 515.

[1] Year 1363. The "aignel" and the "gopil" (lamb and fox) are, however, tolerated. "Rotuli Parliamentorum," vol. ii. p. 281.

[2] " Issues of the Exchequer," ed. Devon, 1837, pp. 142, 147, 189, 209, 6 Ed. III. Richard II. pays 400 pounds for a carriage for the queen, and for a simple cart 2 pounds only. *Ibid.*, pp. 236 and 263.

mourns over "his beauty which has all gone." Richard
II., while still alive, has graven on his tomb that he was
" corpore procerus."[1] The taste of the English for finery
becomes so well known, that to them is ascribed, even
in France, the invention of new fashions. Recalling to
his daughters, in order to teach them modesty, that " the
deluge in the time of Noah happened for the pride and
disguises of men, and mostly of women, who remodelled
their shapes by means of gowns and attire," the Knight
de la Tour Landry gives the English ladies the credit, or
rather the discredit, of having invented the immeasurable
head-dresses worn at that day. It is an evil sign ; in
that country people amuse themselves too much : " In
England many there are that have been blamed, the
report goes, I know not whether it is wrongly or
rightly."[2]

Owing to the attention paid to physical beauty in
England, sculptors now begin—a rare thing at that time
—to have living models, and to copy the nude. In the
abbey of Meaux, " Melsa," near Beverley, on the banks
of the Humber, was seen in the fourteenth century a sight
that would have been rather sought for by the banks of
the Arno, under the indulgent sky of Italy. The abbot
Hugh of Leven having ordered a new crucifix for the

---

[1] The verses chosen by the Black Prince as best suited to his state of mind
(below, p. 353) are found in his will, together with minute details concerning
the carvings with which his tomb must be adorned, and the manner he wishes
to be represented on it, " tout armez de fier de guerre." Stanley, " Historical
Memorials of Canterbury," 1885, p. 132. The tomb of Richard II. at Westminster was built in his lifetime and under his eyes. The original indentures
have been preserved, by which " Nicholas Broker et Godfrey Prest, citeins et
copersmythes de Loundres " agree to have the statues of Richard and Anne
made, such as they are seen to-day with " escriptures en tour la dite
toumbe," April 14, 1395. Another contract concerns the marble masonry ;
both are in the Record Office, " Exchequer Treasury of the recipt," " Mis-
cellanea, ' 3/40.

[2] " Le livre du chevalier de la Tour Landry pour l'enseignement de ses filles,"
ed Montaiglon, Paris, 1854, 12mo, pp. 46 and 98, written in 1371.

convent chapel, the artist " had always a naked man under his eyes, and he strove to give to his crucifix the beauty of form of his model." [1]

One last trait may be added to the others : not only the beauty of live beings, but that also of inanimate things is felt and cared for, the beauty of landscapes, and of trees. In 1350-1 the Commons complain of the cutting down of the large trees overshadowing the houses, those large trees, dear already to English hearts, and point out in Parliament the loss of this beauty, the great " damage, loss, and blemish " that results from it for the dwellings. [2]

In nearly every respect, thus, the Englishman of to-day is formed, and receives his chief features, under the Angevin princes Edward III. and Richard II. : practical, adventurous, a lover of freedom, a great traveller, a wealthy merchant, appreciative of luxury and comfort, an excellent sailor. We have had a glimpse of what he is ; let us now listen to what he says.

[1] " Et hominem nudum coram se stantem prospexit, secundum cujus formosam imaginem crucifixum ipsum aptius decoraret." " Chronica monasterii de Melsa," ed. Bond, Rolls, 1868, vol. iii. p. 35. Hugh of Leven, who ordered this crucifix, was abbot from 1339 to 1349. Thomas of Burton, author of the chronicle, compiled it at the end of the fourteenth century.

[2] The Commons point out that, as the royal purveyors "abatent et ount abatuz les arbres cressauntz entour les mansions des gentz de ladite commune, en grant damage, gast et blemissement de lour mansions, qe plese à Nostre Seigneur le Roi que desoremes tiels arbres ne seront copés ne pris en contre la volonté des seigneurs des ditz mansions."

Answer : " Il semble au conseil qe ceste petition est resonable." " Rotuli Parliamentorum," 25 Ed. III., vol. ii. p. 250.

CHAPTER II.

CHAUCER.

THE new nation had its poet, Geoffrey Chaucer. By his origin, his education, his tastes, his manner of life, as well as by his writings, Chaucer represents the new age; he paints it from nature, and is a part of it. His biography is scarcely less characteristic than his works, for he describes nothing through hearsay or imagination. He is himself an actor in the scenes he depicts; he does not dream, he sees them.

His history is a reflected image of that of the English people in his day. They are enriched by trade, and Chaucer, the son of merchants, grows up among them. The English people no longer repair to Paris in order to study, and Chaucer does not go either; their king wages war in France, and Chaucer follows Edward along the military roads of that country; they put more and more trust in Parliament, and Chaucer sits in Parliament as member for Kent. They take an interest in things of beauty, they are fond of the arts, and want them to be all aglow with ornamentation and bright with smiles; Chaucer is clerk of the king's works, and superintends the repairs and embellishments of the royal palaces. Saxon monotony, the sadness that followed after Hastings, are forgotten past memory; this new England knows how to laugh and also how to smile; she is a merry England, with bursts of joy, and also an England of legends, of sweet songs, and of merciful Madonnas. The England of laughter and the England of smiles are both in Chaucer's works.

I.

Chaucer's life exactly fills the period we have now come to, during which the English people acquired their definitive characteristics : he was born under Edward III. and he died shortly after the accession of Henry of Lancaster. At that time Petrarch and Boccaccio were long since dead, France had no poet of renown, and Chaucer was without comparison the greatest poet of Europe.

His family belonged to the merchant class of the City. His father, John Chaucer, his uncle, Thomas Heyroun, and other relations besides, were members of the Corporation of Wine Merchants, or Vintners. John Chaucer, apparently purveyor to the Court, accompanied Edward III. on his first expedition to the Continent : hence a connection with the royal family, by which the future poet was to profit. The Chaucers' establishment was situated in that Thames Street which still exists, but now counts only modern houses ; Geoffrey was probably born there in 1340, or a little earlier.[1]

Chaucer spent the years of his childhood and youth in London: a London which the great fire of 1666 almost totally destroyed, that old London, then quite young, of

[1] The date 1328 has long but wrongly been believed to be the true one. Chief documents concerning Chaucer, in " Trial Forewords," by Dr. Furnivall, 1871, " Life Records of Chaucer," ed. R. E. G. Kirk, 1900, Chaucer Society. *Cf.* A. A. Kern, "The Ancestry of Chaucer," Baltimore, 1906 ; Miss E. P. Hammond, "Chaucer, a Bibliographical Manual," New York, 1908. One of the municipal ordinances meant to check the frauds of the vintners is signed by several members of the corporation, and among others by John Chaucer, 1342. See Riley, " Memorials of London," p. 211.

which illuminated manuscripts have preserved for us the picturesque aspect. The paternal house was near the river, and by the side of the streamlet called Walbrook, since covered over, but which then flowed in the open air. On the noble river, the waters of which were perhaps not as blue as illuminators painted them, but which were not yet the liquid mud we all know, ships from the Mediterranean and the Baltic glided slowly, borne by the tide. Houses with several stories and pointed roofs lined the water, and formed, on the ground floor, colonnades that served for warehouses, and under which merchandise was landed.[1] The famous London Bridge, built under King John, almost new still, for it was only entering upon its second century and was to live six hundred years, with its many piers, its sharp buttresses, the houses it bore, its chapel of St. Thomas, stood against the line of the horizon, and connected the City with the suburb of Southwark. On that side were more houses, a fine Gothic church, which still exists, hostelries in abundance, for it was the place of arrival for those coming by land; and with the hostelries, places of amusement of every kind, a tradition so well established that most of the theatres in the time of Elizabeth were built there, and notably the celebrated Globe, where Shakespeare's plays were performed. Save for this suburb, the right shore of the Thames, instead of the warehouses of to-day, offered to view the open country, trees, and green meadows. Some way down, on the left bank, rose the walls of the Tower; and further up, towards the interior of the City, the massive pile of St. Paul's stood out above the houses. It was then a Gothic cathedral; Wren, after the great fire, replaced it by the Renaissance edifice we see to-day. The town was sur-

[1] See the view of London, painted in the fifteenth century, obviously from nature, reproduced at the beginning of this vol., from MS. Royal 16 F ii, in the British Museum, showing the Tower, the Bridge, the wharfs, Old St. Paul's, etc.

rounded by walls, portions of which still remain, with
Roman foundations in some places.[1] At intervals gates
opened on the country, defended by bastions, their memory
being preserved at this day by names of streets : Aldgate,
Bishopsgate, &c.

The town itself was populous and busy. The streets,
in which Chaucer's childhood was spent, were narrow,
bordered by houses with projecting stories, with signs
overhanging the way, with "pentys" barring the footpath,
and all sorts of obstructions, against which innumerable
municipal ordinances protested in vain. Riders' heads
caught in the signs, and it was enjoined to make the
poles shorter ; manners being violent, the wearing of arms
was prohibited, but honest folk alone conformed to the
law, thus facilitating matters for the others ; cleanliness
was but indifferent ; pigs ran hither and thither. A decree
of the time of Edward I. had vainly prescribed that they
should all be killed, except those of St. Anthony's Hospital,
which would be recognised by the bell hanging at their
neck : "And whoso will keep a pig, let him keep it in his
own house." Even this privilege was withdrawn a little
later, so elegant were manners becoming.[2]

In this laborious city, among sailors and merchants,
acquiring a taste for adventure and for tales of distant
lands, hearing his father describe the beautiful things to be
seen at Court, Geoffrey grew up, from a child became a
youth, and, thanks to his family's acquaintances, was
appointed, at seventeen, page to Elizabeth, wife of Lionel,
son of Edward III.[3] In his turn, and not as a merchant,

---

[1] Such is the case with a tower in the churchyard of St. Giles's, Cripplegate.

[2] "Et qi pork voedra norir, le norise deinz sa measoun." Four jurymen
were to act as public executors : "Quatuor homines electi et jurati ad inter-
ficiendos porcos inventos vagantes infra muros civitatis." Riley "Munimenta
Gildhallæ," Rolls, 1859, 4 vols. 8vo ; "Liber Albus," pp. 270 and 590.

[3] April, 1357, an information gathered from a fragment of the accounts of
the household of Elizabeth found in the binding of a book.

he had access to the Court and belonged to it. He dressed in the fashion, and received from the Lady Elizabeth a short cloak or paltock, shoes, and a pair of red and black breeches ; cost to the Lady, seven shillings.

In 1359 he took part in the expedition to France, led by the king. It seemed as if it must be a death-blow to the French : the disaster of Poictiers was not yet repaired ; the Jacquerie had just taken place, as well as the Parisian riots and the treason and death of Marcel ; the king of France was a prisoner in London, and the kingdom had for its leader a youth of twenty-two, frail, learned, pious, unskilled in war. It looked as though one had but to take ; but once more the saying of Froissart was verified ; in the fragile breast of the dauphin beat the heart of a great citizen, and the event proved that the kingdom was not "so discomfited but that one always found therein some one against whom to fight." The campaign was a happy one neither for Edward nor for Chaucer. The king of England met with nothing but failures : he failed before Reims, failed before Paris, and was only too pleased to sign the treaty of Brétigny. Chaucer was taken by the French,[1] and his fate would not have been an enviable one if the king had not paid his ransom. Edward gave sixteen pounds to recover his daughter-in-law's page. Everything has its value : the same Edward had spent fifty pounds over a horse called Bayard, and seventy for another called Labryt, which was dapple-grey.

After his return Chaucer was attached to the person of

[1] In the controversy between Sir Richard Scrope and Sir Robert Grosvenor, concerning a question of armorial bearings, Chaucer, being called as witness, declares (1386) that he has seen Sir Richard use the disputed emblems "en France, devant la ville de Retters . . . et issint il [le] vist armez par tout le dit viage tanque le dit Geffrey estoit pris." "The Scrope and Grosvenor controversy, 1385–90," London, 2 vols. fol., vol. i. p. 178. "Retters" is Réthel in Champagne (not Retiers in Brittany, where the expedition did not go). *Cf.* A. F. Emerson, "Chaucer's First Military Service," "Romanic Review," III. No. 4.

Edward in the capacity of valet of the chamber, "valettus cameræ regis"; this is exactly the title that Molière was later to honour in his turn.   His functions consisted in making the royal bed, holding torches, and carrying messages.   A little later he was squire, *armiger*, *scutifer*, and as such served the prince at table, and rode after him in his journeys.[1]   His duties do not seem to have absorbed all his thoughts, for he found time to read many books, to write many poems, to be madly enamoured of a lovely unknown person who did not respond to his passion,[2] to marry "Domicella" or "Damoiselle" Philippa, attached to the service of the queen, then to the service of Constance, second wife of John of Gaunt, Duke of Lancaster—without ceasing however, because he could not, as he assures us, do otherwise, still to love his unknown beauty.[3]

[1] On this see Furnivall, "Chaucer as valet and esquire," Chaucer Society, 1876.

[2] A passage in Chaucer's "Book of the Duchesse" (1369), lines 30 ff., leaves little doubt as to the reality of the unlucky passion he describes.   The poet interrupts the train of his speech to answer a supposed question put to him as to the causes of his depression and "melancolye":

> I holdë hit be a siknesse
> That I have suffred this eight yere,
> And yet my bote is never the nere;
> For ther is phisicien but oon,
> That may me hele.

Proem of the "Book."   See, in connection with this, the "Compleynte unto Pite."   Who was the loved one we do not know; could it be that the poet was playing upon her name in such lines as these:

> For kindly by your heritage right
> Ye been annexed ever unto Bountee? (l. 71).

There were numerous families of Bonamy, Bonenfant, Boncœur.   A William de Boncuor is named in the "Excerpta e Rotulis Finium," of Roberts, vol. ii. pp. 309, 431, 432.

[3] The date of Chaucer's marriage has not been ascertained.   We know that his wife was called Philippa, that one Philippa Chaucer belonged to the queen's household in 1366, and that the Philippa Chaucer, wife of the poet, was at a later date in the service of the Duchess of Lancaster, after having been in the service of the queen.   It seems most likely that the two women

He reads, he loves, he writes, he is a poet. We do not
know whom he loved, but we know what he read and what
he wrote at that time. He read the works which were in
fashion in the elegant society he lived among : romances
of chivalry, love-songs, allegorical poems, from "Roland"
and "Tristan" to the "Roman de la Rose." Poets, even
the greatest, rarely show their originality at twenty, and
Chaucer was no exception to the rule ; he imitated the
writings best liked by those around him, which, at the
Court of the king, were mostly French books. However
it might be with the nation, the princes had remained
French ; the French language was their native tongue; the
beautiful books, richly illustrated, that they kept to divert
themselves with on dull days, in their "withdrawing-room,"
or "chambre de retrait," were French books, of which the
subject for the most part was love. In this respect there
was, even at that time, no difference between the north and
the south. Froissart stays at Orthez, in 1388, with
Monseigneur Gaston Phébus de Foix ; and at Eltham, at the

were the same person : same name, same function, same pension of ten marks,
referred to in the same words in public documents, for example : 1° 42 Ed.
III., 1368, "Philippæ Chaucer cui dominus Rex decem marcas annuatim ad
scaccarium percipiendas pro bono servitio per ipsam Philippam Philippe Regine
Anglie impenso per literas suas patentes nuper concessit. . . ." 2° 4 Ric.
II., 1381, "Philippæ Chaucer nuper uni domicellarum Philippæ nuper
Regine Anglie"—she had died in 1369—"cui dominus Rex Edwardus avus
Regis hujus X marcas annuatim ad scaccarium suum percipiendas pro bono
servitio per ipsam tam eidem domino Regi quam dicte Regine impenso per
literas suas patentes nuper concessit . . . in denariis sibi liberatis per
manus predicti Galfridi mariti sui. . . ." "Life Records," ed. Kirk, pp. 161,
229. Who Philippa was by birth is doubtful, but it seems likely that she
was Philippa Roet, daughter of Sir Payne Roet, who hailed, like the queen
herself, from Hainault—hence her connection with the queen—and sister of
Catherine Roet who became the mistress and then the third wife of John
of Gaunt—hence the favour in which the poet and his family stood with the
Lancastrians. It seems probable, though not absolutely certain, that Thomas
Chaucer, who used at different times both the Chaucer and the Roet arms,
Speaker of the House of Commons under Henry V., was a son or may be
a stepson of the poet. *Cf. Athenæum,* Jan. 27, 1900, May 11, and Oct. 5,
1901 ; "Life Records," *ibid.,* p. lii.

Court of Richard II. in 1394. In each case he uses exactly the same endeavours to please : both personages are men of the same kind, having the same ideal in life, imbued with the same notions, and representing the same civilisation. He finds them both speaking French very well ; Gaston "talked to me, not in his own Gascon, but in fair and good French" ; Richard, too, "full well spoke and read French." The historian was duly recommended to each of them, but he relied especially, to make himself welcome, on a present he had brought, the same in both cases, a French manuscript containing amorous poems, which manuscript "the Comte de Foix saw full willingly ; and every night, after his supper, I read to him from it. But in reading none durst speak nor say a word ; for he wanted me to be well heard."

He takes the same precautions when he goes to England, where he had not been seen for a quarter of a century, and where he scarcely knew any one now : "And I had beforehand caused to be written, engrossed and illuminated and collected, all the amorous and moral treatises that, in the lapse of thirty-four years, I had, by the grace of God and of Love, made and compiled." He awaits a favourable opportunity, and one day when the councils on the affairs of State are ended, "desired the king to see the book that I had brought him. Then he saw it in his chamber, for all prepared I had it ; I put it for him upon his bed. He opened it and looked inside, and it pleased him greatly : and please him well it might, for it was illuminated, written and ornamented and covered in scarlet velvet, with ten silver nails gilded with gold, and golden roses in the middle, and with two great clasps gilded and richly worked in the middle with golden roses.

" Then the king asked me of what it treated, and I told him : of Love.

" With this answer he was much rejoiced, and looked

inside in several places, and read therein, for he spoke and
read French full well ; and then had it taken by one of his
knights, whom he called Sir Richard Credon, and carried
into his withdrawing-room, and treated me better and
better." [1]

Long before this last journey of the illustrious chronicler,
Chaucer was familiar with his poems, and he was acquainted,
as most men around him were, with those of his French
contemporaries : Deguileville, Machault, Des Champs, and
later Granson.[2] He sings like them of love, of spring, of
the field-daisy [3]; he had read with passionate admiration

[1] Book iv. chap. 40.

[2] Froissart declares concerning his own poems that he "les commencha à
faire sus l'an de grâce Nostre Seigneur, 1362." He wrote them "à l'ayde de
Dieu et d'Amours, et à le contemplation et plaisance de pluisours haus et
nobles signours et de pluisours nobles et vaillans dames." MS. Fr. 831 in the
National Library, Paris.—On Guillaume de Deguileville, who wrote about
1330–5, see Ward, "Catalogue of Romances," 1893, vol. ii. p. 558 ; Galpin,
"Public. Mod. Lang. Assn. of America," xxv., and my "Piers Plowman,"
chap. vii. Chaucer imitated from him his "A.B.C.," one of his first
works.—On Machault, who died in 1377, see Hoepffner, "Œuvres,"
Paris, 1908 ff., Thomas, "Romania," x. pp. 325 ff., Kittredge, "Public.
Mod. Lang. Assn. Ama.," xxx. 1.—On Des Champs, see "Œuvres Complètes
publiées d'après le Manuscrit de la Bibliothèque Nationale," by the
Marquis de Queux de St. Hilaire, Société des Anciens Textes, 1878 ff.
(which MS. contains, e.g., 1175 ballads, 171 roundels, and 80 virelais),
and A. Sarradin, "Etude sur Eustache des Champs," Versailles, 1878,
8vo.— On Granson, a knight and a poet slain in a judicial duel, in 1397,
see Piaget, "Granson et ses poésies," "Romania," vol. xix. ; Chaucer imitated
in his later years his "Compleynt of Venus," from a poem of "Graunson,
flour of hem that make in Fraunce."

[3] Chaucer's favourite flower ; he constantly praises it ; it is for him a woman-
flower (see especially the prologue of the "Legend of Good Women "). This
flower enjoyed the same favour with the French models of Chaucer. One of
the ballads of Froissart has for its burden : "Sus toutes flours j'aime la
margherite " (" Le Paradis d'Amour," in "Poésies," ed. Scheler, Brussels,
1870, 3 vols. 8vo), vol. i. p. 49. Des Champs praised the same flower ; Machault
wrote a "Dit de la Marguerite :"

> J'aim une fleur qui s'uevre et qui s'encline
> Vers le soleil, de jour quand il chemine ;
> Et quand il est couchiez soubz sa courtine
>   Par nuit obscure,
> Elle se clost ainsois que le jour fine.

the poem, composed in the preceding century, which was most liked of all the literature of the time, the " Roman de la Rose."

This famous poem was then at the height of a reputation which was to last until after the Renaissance. The faults which deter us from it contributed to its popularity as much as did its merits ; digressions, disquisitions, and sermons did not inspire the terror they do now ; twenty-three thousand lines of moralisation, psychological analysis, abstract dissertations, delivered by personified abstractions, did not weary the young imagination of the ancestors. The form is allegorical : the rose is the maiden whom the lover desires to conquer : this form, which fell later into disfavour, delighted the readers of the fourteenth century for whom it was an additional pleasure to unriddle these easy enigmas.

The Church had helped to bring allegories into vogue ; commentators had early explained the New Testament by the Old, one being an allegory of the other : the adventure of Jonah and the whale was an allegory of the resurrection ; the Bestiaries were series of allegories ; the litanies of the Virgin lists of symbols. The methods of pious authors were adopted by worldly ones ; Love had his religion, his allegories, his litanies, not to speak of his paradise, his hell, and his ten commandments. He had a whole celestial court of personified abstractions, composed of those tenuous and transparent beings who welcome or repel the lover in the garden of the Rose. It was a new religion, this worship of woman, unknown to the ancients ; Ovid no longer sufficed, imitators could not help altering his aim and ideal ; the new cult required a gospel ; that gospel was the " Roman de la Rose." [1]

---

[1] G. de Lorris wrote the first part of the " Roman " betw. 1225 and 1240 ; Jean de Meun finished the second betw. 1279 and 1280. Best ed., by E. Langlois, " Soc. Anc. Textes," 1914 ff. On the sources of the poem see by

The discrepancies in the book did not shock the generality of readers ; art at that time was full of contrasts, and life of contradictions, and the thing was so usual that it went unnoticed. Saints prayed on the threshold of churches, and gargoyles laughed at the saints. Guillaume de Lorris built the porch of his cathedral of Love, and placed in the niches tall, long figures of pure and noble mien. Jean de Meun, forty years later, continued the edifice, and was not sparing of gargoyles, mocking, grotesque, and indecent. Thence followed interminable discussions, some holding for Guillaume, others for Jean, some rejecting the whole romance, others, the most numerous, accepting it all. These dissensions added still more to the fame of the work, and it was so popular that there remain more than two hundred manuscripts of it.[1] The wise biographer of the wise king Charles V., Christine de Pisan, protested in the name of insulted women : "To you who have beautiful daughters, and desire well to introduce them to honest life, give to them, give the Romaunt of the Rose, to learn how to discern good from evil; what do I say, but evil from good! And of what utility, nor what does it profit listeners to hear such horrible things?" The author "never had acquaintance nor association with an honourable or virtuous

the same : "Origines et Sources du Roman de la Rose," Paris, 1891. M. Langlois has traced the originals for 12,000 out of the 17,500 lines of Jean de Meun. *Cf.* Fansler, "Chaucer and the Roman de la Rose," New York, 1914.

[1] One of them has a sort of biographical interest as having belonged to Sir Richard Stury, Chaucer's colleague in one of his missions (see below, p. 284) ; it was afterwards purchased for Thomas, duke of Gloucester, son of Edward III., and is now in the British Museum, MS. Royal 19 B xiii. "Ceste livre est à Thomas fiz au Roy, duc de Glouc', achates dez executeurs Mons' Ric Stury." It has curious miniatures exemplifying the way in which people pictured to themselves at that time Olympian gods and romance heroes. The " Dieu d'amour " figures as a tall person with a tunic, a cloak, and a crown, a bow in his hand and large red wings on his back. See fol. 16, " coment li diex d'amours navra l'amant de ses saietes."

woman"; he has known none save those of "dissolute and evil life," and has taken all the others to be according to that pattern.[1] The illustrious Gerson, in the fifteenth century, did the romance the honour of refuting it by a treatise according to rule ; but the poem was none the less translated into Latin, Flemish, and English, printed a number of times at the Renaissance and rejuvenated and edited by Marot.

There were several English translations, and one of them was the work of our young "Valettus cameræ regis." This translation by Chaucer is lost,[2] but we are aware not only that it existed, but even that it was celebrated ; its merit was known in France, and Des Champs, in sending his own works to Chaucer,[3] congratulates him, above all, on having "planted the rose-tree" in "the isle of giants,"

[1] "A vous qui belles filles avez et bien les désirez à introduire à vie honneste, bailliez leur, bailliez le Rommant de la Rose, pour aprendre à discerner le bien du mal, que diz-je, mais le mal du bien.   Et à quel utilité ne à quoy proufite aux oyans oïr tant de laidures ? " Jean de Meun " oncques n'ot acointance ne hantise de femme honorable ne vertueuse, mais par plusieurs femmes dissolues et de male vie hanter, comme font communément les luxurieux cuida ou faingny savoir que toutes telles feussent car d'autres n'avoit congnoissance." "Débat sur le Rommant de la Rose," in MS. Fr. 604 in the National Library, Paris, fol. 114 and 115.

[2] An incomplete translation of the " Roman " in English verse has come down to us in a single MS. preserved in the Hunterian collection, Glasgow. It is anonymous ; a study of this text, by Lindner and by Kaluza, has shown that it is made up of three fragments of different origin, prosody, and language. The first fragment ends with line 1705, leaving a sentence unfinished ; between the second and third fragments there is a gap of more than 5,000 lines.   The first fragment alone might, on account of its style and versification, be the work of Chaucer, but this is only a surmise, and we have no direct proof of it. The " Romaunt " is to be found in Skeat's edition of the " Complete Works " of Chaucer, 1894, vol. i.   For Fragment I. the French text is given along with the English translation.

[3] Mais pran en gré les euvres d'escolier
Que par Clifford de moy avoir pourras.

For Des Champs, Chaucer is a Socrates, a Seneca, an Ovid, an "aigle très hault," " Œuvres Completes," Paris, 1878 ff., vol. ii. p. 138.

the "angelic land," "Angleterre," and on being there the
god of worldly loves :

> Tu es d'amours mondains dieux on Albie
> Et de la Rose en la terre Angélique . . .
> En bon anglès le livre translatas.

This authority in matters of love which Des Champs
ascribes to his English brother-author, was real. Chaucer
composed then a quantity of amorous poems, in the
French style, for himself, for others, to while away the
time, to allay his sorrows. Of them, said Gower,

> The lande fulfylled is over all.

Most of them are lost ; but we know, from contemporaneous
allusions, that they swarmed, and from himself that he
wrote "many an ympne " to the God of love, " balades,
roundels, virelayes,"

> bokes, songes, dytees,
> In ryme, or elles in cadence,

each and all " in reverence of Love." [1]   A few poems, however, of that early period, have reached us.   They are,
amongst others, his " Compleynte unto Pite "—

> Pite, that I have sought so yore ago
> With herte sore, and ful of besy peyne . . .

—-a rough sketch of a subject that Sidney was to take up
later and bring to perfection, and his " Book of the

---

[1] "Hous of Fame," line 622 ; "Legend of Good Women," line 422,
"Complete Works," 1894, vol. i. pp. 19 and 96. Such was the reputation of
Chaucer that a great many writings were attributed to him—a way to increase
their reputation, not his. The more important of them are : "The Court of
Love"; the "Book of Cupid," otherwise "Cuckoo and Nightingale";
"Flower and Leaf," the "Romaunt of the Rose," such as we have it ; the
"Complaint of a Lover's Life"; the "Testament of Love" (in prose, below
p. 411) ; the "Isle of Ladies," or "Chaucer's Dream"; various ballads.
Most of those works are in "Poetical Works" of Chaucer, ed. Morris ; all oi
them in "Complete Works," ed. Skeat, vii.

Duchesse," composed on the occasion of the death of Blanche of Lancaster, first wife of John of Gaunt.

The occasion is sad, but the setting is exquisite, for Chaucer wishes to raise to the Duchess who has disappeared a lasting monument, that shall prolong her memory, an elegant one, graceful as herself, where her portrait, traced by a friendly hand, shall recall the charms of a beauty that each morning renewed. So lovable was she, and so full of accomplishment,

> That she was lyk to torche bright,
> That every man may take of light
> Ynogh, and hit hath never the lesse.[1]

Already the descriptions have a freshness that no contemporaries equal, and show a care for truth and a gift of observation not often found in the innumerable poems in dream-form left to us by the writers of the fourteenth century.

Tormented by his thoughts and deprived of sleep, the poet has a book brought to him to while away the hours of night, one of those books that he loved all his life, where " clerkes hadde in olde tyme " rimed stories of long ago. The tale, " a wonder thing " though it was, puts him to sleep, and it seems to him that it is morning. The sun rises in a pure sky ; the birds sing on the tiled roof, the light floods the room, which is all painted according to the taste of the Plantagenets. On the walls is represented " al the Romaunce of the Rose " ; the window-glass offers to view the history of Troy ; coloured rays fall on the bed ; outside

> the welken was so fair,
> Blew, bright, clere was the air . . .
> Ne in al the welken was a cloude.

---

[1] And every day hir beaute newed.

(ll. 906, 963.)

A hunt goes by, 'tis the hunt of the Emperor Octavian ; the young man mounts and rides after it under those great trees, " so huge of strengthe, so ful of leves," beloved of the English, amid meadows thick studded with flowers,

> As thogh the erthe envye wolde
> To be gayer than the heven.

A little dog draws near ; his movements are noted with an accuracy that the Landseers of to-day could scarcely excel. The dog would like to be well received, but afraid of being beaten, he creeps up and darts suddenly away :

> Hit com and creep to me as lowe,
> Right as hit hadde me y-knowe,
> Hild doun his heed and joyned his eres,
> And leyde al smothe down his heres.
> I wolde han caught hit, and anoon
> Hit fledde and was fro me goon.

In a glade apart was a knight clothed in black, John of Lancaster. Chaucer does not endeavour to console him ; he knows the only assuagement for such sorrows, and leads him on to speak of the dead. John recalls her grace and gentleness, and praises qualities which carry us back to a time very far from our own. She was not one of those women who, to try their lovers, send them to Wallachia, Prussia, Tartary, Egypt, or Turkey :

> She ne used no suche knakkes smale.[1]

From these " knakkes smale " we may judge what the others must have been. They discourse thus a long

---

[1] "Book of the Duchesse," ll. 339, 406, 391, 1033. John of Gaunt found consolation, however, in marrying two other wives. Blanche was buried with him in old St. Paul's. See a view of their tomb in Dugdale's " St. Paul," reproduced in my "Piers Plowman," p. 92. On Machaut's influence traceable in this poem, see Miss Kitchel, in "Vassar Mediæval Studies," 1923.

while; the clock strikes noon, and the poet awakes, his head on the book which had put him to sleep.

II.

In the summer of 1370 Chaucer left London and repaired to the Continent for the service of the king; this was the first of his diplomatic missions, which succeeded each other rapidly during the ensuing ten years. The period of the Middle Ages was not a period of *nuances*; that *nuance* which distinguishes an ambassador from a messenger was held as insignificant, and escaped observation; the two functions formed but one. "You," said Eustache Des Champs, "you, ambassador and messenger, who go about the world to do your duty at the Courts of great princes, your journeys are not short ones! . . . Don't be in such a hurry; your plea must be submitted to council before an answer can be returned: just wait a little more, my good friend; . . . we must talk of the matter with the chancellor and some others. . . . Time passes and all turns out wrong." [1] Precedents are a great thing in diplomacy; here we find a time-honoured one.

Recourse was often had to men of letters for these mixed functions, and they were filled by the most illustrious writers of the century, Petrarch and Boccaccio in

[1] Vous Ambasseur et messagier,
　Qui alez par le monde es cours
　Des grans princes pour besongnier,
　Vostre voyage n'est pas cours . . .
　Ne soiez mie si hastis !
　Il fault que vostre fait soit mis
　Au conseil pour respondre à plain ;
　Attendez encore mes amis . . .
　Il faut parler au chancelier
　De vostre fait et à plusours . . .
　Temps passe et tout vint arrebours.

" Œuvres Complètes," Société des Anciens Textes, vol. vii. p. 117.

Italy, Chaucer in England, Des Champs in France. The latter, whose career much resembles Chaucer's, has traced the most lamentable pictures of the life led by an "ambassador and messenger" on the highways of Europe: Bohemia, Poland, Hungary; in these regions the king's service caused him to journey. His horse is half dead, and "sits on his knees"[1]; the inhabitants have the incivility to speak only their own language, so that one cannot even order one's dinner; you must needs take what is served: "'Tis ill eating to another's appetite."[2]

The lodging is worse: "No one may lie by himself, but two by two in a dark room, or oftener three by three, in one bed, haphazard." One may well regret sweet France, "where each one has for his money what he chooses to ask for, and at reasonable price: room to himself, fire, sleep, repose, bed, white pillow, and scented sheets."[3]

Happily for Chaucer, it was in Flanders, France, and Italy that he negotiated for Edward and Richard. In December, 1372, he traverses all France, and goes to Genoa to treat with the doge of commercial matters; then

---

[1] De laissier aux champs me manace,
Trop souvent des genoulx s'assiet,
Par ma foy, mes chevaulx se lace.
(*Ibid.*, p. 32.)

[2] Mal fait mangier à l'appétit d'autruy.
(*Ibid.*, p. 81.)

[3] O doulz pais, terre très honorable,
Où chascuns a ce qu'il veult demander
Pour son argent, et à pris raisonnable,
Char, pain et vin, poisson d'yaue et de mer,
Chambre à par soy, feu, dormir, reposer,
Liz, orilliers blans, draps flairans la graine,
Et pour chevaulz, foing, litière et avaine,
Estre servis, et par bonne ordonnance,
Et en seurté de ce qu'on porte et maine;
Tel pais n'est qu'en royaume de France.
(*Ibid.*, p. 79.)

he repairs to Florence, and having thus passed a whole winter far from the London fogs (which already existed in the Middle Ages), he is back to London on May 23rd, 1373. In 1376 a new mission is entrusted to him, this time a secret one, the secret has been well kept to this day ; more missions in 1377 and 1378. "On Trinity Sunday," 1376, says Froissart, "passed away from this world the flower of England's chivalry, my lord Edward of England, Prince of Wales and Aquitaine, in the palace of Westminster by London, and was embalmed and put into a leaden chest." After the obsequies, "the king of England made his children recognise . . . the young *damoisel* Richard to be king after his death." He sends delegates to Bruges to treat of the marriage of his heir, aged ten, with "Madame Marie, daughter of the king of France"; in February other ambassadors are appointed on both sides: "Towards Lent, a secret treaty was made between the two kings for their party to be at Montreuil-on-sea. Thus were sent to Calais, by the English, Messire Guichard d'Angle, Richard Stury, and Geoffrey Chaucer." [1] The negotiation failed, but the poet's services seem nevertheless to have been appreciated, for in the following year he is again on the highways. He negotiates in France, in company with the same Sir Guichard, now become earl of Huntingdon ; and again in Italy, where he has to treat with his compatriot Hawkwood,[2] who led, in the most

---

[1] Book i. chap. 692.

[2] The order for the payment of the expenses of "nostre cher et féal chivaler Edward de Berklé," and "nostre féal esquier Geffray Chaucer," is directed to William Walworth, then not so famous as he was to be, and to the no less notorious John Philpot, mercer and naval leader. Both envoys are ordered "d'aler en nostre message si bien au duc de Melan Barnabo come à nostre cher et foial Johan Haukwode ès parties de Lumbardie, pur ascunes busoignes touchantes l'exploit de nostre guerre," May 12, 1378. Berkeley receives 200 marcs and Chaucer 100 ; the sums are to be paid out of the war subsidy voted by Parliament the year before. The French text of the warrant has been published by Mr. Spont in the *Athenæum* of Sept. 9, 1893. During this

agreeable manner possible, the life of a condottiere for the benefit of the Pope, and of any republic that paid him well.

These journeys to Italy had a considerable influence on Chaucer's mind.   Already in that privileged land the Renaissance was beginning.   Italy had, in that century, three of her greatest poets: the one whom Virgil had conducted to the abode of "the doomed race" was dead; but the other two, Petrarch and Boccaccio, still lived, secluded, in the abode which was to be their last on earth, one at Arqua, near Padua, the other in the little fortified village of Certaldo, near Florence.

In art, it is the century of Giotto, Orcagna, and Andrew of Pisa.   Chaucer saw, all fresh still in their glowing colours, frescoes that time has long faded.   Those old things were then young, and what seems to us the first steps of an art, uncertain yet in its tread, seemed to contemporaries the supreme effort of the audacious, who represented the new times.

Chaucer's own testimony is proof to us that he saw, heard, and learnt as much as possible ; that he went as far as he could, letting himself be guided by " adventure, that is the moder of tydinges."   He arrived without any preconceived ideas, curious to know what occupied men's minds, as attentive as on the threshold of his " Hous of Fame ":

> For certeynly, he that me made
> To comen hider, seyde me,
> I shulde bothe here et see,
> In this place wonder thinges . . .
> For yit peraventure, I may lere
> Some good ther-on, or sumwhat here,
> That leef me were, or that I wente.[1]

---

absence Chaucer appointed to be his representatives or attorneys two of his friends, one of whom was the poet Gower.   " Life Records of Chaucer," iv., ed. Kirk, Chaucer Society, 1900, pp. 215 ff.

[1] ll. 1892, 1890, 1997.

He was thus able to see with his own eyes the admirable activity, owing to which rose throughout Italy monuments where all kinds of contradictory aspirations mingled, and which are nevertheless so harmonious in their *ensemble*, monuments of which Giotto's campanile is the type, wherein we still recognise the Middle Ages, even while we foresee the Renaissance—with Gothic windows and a general aspect that is classic, where the sentiment of realism and everyday life is combined with veneration for antique art, where Apelles is represented painting a triptych of Gothic shape. Pisa had already, at that day, its leaning tower, its cathedral, its baptistery, the exterior ornamentation of which had just been changed, its Campo Santo, the paintings of which were not finished, and were not yet attributed to Orcagna. Along the walls of the cemetery he could examine that first collection of antiques which inspired the Tuscan artists, the sarcophagus, with the story of Phædra and Hippolytus, which Nicholas of Pisa took for his model. He could see at Pistoja the pulpit carved by William of Pisa, with the magnificent nude torso of a woman, imitated from the antique. At Florence the Palazzo Vecchio, which was not yet called thus, was finished ; so were the Bargello, Santa-Croce, Santa-Maria-Novella. Or-San-Michele was being built ; the Loggia of the Lansquenets was scarcely begun ; the baptistery had as yet only one of its famous doors of bronze ; the cathedral disappeared under scaffoldings ; the workmen were busy with the nave and the apse. Giotto's campanile had been finished by his pupil Gaddi, the Ponte Vecchio, which did not deserve that name any better than the palace, had been rebuilt by the same Gaddi, and along the causeway which continued it, through clusters of cypress and olive trees, the road led up to San Miniato, all resplendent with its marbles, its mosaics, and its paintings. On other ranges of hills, amid more cypress and more olive trees, by the side of Roman ruins, arose the church of Fiesole, and half-way to Florence waved in the sunlight the thick foliage overshadowing the villa which, during the great plague had sheltered the young men and young ladies of the " Decameron."

The movement was a general one. Each town strove to emulate its neighbour, not only on the battlefields, which were a very frequent trysting-place, but in artistic progress ; paintings, mosaics, carvings, shone in all the palaces and churches of every city ; the activity was extreme. Giotto, who had his studio, his "botega," in Florence, worked also at Assisi, Rome, and Padua. Sienna was covering the walls of her public palace with frescoes, some figures of which resemble the paintings at Pompeii.[1] An antique statue found within her territory was provoking universal admiration, and was erected on the Gaïa fountain by the municipality ; but the Middle Ages did not lose their rights, and, the republic having suffered reverses, the statue fell into disgrace. The god became nothing more than an idol ; the marble was shattered and carried off, to be treacherously interred in the territory of Florence.[2]

The taste for collections was spreading ; the commerce of antiquities flourished in Northern Italy. Petrarch bought medals, and numbered among his artistic treasures a Madonna of Giotto, " whose beauty," he says in his will, " escaped the ignorant but enraptured the masters of the art." [3] This brightening of the land was the result of concurring wills, nor did it pass unobserved even then ; towns enjoyed their masterpieces, and, like young women, " se miraient en leur beauté."

Figure of " Peace," by Ambrogio Lorenzetti, 1339. See a drawing of it in Müntz, " Les Précurseurs de la Renaissance," Paris, 1882, 4to, p. 29.

[2] Müntz, *ibid.*, p. 30.

[3] " F. Petrarcæ Epistolæ," ed. Fracassetti, Florence, 1859, vol. iii. p. 541.

Contemporaries did not leave to posterity the care of crowning the great poets of the time. Italy, the mother of art, wished the laurel to encircle the brow of the living, not to be simply the ornament of a tomb. Rome had crowned, in 1341, him who, "cleansing the fount of Helicon from slime and marshy rushes, had restored to the water its pristine limpidity, who had opened Castalia's grotto, obstructed by a network of wild boughs, and destroyed the briers in the laurel grove": the illustrious Francis Petrarch.[1] Though somewhat tardy, the honour was no less great for Dante: public lectures on the "Divine Comedy" were instituted in Florence, and the lecturer was Boccaccio.[2]

It was impossible that a mind, from infancy friendly to art and books, should not be struck by this general expansion; the charm of this literary springtime was too penetrating for Chaucer not to feel it; he followed a movement so conformable to his tastes, and we have a proof of it. Before his journeys he was ignorant of Italian literature; now he knows Italian, and has read the great classic authors of the Tuscan land: Boccaccio, Petrarch, and Dante. The remembrance of their works haunts him; the "Roman de la Rose" ceases to be his main literary ideal. He was acquainted with the old classics before his missions;[3] but the tone in which he speaks of them now has changed; to-day it is a tone of veneration; one should kiss their "steppes." He expresses himself about them as Petrarch did; it seems, so great is the resem-

---

[1] Letter of Boccaccio "celeberrimi nominis militi Jacopo Pizzinghe." Corazzini, "Le Lettere di Giovanni Boccaccio," Florence, 1877, 8vo, p. 195.

[2] Chaucer could not be present at the lectures of Boccaccio, who began them on Sunday, October 23, 1373; he had returned to London in May. Disease (probably diabetes) soon obliged Boccaccio to interrupt his lectures; he died in his house at Certaldo on December 21, 1375. See Cochin, in *Revue des Deux Mondes*, July 15, 1888.

[3] On his classical knowledge, see *e.g.* Koch, "Englische Studien," vol. lvii., B. A. Wise, "Influence of Statius upon Chaucer," Baltimore, 1911.

blance, as if we found in his verses an echo of the conversations they very likely had together at Padua in 1373.[1]

In the intervals between his missions Chaucer would return to London, where administrative functions had been entrusted to him. For twelve years, dating from 1374, he was comptroller of the customs, and during the ten first years he was obliged, according to his oath, to write the accounts and to draw up the rolls of the receipts with his own hand: "Ye shall swere that . . . ye shall write the rolles by your owne hande demesned."[2] To have an idea of the work this implies, one should see, at the Record Office, the immense sheets of parchment fastened together, one after the other, which constitute these rolls.[3] After having himself been present at the weighing

---

[1] This meeting, concerning which numerous discussions have taken place, did most probably happen. " I wol," says the clerk of Oxford,

> I wol yow telle a tale which that I
> Lerned at Padowe of a worthy clerk . . .
> He is now deed and nayled in his cheste . . .
> Fraunceys Petrark, the laureat poet. (" Canterb. Tales.")

Such a circumstantial reference is of a most unusual sort ; in most cases, following the example of his contemporaries, Chaucer simply says that he imitates " a book," or sometimes he refers to his models by a wrong or fancy name, such being the case with Boccaccio, whom he calls " Lollius," a name which, however, does duty also with him, at another place, for Petrarch. But on this occasion it seems as if the poet meant to preserve the memory of personal intercourse. We know besides that at that date Chaucer was not without notoriety as a poet on the Continent (Des Champs' praise is a proof of it), and that at the time when he came to Italy Petrarch was not, as usual, at Arqua, but, as Chaucer says, at Padua, where he was busy precisely with his Latin translation of Boccaccio's story of Griselda ; below, p. 333. See my " School for Ambassadors and other Essays," 1924, Appendix.

[2] " The Othe of the Comptroler of the Customes," in Thynne's " Animadversions," Chaucer Society, 1875, p. 131.

[3] None in the handwriting of Chaucer have been discovered as yet ; but some are to be seen drawn, as he was allowed to have them later, by another's hand, under his own responsibility : " per visum et testimonium Galfridi Chaucer."

and verifying of the merchandise, Chaucer entered the
name of the owner, the quality and quantity of the
produce taxed, and the amount to be collected : endless
" rekeninges ! " Defrauders were fined ; one, John Kent,
of London, having tried to smuggle some wools to
Dordrecht, the poet, poet though he was, discovered
the offence ; the wools were confiscated and sold, and
Chaucer received seventy-one pounds four shillings and
sixpence on the amount of the fine John Kent had to
pay.

Chaucer lived now in one of the towers under which
opened the gates of London. The municipality had granted
him lodgings in the Aldgate tower [1] ; his friend the philosopher and logician, Ralph Strode, lived in the same way
in rooms above " Aldrichgate " [2]; both were to quit the
place at any moment if the defence of the town rendered
it necessary. Chaucer lived there twelve years, from 1374
to 1386. There, his labour ended, he would come home
and begin his *other life*, his poet's life, reading, thinking,
remembering. Then all he had known in Italy would
return to his memory, campaniles, azure frescoes, olive
groves, sonnets of Petrarch, poems of Dante, tales of
Boccaccio ; he had brought back wherewithal to move
and to enliven " merry England " herself. Once more
in his tower, whither he returned without speaking to
any one, " domb," he says, " as any stoon," the everyday

---

[1] The lease is dated May 10, 1374 ; Furnivall, " Trial Forewords," p. 1.
Such grants of lodgings in the gates were forbidden in 1386 in consequence of
a panic (described, *e.g.*, in the " Chronicon Angliæ," Rolls, p. 370) caused by
a rumour of the coming of the French. See Riley, " Memorials of London,"
pp. 388, 489.

[2] " Dimissio Portæ de Aldgate facta Galfrido Chaucer.—Concessio de
Aldrichgate Radulphe Strode.—Sursum-redditio domorum supra Aldrichesgate
per Radulphum Strode." Among the " Fundationes et præsentationes
cantariarum . . . shoparum . . . civitati pertinentium." " Liber Albus,"
Rolls, pp. 553, 556, 557. On Ralph Strode, see Gollancz, in Transactions
of the Philological Society, June 3, 1898.

world was done with; his neighbours were to him as though they had lived at the ends of earth [1]; his real neighbours were Dante and Virgil.

He wrote during this period, and chiefly in his tower of Aldgate, the "Lyf of Seinte Cecile," 1373; the "Compleynt of Mars," 1380; a translation of Boethius in prose; the "Parlement of Foules;" "Troilus and Criseyde," 1382; the "Hous of Fame," 1383-4; the "Legend of Good Women," 1385.[2] In all these works the ideal is principally an Italian and Latin one; but, at the same time, we see some beginning of the Chaucer of the last period, who, having moved round the world of letters, will cease to look abroad, and, after the manner of his own

---

[1] Chaucer represents Jupiter's eagle, addressing him thus:

> And noght only fro fer contree
> That ther no tyding comth to thee
> But of thy verray neyghebores,
> That dwellen almost at thy dores,
> Thou herest neither that ne this;
> For whan thy labour doon al is,
> Thou gost hoom to thy hous anoon,
> Thou sittest at another boke,
> Til fully daswed is thy loke,
> And livest thus as an hermyte.

"Hous of Fame," book ii. 1. 647; "Complete Works," iii. p. 20.

[2] All these dates are merely approximative. Concerning the chronology of Chaucer's works, see Ten Brink, "Chaucer Studien," Münster, 1870; Furnivall, "Trial Forewords," 1871, Chaucer Soc.; Koch, "Chronology," Chaucer Soc., 1890; Tatlock (who dates "Troilus" before 1377), "Development and Chronology of Chaucer's Works," 1907; Skeat, "Complete Works of Chaucer," vol. i., "Life" and the introductions to each poem. "Boece" is in vol. ii. of the "Complete Works" (cf. J. Koch in "Anglia," vol. xlvi.). The "Lyf of Seinte Cecile" was transferred by Chaucer to his "Canterbury Tales," where it became the tale of the 2nd nun. The good women of the "Legend" are all love's martyrs: Dido, Ariadne, Thisbe, &c.; it was Chaucer's first attempt to write a collection of stories with a Prologue. In the Prologue Venus and Cupid reproach him with having composed poems where women and love do not appear in a favourable light, such as "Troilus" and the translation of the "Roman de la Rose," which "is an heresye ageyns my lawe." He wrote his "Legend" to make amends.

nation, dropping in a large measure foreign elements, will show himself above all and mainly an Englishman.

At this time, however, he is as yet under the charm of Southern art and of ancient models ; he does not weary of invoking and depicting the gods of Olympus. Nudity, which the image-makers of cathedrals had inflicted as a chastisement on the damned, scandalises him no more than it did the painters of Italy. He sees Venus, " untressed," reclining on her couch, " a bed of golde," clothed in transparent draperies,

> Right with a subtil kerchef of Valence,
> Ther was no thikker cloth of no defence ;

or with less draperies still:

> I saw Beautee withouten any atyr [1];

or again:

> Naked fleting in a see ;

her brows circled with a "rose-garlond white and reed." [2]
He calls her to his aid :

> Now faire blisful, O Cipris,
> So be my favour at this tyme !
> And ye, me to endyte and ryme
> Helpeth, that on Parnaso dwelle
> By Elicon the clere welle. [3]

His " Compleynt of Anelida " is dedicated to

> Thou ferse god of armes, Mars the rede,

---

[1] " Parlement of Foules," ll. 272, 225, " Complete Works," vol. i.
[2] " Hous of Fame," l. 133, *ibid.*, vol. iii.
[3] " Hous of Fame," l. 518.

and to Polymnia :

> Be favourable eek, thou Polymnia,
> On Parnaso that, with thy sustres glade,
> By Elicon, not fer from Cirrea,
> Singest with vois memorial in the shade,
> Under the laurer which that may not fade.[1]

Old books of antiquity possess for him, as they did for the learned men of the Renaissance, or for Petrarch, who cherished a manuscript of Homer without being well able to decipher it, a character almost divine :

> For out of olde feldes, as men seith,
> Cometh al this newe corn fro yeer to yere ;
> And out of olde bokes, in good feith,
> Cometh al this newe science that men lere.[2]

Poggio or Poliziano could not have spoken in more feeling words.

> Glory and honour, Virgil Mantuan,
> Be to thy name ! [3]

exclaims he elsewhere. " Go, my book," he says to his " Troilus and Criseyde,"

> And kis the steppes, wher-as thou seest pace
> Virgile, Ovyde, Omer, Lucan, Stace.[4]

Withal strange discrepancies occur : none can escape entirely the influence of his own time. With Chaucer the goddess of love is also a saint, " Seint Venus " ; her temple

---

[1] " Complete Works," vol. i. p. 365. This beginning is imitated from Boccaccio's " Teseide."

[2] " Parlement of Foules," in " Complete Works," vol. i. p. 336. Chaucer alludes here to a book which " was write with lettres olde," and which contained " Tullius of the dreme of Scipioun."

[3] " Legend of Dido," in " Complete Works," vol. iii. p. 117.

[4] Book v. st. 256.

is likewise a church : " This noble temple . . . this chirche."
Before penetrating into its precincts, the poet appeals to
Christ :

> "O Crist," thought I, " that art in blisse,
> Fro fantom and illusioun
> Me save ! " and with devocioun
> Myn yën to the heven I caste.[1]

This medley was inevitable ; to do better would have been
to excel the Italians, and Dante himself, who places the
Erinnyes within the circles of his Christian hell, or Giotto,
who made Apelles paint a triptych.

As for the Italians, Chaucer borrows from them, sometimes a line, an idea, a comparison, sometimes long passages
very closely translated, or again the plot or the general
inspiration of his tales.   In the " Lyf of Seinte Cecile " a
passage (lines 36–51) is borrowed from Dante's " Paradiso."
The same poet is quoted in the " Parlement of Foules,"
where we find a paraphrase of the famous " Per me si va "[2] ;
another passage is imitated from the " Teseide " of
Boccaccio ; " Anelida and Arcite " contains several stanzas
taken from the same original ; " Troilus and Criseyde " is
an adaptation of Boccaccio's " Filostrato " ; Chaucer introduces into it a sonnet of Petrarch[3] ; the idea of the " Legend
of Good Women " is borrowed from the " De claris Mulieribus " of Boccaccio.   Dante's journeys to the spirit-world
served as models for the " Hous of Fame," where the

---

[1] "Hous of Fame," ll. 469, 473, 492.

> [2] Thorgh me men goon in-to that blisful place . . .
> Thorgh me men goon unto the welle of Grace, &c.

These lines were "over the gate with lettres large y-wroghte," ll. 124, 127.

> [3] S'amor non è, che dunque è quel ch'i sento?

which becomes in Chaucer the " Cantus Troili " :

> If no love is, O God, what fele I so?
> (Book i. stanza 58.)

English poet is borne off by an eagle of golden hue. In it
Dante is mentioned together with the classic authors of
antiquity. Read :

> On Virgil, or on Claudian,
> Or Daunte.[1]

The eagle is not an invention of Chaucer's ; it had already
appeared in the " Purgatorio." [2]

Notwithstanding the quantity of reminiscences of ancient
or Italian authors that recur at every page ; notwithstanding
the story of Æneas related wholly from Virgil, the first
lines being translated word for word [3] ; notwithstanding
incessant allusions and quotations, the " Hous of Fame " [4]
is one of the first poems in which Chaucer shows forth
clearly his own personality. Already we see manifested
that gift for familiar dialogue which is carried so far in
" Troilus and Criseyde," and already appears that sound

[1] l. 449.

[2]
> In sogno mi parea veder sospesa
> Un' aquila nel ciel con penne d'oro
> Con l'ali aperte, ed a calare intesa. . . .
>
> Poi mi parea, che piu rotata un poco,
> Terribil come folgor discendesse,
> E me rapisse suso infino al foco.
> ("Purgatorio," canto ix.)

In Chaucer :

> Me thoughte I saw an egle sore . . .
> Hit was of golde and shoon so bright
> That never saw men such a sighte. . . .
> Me, fleinge, at a swappe he hente,
> And with his sours agayn up wente,
> Me caryinge in his clawes starke.
> (ll. 449, 503, 542.)

[3]
> I wol now singe, if that I can
> The armes, and al-so the man, &c. (l. 142.)

Hereupon follows a complete but abbreviated account of the events in the
Æneid, Dido's story being the only part treated at some length.

[4] "Complete Works," vol. iii. The poem was left unfinished ; it is written
in octosyllabic couplets, with four accents or beats,

and kindly judgment with which the poet will view the things of life in his " Canterbury Tales." Evil does not prevent his seeing good ; the sadness he has known does not make him rebel against fate ; he has suffered and forgiven ; joys dwell in his memory rather than sorrows ; despite his moments of melancholy, his turn of mind makes him an optimist at heart, an optimist like La Fontaine and Addison, whose names often recur to the memory in reading Chaucer. His philosophy resembles the " bonhomme " La Fontaine's ; and several passages in the " Hous of Fame " are like some of Addison's essays.[1]

He is modern, too, in the part he allots to his own self, a self which, far from being odious (" le moi est haïssable," Pascal said), is, on the contrary, charming ; he relates the long vigils in his tower, where he spends his nights in writing, or at other times seated before a book, which he reads until his eyes are dim in his " hermyte's " solitude.

The eagle, come from heaven to be his guide, bears him off where his fancy had already flown, above the clouds, beyond the spheres, to the temple of Fame, built upon an ice mountain. Illustrious names graven in the sparkling rock melt in the sun, and are already almost illegible. The

---

[1] Compare, for example, the beginning of "Hous of Fame," and No. 487 of *The Spectator* (Sept. 18, 1712):

> God turne us every dreem to gode !
> For hit is wonder, by the rode,
> To my wit what causeth swevenes
> Either on morwes or on evenes ;
> And why the effect folweth of somme,
> And of somme hit shal never come ;
> Why this is an avisioun,
> And this a revelacioun . . .
> Why this a fantom, these oracles.

Addison writes : " Tho' there are many authors who have written on Dreams, they have generally considered them only as revelations of what has already happened in distant parts of the world, or as presages of what is to happen in future periods of time," &c,

temple itself is built in the Gothic style of the period, all
bristling with " niches, pinnacles, and statues," and

> . . . ful eek of windowes
> As flakes falle in grete snowes.[1]

There are those rustling crowds in which Chaucer loved
to mix at times, whose murmurs soothed his thoughts,
musicians, harpists, jugglers, minstrels, tellers of tales full
"of weping and of game," magicians, sorcerers and prophets,
curious specimens of humanity. Within the temple, the
statues of his literary gods, who sang of the Trojan war:
Homer, Dares, and also the Englishman Geoffrey of
Monmouth, "English Gaufride," and with them, Virgil,
Ovid, Lucan, Claudian, and Statius. At the command
of Fame, the names of the heroes are borne by the wind
to the four corners of the world; a burst of music celebrates the deeds of the warriors:

> For in fight and blood-shedinge
> Is used gladly clarioninge.[2]

Various companies flock to obtain glory; the poet does
not forget the group, already formed in his day, of the
braggarts who boast of their vices:

> We ben shrewes, every wight,
> And han delyt in wikkednes,
> As gode folk han in goodnes ;
> And joye to be knowen shrewes . . .
> Wherfor we preyen yow, a-rowe,
> That our fame swich be-knowe
> In alle thing right as it is.[3]

As pressing as any, they urgently claim a bad reputation,
a favour which the goddess graciously grants them.

Elsewhere we are transported into the house of news,

[1] l. 1191.   [2] l. 1242.   [3] l. 1830.

noisy and surging as the public square of a populous city
on a day when "something" has happened. People
throng, and crush, and trample each other to see, although
there is nothing to see: Chaucer describes from nature.
There are assembled numbers of messengers, travellers,
pilgrims, sailors, each bearing his bag, full of news, full of
lies :

> " Nost not thou
> That is betid, lo, late or now ? "
> —" No," quod the other, " tel me what."
> And than he tolde him this and that,
> And swoor ther-to that hit was sooth—
> " Thus hath he seyd "—and " thus he dooth "—
> " Thus shal hit be "—" Thus herde I seye "—
> " That shal be found "—" That dar I leye " (state). [1]

Truth and falsehood, closely united, form an inseparable
body, and fly away together. The least little nothing,
whispered in secret in a friend's ear, grows and grows, as
in La Fontaine's fable :

> As fyr is wont to quikke and go,
> From a sparke spronge amis,
> Til al a citee brent up is.[2]

III.

Heretofore Chaucer has composed poems of brightest
hue, chiefly devoted to love, " balades, roundels, virelayes,"
imitations of the " Roman de la Rose," poems inspired by
antiquity, as it appeared through the prism of the Middle
Ages. His writings are superior to those of his English or
French contemporaries, but they are of like kind ; he has
fine passages, charming ideas, but no well-ordered work ;
his colours are fresh but crude, like the colours of illuminations, blazons, or oriflammes ; his nights are of sable, and his
meadows seem of sinople, his flowers are " whyte, blewe,

---

[1] l. 2047.   [2] l. 2078. *Cf.* La Fontaine's " Les Femmes et le Secret."

yelowe, and rede." [1] In "Troilus and Criseyde" we find another Chaucer, far more complete and powerful; he surpasses now even the Italians whom he had taken for his models, and writes the first great poem of renewed English literature.

The fortunes of Troilus had grown by degrees in the course of centuries. Homer merely mentions his name; Virgil devotes three lines to him; Dares, who has seen everything, draws his portrait; Benoit de Sainte-More is the earliest to ascribe to him a love first happy, then tragic; Guido delle Colonne gives authority to Benoit's inventions by transcribing them in Latin; Boccaccio develops the story, adds characters, and makes of it a romance, an elegant tale in which young Italian noblemen, equally handsome, amorous, and unscrupulous, win ladies' hearts, lose them, and discourse subtly about their desires and their mishaps.[2]

Chaucer appropriates the plot,[3] transforms the personages, alters the tone of the narrative, breaks the monotony of it, introduces differences of age and disposition, and moulds in his own way the material that he borrows, like a man now sure of himself, who dares to judge and to criticise; who thinks it possible to improve upon a romance even of Boccaccio's. The literary progress marked by this work is astonishing, not more so, however, than the progress accom-

[1] "Parlement of Foules," l. 186.

[2] Boccaccio's story is told in stanzas of eight lines, and has for its title "Il Filostrato" (love's victim : such was the sense Boccaccio attributed to the word). Text in "Le Opere volgari di Giov. Boccaccio," Florence, 1831, xiii.

[3] "Works," Skeat, vol. ii., variously dated by critics any year betw. 1376 and 1385. It is divided into five books and written in stanzas of seven lines, riming *a b a b b c c.* See the different texts published by the Chaucer Society; also Kittredge, "Chaucer's Language in his Troilus," Chaucer Soc., 1891. Chaucer's poem is dedicated to Gower and to "philosophical Strode" (above, p. 290). About one-third is derived from Boccaccio; some hints are taken from B. de Ste. More and Guido (XII–XIIIth cent.); see Hamilton, "Indebtedness of Chaucer's Troilus to Guido," N.Y., 1903, Rossetti "Troylus and Cressida, compared with Boccaccio's Filostrato," Chaucer Soc., 1893.

plished in the same time by the nation. With the Parliament of Westminster as with Chaucer's poetry, the real
definitive England is beginning.

In Chaucer, indeed, as in the new race, the mingling of
the origins has become intimate and indissoluble. In
"Troilus and Criseyde" the Celt's ready wit, gift of
repartee, and sense of the dramatic; the care for the form
and ordering of a narrative, dear to the Latin races; the
Norman's faculty of observation, are allied to the emotion
and tenderness of the Saxon. This fusion had been
brought about slowly; when however the time came, its
realisation was complete all at once, almost sudden.
Yesterday authors of English tongue could only lisp;
to-day, no longer content to talk, they sing.

In its semi-epic form, the poem of "Troilus and Criseyde"
is connected with the art of the novel and the art of the
drama, to the development of which England was to contribute so highly. It is already the English novel and
drama where the tragic and the comic are blended; where
the heroic and the trivial go side by side, as in real life;
where Juliet's nurse interrupts the lovers leaning over the
balcony of the Capulets, where princesses have no con-
fidants, diminished reproductions of their own selves,
invented to give them their cue; where sentiments
are examined closely, with an attentive mind, fond of
experimental psychology; and where, nevertheless, far
from holding always to subtile dissertations, all that is
material fact is clearly exposed to view, in a good
light, and not merely talked about. The vital parts of
the drama are all exhibited before our eyes and not
concealed behind the scenes; heroes are not all spirit,
neither are they mere images; we are as far from the
crude illuminations of degenerate minstrels as from La
Calprenède's heroic romances; the characters have muscles,
bones and sinews, and at the same time, hearts and souls;

they are real men.   The date of " Troilus and Criseyde"
is a great date in English literature.

The book, like Froissart's collection of poems, treats " of
love."   It relates how Criseyde, or Cressida, the daughter
of Calchas, left in Troy while her father returned to the
Greek camp, loves the handsome knight Troilus, son of
Priam.   Given back to the Greeks, she forgets Troilus,
who is slain.

How came this young woman, as virtuous as she was
beautiful, to love this youth, whom at the opening of the
story she did not even know?   What external circumstances brought them together, and what workings of the
heart made them pass from indifference to doubts and
anxieties, and then to love?   These two orders of
thought are untwined simultaneously, on parallel lines
by Chaucer, that dreamer who had lived so much in
real life, that man of action who had dreamed so many
dreams.

Troilus despised love, and mocked at lovers :

> If knight or squyer of his companye
> Gan for to syke, or lete his eyen bayten
> On any woman that he coude aspye;
> He wolde smyle, and holden it folye,
> And seye him thus, " God wot she slepeth softe
> For love of thee, whan thou tornest ful ofte." [1]

One day, in the temple, he sees Cressida, and his fate is
sealed ; he cannot remove his gaze from her; the wind
of love has swept by ; all his strength has vanished ;
his pride has fallen as the petals fall from a rose ; he
drinks deep draughts of an invincible poison.   Far from
her, his imagination completes what reality had begun :
seated on the foot of his bed, absorbed in thought, he once
more sees Cressida, and sees her so beautiful, depicted in
outlines so vivid, and colours so glowing, that this divine

[1] Book i. st. 28.

image fashioned in his own brain is henceforth the only
one he will behold ; forever will he have before his eyes
that celestial form of superhuman beauty, never more the
real earthly Cressida, the frail daughter of Calchas. Troilus
is ill for life of the love illness.

He has a friend, older than himself, sceptical, trivial,
experienced, " that called was Pandare," Cressida's uncle.
He confides to him his woes, and asks for help. Pandarus,
in Boccaccio, is a young nobleman, sceptical too, but
frivolous, disdainful, elegant, like a personage of Musset.
Chaucer transforms the whole drama and makes room for
the grosser realities of life, by altering the character of
Pandarus.   He makes of him a man of mature years,
devoid of scruples, talkative, shameless, wily, whose
wisdom consists in proverbs chosen among the easiest
to follow, much more closely connected with Molière's
or Shakespeare's comic heroes than with Musset's lovers.
Pandarus is as fond of comparisons as Gros-René, as fond
of old saws as Polonius ; he is coarse and indecent, unin-
tentionally and by nature, like Juliet's nurse.[1] He is totally
unconscious, and thinks himself the best friend in the
world, and the most reserved ; he concludes interminable
speeches by :

> I jape nought, as ever have I joye.

Every one of his thoughts, of his words, of his attitudes is
the very opposite of Cressida's and her lover's, and makes
them stand out in relief by a contrast of shade.   He is all

---

[1] And, as the nurse, gets out of breath, so that he cannot speak :

> . . . O veray God, so have I ronne !
> Lo, nece myn, see ye nought how I swete?

Book ii. st. 210.   Says the Nurse :

> Jesu, what haste ! can you not stay awhile ?
> Do you not see that I am out of breath ?

for tangible and present realities, and does not believe in ever foregoing an immediate and certain pleasure in consideration of merely possible consequences.

With this disposition, and in this frame of mind, he approaches his niece to speak to her of love. The scene, which is entirely of Chaucer's invention, is a true comedy scene ; the gestures and attitudes are minutely noted. Cressida looks down ; Pandarus coughs. The dialogue is so rapid and sharp that one might think this part written for a play, not for a tale in verse. The uncle arrives ; the niece, seated with a book on her knees, was reading a romance.

Ah! you were reading! What book was it? "What seith it? Tel it us. Is it of Love?" It was of Thebes; "this romaunce is of Thebes[1];"she had secured as it seems a very early copy. She excuses herself for indulging in so frivolous a pastime; she would perhaps do better to read "on holy seyntes lyves." Chaucer, mindful above all of the analysis of passions, does not trouble himself about anachronisms; he cares nothing to know if the besieged Trojans could really have drawn examples of virtue from the Lives of the Saints; history matters little to him : let those who take an interest in it look "in Omer or in Dares." The motions of the human heart, that is his real subject, not the march of armies; from the moment of its birth, the English novel is psychological.

With a thousand precautions, and although still keeping to the vulgarity of his rôle, Pandarus manages so as to bring to a sufficiently serious mood the laughter-loving Cressida;

[1] Turned later into English verse by Lydgate, to be read as a supplementary Tale of Canterbury : "Here begynneth the sege of Thebes, ful lamentably told by Johnn Lidgate monke of Bury, annexynge it to ye tallys of Canterbury," MS. Royal 18 D ii. in the British Museum. The exquisite miniatures of this MS. represent Thebes besieged with great guns, fol. 158; Creon's coronation by two bishops wearing mitres and gold copes, fol. 160, see below, p. 499.

he contrives that she shall praise Troilus herself, incidentally, before he has even named him.   With his frivolities
he mingles serious matter, wise and practical advice like
a good uncle, the better to inspire confidence; then he
rises to depart without having yet said what brought him.
Cressida's interest is excited at once, the more so that
reticence is not habitual to Pandarus ; her curiosity,
irritated from line to line, becomes anxiety, almost
anguish, for though Cressida be of the fourteenth century,
and the first of a long line of heroines of romance, with her
appears already the nervous woman.   She starts at the
least thing, she is the most impressionable of beings, " the
ferfullest wight that might be " ;   even the state of the
atmosphere affects her.   What is then the matter ?   Oh !
only this :

> . . . the kinges dere sone,
> The goode, wyse, worthy, fresshe, and free,
> Which alwey for to do wel is his wone,
> The noble Troilus, so loveth thee,
> That, bot ye helpe, it wol his bane be.
> Lo, here is al, what sholde I more seye?
> Do what yow list.[1]

The conversation continues, more and more crafty on the
part of Pandarus ; his friend asks for so little : look less
unkindly upon him, and it will be enough.

But here appears Chaucer's art in all its subtilty.   The
wiles of Pandarus, carried as far as his character will allow,
might have sufficed to make a Cressida of romance yield ;
but it would have been too easy play for the master already
sure of his powers.   He makes Pandarus say a word too
much ; Cressida unmasks him on the spot, obliges him to
acknowledge that in asking less he desired more for his
friend, and now she is blushing and indignant.   Chaucer
does not want her to yield to disquisitions and descriptions;

[1] Book ii. st. 46.

all the cleverness of Pandarus is there only to make us better appreciate the slow inward working that is going on in Cressida's heart ; her uncle will have sufficed to stir her ; that is all, and, truth to say, that is something. She feels for Troilus no clearly defined sentiment, but her curiosity is aroused. And just then, while the conversation is still going on, loud shouts are heard, the crowd rushes, balconies are filled, strains of music burst forth ; 'tis the return, after a victorious sally, of one of the heroes who defend Troy. This hero is Troilus, and in the midst of this triumphal scene, the pretty, frail, laughing, tender-hearted Cressida beholds for the first time her royal lover.

In her turn she dreams, she meditates, she argues. She is not yet, like Troilus, love's prisoner ; Chaucer does not proceed so fast. She keeps her vision lucid ; her imagination and her senses have not yet done their work and reared before her that glittering phantom, ever present, which conceals reality from lovers. She is still mistress of herself enough to discern motives and objections ; she discusses and reviews elevated reasons, low reasons, and even some of those practical reasons which will be instantly dismissed, but not without having produced their effect. Let us not make an enemy of this king's son. Besides, can I prevent his loving me ? His love has nothing un-flattering ; is he not the first knight of Troy after Hector ? What is there astonishing in his passion for me ? If he loves me, shall I be the only one to be loved in Troy ? Scarcely, for

> Men loven wommen al this toun aboute.
> Be they the wers ? Why, nay, withouten doute.

Am I not pretty ? " I am oon of the fayrest " in all " the toun of Troye," though I should not like people to know that I know it :

> Al wolde I that noon wistë of this thought.

21

After all I am free; " I am myn owene woman"; no husband to say to me "chekmat!" And "*par dieux!* I am nought religious!" I am not a nun.

> But right as whan the sonne shyneth brighte
> In March that chaungeth ofte tyme his face
> And that a cloud is put with wind to flighte
> Which over-sprat the sonne as for a space,
> A cloudy thought gan thorugh hir soule pace,
> That over-spradde hir brighte thoughtes alle.[1]

Now she unfolds contradictory arguments supported by considerations equally decisive; she is suffering from that *diboulia* (alternate will) familiar to lovers who are not yet thoroughly in love. There are two Cressidas in her; the dialogue begun with Pandarus is continued in her heart; the scene of comedy is renewed there in a graver key.

Her decision is not taken; when will it be? At what precise moment does love begin? One scarcely knows; when it has come one fixes the date in the past by hypothesis. We say: it was that day, but when that day was the present day, we said nothing, and knew nothing; a sort of "perhaps" filled the soul, delightful, but still only a perhaps. Cressida is in that obscure period, and the workings within her are shown by the impression which the incidents of daily life produce upon her mind. It seems to her that everything speaks of love, and that fate is in league against her with Pandarus and Troilus: it is but an appearance, the effect of her own imagination, and produced by her state of mind; in reality it happens simply that now the little incidents of life impress her more when they relate to love; the others pass so unperceived that love alone has a place. She might have felt anxious about herself if she had discerned this difference between then and now; but the blindness has commenced, she does not observe that the things appertaining to love find easy

[1] Book ii. st. 100 ff.

access to her heart, and that, where one enters so easily, it is usually that the door is open. She paces in her melancholy mood the gardens of the palace ; while she wanders through the shady walks, a young girl sings a song of passion, the words of which stir Cressida to her very soul. Night falls,

> And whyte thinges wexen dimme and donne ;

the stars begin to light the heavens ; Cressida returns pensive ; the murmurs of the city die out. Leaning at her window, facing the blue horizon of Troas, with the trees of the garden at her feet, and bathed in the pale glimmers of the night, Cressida dreams, and as she dreams a melody disturbs the silence : hidden in the foliage of a cedar, a nightingale is heard ; they too, the birds, celebrate love. And when sleep comes, of what will she think in her dreams if not of love?

She is moved, but not vanquished ; it will take yet many incidents ; they will all be small, trivial, insignificant, and will appear to her solemn, superhuman, ordered by the gods. She may recover, at times, before Pandarus, her presence of mind, her childlike laugh, and baffle his wiles : for the double-story continues. Cressida is still able to unravel the best-laid schemes of Pandarus, but she is less and less able to unravel the tangled web of her own sentiments. The meshes draw closer ; now she promises a sisterly friendship : even that had been already invented in the fourteenth century. She can no longer see Troilus without blushing ; he passes and bows : how handsome he is !

> . . . She hath now caught a thorn ;
> She shal not pulle it out this nexte wyke.
> God sende mo swich thornes on to pyke ! [1]

The passion and merits of Troilus, the inventions of

[1] Book ii. st. 182.

Pandarus, the secret good-will of Cressida, a thunderstorm which breaks out opportunely (we know how impressionable Cressida is), lead to the result which might be expected: the two lovers are face to face. Troilus, like a sensitive hero, swoons: for he is extremely sensitive; when the town acclaims him, he blushes and looks down; when he thinks his beloved indifferent he takes to his bed from grief, and remains there all day; in the presence of Cressida, he loses consciousness. Pandarus revives him, and is not slow to perceive that he is no longer wanted:

> For ought I can espyen
> This light nor I ne serven here of nought.

And he goes, adding, however, one more recommendation:

> If ye ben wyse,
> Swowneth not now, lest more folk aryse.[1]

What says Cressida?—What may "the sely larke seye" when "the sparhauk" has caught it? Cressida, however, says something, and, of all the innumerable forms of avowal, chooses not the least sweet:

> Ne hadde I er now, my swete herte dere
> Ben yolde, y-wis, I were now not here![2]

Were they happy?

> But juggeth, ye that han ben at the feste
> Of swich gladnesse.[3]

The gray morn appears in the heavens; the shriek of "the cok, comune astrologer," is heard; the lovers sing their song of dawn.[4] All the virtues of Troilus are increased and

---

[1] Book III. st. 163 and 170.

[2] Book III. st. 173. Boccaccio's Griseida knows none of those nuances of feeling and tenderness. She laughs at newly-wedded maids, and ignores blushes as well as doubts ("Filostrato," III. st. 29 ff.).

[3] Book III. st. 188.

> [4] What me is wo
> That day of us mot make desseveraunce!
>
> (Book III. st. 203, 204.)

intensified by happiness; it is the eternal thesis of poets who are in love with love.

The days and weeks go by: each one of our characters pursues his part. Pandarus is very proud of his; what could one reproach him with? He does unto others as he would be done by; he is disinterested; he has moreover certain principles of honour, that limit themselves, it is true, to recommending secrecy, which he does not fail to do. Can a reasonable woman expect more?

Calchas and the Greeks claim Cressida, and the Trojans decide to give her up. The unhappy young woman faints, but must needs submit. In an excellent scene of comedy, Chaucer shows her receiving the congratulations of the good souls of the town: so she is going to see once more her worthy father, how happy she must be! The good souls insist very much, and pay interminable visits.[1]

She goes, swearing to return, come what may, within ten days. The handsome Diomedes escorts her; and the event proves, what experience alone could teach, and what she was herself far from suspecting, that she loved Troilus, no doubt, above all men, but likewise, and apart from him, love. She is used to the poison, and can no longer do without it; she prefers Troilus, but to return to him is not so easy as she had thought, and to love or not to love is now for her a question of being or being not. Troilus, who from the start had most awful presentiments, feeling that, happen what may, his happiness is over, though yet not doubting Cressida, writes the most pressing letters, and signs them in French, " le vostre T." Cressida replies by little short letters (that she signs " la vostre C."), in which she excuses herself for her brevity. The length of a letter means nothing; besides she never liked to write, and where she is now it is not convenient to do it; let Troilus rest easy, he can count upon her friendship, she will surely

[1] Book iv. st. 98 ff.

return ; true, it will not be in ten days ; it will be when she can.[1]

Troilus is told of his misfortune, but he will never believe it :

> ." Thou seyst nat sooth," quod he, " thou sorceresse !"

A brooch torn from Diomedes which he had given her on the day of parting,

> In remembraunce of him and of his sorwe,

allows him to doubt no more, and he gets killed by Achilles after a furious struggle.

As we have drawn nearer to the catastrophe, the tone of the poem has become more melancholy and more tender. The narrator cannot help loving his two heroes, even the faithless Cressida ; he remains at least merciful for her, and out of mercy, instead of letting us behold her near as formerly, in the alleys or on her balcony, dreaming in the starlight, he shows her only from afar, lost among the crowd in which she has chosen to mix, the crowd in every sense, the crowd of mankind and the crowd of sentiments, all commonplace. Let us, he thinks, remember only the former Cressida.

He ends with reflections which are resigned, almost sad, and he contemplates with a tranquil look the juvenile passions he has just depicted. Troilus, resigned too, beholds, from heaven, the field under the walls of Troy,

> [1] Yet preye I yow on yvel ye ne take,
> That it is short which that I to yow wryte ;
> I dar not, ther I am, wel lettres make,
> Ne never yet ne coude I wel endyte.
> Eek greet effect men wryte in place lyte.
> Thentente is al, and nought the lettres space
> And fareth now wel, God have you in his grace.
>   La vostre C.

Book v. st. 233. Troilus had written at great length, of course, "the papyr al y-pleynted." St. 229.

where he was slain, and smiles at the remembrance of his miseries ; and Chaucer, transforming Boccaccio's conclusion like all the rest, addresses a touching appeal, and wise, even religious advice, to you,

O yonge fresshe folkes, he or she,
In which that love up groweth with your age.[1]

This return to seriousness is quite as noteworthy as the mixture of everyday life, added by the poet to the idea borrowed from his model. By these two traits, which will be seen again from century to century, in English literature, Chaucer manifests his true English character ; and if we wish to see precisely in what consists the difference between this temperament and that of the men of the South, whom Chaucer was nevertheless so akin to, let us compare this conclusion with that of the " Filostrato " as translated at the same time into French by Pierre de Beauveau: " You will not believe lightly those who give you ear ; young women are wilful and lovely, and admire their own beauty, and hold themselves haughty and proud amidst their lovers, for vain-glory of their youth ; who, although they be gentle and pretty more than tongue can say, have neither sense nor firmness, but are variable as a leaf in the wind." Unlike Chaucer, Pierre de Beauveau contents himself with such graceful moralisation,[2] which

[1] Book v. st. 263.

[2] Pierre de Beauveau's translation of the passage (in Moland and d'Héricault, " Nouvelles françoises en prose, du XIVe Siècle," 1858, p. 303) does not differ much from the original. Here is the Italian text :

Giovane donna è mobile, e vogliosa
È negli amanti molti, e sua bellezza
Estima piu ch'allo specchio, e pomposa
Ha vanagloria di sua giovinezza ;
La qual quanto piaccevole e vezzosa
È piu, cotanto più seco l'apprezza ;
Virtù non sente ni conoscimento,
Volubil sempre come foglia al vento.

(" Opere Volgari," Florence, 1831, vol. xiii. p. 253.)

will leave no very deep impression on the mind, and which indeed could not, for it is itself as light as "a leaf in the wind."

IV.

After 1379 Chaucer ceased to journey on the Continent, and until his death he lived in England an English life. He saw then several aspects of that life which he had not yet known from personal experience. After having been page, soldier, prisoner of the French, squire to the king, negotiator in Flanders, France, and Italy, he entered Westminster the 1st of October, 1386, as member of Parliament; the county of Kent had chosen for its representatives: "Willielmus Betenham" and "Galfridus Chauceres."[1] It was one of the great sessions of the reign, and one of the most stormy; the ministers of Richard II. were impeached, and among others the son of the Hull wool merchant, Michel de la Pole, Chancellor of the kingdom. For having remained faithful to his protectors, the king and John of Gaunt, Chaucer, looked upon with ill favour by the men then in power, of whom Gloucester was the head, lost his places and fell into want. Then the wheel of Fortune revolved, and new employments offered a new field to his activity. At the end of three years, Richard, having dismissed the Council which Parliament had imposed upon him, took the authority into his own hands, and the poet, soldier, member of Parliament, and diplomat, was appointed clerk of the royal works (1389). For two years he had to attend to the constructions and repairs at Westminster, at the Tower, at Berkhamsted, Eltham, Sheen, at St. George's Chapel, Windsor, and in many others of those castles which he

[1] "Return of the names of every member [of Parliament]," 1878, fol. a Blue Book, p. 229.

had described, with "pinacles, imageries, and tabernacles," and

> ful eek of windowes
> As flakes falle in grete snowes.[1]

His great literary occupation, during that time, was the composition of his famous "Canterbury Tales."[2] Experience had ripened him ; he had read all there was to read, and seen all there was to see ; he had visited the principal countries where civilisation had developed: he had observed his compatriots at work on their estates and in their parliaments, in their palaces and in their shops. Merchants, sailors, knights, pages, learned men of Oxford and suburban quacks, men of the people and men of the Court, labourers, citizens, monks, priests, sages and fools, heroes and knaves, had passed in crowds beneath his scrutinising gaze ; he had associated with them, divined them, and understood them ; he was prepared to describe them all.

On an April day, in the reign of Richard II., in the noisy suburb of Southwark, the place for departures and arrivals, with streets bordered with inns, encumbered with horses and carts, resounding with cries, calls, and barks, one of those mixed troops, such as the hostelries of that time often gathered together, seats itself at the common board, in the hall of the " Tabard, faste by the Belle"[3] ; the inns were all close to each other. It was springtime, the season of fresh flowers, the season of love, the season, too, of pilgrimages. Knights returned from the wars go to render thanks to the saints for having let them

---

[1] "Hous of Fame," l. 1189.

[2] "Complete Works," ed. Skeat, Oxford, 1894, 7 vols. 8vo, vol. iv.

[3] The " Tabard," a sleeveless overcoat, then in general use, was, like the " Bell," a frequent sign for inns. The Tabard Inn, famous in Chaucer's day, was situated in the Southwark High Street. Often repaired and restored, rebaptized the "Talbot," it lasted till the nineteenth century.

behold again their native land ; invalids render thanks for their restoration to health ; others go to ask Heaven's grace. Does not every one need it ? Every one is there ; all England.

There is a knight who has warred, all Europe over, against heathens and Saracens. It was easy to meet them ; they might be found in Prussia and in Spain, and our "verray parfit gentil knight" had massacred enormous numbers of them " at mortal batailles fiftene " for " our faith." Next to him, a squire who had, like Chaucer, fought in France, with May in his heart, a song upon his lips, amorous, elegant, charming, embroidered as a meadow —"as it were a mede "—with white and red flowers ; a stout merchant, who looked so rich, was so well furred, and "fetisly" dressed that

> Ther wiste no wight that he was in dette;

a modest clerk, who had come from the young University of Oxford, poor, patched, threadbare, with hollow cheeks, mounted on a lean horse, and whose little all consisted in

> Twenty bokes, clad in blak and reed ;

an honest country franklin, with " sangwyn " visage and beard white " as is the dayesye," a sort of fourteenth-century Squire Western, kindly, hospitable, good-humoured, holding open table, with fish and roasts and *sauce piquante* and beer all day long, so popular in the county that,

> Ful ofte tyme he was knight of the shire ;

a shipman who knew every creek, from Scotland to Spain, and had encountered many a storm, with his good ship " the Maudelayne,"

> With many a tempest hadde his berd been shake ;

a physician who had driven a thriving trade during the
plague, learned, and acquainted with the why and the
wherefore of every disease,

> Were it of hoot or cold, or moiste or drye ;

who knew by heart Hippocrates and Galen, but was on
bad terms with the Church, for

> His studie was but litel on the Bible.

With them, a group of working men from London, a
haberdasher, a carpenter, dyer, weaver, and cook ; people
from the country, a ploughman, a miller,

> His mouth as greet was as a great forneys,

a group of men-at-law devoured with cares, close shaven,
bitter of speech—

> Ful longe were his legges, and ful lene,
> Y-lyk a staf, ther was no calf y-sene—

bringing out their Latin on every occasion, terrible as
adversaries, but easy to win over for money, and after all,
as Chaucer himself says, "les meilleurs fils du monde":

> A bettre felawe sholde men noght finde.

Then a group of Church-folk, men and women, of every
garb and every character, from the poor parish priest, who
lives like a saint, obscure and hidden, visiting, in rain and
cold, the scattered cottages of his peasants, forgetting to
receive his tithes, a model of abnegation, to the hunting
monk, dressed like a layman, big, fat, with a head as shiny
as a ball, who will make one day the finest abbot in the
world, to the degenerate friar, who lives at the expense
of others, physician become poisoner, who destroys souls
instead of healing them, and to the pardoner, a rascal

of low degree, who bestows heaven at random by his own
" heigh power" on whoever will pay, and who manufac-
tures precious relics out of pieces from his " old breech."
Finally there are nuns, reserved, quiet, neat as ermines,
who are going to hear on the way enough to scandalise
them all the rest of their lives. Among them, Madame
Eglantine, the prioress, with her French of Stratford,

For Frensh of Paris was to hir unknowe,

who imitated the style of the Court, and, consequently,

Ne wette hir fingres in hir sauce depe.

She was "so pitous" that she wept to see a mouse caught,
or if one of her little dogs died. Can one be more
"pitous"?

All those personages there were, and many more besides.
There was the Wife of Bath, that incomparable gossip,
screaming all the louder as she was " som-del deef." There
was the jovial host, Harry Bailey, used to govern and
command, and to drown with his brazen voice the tumult
of the common table. There is also a person who looks
thoughtful and kindly, who talks little but observes
everything, and who is going to immortalise the most
insignificant words pronounced, screamed, grumbled, or
murmured by his companions of a day, namely, Chaucer
himself. With its adventurers, its rich merchants, its
Oxford clerks, its members of Parliament, its workmen,
its labourers, its saints, its great poet, it is indeed the
new England, joyous, noisy, radiant, all youthful and full
of life, that sits down, this April evening, at the board of
" the Tabard faste by the Belle." Where are now the
Anglo-Saxons? But where are the last year's snows?
April has come.

The characters of romance, the statues on cathedrals, the

figures in missals, had mostly been heretofore lank and
lean, or awkward or stiff; especially those due to English
craftsmen. Owing to one or the other of these traits, such
representations were not true to nature. Now we have, in
an English poem, a number of human beings, drawn from
the original, whose movements are supple, whose types are
as varied as in real life, depicted exactly as they were in
their sentiments and in their dress, so that it seems we
see them, and when we part the connection is not broken.
The acquaintances made at "the Tabard faste by the Belle"
are not of those that can be forgotten ; they are life-long
remembrances.

Nothing is omitted which can serve to fix, to anchor in
our memory, the vision of these personages. A half-line,
that unveils the salient trait of their characters, becomes
impossible to forget ; their attitudes, their gestures, their
clothes, their warts, the tones of their voices, their defects
of pronunciation—

Somwhat he lipsed for his wantonnesse—

their peculiarities, the host's red face and the reeve's
yellow one, their elegances, their arrows with peacock
feathers, their bagpipes, nothing is left out ; their horses
and the way they ride them are described ; Chaucer even
peeps inside their bags and tells us what he finds there.

So the new England has its Froissart, who is going to
tell feats of arms and love stories glowing with colour, and
take us hither and thither, through highways and byways,
giving ear to every tale, observing, noting, relating? This
young country has Froissart and better than Froissart.
The pictures are as vivid and as clear, but two great
differences distinguish the ones from the others : humour
and sympathy. Already we find humour well developed
in Chaucer ; his sly jests penetrate deeper than French
jests ; he does not go so far as to wound, but he does more

than merely prick skin-deep ; and in so doing, he laughs
silently to himself.   There was once a merchant,

That riche was, for which men helde him wys.[1]

The " Sergeant of Lawe " was a busy man indeed :

No wher so bisy a man as he ther nas,
And yet he semed bisier than he was.

Moreover, Chaucer sympathises ; he has a quivering
heart that tears move, and that all sufferings touch, those
of the poor and those of princes.   The rôle of the people,
so marked in English literature, affirms itself here, from
the first moment.   " There are some persons," says, for
his justification, a French author, " who think it beneath
them to bestow a glance on what opinion has pronounced
ignoble ; but those who are a little more philosophic, who
are a little less the dupes of the distinctions that pride
has introduced into the affairs of this world, will not be
sorry to see the sort of man there is inside a coach-
man, and the sort of woman inside a petty shopkeeper."
Thus, by a great effort of audacity, as it seems to him,
Marivaux expresses himself in 1731.[2]   Chaucer, even in
the fourteenth century, is curious to see the sort of man a
cook of London may be, and the sort of woman a Wife of
Bath is.   How many wretches perish in Froissart !   What
blood ; what hecatombs ; and how few tears !   Scarcely
here and there, and far apart, words absently spoken about
so much suffering : " And died the common people of
hunger, which was great pity." [3]   Why lament long, or
marvel at it ?   It is the business and proper function of
the common people to be cut to pieces ; they are the raw

---

[1] Beginning of the " Shipmannes Tale."
[2] " Vie de Marianne," Paris, 1731–41.
[3] Book i. chap. 81, Luce's edition.

material of feats of arms, and as such only figure in the narrative.

They figure in Chaucer's narrative, because Chaucer *loves* them; he loves his plowman, "a true swinker and a good," who has strength enough and to spare in his two arms, and helps his neighbours for nothing; the poet suffers at the thought of the muddy lanes along which his poor parson must go in winter, through the rain, to visit a distant cottage. His sympathy is broad; he loves, as he hates, with all his heart.

One after another, all these persons of such diverse conditions have gathered together, twenty-nine in all. For a few days they have the same object in view, and are going to live a common life. Fifty-six miles from London is the shrine, famous through all Europe, which contains the remains of Henry the Second's former adversary, the Archbishop Thomas Becket, assassinated in his cathedral, and canonised.[1] Mounted each on his steed, either good or bad, the knight on a beast sturdy, though of indifferent appearance; the hunting monk on a superb palfrey, "as broun as is a berye"; the Wife of Bath sitting astride her horse, armed with great spurs and showing her red stockings, they set out, taking with them mine host of the "Tabard," and there they go, at an easy pace, along the sunny road lined with hedges, among the gentle undulations of the soil. They will cross the Medway; they will pass beneath the walls of Rochester's gloomy keep, then one of the principal fortresses of the kingdom, but sacked recently by revolted peasantry; they will see the cathedral built a little lower down, and, as it were, in its shade. There are women and bad riders in the group; the miller has drunk too much, and can hardly sit

---

[1] The canonisation took place shortly after the death of the archbishop, 1170–73. See Dean Stanley, "Historical Memorials of Canterbury," ch. iv. ; "English Wayfaring Life," 1920, pp, 348 ff.

in the saddle; the way will be long.[1] To make it seem
short, each one will relate two tales, and the troop, on its
return, will honour by a supper the best teller.

Under the shadow of great romances, shorter stories
had sprung up. The forest of romance was now losing
its leaves, and the stories were expanding in the sunlight.
The most celebrated collection was Boccaccio's, written in
delightful Italian prose, a many-sided work, edifying and
licentious at the same time, a work audacious in every way,
even from a literary point of view. Boccaccio knew it,
and justified his doings. To those who reproached him
with having busied himself with "trifles," neglecting "the
Muses of Parnassus," he replied : Who knows whether I
have neglected them so very much ? "Perhaps, while I
wrote those tales of such humble mien, they may have
come sometimes and seated themselves at my side."[2]
They bestowed the same favour on Chaucer.

The idea of "Troilus and Criseyde," borrowed from
Boccaccio, had been transformed ; the general plan and
the setting of the "Tales" are modified more profoundly
yet. In Boccaccio, it is always young noblemen and ladies
who talk : seven young ladies, "all of good family, beautiful, elegant, and virtuous," and three young men, "all three
affable and elegant," whom the misfortunes of the time
"did not affect so much as to make them forget their
amours." The great plague has broken out in Florence ;
they seek a retreat "wherein to give themselves up to
mirth and pleasure"; they fix upon a villa half-way to
Fiesole, now villa Palmieri.

"A fine large court, disposed in the centre, was sur-

---

[1] A map of the road from London to Canterbury, drawn in the seventeenth
century, but showing the line of the old highway, has been reproduced by
Dr. Furnivall in his "Supplementary Canterbury Tales—I. The Tale of
Beryn," Chaucer Society, 1876, 8vo.

[2] "E forse a queste cose scrivere, quantunque sieno umilissime, si sono elle
venute parecchi volte a starsi meco." Prologue of "Giornata Quarta."

rounded by galleries, halls and chambers all ornamented with the gayest paintings. The dwelling-house rose in the midst of meadows and magnificent gardens, watered by cool streams ; the cellars were full of excellent wines." Every one is forbidden, " whencesoever he may come, or whatever he may hear or see, to bring hither any news from without that be not agreeable." They seat themselves "in a part of the garden which the foliage of the trees rendered impenetrable to the sun's rays," at the time when, "the heat being in all its strength, one heard nothing save the cicadæ singing among the olive-trees." Thanks to the stories they relate to each other, they pleasantly forget the scourge which threatens them, and the public woe ; yonder it is death ; here they play.

Chaucer has chosen for himself a plan more humane, and truer to nature. It is not enough for him to saunter each day from a palace to a garden ; he is not content with an alley, he must have a road. He puts his whole troop of narrators in motion ; he stops them at the inns, takes them to drink at the public-houses, obliges them to hurry their pace when evening comes, causes them to make acquaintance with the passers-by. His people move, bestir themselves, listen, talk, scream, sing, exchange compliments, sometimes blows ; for if his knights are real knights, his millers are real millers, who swear and strike as in a mill.

The interest of each tale is doubled by the way in which it is told, and even by the way it is listened to. The knight delights his audience, which the monk puts to sleep and the miller causes to laugh ; one is heard in silence, the other is interrupted at every word. Each story is followed by a scene of comedy, lively, quick, unexpected, and amusing ; they discuss, they approve, they lose their tempers ; no strict rules, but all the independence of the high-road, and the unforeseen of real life ; we are not sauntering in alleys ! Mine host himself, with his deep voice and his peremptory

22

decisions, does not always succeed in making himself obeyed. After the knight's tale, he would like another in the same style to match it; but he will have to listen to the miller's, which, on the contrary, will serve as a contrast. He insists ; the miller shouts, he shouts "in Pilates vois," he threatens to leave them all and "go his wey" if they prevent him from talking. "Wel," says the host,

> " Tel on, a devel wey !
> Thou art a fool, thy wit is overcome."

What would Donna Pampinea and Donna Filomena have said, hearing such words ?

At other times the knight is obliged to interfere, and then the tone is very different. He does not have to scream ; a word from him is enough, and the storms are calmed. Moreover, the host himself becomes more gentle at times ; this innkeeper knows whom he has to deal with ; with all his bluntness, he has a rude notion of differences and distances. His language is the language of an innkeeper; Chaucer never commits the fault of making him step out of his rôle ; but the poet is too keen an observer not to discern *nuances* even in the temper of a jovial host. One should see with what politeness and what salutations and what embarrassed compliments he informs the abbess that her turn has come to relate a story :

> " My lady Prioresse, by your leve,
> So that I wist I sholde yow nat greve,
> I wolde demen that ye telle sholde
> A tale next, if so were that ye wolde.
> Now wol ye vouche-sauf, my lady dere ? "
> —" Gladly," quod she, and seyde as ye shal here.

The answer is not less suitable than the request.

Thus, in these little scenes, we see, put into action, the descriptions of the prologue ; the portraits step out of their frames and come down into the street ; their limbs have become at once supple and active ; the blood courses through their veins; life fills them to the end of their fingers. No sooner are they on their feet than they turn somersaults or make courtesies; and by their words they charm, enliven, edify, or scandalise. Their personality is so accentuated that it makes them unmanageable at times; their temper rules them; they are not masters of their speech. The friar wants to tell a story, but he is so blinded by anger that he does not know what he is saying; he stammers, he chokes, and his narrative remains shape-less; the pardoner is so closely bound to his profession that he cannot for a moment move out of it; shirt and skin make one, to use a familiar phrase of Montaigne's; his tale resembles a sermon, and he concludes as though he were in church:

> Now, goode men, God forgeve yow your trespas . . .
> I have relikes and pardon in my male
> As faire as any man in Engelond . . .
> It is an honour to everich that is heer,
> That ye mowe have a suffisant pardoneer
> Tassoille yow, in contree as ye ryde,
> For aventures which that may bityde.
> Peraventure ther may falle oon or two
> Doun of his hors, and breke his nekke atwo.
> Look what a seuretee is it to yow alle
> That I am in your felaweship y-falle,
> That may assoille yow, bothe more and lasse,
> Whan that the soule shal fro the body passe.
> I rede that our hoste heer shal biginne,
> For he is most envoluped in sinne.
> Com forth sir hoste, and offre first anon,
> And thou shalt kisse the reliks everichon,
> Ye, for a grote! unbokel anon thy purs ! [1]

A most happy idea! Mine host makes a reply which cannot be repeated.

In other cases the personage is so wordy and impetuous that it is impossible to stop him, or set him right, or inter-rupt him; he cannot make up his mind to launch into his

[1] "Pardoner's Tale," ll. 904, 920, 931.

narrative ; he must needs remain himself on the stage and talk about his own person and belongings ; he alone is a whole comedy.   One must perforce keep silence when the Wife of Bath begins to talk, irresistible gossip, chubby-faced, over-fed, ever-buzzing, inexhaustible in speech, never-failing in arguments, full of glee.   She talks about what she knows, about her specialty ; her specialty is matrimony ; she has had five husbands, "three of hem were gode and two were badde ; " the last is still living, but she is already thinking of the sixth, because she does not like to wait, and because husbands are perishable things ; they do not last long with her ; in her eyes the weak sex is the male sex.   She is not going to break her heart about a husband who gives up the ghost ; her conscience is easy ; the spouse departs quite ready for a better world :

> By God, in erthe I was his purgatorie,
> For which I hope his soule be in glorie.

Some praise celibacy, or reason about husbands' rights ; the merry gossip will answer them.   She discusses the matter thoroughly ; sets forth the pros and cons ; allows her husband to speak, then speaks herself ; she has the best arguments in the world ; her husband, too, has ex-cellent ones, but it is she who has the very best.   She is a whole *École des Maris* in herself.

The tales are of every sort,[1] and taken from everywhere.

---

[1] The setting of the tales into their most likely order (contested since on some points, *e.g.*, by S. Moore), is due to Bradshaw and Furnivall ; see Furnivall's "Temporary Preface" for the "Six-text edition of Chaucer's Canterbury Tales," Chaucer Society, 1868.   The order, subject, and originals of the tales are as follows :—

1st Day.   London to Dartford, 15 miles.—Tale of the Knight, history of Palamon and Arcyte, derived from Boccaccio's "Teseide."—Tale of the Miller : story of Absolon, Nicholas and Alisoun the carpenter's wife, source unknown.—Reeve's tale, imitated from the French fabliau of Gombert and the two clerks (above, p. 155) ; same tale in Boccaccio, ix. 6, from whom La Fontaine took it : "le Berceau."—Cook's tale, unfinished ; the tale of Gamelyn attributed by some MSS. to the Cook seems to be simply an old

Chaucer never troubled himself to invent any; he received them from all hands, but he modelled them after his own fashion, and adapted them to his characters. They

story which Chaucer intended to remodel; it would suit the Yeoman better than the Cook (in " Complete Works," as an appendix to vol. iv.).

2nd Day. Stopping at Rochester, 30 miles.—Tale of the Man of Law: history of the pious Constance, from the French of Trivet, an Englishman who wrote also Latin chronicles, &c., same story in Gower, who wrote it ab. 1393.— Shipman's tale: story of a merchant of St. Denys, his wife, and a wicked monk, from some French fabliau, or from "Decameron," viii. 1.—Tale of the Prioress: a child killed by Jews, from the French of Gautier de Coinci.—Tales by Chaucer: Sir Thopas, a caricature of the romances of chivalry; story of Melibeus, from a French version of the " Liber consolationis et consilii " of Albertano of Brescia, thirteenth century.—Monk's tale : " tragedies " of Lucifer, Adam, Sampson, Hercules, Nebuchadnezzar, Belshazzar, Zenobia, Pedro the Cruel, Pierre de Lusignan king of Cyprus, Barnabo Visconti (d. 1385), Hugolino, Nero, Holofernes, Antiochus, Alexander, Cæsar, Crœsus ; from Boccaccio, Machault, Dante, the ancients, &c.—Tale of the Nun's Priest: Story of Chauntecleer, same story in " Renart " and in Marie de France.

3rd Day. Rest at Ospringe, 46 miles.—Tale of the Physician : Appius and Virginia, from Titus Livius and the " Roman de la Rose ; " same story in Gower.—Pardoner's tale : three young men find a treasure, quarrel over it and kill each other, an old legend, of which, however, we have no earlier version than the one in the " Cento Novelle antiche," nov. 82.—Tale of the Wife of Bath : story of the young knight saved by an old sorceress, whom he marries and who recovers her youth and beauty ; the first original of this old legend is not known ; same story in Gower (Story of Florent), and in Voltaire : " Ce qui plait aux Dames."—Friar's tale : a summoner taken away by the devil, from one of the old collections of *exempla.*—Tale of the Summoner (somnour, sompnour) : a friar ill-received by a moribund ; a coarse, popular story, a version of which is in "Til Ulespiegel."—Clerk of Oxford's tale: story of Griselda from Petrarch's Latin version of the last tale in the " Decameron."—Merchant's tale : old January beguiled by his wife May and by Damian ; there are several versions of this story, one in the "Decameron," vii. 9, which was made use of by La Fontaine, ii. 7.

4th Day. Reach Canterbury, 56 miles.—Squire's tale : unfinished story of Cambinscan, king of Tartary ; in part from the French romance of " Cleomades."—Franklin's tale : Aurelius tries to obtain Dorigen's love by magic ; from a Breton lay, same story in Boccaccio's "Filocolo," iv. 4, and " Decameron," x. 5.—Tale of the second nun : story of St. Cecilia, from the Golden Legend.— Tale of the Canon's Yeoman : frauds of an alchemist (from Chaucer's personal experience ?).—Maniple's tale : a crow tells Phœbus of the faithlessness of the woman he loves ; from Ovid, to be found also in Gower.—Parson's tale, from both the " Somme des Vices et des Vertus " of Friar Lorens, 1279, and, according to Liddell, the " Clensyng of Manne's Sowle " ("Furnivall Miscell.," 255).

are borrowed from France, Italy, ancient Rome; the knight's tale is taken from Boccaccio, that of the nun's priest is imitated from the " Roman de Renart " ; that of " my lord the monk" from Latin authors and from Dante, "the grete poete of Itaille." The miller, the reeve, the somnour, the shipman, relate coarse stories, and good Chaucer pretends to be embarrassed by their licentiousness, and offers excuses. It is not he who talks, it is his road-companions ; and it is the Southwark beer which inspires them, not he ; you must blame the Southwark beer. The manners of the people of the lower classes, their loves, their animosities and their jealousies, are described to the life in these narratives. We see how the jolly Absolon goes to work to charm the carpenter's wife, who prefers Nicholas ; he makes music under her windows, and brings her little presents ; he is careful of his attire, wears "hoses rede," spreads out hair that shines like gold,

> He kempte hise lokkes brode, and made him gay.

If on a feast-day they play a Mystery on the public place before the church, he gets the part of Herod allotted to him : who could resist a person so much in view ? Alison resists, however, not out of virtue, but because she prefers Nicholas. She does not require fine phrases to repel Absolon's advances ; village-folk are not so ceremonious :

> Go forth thy wey, or I wol caste a ston.

Blows abound in stories of that kind, and the personages go off with "their back as limp as their belly," as we read in one of the narratives from which Chaucer drew his inspiration.

Next to these great scenes of noise there are little familiar scenes, marvellously observed, and described to

perfection ; scenes of home-life that might tempt the pencil
of a Dutch painter ; views of the mysterious laboratory
where the alchemist, at once duped and duping, surrounded
with retorts, " cucurbites and alembykes," his clothes burnt
to holes, seeks to discover the philosopher's stone. They
heat, they watch, they stir the mixture ;

> The pot to-breketh, and farewel ! al is go !

Then they discuss ; it is the fault of the pot, of the fire,
of the metal ; it is just as I thought ;

> Som seyde, it was long on the fyr-making,
> Som seyde, nay ! it was on the blowing. . . .
> " Straw," quod the thridde, " ye been lewede and nyce,
> It was nat tempred as it oghte be."

A fourth discovers a fourth cause: " Our fyr was nat
maad of beech." What wonder, with so many causes for
a failure, that it failed ? We will begin over again.[1]

Or else, we have representations of those interested
visits that mendicant friars paid to the dying. The friar,
low, trivial, hypocritical, approaches :

> " Deus hic," quod he, " O Thomas, freend, good day."

He lays down his staff, wallet, and hat ; he takes a seat,
the cat was on the bench, he makes it jump down ; he
settles himself ; the wife bustles about, he allows her to,
and even encourages her. What could he eat ? Oh !
next to nothing, a fowl's liver, a pig's head roasted, the
lightest repast ; his " stomak is destroyed ; "

> My spirit hath his fostring in the Bible.

---

[1] " Complete Works," vol. iv. p. 538. The canon and his man join the
pilgrims during the fourth day's journey. Contrary to Chaucer's use, such a
keen animosity appears in this satire of alchemists that it seems as if the poet,
then rather hard up, had had himself a grudge against such quacks.

He thereupon delivers to the sick man a long and interested sermon, mingled with Latin words, in which the verb " to give" comes in at every line : whatever you do, don't give to others, give to me ; give to my convent, don't give to the convent next door :

> A ! yif that covent half a quarter otes !
> A ! yif that covent four and twenty grotes !
> A ! yif that frere a peny and let him go. . . .
> Thomas, of me thou shalt nat ben y-flatered ;
> Thou woldest han our labour al for noght.[1]

Pay then, give then, give me this, or only that ; Thomas gives less still.

Familiar scenes, equally true but of a more pleasing kind, are found in other narratives, for instance in the story of Chauntecleer the cock, so well localised with a few words, in a green, secluded country nook :

> A poure widwe, somdel stope in age
> Was whylom dwelling in a narwe cotage,
> Bisyde a grove, standing in a dale.

Her stable, her barn-yard are described ; we hear the lowing of the cows and the crowing of the cock ; the tone rises little by little, and we get to the mock-heroic style.   Chauntecleer the cock,

> In al the land of crowing nas his peer.
> His vois was merier than the mery orgon
> On messe-days that in the chirche gon ;
> Wel sikerer was his crowing in his logge
> Than is a clokke, or an abbey orlogge. . . .
> His comb was redder than the fyn coral,
> And batailed, as it were a castel-wal !

---

[1] iv, p. 379. Compare the mendicant friar in Diderot, who drew him from nature, centuries later ; it is the same sort of nature. Friar John "venait dans notre village demander des œufs, de la laine, du chanvre, des fruits à chaque saison." Friar John "ne passait pas dans les rues que les pères, les mères et les enfants n'allassent à lui et ne lui criassent : Bonjour, frère Jean, comment vous portez vous, frère Jean ? Il est sûr que quand il entrait dans une maison, la bénédiction du ciel y entrait avec lui." "Jacques le Fataliste et son Maître," ed. Asseline, p. 46.

He had a black beak, white " nayles," and azure legs ; he reigned unrivalled over the hens in the barn-yard. One of the hens was his favourite, the others filled subalternate parts. One day—

> This storie is al-so trewe, I undertake
> As is the book of Launcelot de Lake,
> That wommen holde in ful gret reverence,

—he was looking for " a boterflye," and what should he see but a fox ! " Cok, cok ! " he cries, with a jump, and means to flee.

> " Gentil sire, allas ! wher wol ye gon ?
> Be ye affrayed of me that am your freend ? "

says the good fox ; I came only to hear you sing ; you have the family talent :

> My lord your fader (God his soule blesse !),

sang so well ; but you sing better still. To sing better still, the cock shuts his eye, and the fox bears him off. Most painful adventure ! It was a Friday : such things always befall on Fridays.

> O Gaufred, dere mayster soverayn,
> That whan the worthy King Richard was slayn
> With shot, compleynedest his deth so sore,
> Why ne had I now thy sentence and thy lore,
> The Friday for to chide, as diden ye ? [1]

Great commotion in the barn-yard ; and here we find a picture charming for its liveliness : " Out ! harrow ! and weyl-away ! Ha, ha, the fox ! " every one shrieks, yells, runs ; the dogs bark,

> Ran cow and calf, and eek the verray hogges ;

---

[1] " Complete Works," vol. iv. p. 285 ; on Geoffrey de Vinesauf and Richard Cœur-de-Lion, see above, p. 180.

the ducks scream,

> The gees for fere flowen over the trees,

and the bees come out of their hives.   The prisoner is delivered; he will be more prudent another time; order reigns once more in the domains of Chauntecleer.

Side by side with such tales of animals, we have elegant stories of the Round Table, borrowed from the lays of "thise olde gentil Britons," and which carry us back to a time when,

> In tholde dayes of the King Arthour
> Of which that Britons speken greet honour,
> Al was this land fulfild of fayerye ;
> The elf-queen, with hir joly companye,
> Daunced ful ofte in many a grene mede ;

oriental legends, which the young squire will relate, with enchantments, magic mirrors, a brass horse that transports its rider through the air, here or there according as one touches a peg in its ears, an ancestor doubtless of "Clavilegno," the steed of Don Quixote in the Duchesse's park ; biographies of Appius and Virginia, of Cæsar, of Nero, of Holophernes, of Hugolino in the tower of hunger, taken from Roman history, the Bible and Dante ; adventures of chivalry, in which figures Theseus, duke of Athens, where blood flows profusely, and we have all the digressions and embellishments which still continued to please great men and great ladies, and that is why the story is told by the knight, and Chaucer retains purposely all the faults of that particular sort of story.   In opposition to his usual custom, he contents himself here with lending a little life to illuminations of manuscripts.[1]

---

[1] See for example his description of a young lady gathering flowers at dawn in a garden, at the foot of a "dongeoun," Knight's Tale, l. 190, "Complete Works," iv. p. 31.

Grave personages relate grave stories, like canticles or
sermons, coloured as with the light of stained glass,
perfumed with incense, accompanied by organ music :
story of the pious Constance, of St. Cecilia, of a child
killed by the Jews ; dissertations of dame Prudence (a
tale of wondrous dulness,[1] which Chaucer modestly
ascribes to himself) ; story of the patient Griselda ; discourse of the poor parson. A while ago we were at the
inn ; now we are in church ; in the Middle Ages striking
colours and decided contrasts were best liked ; the faded
tints that have since been in fashion, mauve, cream, old-
green, did not touch any one ; and we know that Chaucer,
when he was a page, had a superb costume, of which one
leg was red and the other black. Laughter was inextinguishable ; it rose and fell and rose again, rebounding
indefinitely ; despair was immeasurable ; the sense of
measure was rare ; its propagation was to be one of
the results of the Renaissance. Panegyrics and satires
were readily carried to the extreme. Old-fashioned
logic, still taught in the schools, had been producing
its effect ; it pleased many a writer to draw apart one
single quality or characteristic and descant upon it,
neglecting all the rest. Thus it is that Griselda becomes
Patience, and Janicola Poverty, and that by an easy
and imperceptible transition the abstract personages of
novels and moralities are created : Cowardice, Valiance,
Vice. Those typical beings, whose names alone make us
shudder, were considered perfectly natural ; and, indeed,

[1] But very popular, derived from the "Liber Consolationis" of Albertano of
Brescia, written ab. 1246, ed. Thor Sundby, Chaucer Society, 1873. It was
translated into French (several times), Italian, German, Dutch. French text
in MS. Reg. 19, C vii. in the British Museum : " Uns jouvenceauls appelé
Melibée, puissant et riches ot une femme nommé Prudence, et de celle femme
ot une fille. Advint un jour. . . ." "A young man," says Chaucer, whose
tale is also in prose, " called Melibeus, mighty and riche, bigat up-on his wyf
that called was Prudence, a doghter which that called was Sophie. Upon a
day befel. . . ." (iv. 119).

they bore a striking resemblance to Griselda, Janicola, and other heroes of the most popular stories.

The success of Griselda is a proof of it. That poor girl, married to the marquis of Saluces, who repudiates her in order to try her patience, and then gives her back her position of wife, enjoyed an immense popularity. Boccaccio had related her misfortunes in the " Decameron "; Petrarch thought the story so beautiful that it appeared to him worthy of that supreme honour, a Latin translation : Chaucer translated it in his turn from Latin into English, and made of it his Clerk of Oxford's tale ; [1] it was turned several times into French.[2] Pinturicchio represented the adventures of Griselda in a series of pictures, now preserved in the National Gallery ; the story furnished the subject of plays in Italy, in France, and in England.[3]   These

[1] Unlike most of the tales, this one is written in stanzas, Chaucer's favourite seven-line stanza, riming *a b a b b c c.*

[2] It is to be found in the " Ménagier de Paris," ab. 1393, the author of which declares that he will " traire un exemple qui fut ja pieça translaté par maistre François Petrarc qui à Romme fut couronné poète " (" Ménagier," 1846, vol. i. p. 99).   The same story finds place in " Melibeus," MS. Reg. 19 C vii. in the British Museum, fol. 140.   Another French translation was printed ab. 1470: " La Patience Griselidis Marquise de Saluces."   Under Louis XIV., Perrault wrote a metrical version of the same story : " La Marquise de Saluces ou la patience de Griselidis," Paris, 1691, 12mo.   A number of ballads in all countries were devoted to Griselda ; the popularity of an English one is shown by the fact of other ballads being " to the tune of Patient Grissel."   One of Miss Edgeworth's novels has for its title and subject : " The Modern Griselda."

[3] One in French was performed at Paris in 1395 (" Estoire de Griselidis . . . par personnages," MS. Fr. 2203 in the National Library, Paris), and was printed at the Renaissance, by Bonfons, ab. 1550: "Le Mystère de Griselidis"; one in German was written by Hans Sachs in 1550.   In Italy it was the subject of an opera by Apostolo Zeno, 1620.   In England, Henslowe, on the 15th of December, 1599, lends three pounds to Dekker, Chettle and Haughton for their " Pleasant comodie of Patient Grissil," printed in 1603, reprinted by the Shakespeare Society, 1841.   The English authors drew several hints from the French play, but theirs is the best written on the subject (parts of Julia, the witty sister of the Marquis, of Laureo, the poor student, brother of Griselda, as proud as she is humble, &c.).

exaggerated descriptions were just what went to the very heart; people wept over them in the fourteenth century as over Clarissa in the eighteenth. Petrarch, writing to Boccaccio about Griselda, uses almost the same terms as Lady Bradshaigh, writing to Richardson about Clarissa:

"Had you seen me, I surely should have moved your pity. When alone, in agonies would I lay down the book, take it up again, walk about the room, let fall a flood of tears, wipe my eyes, read again—perhaps not three lines—throw away the book, crying out: 'Excuse me, good Mr. Richardson, I cannot go on; it is your fault, you have done more than I can bear.'" [1]

I made "one of our mutual friends, a Paduan," writes Petrarch, "a man of elevated mind and vast learning, read this story. He had hardly got half through, when suddenly he stopped, choking with tears; a moment after, having composed himself, he took up the narrative once more to continue reading, and, behold, a second time sobs stopped his utterance. He declared it was impossible for him to continue, and he made a person of much instruction, who accompanied him, finish the reading." About that time, in all probability, Petrarch, who, as we see in the same letter, liked to renew the experience, gave the English poet and negotiator, who had come to visit him at Padua, this tale to read,[2] and Chaucer, for that very reason less free than with most of his other stories, scarcely altered anything in Petrarch's text. With him as with his model, Griselda is Patience, nothing more; everything is sacrificed to that virtue; Griselda is neither woman nor mother; she is only the patient spouse, Patience made wife. They take her daughter from her, to be

---

[1] Lady Bradshaigh to Richardson, January 11, 1749. "Correspondence of Samuel Richardson," ed. Barbauld, London, 1804, 6 vols. 12mo, vol. iv. p. 240.

[2] Above, p. 289, n. 1.

killed, as they tell her, by order of the marquis. So be it, replies Griselda :

> " Goth now," quod she, "and dooth my lordes heste ;
> But o thing wil I preye yow of your grace,
> That, but my lord forbad yow, atte leste,
> Burieth this litel body in som place,
> That bestes ne no briddes it to-race."
> But he no word wol to that purpos seye,
> But took the child and wente upon his weye.[1]

Whereupon every one goes into ecstasies, and is greatly affected. The idea of entreating her husband, of throwing herself at his feet, of trying to move him, never enters her mind ; she would no longer be playing her part, which is not to be a mother, but to be : Patience.

Chaucer left his collection of tales uncompleted ; we have less than the half of it ; but he wrote enough to show to the best his manifold qualities. There appear in perfect light his masterly gifts of observation, of comprehension, and of sympathy ; we well see with what art he can make his characters stand forth, and how skilfully they are chosen to represent all contemporaneous England. The poet shows himself full of heart, and at the same time full of sense ; he is not without suspicion that his pious stories, indispensable to render his picture complete, may offend by their monotony and exaggerated good sentiments. In giving them place in his collection, he belongs to his time and helps to make it known ; but a few mocking notes, scattered here and there, show that he is superior to his epoch, and that, in spite of his long dissertations and his digressions, he has, what was rare at that period, a certain notion, at least theoretical, of the importance of proportion. He allows his heroes to speak, but he is not their dupe ; in fact he is so little their dupe that sometimes he can stand their talk no longer, and interrupts

[1] " Complete Works," vol. iv. p. 406.

them or laughs at them to their very face. He laughs in the face of the tiresome Constance, on the night of her wedding; he shows us his companions riding drowsily on their horses to the sound of the monk's solemn stories, and hardly preserved from actual slumber by the noise of the horses' bells. He allows the host abruptly to interrupt him when, to satirise the romances of chivalry, he relates, in "rym dogerel," the feats of arms and marvellous adventures of the matchless Sir Thopas.[1] Before we could even murmur the word "improbable," he warns us that the time of Griseldas has passed, and that there exist no more such women in our day. As the pilgrims draw near Canterbury, and it becomes seemly to finish on a graver note, he causes his poor parson to speak, and the priest announces beforehand that his discourse will be a sermon, a real sermon, with a text from Scripture: "Incipit sermo," says one of the manuscripts. He will speak in prose, as in church:

> Why sholde I sowen draf out of my fest,
> Whan I may sowen whete if that me lest?

All agree, and it is with the assent of his companions, who become more serious as they approach the holy city, that he commences, for the good of their souls, his ample "meditation." The coarse story told by the miller had been justified by excuses no less appropriate to the man and to the circumstances. The man was a clown, and chanced to be drunk; now the man is a saint, and, as it happens, they are just nearing the place of pilgrimage.

The good sense which caused the poet to write his "Canterbury Tales" according to a plan so conformable to

[1] Listeth, lordes, in good entent,
And I wol telle verrayment
Of mirthe and of solas, &c.

The caricature of the popular heroic stories of the day is extremely close (see below, p. 347).

reason and to nature, is one of the most eminent of
Chaucer's qualities.   It reveals itself in the details as in
the whole scheme, and inspires him, in the midst of his
most fanciful inventions, with reassuring remarks which
show that earth and real life are not far away, and that we
are not in danger of falling from the clouds.   He reminds
us at an opportune moment that there is a certain nobility,
the highest of all, which cannot be bequeathed in a will;
that the corrupt specimens of a social class should not
cause the whole class to be condemned :

Of every ordre som shrewe is, parde ;[1]

that, in the education of children, parents should be careful not to treat them too soon as men ; if one takes them
to merry-makings before time, they become "to sone rype
and bold, . . . which is ful perilous."   He expresses himself very freely about great captains, each of whom would
have been called "an outlawe or a theef" had they done
less harm.   This last idea is put forth in a few lines of a
humour so truly English [2] that it is impossible not to think
of Swift and Fielding ; and, indeed, Fielding can the more
appropriately be named here as he has devoted all his
novel of "Jonathan Wild the Great" to the expounding of
exactly the same thesis.

Finally, we owe to this same common sense of Chaucer's
a thing more remarkable yet : namely, that with his know-

---

[1] Tale of the Canon's Yeoman, l. 995.

[2] . . . For the tyrant is of gretter might,
By force of meynee for to sleen doun-right,
And brennen hous and hoom, and make al plain,
Lo ! therfor is he cleped a capitain ;
And, for the outlawe hath but smal meynee,
And may nat doon so greet an harm as he,
Ne bringe a contree to so greet mescheef,
Men clepen him an outlawe or a theef.
(Maunciple's tale, in "Complete Works," iv. p. 562.)

ledge of Latin and of French, and living in a circle where
those two languages were in great favour, he wrote solely
in English. His prose, like his verse, his " Treatise on the
Astrolabe " like his tales, are in English. He belongs to the
English nation, and that is why he writes in that language ;
a reason of that sort is sufficient for him : " Suffyse to thee
thise trewe conclusiouns in English, as wel as suffyseth to
thise noble clerkes Grekes thise same conclusiouns in
Greek, and to Arabiens in Arabik, and to Jewes in Ebrew,
and to the Latin folk in Latin." Chaucer, then, will make
use of plain English, " naked wordes in English " ; he will
employ the national language, the king's English—" the
king that is lord of this langage." [1] And he will use it, as
in truth he did, to express exactly his thoughts and not
to embellish them ; he hates travesty, he worships truth ;
he wants words and things to be in the closest possible
relation :

> The wordes mote be cosin to the dede. [2]

The same wisdom is again the cause why Chaucer does
not spend himself in vain efforts to attempt impossible
reforms, and to go against the current. It has been made
a subject of reproach to him in our day ; and some, from
love of the Saxon past, have been indignant at the number
of French words Chaucer uses ; why did he not go
back to the origins of the language ? But Chaucer was not
one of those who, as Milton says, think " to pound up the
crows by shutting their park gates ; " he employed the
national tongue, as it existed in his day ; the proportion
of French words is not greater with him than with the
mass of his contemporaries. The words he made use of
were living and fruitful, since they are still alive, they
and their families ; the proportion of those that have
disappeared is wonderfully small, seeing the time that has

[1] " A Treatise on the Astrolabe " in " Complete Works," vol. iii. p. 175.
[2] " General Prologue," l. 742.

elapsed. As to the Anglo-Saxons, he retained, as did
the nation, but without being aware of it, something of
their grave and powerful genius ; it is not his fault if he
ignored these ancestors ; every one in his day ignored them,
even such thinkers as Langland, in whom lived again
with most force the spirit of the ancient Germanic race.
The tradition was broken ; in the literary past one went
back to the Conquest, and thence without transition to
" thise olde gentil Britons." In his enumeration of celebrated bards, Chaucer gives a place to Orpheus, to Orion,
and to the " Bret Glascurion " ; but no author of any
" Beowulf" is named by him. Shakespeare, in the same
manner, will derive inspiration from the national past ; he
will go back to the time of the Roses, to the time of the
Plantagenets, to the time of Magna Charta, and, passing
over the Anglo-Saxon period, he will take from the Britons
the stories of Lear and of Cymbeline.

The brilliancy with which Chaucer used this new tongue,
the instant fame of his works, the clear proof afforded by his
writings that English could fit the highest and the lowest
themes, assured to that idiom its definitive place among the
great literary languages. English still had, in Chaucer's
day, a tendency to resolve itself into dialects, as, in the
time of the Conquest, the kingdom had still a tendency to
resolve itself into sub-kingdoms. Chaucer knew this, and
was concerned about it ; he was anxious about those
differences of tongue, of orthography, and of vocabulary ;
he did all in his power to regularise these discordances ; he
had set ideas on the subject ; and, what was rare in those
days, the whims of copyists made him shudder. Nothing
shows better the faith he had in the English tongue, as
a literary language, than his reiterated injunctions to the
readers and scribes who shall read his poems aloud or copy
them. He experiences already, concerning his work, the
anxieties of the poets of the Renaissance :

And for ther is so greet diversitee
In English, and in writyng of our tonge,
So preye I God, that noon miswryte thee,
Ne thee mysmetre for defaute of tonge,
And red wher-so thou be, or elles songe,
That thou be understonde I God beseche ! [1]

Chaucer himself looked over the transcriptions done
from his original manuscripts by his amanuensis Adam ;
he corrected with minute care every fault ; he calls down
all manner of woe upon the " scriveyn's " head, if, copying once more " Boece " or " Troilus," he leaves as many
errors again.[2] We seem to hear Ronsard himself addressing
his supplications to the reader : " I implore of you one
thing only, reader, to pronounce well my verses and suit
your voice to their passion . . . and I implore you again,
where you will see this sign : (!) to raise your voice a little,
to give grace to what you read." [3]

Chaucer's efforts were not exercised in vain ; they assisted
the work of concentration. After him, the dialects lost
their importance ; the one he used, the East Midland
dialect, has since become the language of the nation.

His verse, too, is the verse of the new literature, formed
by a compromise between the old and the new prosody.
Alliteration, which is not yet dead, and which is still used
in his time, he does not like ; its jingle seems to him
ridiculous :

I can nat geste—run, ram, ruf—by lettre.[4]

---

[1] " Troilus," Book v. st. 257.

[2] " Chaucer's wordes unto Adam, his owne Scriveyn," in " Complete Works,"
vol. i. p. 379.

[3] " Je te suppliray seulement d'une chose, lecteur, de vouloir bien prononcer mes vers et accomoder ta voix à leur passion . . . et je te supplie
encore de rechef, où tu verras cette marque : (!) vouloir un peu eslever ta voix
pour donner grâce à ce que tu liras." Preface of the " Franciade.'

[4] So says the Parson, who adds :

Ne, God wot, rym holde I but litel bettre.

Parson's Prologue, l. 43. It will be observed that while *naming* simply
rime, he *caricatures* alliteration.

Ridiculous, too, in his eyes is the " rym dogerel " of the popular romances of which " Sir Thopas " is the type. His verse is the rimed verse, with a fixed number of accents or beats, and a variable number of syllables. Nearly all the " Tales " are written in heroic verse, riming two by two in couplets and containing five accentuated syllables.

The same cheerful, tranquil common sense which made him adopt the language of his country and the usual versification, which prevented him from reacting with excess against received ideas, also prevented his harbouring, out of patriotism, piety, or pride, any illusions about his country, his religion, or his time. He belonged to them, however, as much as any one, and loved and honoured them more than anybody. Still the impartiality of judgment of this former prisoner of the French is wonderful, superior even to Froissart's, who, the native of a border-country, was by birth impartial, but who, as age crept on, showed in the revision of his " Chronicles " decided preferences. Towards the close of the century Froissart, like the Limousin and the Saintonge, counts among the resumptions made by France. Chaucer, from the beginning to the end of his career, continues the same, and the fact is all the more remarkable because his turn of mind, his inspiration and his literary ideal, become more and more English as he grows older. He remains impartial, or, rather, outside the great dispute, in which, however, he had actually taken part ; his works do not contain a single line directed against France, nor even any praise of his country in which it is extolled as the successful rival of its neighbour.

For this cause Des Champs, a great enemy of the English, who had not only ravaged the kingdom in general but burnt down his own private country house, made an exception in his hatred, and did homage to the wisdom and genius of the " noble Geoffrey Chaucer," the ornament of the " kingdom of Eneas," England.

V.

The composition of the "Canterbury Tales" occupied the last years of Chaucer's life. During the same period he also wrote his "Treatise on the Astrolabe" in prose, for the instruction of his son Lewis,[1] and a few detached poems, melancholy pieces in which he talks of shunning the world and the crowd, asks the prince to help him in his poverty, withdraws into his inner self, and becomes graver and more and more resigned :

> Fle fro the prees, and dwelle with sothfastnesse,
> Suffyce unto thy good, though hit be smal. . . .
> Forth, pilgrim, forth ! Forth, beste out of thy stal ! . . .
> Hold the hye wey, and lat thy gost thee lede :
> And trouth shal delivere, hit is no drede.[2]

In spite of this melancholy, he was at that time the un-contested king of English letters ; a life-long friendship bound him to Gower[3] ; the young poets, Hoccleve, Scogan, Lydgate, came to him and proclaimed him their master. His face, the features of which are known to us, thanks to the portrait we owe to Hoccleve, had gained an expression of gentle gravity ; he liked better to listen than to talk, and, in the "Canterbury Tales," the host rallies him on his pensive air and downcast eyes :

> " What man artow ? " quod he ;
> " Thou lokest as thou woldest finde an hare,
> For ever up-on the ground I see thee stare."

---

[1] 1391, in "Complete Works," vol. iii. On that other, *possible* son of Chaucer, Thomas, see *ibid.*, vol. i. p. xlviii., and above, p. 273.

[2] "Truth," or "Balade de bon Conseyl," in "Complete Works," vol. i. p. 390. Belonging to the same period : "Lak of Stedfastnesse" (advice to the king himself) ; "L'Envoy de Chaucer à Scogan" ; "L'Envoy de Chaucer à Bukton," on marriage, with an allusion to the Wife of Bath ; "The Compleynt of Venus" ; "The Compleint of Chaucer to his empty purse," &c., all in vol i. of "Complete Works."

[3] It has been said, but without sufficient cause, that this friendship came to an end some time before the death of Chaucer.

Age had bestowed on him a corpulency which made him a match for Harry Bailey himself.[1]

When Henry IV. mounted the throne, within the four days that followed his accession, he doubled the pension of the poet (Oct. 3, 1399), who then hired, for two pounds thirteen shillings and four pence a year, a house in the garden of St. Mary's, Westminster. The lease is still preserved in the archives of the Abbey.[2] He passed away in the following year, in that tranquil retreat, and was interred at Westminster, not far from the sepulchres where slept his patrons, Edward III. and Richard II., in that wing of the transept which has since been called the Poets' Corner, where we saw Browning's coffin lowered, and where, not long after, Tennyson's was laid.

No English poet enjoyed a fame more constantly equal to itself. In the fifteenth century writers did scarcely anything but lament and copy him : " Maister deere," said Hoccleve,

> O maister deere and fadir reverent,
> Mi maister Chaucer, flour of eloquence,
> Mirour of fructuous entendement,
> O universal fadir of science,
> Allas that thou thyn excellent prudence
> In thi bed mortel mightist noght byquethe ! [3]

At the Renaissance Caxton printed twice the " Canterbury Tales "[4] and a number of his minor works. Henry VIII. made an exception in favour of Chaucer

---

[1] He in the waast is shape as wel as I.

(Prologue to Sir Thopas.)

[2] To be seen (1894) under glass in the Chapter House.

[3] "Hoccleve's Works," ed. Furnivall, E.E.T.S., 1892, vol. i. p. xxi.

[4] Once ab. 1478, then ab. 1484 ; this last ed. is illustrated. See in my "English Novel in the time of Shakespeare," p. 45, a facsimile of the woodcut representing the pilgrims seated at the table of the Tabard inn. Caxton printed also "Boethius," "Hous of Fame," "Troilus," etc. *Cf.* Greg, "Early printed editions of the 'Canterb. Tales,'" in "Publications of the Mod. Lang. Assn. of America," xxxix, 737.

when prohibiting " printed bokes, printed balades, . . . and other fantasies." [1] " The fine courtier," says Wilson in his " Arte of Rhetorique," " will talke nothing but Chaucer." Under Elizabeth, Thynne annotated him,[2] Spenser declared that he " of Tityrus," that is of Chaucer, "his songs did lere," [3] and Sidney exalted him to the skies.[4] In the seventeenth century Dryden rejuvenates his tales ; in the eighteenth century the admiration is universal, and extends to Pope and Walpole.[5] In our time the learned men of all countries have applied themselves to the task of commentating his works and of disentangling his biography ; a Society has been founded to publish the best texts of his writings,[6] and but lately his " Legend of Good Women " inspired with an exquisite poem the Laureate who sleeps to-day close to the great ancestor, beneath the pavement of the famous Abbey.

[1] " Animadversions uppon the Annotacions and corrections of some imper-fections of impressiones of Chaucers workes . . ." by Francis Thynne, ed. Furnivall and Kingsley, Chaucer Society, 1876, p. xiv

[2] *Ibid.*

[3] "Shepheard's Calender," December.

[4] " Of whom, truly I know not, whether to mervaile more, either that he in that mistie time could see so clearly, or that wee in this cleare age walke so stumblingly after him." " Apologie for Poetrie," ed. Arber, p. 62.

[5] On Chaucer's fame see "Five hundred years of Chaucer criticism and allusion," by Miss Caroline F. E. Spurgeon, 4 vols., 1915 ff. See also Lounsbury's " Studies in Chaucer, his life and writings," London, 1892, 3 vols. 8vo, vol. iii. ch. vii. : " Chaucer in Literary History."

[6] The Chaucer Society, founded by Dr. Furnivall, which has issued among other publications : the " Six-text edition of the Canterbury Tales " ; " Life Records of Chaucer " ; various " Essays " on questions concerning the poet's works ; a collection of "Originals and Analogues" illustrative of the "Canter-bury Tales," &c. Among modern tributes paid to Chaucer may be added, besides many studies by *e.g.* Lounsbury, Pollard, Legouis, Kittredge, R. K. Root, &c., Wordsworth's modernisation of part of " Troilus " (John Morley's ed., p. 165), and Lowell's admirable essay in his " Study Windows." On Chaucer's times, see *e g.* G. G. Coulton, " Chaucer and his England," London, 1st ed. 1908 ; Dorothy Hughes, " Illustrations of Chaucer's England," New York, 1918.

CHAPTER III.

THE GROUP OF POETS.

THE nation was young, virile, and productive. Around Chaucer was a whole swarm of poets ; he towers above them as an oak towers above a coppice ; but the oak is not isolated like those great trees sometimes seen alone, beneath the sun, in the midst of an open country. Chaucer is without peer but not without companions ; and, among those companions, one at least deserves to be ranked very near him.

He has companions of all kinds, nearly as diverse as those with whom he had associated on the road to Canterbury. Some are continuators of the old style, and others are reformers ; some there are, filled with the dreamy spirit of the Anglo-Saxons ; there are others who care little for dreams and theories, who are of the world, and will not leave the earth ; some who sing, others who hum, others who talk. Certain poems are like clarions, and celebrate the battle of Crécy, of which Chaucer had not spoken ; others resemble lovers' serenades ; others a dirge for the dead.

I.

The old styles are continued ; the itinerant poets, jugglers, and minstrels have not disappeared ; on the contrary, they are more numerous than ever. " Merry

England " favours them ; they continue to play, as under
the first Angevins,[1] a very considerable and multiple part,
which it is difficult to estimate. Those people, with their
vast memory, are like perambulating libraries; they instruct,
they amuse, they edify. Passing from county to county,
hawking news, composing satirical songs, they fill also
the place of a daily gazette ; they represent public opinion,
sometimes create it, and often distort it : they are living
newspapers. They furnish their auditors with information
about the misdeeds of the Government, which, from time to
time, seizes the most talkative, and imprisons them to keep
them silent. The king has minstrels in his service ; they
are great personages in their way, pensioned by the prince
and despising the others. The nobles also keep some in
their pay, which does not prevent their welcoming those
who pass ; they feast them when they have sung well, and
give them furred robes and money.[2]

They continue to prosper in the following century.
We see at that time the king of England's minstrels,
clever people and well taught, protesting against the
increasing audacity of sham minstrels, whose ignorance
casts discredit on the profession. " Uncultured peasants,"
says the king in a vengeful statute, " and workmen of
different kinds in our kingdom of England . . . have given
themselves out to be our own minstrels."[3] Without any

[1] See above, p. 162.

[2] Against those practices Langland strongly protests in his " Visions," text
C. x. 133 ; xvi. 200. See following Chapter.

[3] Rymer, " Fœdera," April 24, 1469. The classic instrument of the
minstrel was the vielle or viol, a sort of violin, which only true artists knew
how to use well (one is reproduced in " English Wayfaring Life," p. 202).
Therefore many minstrels early replaced this difficult instrument by the
common tabor, which sufficed to mark the cadence of their chants. Many
other musical instruments were known in the Middle Ages ; a list of them
has been drawn up by H. Lavoix : " La Musique au temps de St. Louis," in
G. Raynaud's " Recueil des motets français des XIIe et XIIIe Siècles," vol. ii.
p. 321.

experience or understanding of the art, they go from place to place on festival days, and gather all the money that should have enriched the true artists, those who really devote themselves to their profession and ply no manual craft. Vain efforts ; decline was imminent ; minstrels were not to recover their former standing. The Renaissance and the Reformation came ; and, owing to the printing-press, gay scavoir found other means of spreading through the country. In the sixteenth century, it is true, minstrels still abound, but they are held in contempt ; right-minded people, like Philip Stubbes, have no terms strong enough to describe " suche drunken sockets and bawdye parasits as range the cuntreyes, ryming and singing of uncleane, corrupt, and filthie songes in tavernes, ale-houses, innes, and other publique assemblies. . . . Every towne, citie, and countrey is full of these minstrelles to pype up a dance to the devill ; but of dyvines, so few there be as they maye hardly be seene." [1]

Before this awful time comes for them, however, the minstrels thrive under the last Plantagenets. Their bill is a varied one, and includes the best and the worst ; they sometimes recite the " Troilus " of Chaucer,[2] and sometimes the ancient romances of chivalry, altered, spoiled, shorn of all their poetry. Chaucer had ridiculed these versions of the old heroic stories, written in tripping verses, but in vain. Throughout his life, after as well as before " Sir Thopas," he could wonder and laugh at the success of stories, composed in the very style of his own burlesque poem, about heroes who, being all peerless, are necessarily all alike. One is " stalworthe and wyghte," another " hardy and wyght,"

---

[1] "Anatomy of Abuses," ed. Furnivall, London, 1877–79, 8vo, pp. 171, 172. *Cf.* further, vol. ii. p. 408.

[2] Chaucer himself expected his poem to be said or *sung:*

> And red wher-so thou be, or elles songe ;
> That thou be understonde, I God beseche ! (V. 257).

a third also "hardy and wyght"; and the fourth, fifth,
and hundredth are equally brave and invincible. They
are called Isumbras, Eglamour, Degrevant[1]; but they
differ in their names and in nothing more. The booksellers
of the Renaissance who printed their histories could make
the same woodcut on the cover serve for all their portraits.
By merely altering the name beneath, they changed all
there was to change; one and the same block did duty in
turn for Romulus or Robert the Devil.[2] Specimens of this
facile art swarm indefinitely; they are scattered over the
country, penetrate into hamlets, find their way into cottages, and make the people acquainted with the doughty
deeds of Eglamour and of Roland. We now find ourselves really in the copse.

In the middle of the copse are trees of finer growth.
Some among the poets, while conforming to the old style,
improve upon their models as they proceed; they add an
original note of their own, and on that account deserve to
be listened to. Far above those empty, tripping metrical
stories, and superior even to "Morte Arthure" and to
"William of Palerne,"[3] written in English verse at the

[1] I wille yow telle of a knyghte
That bothe was stalworthe and wyghte. (*Isumbras.*)

Y schalle telle yow of a knyght
That was bothe hardy and wyght. (*Eglamour.*)

And y schalle karppe off a knyght
That was both hardy and wyght. (*Degrevant.*)

"The Thornton Romances," ed. Halliwell (Camden Society, 1844, pp. 88,
121, 177), from a MS. preserved in the cathedral of Lincoln, that contains
romances, recipes, prayers, &c., copied in the first half of the fifteenth century,
on more ancient texts. *Cf.* Ritson, "Ancient metrical Romances," ed. Goldsmid, 1884, 3 vols., Ward's "Catalogue of MS. Romances," 1883, i. 760 ff.

[2] See in "English Novel in the Time of Shakespeare," pp. 57 and 65,
facsimiles of woodcuts which served about 1510 and 1560 to represent, the
first, Romulus, Robert the Devil, &c., the second, Guy of Warwick, Graund
Amoure, and the "Squyr of Lowe Degre."

[3] Both published by the E.E.T.S.: "Morte Arthure." ed. Brock, 1871;

time of Chaucer, ranks "Sir Gawayne and the Green Knight," [1] being incomparably the best specimen of the style. Instead of puppets with jerky movements, and wooden joints that we hear crack, the English poet shows in this work real men and women, with supple limbs and red lips; elegant, graceful, and charming to behold. These knights and ladies in their well-fitting armour or their tight dresses, whom we see stretched in churches on their fourteenth century tombs, have come back to life; and now they move, gaze on each other, love again.

On Christmas Day, in presence of Arthur and his whole Court, Sir Gawayne cuts off the head of the Green Knight. This giant knight is doubtlesss an enchanter, for he stoops, picks up his head, and, remounting his horse, bids Sir Gawayne meet him a year hence at the Green Chapel, where he will give him blow for blow.

The year passes. Gawayne leaves the Court with his horse "Gringolet," and without quitting England, rides

"William of Palerne," ed. Skeat, 1867; see also "Parlement of the three Ages" (of man), ed. Gollancz, 1915, "Patience," same ed. 1914; all in alliterative verse, XIVth cent.

[1] The MS. containing this poem, "Pearl," &c., Cotton, Nero A 10, in the B.M., in a good handwriting of the fourteenth century, has been pub. in facsimile by Gollancz, E.E.T.S., 1923. Some curious, though not fine, miniatures: the Green Knight leaving the Court, his head in his hand; Gawayne and his hostess; the scene at the Green Chapel, &c. Ed., *e.g.*, R. Morris: "Sir Gawayne and the Green Knight," 1864, Gollancz, 1912, both E.E.T.S. The date assigned to the poem by Morris (1320–30) seems to be too early; the work belongs more probably to the second half of the century. The immediate original of the tale is not known; it was, however, certainly a French poem. See Ward, "Catal. of Romances," 1883, p. 387, G. Paris, "Hist. Litt. de la France," vol. xxx, Wells, "Manual of Middle English," 1916, p. 54. "Sir Gawayne" has been, on very doubtful grounds, attributed by some to that misty Huchoun mentioned, as the author of several works, by Wyntoun in his "Original Chronicle" (ed. Amours, 1903 ff., iv. 19) and credited by his champions, Mr. G. Neilson especially, with most of the fourteenth-century poems of value, English or Scottish, that have come down to us without a name. See Append. I., below, p. 526. Same period and family of writings, the weird Scottish poem "The Awntyrs off Arthure," Amours, "Scottish Alliterative Poems," 1897, Scot. Text Society.

through unknown lands, having no one to speak to save
God. He reaches the gate of a splendid castle, and is
welcomed by a knight of ordinary stature, under whose
present appearance he does not recognise his adversary
the giant. Three days are left before the date of the tryst ;
they are spent in amusements. The knight goes daily to
hunt ; he agrees to give all his game to his guest, who
remains at home with the lady of the castle, the most
beautiful woman ever seen, on condition that Gawayne, in
his turn, will give him what he has taken during his
absence. Every night they gaily sup in the hall ; a bright
light burns along the walls, the servants set up wax torches,
and serve at table. The meal is cheered by music and
" caroles newe,"[1] jests, and the laughter of ladies.[2] At
three o'clock each morning the lord of the castle rises,
hears mass, and goes a-hunting. Gawayne is awakened
from sleep by his hostess ; she enters his room, with easy
and graceful movements, dressed in a " mery mantyle " and
furred gown, trailing on the floor, but very low in the
neck :

> Hir breste bare bifore, and bihinde eke.

She goes to the window, opens it, and says, " with hir riche
wordes " :

> A ! mon, hou may thou sleep,,
> This morning is so clere ! [3]

She seats herself, and refuses to go. Gawayne is assailed

---

[1] Much glam and gle glent up ther-inne,
Aboute the fyre upon flat (floor) and on fele (many) wyse,
At the soper and after, mony athel songez,
As coundutes of Kryst-masse and caroles newe. . . .

[2] With merthe and mynstralsye, wyth metez at hor wylle,
Thay maden as mery as any men moghten
With laghyng of ladies, with lotes of bordes (play upon words).
(l. 1952.)

[3] l. 1746.

by terrible temptations. The thought of the Green Chapel, fortunately, helps him to overcome them, and the first, second, and third night his fair friend finds him equally coy. She kisses him once, twice, thrice, and jeers at him for forgetting each day what she had taught him on the previous one, namely, to kiss. When the hunter returns in the evening, Gawayne gives him the kisses he has received in exchange for the spoils of the chase: a buck, a boar, and a fox. He had, however, accepted besides a marvellous belt, which protected the wearer from all danger, but he says nothing about this, and puts it on : " Aux grands cœurs donnez quelques faiblesses," our author obviously thinks, with Boileau.

On the fourth day Gawayne starts with a guide, and reaches the Green Chapel ; the Green Giant is there, ready to give him back the blow received a year before. Gawayne stoops his head under the dreadful axe, and just as it falls cannot help bending his shoulders a little. You are not that Gawayne, says the giant, held in such high esteem. At this, Arthur's knight straightens himself ; the giant lifts his axe again and strikes, but only inflicts a slight wound. All is now explained : for the kisses Gawayne should have received mortal blows, but he gave them back ; he kept the belt, however, and this is why he will bear through life a scar on his neck. Vexed, he throws away the belt, but the giant returns it to him, and consoles him by admitting that the trial was a superhuman one, that he himself is Bernlak de Haut-Désert, and that his guest has been the sport of " Morgan the fairy," the companion of his hostess :

Thurgh myght of Morgne la Faye that in my hous lenges (dwells).

Gawayne declares that should he ever be tempted by pride, he need only look at the belt, and the temptation will vanish. He rejoins Arthur's court and his peers, and tells his adventures, which afford food for laughter and for admiration.

The poem is anonymous. The same manuscript contains another, on a totally different subject, which seems to be by the same author, and which has been called " The Pearl ; "[1] it is a song of mourning. It must have been written some time after the sad event which it records, when the bitterness of sorrow had softened. The landscape is bathed in sunlight, the hues are wonderfully bright. The poet has lost his daughter, his pearl, who is dead ; his pearl has fallen in the grass, and he has been unable to find it ; he cannot tear himself away from the spot where she had been. He entered in that arbour green ; it was August, that sunny season, when the corn has just fallen under the sickle ; there the pearl had " trendeled doun " among the glittering, richly-coloured plants, gilly-flowers, gromwell seed, and peonies, splendid in their hues, sweeter in their smell.[2] He sees a forest,

[1] " Pearl," ed. Gollancz, London, 1921, in alliterated stanzas riming *a b a b a b a b b c b c*. " Pearl," " Gawayne," " Cleanness " (ed. Gollancz, 1922), and " Patience," the two last of lesser merit (" Early Engl. Allit. Poems," ed. Morris, E.E.T.S., 1864), all in MS. Cotton A 10, are of the 2nd nalf of the XIVth cent. and have been doubtfully attributed to the same unknown writer. According to Profs. Brown and Schofield (who pointed out the similitude of the theme with that of Boccaccio's Egl. 14, " Publications Mod Lang. Assn." 1909, p. 651), the author of " Pearl " was a priest, and the pearl was not his daughter but " clean maidenhood." If admitted, their tests would go far towards proving Rolle of Hampole a priest and Gower too. As for maidenhood, it is not clear why the supposed priest should weep for the loss thereof, describing the same as being " not two yer old," and " nerre " him " then aunte or nece." *Cf.* Coulton, " Mod. Lang. Rev.," ii. 39 ; Gollancz, " Boccaccio's Olympia," 1914.

[2] I entred in that erber grene,
In Auguste in a hygh seysoun,
Quen corne is corven with crokez kene ;
On huyle ther perle it trendeled doun ;
Schadowed this wortes (plants) full schyre and schene,
Gilofre, gyngure and gromylyoun,
And pyonys powdered ay betwene.
Yif hit wacz semly on to sene,
A fayrre flayr yet fro hit flot. (St. 4.)

rocks that glisten in the sun, banks of crystal ; birds sing in the branches, and neither cistern nor guitar ever made sweeter music. The sound of waters, too, is heard ; a brook glides over pebbles shining like the stars in a winter's night, at the hour when the weary sleep.[1]

So great is the beauty of the place that the father's grief is soothed, and he has a marvellous vision. On the opposite side of the stream he sees a maiden clothed in white ; and as he gazes he suddenly recognises her : O pearl art thou in sooth my pearl, so mourned and wept for through so many nights? Touching and consoling is the answer : Thou hast lost no pearl, and never hadst one ; that thou lost was but a rose, that flowered and faded ; now only has the rose become a pearl for ever.[2] The father follows his child to where a glimpse can be caught of the Celestial City, with its flowers and jewels, the mystic lamb, and the procession of the elect ; it seems as if the poet were describing beforehand, figure by figure, Van Eyck's painting at St. Bavon of Ghent.

II.

An immense copse surrounds the oak. About Chaucer swarm, innumerable, minstrels, anonymous poets, riming clerks, knightly ballad makers.[3] The fragile works of

[1] As stremande sternes quen strothe men slepe,
 Staren in welkyn in wynter nyght. (St. 10.)

[2] For that thou lestes wacs bot a rose,
 That flowred and fayled as kynde hit gefe. (St. 23.)

[3] The principal collections containing lyrical works and popular ballads of that period are : " Ancient Songs and Ballads from the reign of Henry II. to the Revolution," collected by John Ritson, revised by W. C. Hazlitt, London, 1877, 12mo ; " Specimens of Lyric Poetry, composed in England in the reign of Edward I.," ed. Th. Wright, Percy Society, 1842, 8vo ; " Reliquiæ Antiquæ, scraps from ancient MSS. illustrating chiefly Early English Literature," ed. T. Wright and J. O. Halliwell, London, 1841-43, 2 vols. 8vo ;

these riming multitudes are for the most part lost, yet great quantities of them still exist. They are composed by everybody, and written in the three languages used by the English ; some being in French, some in English, some in Latin.

The Plantagenets were an art-loving race. Edward III. never thought of cost when it came to painting and gilding the walls of St. Stephen's Chapel ; Richard II. disliked a want of conformity in architectural styles, and, having the conscience of an artist, gave an example rare in the Middle Ages, for he continued Westminster Abbey in the style of Henry III. Kings and princes were enamoured of poetry. The hero of Poictiers inserted in his will a piece of poetry in French, requesting that the lines should be graven on his tomb, where they can still be read in Canterbury Cathedral : " Such as thou wast, so was I ; of death I never thought so long as I lived. On earth I enjoyed ample wealth, and I used it with great splendour, land, houses, and treasure, cloth, horses, silver and gold ; but now I am poor and bereft, I lie under earth, my great beauty is all gone. . . . And were you to see me now, I do not think you would believe that ever I was a man." [1]

" Political Songs of England, from the reign of John to that of Edward II." ed. Th. Wright, Camden Society, 1839, 4to ; " Songs and Carols now first printed from a MS. of the XVth Century," ed. Th. Wright, Percy Society, 1847, 8vo ; " Political Poems and Songs, from Edward III. to Richard III.," ed. Th. Wright, Rolls, 1859-61, 2 vols. 8vo ; " Political, Religious and Love Poems," ed. Furnivall, London, Early English Text Society, 1866, 8vo ; " Bishop Percy's Folio MS." ed. J. W. Hales and F. J. Furnivall, Ballad Society, 1867 8vo ; " The English and Scottish Popular Ballads," ed. F. J. Child, Boston, 1882 ff. Useful indications will be found in H. L. D. Ward's " Catalogue of MS. Romances in the British Museum," vol. i. 1883. *Cf.* further, II. 405 ff.

[1] Tiel come tu es je autie fu,
Tu seras til come je su.
De la mort ne peusay-je mie
Tant come j'avoy la vie.
En terre avoy grand richesse
Dont je y fis grand noblesse,

The nobles followed suit ; some put their passions into verse ; others had not sufficient skill for such delicate pastimes and merely copied for their beloved those ready-made ballads, of which professional poets supplied ready-made collections ; just as sermons were written for the benefit of obtuse parish priests, under the significant title of " Dormi Secure " [1] (Sleep in peace, to-morrow's sermon is ready). We find likewise in English manuscripts such rubrics as the following : " Loo here begynnethe a Balade whiche that Lydegate wrote at the request of a squyer y^t served in Love's court." [2]   In their most elegant language, with all the studied refinement of the flowery style, the professional poets amplified, embellished, and spoilt : " ce mot, le mot des dieux et des hommes : je t'aime ! " We are not even in the copse now, and we must stoop close to earth in order to see these blossoms of a day.

> Terre, mesons et grand tresor . . .
> Mes ore su-je povres et cheitifs,
> Perfond en la terre gys,
> Ma grand beauté est tout alée . . .
> Et si ore me veissez
> Je ne quide pas qe vous deeisez
> Qe j'eusse onqes hom esté.

Text in Stanley, " Historical Memorials of Canterbury," but drawn from the " Castoiement d'un père à son fils," tale 28, as shown by Kastner.   See J. Tait, *Athenæum*, June 16, 1900.

[1] Compiled in France in 1395.   Lecoy de la Marche, " la Chaire française au moyen âge," 2nd ed., Paris, 1886, 8vo, p. 334.

[2] MS. R. iii. 20, in the Library of Trinity College, Cambridge, fol. 33.   In the same MS., *e g.* : " A roundell made . . . by my lorde therlle of Suffolk " :

> Quel desplaysier, quel courous, quel destresse,
> Quel griefs, quelx mauls viennent souvent d'amours, &c. (fol. 36).

The author is the famous Earl, afterwards Duke of Suffolk (on whom see MacCracken, " Publ. Mod. Lang. Assn. Ama," xxvi, 141), who was beaten by Joan of Arc, who married Alice, daughter of Thomas Chaucer, and was beheaded in 1450.   For ballads of the same kind, by Gower, see below, p. 367. The same taste reigned in France ; to say nothing of Charles d'Orléans, Pierre de Beauveau writes : " Le joyeulx temps passé souloit estre occasion que je faisoie de plaisant diz et gracieuses chançonnetes et balades."   " Nouvelles Françoises du XIVe Siècle," ed. Moland and d'Héricault, 1858, p. 303.

Among men of the people, and plain citizens, as well as at Court, the taste for ballads and songs imported from France became general in the fourteenth century. In the streets of London, mere craftsmen could be heard singing French burdens : for in spite of the progress of the national tongue, French was not yet entirely superseded in Great Britain. Langland in his Visions has London workmen who sing : " Dieu vous sauve dame Emma." [1] Chaucer's good parson bears witness to the popularity of another song, and declares in the course of his sermon : " Wel may that man that no good werke ne dooth, singe thilke newe Frenshe song : " J'ay tout perdu mon temps et mon labour." [2]

In imitation of what was done in the northern provinces of France, a *Pui* had been founded in London, that is an association established for the purpose of encouraging the art of the *chanson*, which awarded prizes to the authors of the best verses and the best music.[3] In the fourteenth century the Pui of London was at the height of its prosperity ; it included both foreign and English merchants. It had been instituted so that "jolity, peace, courtesy, gentleness, debonairity, and love without end might be maintained, all good promoted, and evil prevented." These merchants of divers countries evidently agreed in thinking that music softens the manners, and tried to extinguish their quarrels by songs. At the head of the Pui was a

---

[1] " Visions concerning Piers Plowman," A. Prol. l. 103, written about 1362–3. See following Chapter.

[2] " Parson's Tale."—" Complete Works," vol. iv. p. 581.

[3] " Munimenta Gildhallæ Londiniensis."—" Liber albus, Liber custumarum ; Liber Horn," Rolls, 1859, ed. Riley. The regulations (in French) relating to the Pui are drawn from the " Liber Custumarum," compiled in 1320 (14 Ed. II.), pp. 216 ff. " The poetical competitions called *puis*," established in the north of France, " seem to have given rise to German and Dutch imitations, such as the *Master Singers* and the *Chambers of Rhetoric*." G. Paris, " Littérature française au moyen âge," paragraph 127. To these we can add the English imitation which now occupies us.

"prince" surrounded by twelve "compaignouns," elected by the brotherhood, whose mission included the duty of pacifying the squabblers. Each year a new prince was chosen and solemnly enthroned. On the appointed day "the old prince and his companions must go from one end of the hall to the other, singing ; the old prince will bear on his head the crown of the Pui, and have in his hand a gilt cup full of wine. And when they shall have gone all round, the old prince must give the one they have elected to drink, and also give him the crown, and that one shall be prince."

To pass judgment on *chansons* is no trifle, and the deed is surrounded by every precaution befitting so important a sentence. The decision rests with the old prince and the new, assisted by about fifteen "of the most knowing among the companions," who are all obliged to take a solemn oath : "They must find which is the best song, to the best of their capacity, under oath that they will not fail for love, for hate, for favour, for promise, for neighbourhood, for lineage, for any tie old or new, or for any reason whatsoever." Moreover, two or three judges shall be appointed "who are skilled in singing and music," to examine the tune of the song : "For unless it be accompanied by music, a written text cannot be called a *chanson*, neither can a *chanson royale* be crowned unless it be accompanied with the sweetness of melodious singing." The winner is to receive the crown, and his composition, copied and fairly written out, will be posted up in the hall, under the prince's coat of arms : "The prince shall cause to be fastened under his coat of arms the song crowned on the day he was chosen to be the new prince, clearly written, and correctly, without fault."

At one time the Pui society was nearly ruined, owing to the expense incurred for decking the hall. In future it will be more moderate: "It is agreed henceforth that the

part of the hall where the feast of the Pui is held, be not
hung with silk or cloth of gold, neither shall the hall itself
be draped, but only fairly garnished with green boughs,
the floor strewn with rushes, benches prepared, as befits
such a feast royal ; only the seat for the singers who are
to sing the *chansons royales* shall be covered with cloth of
gold."

After the competition, all dine together. Here is the
bill of fare for the feast : " And the bill of fare is thus
ordained ; be all the companions liberally served, the
poorest as well as the richest, after this fashion, to wit,
that to them be served good bread, good ale and good
wine, and then potage and a course of strong meat, and
after that a double roast in a dish, and cheese, and nothing
else." Women were not admitted to these gatherings, and
so that slanderers might not say it was for fear of quarrels,
or worse, we are told by the society itself that it was to
teach the members to " honour, cherish, and praise them as
much in their absence as in their presence."

No feast was complete in the Middle Ages without a
procession or progress through the streets ; the amusement
was thus shared by the people. The members of the Pui
did not fail in this : " As soon as they shall have given the
crown to the best singer, they shall mount their horses
and ride through the town, and then accompany their new
prince to his hostel, and there all get down, and dance
before departing ; and drink once, and return each to his
hostel." With its songs and music, its kind purpose, its
crowns and green branches, this association seems like a
peaceful and verdant corner of Arcadia in the midst of
London City : peaceful and merry in spite of mercantile
jealousies and international hatreds.

This oasis is all the more charming to the sight because
it is only an oasis. Such sentiments were too courteous
to be very common. While our friends of the Pui en-

deavour to cherish and praise women even in their absence, other makers of songs follow another mediæval tradition and satirise them mercilessly. Triads were dedicated to them, which were nothing but slanderous litanies :

> Herfor, and therfor, and therfor I came
> And for to preysse this praty woman.
> There wer three wylly, three wyly ther wer,
> A fox, a fryyr and a woman.
> Ther wer three angry, three angry ther wer :
> A wasp a wesyll and a woman.[1]

So the litany continues, very different from the litany of the beauties of woman sung in the same period, perhaps by the same men. Friars, monks, and fops who adopt absurd fashions, and wear hose so tight that they cannot stoop for fear of bursting them,[2] are, with women, the subjects of these satirical songs :

> Preste, ne monke, ne yit chanoun,
> Ne no man of religioun,
> Gyfen hem so to devocioun
>   As done thes holy frers,
> For summe gyven ham chyvalry,
> Somme to riote and ribaudery ;
> Bot ffrers gyven ham to grete study
>   And to grete prayers.[3]

An account follows of doings, studies, and prayers, by no means edifying, and which recalls Chaucer rather than St. Francis.

---

[1] " Songs and Carols now first printed," ed. Th. Wright, Percy Society, 1847, 8vo, p. 4.

[2]   For hortyng of here hosyn
>   Non inclinare laborant.

In the same piece, large collars, wide sleeves, big spurs are satirised. Th. Wright, " Political Poems and Songs from Ed. III. to Ric. III.," Rolls, 1859, 2 vols. 8vo, vol. i. p. 275.

[3] " Political Poems," *ibid.*, vol. i. p. 263.

III.

The tone becomes more elevated ; and then we have
forest songs in honour of the outlaw Robin Hood.[1] The
satire ceases to be simply mocking ; the singer's laughter
no longer consoles him for abuses ; he wants reforms ; he
chides and threatens. In his speech to the rebel peasants
in 1381, the priest John Ball takes from a popular song
the burden that comprises his whole theory :

> Whan Adam dalf and Eve span,
> Who was thanne the gentilman ?[2]

The anonymous poet makes the dumb peasant speak,
describe his woes, and draw up a list of his complaints.
By way of reply, anonymous clerks compose songs, half
English and half Latin, a favourite mixture at that time,
in which they express their horror of the rebels.[3] Others
sound the praises of the English heroes of the Hundred
Years' War.

Contrary to what might be supposed, the number of
these last songs is not great, and their inspiration not
exalted. The war, as has been seen, was a royal and not
a national one ; and it happened, moreover, that none of

---

[1] The greater part of those that have come down to us are of the fifteenth and
sixteenth centuries ; but Robin was very popular, and his praises were sung
as early as the fourteenth century. The lazy parson in Langland's Visions
confesses that he is incapable of chanting the services :

> But I can rymes of Robin Hood · and Randolf erle of Chestre.

Ed. Skeat, text B. v. 402. See above, p. 224.

[2] Walsingham, " Historia Anglicana," Rolls, vol. ii p. 32. See a XIVth
century English miniature representing Adam and Eve, so occupied, reproduced in " English Wayfaring Life," p. 283.

[3] Nede they fre be most,
> Vel nollent pacificari, &c.

" Political Poems," vol. i. p. 225. Satire of the heretical Lollards : " Lollardi
sunt zizania," &c. *Ibid.*, p. 232 ; of friars become peddlers, p. 264.

the famous poets of the time saw fit to celebrate Crécy and Poictiers. We have, therefore, nothing but rough sketches, akin to later-day popular prints, barbarous in design, and coarse in colouring, but of strong intent. Clerks, in their Latin, pursue France and Philip de Valois, with opprobrious epithets :

> Lynxea, viperea, vulpina, lupina, medea,
> Callida, syrena, crudelis, acerba, superba.

Such is France according to them, and as to her king, his fate is predicted in the following pun :

> O Philippus Valeys, Xerxes, Darius, Bituitus,
> Te faciet *maleys* Edwardus, aper polimitus.[1]

To which the French replied :

> Puis passeront Gauloys le bras marin,
> Le povre Anglet destruiront si par guerre,
> Qu'adonc diront tuit passant ce chemin :
> Ou temps jadis estoit ci Angleterre.[2]

But both countries have survived, for other quarrels, other sorrows, and other glories.

The battles of Edward III. were also celebrated in a series of English poems, that have been preserved for us in a single manuscript, together with the name of their author, Laurence Minot,[3] concerning whom nothing is

---

[1] " Political Poems," *ibid.*, vol. i. pp. 26 ff.

[2] Ballad by Eustache des Champs, " Œuvres Complètes," ii. p. 34.

[3] "The Poems of Laurence Minot," ed. J. Hall, Oxford, 1887, 8vo, eleven short poems on the battles of Edward III. Adam Davy may also be classed among the patriotic poets : " Davy's five dreams about Edward II.," ed. Furnivall, Early English Text Society, 1878, 8vo. They are dreams interspersed with prophecies ; the style is poor and aims at being apocalyptic. Edward II. shall be emperor of Christendom, &c. Various pious works, a life of St. Alexius, a poem on the signs betokening Doomsday, &c., have been attributed to Davy without sufficient reason. See on this subject, Furnivall, *ibid.*, who gives the text of these poems.

known. In his rude verse, where alliteration is sometimes combined with rime, both being very roughly handled, Minot follows Edward step by step, and extols his prowess with the best will, but in the worst poetry. Grand subjects do not need magnifying ; and when magnified by unskilful artists they run the risk of recalling the Sir Thopas example : this risk Edward incurs at the hands of Laurence Minot. On the other hand absurd and useless expletives, "suth to saine," " i-wis," and especially "both day and night" continually help Minot to eke out his rimes ; and the reader is sorely tempted uncourteously to agree with him when he exclaims :

Help me God, my wit es thin ![1]

Besides these war-songs, and at the same time, laments are heard, as in former days, sad and desponding accents. Defeats have succeeded to victories, and they contribute to raise doubts as to the validity of Edward's claims.[2] What if, after all, this ruinous war, the issue of which is uncertain, should turn out to be an unjust war as well ? Verses are even composed on the subject of wrongs done to inoffensive people in France : " Sanguis communitatis Franciæ quæ nihil ei nocebat quæritur apud Deum." [3]

In war literature the Scots did not fare better than the French at the hands of their neighbours. At this time, and for long after, they were still the foe, just as the Irish or French were. Following the example given by the latter, the Scots replied ; several of their replies, being in English, take rank in the literature of England. The most energetic is the semi-historical romance called "The Bruce"; it is the best of the patriotic poems deriving their inspiration from the wars of the fourteenth century.

---

[1] *Ibid.*, p. 21.
[2] Vices and faults of Edward : "Political Poems," vol. i. pp. 159, 172, &c.
[3] "Political Poems," vol. i. p. 172.

"The Bruce," composed about 1375 by John Barbour,[1] is divided into twenty books; it is written in the dialect spoken in the south of Scotland from Aberdeen to the frontier, the dialect employed later by James I. and Sir David Lyndesay, who, like Barbour himself, called it "inglis." Barbour's verse is octo-syllabic, forming rimed couplets; it is the same as Chaucer's in his "Hous of Fame."

Barbour's intention is to write a true history; he thus expects, he says, to give twofold pleasure: firstly because it is a history, secondly because it is a true one. But where passion has a hold it is rare that Truth reigns paramount, and Barbour's feeling for his country is nothing short of passionate love; so much so that, when a legend is to the credit of Scotland, his critical sense entirely disappears, and miracles become for him history. Thus with monotonous uniformity, throughout his poem a handful of Scotchmen rout the English multitudes; the highlanders perform prodigies, and the king still surpasses them in valour; everything succeeds with him as in a fairy tale. This love of the soil, of its rocks and its lochs, of its clans and their chieftains, brings to mind the most illustrious of the literary descendants of Barbour, Walter Scott, who more than once borrowed from "The Bruce" the subjects of his stories.[2]

---

[1] "The Bruce, or the book of the most excellent . . . Prince Robert de Broyss, King of Scots," ed. Skeat, E.E.T.S., 1879–89; ed. MacKenzie, 1909. Barbour, having received safe conducts from Edward III., studied at Oxford, 1357, 1364, and visited France, 1365, 1368. He enjoyed a royal pension and d. archdeacon of Aberdeen, ab. 1395. He had written also a "Stewartis Oryginale" (lost) carrying back his Kings' genealogy to Dardanus. Fragments on Troy (from Guido, ed. Horstmann, Heilbronn, 1882) and "Legends of the Saints" (ed. Metcalfe, Edinb. 1896, 3 vols.) have *e.g.* been also attributed to him. *Cf.* G. Neilson, "Barbour," poet and translator, 1900.

[2] "The incidents on which the ensuing novel mainly turns are derived from the ancient metrical chronicle of the Bruce by Archdeacon Barbour," &c "Castle Dangerous," Introd.—"The authorities used are chiefly those . . . of Archdeacon Barbour. . . . " "Lord of the Isles," Advert. to 1st ed.

Besides the love of their land, the two compatriots have in common a taste for picturesque anecdotes, and select them with a view of making their heroes popular; the sense of humour is not developed to an equal degree, but it is of the same quality in both; and the same kind of happy answers are enjoyed by the two. Barbour delights, and with good reason, in preserving the account of the fight in which the king, traitorously attacked by three men while alone in the mountains, "by a wode syde," smites them "rigorously," and kills them all, and, when congratulated on his return :

> " Perfay," said he,
> " I slew bot ane forouten ma,
> God and my hound has slane the twa." [1]

Barbour likes to show the king, simple, patriarchal and valorous, stern to his foes, and gentle to the weak. He makes him halt his army in Ireland, because the screams of a woman have been heard ; it is a poor laundress in the pangs of child-birth ; the march is interrupted ; a tent is spread, under which the poor creature is delivered in peace. [2]

To England's threats Barbour replies by challenges, and by his famous apostrophe to liberty :

> A ! fredome is a noble thing ! . . . [3]

Some people, continues the good archdeacon, who cannot long keep to the lyric style, have compared marriage to bondage, but they are unexperienced men who know nothing about it ; of course marriage is the worst state in which it is possible to live, the thing is beyond discussion ; but in bondage one cannot live, one dies.

---

[1] Book vii. line 483.　　[2] Book xvi. line 270.　　[3] Book i. line 225.

IV.

A little above the copse another head rises; that of Chaucer's great friend, John Gower. Unlike Chaucer, Gower hates and despises the common people; when he allows them room in his works, the place assigned to them is an unenviable one. He is aristocratic and conservative by nature, so that he belongs to older England as much as to the new nation, and is the last in date of the recognisable representatives of Angevin Britain. Like the latter, Gower hesitates between several idioms; he is not sure that English is the right one; he is tri-lingual, just as England had been; he writes long poems in Latin and English, and when he addresses himself to "the universality of all men" he uses French. His French savours a little "of Stratford," he knows it and confesses it; but nothing shows better how truly he belongs to the England of bygone times, the half-French England of former days: he excuses himself and persists. "And if I stumble in my French, forgive me my mistakes; English I am; and beg on this plea to be excused." [1]

Gower was rich and of good family. His life was a long one; born about 1330, he died in 1408. He was related to Sir Robert Gower; he owned manors in Kent and elsewhere. He was known to the king, and to the royal family, but undertook no public functions. To him as we have seen, and to Strode, Chaucer offered his "Troilus":

> O moral Gower, this book I directe
> To thee and to the philosophical Strode,
> To vouchen sauf, ther nede is, to corecte
> Of your benignitees and zeles gode.   (v. 266.)

---

[1] Et si jeo n'ai de François la faconde,
Pardonetz moi qe jeo de ceo forsvoie ;
Jeo suis Englois, si quier par tiele voie
Estre excusé.

"Traitié . . . pour essampler les amantz marietz," "Complete Works of John Gower," ed. G. C. Macaulay, Oxford, 1899 ff., i. 391. See Appendix II.

Gower, in his turn, represents Venus addressing him as
follows :

> . . . Gret wel Chaucer whan ye mete
> As mi disciple and mi poete,
> For in the floures of his youthe
> In sondri wise, as he well couthe,
> Of ditees and of songes glade,
> The whiche he for mi sake made,
> The lond fulfild is overal.

Gower was exceedingly pious. When old age came he
retired within the precincts of the priory of St. Mary
Overy's (now St. Saviour), in that same suburb of Southwark where Chaucer preferred to frequent the "Tabard,"
and he spent his last years there with his wife in devout
observances. He became blind in 1400, eight years before
his death. He bequeathed to his wife three cups, two salt-
cellars, twelve silver spoons, all his beds and chests, the
income of two manors, etc.; he left a number of pious
legacies in order to have lamps kept burning, and masses
said for his soul. He gave the priory two chasubles of
silk, a large missal, a chalice, a martyrology he had caused
to be copied for this purpose; he asked to be buried in
the chapel of St. John the Baptist at St. Mary Overy's;
which was done. His tomb, restored and repainted, still
exists. He is represented lying with his hands raised as
if for prayer, his thick locks are bound by a fillet adorned
with roses, and the inscription : "Merci ihs," Jesus, Saviour
of men, have mercy. The head of the plump, round-
cheeked poet rests on his three principal works; he wears
about his neck a collar of interwoven SS, together with the
swan, emblem of Henry IV.[2]

---

[1] "Confessio Amantis," "Complete Works," vol. iii. p. 466.

[2] Henry, then earl of Derby, had given him a collar in 1393; the swan was
the emblem of Thomas, duke of Gloucester, Henry's uncle, assassinated in
1397; Henry adopted it from that date. A view of Gower's tomb is, *e.g.*,
in my "Piers Plowman," 1894, p. 46. When Gower's tomb was displaced
in 1832, no care was taken of his bones which "disappeared."

The worthy man wrote immoderately, and in especial three great poems : the " Speculum Meditantis," in French ; the " Vox Clamantis," in Latin ; the " Confessio Amantis," in English. The first was long lost ; the loss was not very great. It has been recently discovered ; the gain is not considerable. We knew on contemporary evidence that Gower treated there of the vices and virtues of his day ; but he had told pretty clearly elsewhere what he thought of them, and, even had he not, it would have been easy to guess, for he was too right-minded a man not to have thought of them all the evil possible. The text now recovered by Mr. G. C. Macaulay shows how well justified was the good opinion generally held of " moral Gower's " morality. [1]

Besides this long, very long poem (some 31,000 lines in its original shape), Gower wrote, also in French, 5[1] ballads for unmarried lovers and 18 for married ones : Court poems, they are, imitations of Petrarch,[2] the light verses of a well-taught man. He promises eternal service

---

[1] For his discovery, his identification of the " Speculum Meditantis " (*alias* "hominis") with the " Mirrour de l'Omme," written ab. 1375, and his excellent edition so greatly needed of Gower's Complete Works, Mr. Macaulay deserves the thanks of every student. " The ' Speculum Meditantis,' " I wrote in 1894. " was sure to much resemble those works of moralisation (hence Chaucer's ' moral Gower '), numerous in French mediæval literature, which were called ' bibles.' "   So it does, recalling besides, as Mr. Macaulay has shown, I. xlvii., such kindred works as the " Somme des Vices et Vertus " and the " Manuel des Pechiez."   See " La Bible Guiot de Provins " (Barbazan and Méon, " Fabliaux," ii. 307) :

> Dou siécle puant et orrible
> M'estuet commencier une bible.

" On this stinking and horrid world, I want to begin a bible ; " and Guiot reviews all classes of society, all trades and professions, and blames everything and everybody ; Gower does the same ; everything for both is " puant." Rome is not spared : " Rome nos suce et nos englot," says Guiot ; so says Gower too, in his chapter on " la Court de Rome," ll. 18421 ff. He appropriately chose, as fitting his subject perfectly, what is perhaps the most monotonous stanza in French prosody : *aab aab bba bba.*

[2] Jeo ris en plour et en santé languis . . .
Ars en gelée et en chalour frémis—

to his "douce dame," his "douce dame" being no one in particular. He writes for others, and they are welcome to draw from his works : " The love-songs thus far are composed specially for those who expect love favours through marriage. . . . The ballads from here to the end of the book are common to all, according to the properties and conditions of lovers who are diversely wrought upon by fickle love." ¹ Here and there some fine similes are found in which figure the chameleon, for instance, who was supposed to live on air alone, or the hawk : " Chameleon a proud creature is, that lives upon air without more ; thus may I say in like fashion only through my hopes born of love is my soul's life preserved." ²

Gower's principal poem in Latin, the " Vox Clamantis," deals with the great rising of 1381, which had imperilled the Crown and the whole social order.³ Being a landowner in Kent, he was in the best situation fully to appreciate the danger.

Vol. i. p. 345. No passage in Petrarch has been oftener imitated. Villon wrote :

> Je meurs de soif auprès de la fontaine . . .
> Je ris en pleurs et attens sans espoir, &c.

¹ Vol. i. pp. 242, 243.

² Camelion est une beste fiere
Qui vit tansoulement de l'air sanz plus ;
Ensi pour dire en mesme la maniere,
De soul espoir qe j'ai d'amour conçuz
Sont mes pensers en vië sustenuz.

Ballad xvi ; what a chameleon is, is thus explained in a Vocabulary of the fifteenth century : " Hic gamelion, animal varii coloris et sola aere vivit—*a buttyrfle* " (Th. Wright, " Vocabularies," 1857, 4to, p. 220).

³ According however to Mr. Macaulay, IV. xxxi., Gower had possibly written before that the main part of his poem, and he added after what is now his first book, the only one which directly concerns the rising. Mr. M. has for the first time shown how ample were Gower's borrowings : " He repeatedly takes . . . passages of 8, 10 or even 20 lines from the ' Aurora ' of Peter Riga, from the poem of Alex. Neckham ' De vita Monachorum,' from the ' Speculum Stultorum ' or from the ' Pantheon.' " Gower wrote also in Latin verse "Chronica Tripartita " (wherein he relates with great severity, the reign of Richard II., from 1387 to its end), and a few shorter poems.

In order to treat this terrible subject, Gower, who is not inventive, adopts the form of a dream, just as if it were a new " Romaunt of the Rose." It is spring-time, and he falls asleep. Let us not mind it overmuch, we shall soon do likewise ; but our slumber will be a broken one ; in the midst of the droning of his sermon, Gower suddenly screams, roars, flies into a passion—" Vox Clamantis ! " His hearers open an eye, wonder where they are, recognise Gower, and go off to sleep again.

Gower heaps up enormous and vague invectives ; he fancies his style resembles that of the apostle in Patmos. Animals and monsters fight and yell ; the common people have been turned into beasts, oxen, hogs, dogs, foxes, flies, frogs ; all are hideous or dangerous. Cursing as he goes along, Gower drives before him, with hissing distichs the strange herd of his monsters, who " dart sulphureous flames from the cavern of their mouth." [1]

These disasters are caused by the vices of the time, and Gower lengthily, patiently, complacently, draws up an interminable catalogue of them. A University education has taught him the importance of correct divisions ; he divides and subdivides, as he had done before in his " Mirour de l'Omme." Firstly, there are the vices of churchmen ; these vices are of different kinds, as are ecclesiastics themselves ; he re-divides and re-subdivides. Some parsons " give Venus the tithes that belong to God"; others are the terror of hares : " lepus visa pericla fugit," and hearken to no chime but the " vociferations" of the

---

[1] P. 31.   He jeers at the vulgarity of their names :

> Hudde ferit, quos Judde terit, dum Tebbe minatur . . .
> Hogge suam pompam vibrat, dum se putat omni
>   Majorem Rege nobilitate fore.
> Balle propheta docet, quem spiritus ante malignus
>   Edocuit . . . (iv. p. 44.)

The famous John Ball is here referred to, the apostle of the revolt, who died quartered. See below, p. 413.

hounds [1]; others practise trade. Knights are too fond
of women "with golden locks"; peasants are slothful;
merchants, rapacious and dishonest; they make "false
gems out of glass."[2] The king himself does not escape a
lecture : let him be upright, pious, merciful, and choose his
ministers with care ; let him beware of women : " Thou
art king, let one sole queen suffice thee."[3]

In one particular, however, this sermon is a remarkable
one. What predominates in these long tirades of poor
verses is an intense feeling of horror and dismay ; the
quiet Gower, and the whole community to which he belonged, have suddenly been brought face to face with
something unusual and terrifying even for that period.
The earth shook, and a gulf opened ; hundreds of victims,
an archbishop of Canterbury among them, disappeared,
and the abyss still yawns ; the consternation is general,
and no one knows what remedy to expect. Happily the
two edges of the chasm have at last united ; it has closed
again, hiding in its depths a heaving sea of lava, the
rumblings of which are still heard, and give warning that
it may burst forth at some future day. Gower, in the
meantime, scans his distichs.

Chaucer wrote in English, naturally, his sole reason
being that it was the language of the country. Gower,
when he uses this idiom,[4] offers explanations :

---

[1] Est sibi crassus equus, restatque scientia macra . . .
　　Ad latus et cornu sufflans gerit, unde redundant
　　　　Mons, nemus, unde lepus visa pericla fugit. . . .
　　Clamor in ore canum, dum vociferantur in unum,
　　　　Est sibi campana psallitur unde Deo.
　　Stat sibi missa brevis devocio longaque campis,
　　　　Quo sibi cantores deputat esse canes. (iv. p. 147.)

[2] Conficit ex vitris gemmas oculo pretiosas. (iv. p. 223.)

[3] Rex es, regina satis est, tibi sufficit una. (iv. p. 256.)

[4] " Confessio Amantis," " Complete Works," vols. ii., iii. Gower left also
a short poem in English in " Praise of Peace," vol. iv. p. 481. The " Con-

25

> And for that fewe men endite
> In oure englisshe, I thenke make,
> A bok for Engelondes sake.[1]

He has no idea to what extent this apology, so common a hundred years before, is now out of place after the "Troilus" of Chaucer. His English book is a lengthy compilation, written at the request of the young King Richard,[2] wherein Gower seeks both to amuse and to instruct, giving as he does,

> Somwhat of lust, somewhat of lore.

In his turn, and after Boccaccio, he invents a plot that will allow him to insert a whole series of tales and stories into one single work, compositions of this sort being the fashion. Gower's collection contains a hundred and twelve short stories, two or three of which are very well told; one, the adventure of Florent, being, perhaps, related even better than in Chaucer.[3] The rest resembles the Gower of the "Vox Clamantis."

---

fessio" is written in octo-syllabic couplets, with four accents. This poem should be compared with French compilations of the same type, and especially with the "Castoiement d'un père à son fils," early thirteenth century, a series of tales in verse, told by the father to castigate and edify the son: Barbazan and Méon, "Fabliaux," Paris, 1808, vol. ii. An English version (late XVth cent.) has been discovered at Worcester by W. H. Hulme, 1906.

[1] Vol. ii. p. 2.

[2] Gower seems to have begun working at his "Confessio" ab. 1386; his first version was finished 1390; his last 1393 (vol. II. xxi ff.). In the latter, having openly taken the side of the future Henry IV. (which was very bold of him), he suppressed every flattering allusion to Richard. In the first version, instead of,

> A bok for Engelondes sake,

he had written:

> A bok for King Richardes sake.

[3] Vol. ii. pp. 74 ff. In Chaucer, the story is told by the Wife of Bath.

What will be the subject of this philosopher's talk? He
will tell us of a thing :

> . . . wherupon the world mot stonde,
> And hath don sithen it began,
> And schal whil ther is any man,
> And that is love.[1]

In order to treat of this subject, and of many others,
Boccaccio had conceived the idea of his gathering in the
villa near Florence, and Chaucer that of his pilgrimage.
Moral Gower remains true to his character, and imagines
a confession. The lover seeks a priest of Venus, a worthy
and very learned old man, called Genius, who had already
figured as confessor in the "Roman de la Rose" (and was
to appear again in Marot) [2] : "Benedicite," says the priest ;
"Dominus," answers the lover ; and a miniature shows the
lover in a pink gown, kneeling in a meadow at the feet of
Genius, a tonsured monk in frock and cowl.[3]

We find ourselves again among vices and virtues, classi-
fications, divisions, and subdivisions. Genius condemns the
vices (those of his goddess included, for he is a free-speaking
priest). He hates, above all things, Lollardry, "this new
tapinage," and he commends every virtue ; the stories come
in by way of example. Mind what your eyes do, witness
Actæon ; and your ears, witness the Sirens. He passes on
to the seven deadly sins which were apparently studied in

---

[1] Beginning of Book I.

[2] Already had been seen in the "Roman" :

> Comment Nature la déesse
> A son prêtre se confesse . . .
> "Génius, dit-elle, beau prêtre,
> D'une folie que j'ai faite,
> A vous m'en vuel faire confesse ; "

and taking confession as a pretext, she explains the various systems of the
universe at great length. *Cf.* Marot, "Le Temple de Cupido."

[3] In MS. Egerton, 1991, fol. 7, in the British Museum, reproduced in my
"Piers Plowman," p. 11.

the seminary where this priest of Venus learnt theology. After the deadly sins the mists and marvels of the " Secretum Secretorum " fill the scene. At last the lover begs for mercy ; he writes Venus a letter : " with the teres of min eye in stede of inke." Venus, being a goddess, deciphers the watery scrawl, hastens to the spot, and laughs at this shivering lover, whom age and wrinkles have still left a lover. Gower then decides to withdraw, and make, as he says, " beau retraite." In a last vision, the poor " olde grisel " gazes upon the series of famous loving couples, who give themselves up to the delight of dancing, in a paradise, where one could scarcely have expected to find them together : Tristan and Iseult, Paris and Helen, Troilus and Cressida, Samson and Dalila, David and Bathsheba, and the wise Solomon who has for himself alone a hundred or so of " Jewes eke and Sarazines."

In spite of the immense difference in their merit, the names of Chaucer and Gower were constantly coupled. James of Scotland, Skelton, Dunbar, always mention them together. The " Confessio," of which some forty manuscripts are known, was printed by Caxton in 1483, and twice by Berthelet, in 1532 and 1554. Under Elizabeth we find Gower on the stage ; he figures in " Pericles," and recites the prologue of this play, the plot of which is borrowed from his poem.[1]

---

[1] On a Spanish translation of the " Confessio " made apparently from a Portuguese one, in Gower's lifetime, and to be found in a MS. at the Escorial, see " Complete Works," II. clxvii. " This double translation into contemporary languages of the continent must denote," says Mr. Macaulay, p. vii, "that the writer's fame was not merely insular in his lifetime." Too much however should not be made of the fact, which seems to be due to the accident of an English canon, Robert Payn by name, living in Lisbon, and choosing to translate a work which reminded him of his country.

CHAPTER IV.

WILLIAM LANGLAND AND HIS VISIONS.

GOWER'S books were made out of books. Chaucer's friend carries us in imagination to the paradise of Eros, or to a Patmos of his own invention, from whence he foretells the end of the world; but whatever he does or says we are always perfectly aware of where we are: we are in his library.

It is quite different with another poet of this period, a mysterious and intangible personage, whose very name is doubtful, whose writings had great influence, and that no one appears to have seen, concerning whom we possess no contemporaneous information. Like Gower, strong ties bind him to the past; but Gower is linked to Angevin England, and William Langland, if such be really his name, to the dreamy England of the Saxons and Scandinavians. His books are not made out of books; they are made of real life, of things seen, of dreams dreamt, of feelings actually experienced. He is the exact opposite of Gower, he completes Chaucer himself. When the "Canterbury Tales" are read, it seems as though all England were described in them; when the Visions of Langland are opened, it is seen that Chaucer had not said everything.

Langland is without comparison the greatest poet after Chaucer in the mediæval literature of England.

I.

His Visions have been preserved for us in a considerable number of manuscripts. They differ greatly from each other; Langland appears to have absorbed himself in his work, continually remodelling and adding to it. No poem has been more truly lived than this one; it was the author's shelter, his real house, his real church; he always came back there to pray, to tell his sorrows—to live in it. Hence strange incoherencies, and at the same time many unexpected lights. The spirit by which Langland is animated is the spirit of the Middle Ages, powerful, desultory, limitless. A classic author makes a plan, establishes noble proportions, conceives a definite work, and completes it; the poet of the Middle Ages, if he makes a plan, rarely keeps to it; he alters it as he goes along, adding a porch, a wing, a chapel to his edifice: a cathedral in mediæval times was never finished. Some authors, it is true, were already touched by classic influence, and had an idea of measure; such was the case with Chaucer, but not with Langland; anything and everything finds place in his work. By collecting the more characteristic notes scattered in his poem, sketch-books full of striking examples might be formed, illustrative of English life in the fourteenth century, to compare with Chaucer's, of the political and religious history of the nation, and also of the biography of the author.

Allusions to events of the day which abound in the poem enable us to date it. Three principal versions exist,[1] without counting several intermediate remodellings;

---

[1] Mr. Skeat has given two excellent editions of these three texts (called texts A. B. and C.): 1º "The Vision of William concerning Piers Plowman,

the first contains twelve cantos or *passus*, the second twenty, the third twenty-three ; their probable dates are 1362–3, 1376–7, and 1398–9.[1]

The numerous allusions to himself made by the author, principally in the last text of his poem, when, according to the wont of old men, he chose to tell the tale of his past life, allow us to form an idea of what his material as well as moral biography must have been. He was probably born in 1331 or 1332, at Cleobury, or rather Ledbury, eight miles from Malvern,[2] not far from the border of Wales. He was (I think) of low extraction, and appears to have escaped bondage owing to the help of patrons who were pleased by his ready intelligence. From childhood he was used to peasants and poor folk ; he describes their habits as one familiarised with them, and their cottages as one who knows them well. His life oscillated chiefly between two localities, Malvern and London. Even when he resides in the latter place, his thoughts turn to Malvern, to its hills and verdure ; he imagines himself there ; for tender ties, those ties that bind men to mother earth, and which are only formed in childhood, endear the place to him. A convent and a school formerly

together with Vita de Dowel, &c., London, E.E.T.S., 1867–84, 4 vols. ; 2° "The Vision of William concerning Piers Plowman, in three parallel texts, together with Richard the Redeless," Oxford, 1886, 2 vols. Prof. Manly has ventured the opinion, untenable as I think, that the Vision was the work not of one but of five authors ("Cambr. Hist. of Engl. Lit." vol. ii.). On the discussion which ensued, see *e.g.* "The Piers Plowman Controversy," E.E.T.S., 1910 ; R. W. Chambers, in "Essays by Members of the Engl. Assoc.," ix. 50, and in "Modern Lang. Rev.," Ap. 1919.

[1] The reasons for these dates are given in my "Piers Plowman" (some passages from which are reproduced in this chapter), and in a paper I published in the *Revue Critique*, Oct. 25th, and Nov. 1, 1879. Mr. Skeat assigns the date of 1393 to the third text, adding, however, "I should not object to the opinion that the true date is later still." I have adduced proofs of this final revision having taken place in 1398 or shortly after.

[2] Letters of Canon Bannister and of Mr. A. H. Bright, "Times Lit. Supplt.," Sept. 2, 1922, March 12, 1925.

existed at Malvern, and there in all likelihood Langland first studied.

The church where he came to pray still exists, built of red sandstone, a structure of different epochs, where the Norman style and perpendicular Gothic unite. Behind the village rise steep hills, covered with gorse, ferns, heather, and moss. Their highest point quite at the end of the chain, towards Wales, is crowned by Roman earthworks. From thence can be descried the vast plain where flows the Severn, crossed by streams bordered by rows of trees taking blue tints in the distance, spotted with lights and shadows, as the clouds pass in the ever-varying sky. Meadows alternate with fields of waving grain; the square tower of Worcester rises to the left, and away to the east those mountains are seen that witnessed the feats of Arthur. This wide expanse was later to give the poet his idea of the world's plain, " a fair feld ful of folke," where he will assemble all humanity, as in a Valley of Jehoshaphat. He enjoys wandering in this "wilde wildernesse," attracted by " the layes the levely foules made."

From childhood imagination predominates in him; his intellectual curiosity and facility are very great. He is a vagabond by nature, both mentally and physically; he roams over the domains of science as he did over his beloved hills, at random, plunging into theology, logic, law, astronomy, "an harde thynge"; or losing himself in reveries, reading romances of chivalry, following Ymagynatyf, who never rests: " Idel was I nevere." He studies the properties of animals, stones, and plants, a little from nature and a little from books; now he talks as Euphues will do later, and his animal mythology will cause a smile; and now he speaks as one country-bred, who has seen with his own eyes, like Burns, a bird build her nest, and has patiently watched her do it. Sometimes the animal is a living one, that leaps from bough to bough in the sunlight;

at others, it is a strange beast, fit only to dwell among the stone foliage of a cathedral cornice.

He knows French and Latin ; he has some tincture of the classics ; he would like to know everything:

> Alle the sciences under sonne · and alle the sotyle craftes,
> I wolde I knewe and couth · kyndely in myne herte ! [1]

But, in that as in other things, his will is not on a par with his aspirations : this inadequacy was the cause of numberless disappointments. Thou art, Clergye says most appropriately, one of those who want to know but hate to study :

> The wer lef to lerne · but loth for to stodie.[2]

Even in early youth his mind seems to lack balance ; being as yet a boy, he is already a soul in trouble.

His dreams at this time were not all dark ones ; radiant apparitions came to him. Thou art young and lusty, said one, and hast years many before thee to live and to love ; look in this mirror, and see the wonders and joys of love. I shall follow thee, said another, till thou becomest a lord, and hast domains.[3] But one by one the lights faded around him ; his patrons died, and this was the end of his ambitions ; for he was not one of those men able by sheer strength of will to make up for outside help when that fails them. His will was diseased ; an endless grief began for him. Being dependent on his " Clergye " for a liveli-

---

[1] B. xv. 48.   [2] A. xii. 6.

[3] *Concupiscencia carnis* · colled me aboute the nekke,
And seyde, " Thou art yonge and yepe · and hast yeres yn
Forto lyve longe · and ladyes to lovye.
And in this myroure thow myghte se · myrthes ful manye
That leden the wil to lykynge · al thi lyf-tyme."
    The secounde seide the same · " I shal suwe thi wille ;
Til thow be a lorde and have londe." (B. xi. 16.)

hood, he went to London, and tried to earn his daily bread by means of it, of "that labour" which he had "lerned best." [1]

Religious life in the Middle Ages had not those well-defined and visible landmarks to which we are accustomed. Nowadays one either is or is not of the Church ; formerly, no such obvious divisions existed. Religious life spread through society, like an immense river without dykes, swollen by innumerable affluents, whose subterranean penetrations impregnated even the soil through which they did not actually flow. From this arose numerous situations difficult to define, bordering at once on the world and on the Church, a state of things with which there is no analogy now, except in Rome itself, where the religious life of the Middle Ages still partly continues.

Numerous semi-religious and slightly renumerative functions were accessible to clerks, who were not, however, obliged to renounce the world on that account. The great thing in the hour of death being to ensure the salvation of the soul, men of fortune continued, and sometimes began, their good works at that hour. They endeavoured to win Paradise by proxy; they left directions in their will that, by means of lawful hire, soldiers should be sent to battle with the infidel ; and they also founded what were called "*chantries.*" A sum of money was left by them in order that masses, or the service for the dead, or both, should be chanted for the repose of their souls.

The number of these chantries was countless ; every arch in the aisles of the cathedrals contained some, where the service for the dead was sung ; sometimes separate edifices were built with this view. A priest celebrated masses when the founder had asked for them ; and clerks performed the office of choristers, having, for the most part, simply received the tonsure, and not being

[1] C. vi. 42.

necessarily in holy orders. It was, for them all, a career, almost a trade ; giving rise to discussions concerning salaries, and even to actual strikes. These services derived the name under which they commonly went from one of the words of the liturgy sung ; they were called *Placebos* and *Diriges.* The word "dirge" has passed into the English language, and is derived from the latter.

To psalmody for money, to chant the same words from day to day and from year to year, transforming into a mere mechanical toil the divine gift and duty of prayer, could not answer the ideal of life conceived by a proud and generous soul filled with vast thoughts. Langland, however, was obliged to curb his mind to this work ; *Placebo* and *Dirige* became his *tools* :

The lomes that ich laboure with · and lyflode deserve.[1]

Like many others whose will is diseased, he condemned the abuse and profited by it. The fairies at his birth had promised riches, and he was poor ; they had whispered of love, and an unsatisfactory marriage had closed the door on love, and debarred him from preferment to the highest ecclesiastical ranks. Langland lives miserably with his wife Catherine and his daughter Nicolette, in a house in Cornhill, not far from St. Paul's, the cathedral of many chantries,[2] and not far from that tower of Aldgate, to which about this time that other poet, Chaucer, directed his steps, he, too, solitary and lost in dreams.

Langland has depicted himself at this period of his existence a great, gaunt figure, dressed in sombre garments with large folds, sad in a grief without end, bewailing the

---

[1] C. vi. 45.

[2] On which see W. S. Simpson, "St. Paul's Cathedral and old City life," London, 1894, 8vo, p. 95 : "The chantry priests of St. Paul's." A list of those chantries in a handwriting of the fourteenth century has been preserved ; there are seventy-three of them. *Ibid.*, p. 99.

lost protectors of his childhood and his vanished illusions, seeing but clouds on the horizon of his life. He begins no new friendships ; he forms ties with no one ; he follows the crowded streets of the city, elbowing lords, lawyers, and ladies of fashion ; he greets no one. Men wearing furs and silver pendants, rich garments and collars of gold, brush past him, and he knows them not. Gold collars ought to be saluted, but he does not do it ; he does not say to them: " God loke yow, Lordes ! " But then his air is so absent, so strange, that instead of quarrelling with him people shrug their shoulders, and say : He is " a fole " ; he is mad.[1] Mad ! the word recurs again and again under his pen, the idea presents itself incessantly to his mind, under every shape, as though he were possessed by it : " fole," " frantyk," " ydiote ! " He sees around him nothing but dismal spectres : Age, Penury, Disease.

To these material woes are added mental ones. In the darkness of this world shines at least a distant ray, far off, beyond the grave. But, at times, even this light wavers ; clouds obscure and apparently extinguish it. Doubts assail the soul of the dreamer ; theology ought to elucidate, but, on the contrary, only darkens them :

> The more I muse there-inne · the mistier it seemeth,
> And the depper I devyne · the derker me it thinketh.[2]

How is it possible to reconcile the teachings of theology with our idea of justice ? And certain thoughts constantly recur to the poet, and shake the edifice of his faith ; he drives them away, they reappear ; he is bewitched by them and cannot exorcise these demons. Who had a more elevated mind than Aristotle, and who was wiser than Solomon ? Still they are held by Holy-Church " bothe

---

[1] C. beginning of passus vi. ; B. beginning of passus xv. : " My witte wex and wanyed til I a fole were."   [2] B. x. 181.

ydampned!" and on Good Friday, what do we see? A
felon is saved who had lived all his life in lies and thefts;
he was saved at once "with-outen penaunce of purgatorie."
Adam, Isaiah, and all the prophets remained "many longe
yeres" with Lucifer, and—

A robbere was yraunceouned · rather than thei alle ! [1]

He wishes he had thought less, learnt less, "conned"
fewer books, and preserved for himself the quiet, "sad
bileve" of "plowmen and pastoures"; happy men who
can, he says in a striking line,

Percen with a *pater noster* · the paleys of hevene ! [2]

In the midst of these trials and sorrows, Langland had
one refuge: his book. His poem made up for those
things which life had denied him. Why make verses, why
write, said Ymagynatyf to him; are there not "bokes
ynowe?" [3] But without his book, Langland could not
have lived, like those fathers whose existence is bound up
in that of their child, and who die if he dies. When he
had finished it, and though his intention was never to
touch it again, for in it he announced his own death, he
still began it over again, once, twice; he worked at it all
his life.

What was the end of that life? No one knows. Some
indications tend to show that in his later years he left

[1] B. x. 420.

[2] . . . None sonner saved · ne sadder of bileve,
Than plowmen and pastoures · and pore comune laboreres.
Souteres and shepherdes · suche lewed jottes
Percen with a *pater-noster* · the paleys of hevene,
And passen purgatorie penaunceles · at her hennes-partynge,
In-to the blisse of paradys · for her pure byleve,
That inparfitly here · knewe and eke lyved. (B. x. 458.)

[3] And thow medlest with makynges · and myghtest go sey thi sauter,
And bidde for hem that giveth the bred · for there ar bokes ynowe
To telle men what Dowel is. . . . (B. xii. 16.)

London, where he had led his troubled life to return to the
Western country.[1]   There we should like to think of him,
soothed, healed, resigned, and watching that sun decline in
the west which he had seen rise, many years before, "in a
somere seyson."

II.

In this summer season, in the freshness of the morning,
to the musical sound of waters, " it sowned so murrie," the
poet, lingering on the summit of Malvern hills, falls asleep,
and the first of his visions begins.   He contemplates

> Al the welthe of this worlde · and the woo bothe ;

and, in an immense plain, a " feld ful of folke," he notices
the bustle and movements of mankind,

> Of alle maner of men · the mene and the riche.

Mankind is represented by typical specimens of all
sorts : knights, monks, parsons, workmen singing French
songs, cooks crying : Hot pies ! " Hote pyes, hote ! " pardoners, pilgrims, preachers, beggars, janglers who will not
work, japers and " mynstralles " that sell " glee."   They
are, or nearly so, the same beings Chaucer assembled at
the " Tabard " inn, on the eve of his pilgrimage to Canterbury.   This crowd has likewise a pilgrimage to make, not,
however, on the sunny high-road that leads from Southwark to the shrine of St. Thomas.   No, they journey
through abstract countries, and have to accomplish, some
three hundred years before Bunyan's Christian, their
pilgrim's progress in search of Truth and of Supreme
Good.

[1] He seems to have written at this time the fragment called by Mr. Skeat :
" Richard the Redeless," and attributed by the same with great probability
to our author.

A lady appears, who explains the landscape and the vision ; she is Holy-Church. Yonder tower is the tower of Truth. This castle is the "Castel of Care" that contains "Wronge." Holy-Church points out how mankind ought to live, and teaches kings and knights their duties with regard to Truth.

Here comes Lady Meed, a lady of importance, whose friendship means perdition, yet without whom nothing can be done, and who plays an immense part in the world. The monosyllable which designates her has a vague and extended signification ; it means both reward and bribery. Disinterestedness, the virtue of noble minds, being rare in this world, scarcely anything is undertaken without hope of recompense, and what man, toiling solely with a view to recompense, is quite safe from bribery ? So Lady Meed is there, beautiful, alluring, perplexing ; to get on without her is impossible, and yet it is hard to know what to do with her. She is about to marry "Fals" ; the friends and witnesses have arrived, the marriage deed is drawn up; the pair are to have the "Erldome of Envye," and other territories that recall the worst regions of the celebrated map of the Tendre. Opposition is made to the marriage, and the whole wedding party starts for Westminster, where the cause is to be determined ; friends, relations, bystanders ; on foot, on horseback, and in carriages ; a singular procession !

The king, notified of the coming of this *cortège*, publicly declares he will deal justice to the knaves, and the procession melts away; most of the friends disappear at a racing pace through the lanes of London. The poet hastens to lodge the greatest scoundrels with the people he hates, and has them received with open arms. "Gyle" is welcomed by the merchants, who dress him as an apprentice, and make him wait on their customers. "Lyer" has at first hard work to find shelter ; he hides in the obscure holes of the alleys, "lorkynge thorw lanes"; no door opens, his felonies are too notorious.   At last, the pardoners "hadden pite and pullede hym to house"; they washed him and clothed him and sent him to church on Sundays with bulls and seals appended, to sell "pardons for pans" (pence).   Then leeches send him letters to say that if he would assist them "waters to loke," he should be well received; spicers have an interview with him; minstrels and messengers keep him "half a yere and eleve dayes"; friars dress him as a friar, and, with them, he forms the friendliest ties of all.[1]

Lady Meed appears before the king's tribunal; she is beautiful, she looks gentle, she produces a great effect; she is Phryne before her judges with the addition of a garment.   The judges melt, they cheer her, and so do the clerks, the friars, and all those that approach her.   She is so pretty! and so kind!   Anything you will, she wills it too; no one feels bashful in her presence; she is indeed so kind.   A friar offers her the boon of an absolution, which he will grant her "himself"; but she must do good to the brotherhood: We have a window begun that will cost us dear; if you would pay for the stained glass of the gable, your name should be engraved thereon, and to heaven would go your soul.   Meed is willing.   The king appears and examines her; he decides to marry her, not to Fals, but to the knight Conscience.   Meed is willing; she is always willing.

The knight comes, refuses, and lays bare the ill-practices of Meed, who corrupts all the orders of the kingdom, and has caused the death of "yowre fadre" (your father, King Edward II.).   She would not be an amiable spouse; she is as "comune as the cart-wey."   She connives with the Pope in the presentation to benefices; she obtains bishoprics for fools, "theighe they be lewed."

[1] C. iii. 211 ff.

Meed weeps, which is already a good answer ; then, having recovered the use of speech, she defends herself cleverly.   The world would fall into a torpor without Meed ; knights would no longer care for kings ; priests would no longer say masses; minstrels would sing no more songs ;   merchants would not trade ; and even beggars would no longer beg.

The knight tartly replies : There are two kinds of Meed ; we knew it ; there is reward, and there is bribery, but they are always confounded.   Ah ! if Reason reigned in this world instead of Meed, the golden age would return ; no more wars ; no more of these varieties of tribunals, where Justice herself gets confused.   At this Meed becomes "wroth as the wynde." [1]

Enough, says the king ; I can stand you no longer ; you must both serve me :

> " Kisse hir," quod the kynge · " Conscience, I hote (bid)."
> —" Nay bi Criste ! " [2]

the knight answers, and the quarrel continues.   They send for Reason to decide it.   Reason has his horses saddled ; they have interminable names, such as " Suffre-til-I-see-my-time."   Long before the day of the Puritans, our visionary employs names equivalent to sentences; we meet, in his poem, with a little girl, called Behave-well-or-thy-mother-will-give-thee-a-whipping,[3] scarcely a practical name for everyday life ; another personage, Evan the Welshman, rejoices in a name six lines long.

Reason arrives at Court ; the dispute between Meed and Conscience is dropped and forgotten, for another one has arisen.   "Thanne come Pees into Parlement ; " Peace

---

[1] B. iii. 328.   [2] B. iv. 3.
[3] Daughter of Piers Plowman :

Hus douhter hihte Do-ryght-so- · other-thy-damme-shal-the-bete.

(C. ix. 81.

presents a petition against Wrong, and enumerates his evil actions. He has led astray Rose and Margaret ; he keeps a troup of retainers who assist him in his misdeeds ; he attacks farms, and carries off the crops ; he is so powerful that none dare stir or complain. These are not vain fancies ; the Rolls of Parliament, the actual Parliament that was sitting at Westminster, contain numbers of similar petitions, where the real name of Wrong is given, and where the king endeavours to reply, as he does in the poem, according to the counsels of Reason.

Reason makes a speech to the entire nation, assembled in that plain which is discovered from the heights of Malvern, and where we found ourselves at the beginning of the Visions.

Then a change of scene. These scene-shiftings are frequent, unexpected, and rapid as in an opera. "Then, . . ." says the poet, without further explanation : then the scene shifts ; the plain has disappeared ; a new personage, Repentance, now listens to the Confession of the Deadly Sins. This is one of the most striking passages of the poem ; in spite of their abstract names, these sins are tangible realities ; the author describes their shape and their costumes ; some are bony, others are tun-bellied ; singular abstractions with warts on their noses! We were just now in Parliament, with the victims of the powerful and the wicked ; we now hear the general con-fession of England in the time of the Plantagenets.[1]

That the conversion may be a lasting one, Truth must be sought after. Piers Plowman appears, a mystic person-age, a variable emblem, that here simply represents the man of "good will," and elsewhere stands for Christ him-self. He teaches the way ; gates must be entered, castles encountered, and the Ten Commandments will be passed

[1] See in particular Gloton's confession, with a wonderfully realistic descrip-tion of an English tavern, C. vii. 350.

through. Above all, he teaches every one his present
duties, his active and definite obligations; he protests
against useless and unoccupied lives, against those who
have since been termed "dilettanti," for whom life is a
sight, and who limit their function to being sight-seers, to
amusing themselves and judging others. All those who
live upon earth have actual practical duties, even you,
lovely ladies:

> And ye lovely ladyes · with youre longe fyngres.

All must defend, or till, or sow the field of life. The
ploughing commences, but it is soon apparent that some
pretend to labour and labour not; they are lazy or talkative, and sing songs. Piers succeeds in mastering them
by the help of Hunger. Thanks to Hunger and Truth,
distant possibilities are seen of a reform, of a future
Golden Age, an island of England that shall be similar to
the island of Utopia, imagined later by another Englishman.

The vision rises and fades away; another vision and
another pilgrimage commence, and occupy all the re-
mainder of the poem, that is, from the eleventh to the
twenty-third passus (C. text). The poet endeavours to
join in their dwellings Dowel, Dobet, and Dobest; in other
terms: Good-life, Better-life, and Best-life. All this part
of the book is filled with sermons, most of them energetic,
eloquent, spirited, full of masterly touches, leaving an
ineffaceable impression on the memory and the heart:
sermon of Study on the Bible and on Arts and Letters;
sermons of Clergye and of Ymagynatyf, dialogue
between Hawkyn (active life) and Patience; sermons of
Faith, Hope, and Charity. Several visions are inter-
mingled with these sermons: visions of the arrival of
Christ in Jerusalem, and of the Passion; visions of hell

attacked by Jesus, and defended by Satan and Lucifer with guns, "brasene gonnes," a then recent invention, which appeared particularly diabolical. Milton's Satan, in spite of having had three hundred years in which to improve his tactics, will find nothing better; his batteries are ranged in good order; a seraph stands behind each cannon with lighted match; at the first discharge, angels and archangels fall to the ground:

> By thousands, Angel on Archangel rolled.

They are not killed, but painfully suffer from a knowledge that they look ridiculous: "an indecent overthrow," they call it. The fiends, exhilarated by this sight, roar noisily, and it is hard indeed for us to take a tragical view of the massacre.[1]

In the Visions, Christ, conqueror of hell, liberates the souls that await his coming, and the poet awakes to the sounds of bells on Easter morning.

The poem ends amid doleful apparitions; now comes Antichrist, then Old Age, and Death. Years have fled, death draws near; only a short time remains to live; how employ it to the best advantage? (Dobet). Advise me, Nature! cries the poet. "Love!" replies Nature:

> "Lerne to love," quod Kynde · "and leve of alle othre."

III.

Chaucer, with his genius and his manifold qualities, his gaiety and his gracefulness, his faculty of observation and that apprehensiveness of mind which enables him to sympathise with the most diverse specimens of humanity, has drawn an immortal picture of mediæval England. In cer-

---

[1] "Paradise Lost," canto vi. 601; invention of guns, 470.

tain respects, however, the description is incomplete, and one must borrow from Langland some finishing touches.

We owe to Chaucer's horror of vain abstractions the individuality of each one of his personages ; all classes of society are represented in his works ; but the types which impersonate them are so clearly characterised, their singleness is so marked, that on seeing them we think of them alone and of no one else. We are so absorbed in the contemplation of this or that man that we think no more of the class, the *ensemble*, the nation.

The active and actual passions of the multitude, the subterranean lavas which simmer beneath a brittle crust of good order and regular administration, all the latent possibilities of volcanoes which this inward fire betokens, arc, on the contrary, always present to the mind of the visionary ; rumblings are heard, and they herald the earthquake. The vehement and passionate England that produced the great rising of 1381, and the heresy of Wyclif, that later on will give birth to the Cavaliers and Puritans, is contained in essence in Langland's work ; we divine, we foresee her. Chaucer's book is, undoubtedly, not in contradiction to that England, but it screens and allows her to be forgotten. In their anger Chaucer's people exchange blows on the highway ; Langland's crowds in their anger sack the palace of the Savoy, and storm the Tower of London.

Langland thus shows us what we find in none of his contemporaries : crowds, groups, classes, living and true to nature ; the merchant class, the religious world, the Commons of England. He is, above all, the only author who gives a sufficient and contemporaneous idea of that grand phenomenon, the power of Parliament. Chaucer, who was himself a member of that assembly, sends his franklin there ; he mentions the fact, and nothing more ; the part played by the franklin in that group, amid that concourse of human beings, is not described. On the other hand, an admirable picture represents him keeping open house, and ordering capons, partridges, and "poynant sauce" in abundance. At home, his personality stands out in relief; but yonder, at Westminster, the franklin was doubtless lost in the crowd ; and crowds had little interest for Chaucer.

In two documents only does that power appear great and impressive as it really was, and those documents are: the Rolls wherein are recorded the acts of Parliament, and the poem of William Langland. No one before him, none of his contemporaries, had seen so clearly how the matter stood. The whole organisation of the English State is summed up in a line of admirable conciseness and energy, in which the poet shows the king surrounded by his people :

> Knyghthod hym ladde,
> Might of the comunes · made hym to regne.[1]

The power of the Commons is always present to the mind of Langland ; he observes the impossibility of doing without them. When the king is inclined to stretch his prerogative beyond measure, when he gives in his speeches a foretaste of the theory of divine right, when he speaks as did Richard II. a few years after, and the Stuarts three centuries later, when he boasts of being the ruler of all, of being "hed of lawe," while the Clergy and Commons are but members of the same, Langland stops him, and through the mouth of Conscience, adds a menacing clause :

> "In condicioun," quod Conscience, · "that thow konne defende
> And rule thi rewme in resoun · right wel, and in treuth."[2]

The deposition of Richard, accused of having stated, nearly in the same terms, "that he dictated from his lips the laws of his kingdom,"[3] and the fall of the Stuarts, are contained, so to say, in these almost prophetic words.

---

[1] B. Prol. 112. [2] B. xix. 474.
[3] "Rotuli Parliamentorum," vol. iii. p. 419. See above, p. 253.

On nearly all the questions which agitate men's minds in the fourteenth century, Langland agrees with the Commons, and, as we follow from year to year the Rolls of Parliament, petitions or decisions are found inspired by the same views as those Langland entertained ; his work at times reads like a poetical commentary of the Rolls. Langland, as the Commons, is in favour of the old division of classes, of the continuance of bondage, and of the regulation of wages by the State ; he feels nothing but hatred for Lombard and Jew bankers, for royal purveyors, and forestallers. In the same way as the Commons, he is in favour of peace with France ; his attention is concentrated on matters purely English ; distant wars fill him with anxiety. He would willingly have kept to the peace of Brétigny, he hopes the Crusades may not recommence. He is above all *insular.* Like the Commons he recognises the religious authority of the Pope, but protests against the Pope's encroachments, and against the interference of the sovereign-pontiff in temporal matters. The extension of the papal power in England appears to him excessive ; he protests against appeals to the Court of Rome ; he is of opinion that the wealth of the Church is hurtful to her ; he shares the sentiments of the Commons of the Good Parliament towards what they do not hesitate to term the sinful city of Avignon : " la peccherouse cité d'Avenon."[1] He is indignant with the bishops, masters, and doctors that allow themselves to become domesticated, and :

> . . . serven as servantz · lordes and ladyes,
> And in stede of stuwardes · sytten and demen (judge).[2]

Going down in this manner, step by step, Langland reaches the strange, grimacing, unpardonable herd of liars, knaves and cheats who traffic in holy things, absolve for money, sell heaven, deceive the simple, and appear as if

---

[1] Good Parliament of 1376 on which, *infra*, p. 419.   [2] B. Prol. 95.

they "hadden leve to lye al here lyf after."[1] In this nethermost circle of his hell, where he scourges them with incessant raillery, the poet confines pell-mell all these glutted unbelievers. Like hardy parasitical plants, they have disjoined the tiles and stones of the sacred edifice, so that the wind steals in, and the rain penetrates : shameless pardoners they are, friars, pilgrims, hermits, with nothing of the saint about them save the garb, whose example, unless a stop is put to it, will teach the world to despise clerical dress, those who wear it, and the religion, even, that tolerates and supports them.

At this depth, and in the dim recesses where he casts the rays of his lantern, Langland spares none ; his ferocious laugh is reverberated by the walls, and the scared night-birds take to flight. His mirth is not the mirth of Chaucer, itself less light than the mirth of France ; not the joyous peal of laughter which rang out on the Canterbury road, welcoming the discourses of the exhibitor of relics, and the far from disinterested sermons of the friar to sick Thomas. It is a woful and terrible laugh, harbinger of the final catastrophe and doom. What they have heard in the plain of Malvern, the accursed ones will hear again in the Valley of Jehoshaphat.

They have now no choice, but must come out of their holes ; and they come forward into the light of day, hideous and grotesque, saturated with the moisture of their dismal vaults ; the sun blinds them, the fresh air makes them giddy ; they present a sorry figure. Unlike the pilgrims of Canterbury, they derive no benefit from the feelings of indulgence that softens our hearts on a gay April morn ; they will learn to know the difference between the laugh that pardons and the laugh that kills. Langland takes them up, lets them fall, and takes them up again ; he never wearies of this cruel sport ; he presents

[1] B. Prol. 49.

them to us now separately, and now collectively: packs of pilgrims, "eremytes on an hep," pilgrims that run to St. James's in Spain, to Rome, to Rocamadour in Guyenne, who have paid visits to every saint. But have they ever sought for St. Truth? No, never! Will they ever know the real place where they might find St. James? Will they suspect that St. James should

> be souht · ther poure syke lyggen (lie)
> In prisons and in poore cotes? [1]

They seek St. James in Spain, and St. James is at their gates; they elbow him each day, and they recognise him not.

What sight can comfort us for these sad things? That of the poor and disinterested man, of the honest and courageous labourer. Langland here shows himself truly original: the guide he has chosen differs as much from the Virgil of Dante as from the Lover that Guillaume de Lorris follows through the paths of the Garden of the Rose. The English visionary is led by Piers Plowman; Piers is the mainspring of the State; he realises that ideal of disinterestedness, conscience, reason, which fills the soul of our poet; he is the real hero of the work. Bent over the soil, patient as the oxen that he goads, he performs each day his sacred task; the years pass over his whitening head, and, from the dawn of life to its twilight, he follows ceaselessly the same endless furrow, pursuing behind the plough his eternal pilgrimage.

Around him the idle sleep, the careless sing; they pretend to cheer others by their humming; they trill: "Hoy! troly lolly!" Piers shall feed every one, except these useless ones; he shall not feed "Jakke the jogeloure and Jonet . . . and Danyel the dys-playere and Denote the baude, and frere the faytoure, . . ." for, all whose name is entered "in

---

[1] B. Prol. 46; xii. 37; v. 57; C. v. 122.

the legende of lif" must take life seriously.[1]   There is no place in this world for people who are not in earnest ; every class that is content to perform its duties imperfectly and without sincerity, that fulfils them without eagerness, without passion, without pleasure, without striving to attain the best possible result and do better than the preceding generation, will perish.   So much the more surely shall perish the class that ceases to justify its privileges by its services : this is the great law propounded in our own day by Taine.   Langland lets loose upon the indolent, the careless, the busybodies who talk much and work little, a foe more terrible and more real then than now : Hunger.   Piers undertakes the care of all sincere people, and Hunger looks after the rest.   All this part of the poem is nothing but an eloquent declaration of man's duties, and is one of the finest pages of this " Divine Comedy " of the poor.

IV.

Langland speaks as he thinks, impetuously ; a sort of dual personality exists in him ; he is the victim and not the master of his thought.   And his thought is so completely a separate entity, with wishes opposed to his desires, that it appears to him in the solitudes of Malvern ; and the melody of lines heard not long ago occurs to the memory :

> Je marchais un jour à pas lents
> Dans un bois, sur une bruyère ;
> Au pied d'un arbre vint s'asseoir
> Un jeune homme vêtu de noir
> Qui me ressemblait comme un frère. . . . [2]

Filled with a similar feeling, the wandering dreamer had met, five hundred years before, in a "wilde wildernesse

---

[1] B. vi. 71 ; C. ix. 122.   [2] Musset, " Nuit de Décembre."

and bi a wode-syde," a "moche man" who looked like
himself; who knew him and called him by name :

> And thus I went wide-where · walkyng myne one (alone),
> By a wilde wildernesse · and bi a wode-syde . . .
> And under a lynde uppon a launde · lened I a stounde. . . .
> A moche man, as me thoughte · and lyke to my-selve
> Come and called me · by my kynde name,
> "What artow," quod I tho (then) · "that thow my name knowest?"
> "That thow wost wel," quod he · "and no wyghte bettere."
> "Wote I what thow art?" · "Thought," seyde he thanne,
> "I have suwed (followed) the this sevene yere · sey thow me no
> rather (sooner)?" [1]

"Thought" reigns supreme, and does with Langland
what he chooses. Langland is unconscious of what he is
led to; his visions are for him real ones; he tells them as
they rise before him; he is scarcely aware that he invents;
he stares at the sight, and wonders as much as we do;
he can change nothing; his personages are beyond his
reach. There is therefore nothing prepared, artistically arranged, or skilfully contrived, in his poem; the deliberate
hand of a man of the craft is nowhere to be seen. He
obtains artistic effects, but without seeking for them; he
never selects or co-ordinates; he is suddenly led, and
leads us, from one subject to another, without any better
transition than an "and thanne" or a "with that." And
"thanne" we are carried a hundred miles away, among
entirely different beings, and frequently we hear no more
of the first ones. Or sometimes, even, the first reappear,
but they are no longer the same; Piers Plowman personifies
now the honest man of the people, now the Pope, now
Christ. Dowel, Dobet, and Dobest have two or three
different meanings. The art of transitions is as much dis-
pensed with in his poem as at the opera : a whistle of the
scene-shifter—an "and thanne" of the poet – the palace of
heaven fades away, and we find ourselves in a smoky
tavern in Cornhill.

[1] B. viii. 62.

Clouds pass over the sky, and sometimes sweep by the earth ; their thickness varies, they take every shape : now they are soft, indolent mists, lingering in mountain hollows, that will rise towards noon, laden with the scent of flowering lindens ; now they are storm-clouds, threatening destruction and rolling with thunder. Night comes on, and suddenly the blackness is rent by so glaring a light that the plain assumes for an instant the hues of mid-day ; then the darkness falls again, deeper than before.

The poet moves among realities and abstractions, and sometimes the first dissolve in fogs, while the second condense into human beings, tangible and solid. On the Malvern hills, the mists are so fine, it is impossible to say : here they begin and here they end ; it is the same in the Visions.

In the world of ethics, as among the realities of actual life, Langland excels in summing up in one sudden memorable flash the whole doctrine contained in the nebulous sermons of his abstract preachers ; he then attains to the highest degree of excellence, without striving after it. In another writer, the thing would have been premeditated, and the result of his skill and cunning ; here the effect is as unexpected for the author as for the reader. He so little pretends to such felicities of speech that he never allows the grand impressions thus produced to last any time ; he utilises them, he is careful to make the best of the occasion. It seems as if he had conjured the lightning from the clouds unawares, and he thinks it his duty to turn it to use. The flash had unveiled the uppermost summits of the realm of thought, and there will remain in our hands a flickering rushlight that can at most help us upstairs.

The passionate sincerity which is the predominant trait of Langland's character greatly contributed to the lasting influence of his poem. Each line sets forth his unconquerable aversion for all that is mere appearance and show, self-interested imposture ; for all that is antagonistic to conscience, abnegation, sincerity. Such is the great and fundamental indignation that is in him ; all the others are derived from this. For, while his mind was impressed with the idea of the seriousness of life, he happened to live when the mediæval period was drawing to its close ; and, as usually happens towards the end of epochs, people no longer took in earnest any of the faiths and feelings which had supplied foregoing generations with their strength and motive power. He saw with his own eyes knights preparing for war as if it were a hunt ; learned men consider the mysteries of religion as fit subjects to exercise one's minds in after-dinner discussions ; the chief guardians of the flock busy themselves with their "owelles" only to shear, not to feed them. Meed was everywhere triumphant ; her misdeeds had been vainly denounced ; her reign had come ; under the features of Alice Perrers she was now the paramour of the king !

At all such men and at all such things, Langland thunders anathema. Lack of sincerity, all the shapes and sorts of "faux semblants," or "merveilleux semblants," as Rutebeuf said, fill him with inextinguishable hatred. In shams and "faux semblants" he sees the criterion of good and evil, the touchstone of right and wrong, the main difference between the worthy and the unworthy. He constantly recurs to the subject by means of his preachings, epigrams, portraits, caricatures ; he broadens, he magnifies and multiplies his figures and his precepts, so as to deepen our impression of the danger and number of the adherents of "Fals-Semblant." By such means, he hopes, we shall at last hate those whom he hates. Endlessly, therefore, in season and out of season, among the mists, across the streets, under the porches of the church, to the drowsy chant of his orations, to the whistle of his satires, ever and ever again, he conjures up before our eyes the hideous grinning face of " Fals-Semblant," the insincere. Fals-Semblant is never named by name ; he assumes all names and shapes ; he is the king who reigns contrary to conscience, the knight perverted by Lady Meed, the heartless man of law, the merchant without honesty, the friar, the pardoner, the hermit, who under the garment of saints conceal hearts that will rank them with the accursed ones. Fals-Semblant is the pope who sells benefices, the histrion, the tumbler, the juggler, the adept of the vagrant race, who goes about telling tales and helping his listeners to forget the seriousness of life. From the un-worthy pope down to the lying juggler, all these men are the same man. Deceit stands before us ; God's vengeance be upon him ! Whenever and wherever Langland detects Fals-Semblant, he loses control over himself ; anger blinds him ; it seems as if he were confronted by Antichrist.

No need to say whether he is then master of his words, and able to measure them. With him, in such cases, no *nuances* or extenuations are admissible ; you are with or against Fals-Semblant ; there is no middle way ; a com-promise is a treason ; and is there anything worse than a traitor ? And thus he is led to sum up his judgment in such lines as this :

He is worse than Judas · that giveth a japer silver.[1]

If we allege that there may be some shade of exaggera-tion in such a sentence, he will shrug his shoulders. The doubt is not possible, he thinks, and his plain proposition is self-evident.

No compromise ! Travel through life without bending ; go forward in a straight line between the high walls of duty. Perform your own obligations ; do not perform the

[1] B. ix. 90.

obligations of others. To do your duty over-zealously, to take upon you the duty of others, would trouble the State ; you approach, in so doing, the borderland of Imposture. The knight will fight for his country, and must not lose his time in fasting and in scourging himself. A fasting knight is a bad knight.

Many joys are allowed. They are included, as a bed of flowers, between the high walls of duty ; love-flowers even grow there, to be plucked, under the blue sky. But take care not to be tempted by that wonderful female Proteus, Lady Meed, the great corruptress. She disappears and reappears, and she, too, assumes all shapes ; she is everywhere at the same time ; it seems as if the serpent of Eden had become the immense reptile that encircles the earth.

This hatred is immense, but stands alone in the heart of the poet. Beside it there is place for treasures of pity and mercy ; the idea of so many Saracens and Jews doomed wholesale to everlasting pain repels him ; he can scarcely accept it ; he hopes they will be all converted, and " turne in-to the trewe feithe " ; for " Cryste cleped us alle. . . . Sarasenes and scismatikes . . . and Jewes." [1] There is something pathetic, and tragic also, in his having to acknowledge that there is no cure for many evils, and that, for the present, resignation only can soothe the suffering. With a throbbing heart he shows the unhappy and the lowly, who must die before having seen the better days that were promised, the only talisman that may help them : a scroll with the words, " Thy will be done ! " [2]

The truth is that there was a tender heart under the rough and rugged exterior of the impassioned, indignant,

---

[1] B. xi. 114
[2] But I loked what lyflode it was · that Pacience so preysed,
And thanne was it a pece of the *Pater noster* · " *Fiat voluntas tua.*"
(B. xiv. 47.)

suffering poet ; and thus he was able to sum up his life's ideal in this beautiful motto : *Disce, Doce, Dilige ;* in these words will be found the true interpretation of Dowel, Dobet, and Dobest : " Learn, Teach, Love." [1]

The poet's language is, if one may use the expression, like himself, above all, sincere. Chaucer wished that words were " cosyn to the dede ; " Langland holds the same opinion. While, in the mystic parts of his Visions, he uses a superabundance of fluid and abstract terms, that look like morning mists and float along with his thoughts, his style becomes suddenly sharp, nervous, and sinewy when he comes back to earth and moves in the world of realities. Let some sudden emotion fill his soul, and he will rise again, not in the mist this time, but in the rays of the sun ; he will soar aloft, and we shall wonder at the grandeur of his eloquence. Whatever be his subject, he will coin a word, or distort a meaning, or cram into an idiom more meaning than grammar, custom, or dictionary allow, rather than leave a gap between word and thought ; both must be fused together, and made one. If the merchants were honest, they would not " timber " so high—raise such magnificent houses.[2]   In other parts he uses realistic terms, noisy, ill-favoured expressions, which it is impossible to quote.

His vocabulary of words is the normal vocabulary of the period, the same nearly as Chaucer's. The poet of the " Canterbury Tales " has been often reproached with having used his all-powerful influence to obtain rights of citizenship in England for French words ; but the accusation does not stand good, for Langland did not write for courtly men, and the admixture of French words is no less considerable in his work.

[1] B. xiii. 137.
[2] Thei timbrede not so hye.
(A. iii. 76.)

The Visionary's poem offers a combination of several dialects ; one, however, prevails ; it is the Midland dialect. Chaucer used the East-Midland, which is nearly the same, and was destined to survive and become the English language.

Langland did not accept any of the metres used by Chaucer ; he preferred to remain in closer contact with the past of his kin. Rime, the main ornament of French verse, had been adopted by Chaucer, but was rejected by Langland, who, like several of his contemporaries, gave to his lines the ornament best liked by Anglo-Saxons, Germans, and Scandinavians, namely, alliteration.[1]

While their author continued to live obscure and un-known, the Visions, as soon as written, were circulated, and acquired considerable popularity throughout England. In spite of the time that has elapsed, and numberless destructions, there still remain forty-five manuscripts of the poem, more or less complete. " Piers Plowman " soon became a sign and a symbol, a sort of password, a personification of the labouring classes, of the honest and courageous workman. John Ball invoked his authority in his letter to the rebel peasants of the county of Essex in 1381.[2] The name of Piers figured as an attraction on the title of numerous treatises : there existed, as early as the fourteenth century, " Credes " of Piers Plowman, " Com-playntes " of the Plowman, &c. Piers' credit was made

---

[1] Langland's lines usually contain four accentuated syllables, two in each half line ; the two accentuated syllables of the first half line, and the first accentuated syllable of the second half line are alliterated, and commence by the same " rime-letter : "

I *sh*όpe me in *sh*roúdes · as I a *sh*épe wére. (B. Prol. 2.)

It is not necessary for alliteration to exist that the letters be exactly the same ; if they are consonants, nothing more is wanted than a certain similitude in their sounds ; if they are vowels even less suffices : it is enough that all be vowels. On alliterative poems of the period, *supra*, p. 348.

[2] Walsingham, " Historia Anglicana," vol. ii. p. 33. Rolls.

use of at the time of the Reformation, and in his name were demanded the suppression of abuses and the transformation of the old order of things ;[1] he even appeared on the stage ; Langland would have been sometimes greatly surprised to see what tasks were assigned to his hero.

Chaucer and Langland, the two great poets of the period, represent excellently the English genius, and the two races that have formed the nation. One more nearly resembles the clear-minded, energetic, firm, practical race of the latinised Celts, with their fondness for straight lines ; the other resembles the race which had the deepest and especially the earliest knowledge of tender, passionate, and mystic aspirations, and which lent itself most willingly to the lulls and pangs of hope and despair, the race of the Anglo-Saxons. And while Chaucer sleeps, as he should, under the vaults of Westminster, some unknown tuft of Malvern moss perhaps covers, as it also should, the ashes of the dreamer who followed "Treuthes Pilgryme atte Plowe."

[1] "Pierce the Ploughman's Crede," ed. Skeat, Oxford, Clar. Press, 1906, written ab. 1394 in the same metre as the "Visions," by a different author. A poor man who knows only his *Pater* and *Ave* wants to learn his *Crede*, and applies to the different monastic orders who fail to satisfy him, but honest Piers Plowman does.—"The Plowman's Tale" (in "Complete Works of Chaucer," vol. vii. Supplement), in strongly alliterated riming stanzas ; wrongly attributed in the sixteenth century to Chaucer, and since to the author of the "Crede" ; being probably "a Lollard piece of the fourteenth century" which underwent "two successive expansions in the sixteenth century, both with the object of adapting it to the needs of contemporary controversy" (H. Bradley, in *Athenæum*, July 12, 1902). *Cf.* the remarkable alliterative poem "Death and Liffe" (xvth cent.?), ed. Hanford and Steadman, "Studies in Philology," University of N. Carolina, 1918.

CHAPTER V.

PROSE.

FOR a long time, and up to our days, the title and dignity of " Father of English prose" has been borne by Sir John Mandeville, of St. Albans, knight, who, "in the name of God glorious," left his country in the year of grace 1322, on Michaelmas Day, and returned to Europe after an absence of thirty-four years, twice as long as Robinson Crusoe remained in his desert island.

This title belongs to him no longer. The good knight of St. Albans, who had seen and told so much, has dwindled before our eyes, has lost his substance and his outline, and has vanished like smoke in the air. His coat of mail, his deeds, his journeys, his name : all are smoke. He first lost his character as a truthful writer ; then out of the three versions of his book, French, English, and Latin, two were withdrawn from him, leaving him only the first. Existence now has been taken from him, and he is left with nothing at all. Sir John Mandeville, knight, of St. Albans, who crossed the sea in 1322, is, as an author, a myth, and never existed. He has joined, in the kingdom of the shades and the land of nowhere, his contemporary the famous " Friend of God of the Oberland," who some time ago also ceased to have existed.

One thing however remains, and cannot be blotted out : namely, the book of travels bearing the name of Mandeville, the translation of which is one of the best and oldest specimens of simple and flowing English prose.

I.

The same phenomenon already pointed out in connection with the Anglo-Saxons occurs again with regard to the new English people. For a long time (and not to speak of practical, useful works), poetry alone seems worthy of being remembered ; most of the early monuments of the new language for the sake of which the expense of parchment is incurred are poems ; verse is used, even in works for which prose would appear much better fitted, such as history. Robert of Gloucester writes his chronicles in English verse, just as Wace and Benoit de Sainte-More had written theirs in French verse. After some while only it is noticed that there is an art of prose, very delicate, very difficult, well worthy of care, and that it is a mistake to look upon it in the light of a vulgar instrument, on which every one can play without having learnt how, and to confine oneself to doing like Molière's Monsieur Jourdain " de la prose sans le savoir."

At the epoch at which we have arrived, and owing to the renovation and new beginnings occasioned by the Conquest, English prose found itself far behind the French. In the fourteenth century if French poets are poor, prose-writers are excellent ; as early as the twelfth and thirteenth there were, besides Joinville, many charming tale writers who had told in prose delightful things, the loves of Aucassin and Nicolette, for example ; now, without speaking of the novelists of the day, there is Froissart, and to name him is to say enough ; for every one has read at least a few pages of him, and a single page of Froissart, taken haphazard in his works, will cause him to be loved. The language glides on, clear, limpid, murmuring like spring water ; and yet, in spite of its natural flow, art already appears. Froissart selects and chooses ; the title of " historian," which he gives himself, is no mean one in his eyes, and he strives to be worthy of it. The spring bubbles up in the depths of the wood, and without muddying the water the artist knows how to vary its course at times, to turn it off into ready prepared channels, and make it gush forth in fountains.

In England nothing so far resembles this scarcely perceptible and yet skilful art, a mixture of instinct and method, and many years will pass before prose becomes, like verse, an art. In the fourteenth century English prose is used in most cases for want of something better, from necessity, in order to be more surely understood, and owing to this its monuments are chiefly translations, scientific or religious treatises, and sermons. An English Froissart would at that time have used Latin ; several of the chronicles composed in monasteries, at St. Albans and elsewhere, are written in a brisk and lively style, animated now by enthusiasm and now by indignation ; men and events are freely judged ; characteristic details find their place ; the personages live, move, talk : all those chronicles, however, are in Latin. Walsingham's account of the revolt of the peasants in 1381, for example, well deserves to be read, with the description of the taking of London that followed, the sack of the Tower and the Savoy Palace, the assassination of the archbishop,[1] the heroic deed of the peasant Grindecobbe who, being set free on condition that he should induce the rebels to submit, meets them and says : " Act to-day as you would have done had I been beheaded yesterday at Hertford," [2] and goes back to his

---

[1] " Historia Anglicana," vol. i. pp. 453 ff. By the same : " Gesta abbatum monasterii Sancti Albani," 3 vols., " Ypodigma Neustriæ," 1 vol. ed. Riley, Rolls, 1863, 1876.

[2] *Ibid.*, vol. ii. p. 27. See above, p. 201.

prison to suffer death.   Every detail is found there, even
the simple picturesque detail ; the rebels arm themselves
as they can, with staves, rusty swords, old bows blackened
by smoke, arrows " on which only a single feather
remained."   The account of the death of Edward III. in
the same annals is gloomy and tragic and full of grandeur.
In the " Chronicon Angliæ," [1] the anonymous author's
burning hatred for John of Gaunt inspires him with some
fiery pages: all of which would count among the best of
old English literature, had these historians used the
national idiom.   The prejudice against prose continued ;
to be admitted to the honours of parchment it had first to
be ennobled ; and Latin served for that.

Translations begin to appear, however, which is already
an improvement.   Pious treatises had been early turned
into English.   John of Trevisa, born in Cornwall, vicar of
Berkeley, translates at a running pace, with numerous
errors, but in simple style, the famous Universal History,
" Polychronicon," of Ralph Higden,[2] and the scientific
encyclopædia, " De Proprietatibus Rerum," [3] of Bartholomew the Englishman.   The first of these works was finished
in 1387, and had at the Renaissance the honour of being
printed by Caxton ; the second was finished in 1398.

The anonymous English translation of the Travels of
Mandeville enjoyed still greater popularity.[4]   It has been
found to-day that the original text of the " Travels " was

[1] "Chronicon Angliæ," 1328–88, Rolls, ed. Maunde Thompson, 1874, 8vo.
Mr. Thompson has proved that, contrary to the prevalent opinion, Walsingham
has been copied by this chronicler instead of copying him.   But the book is
an important one on account of the passages referring to John of Gaunt, which
are not found elsewhere.   *Infra*, pp. 419, 424.

[2] " Polychronicon Ranulphi Higden . . . with the English translation of
John Trevisa," ed. Babington and Lumby, Rolls, 1865, 8 vols. 8vo.

[3] See above, p. 195.

[4] " The buke of John Maundeuill, being the travels of Sir John Mandeville,
Knight, 1322–56, from . . . Eg. MS. 1982 in the Brit. Mus., ed. together
with the French text," by G. F. Warner ; Roxb. Club, 1889.   In the introduction will be found the series of proofs showing that no Mandeville wrote

compiled in French at Liège, either by Jean de Bourgogne, *alias* John-with-the-Beard, "Joannes-ad-Barbam," author of a treatise on the plague, 1365, or more probably by the contemporary mystificator and pretended chronicler, Jean d'Outremeuse: one more hoax perpetrated by him, all of them remarkably successful.[1] One or the other of the two Johns invented the character of Mandeville as Swift invented Gulliver, and Defoe Robinson Crusoe. Now that the imposture is discovered, the least we can do is to acknowledge the skill of its author: for five centuries Europe has believed in Mandeville, and the wonder is all the greater, seeing that the deviser thereof was not content with merely making his hero travel to a desert island; that would have been far too simple. No, he unites beforehand a Crusoe and a Gulliver in one; it is Crusoe at Brobdingnag; the knight comes to a land of giants; he does not see the giants, it is true, but he sees their sheep (the primitive sheep of Central Asia); elsewhere the inhabitants feed on serpents and hiss as serpents do; some men have dogs' faces; others raise above their head an enormous foot, which serves them for a parasol. Gulliver was not to behold anything more strange. Still the whole was accepted: with enthusiasm by the readers of the Middle Ages; with kindness and goodwill by the critics of modern times. The most obvious lies were

the "Travels." Text in mod. spelling, ed. Pollard, 1900. The English translation was made before 1400, and twice revised at the beginning of the fifteenth century. On the passages borrowed from "Mandeville" by Christine de Pisan, in her "Chemin de long Estude," see Toynbee, "Romania," xxi. 229.

[1] Hamelius has adduced serious reasons for the authorship of Jean d'Outremeuse. See his ed. of the "Travels," E.E.T.S., 1919-23, his art. in the "Quarterly Review," vol. 227, p. 331. *Cf.* Kurth, "Etude critique sur Jean d'Outremeuse," in "Mémoires de d'Académie de Belgique," 2nd ser. vol. vii. On Jean de Bourgogne, see Pirenne, in the Belgian "Biographie Nationale," *suh verbo* Mandeville; Delisle, "Catalogue des Fonds Libri et Barrois," 1888, p. 251.

excused and even justified, and the success of the book was such that there remain about three hundred manuscript copies of it, whereas of the authentic travels of Marco Polo there exist only seventy-five. " Mandeville " had more than twenty-five editions in the fifteenth century and Marco Polo only five.[1]

Nothing, indeed, is more cleverly persuasive than the manner in which the author introduces his hero. His traveller is an honest man, somewhat naïve and credulous perhaps, but one who does not lack good reasons to justify if need be his credulity ; he has read much, and does not hide the use he makes of others' journals. He reports what he has seen and what others have seen. For his aim is a practical one ; he wants to write a guide book, and receives information from all comers. The information sometimes is very peculiar ; but Pliny is the authority : who shall be believed if Pliny is not trusted ? After a description of wonders, the knight takes breathing time and says : Of course you won't believe me ; nor should I have believed myself if such things had been told me, and if I had not seen them.[2] He felt so sure of his own honesty that he challenged criticism ; this disposition was even one of the causes why he had written in French : " And know you that I should have turned this booklet into Latin in order to be more brief : but for the reason that many understand better romance," that is French, " than Latin, I wrote in romance, so that everybody will be able to understand it, and that the lords, knights, and other noblemen, who know little Latin or none, and have been over the sea, perceive and understand whether I speak truth or not. And if I make mistakes in my narrative for want of memory or for any cause, they will be able to check and correct me : for things seen long ago

[1] Warner, *ibid.*, p. v.
[2] Same excuse in the no less fabulous Letter of Alexander to Aristotle.

may be forgotten, and man's memory cannot embrace and keep everything." [1]

And so the sail is spread, and being thus amply supplied with oratorical precautions, our imaginary knight sets out on his grand voyage of discovery through the books of his library. Having left St. Albans to visit Jerusalem, China, the country of the five thousand islands, he journeys and sails through Pliny, Marco Polo, Odoric de Pordenone,[2] Albert d'Aix, William of Boldensele, Pierre Comestor, Jacques de Vitry, bestiaries, tales of travels, collections of fables, books of dreams, patching together countless marvels, but yet, as he assures us, omitting many so as not to weary our faith : It would be too long to say all; "y seroit trop longe chose à tot deviser." With fanciful wonders are mingled many real ones, which served to make the rest believed in, and were gathered from well-informed authors ; thus Mandeville's immense popularity served at least to vulgarise the knowledge of some curious and true facts. He describes, for example, the artificial hatching of eggs in Cairo; a tree that produces "wool" of which clothing is made, that is to say the cotton-plant ; a country of Asia where it is a mark of nobility for the women to have tiny feet, on which account they are bandaged in their infancy, that they may only grow to half their natural size ; the magnetic needle which points out the north to mariners ; the country of the five thousand islands

---

[1] " Et sachies que je eusse cest livret mis en latin pour plus briefment deviser, mais pour ce que plusieurs entendent miex roumant que latin, j'e l'ay mis en roumant par quoy que chascun l'entende, et que les seigneurs et les chevalers et les autres nobles hommes qui ne scevent point de latin ou pou, qui ont esté oultre mer sachent et entendent se je dis voir ou non et se je erre en devisant pour non souvenance ou autrement que il le puissent adrecier et amender, car choses de lonc temps passées par la veue tournent en oubli et mémoire d'omme ne puet tout mie retenir ne comprendre." MS. fr. 5637 in the National Library, Paris, fol. 4, fourteenth century.

[2] On Odoric and Mandeville, see H. Cordier, " Odoric de Pordenone," Paris, 1891, Introduction.

(Oceania) ; the roundness of the earth, which is such that
the inhabitants of the Antipodes have their feet directly
opposite to ours, and yet do not fall off into space any
more than the earth itself falls there, though of much
greater weight. People who start from their own country,
and sail always in the same direction, finally reach a land
where their native tongue is spoken : they have come back
to their starting-point.

In the Middle Ages the English were already pas-
sionately fond of travels ; Higden and others had, as has
been seen, noted this trait of the national character. This
account of adventures attributed to one of their compatriots could not fail therefore greatly to please them ;
they delighted in Mandeville's book ; it was popular
at once,[1] soon became one of the classics of the English
language, and served, at the time of its appearance, to
vulgarise in England the use of that simple and easy-
going prose of which it was a model in its day, the best
that had been seen till then.[2]

Various scientific and religious treatises were also written

---

[1] A part of it was even put into verse : " The Commonyng of Ser John
Mandeville and the gret Souden ;" in " Remains of the early popular Poetry
of England," ed. Hazlitt, London, 1864, 4 vols. 8vo, vol. i. p. 153.

[2] Here is a specimen of this style ; it is the melancholy end of the work, in
which the weary traveller resigns himself, like Robinson Crusoe, to rest at
last : " And I John Maundevyll, knyght aboveseyd alle though I be unworthi,
that departed from oure contrees and passed the see the yeer of grace 1322,
that have passed many londes and many yles and contrees, and cerched manye
fulle strange places, and have ben in many a full gode honourable companye
and a many a faire dede of armes, alle be it that I dide none my self, for myn
unable insuffisance ; And now I am comen hom, mawgre myself, to reste ;
for gowtes artetykes that me distreynen, that diffynen the ende of my labour,
agenst my wille God knowethe. And thus taking solace in my wreched reste,
recordynge the tyme passed, I have fulfilled theise thinges and putte hem
wryten in this boke, as it wolde come into my mynde, the yeer of grace 1356
in the 34 yeer that I departede from oure contrees. Werfore I preye to alle
the rederes and hereres of this boke, yif it plese hem that thei wolde
preyen to God for me, and I shalle preye for hem." Ed. Hamelius, 1919,
p. 210.

in prose ; those of Richard Rolle, hermit of Hampole,
count amongst the oldest and most remarkable. We owe
several to Chaucer ; they pass unnoticed in the splendour
of his other works, and it is only fair they should. Chaucer
wrote in prose his tale of the parson, and his tale of Melibeus, both taken from the French, his translation of
Boethius,[1] and his treatise on the Astrolabe. His prose is
laboured and heavy, sometimes obscure ; he, whose
poetical similes are so brilliant and graceful, comes to
write, when he handles prose, such phrases as this : " And,
right by ensaumple as the sonne is hid whan the sterres ben
clustred (that is to seyn, whan sterres ben covered with
cloudes) by a swifte winde that highte Chorus, and that the
firmament stant derked by wete ploungy cloudes, and that
the sterres nat apperen up-on hevene, so that the night
semeth sprad up-on erthe : yif thanne the wind that highte
Borias, y-sent out of the caves of the contree of Trace,
beteth this night (that is to seyn, chaseth it a-wey, and
discovereth the closed day) : than shyneth Phebus y-shaken
with sodein light, and smyteth with his bemes in mervelinge
eyen."[2] Chaucer, the poet, in the same period of his life,
perhaps in the same year, had expressed, as we have seen,
the same idea thus :

> But right as whan the sonne shyneth brighte
> In march that chaungeth ofte tyme his face,
> And that a cloud is put with wind to flighte
> Which over-sprat the sonne as for a space,
> A cloudy thought gan thorugh hir soule pace,
> That over-spradde hir brighte thoughtes alle.[3]

Accustomed to poetry, Chaucer sticks fast in prose, the
least obstacle stops him ; he needs the blue paths of the
air. High-flying birds are bad walkers.

[1] Curiously imitated by Thos. Usk (hanged for treason in 1388) in his
"Testament of Love," a semi-religious treatise in rather cumbrous English
prose ; text in " Complete Works of Chaucer," vol. vii. Supplt.

[2] " Boethius," in " Complete Works," vol. ii. p. 6.

[3] "Troilus," II. 100 ; above, p. 306. *Cf.* " De Consolatione," m. HI.

II.

Under a different form, however, prose progressed in England during the course of the fourteenth century. This form is the oratorical.

The England of Chaucer and Langland, that poetical England whose prose took so long to come to shape, was already, as we have seen, the parliamentary England that has continued up to this day. She defended her interests, bargained with the king, listened to the speeches, sometimes very modest ones, that the prince delivered, and answered by remonstrances, sometimes very audacious. The affairs of the State being even then the affairs of all, every free man discussed them ; public life had developed to an extent with which nothing in Europe could be compared ; even bondmen on the day of revolt were capable of assigning themselves a well-determined goal, and working upon a plan. They destroy the Savoy as a means of marking their disapprobation of John of Gaunt and his policy ; but do not plunder it, so as to prove they are fighting for an idea : " So that the whole nation should know they did nothing for the love of lucre, death was decreed against any one who should dare to appropriate anything found in the palace. The innumerable gold and silver objects there must be chopped up in small pieces with a hatchet, and the pieces thrown into the Thames or the sewers ; the cloths of silk and gold must be torn. And it was done so." [1]

Many eloquent speeches were delivered at this time,

---

[1] " Et ut patesceret totius regni communitati eos non respectu avaritiæ quicquam facere, proclamari fecerunt sub pœna decollationis, ne quis præsumeret aliquid vel aliqua ibidem reperta ad proprios usus servanda contingere, sed ut vasa aurea et argentea, quæ ibi copiosa habebantur, cum securibus minutatim confringerent et in Tamisiam vel in cloacas projicerent, pannos aureos et holosericos dilacerarent. . . . Et factum est ita." Walsingham, " Historia Anglicana," vol. i. p. 457 (Rolls).

vanished words, the memory of which is lost; the most impassioned, made on heaths or in forest glades, are only known to us by their results : these burning words called armed men out of the earth. These speeches were in English ; no text of them has been handed down to us; of one, however, the most celebrated of all, we have a Latin summary ; it is the famous English harangue made at Blackheath, by the rebel priest, John Ball, at the time of the taking of London.[1]

Under a quieter form, which might already be called the "parliamentary" form, but often with astonishing boldness and eloquence, public interests are discussed during this century, but nearly always in French at the palace of Westminster. There, documents abound ; the Rolls of Parliament, an incomparable treasure, have come down to us, and nothing is easier than to attend, if so inclined, a session in the time of the Plantagenets. Specimens of questions and answers, of Government speeches and speeches of the Opposition, have been preserved. Moreover, some of the buildings where these scenes took place still exist to-day.[2]

---

[1] "Ad le Blakeheth, ubi ducenta millia communium fuere simul congregata hujuscemodi sermonem est exorsus :

> Whann Adam dalfe and Eve span
> Who was thanne a gentil man ?

Continuansque sermonem inceptum, nitebatur, per verba proverbii quod pro themate sumpserat, introducere et probare, ab initio omnes pares creatos a natura, servitutem per injustam oppressionem nequam hominum introductam, contra voluntatem Dei ; quia si Deo placiusset servos creasse utique in principio mundi constituisset quis servus, quisve dominus futurus fuisset." Let them therefore destroy nobles and lawyers, as the good husbandman tears up the weeds in his field ; thus shall liberty and equality reign : "Sic demum . . . esset inter eos æqua libertas, par dignitas, similisque potestas." "Chronicon Angliæ," ed. Mau. de Thompson (Rolls), 1874, 8vo, p. 321 ; Walsingham, vol. ii. p. 32.

[2] "Rotuli Parliamentorum, ut et petitiones et placita in Parliamento," London, 7 vols. fol. (one volume contains the index).

First of all, and before the opening of the session, a "general proclamation" was read in the great hall of Westminster, that hall built by William Rufus, the woodwork of which was replaced by Richard II., and that has been lately cleared of its cumbrous additions.[1] This proclamation forbids each and all to come to the place where Parliament sits, "armed with hoquetons, armor, swords, and long knives or other sorts of weapons;" for such serious troubles have been the result of this wearing of arms that business has been impeded, and the members of Parliament have been "effreietz," frightened, by these long knives. Then, descending to lesser things, the proclamation goes on to forbid the street-boys of London to play at hide-and-seek in the palace, or to perform tricks on the passers-by, such as "to twitch off their hoods" for instance, which the proclamation in parliamentary style terms improper games, "jues nient covenables." But as private liberty should be respected as much as possible, this prohibition is meant only for the duration of the session.[2]

On the day of the opening the king repairs to the place of the sittings, where he not unfrequently finds an empty room, many of the members or of the "great" having been delayed on the way by bad weather, bad roads, or other impediments.[3] Another day is then fixed upon for the solemn opening of the business.

All being at last assembled, the king, the lords spiritual and temporal and the Commons, meet together in the "Painted Chamber." The Chancellor explains the cause of the summons, and the questions to be discussed. This

---

[1] Richard restored it entirely, and employed English master masons, "Richard Washbourn" and "Johan Swalwe." The indenture is of March 18, 1395; the text of it is in Rymer, 1705, vol. vii. p. 794.

[2] "Rotuli Parliamentorum," vol. ii. p. 103.

[3] Ex. 13 Ed. III., 17 Ed. III., "Rotuli Parliamentorum," vol. ii. pp. 107, 135.

is an opportunity for a speech, and we have the text of
a good many of them. Sometimes it is a simple, clear,
practical discourse, enumerating, without any studied
phrases or pompous terms, the points that are to be
treated ; sometimes it is a flowery and pretentious oration,
adorned with witticisms and quotations, and compliments
addressed to the king, as is for instance the speech (in
French) of the bishop of St. David's, Adam Houghton,
Chancellor of England in 1377 :

"Lords and Gentlemen, I have orders from my lord the
Prince here present, whom God save," the youthful Richard,
heir to the throne, "to expound the reason why this Parliament was summoned. And true it is that the wise suffer
and desire to hear fools speak, as is affirmed by St. Paul in
his Epistles, for he saith : *Libenter suffertis insipientes cum
sitis ipsi sapientes.* And in as much as you are wise and
I am a fool, I understand that you wish to hear me speak.
And another cause there is, which will rejoice you if you
are willing to hear me. For the Scripture saith that every
messenger bringing glad tidings, must be always welcome ;
and I am a messenger that bringeth you good tidings,
wherefore I must needs be welcome."

All these pretty things are to convey to them that the
king, Edward III., then on the brink of the grave, is not
quite so ill as reported, which should be a cause of satisfaction for his subjects. Another cause of joy, for
everything seems to be considered as such by the worthy
bishop, is this illness itself ; "for the Scripture saith : *Quos
diligo castigo,* which proves that God him loves, and that
he is blessed of God." The king is to be a "vessel of
grace," *vas electionis.*[1] The Chancellor continues thus at
length, heedless of the fact that the return of Alice Perrers
to the old king belies his Biblical applications.

Simon Sudbury, Archbishop of Canterbury, who was to

[1] "Rotuli Parliamentorum," vol. ii. p. 361.

die such a dreadful death, from the eighth blow of the axe, after having lost the hand which he carried to the first wound, spoke in much the same style. He opened in these terms the first parliament of Richard II. :

"*Rex tuus venit tibi.*—Lords and Gentlemen, the words which I have spoken signify in French : Your king comes to thee.—And thereupon, the said archbishop gave several good reasons agreeing with his subject, and divided his said subject in three parts, as though it had been a sermon."

In truth it is a sermon ; the Gospel is continually quoted, and serves for unexpected comparisons. The youthful Richard has come to Parliament, just as the Blessed Virgin went to see St. Elizabeth ; the joy is the same : "*Et exultavit infans in utero ejus.*" [1]

Fortunately, all did not lose themselves in such flowery mazes. William Thorpe, William of Shareshull, William of Wykeham, John Knyvet, &c., make business-like speeches, simple, short, and to the point : "My Lords, and you of the Commons," says Chancellor Knyvet, "you well know how after the peace agreed upon between our lord the King and his adversaries of France, and openly infringed by the latter, the king sent soldiers and nobles across the sea to defend *us*, which they do, but are hard pressed by the enemy. If they protect us, we must help them."

The reasoning is equally clear in Wykeham's speeches, and with the same skill he makes it appear as if the Commons had a share in all the king's actions: "Gentlemen,

---

[1] "Seigneurs et Sires, ces paroles qe j'ay dist sont tant à dire en Franceys, vostre Roi vient à toy." *Ibid.*, vol. iii. p. 3. A speech of the same kind adorned with puns was made by Thomas Arundel, Archbishop of Canterbury, to open the first Parliament of Henry IV. : " Cest honorable roialme d'Angleterre q'est le pluis habundant Angle de richesse parmy tout le monde, avait estée par longe temps mesnez, reulez et governez par enfantz et conseil de vefves. . . ." 1399, *Ibid.*, p. 415.

you well know how, in the last Parliament, the king, *with
your consent*, again took the title of King of France. . . ." [1]

These speeches being heard, and the "receivers" and
"triers" of petitions having been appointed,[2] the two
houses divided, and deliberated apart from each other ; the
Lords retired " to the White Chamber " ; the Commons
remained " in the Painted Chamber." At other times " the
said Commons were told to withdraw by themselves to
their old place in the Chapter House of Westminster
Abbey,"[3] that beautiful Chapter House still in existence,
which had been built under Henry III.

Then the real debates began, interrupted by the most
impassioned speeches. They were not reported, and only
a faint echo has reached us. Traces of the sentiments
which animated the Commons are found, however, in
the petitions they drew up, which were like so many
articles of the bargains entered into by them. For they did
not allow themselves to be carried away by the eloquent
and tender speeches of the Government orators ; they were
practical and cold-blooded ; they agreed to make concessions provided concessions were made to them, and they
added an annulling clause in case the king refused : " In
case the conditions are not complied with, they shall not
be obliged to grant the aid."[4] The discussions are long

---

[1] " Rotuli Parliamentorum." Speech of Knyvet, vol. ii. p. 316 ; of Wykeham, vol. ii. p. 303. This same Knyvet opens the Good Parliament of 1376
by a speech equally forcible. He belonged to the magistracy, and was greatly
respected ; he died in 1381.

[2] Ex : " Item, meisme le jour (that is to say the day on which the general
proclamation was read) fut fait une crie qe chescun qi vodra mettre petition à
nostre seigneur le Roi et à son conseil, les mette entre cy et le lundy prochein
à venir. . . . Et serront assignez de receivre les pétitions . . . les sousescrit*."
Ibid., vol. ii. p. 135.

[3] *Ibid.*, vol. ii. pp. 136, 163. " Fut dit à les ditz Communes de par le
Roy, q'ils se retraiassent par soi à lour aunciene place en la maison du chapitre
de l'abbeye de Westm', et y tretassent et conseillassent entre eux meismes."

[4] Vol. ii. p. 107, second Parliament of 1339.

and minute in both houses ; members do not meet for
form's sake ; decisions are not lightly taken : " Of which
things," we read in the Rolls, " they treated at length."[1]
In another case, the Commons, from whom a ready-made
answer was expected, announce that " they wish to talk
together," and they continue to talk from the 24th of
January to the 19th of February.[2]   Only too glad was the
Government when the members did not declare " that they
dare not assent without discussing the matter with the
Commons of their shire," [3] that is to say, without consulting
their constituents.   And this they do, though William de
la Pole and others, sent " by our lord the king from thence
(that is from France) as envoys," had modestly explained
the urgency of the case, and " the cause of the long stay the
king had made in these aforesaid parts, without riding
against his enemies," [4] this cause being lack of money.

When the Commons have at last come to a decision,
they make it known in the presence of the Lords through
the medium of their Speaker, or, as he was called in the
French of the period, the one who had the words for
them : " Qui avoit les paroles pur les Communes d'Engleterre en cest Parlement." [5]   In these replies especially, and
in the petitions presented at the same time, are found traces
of the vehemence displayed in the Chapter House.   The

---

[1] " Ils tretèrent longement," *Ibid.*, ii. p. 104.

[2] " Sur quele demonstrance il respoundrent q'il voleient parler ensemble et
treter sur cest bosoigne. . . . Sur quel bosoigne ceux de la Commune demorè-
rent de lour respons doner tant qe à Samedi, le XIX. jour de Feverer."   A.D.
1339, " Rotuli Parliamentorum," vol. ii. p. 107.

[3] " Ils n'osoront assentir tant qu'ils eussent conseillez et avysez les Communes de lour pais."   They promise to do their best to persuade their constituents.   A.D. 1339 ;   " Rotuli Parliamentorum," vol. ii. p. 104.

[4] " Et les nuncia auxi la cause de la longe demore quele il avoit faite es
dites parties saunz chivaucher sur ses enemys ; et coment il le covendra faire
pur defaute d'avoir."   " Rotuli Parliamentorum," vol. ii. p. 103, first Parliament of 1339.

[5] 51 Ed. III., " Rotuli Parliamentorum," ii. p. 374.

boldness of the answers and of the remonstrances is extra-ordinary, and from their tone can be conceived with what power and freedom civil eloquence, of which England has since produced so many admirable specimens, must have shone, even at that distant epoch.

The most remarkable case is that of the Good Parlia-ment of 1376, in which, after having deliberated apart, the Commons join the other house, and by the mouth of their Speaker, Peter de la Mare, bring in their bill of complaints against royalty : " And after that the aforesaid Commons came to Parliament, openly protesting that they were as willing and determined to help their noble liege lord . . . as any others had ever been, in any time past. . . . But they said it seemed to them an undoubted fact, that if their liege lord had always had around him loyal counsellors and good officers . . . our lord the king would have been very rich in treasure, and therefore would not have had such great need of burdening his Commons, either with subsidy, talliage, or otherwise. . . ." A special list of grievances is drawn up against the principal prevaricators ; their names are there, and their crimes ; the king's mis-tress, Alice Perrers, is not forgotten. Then follow the petitions of the Commons, the number of which is enormous, a hundred and forty in all, in which abuses are pointed out one by one.[1]

[1] " Rotuli Parliamentorum," vol. ii. p. 323. This speech created a great stir ; another analysis of it exists in the " Chronicon Angliæ" (written by a monk of St. Albans, the abbot of which, Thomas de la Mare, sat in Parlia-ment) : " Quæ omnia ferret æquanimiter [plebs communis] si dominus rex noster sive regnum istud exinde aliquid commodi vel emolumenti sumpsisse videretur ; etiam plebi tolerabile, si in expediendis rebus bellicis, quamvis gestis minus prospere, tanta pecunia fuisset expensa. Sed palam est, nec regem commodum, nec regnum ex hac fructum aliquem percepisse. . . . Non enim est credibile regem carere infinita thesauri quantitate si fideles fuerint qui ministrant ei" (p. 73). The drift of the speech is, as may be seen, exactly the same as in the Rolls of Parliament. Another specimen of pithy eloquence will be found in the apostrophe addressed to the Earl of Stafford by John Philpot, a mercer of London, after his naval feat of 1378. *Ibid.*, p. 200.

Formerly, say the Commons, " bishoprics, as well as other benefices of Holy Church, used to be, after true elections, in accordance with saintly considerations and pure charity, assigned to people found to be worthy of clerical promotion, men of clean life and holy behaviour, whose intention it was to stay on their benefices, there to preach, visit, and shrive their parishioners. . . . And so long as these good customs were observed, the realm was full of all sorts of prosperity, of good people and loyal, good clerks and clergy, two things that always go together. . . ." The encroachments of the See of Rome in England are, for all right-minded people, " great subject of sorrow and of tears." Cursed be the "sinful city of Avignon," where simony reigns, so that " a sorry fellow who knows nothing of what he ought and is worthless " will receive a benefice of the value of a thousand marcs, " when a doctor of decree and a master of divinity will be only too glad to secure some little benefice of the value of twenty marcs." The foreigners who are given benefices in England "will never see their parishioners . . . and more harm is done to Holy Church by such bad Christians than by all the Jews and Saracens in the world. . . . Be it again remembered that God has committed his flock to the care of our Holy Father the Pope, that they might be fed and not shorn." [1] The Commons fear nothing ; neither king nor Pope could make them keep silence. In their mind the idea begins to dawn that the kingdom is theirs, and the king too ; they demand that Richard, heir to the throne, shall be brought to them ; they wish to see him ; and he is shown to them.[2]

In spite of the progress made by the English language, French continued to be used at Westminster. It remained as a token of power and an emblem of authority, just as modern castles are still built with towers, though not meant

---

[1] " Rotuli Parliamentorum," ii. pp. 337 ff.   [2] June 25, 1376.

to be defended by cannon. It was a sign, and this sign has subsisted, since the formula by which the laws are ratified is still in French at the present time. English, nevertheless, began to make an appearance even at Westminster. From 1363,[1] the opening speeches are sometimes in English ; in 1399, the English tongue was used in the chief acts and discourses relating to the deposition of Richard. On Monday, the 29th of September, the king signed his act of resignation ; on the following day a solemn meeting of Parliament took place, in presence of all the people, in Westminster Hall ; the ancient throne containing Jacob's stone, brought from Scotland by Edward I., and which can still be seen in the abbey, had been placed in the hall, and covered with cloth of gold, " cum pannis auri." Richard's act of resignation was read " first in Latin, then in English," and the people showed their approbation of the same by applause. Henry then came forward, claimed the kingdom, in English, and seated himself on the throne, in the midst of the acclamations of those present. The Archbishop of Canterbury delivered an oration, and the new king, speaking again, offered his thanks in English to " God, and yowe Spirituel and Temporel, and alle the Astates of the lond."[2] There is no more memorable sign of the changes that had taken place than

---

[1] The speech of this year was made "en Engleis," by Simon, bishop of Ely; but the Rolls give only a French version of it : " Le prophet David dit que . . ." &c., vol. ii. p. 283.

[2] " Sires, I thank God, and yowe Spirituel and Temporel and alle the Astates of the lond ; and do yowe to wyte, it es noght my will that no man thynk y[t] be waye of conquest I wold disherit any man of his heritage, franches, or other ryghtes that hym aght to have, no put hym out of that that he has and has had by the gude lawes and custumes of the Rewme : Except thos persons that has ben agan the gude purpose and the commune profyt of the Rewme." " Rotuli Parliamentorum," vol. iii. p. 423. In the fifteenth century the Parliamentary documents are written sometimes in French, sometimes in English; French predominates in the first half of the century, and English in the second.

the use made of the English language on an occasion like this, by a prince who had no title to the crown but popular favour.

III.

All these translators were necessarily wanting in originality (less, however, than they need have been), and all these orators spoke for the most part in French. In their hands, English prose could not be perfected to a very high degree. It progressed, however, owing to them, but owing much more to an important personage, who made common English his fighting weapon, John Wyclif, to whom the title of " Father of English prose" rightfully belongs, now that Mandeville has dissolved in smoke. Wyclif, Langland, and Chaucer are the three great figures of English literature in the Middle Ages.

Wyclif belonged to the rich and respected family of the Wyclifs, lords of the manor of Wyclif, in Yorkshire.[1] He was born about 1320, and devoted himself early to a scientific and religious calling. He studied at Oxford, where he soon attracted notice, being one of those men of character who occupy from the beginning of their lives, without seeking for it, but being, as it seems, born to it, a place apart, amid the limp multitude of men. The turn of his mind, the originality of his views, the firmness of his will, his learning, raised him above others ; he was one of those concerning whom it is at once said they are "some one ; " and several times in the course of his existence he saw the University, the king, the country even, turn to him when " some one " was needed.

He was hardly thirty-five when, the college of Balliol at

---

[1] On Wyclif's family, see " The Birth and Parentage of Wyclif," by L. Sergeant, *Athenæum*, March 12 and 26, 1892. This spelling of his name is the one which appears oftenest in contemporary documents. (Note by F. D. Matthew, *Academy*, June 7, 1884.)

Oxford having lost its Master, he was elected to the post. In 1366 Parliament ruled that the Pope's claim to the tribute promised by King John should no longer be recognised, and Wyclif was asked to draw up a pamphlet justifying the decision.[1] In 1374 a diplomatic mission was entrusted to him, and he went to Bruges, with several other "ambassatores," to negotiate with the Pope's representatives.[2] He then had the title of doctor of divinity.

Various provincial livings were successively bestowed upon him: that of Fillingham in 1361 ; that of Ludgarshall in 1368 ; that of Lutterworth, in Leicestershire, in 1374, which he kept till his death. He divided his time between his duties as rector, his studies, his lectures at Oxford, and his life in London, where he made several different stays, and preached some of his sermons.

These quiet occupations were interrupted from time to time owing to the storms raised by his writings. But so great was his fame, and so eminent his personality, that he escaped the terrible consequences that heresy then involved. He had at first alarmed religious authority by his political theories on the relations of Church and State, next on the reformation of the Church itself; finally he created excessive scandal by attacking dogmas and by discussing the sacraments. Summoned a first time to answer concerning his doctrines, he appeared in St. Paul's, in 1377, attended by the strange patrons that a common animosity against the high dignitaries of the Church had gained for him ; John of Gaunt, Duke of Lancaster, and Lord Henry Percy accompanied him. The duke, little troubled by

---

[1] "Determinatio quedam magistri Johannis Wyclyff de Dominio contra unum monachum." The object of this treatise is to show "quod Rex potest juste dominari regno Anglie negando tributum Romano pontifici." The text will be found in John Lewis : "A history of the life and sufferings of . . . John Wiclif," 1720, reprinted Oxford, 1820, 8vo, p. 349.

[2] "Ambassatores, nuncios et procuratores nostros speciales." Lewis, *ibid.*, p. 304.

scruples, loudly declared, in the middle of the church, that he would drag the bishop out of the cathedral by the hair of his head. These words were followed by an indescribable tumult. Indignant at this insult, the people of the City drove the duke from the church, pursued him through the town, and laid siege to the house of John of Ypres, a rich merchant with whom he had gone to sup. Luckily for the prince, the house opened on the Thames. He rose in haste, knocking his legs against the table, and, without stopping to drink the cordial offered him, slipped into a boat and fled, as fast as oars could carry him, to his sister-in-law's, the Princess of Wales, at Kennington.[1] The summoning of Wyclif thus had no result.

But the Pope, in the same year, launched against the English theologian bulls branding eighteen erroneous propositions contained in his writings, and enjoining that the culprit should be put in prison if he refused to retract. The University of Oxford, being already a power at that time, proud of its privileges, jealous in maintaining solidarity between its members, imbued with those ideas of opposition to the Pope which were increasing in England, considered the decree as an exorbitant exercise of authority. It examined the propositions, and declared them to be orthodox, though capable of wrong interpretations, on which account Wyclif should go to London and explain himself.[2]

He is found, therefore, in London in the beginning of

---

[1] All these details are found in the "Chronicon Angliæ," 1328–88, ed. Maunde Thompson, Rolls, 1874, 8vo, p. 123, one of the rare chronicles the MS. of which was not expurgated, in what relates to John of Gaunt, at the accession of the Lancasters. (See above, p. 406.)

[2] This extreme leniency caused an indignation of which an echo is found in Walsingham : "Oxoniense studium generale," he exclaims, "quam gravi lapsu a sapientiæ et scientiæ culmine decidisti ! . . . Pudet recordationis tantæ impudentiæ, et ideo supersedeo in husjusmodi materia immorari, ne materna videar ubera decerpere dentibus, quæ dare lac, potum scientiæ, consuevere." "Historia Anglicana Rolls, vol. i. p. 345, year 1378.

1378 ; the bishops are assembled in the still existing chapel of Lambeth Palace. But by one of those singularities that allow us to realise how the limits of the various powers were far from being clearly defined, it happened that the bishops had received positive orders not to condemn Wyclif. The prohibition proceeded from a woman, the Princess of Wales, widow of the Black Prince. The prelates, however, were spared the trouble of choosing between the Pope and the lady ; for the second time Wyclif was saved by a riot ; a crowd favourable to his ideas invaded the palace, and no sentence could be given. Any other would have appeared the more guilty ; he only lived the more respected. He was then at the height of his popularity ; a new public statement that he had just issued in favour of the king against the Pope had confirmed his reputation as advocate and defender of the kingdom of England.[1]

He resumed, therefore, in peace his work of destruction, and began to attack dogmas. Besides his writings and his speeches, he used, in order to popularise his doctrines, his "simple priests," or "poor priests," who, without being formed into a religious order, imitated the wandering life of the friars, but not their mendicity, and strove to attain the ideal which the friars had fallen short of. They went about preaching from village to village, and the civil authority was alarmed by the political and religious theories expounded to the people by these wanderers, who journeyed " from county to county, and from town to

---

[1] See in the "Fasciculi Zizaniorum magistri Johannis Wyclif cum tritico," ed. Shirley, Rolls, 1858, 8vo, p. 258 : " Responsio magistri Johannis Wyccliff ad dubium infra scriptum, quæsitum ab eo, per dominum regem Angliæ Ricardum secundum et magnum suum consilium anno regni sui primo." The point to be elucidated was the following : " Dubium est utrum regnum Angliæ possit legitime, imminente necessitate suæ defensionis, thesaurum regni detinere, ne deferatur ad exteros, etiam domino papa sub pœna censurarum et virtute obedientiæ hoc petente."

town, in certain habits under dissimulation of great holi·
ness, without license of our Holy Father the Pope, or of
the ordinary of the diocese." [1]   Wyclif justified these
unlicensed preachings by the example of St. Paul, who,
after his conversion, "preechide fast, and axide noo leve of
Petir herto, for he hadde leve of Jesus Crist." [2]

From this time forth Wyclif began to circulate on the
sacraments, and especially on the Eucharist, opinions that
Oxford even was unable to tolerate ; the University condemned them.   Conformably to his own theory, which
tended, as did that of the Commons, towards a royal
supremacy, Wyclif appealed not to the Pope but to the
king, and in the meantime refused to submit.   This was
carrying boldness very far.   John of Gaunt separates from
his *protégé;* Courtenay, bishop of London, calls together a
Council which condemns Wyclif and his adherents (1382);
the followers are pursued, and retract or exile themselves ;
but Wyclif continues to live in perfect quiet.   Settled at
Lutterworth, from whence he now rarely stirred, he wrote
more than ever, with a more and more caustic and daring
pen.   The papal schism, which had begun in 1378, had
cast discredit on the Holy See ; Wyclif's work was made
the easier by it.   At last Urban VI., the Pope whom
England recognised, summoned him to appear in his
presence, but an attack of paralysis came on, and Wyclif
died in his parish on the last day of the year 1384.
"Organum diabolicum, hostis Ecclesiæ, confusio vulgi,

[1] "Statutes of the Realm," 5 Rich. II., st. 2, chap. 5. Walsingham thus
describes them : "Congregavit . . . comites . . . talaribus indutos vestibus
de russeto in signum perfectionis amplioris, incedentes nudis pedibus, qui suos
errores in populo ventilarent, et palam ac publice in suis sermonibus prædicarent."   "Historia Anglicana," *sub anno* 1377, Rolls, vol. i. p. 324.   A
similar description is found (they present themselves, "sub magnæ sanctitatis
velamine," and preach errors "tam in ecclesiis quam in plateis et aliis locis
profanis") in the letter of the archbishop of Canterbury, of May 28, 1382,
"Fasciculi," p. 275.

[2] "Select English Works," ed. T. Arnold, Oxford, 1869, vol. i. p. 176.

hæreticorum idolum, hypocritarum speculum, schismatis incentor, odii seminator, mendacii fabricator"[1] : such is the funeral oration inscribed in his annals, at this date, by Thomas Walsingham, monk of St. Albans. By order of the Council of Constance, his ashes were afterwards thrown to the winds, and the family of the Wyclifs of Wyclif, firmly attached to the old faith, erased him from their genealogical tree. When the Reformation came, the family remained Catholic, and this adherence to the Roman religion seems to have been the cause of its decay : " The last of the Wyclifs was a poor gardener, who dined every Sunday at Thorpe Hall, as the guest of Sir Marmaduke Tunstall, on the strength of his reputed descent."[2]

IV.

Wyclif had begun early to write, using at first only Latin.[3] Innumerable treatises of his exist, many of which

---

[1] " Historia Anglicana," Rolls, vol. ii. p. 119. Elsewhere, in another series of unflattering epithets ("old hypocrite," "angel of Satan," &c.), the chronicler had allowed himself the pleasure of making a little pun upon Wyclif's name : " Non nominandus Joannes Wicliffe, vel potius Wykbeleve." Year 1381 vol. i. p. 450.

[2] L. Sergeant, " The Birth and Parentage of Wyclif," in the *Athenæum* of March 12, 1892.

[3] The Wyclif Society, founded in London by Dr. Furnivall, has published a great part of the Latin works of Wyclif : " Polemical Works in Latin," ed. Buddensieg, 1883, 8vo ; "Joannis Wyclif, de compositione Hominis," ed. R. Beer, 1884 ; " Tractatus de civili Dominio . . . from the unique MS. at Vienna," ed. R. Lane Poole, 1885 ff. ; " Tractatus de Ecclesia," ed. Loserth, 1886 ; " Dialogus, sive speculum Ecclesie militantis," ed. A. W. Pollard, 1886 ; "Tractatus de benedicta Incarnatione," ed. Harris, 1886 ; " Sermones," ed. Loserth and Matthew, 1887 ; " Tractatus de officio Regis," ed Pollard and Sayle, 1887 ; " De Dominio divino libri tres, to which are added the first four books of the treatise ' De pauperie Salvatoris,' by Richard Fitzralph, archbishop of Armagh," ed. R. L. Poole, 1890 ; " De Ente prædicamentali," ed. R. Beer, 1891 " De Eucharistia tractatus maior ; accedit tractatus de Eucharistia et Pœnitentia," ed. Loserth and Matthew, 1892 ; " Tractatus de Logica," ed. Dzierwicki, 1893-99.

Among the Latin works published outside of the Society, see " Tractatus de

are still unpublished, written in a Latin so incorrect and
so English in its turns that "often the readiest way of
understanding an obscure passage is to translate it into
English." [1] He obviously attracted the notice of his contemporaries, not by the elegance of his style, but by the
power of his thought.

His thought deserved the attention it received. His
mind was, above all, a critical one, opposed to formulas,
to opinions without proofs, to traditions not justified by
reason. Precedents did not overawe him, the mysterious
authority of distant powers had no effect on his feelings.
He liked to look things and people in the face, with a
steady gaze, and the more important the thing was and the
greater the authority claimed, the less he felt disposed to
cast down his eyes.

Soon he wished to teach others to open theirs, and to
see for themselves. By "others" he meant every one, and
not only clerks or the great. He therefore adopted the
language of every one, showing himself in that a true
Englishman, a partisan of the system of free investigation,
so dear since to the race. He applied this doctrine to all
that was then an object of faith, and step by step, passing
from the abstract to the concrete, he ended by calling for
changes, very similar to those England adopted at the
Reformation, and later on in the time of the Puritans.

His starting-point was as humble and abstract as his conclusions were, some of them, bold and practical. A super-

officio pastorali," ed. Lechler, Leipzig, 1863, 8vo ; "Trialogus cum supple-
mento Trialogi," ed. Lechler, Oxford, 1869, 8vo ; "De Christo et suo Adver-
sario Antichristo," ed. R. Buddensieg, Gotha, 1880, 4to. Many documents
by or concerning Wyclif are to be found in the "Fasciculi Zizaniorum magistri
Joannis Wyclif cum tritico," ed. Shirley, Rolls, 1858 (compiled by Thomas
Netter, fifteenth century). *Cf.* Shirley, "A Catalogue of the Original Works
of John Wyclif," Oxford, 1865 ; Maunde Thompson, "Wycliffe Exhibition
in the King's Library," 1884 ; Trevelyan, "England in the Age of Wyclif,"
1st. ed., 1899 ; Gairdner, "Lollardry and the Reformation," 4 vols, 1908–13.
    [1] R. Lane Poole, "Wycliffe and Movements for Reform," 1889, p. 85.

human ideal had been proposed by St. Francis to his disciples ; they were to possess nothing, but beg their daily bread and help the poor. Such a rule was good for apostles and angels ; it was practised by men. They were not long able to withstand the temptation of owning property, and enriching themselves ; in the fourteenth century their influence was considerable, and their possessions immense. Thin subterfuges were resorted to in order to justify this change : they had only the usufruct of their wealth, the real proprietor being the Pope. From that time two grave questions arose and were vehemently discussed in Christendom : What should be thought of the poverty and mendicity of Christ and his apostles ? What is property, and what is the origin of the power whence it proceeds ?

In the first rank of the combatants figured, in the fourteenth century, an Englishman, Richard Fitzralph, archbishop of Armagh, " Armachanus," who studied the question of property, and contested the theory of the friars in various sermons and treatises, especially in his work : "De pauperie Salvatoris," composed probably between 1350 and 1356.[1]

Wyclif took his starting-point from the perfectly orthodox writings of Fitzralph, and borrowed from him nearly the whole of his great theory of " Dominium," or lordship, power exercised either over men, or over things, domination, property, possession. But he carried his conclusions much farther, following the light of logic, as was the custom of schools, without allowing himself to be hindered by the radicalism of the consequences and the material difficulties of the execution.

The theory of " Dominium," adopted and popularised by

---

[1] On this treatise, and on the use made of it by Wyclif, see : " Johannis Wycliffe De Dominio divino libri tres. To which are added the first four books of the treatise ' De pauperie Salvatoris,' by Richard Fitzralph," ed. R. Lane Poole, 1890. The " De Dominio divino," of Wyclif, seems to have been written about 1366 ; his " De Dominio Civili," about 1372.

Wyclif, is an entirely feudal one. According to him all lordship comes from God ; the Almighty bestows it on man as a fief, in consideration of a service or condition : the keeping of His commandments. Deadly sin breaks the contract, and deprives the tenant of his right to the fief ; therefore no man in a state of deadly sin possesses any of the lordships called property, priesthood, royalty, magistracy. All which is summed up by Wyclif in his proposition : any "dominium" has grace for its foundation. By such a theory, the whole social order is shaken ; neither Pope nor king is secure on his throne, nor priest in his living, nor lord in his estate.

The confusion is all the greater from the fact that a multitude of other subversive conclusions are appended to this fundamental theory : While sinners lose all lordship, the good possess all lordship ; to man, in a state of "gratia gratificante," belongs the whole of what comes from God ; "in re habet omnia bona Dei."[1]   But how can that be ? The easiest thing in the world, replies Wyclif, whom nothing disturbs : all goods should be held in common, "Ergo omnia debent esse communia "[2] ; wives should be alone excepted.—The Bible is a kind of Koran in which everything is found ; no other law should be obeyed save that one alone ; civil and canonical laws are useless if they agree with the Bible, and criminal if they are opposed to it.[3]—Royalty is not the best form of government; an aristocratic system is better, similar to that of the Judges in Israel.[4]—Neither heirship nor popular election is sufficient

---

[1] "Quilibet existens in gratia gratificante, finaliter nedum habet jus, sed in re habet omnia bona Dei."   "De Dominio Civili," chap. i. p. 1.

[2] "De Dominio Civili," chap. xiv. p. 96, chap. xvii. pp. 118–120.

[3] "Vel esset lex superaddita in lege evangelica implicata, vel impertinens, vel repugnans."   "De Dominio Civili," chap. xvii.

[4] The worst is the ecclesiastical form : " Pessimum omnium est quod prelati ecclesie secundum tradiciones suas immisceant se negociis et solicitudinibus civilis dominii."   Chap. xxvii. p. 195.

for the transmission of the crown ; grace is needed besides.[1]
—The bequeathing to the Church of estates which will
become mortmain lands is inadmissible : " No one can
transmit more rights than he possesses, and no one is
personally possessed of rights of civil lordship extending
beyond the term of life." [2]—If the convent or the priest
make a bad use of their wealth, the temporal power will
be doing " a very meritorious thing " in depriving them
of it.[3]

The whole order of things is unhinged, and we are
nearing chaos. It is going so far that Wyclif cannot
refrain from inserting some of those slight restrictions
which the logicians of the Middle Ages were fond of
slipping into their writings. In time of danger this was
the secret door by which they made their escape, turning
away from the stake. Wyclif is an advocate of communism;
but he gives to understand that it is not for now ; it is a
distant ideal. After us the deluge! Not so, answer the
peasants of 1381 ; the deluge at once : " Omnia debent
esse communia ! "

If all lordship vanishes through sin, who shall be judge
of the sin of others ? All real lordship vanishes from the
sinner, answered Wyclif, but there remains to him, by the
permission of God, a power *de facto*, that it is not given us
to remove ; evil triumphs, but with God's consent ; the
Christian must obey the wicked king and bishop : " Deus
debet obedire diabolo." [4] But the dissatisfied only adopted
the first part of the theory, and instead of submitting to
Simon Sudbury, their archbishop, of whom they disap-
proved, they cut off his head.

These were certainly extreme and exceptional consequences, to which Wyclif only contributed in a slight

---

[1] Chap. xxx. p. 212. [2] Chap. xxxv. p. 250. [3] Chap. xxxvii. p. 266.
[4] A conclusion pointed out as heretical by the archbishop of Canterbury
in his letter of 1382. " Fasciculi," p. 278.

measure.　The lasting and permanent result of the doctrine was to strengthen the Commons of England in the aim they already had in view, namely, to diminish the authority exercised over them by the Pope, and to loosen the ties that bound the kingdom to Rome.　Wyclif pointed out that, contrary to the theory of Boniface VIII. (bull " Unam Sanctam "), there does not exist in this world one single supreme and unequalled sovereignty ; the Pope is not the sole depositary of divine power.　Since all lordship proceeds from God, that of the king comes from Him, as well as that of the Pope ; kings themselves are " vikeris of God " ; beside the Pope, and not below him, there is the king.[1]

V.

The English will thus be sole rulers in their island. They must also be sole keepers of their consciences, and for that Wyclif is to teach them free investigation.　All, then, must understand him ; and he begins to write in English.　His English works are numerous ; sermons, treatises, translations ; they fill volumes.[2]

Before all the Book of truth was to be placed in the hands of everybody, so that none need accept without check the interpretations of others.　With the help of a few disciples, Wyclif began to translate the Bible into

---

[1] " Kingis and lordis schulden wite that thei ben mynystris and vikeris of God, to venge synne and ponysche mysdoeris."　" Select English Works," ed. Arnold, vol. iii. p. 214.

[2] The principal ones will be found in : T. Arnold, "Select English Works of John Wyclif," Oxford, 1869–71, 3 vols. 8vo ; F. D. Matthew, " The English Works of Wyclif, hitherto unprinted," London, Early English Text Society, 1880, 8vo. (Many of the pieces in this last collection are not by Wyclif, but are the work of his followers.　In the first, too, the authenticity of some of the pieces is doubtful.)　See also : " Wyclyffe's Wycket, which he made in Kyng Richard's days the Second (a famous sermon on the Eucharist), Nuremberg, 1546, 4to ; Oxford, ed. T. P. Pantin, 1828.

English. To translate was not forbidden ; several versions had been made before, without the Church interfering in any way. There existed various ones, complete or partial, in different languages ; a complete one in French, written in the thirteenth century,[1] and several partial ones in English. The fourteenth century complete English version due to Wyclifites includes the whole of the canonical books, and even the Apocrypha. The greater part of the Old Testament was almost certainly the work of Wyclif's disciple, Nicholas of Hereford. The task was an immense one, the need pressing ; the attempt suffered from the author's haste. A revision of the work was undertaken by, probably, J. Purvey, prefaced with an eloquent and strongly Wyclifite Prologue, and finished about 1388.[2]

No attempt at elegance is found in this translation ; the language is rugged, and on that account the better adapted to the hieratic directness of the holy Word. Harsh though it be, we feel, however, that it is tending towards improvement ; the meaning of the terms becomes more precise, owing to the necessity of giving to the sacred phrases their exact signification; the effort is not always successful, but it is a continued one, and it is an effort in the right direction. It was soon perceived that, as we read in the Prologue, the common people, "the lewid puple, crie[d] aftir holi writ to kunne it and kepe it." In spite of years and of many causes of destruction, there remain 170

---

[1] S. Berger, " La Bible française au moyen âge," Paris, 1884, p. 120. This version was circulated in England, and was recopied by English scribes. A copy (incomplete) by an English hand is preserved in the Univ. Libr. Cambridge ; P. Meyer, " MSS. français de Cambridge," " Romania," 1886, p. 265.

[2] "The Holy Bible . . . by John Wycliffe and his followers," ed. J. Forshall and Sir Fred. Madden, Oxford, 1850, 4 vols. 4to. On the share of Wyclif, Hereford, &c., in the work, see pp. xi, xvi, xvii, xx, xxiv ; Maunde Thompson, " Wycliffe Exhibition," 1884, p. xviii; Abbot, later Cardinal, Gasquet, " The O. E. Bible," 1897; F G. Kenyon, " Our Bible," 4th ed. 1903, pp. 204 ff. ; F. D. Matthew, in " Historic. Rev.," vol. x. 1895 an anon. art. in the " Church Quarterly Rev ," Jan., 1901. See *infra*, Append. II, p. 536.

manuscripts, more or less complete, of this Bible. For some time, it is true, no check had been given to the work of copying and translating. In 1408 only the Oxford council forbade any one to compose any translation "of his own authority" and to read any made in the time of Wyclif and since, until the work be approved by the Church.[1] In the England of the Plantagenets could be foreseen the England of the Tudors, under whom 326 editions of the Bible were printed in less than a century, from 1525 to 1600.

But Wyclif's greatest influence on the development of prose was exercised through his sermons and treatises. In these, the reformer gives himself full scope ; he alters his tone at need, employs all means, from the most impassioned eloquence down to the most trivial pleasantry, fit to delight men of the lower class. Put to such varied uses, prose could not but become a more workable instrument. True it is that Wyclif never seeks after artistic effect in his English, any more than in his Latin. His sermons regularly begin by : "This gospel tellith. . . . This gospel techith alle men that . . ." and he continues his arguments in a clear and measured style, until he comes to one of those burning questions about which he is battling ; then his irony bursts forth, he uses scathing similes ; he thunders against those "emperoure bishopis," absorbed by worldly cares ; his speech is short and haughty ; he knows how to condense his whole theory in one brief, clear-cut phrase, easy to remember, that every one will know by heart, and which it will not be easy to answer. Why are the people preached to in a foreign tongue ? Christ, when he was with his apostles, "taughte hem oute this prayer, bot be thou syker, nother in Latyn nother in Frensche, bot in the langage that they usede to speke."

<hr />

[1] Labbe, "Sacrorum Conciliorum Collectio," xxvi. 1038 On partial Engl. transl. see Miss Paues, "A 14th Cent. Engl. Biblical Version," Cam. Univ. Press.

How should popes be above kings? "Thus shulden popis be suget to kynges, for thus weren bothe Crist and Petre."[1] How believe in indulgences sold publicly by pardoners on the market-places, and in that inexhaustible "treasury" of merits laid up in heaven that the depositaries of papal favour are able to distribute at their pleasure among men for money? Each merit is rewarded by God, and consequently the benefit of it cannot be applicable to any one who pays: "As Peter held his pees in grauntinge of siche thingis, so shulden thei holden ther pees, sith thei ben lasse worth than Petir."[2]

Next to these brief arguments are familiar jests, gravely uttered, with scarcely any perceptible change in the expression of the lips, jests that Englishmen have been fond of in all times. If he is asked of what use are the "letters of fraternity," sold by the friars to their customers, to give them a share in the superabundant merits of the whole order, Wyclif replies with a serious air: "Bi siche resouns thinken many men that this lettris mai do good for to covere mostard pottis."[3]

It is difficult to follow him in all the places where he would fain lead us. He terrified the century by the boldness of his touch; when he was seen to shake the frail holy thing with a ruthless hand, all eyes turned away, and his former protectors withdrew from him.[4] He did not, however, carry his doubt to the extreme end; according to his doctrine the *substance* of the host, the particle of matter, is not the matter itself, the living flesh of the body that Jesus Christ had on earth; this substance is bread; only by a miracle which is the effect of consecration, the body of Christ is present sacramentally; that is to say, all the

---

[1] "Select English Works," vol. iii. p. 100; *Ibid.*, ii. p. 296.
[2] *Ibid.*, i. p. 189. [3] *Ibid.*, i. p. 381.
[4] His adversaries, perhaps exaggerating his sayings, attribute to him declarations like the following: "Quod sacramentum illud visibile est infinitum abjectius in natura, quam sit panis equinus, vel panis ratonis; immo, quod verecundum est dicere vel audire, quod stercus ratonis." "Fascic. Ziz." 108.

benefits, advantages, and virtues which emanate from it
are attached to the host as closely as the soul of men is
united to their body.[1]

The other sacraments,[2] ecclesiastical hierarchy, the tithes
collected by the clergy, are not more respectfully treated
by him.   These criticisms and teachings had all the more
weight owing to the fact that they were delivered from a
pulpit and fell from the lips of an authorised master, whose
learning was acknowledged even by his adversaries: "A very
eminent doctor, a peerless and incomparable one," says
the continuator of Knighton.[3]   Still better than Langland's
verses, his forcible speech, by reason of his station,
prepared the way for the great reforms of the sixteenth
century.   He already demands the confiscation of the
estates of the monasteries, accomplished later by Henry
VIII.   He appeals constantly to the secular arm, hoping
by its means to bring back humility by force into the
heart of prelates.

----

[1] "Ille panis est bene miraculose, vere et realiter, spiritualiter, virtualiter et
sacramentaliter corpus Christi.   Sed grossi non contentantur de istis modis, sed
exigunt quod panis ille, vel saltem per ipsum, sit substantialiter et corporaliter
corpus Christi; sic enim volunt, zelo blasphemorum, Christum comedere, sed non
possunt. . . . Ponimus venerabile sacramentum altaris esse naturaliter panem
et vinum, sed sacramentaliter corpus Christi et sanguinem."   "Fasciculi," pp.
122, 125; Wyclif's statement of his beliefs after his condemnation by the
University in 1381.   Again, in his sermons : " Thes ben to rude heretikes that
seien thei eten Crist bodili, and seien thei parten ech membre of him, nekke,
bac, heed and foot. . . . This oost is breed in his kynde as ben other oostes
unsacrid, and sacramentaliche Goddis bodi."   "Select English Works," vol. ii.
p. 169.   This is very nearly the theory adopted later by Latimer, who declares
" that there is none other presence of Christ required than a spiritual presence ;
and that presence is sufficient for a Christian man ; " there remains in the host
the substance of bread.   "Works," Parker Society, 1844, vol. ii. p. 250.

[2] Auricular confession, that " rowninge in preestis eere," is not the true one,
according to Wyclif; the true one is that made to God.   "Select English
Works," vol. i. p. 196.

[3] "Doctor in theologia eminentissimus in diebus illis, in philosophia nulli
reputabatur secundus, in scolasticis disciplinis incomparabilis."   "Chronicon
W. de Knighton," ed. Lumby, Rolls, ii. 151.

He feels the realisation of his dream to be so remote that he is misled into defending chimerical schemes. He wishes the wealth of the clergy to be taken from them and bestowed upon poor, honest, brave, trustworthy gentlemen, who will defend the country ; and he does not perceive that these riches would have fallen principally into the hands of turbulent and grasping courtiers, as happened in the sixteenth century.[1] He is carried away by his own reasonings, so that the utopian or paradoxical character of his statements escape him. Wanting to minimise the power of the popes, he protests against the rules followed for their election, and goes on to say concerning the vote by ballot : " Sith ther ben fewe wise men, and foolis ben without noumbre, assent of more part of men makith evydence that it were foli." [2]

His disciples, *Lollards* as they were usually called, a name the origin of which has not been cleared, survived him, and his simple priests continued, for a time, to propagate his doctrines. The master's principal propositions were even found one day in 1395, posted up on the door of St. Paul's Cathedral, in the heart of London. Among them figure declarations that, at a distance of three centuries, seem a foreshadowing of the theories of the Puritans ; one for instance, affirming " that the multitude of useless arts allowed in the kingdom are the cause of sins without number." Among the forbidden arts are included that of the goldsmiths, and another art of which, however, the Puritans were to make a somewhat notorious use, that of the armorers.[3]

At the University, the followers of Wyclif were numerous ; in the country they continued to increase until the end of the fourteenth century. Energetic

---

[1] "Select English Works," vol. iii. pp. 216, 217.   [2] *Ibid.*, ii. p. 414.
[3] Conclusion No. 12. " Henrici de Blandeforde. . . . Annales," ed. Riley, Rolls, 1866, p. 174.

measures were adopted in the beginning of the fifteenth ; the statute " De hæretico comburendo " was promulgated in 1401 (but at first arely applied) ; the master's books were condemned and pro..ibited ; from that time Wyclifism declined, and mere traces of its survival can be found at the period when the Reformation was introduced into England.

By a strange fate Wyclif's posterity continued to flourish outside of the kingdom.   Bohemia had just given a queen to England, and used to send students every year from its University of Prague to Paris and to Oxford.   In that country the Wyclifite tenets found a multitude of adepts ; the Latin works of the thinker were transcribed by Czech students, and carried back to their own land ; several writings of Wyclif exist only in Czech copies. His most illustrious disciple, John Hus, rector of the University of Prague, was burnt at the stake, by order of the Council of Constance, on the 6th of July, 1415. But the doctrine survived ; it was adopted with modifications by the Taborites and the Moravian Brethren, and borrowed from them by the Waldenses [1] ; the same Moravian Brethren who, owing to equally singular vicissitudes, were to become an important factor in the English religious movement of the eighteenth century : the Wesleyan movement.   In spite of differences in their doctrines, the Moravian Brethren and the Hussites stand as a connecting link between Wesley and Wyclif.[2]

---

[1] "The old belief that the Waldenses (or Vaudois) represent a current of tradition continuous from the assumed evangelical simplicity of the primitive church has lost credit. . . . The imagined primitive Christianity of these Alpine congregations can only be deduced from works which have been shown to be translations or adaptations of the Hussite manuals or treatises." " Wycliffe," by Reginald Lane Poole, 1889, p. 174.   *Cf.* J. Loserth, " Hus und Wiclif," Leipzig, 1884.

[2] The great crisis in Wesley's religious life, what he terms his " conversion," took place on the 24th of February, 1738, under the influence of the Moravian Peter Böhler, who had convinced him, he says in his Journal, " of the want of that faith whereby we are saved."

CHAPTER VI.

THE STAGE.

I.

DRAMATIC art, in which the English people was to find one of the most brilliant of its literary glories, was evolved slowly from distant and obscure origins.

In England, as in the rest of Europe, the sources of modern drama were of two sorts : there were civil and religious sources.

The desire for amusement and the craving for laughable things never disappeared entirely, even in the darkest days ; the sources of the lay drama began to spring and flow, owing to no other cause. The means formerly employed to amuse and raise a laugh cannot be expected to have shown much refinement. No refinement is to be found in them ; all means were considered good which ensured success ; kicks were among the simplest and oftenest resorted to, but not at all among the grossest ; others were worse, and were much more popular. Let us not wonder overmuch : some of them have recovered again, quite recently, a part of their pristine popularity. They were used by jugglers or players, " joculatores," nomadic sometimes, and sometimes belonging to the household of the great. The existence of such men is testified to from century to century, during the whole of the Middle Ages, mainly by the blame and condemnation they constantly incurred : and so it is that the best information concerning these men is not to be sought for in the monuments of the gay literature, but rather in pious treatises and in the acts of Councils.

Treatises and Councils, however, might to our advantage have been even more circumstantial ; the pity is that they, naturally enough, consider it below their dignity to descend to very minute particulars ; it is enough for them to give an enumeration, and to condemn in one phrase all the mimes, tumblers, histrions, wrestlers, and the rest of the juggling troup. Sometimes, however, a few particulars are added ; the peculiar tricks and the scandalous practices of the ill-famed race are mentioned ; and an idea can thus be formed of our ancestors' amusements. John of Salisbury in the twelfth century alludes to a variety of pastimes, and while protesting against the means used to produce laughter, places them on record : a heavy laughter indeed, noisy and tumultuous, Rabelais' laughter before Rabelais. Of course, "such a modest hilarity as an honest man would allow himself" is not to be reproved, and John did not forbid this moderate way of enjoyment ; but the case is different with the jugglers and tumblers : "much better it would be for them to do nothing than to act so wickedly." [1]

[1] " Nostra ætas prolapsa ad fabulas et quævis inania, non modo aures et cor prostituit vanitati, sed oculorum et aurium voluptate suam mulcet desidiam. . . . Nonne piger desidiam instruit et somnos provocat instrumentorum suavitate, aut vocum modulis, hilaritate canentium aut fabulantium gratia, sive quod turpius est ebrietate vel crapula? . . . . Admissa sunt ergo spectacula et infinita tyrocinia vanitatis, quibus qui omnino otiari non possunt perniciosius occupentur. Satius enim fuerat otiari quam turpiter occupari. Hinc mimi, salii vel saliares, balatrones, æmiliani, gladiatores, palæstritæ, gignadii, præstigiatores, malefici quoque multi et tota joculatorum scena procedit. Quorum adeo error invaluit, ut a præclaris domibus non arceantur, etiam illi qui obscenis partibus corporis oculis omnium eam ingerunt turpitudinem, quam erubescat videre vel cynicus. Quodque magis mirere, nec tunc ejiciuntur, quando tumultuantes inferius crebro sonitu aerem fœdant, et turpiter inclusum turpius produnt . . . Jucundum quidem est et ab honesto non recedit virum probum quandoque modesta hilaritate mulcere." " Policraticus," Book I. chap. viii., in " Opera Omnia," ed. Giles, Oxford, 1848, vol. iii. p. 42. Above, p. 188.

No doubt was possible. The jesters did not care in the least to keep within the bounds of "a modest hilarity"; nor did their audience, for in the fourteenth century we find these same men described in the poem of Langland, and they have not altered in any way [1]; their tricks are the same, the same shameful exhibitions take place with the same success ; for two hundred years they have been laughed at without intermission. Many things have come and gone ; the nation has got tired of John's tyranny, of Henry the Third's weakness, of the Pope's supremacy, but the histrions continue to tumble and jump ; " their points being broken, down fall their hose," (to use Shakespeare's words), and the great at Court are convulsed with laughter on their benches.

Besides their horseplay, jugglers and histrions had, to please their audience, retorts, funny answers, witticisms, merry tales, which they acted rather than told, for gestures accompanied the delivery. This part of the amusement, which came nearest the drama, sharp repartees, impromptu dialogues, is the one we know least about. Voices have long been silent, and the great halls which heard them are now but ivy-clad ruins, yielding no echo. Some idea, however, can be formed of what took place.

First we know from innumerable testimonies that those histrions spoke and told endless nonsense ; they have been often enough reproached with it for no doubt to remain as to their talking. Then there is superabundant proof of the relish with which men enjoyed, in the Middle Ages, silly, teazing or puzzling answers ; the questioner remaining at the end rolled up in the repartees, gasping as a fly caught in a spider's web. The Court fool or buffoon had for his principal merit his clever knack of returning witty or confusing answers ; the best of them were preserved ; itinerant minstrels remembered and

[1] C. xvi. 205.

repeated them ; clerks turned them into Latin, and gave them place in their collections of *exempla*. They afforded amusement for a king, an amusement of a mixed sort, sometimes :

—Why, says the king, are there no longer any Rolands?

—Because, the fool answers the king, there are no longer any Charlemagnes.[1]

Walter Map, as we saw, was so fond of happy answers that he formed a book of a.l those he heard, knew, or made in his day. The fabliau of the "Jongleur d'Ely," written in England in the thirteenth century, is a good specimen of the word-fencing at which itinerant amusers were expert. The king is unable to draw from the jongleur any answer to any purpose : What is his name?—The name of his father.—Whom does he belong to?—To his lord.—How is this river called?—No need to call it; it comes of its own accord.—Does the jongleur's horse eat well?—"Certainly yes, my sweet good lord, he can eat more oats in a day than you would do in a whole week."[2]

This is a mere sample of an art that lent itself to many uses, and to which belonged debates, "estrifs," "dis-

---

[1] " De Mimo et Rege Francorum," in Wright, " Latin Stories," 1842, No. cxxxvii.

[2]   Le roi demaund par amour :
        Ou qy estes vus, sire Joglour?
        E il respount sauntz pour :
        Sire, je su ou mon seignour.
        Quy est toun seignour? fet le Roy.
        Le baroun ma dame, par ma foy. . . .
        Quei est le eve apelé, par amours ?
        L'em ne l'apele pas, eynz vint tous jours.

Concerning the horse :

        Mange il.bien, ce savez dire.
        Oïl certes, bel douz sire ;
        Yl mangereit plus un jour d'aveyne
        Que vus ne frez pas tote la semeyne.

Montaiglon and Raynaud, " Recueil général des Fabliaux," vol. ii. p. 243.

putoisons," "jeux-partis," equally popular in England and
in France. Some specimens of it are as old as the time
of the Anglo-Saxons, such as the "Dialogue of Salomon
and Saturnus." [1] There are found in the English language
debates or dialogues between the Owl and Nightingale,
thirteenth century; the Thrush and Nightingale; the Fox
and Wolf, time of Edward I.; the Carpenter's Tools, and
others.[2] Collections of silly answers were also made in
England; one of them was composed to the confusion of
the inhabitants of Norfolk; another in their honour and
for their defence.[3] The influence of those estrifs, or
debates, on the development of the drama cannot be
doubted; the oldest dramatic fragment in the English
language is nothing but an estrif between Christ and
Satan. The author acknowledges it himself:

A strif will I tellen on,

says he in his prologue. [4]

Debates enjoyed great favour in castle halls; impromptu ones which, as Cathos and Madelon said,
centuries later, "exerçaient les esprits de l'assemblée,"
were greatly liked; they constituted a sort of society
game, one of the oldest on record. A person among

---

[1] "Dialogue of Salomon and Saturnus," in prose, ed. Kemble, Ælfric
Society, 1848, 8vo. See also the "estrif" between Joseph and Mary in
"Cynewulf's Christ," ed. Gollancz, 1892, p. 17; above, p. 75.

[2] "The Owl and the Nightingale," ed. Atkins, Cambr. 1922. "The Thrush
and the Nightingale"; "Of the Vox and the Wolf" (above, p. 228); "Debate
of the Carpenter's Tools," in Hazlitt, "Remains of the early Popular Poetry of
Engl.," 1864, 4 vols., i. 50, 58, 79. *Cf.* above, p. 230. On the orig. of the *genre*,
see Hanford and Steadman, "Studies in Philol." Univ. of N. Carol., xv. 232.

[3] "Anonymi Petroburgensis Descriptio Norfolcensicum" (end of the twelfth
century); "Norfolchiæ Descriptionis Impugnatio," in Latin verse, with some
phrases in English, in Th. Wright, "Early Mysteries and other Latin Poems
of the XIIth and the XIIIth centuries," London, 1838, 8vo.

[4] "Harrowing of Hell." This work consists in a dramatic dialogue or
scene, but it was not meant to be represented. Time of Henry III.; text in
Pollard, "English Miracle Plays," Oxford, 7th ed., 1923, p. 166.

those present was chosen to answer questions, and the amusement consisted in putting or returning questions and answers of the most unexpected or puzzling character. This was called the game of the " King who does not lie," or the game of the " King and Queen." [1] By a phenomenon which has been observed in less remote periods, after-dinner conversations often took a licentious turn ; in those games love was the subject most willingly discussed, and it was not, as a rule, treated from a very ethereal point of view ; young men and young ladies exchanged on those occasions observations the liberty of which gave umbrage to the Church, who tried to interfere ; bishops in their Constitutions mentioned those amusements, and forbade to their flock such unbecoming games as " ludos de Rege et Regina ; " Walter de Chanteloup, bishop of Worcester, did so in 1240. [2] Some of that freedom of speech survived, however, through the Middle Ages up to the time of Shakespeare ; while listening to the dialogues of Beatrix and Benedick one wonders sometimes whether they are not playing the game " de Rege et Regina."

Parody also helped in its way to the formation of the drama. People had a fondness for masking, for the imitation of other people ; for the caricaturing of some grave person

---

[1] This game is described in the (very coarse) fabliau of the " Sentier batu " by Jean de Condé, fourteenth century :

> De plusieurs deduis s'entremistrent
> Et tant c'une royne fistrent
> Pour jouer au Roy qui ne ment.
> Ele s'en savoit finement
> Entremettre de commander
> Et de demandes demander.

Montaiglon and Raynaud, "Recueil général des Fabliaux," iii. 248. *Cf.* Bretex, "Tournois de Chauvenci," 1285 ; ed. Delmotte, Valenciennes, 1835, l. 2948.

[2] " Prohibemus etiam clericis ne intersint ludis inhonestis, vel choreis, vel ludant ad aleas, vel taxillos ; nec sustineant ludos fieri de rege et regina," &c. "Constitutiones Walteri de Cantilupo, promulgatæ . . . A.D. 1240," art. xxxviii., in Labbe, "Sacrorum conciliorum . . . Collectio," vol. xxiii. col. 538.

or of some imposing ceremony, mass for example ; for the
reproduction of the song of birds or the noise of a storm,
gestures being added to the noise, the song, or the words.
Some jugglers excelled in this ; they were live gargoyles
and were paid " the one to play the drunkard, another the
fool, a third to imitate the cat." The great minstrels,
"grans menestreus," had a horror of those gargoyles, the
shame of their profession ;[1] noblemen, however, did not
share these refined, if not disinterested, feelings, and asked
to their castles and freely rewarded the members of the
wandering tribe who knew how to imitate the drunkard,
the fool, or the cat.

On histrionic liberties introduced even into church
services, Aelred, abbot of Rievaulx in the twelfth century,

---

[1] The two sorts are well described by Baudouin de Condé in his " Contes
des Hiraus," thirteenth century. The author meets a servant and asks him
questions about his master :

> Dis-moi, par l'âme de ton père,
> Voit-il volentiers menestreus ?
> —Oïl voir, biau frère, et estre eus
> En son hostel à grant solas. . . .
> . . . Et quant avient
> C'aucuns grans menestreus là vient,
> Maistres en sa menestrandie,
> Qui bien viele ou ki bien die
> De bouce, mesires l'ascoute
> Volentiers. . . .
> Mais peu souvent i vient de teus,
> Mais des félons et des honteus,

who speak but nonsense and know nothing, and who, however, receive bread,
meat, and wine,

> . . . l'un por faire l'ivre,
> L'autre le cat, le tiers le sot ;
> Li quars, ki onques rien ne sot
> D'armes s'en parole et raconte
> De ce preu duc, de ce preu conte.

" Dits et Contes de Baudouin de Condé," ed. Scheler, Brussels, 1866, 3 vols.
8vo, vol. i. p. 154.

gives some unexpected particulars. He describes the movements and attitudes of certain chanters by which they "resembled actors": so that we thus get information on both at the same time. Chanters are found in various churches, he says, who with inflated cheeks imitate the noise of thunder, and then murmur, whisper, allow their voice to expire, keeping their mouth open, and think that they give thus an idea of the death or ecstasy of martyrs. Now you would think you hear the neighing of horses, now the voice of a woman. With this "all their body is agitated by histrionic movements"; their lips, their shoulders, their fingers are twisted, shrugged, or spread out as they think best to suit their delivery. The audience, filled with wonder and admiration at those inordinate gesticulations, at length bursts into laughter: "It seems to them they are at the play and not at church, and that they have only to look and not to pray."[1]

The transition from these various performances to little dramas or interludes, which were at first nothing but tales turned into dialogues, was so natural that it could scarcely attract any notice. Few specimens have survived; an English one, however, is extant, dating from the time of Edward I., and shows that this transition had then taken place. It consists in the dramatising of one of the most absurd and most popular tales told by wandering minstrels,

---

[1] "Ad quid illa vocis contractio et infractio? Hic succinit, ille discinit. . . . Aliquando, quod pudet dicere, in equinos hinnitus cogitur; aliquando virili vigore deposito in femineæ vocis gracilitates acuitur. . . . Videas aliquando hominem aperto ore quasi intercluso habitu expirare, non cantare, ac ridiculosa quadam vocis interceptione quasi minitari silentium; nunc agones morientium, vel extasim patientium imitari. Interim histrionicis quibusdam gestibus totum corpus agitatur, torquentur labia, rotant, ludunt humeri; et ad singulas quasque notas digitorum flexus respondet. Et hæc ridiculosa dissolutio vocatur religio! . . . Vulgus . . . miratur . . . sed lascivas cantantium gesticulationes, meretricias vocum alternationes et infractiones, non sine cachinno risuque intuetur, ut eos non ad oratorium sed ad theatrum, nec ad orandum sed ad spectandum æstimes convenisse." "Speculum Charitatis," Book ii. chap. 23, in Migne's "Patrologia," vol. cxcv. col. 571.

the story, namely, of the Weeping Bitch. A woman or maid rejects the love of a clerk ; an old woman (Dame Siriz in the English prose text) calls upon the proud one, having in her hands a little bitch whom she has fed with mustard, and whose eyes accordingly weep. The bitch, she says, is her own daughter, so transformed by a clerk who had failed to touch her heart ; the young woman at once yields to her lover, fearing a similar fate. There exist French, Latin, and English versions of this tale, one of the few which are of undoubted Hindu origin. The English version seems to belong to the thirteenth century.[1]

The turning of it into a drama took place a few years later. Nothing was easier ; this fabliau, like many others, was nearly all in dialogues ; to make a play of it, the jongleur had but to suppress some few lines of narrative ; we thus have a drama, in rudimentary shape, where a deep study of human feelings must not be sought for.[2] Here is the conversation between the young man and the young maid when they meet :

Clericus.	Damishel, reste wel.
Puella.	Sir, welcum, by Saynt Michel !
Clericus.	Wer esty (is thy) sire, wer esty dame ?
Puella.	By Gode, es noner her at hame.
Clericus.	Wel wor suilc (such) a man to life That suilc a may (maid) mihte have to wyfe !
Puella.	Do way, by Crist and Leonard. . . . Go forth thi way, god sire, For her hastu losye al thi wile.

---

[1] Latin text in " The Exempla . . . of Jacques de Vitry," thirteenth century, ed. T. F. Crane, London, 1890, 8vo, p. 105 (No. ccl.), and in Th. Wright, " A Selection of Latin Stories," 1842, Percy Society, p. 16 : " De Dolo et Arte Vetularum." French text in Barbazan and Méon, " Fabliaux," vol. ii., included into the " Castoiement d'un père à son fils," thirteenth century. English text in Th. Wright, " Anecdota Literaria," London, 1844, 8vo, p. 1 ; the title is in French : " Ci commence le fables et le cointise de dame Siriz."

[2] Text in Wright and Halliwell, " Reliquiæ Antiquæ," 1841, 2 vols., vol. i. p. 145. " Hic incipit interludium de Clerico and Puella." Above, p. 225.

After some more supplications, the clerk, who is a student at the University, goes to old Helwis (Siriz in the prose tale) and then the author, more accustomed, it seems, to such persons than to the company of young maidens, describes with some art the hypocrisy of the matron. Helwis will not interfere ; she leads a holy life, and what is asked of her will disturb her from her pious observances. Her dignified scruples are removed at length by the plain offer of a reward.

In this way, some time before Chaucer's birth, the lay drama came into existence in Shakespeare's country.

Other stories of the same sort were also turned into plays ; we have none of them, but we know that they existed. An Englishman of the fourteenth century calls the performance of them "pleyinge of japis,"[1] by opposition to the performance of religious dramas.

Other amusements again, of a strange kind, helped in the same early period to the formation of the drama. A particularly keen pleasure was afforded during the Middle Ages by songs, dances, and carols, when performed in consecrated places, such as cemeteries, cloisters, churches. A preference for such places may seem scarcely credible ; still it cannot be doubted, and is besides easily explainable. To the unbridled instincts of men as yet half tamed, the Church had opposed rigorous prescriptions which were enforced wholesale. To resist excessive independence, excessive severity was needful ; buttresses had to be raised equal in strength to the weight of the wall. But from time to time a cleft was formed, and the loosened passions burst forth with violence. Escaped from the bondage of discipline, men found inexpressible delight in violating all

---

[1] "Here bigynnis a tretise of Miraclis Pleyinge," end of fourteenth century, in Wright and Halliwell, "Reliquiæ Antiquæ," vol. ii. p. 46. Elsewhere in the same treatise, "to pley in rebaudye" is opposed to "pley in myriclis," p. 49.

prohibitions at once ; the day for the beast had come, and, it challenged the angel in its turn.

The propelling power of passions so repressed was even increased by certain weird tastes very common at that period, and by the merry reactions they caused. Now oppressed by, and now in revolt against, the idea of death, the faithful would at times answer threats with sneers ; they found a particular pleasure in evolving bacchanalian processions among the tombs of churchyards, not only because it was forbidden, but also on account of the awful character of the place. The watching of the dead was also an occasion for orgies and laughter. At the University, even, these same amusements were greatly liked ; students delighted in singing licentious songs, wearing wreaths, carolling and deep drinking in the midst of churchyards. Councils, popes, and bishops never tired of protesting, nor the faithful of dancing. Be it forbidden, says In- nocent III. at the beginning of the thirteenth century, to perform "theatrical games" in churches. Be this prohibition enforced, says Gregory IX. a little later.[1] Be it forbidden, says Walter de Chanteloup, bishop of Worcester, to perform "dishonest games" in cemeteries and churches, especially on feast days and on the vigils of saints.[2] Be it forbidden, says the provincial council of Scotland in 1225, "to carol and sing songs at the funeral of the dead ; the tears of others ought not to be an occasion for laughter."[3] Be it forbidden, the University

---

[1] "Ludi theatrales, etiam prætextu consuetudinis in ecclesiis vel per clericos fieri non debent." Decretal of Innocent III., year 1207, included by Gregory IX. in his "Compilatio." Richter and Friedberg, "Corpus Juris Canonici," Leipzig, 1879, vol. ii. p. 453.

[2] "Constitutiones Walteri de Cantilupo, A.D. 1240," in Labbe's "Sacrorum Conciliorum . . . Collectio," vol. xxiii. col. 526.

[3] Wilkins, "Concilia Magnæ Britanniæ," London, 1737, 4 vols. fol., vol. i. p. 617, Nos. lxxiv., lxxv. The same prohibition is made by Walter de Chanteloup, *ut supra*, art. lv. The custom was a very old one, and existed already in Anglo-Saxon times ; see " Ælfric's Lives of Saints," 1881, E.E.T.S., p. 461.

of Oxford decrees in the same century, to dance and sing in churches, and wear there disguises and wreaths of flowers and leaves.[1]

The year was divided by feasts ; and those feasts, the importance of which in everybody's eyes has gradually dwindled, were then great events ; people thought of them long before, saw them in the distance, towering above the common level of days, as cathedrals above houses. Every-day life was arrested, and it was a time for rejoicings, of a religious, and sometimes of an impious, character : both kinds helped the formation of drama, and they were at times closely united. On such great occasions, more than ever, the caricature and derision of holy things increased the amusement. Christmas-time had inherited the licence as well as it occupied the date of the ancient Roman saturnalia; and whatever be the period considered, be it early or late in the Middle Ages, it will be found that the anniversary was commemorated, piously and merrily, by adoring and sneering multitudes. For the one did not prevent the other ; people caricatured the Church, her hierarchy and ceremonials, but did not doubt her infalli-bility; they laughed at the devil and feared him. "Priests, deacons, and sub-deacons," says the Pope, are bold enough, on those mad days, "to take part in unbecoming bacchanals, in the presence of the people, whom they ought rather to edify by preaching the Word of God."[2] In those bacchanals parodies of the Church prayers were in-

---

[1] " . . . Ne quis choreas cum larvis seu strepitu aliquo in ecclesiis vel plateis ducat, vel sertatus, vel coronatus corona ex foliis arborum, vel florum vel aliunde composita, alicubi incedat . . . prohibemus," thirteenth century, "Munimenta Academica," ed. Anstey, Rolls, 1868, p. 18.

[2] Decretal of Innocent III., reissued by Gregory IX.: " In aliquibus anni festivitatibus, quæ continue natalem Christi sequuntur, diaconi, presbyteri ac subdiaconi vicissim insaniæ suæ ludibria exercere præsumunt, per gesticula-tionum suarum debacchationes obscœnas in conspectu populi decus faciunt clericale vilescere, quem potius illo tempore verbi Dei deberent prædicatione mulcere." Richter and Friedberg, "Corpus Juris Canonici," vol. ii. p. 453.

troduced ; a Latin hymn on the Nativity was transposed
line for line, and became a song in honour of the good ale.
Here, as a sample, are two stanzas, both of the original and
of the parody, this last having, as it seems, been composed
in England :

Letabundus	Or i parra :
Exultet fidelis chorus,	La Cerveise nos chantera
Alleluia !	*Alleluia !*
Regem Regum	Qui que en beit,
Intacte perfundit thorus :	Se tele seit com estre deit,
Res miranda !	*Res miranda !*
Angelus consilii	Bevez quant l'avez en poing ;
Natus est de Virgine,	Bien est droit, car mout est loing
Sol de Stella,	*Sol de Stella ;*
Sol occasum nesciens,	Bevez bien et bevez bel,
Stella semper rutilans,	El vos vendra del tonel
Semper clara.	*Semper clara.*

"You will see ; the ale will make us sing, Alleluia ! all
of us, if the ale is as it should be, a wonderful thing ! (Res
miranda). Drink of it when you hold the jug ; 'tis a most
proper thing, for it is a good long way from sun to star
(Sol de Stella) ; drink well ! drink deep ! it will flow for
you from the tun, ever clear ! (Semper clara)." [1]

So rose from earth at Christmastide, borne on the same

---

[1] Thirteenth century. See Gaston Paris, " Romania," vol. xxi. p. 262.
Songs of a much worse character were also sung at Christmas. To deter his
readers from listening to any such Gascoigne writes (first half of the fifteenth
century) : "Cavete et fugite in hoc sacro festo viciosa et turpia, et præcipue
cantus inhonestos et turpes qui libidinem excitant et provocant . . . et
ymagines imprimunt in mente quas expellere difficillimum est. Novi ego,
scilicet Gascoigne, doctor sacræ paginæ qui hæc scripsi, unum magnum et
notabilem virum talem cantum turpem in festo Natalis audivisse." He could
never forget the shameful things he had heard, and fell on that account into
melancholy, by which he was driven to death. " Loci e libro veritatum . . .
passages selected from Gascoigne's Theological Dictionary," ed. Thorold Rogers,
Oxford, 1881, 4to. On the Christmas festivities at the University and on the
" Rex Natalicius " (sixteenth century and before), see C. R. L. Fletcher,
" Collectanea," Oxford, 1885, 8vo, p. 39.

winds, angels and demons, and the ancient feast of Saturn was commemorated at the same time as Christ's. In the same way, again, the scandalous feasts of the Fools, of the Innocents, and of the Ass, were made the merrier with grotesque parodies of pious ceremonies ; they were celebrated in the church itself, thus transformed, says the bishop of Lincoln, Grosseteste, into a place for pleasure and folly : God's house was defiled by the devil's inventions. He forbade, in consequence, the celebration of the feast of Fools, " festum Stultorum," on the day of Circumcision in his cathedral, and then in the whole diocese. [1]

The feast of the Innocents was even more popular in England. The performers had at their head a " boy bishop," and this diminutive prelate presided, with mitre on his head, over the frolics of his madcap companions. The king would take an interest in the ceremony ; he would order the little dignitary to be brought before him, and give him a present. Edward II. gave six shillings and eight pence to the young John, son of Allan Scroby, who had played the part of the " boy bishop " in the royal chapel ; another time he gave ten shillings ; Richard II., more liberal, gave a pound.[2] Nuns even were known to

---

[1] "Cum domus Dei, testante propheta Filioque Dei, domus sit orationis, nefandum est eam in domum jocationis, scurrilitatis et nugacitatis convertere, locumque Deo dicatum diabolicis adinventionibus execrare ; cumque circumcisio Domini nostri Jesu Christi prima fuerit nec modicum acerba ejusdem passio, signum quoque sit circumcisionis spiritualis qua cordium præputia tolluntur . . . execrabile est circumcisionis Domini venerandam solemnitatem libidinosarum voluptatum sordibus prophanare : quapropter vobis mandamus in virtute obedientiæ firmiter injungentes, quatenus Festum Stultorum cum sit vanitate plenum et voluptatibus spurcum, Deo odibile et dæmonibus amabile, ne de cætero in ecclesia Lincolniensi, die venerandæ solemnitatis circumcisionis Domini permittatis fieri." "Epistolæ," ed. Luard, Rolls, 1861, p. 118, year 1236 (?). Same defence for the whole diocese, p. 161.

[2] "Wardrobe Accounts," in "Archæologia," vol. xxvi. p. 342 ; "Issue Roll of Thomas de Brantingham," ed. Devon, 1835, p. xlvi ; "Issues of the Exchequer," ed. Devon, p. 222, 6 Rich. II. Text of the Sarum office "De Episcopo Puerorum," in Chambers, "Mediæval Stage," 1903, ii. 283.

forget on certain occasions their own character, and to carol with laymen on the day of the Innocents, or on the day of Mary Magdalen, to commemorate the life of their patroness–in its first part as it seems.[1]

The passion for sightseeing, which was then very keen, and which was to be fed, later, mainly on theatrical entertainments, was indulged in during the Middle Ages in various other ways. Processions were one of them ; occasions were numerous, and causes for them were not difficult to find. Had the *Pui* of London awarded the crown to the writer of the best *chanson?* a procession was formed in the streets in honour of the event. A marriage, a pilgrimage to Palestine, a patronal feast, were sufficient motives ; gilds and associations donned their liveries, drew their insignia from their chest, and paraded the streets, including in the "pageant," when the circumstance allowed of it, a medley of giants and dwarfs, monsters, gilt fishes, and animals of all sorts. On grand days the town itself was transformed ; with its flower-decked houses, its tapestries and hangings, it gave, with some more realism about it, the impression we receive from the painted scenery of an opera.

The town at such times was swept with extraordinary care ; even "insignificant filth" was removed, Matthew Paris notes with wondering pen in 1236.[2] The procession moved forward, men on horseback and on foot, with unfurled banners, along the decorated streets, to the sound of bells ringing in the steeples. At road-crossings the procession stopped ; after having been a sight, the members of it became in their turn sightseers. Wonders had been prepared to please them : here a forest with wild beasts

---

[1] "Inhibemus ne de cetero in festis Innocentium et Beate Marie Magdalene ludibria exerceatis consueta, induendo vos scilicet vestis secularium aut inter vos, seu cum secularibus, choreas ducendo, nec extra refectorium comedatis," &c. Eudes Rigaud, archbishop of Rouen, to the nuns of Villarciaux, thirteenth century. "Registrum Visitationum," ed. Bonnin, 1842, 4to, p. 44

[2] "Historia Major," Rolls, vol. iii. p. 336.

and St. John the Baptist; elsewhere scenes from the
Bible, or from knightly romances, the "pas de Saladin,"
for example, where the champion of England, Richard
Cœur-de-Lion, fought the champion of Islam. At
times it was a dumb-show, a sort of *tableau vivant*, at
others actors moved but did not speak; at others again
they did both, and complimented the king. A day came
when the compliments were cut into dialogues; such
practice was frequent in the fifteenth century, and it
approached very near to the real drama.

In 1236, Henry III. of England having married Aliénor
of Provence made a solemn entry into his capital. On
this occasion were gathered together "so many nobles, so
many ecclesiastics, such a concourse of people, such a
quantity of histrions, that the town of London could
scarcely hold them in her ample bosom—*sinu suo capace.*
—All the town was adorned with silk banners, wreaths,
hangings, candles and lamps, mechanisms and inventions
of extraordinary kinds." [1]

The same town, fond above all others of such exhibitions, and one of the last to preserve vestiges of them in
her Lord Mayor's Show, outdid all that had been seen
before when, on the 29th of August, 1393, Richard II.
made his entry in state, after having consented to receive
the citizens again into his favour. [2] The streets were lined
with cloth of gold and purple; "sweet smelling flowers"
perfumed the air; tapestries with figures hung from the
windows; the king was coming forth, splendid to look
at, very proud of his good looks, "much like Troilus;"
queen Anne took part also in the procession. Various scenes
stopped the progress and delighted the onlookers; one

---

[1] Matthew Paris, *ibid.*

[2] Described by Richard of Maidstone (d. 1396) in a Latin poem : "Richardi
Maydiston de Concordia inter Regem Ricardum II. et civitatem London," in
the "Political Poems and Songs" of Wright, Rolls, vol. i. p. 282.

had an unforeseen character. The queen was nearing the
gate of the bridge, the old bridge with defensive towers and
gates, and two cars full of ladies were following her, when
one of the cars, "of Phaetonic make" says the classical-
minded narrator, suddenly broke. Grave as saints, beautiful as angels, the ladies, losing their balance, fell head
downwards; and the crowd, while full of admiration for
what they saw, "could not suppress their laughter." The
author of the description calls it, as Fragonard would have
done, "a lucky chance," *sors bona;* but there was nothing
of Fragonard in him except this word: he was a Carmelite
and Doctor of Divinity.

Things having been set right again, the procession
entered Cheapside, and there was seen an "admirable
tower"; a young man and a young maiden came out of
it, addressed Richard and Anne, and offered them crowns;
at the Gate of St. Paul's a concert of music was heard; at
Temple Bar, "barram Templi," a forest had been arranged
on the gate, with animals of all sorts, serpents, lions, a bear,
a unicorn, an elephant, a beaver, a monkey, a tiger, a bear,
"all of which were there, running about, biting each other,
fighting, jumping." Forests and beasts were supposed to
represent the desert where St. John the Baptist had lived.
An angel was let down from the roof, and offered the king
and queen a little diptych in gold, with stones and enamel
representing the Crucifixion; he made also a speech. At
length the queen, who had an active part to play in
this opera, came forward, and, owing to her intercession,
the king, with due ceremony, consented to bestow his
pardon on the citizens.

Many other examples might be adduced; feasts were
numerous, and for a time caused all pain to be forgotten:
"oubliance était au voir," as Froissart says so well on an
occasion of this sort.[1] There were also for the people the

---

[1] Entry of Isabeau of Bavaria into Paris, in 1384.

May celebrations with their dances and songs, the imper-
sonation of Robin Hood, later the performance of short
plays of which he was the hero [1] ; and again those chimes,
falling from the steeples, filling the air with their joyous
peals. At Court there were the "masks" or "ballets" in
which the great took part, wrapped in starry draperies,
disguised with gold beards, dressed in skins or feathers,
as were at Paris King Charles VI. and his friends on
the 29th of January, 1392, in the famous Ballet of
Wild Men, since called, from the catastrophe which
happened, "Ballet des Ardents" (of men on fire). The
taste for ballets and Masks was one of long duration ;
the Tudors and Stuarts were as fond of them as the
Plantagenets, so much so that a branch apart in dramatic
literature was created on this account, and it includes in
England such graceful and touching masterpieces as the
"Sad Shepherd" of Ben Jonson and the "Comus" of
Milton.

II.

While joculators gave a foretaste of farce and comedy in
castle halls, while romantic drama was foreshadowed in the
"Pas de Saladin" and the "Taking of Troy," and the
pastoral drama began with May games, other sources of
the modern dramatic art were springing up in the shadow
of the cloister and under the naves of churches.

The imitation of any action is a step towards drama.
Conventional, liturgical, ritualistic as the imitation was,
still there was an imitation in the ceremony of mass ; and

---

[1] On the popularity of Robin Hood in the fourteenth century, see above, p.
224. In the fifteenth century he was the hero of plays performed during the
May festivities : " Rece[d] for the gathering of the May-pole called Robin Hood,
on the fair day, 19s." Accounts of the church of St. Lawrence at Reading,
1499, *Academy*, October 6, 1883, p. 231. Samples of Robin Hood dialogues,
in Manly, "Pre-Shaksperean Drama," Boston, 1897, vol. i.

mass led to the religious drama, which was therefore, at starting, as conventional, liturgical, and ritualistic as could be. Its early beginning is to be sought for in the antiphoned parts of the service, and then it makes one with the service itself. In a similar manner, outside the Church, lay drama had begun with the alternate *chansons*, debates, poetical altercations of the singers of facetious or love songs. A great step was made when, at the principal feasts of the year, Easter and Christmas, the chanters, instead of giving their responses from their stalls, moved in the Church to recall the action commemorated on that day; additions were introduced into the received text of the service; religious drama begins then to have an existence of its own.

"'Tell us, shepherds, whom do you seek in this stable? —They will answer: 'Christ the Saviour, our Lord.'"

Such is the starting-point; it dates from the tenth century; from this is derived the play of Shepherds, of which many versions have come down to us. One of them, followed in the cathedral of Rouen, gives a minute account of the performance as it was then acted in the midst of the religious service: "Be the crib established behind the altar, and be the image of the Blessed Mary placed there. First a child, from before the choir and on a raised platform, representing an angel, will announce the birth of the Saviour to five canons or their vicars of the second rank; the shepherds must come in by the great gate of the choir. . . . As they near the crib they sing the prose *Pax in terris*. Two priests of the first rank, wearing a dalmatic, will represent the midwives and stand by the crib." [1]

These adventitious ornaments were greatly appreciated, and from year to year they were increased and perfected.

---

[1] "Quem quæritis in præsepe, pastores? Respondent: Salvatorem Christum Dominum." Petit de Julleville, "Histoire du Théâtre en France.—Les Mystères," 1880, i. 25, 26. *Cf.* A. W. Ward, "Hist. of Engl. Dramatic Lit.," Oxf., 3 vols., E. K. Chambers, "Mediæval Stage," 1903, 2 vols., Krestmann, "The liturgical element in the Mediæval Drama," Minneapolis, 1916.

Verse replaced prose ; the vulgar idiom replaced Latin ;
open air and the public square replaced the church nave
and its subdued light.   It was no longer necessary to have
recourse to priests wearing a dalmatic in order to represent
midwives ; the feminine parts were performed by young
boys dressed as women : this was coming much nearer
nature, as near in fact as Shakespeare did, for he never
saw any but boys play the part of his Juliet.   There were
even cases in which actual women were seen on the
mediæval stage.   These ameliorations, so simple, summed
up in a phrase, were the work of centuries, but the tide
when on the flow was the stronger for waiting.   The
drama left the church, because its increased importance
had made it cumbersome there, because it was badly seen
and because having power it wanted freedom.

Easter was the occasion for ornaments and additions
similar to those introduced into the Christmas service.[1]
The ceremonies of Holy Week, which reproduced each
incident in the drama of the Passion, lent themselves
admirably to it.   Additions following additions, the whole
of the Old Testament ended by being grouped round and
tied to the Christmas feast, and the whole of the New
Testament round Easter.   Both were closely connected,
the scenes in the one being interpreted as symbols of the
scenes in the other ; complete cycles were thus formed, representing in two divisions the religious history of mankind
from the Creation to Doomsday.   Once severed from the
church, these groups of plays often got also separated
from the feast to which they owed their birth, and were

---

[1] Same beginning (and even earlier according to K. Young, " Publ. Mod.
Lang. Assn. of America," xxix. 1).—" Quem queritis in sepulchro o
Christicole ?—Jesum Nazarenum crucifixum o celicole.—Non est hic, surrexit
sicut predixerat ; ite nunciate quia surrexit.   Alleluia."   In use at Limoges,
eleventh century.   Carl Lange, " Die lateinischen Osterfeiern," Munich, 1887,
p. 22.   Text of the " Dublin Quem Quæritis," XVth century, in Chambers,
" Mediæval Stage," 1903, ii. 315.

represented at Whitsuntide, on Corpus Christi day, or on the occasion of some other solemnity.

As the taste for such dramas was spreading, a variety of tragic subjects, not from the Bible, were turned into dialogues : first lives of saints ; later, in France, some few subjects borrowed from history or romance : the story of Griselda, the raising of the siege at Orléans by Joan of Arc, &c.[1] The English adhered more constantly to the Bible.[2] Dramas drawn from the lives of saints were usually called Miracles ; those derived from the Bible, Mysteries ; but these appellations had nothing very definite and were often used one for the other.

The religious drama was on the way to lose its purely liturgical character when the conquest of England had taken place. Under the reign of the Norman and Angevin kings, the taste for dramatic performances increased considerably; within the first century after Hastings we find them numerous and largely attended.

The oldest representation the memory of which has come down to us took place at the beginning of the twelfth century, and had for its subject the story of that St. Catherine of Alexandria whom the Emperor Maximinus caused to be beheaded after she had converted the fifty orators entrusted with the care of bringing her back to paganism by dint of their eloquence. The fifty orators received baptism, and were burnt alive.[3] The representation was managed by a Mancel of good family called Geoffrey, whom Richard, abbot of St. Albans,

[1] "Ci comence l'estoire de Griselidis ;" MS. fr. 2203, National Library, Paris, dated 1395, outline drawings (privately printed, Paris, 1832). "Le Mistère du siège d'Orléans," ed. Guessard and Certain, Paris, 1862.

[2] Concerning English "Saint-plays" on St. George, St. Thomas of Canterbury, &c.; see Chambers, "Mediæval Stage," ii. 132. *Cf.* Manly, "Pre-Shaksperean Drama," vol. i.

[3] This story was very popular during the Middle Ages, in France and in England. It was, *e g.*, the subject of a poem in English verse, XIIIth century : "The Life of St. Katherine," ed. Einenkel, E.E.T.S., 1884.

had asked to come from France to be the master of the Abbey school. But as he was late in starting, he found on his coming that the school had been given to another ; in his leisure he caused to be represented at Dunstable a play, or miracle, of St. Catherine, "quendam ludum de Sancta Katerina quem miracula vulgariter appellamus." He borrowed from the sacristan at St. Albans the Abbey copes to dress his actors in ; but the night following upon the performance, the fire consumed his house; all his books were burnt, and the copes too: "Wherefore, not knowing how to indemnify God and St. Albans, he offered his own person as a holocaust and took the habit in the monastery. This explains the zeal with which, having become abbot, he strove to enrich the convent with precious copes." For he became abbot, and died in 1146, after a reign of twenty-six years,[1] and Matthew Paris, to whom we owe those details, and whose taste for works of art is well known, gives a full enumeration of the splendid purple and gold vestments, adorned with precious stones, with which the Mancel Geoffrey enriched the treasury of the Abbey.[2]

A little later in the same century, Fitzstephen, who wrote under Henry II., mentions as a common occurrence the "representations of miracles" held in London.[3] In the following century, under Henry III., some were written in the English language.[4] During the fourteenth century, in

---

[1] "Vitæ . . . viginti trium abbatum Sancti Albani," in "Matthæi Paris monachi Albanensis [Opera]," London, 1639-40, 2 vols. fol., vol ii. p. 56 "Gaufridus decimus sextus [abbas]."

[2] *Ibid.*, p. 64.

[3] He writes, twelfth century: "Londonia pro spectaculis theatralibus pro ludis scenicis, ludos habet sanctiores, representationes miraculorum . . ." "Descriptio nobilissimæ civitatis Londoniæ," printed with Stow's "Survey of London," 1599, 4to.

[4] This can be inferred from the existence of that "estrif" tne "Harrowing of Hell," written in the style of mysteries, which has come down to us, and belongs to that period. See above, p. 443. Religious dramas were written in Latin by subjects of the kings of England, and, among others, by Hilary, a

the time of Chaucer, mysteries were at the height of their popularity ; their heroes were familiar to all, and the sayings of the same became proverbs. Kings themselves journeyed in order to be present at the representations ; Chaucer had seen them often, and the characters in his tales make frequent allusions to them ; his drunken miller cries "in Pilates vois " ; "Jolif Absolon" played the part of "king Herodes," and is it to be expected that any Alisoun could resist king Herodes ? The Wife of Bath, dressed in her best garments, goes "to pleyes of miracles," and there tries to make acquaintances that may be turned into husbands when she wants them. "Hendy Nicholas" quotes to the credulous carpenter the example of Noah, whose wife would not go on board, and who regretted that he had not built a separate ship for "hir-self allone."

A treatise, written in English at this period, against such representations, shows the extreme favour in which they stood with all classes of society.[1] The enthusiasm was so general and boundless that it seems to the author indispensable to take the field and retort (for the question was keenly disputed) the arguments put forward to justify the performance of mysteries. The works and miracles of Christ, he observes, were not done in jest ; He did them ' ernystfully," and we use them "in bourde and pleye !" It is treating with great familiarity the Almighty, who may well say : " Pley not with me, but pley with thi pere." Let us beware of His revenge ; it well may happen that "God takith more venjaunce on us than a lord that sodaynly sleeth his servaunt for he pleyide to homely

disciple of Abélard, twelfth century, who seems to have been an Anglo-Norman ; " Hilarii versus et Ludi," ed. Champollion-Figeac, Paris, 1838. A few lines in French are mixed with his Latin.

[1] " Here bigynnis a tretise of miraclis pleyinge," in Wright and Halliwell, " Reliquiæ Antiquæ," London, 1842, vol. ii. p. 42 ; end of fourteenth century.

with hym ; " and yet the lord's vengeance cannot be considered a trifling one.

What do the abettors of mysteries answer to this ? They answer that " thei pleyen these myraclis in the worschip of God " ; they lead men to think and meditate ; devils are seen there carrying the wicked away to hell ; the sufferings of Christ are represented, and the hardest are touched, they are seen weeping for pity ; for people wept and laughed at the representations, openly and noisily, " wepynge bitere teris." Besides, there are men of different sorts, and some are so made that they cannot be converted but by mirthful means, " by gamen and pley " ; and such performances do them much good. Must not, on the other hand, all men have " summe recreatioun " ? Better it is, " or lesse yvele, that thei han thyre recreacoun by pleyinge of myraclis than bi pleyinge of other japis." And one more very sensible reason is given : " Sithen it is leveful to han the myraclis of God peyntid, why is not as wel leveful to han the myraclis of God pleyed . . . and betere thei ben holden in mennus mynde and oftere rehersid by the pleyinge of hem than by the peyntynge, for this is a deed bok, the tother a quick."

To those reasons, which he does not try to minimise, but on the contrary presents very forcibly, the fair-minded author answers his best. These representations are too amusing ; after such enjoyments, everyday life seems plain and dull ; women of " yvil continaunse," Wives of Bath maybe, or worse, flock there and do not remain idle. The fact that they come does not prevent the priests from going too ; yet it is " uttirly " forbidden them " not onely to been myracle pleyere but also to heren or to seen myraclis pleyinge." But they set the decree at nought and " pleyn in entirlodies," and go and see them : " The prestis that seyn hemsilf holy, and besien hem aboute siche pleyis, ben verry ypocritis and lyeris." All bounds have

been overstepped ; it is no longer a taste, but a passion ;
men are carried away by it ; citizens become avaricious
and grasping to get money in view of the representations
and the amusements which follow: "To peyen ther rente
and ther dette thei wolen grucche, and to spende two so
myche upon ther pley thei wolen nothinge grucche."
Merchants and tradesmen "bygilen ther neghbors, in
byinge and sellyng," that is "hideous coveytise," that is
"maumetrie"; and they do it "to han to spenden on
these miraclis."

Many documents corroborate these statements and
show the accuracy of the description. The fondness of
priests for plays and similar pastimes is descanted upon
by the Council of London in 1391.[1] A hundred years
earlier an Englishman, in a poem which he wrote in
French, had pointed out exactly the same abuses: from
which can be perceived how deeply rooted they were.
Another folly, William de Wadington[2] had said, has been
invented by mad clerks ; it consists in what is called
Miracles ; in spite of decrees they disguise themselves
with masks, "li forsené!"[3] Purely liturgical drama, of

---

[1] "Item quod tabernas, spectacula aut alia loca inhonesta, seu ludos
noxios at illicitos non frequentent, sed more sacerdotali se habeant et in
gestu, ne ipsorum ministerium, quod absit, vituperio, scandalo vel despectui
habeatur." Labbe, vol. xxvi. col. 767. The inhibition is meant for priests
of all sorts : "presbyteri stipendarii aut alii sacerdotes, propriis sumptibus seu
alias sustentati." Innocent III. and Gregory IX. had vainly denounced the
same abuses, and tried to stop them : "Clerici officia vel commercia sæcularia
non exerceant, maxime inhonesta. Mimis, joculatoribus et histrionibus non
intendant. Et tabernas prorsus evitent, nisi forte causa necessitatis in itinere
constituti." Richter and Friedberg, "Corpus Juris Canonici," ii. p. 454.

[2] "Roberd of Brunne's Handlyng Synne (written A.D. 1303), with the French
treatise on which it is founded, 'Le Manuel des Pechiez,' by William de
Wadington," ed. Furnivall, Roxburghe Club, 1862, 4to, pp. 146 ff.

[3] Un autre folie apert
Unt les fols clercs contrové,
Qe " miracles " sunt apelé ;
Lur faces unt la déguisé
Par visers, li forsené.

course, is permissible (an additional proof of its existence in England) ; certain representations can be held, "provided they be chastely set up and included in the Church service," as is done when the burial of Christ or the Resurrection is represented "to increase devotion." [1]　But to have "those mad gatherings in the streets of towns, or in the cemeteries, after dinner," to prepare for the idle such meeting-places, is a quite different thing ; if they tell you that they do it with good intent and to the honour of God, do not believe them ; it is all "for the devil." If players ask you to lend them horses, equipments, dresses, and ornaments of all sorts, don't fail to refuse.　For the stage continued to live upon loans, and the example of the copes of St. Albans destroyed by fire had not deterred convents from continuing to lend sacred vestments to actors.[2]　In the case of sacred vestments, says William, "the sin is much greater."　In all this, as well as in all sorts of dances and frolics, a heavy responsibility rests with the minstrels ; they ply a dangerous trade, a "trop perilus mester" ; they cause God to be forgotten, and the vanity of the world to be cherished.

Not a few among these English dramas, so popular

[1] Fere poent representement,
Mes qe ceo seit chastement
En office de seint église
Quant hom fet la Deu servise,
Cum Jesu Crist le fiz Dee
En sepulcre esteit posé,
Et la resurrectiun
Pur plus aver devociun.

[2] Ki en lur jus se délitera,
Chivals ou harneis les aprestera,
Vesture ou autre ournement,
Sachez il fet folement.
Si vestemens seient dediez,
Plus grant d'assez est le pechez ;
Si prestre ou clerc les ust presté
Bien dust estre chaustié.

in former days, have come down to us. Besides separate
pieces, histories of saints (very scarce in England), or fragments of old series, several collections have survived, the
property whilom of gilds or municipalities. A number
of towns kept up those shows, which attracted visitors, and
were at the same time edifying, profitable, and amusing.
From the fourteenth century the performances were in
most cases intrusted to the gilds, each craft having as
much as possible to represent a play in accordance with
its particular trade. Shipwrights represented the building
of the ark; fishermen, the Flood; goldsmiths, the coming
of the three kings with their golden crowns; wine merchants, the marriage at Cana, where a miracle took place
very much in their line. In other cases the plays were
performed by gilds founded especially for that purpose:
gild of Corpus Christi, of the Pater Noster, &c. This last
had been created because " once on a time, a play setting
forth the goodness of the Lord's Prayer was played in the
city of York, in which play all manner of vices and sins
were held up to scorn and the virtues were held up to
praise. This play met with such favour that many said:
' Would that this play could be kept in this city, for the
health of souls and for the comfort of citizens and neighbours!' Hence the keeping up of that play in times to
come " (year 1389).[1]

In a more or less complete state, the cycles of mysteries
performed at Chester, Wakefield (?), York, and an indeter-
minate city have been preserved, without speaking of fragments of other series. Most of those texts date back from
the fourteenth century, but have been remodelled at a later
date.[2] Old mysteries did not escape the hand of the

[1] Miss L. Toulmin Smith, " English Gilds," London, 1870, E.E.T.S., p. 139
[2] The principal monuments of the English religious stage are the following:
"Chester Plays," ed. Th. Wright, Shahesp. Soc., 1843-7, 2 vols., or ed.
Deimling and Matthews, E.E.T.S., 1893 ff. (possibly adapted from an Anglo-
Norman original, not recovered yet; originally written XIVth century);

improvers, any more than old churches, where any one who pleased added paintings, porches, and tracery, according to the fashion of the day.

These dramatic entertainments, which thrilled a whole town, to which flocked, with equal zeal, peasants and craftsmen, citizens, noblemen, kings and queens, which it took the Reformation more than half a century to kill, enlivened with incomparable glow the monotonous course of days and weeks. The occasion was a grand one; preparation was begun long beforehand; it was an

"The Pageant of the Company of Sheremen and Taylors in Coventry . . . together with other Pageants," ed. Th. Sharp, Coventry, 1817, 4to. By the same: "A dissertation on the Pageants or Dramatic Mysteries anciently performed at Coventry," Coventry, 1825, 4to (illustrated) ;

"Ludus Coventriæ," ed. Halliwell, Shakespeare Society, 1841 ; ed. Miss Block, E.E.T.S., 1922. There is no proof of those plays having been performed at Coventry. Some are now calling them Hegge plays from a former owner, but it would seem fairer, if a change were made, to call them Cotton plays from that other owner who gave them to the nation ;

"Towneley Plays," ed. England and Pollard, E.E.T.S., 1897, performed probably at Wakefield (see Peacock, "Anglia," xii., and "Times Lit. Suppt.," March 5, 1925), early fifteenth century ;

"York Plays, the plays performed by the crafts or mysteries of York on the day of Corpus Christi, in the 14th, 15th, and 16th centuries," ed. L. Toulmin Smith, Oxford, 1885. Five of those plays are from the same originals as the Towneleys ;

"The Digby Mysteries," ed. Furnivall, New Shakspere Society, 1882 ;

"Play of Abraham and Isaac" (fourteenth century), in the "Boke of Brome, a commonplace book of the xvth century," ed. Lucy Toulmin Smith, 1886, 8vo.—"Play of the Sacrament" (story of a miracle, a play of a type scarce in England; *infra*, 485, note), ed. Whitley Stokes, Philol. Soc. Transact., Berlin, 1860–61, p. 101.—"A Mystery of the Burial of Christ"; "A Mystery of the Resurrection": "This is a play to be played on part on gudfriday afternone, and the other part opon Esterday afternone," in Wright and Halliwell, "Reliquiæ Antiquæ," 1841-3, vol. ii. pp. 124 ff., from a MS. of the beginning of the sixteenth century.—See also "The ancient Cornish Drama," three mysteries in Cornish, fifteenth century, ed. Norris, Oxford, 1859, 2 vols. 8vo (with a translation).—For extracts, see A. W. Pollard, "English Miracle Plays, Moralities and Interludes," Oxford, 7th ed., 1923.

On the various English cycles, see A. Hohlfield, "Anglia," xi. p. 219, Ch. Davidson, "Studies in the English Mystery Plays," Yale University, 1892, Chambers, "Mediæval Stage," 1903, with a complete tabulation of representations, notes on MSS., &c., ii. pp. 329, 407.

important affair, an affair of State. Gilds taxed their members to secure a fair representation of the play assigned to them ; they were fined by the municipal authority in case they proved careless and inefficient, or were behind their time to begin.

Read as they are, without going back in our minds to times past and taking into account the circumstances of their composition, mysteries might be judged a gross, childish, and barbarous production. Still, they are worthy of great attention, as showing a side of the soul of ancestors, who in all this did *their very best.* For those performances were not got up anyhow : they were the result of prolonged care and attention. Not any man who wished was accepted as an actor ; some experience of the art was expected ; and in some towns even examinations took place. At York a decree of the Town Council ordains that long before the appointed day, "in the tyme of lentyn" (while the performance itself took place in summer, at the Corpus Christi celebration) " there shall be called afore the maire for the tyme beyng four of the moste connyng discrete and able players within this Citie, to serche, here and examen all the plaiers and plaies and pagentes thrughoute all the artificers belonging to Corpus Christi plaie. And all suche as thay shall fynde sufficiant in personne and connyng, to the honour of the Citie and worship of the saide craftes, for to admitte and able ; and all other insufficiant personnes, either in connyng, voice, or personne to discharge, ammove and avoide." All crafts were bound to bring "furthe ther pageantez in order and course by good players, well arayed and openly spekyng, upon payn of lesying 100 s. to be paide to the chambre without any pardon."[1] These texts belong to the fifteenth century, but there are older ones; and they show that from the beginning the difference between good and bad actors was

[1] " York Plays," pp. xxxiv, xxxvii.

appreciated and great importance was attached to the gestures and delivery. The Mystery of "Adam" (in French, the work, it seems, of a Norman), which belongs to the twelfth century, commences with recommendations to players : "Be Adam well trained so as to answer at the appropriate time, without any slackness or haste. The same with the other actors ; let them speak in sedate fashion, with gestures fitting the words ; be they mindful not to add or suppress a syllable in the verses ; and be their pronunciation constantly clear."[1] The amusement afforded by such exhibitions, the personal fame acquired by good actors, suddenly drawn from the shadow in which their working lives had been spent till then, acted so powerfully on craftsmen that some would not go back to the shop, and, leaving their tools behind them, became professional actors ; thus showing that there was some wisdom in the reproof set forth in the "Tretise of Miraclis pleyinge."

Once emerged from the Church, the drama had the whole town in which to display itself ; and it filled the whole town. On such days the city belonged to dramatic art ; each company had its cars or scaffolds, *pageants* (placed on wheels in some towns), each car being meant to represent one of the places where the events in the play happened. The complete series of scenes was exhibited at the main crossings, or on the principal squares or open spaces in the town. The inhabitants of neighbouring houses sat thus as in a front row, and enjoyed a most enviable privilege, so enviable that it was indeed envied, and at York, for example, they had to pay for it. After

[1] This preliminary note is in Latin : " Sit ipse Adam bene instructus quando respondere debeat, ne ad respondendum nimis sit velox aut nimis tardus, nec solum ipse, sed omnes persone sint. Instruantur ut composite loquentur ; et gestum faciant convenientem rei de qua loquuntur, et, in rithmis nec sillabam addant nec demant, sed omnes firmiter pronuncient." "Adam, Mystère du XII⁰. Siècle," ed. Palustre, Paris, 1877, 8vo.

1417 the choosing of the places for the representations was regulated by auction, and the plays were performed under the windows of the highest bidders. In other cases the scaffolds were fixed ; so that the representation was performed only at one place.

The form of the scaffolds varied from town to town. At Chester "these pagiantes or cariage was a highe place made like a house with two rowmes beinge open on ye tope: the lower rowme they apparrelled and dressed them selves ; and in the higher rowme they played : and they stoode upon six wheeles. And when they had done with one cariage in one place, they wheeled the same from one streete to an other." [1] In some cases the scaffolds were not so high, and boards made a communication between the raised platform and the ground ; a horseman could thus ride up the scaffold : " Here Erode ragis in the pagond and in the strete also." [2]

Sometimes the upper room did not remain open, but a curtain was drawn, according to the necessity of the action. The heroes of the play moved about the place, and went from one scaffold to another ; dialogue then took place between players on the ground and players on the boards : " Here thei take Jhesu and lede hym in gret hast to Herowde ; and the Herowdys scaffald xal unclose, shewyng Herowdes in astat, alle the Jewys knelyng except Annas and Cayaphas." Chaucer speaks of the " scaffold hye " on which jolif Absolon played Herod;[3] king Herod in fact was always enthroned high above the common rabble.

The arrangements adopted in England differed little, as we see, from the French ones ; and it could scarcely be otherwise, as the taste for these dramas had been imported

---

[1] " Digby Myst.", p. xix.   [2] " The Pageants of Coventry," ed. Sharp.
[3] " Coventry Mysteries," Trial of Christ. See my " Note on Pageants and scaffolds hye," " Furnivall Miscellany," p. 183 ; A. F. Leach, " Some English Plays," *ibid.*, 224, 228.

by the Normans and Angevins. Neither in England nor in France were there ever any of those six-storied theatres described by the brothers Parfait, each story being supposed to represent a different place or country. To keep to truth, we should, on the contrary, picture to ourselves those famous buildings stretched all along on the ground, with their different compartments scattered round the public square.

But we have better than words and descriptions to give us an idea of the sight; we have actual pictures, offering to view all the details of the performances. An exquisite miniature of Jean Fouquet, preserved at Chantilly, which has never been studied as it ought to be with reference to this question, has for its subject the life of St. Apollinia. Instead of painting a fancy picture, Fouquet has chosen to represent the martyrdom of the saint as it was acted in a miracle play.[1] The main action takes place on the ground; Apollinia is there, in the middle of the executioners.

---

[1] The French drama written on this subject is lost (it is, however, mentioned in the catalogue of a bookseller of the fifteenth century; see "Les Mystères," by Petit de Julleville, vol. ii. chap. xxiii., "Mystères perdus"); but the precision of details in the miniature is such that I had no difficulty in identifying the particular version of the story followed by the dramatist. It is an apocryphal life of Apollinia, in which is explained how she is the saint to be applied to when suffering toothache. This episode is the one Fouquet has represented. Asked to renounce Christ, she answers: "'Quamdiu vixero in hac fragili vita, lingua mea et os meum non cessabunt pronuntiare laudem et honorem omnipotentis Dei.' Quo audito jussit [imperator] durissimos stipites parari et in igne duros fieri et præacutos ut sic dentes ejus et per tales stipites læderent, radices dentium cum forcipe everentur radicitus. In illa hora oravit S. Apollinia dicens: 'Domine Jesu Christe, precor te ut quicumque diem passionis meæ devote peregerint . . . dolorem dentium aut capitis nunquam sentiant passiones.'" The angels thereupon (seated on wooden stairs, in Fouquet's miniature) come down and tell her that her prayer has been granted. "Acta ut videntur apocrypha S. Apolloniæ," in Bollandus, "Acta Sanctorum," Antwerp, vol. ii. p. 280, under the 9th Feb. See also the sixteenth century MS. of the Valenciennes Passion, MS. fr. 15,236, National Libr., and the model in the Opéra Museum, Paris. *Cf.* "Shakesp. in France," p. 63, and Cohen, "Mise en scène au Moyen-âge," 1906.

Round the place are scaffolds with a lower room and an upper room, as at Chester, and there are curtains to close them. One of those boxes represents Paradise; angels with folded arms, quietly seated on the wooden steps of their stairs, await the moment when they must speak; another is filled with musicians playing the organ and other instruments; a third contains the throne of the king. The throne is empty; for the king, Julian the apostate, his sceptre, adorned with *fleurs-de-lys*, in his hand, has come down his ladder to take part in the main action. Hell has its usual shape of a monstrous head, with opening and closing jaws; it stands on the ground, for the better accommodation of devils, who had constantly to interfere in the drama, and to keep the interest of the crowd alive, by running suddenly through it, with their feathers and animals' skins, howling and grinning; "to the great terror of little children," says Rabelais, who, like Chaucer, had often been present at such dramas. Several devils are to be seen in the miniature; they have cloven feet, and stand outside the hell-mouth; a buffoon also is to be seen, who raises a laugh among the audience and shows his scorn for the martyr by the means described three centuries earlier in John of Salisbury's book, exhibiting his person in a way " quam erubescat videre vel cynicus."

Besides the scaffolds, boxes or " estableis " meant for actors, others are reserved for spectators of importance, or those who paid best. This commingling of actors and spectators would seem to us somewhat confusing; but people were not then very exacting; with them illusion was easily caused, and never broken. This magnificent part of the audience, besides, with its rich garments, was itself a sight; and so little objection was made to the presence of beholders of that sort that we shall find them seated on the Shakesperean stage as well as on the stage of Corneille and of Molière. "I was on the stage, meaning to listen to

the play . . ." says the Éraste of "Les Facheux." In the
time of Shakespeare the custom followed was even more
against theatrical illusion, as there were gentlemen not
only on the sides of the scene, but also behind the actors ;
they filled a vast box in the rear of the platform.

The dresses were rich : this is the best that can be said
of them. Saints enwreathed their chins with curling beards
of gold ; God the Father was dressed as a pope or a bishop.
For good reasons the audience did not ask much in the way
of historical accuracy ; all it wanted was *signs*. Copes and
tiaras were in its eyes religious signs by excellence, and in
the wearer of such they recognised God without hesitation.
The turban of the Saracens, Mahomet the prophet of the
infidels, were known to the mob, which saw in them the
signs and symbols of irreligiousness and impiety. Herod,
for this cause, wore a turban, and swore premature oaths
by "Mahound." People were familiar with symbols, and
the use of them was long continued. The painters at the
Renaissance represented St. Stephen with a stone in his
hand and St. Paul with a sword, which stone and sword
stood for symbols, and the sight of them evoked all the
doleful tale of their sufferings and death.

The authors of mysteries did not pay, as we may well
believe, great attention to the rule of the three Unities.
The events included in the French mystery of the "Vieil
Testament" had not taken place in one day, but in four
thousand years. The most distant localities were represented next to each other : Rome, Jerusalem, Marseilles.
The scaffolds huddled close together scarcely gave an idea
of geographical realities ; the imagination of the beholders
was expected to supply what was wanting : and so it did.
A few square yards of ground (sometimes, it must be acknowledged, of water) were supposed to be the Mediterranean ; Marseilles was at one end, and Jaffa at the other.
A few minutes did duty for months, years, or centuries.

Herod sends a messenger to Tiberius ; the tetrarch has scarcely finished his speech when his man is already at Rome, and delivers his message to the emperor. Noah gets into his ark and shuts his window ; here a silence lasting a minute or so ; the window opens, and Noah declares that the forty days are past (" Chester Plays ").

To render, however, his task easier to the public, some precautions were taken to let them perceive where they were. Sometimes the name of the place was written on a piece of wood or canvas, a clear and honest means.[1] It worked so successfully that it was still resorted to in Elizabethan times ; we see " Thebes written in great letters upon an olde doore," says Sir Philip Sidney, and without asking for more we are bound " to beleeve that it is Thebes." In other cases the actor followed the sneering advice Boileau was to express later, and in very simple fashion declared who he was : I am Herod ! I am Tiberius ! Or again, when they moved from one place to another, they named both : now we are arrived, I recognise Marseilles ; " her is the lond of Mercylle." [2] Most of those inventions were long found to answer, and very often Shakespeare had no better ones to use. The same necessities caused him to make up for the deficiency of the scenery by his wonderful descriptions of landscapes, castles, and wild moors. All that poetry would have been lost had he had painted scenery at his disposal.

Some attempts at painted scenery were made, it is true, but so plain and primitive that the thing again acted as a symbol rather than as the representation of a place. A

---

[1] What the place is—

. . . Vous le povez congnoistre
Par l'escritel que dessus voyez estre.

Prologue of a play of the Nativity, performed at Rouen, 1474 ; Petit de Julleville, " Les Mystères," vol. i. p. 397. *Cf.* " Shakespeare in France," p. 67.
" Digby Mysteries," ed. Furnivall, p. 127.

throne meant the palace of the king. God divides light from darkness: "Now must be exhibited a sheet painted, know you, one half all white and the other half all black." The creation of animals comes nearer the real truth: "Now must be let loose little birds that will fly in the air, and must be placed on the ground, ducks, swans, geese . . . with as many strange beasts as it will have been possible to secure." But truth absolute was observed when the state of innocence had to be represented: "Now must Adam rise all naked and look round with an air of admiration and wonder."[1] Beholders doubtless returned his wonder and admiration. In the Chester Mysteries a practical recommendation is • made to the actors who personate the first couple: "Adam and Eve shall stande nakede, and shall not be ashamed."[2] The proper time to be ashamed will come a little later. The serpent steals "out of a hole"; man falls: "Now must Adam cover himself and feign to be ashamed. The woman must also be seized with shame, and cover herself with her hands."[3]

If painted scenery was greatly neglected, machinery received more attention. That characteristic of modern times, yeast through which the old world has been transformed, the hankering after the unattainable, which caused so many great deeds, had also smaller results; it affected these humble details. Painted canvas was neglected, but people laboured at the inventing of machinery. While a sheet half white and half black was hung to represent light and chaos, in the drama of "Adam," so early as the

---

[1] "Mystère du vieil Testament," Paris, 1542, with curious cuts, "pour plus facile intelligence." Many other editions; one modern one by Baron J. de Rothschild, Société des Anciens Textes Français, 1878 ff.

[2] "Chester Plays," ii.

[3] "Adoncques doit Adam couvrir son humanité, faignant avoir honte. Icy se doit semblablement vergongner la femme et se musser de sa main." "Mystère du vieil Testament."

twelfth century, a self-moving serpent, " serpens artificiose compositus," tempted the woman in Paradise. Dazzled Eve offered but small resistance. Elsewhere an angel carried Enoch " by a subtile engine" into Paradise. In the Doomesday play of the Chester Mysteries, "Jesus was to come down as on a cloud, if that could be managed." But sometimes it could not ; in Fouquet's miniature the angels have no other machinery but a ladder to allow them to descend from heaven to earth. In the " Mary Magdalene" of the Digby Mysteries a boat appeared with mast and sail, and carried to Palestine the King of Marseilles.

Hell was in all times most carefully arranged; and it had the best machinery. The mouth opened and closed, threw flames from its nostrils, and let loose upon the crowd devils armed with hooks and emitting awful yells. From the back of the mouth appalling noises were heard, being meant for the moans of the damned. These moans were produced by a simple process : pots and frying-pans were knocked against each other. In " Adam," the heroes of the play are taken to hell, there to await the coming of Christ ; and the scene, according to the stage direction in the manuscript, was to be represented thus : " Then the Devil will come and three or four devils with him with chains in their hands and iron rings which they will put round the neck of Adam and Eve. Some push them and others draw them toward hell. Other devils awaiting them by the entrance jump and tumble as a sign of their joy for the event." After Adam has been received within the precincts of hell, " the devils will cause a great smoke to rise ; they will emit merry vociferations, and knock together their pans and caldrons so as to be heard from the outside. After a while, some devils will come out and run about the place." Pans were of frequent use ; Abel had one under his tunic, and Cain, knocking on it, drew forth lugubrious sounds, which went to the heart of the audience.

The machinery became more and more complicated toward the time of the Renaissance ; but much money was needed, and for long the Court or the municipalities could alone use them.   In England fixed or movable scenery reaches great perfection at Court: Inigo Jones shows a genius in arranging elegant decorations ; some of his sketches have been preserved.[1]   But such splendid inventions were too costly to be transferred to the stages for which Shakespeare wrote ; and he never used any other magic but that of his poetry.   Inigo Jones had fine scene-shiftings with the help of his machinists, and Shakespeare with the help of his verses ;   these last have this advantage, that they have not faded, and can still be enjoyed to the full.

III.

Whatever may be thought of so much simplicity, childishness, or barbarity, of those ivy-clad ruins the forms of which can scarcely be discerned, they must be subjected to a closer inspection ; and if there were no other, this one consideration would be enough to incline us to it : while in the theatre of Bacchus the tragedies of Sophocles were played once and no more, the Christian drama, remodelled from century to century, was represented for four hundred years before immense multitudes ; and this is a unique phenomenon in the history of literature.

The fact may be ascribed to several causes, some of which have already been pointed out.   The desire to see was extremely keen, and there was seen all that could be wished : the unattainable, the unperceivable, miracles, the king's Court, earthly paradise, all that had been heard of

[1] See R. T. Blomfield, *Portfolio*, May, June, July, 1889.   See also, Inigo Jones, "Designs for Masques and Plays," Walpole Soc., 1914.   *Cf. infra*, iii, 23.

or dreamt about. Means of realisation were rude, but the public held them satisfactory.

What feasts were in the year, sacraments were in the existence of men ; they marked the great memorable stages of life. A complete net of observances and religious obligations surrounded the months and seasons ; bells never remained long silent ; they rang less discreetly than now, and were not afraid to disturb work or talk by their chant. At each period of the day they recalled that there were prayers to say, and to those even who did not pray they recalled the importance of religion. Existences were thus impregnated with religion ; and religion was in its entirety explained, made accessible and visible, in the Mysteries.

The verses spoken by the actors did not much resemble those in Shakespeare ; they were, in most cases, mere tattle, scarcely verses ; rime and alliteration were some-times used both together, and both anyhow. And yet the emotion was deep ; in the state of mind with which the spectators came, nothing would have prevented their being touched by the affecting scenes, neither the lame verse nor the clumsy machinery ; the cause of the emotion was the subject, and not the manner in which the subject was represented. All the past of humanity and its eternal future were at stake ; players, therefore, were sometimes interrupted by the passionate exclamations of the crowd. At a drama lately represented on the stage of the Comédie Française, one of the audience astonished his neighbours by crying : " Mais signe donc ! Est-elle bête ! . . ." In the open air of the public place, at a time when manners were less polished, many such interjections interrupted the performance ; many insulting apostrophes were addressed to Eve when she listened to the serpent ; and the serpent spoke (in the Norman drama of " Adam ") a language easy to understand, the language of everyday life :

" *Diabolus.*—I saw Adam ; he is an ass.

" *Eva.*—He is a little hard.

" *Diabolus.*—We shall melt him ; but at present he is harder than iron."

But thou, Eve, thou art a superior being, a delicate one, a delight for the eyes. " Thou art a little tender thing, fresher than the rose, whiter than crystal, or snow falling on the ice in a dale. The Creator has ill-matched your couple ; thou art too sweet ; man is too hard. . . . For which it is very pleasant to draw close to thee. Let me have a talk with thee." [1]

And for such cajolery, for such folly, thought the crowd, for this sin of our common mother, we sweat and we suffer, we observe Lent, we experience temptations, and under our feet this awful hell-mouth opens, in which, maybe, we shall some day fall. Eve, turn away from the serpent !

Greater even was the emotion caused by the drama of the Passion, the sufferings of the Redeemer, all the details of which were familiar to everybody. The indignation was so keen that the executioners had difficulty sometimes in escaping the fury of the multitude.

The Middle Ages were the age of contrasts ; what measure meant was then unknown. This has already been noticed with reference to Chaucer; the cleverest *compensated*, as Chaucer did, their Miller's tales with stories of Griselda.

---

[1] *Diabolus.*   Jo vis Adam, mais trop est fols.

Eva.   Un poi est durs.

Diabolus.   Il serra mols ;
Il est plus durs que n'est un fers . . .
Tu es fieblette et tendre chose,
Et es plus fresche que n'est rose ;
Tu es plus blanche que cristal,
Que nief qui chiet sor glace en val.
Mal cuple en fist le criatur ;
Tu es trop tendre et il trop dur . . .
Por ço fait bon se treire à tei ;
Parler te voil.   (" Adam," as above, 468, n. 1.)

When they want to be tender the authors of Mysteries fall often into that mawkish sentimentality relished by the barbarian or the crude man of the people. A feeling for measure is a produce of civilisation, and men in the rough ignore it. Those street daubers, who draw on the flags of the London side-walks, always represent heartrending scenes, or scenes of a sweetness unspeakable : here are fires, storms, and disasters ; now a soldier, in the middle of a battle, forgets his own danger, and washes the wound of his horse ; then a cascade under an azure sky, amidst a spring landscape, with a blue bird flying about. Many such drawings might be detected in Dickens, many also in the mysteries. After a truly moving scene between Abraham and his son, the pretty things Isaac does and says, his prayer not to see the sword so keen, cease to touch, and come very near making us laugh. The contrast between the fury of Herod and the sweetness of Joseph and Mary is similarly carried to an extreme. This same Joseph who, a minute ago, insulted his wife in words impossible to quote, has now become such a suave and gentle saint that one can scarcely believe the same man addresses us. He is packing before his journey to Egypt ; he will take his tools with him, his " *smale* instrumentes." [1] Is there anything more touching ? Nothing, except perhaps the appeal of the street painter, calling our attention to the fact that he draws " on the *rude* stone." How could the passer-by not be touched by the idea that the stone is so hard ? In the Middle Ages people melted at this, they were moved, they wept ; and all at once they were in a mood to enjoy the most enormous buffooneries. These fill a large place in the Mysteries, and beside them shine scenes of real comedy, evincing great accuracy of observation.

[1] All my smale instrumentes is putt in my pakke.

("Digby Mysteries," p. 11.)

The personages worst treated in Mysteries are usually the kings; they are mostly represented as grotesque and mischievous beings. The playwrights would have given as their excuse that their kings were miscreants, and that black was not dark enough to paint such faces. But to this commendable motive was added a sly pleasure felt in caricaturing those great men, not only because they were heathens, but also because they were kings ; for when Christian princes and lords appear on the stage, the satire is often continued. Thus Lancelot of the Lake appears unexpectedly at the Court of king Herod, and after much rant the lover of queen Guinevere draws his invincible sword and massacres the Innocents (" Chester Plays ").

Herod, Augustus, Tiberius, Pilate, Pharaoh, the King of Marseilles, always open the scenes where they figure with a speech, in which they sound their own praise. It was an established tradition ; in the same way as God the Father delivered a sermon, these personages made what the manuscripts technically call " their boast." They are the masters of the universe ; they wield the thunder ; everybody obeys them ; they swear and curse unblushingly (by Mahomet) ; they are very noisy. They strut about, proud of their fine dresses and fine phrases, and of their French, French being there again a token of power and authority. The English Herod could not claim kinship with the Norman Dukes, but the subjects of Angevin monarchs would have shrugged their shoulders at the representation of a prince who did not speak French. It was for them the sign of princeship, as a tiara was the sign of godhead. Herod therefore spoke French, a very mean sort of French, it is true, and the Parliament of Paris which was to express later its indignation at the faulty grammar of the "Confrères de la Passion" would have suffered much if it had seen what became of the noble language of France on the scaffolds at Chester. But it did not matter ; any words were enough, in the same way as any sword would do as an emblem for St. Paul.

One of the duties of these strutting heroes was to maintain silence. It seemed as if they had a privilege for noise making, and they repressed encroachments ; their task was not an easy one. Be still, "beshers," cries Augustus ; "beshers" means "beaux sires" in the kingly French of the Mysteries :

> Be styll, beshers, I commawnd yow,
> That no man speke a word here now
>> Bot I my self alon ;
> And if ye do, I make a vow,
> Thys brand abowte youre nekys shalle bow,
>> Ffor thy by styll as ston.[1]

Silence! cries Tiberius.   Silence! cries Herod :

> Styr not bot ye have lefe,
> Ffor if ye do, I clefe
>> You smalle as flesh to pott.[2]

Pilate knows Latin, and parades this accomplishment before the audience :

> Stynt, I say! gyf men place, quia sum dominus dominorum !
> He that agans me says, rapietur lux oculorum.[3]

And each of them hereupon moves about his scaffold, and gives the best idea he can of the magnitude of his power :

> Above all kynges under the cloudys crystall,
> Royally I reigne in welthe without woo . . .
> I am Kyng Herowdes.[4]

---

[1] "Towneley Mysteries."   [2] *Ibid.*—Magnus Herodes.
[3] "Towneley Mysteries."—Processus Talentorum.
[4] "Digby Mysteries."—Candlemas Day, p. 3.

32

Be it known, says another:

> That of heven and hell chyff rewlar am I,
> To wos magnyfycens non stondyt egall,
> For I am soveren of al soverens.[1]

Make room, says a third:

> A-wantt, a-want the, on-worthy wrecchesse!
> Why lowtt ye nat low to my lawdabyll presens? . . .
> I am a sofereyn semely, that ye se butt seyld;
> Non swyche onder sonne, the sothe for to say . . .
> I am kyng of Marcylle![2]

Such princes fear nothing, and are never abashed; they are on familiar terms with the audience, and interpellate the bystanders, which was a sure cause of merriment, but not of good order.   Octavian, being well pleased with the services of one of his men, tells him:

> Boye, their be ladyes many one,
> Among them all chose thee one,
> Take the fayrest, or els none,
> And freely I geve her thee.[3]

Every lord bows to my law, observes Tiberius:

> Is it nat so?   Sey yow all with on showte.

and a note in the manuscript has: "Here answerryt all the pepul at ons, 'Ya, my lord, ya.'"[4]   All this was performed with appropriate gesture, that is, as wild as the words they went with, a tradition that long survived.   Shakespeare complained, as we know, of the delivery of those actors who "out-heroded Herod."

The authors of English Mysteries had no great experience of Courts; they drew their caricatures somewhat haphazard.   They were neither very learned nor very careful;

---

[1] "Digby Mysteries."—Mary Magdalen, p. 55.   [2] *Ibid.*, p. 90.
[3] 'Chester Plays."—Salutation and Nativity.
[4] "Digby Mysteries," p. 56.

anachronisms and mistakes swarm under their pen. While Herod sacrifices to Mahomet, Noah invokes the Blessed Virgin, and the Christmas shepherds swear by "the death of Christ," whose birth is announced to them at the end of the play.

The psychology of these dramas is not very deep, especially when exalted personages and the more refined feelings have to be described. The authors of Mysteries speak then at random and describe by hearsay ; they have seen their models only from afar, and are not familiar with them. When they have to show how it is that young Mary Magdalen, as virtuous as she was beautiful, consents to sin for the first time, they do it in the plainest fashion. A "galaunt" meets her and tells her that he finds her very pretty, and loves her. "Why, sir," the young lady replies, "wene you that I were a kelle (prostitute)?" Not at all, says the other, but you are so pretty! Shall we not dance together? Shall we drink something?

> Soppes in wyne, how love ye ?

Mary does not resist those proofs of true love, and answers:

> As ye dou, so doth me ;
> I am ryth glad that met be we ;
> My love in yow gynnyt to close.

Then, "derlyng dere," let us go, says the "galaunt."

> *Mary.* Ewyn at your wyl, my dere derlyng !
> Thow ye wyl go to the worldes eynd,
> I wol never from yow wynd (turn).[1]

---

[1] "Digby Mysteries," pp. 74, 75. After living wickedly Mary Magdalen repents, comes to Marseilles, converts the local king and performs miracles. This legend was extremely popular ; it was told several times in French verse during the thirteeeth century ; see A. Schmidt, "Guillaume, le Clerc de Normandie, insbesondere seine Magdalenenlegende," in "Romanische Studien,"

Clarissa Harlowe will require more forms and more time; here twenty-five verses have been enough. A century and a half divides " Mary Magdalene" from the dramatised story of the " Weeping Bitch"; the interpretation of the movements of the feminine heart has not greatly improved, and we are very far as yet from Shakespeare and Richardson.

But truth was more closely observed when the authors spoke of what they knew by personal experience, and described men of the poorer sort with whom they were familiar. In this lies the main literary merit of the Mysteries; there are to be found the earliest scenes of real comedy in the history of the English stage.

This comedy of course is very near farce : in everything people then went to extremes. Certain merry scenes were as famous as the rant of Herod, and they have for centuries amused the England of former days. The strife between husband and wife : Noah and his wife, Pilate and his wife, Joseph and Mary, this last a very shocking one, were among the most popular.

In all the collections of English Mysteries Noah's wife is an untamed shrew, who refuses to enter the ark. In the York collection, Noah being ordered by " Deus " to build his boat, wonders somewhat at first :

> A ! worthy lorde, wolde thou take heede,
> I am full olde and oute of qwarte.

He sets to work, however; rain begins; the time for sailing has arrived: Noah calls his wife; she does not come. Get into the ark and " leve the harde lande ? "

vol. iv. p. 493; Doncieux, " Fragment d'un Miracle de Sainte Madeleine, texte restitué," in " Romania," 1893, p. 265. There was also a drama in French based on the same story: " La Vie de Marie Magdaleine . . . Est à xxii. personages," Lyon, 1605, 12mo (belongs to the fifteenth century).

This she will not do. She meant to go this very day to
town, and she will:

Doo barnes, goo we and trusse to towne.

She does not fear the flood ; Noah remarks that the rain
has been terrific of late, and has lasted many days, and
that her idea of going just then to town is not of the
wisest. The lady is not a whit pacified ; why have made
a secret of all this to her ? Why had he not consulted
her ? It turns out that her husband had been working at
the ark for a hundred years, and she did not know of it !
Life in a boat is not at all pleasant ; anyhow she will
want time to pack ; also she must take her gossips with
her, to have some one to talk to during the voyage.
Noah, who in building his boat has given some proof of
his patience, does not lose courage ; he receives a box on
the ear ; he is content with saying:

I pray the, dame, be stille.

The wife at length gets in, and, as we may believe,
stormy days in more senses than one are in store for the
patriarch.[1]

St. Joseph is a poor craftsman, drawn to the life,
using the language of craftsmen, having their manners,
their ignorances, their aspirations. Few works in the whole

---

[1] "York Plays," viii., ix. See also, *e.g.*, as specimens of comical scenes,
the discussions between the quack and his man in the "Play of the Sacrament": "Yᵉ play of yᵉ conversyon of ser Jonathas yᵉ Jewe by myracle of yᵉ
blyssed sacrament." Master Brundyche addresses the audience as if he were
in front of his booth at a fair. He will cure the diseases of all present.
Be sure of that, his man Colle observes,

What dysease or syknesse yᵗ ever ye have,
He wyll never leve yow tylle ye be in your grave.

Ed. Whitley Stokes, Philological Society, Berlin, 1860-61, p. 127 (fifteenth
century).

range of mediæval literature contain better descriptions of
the workman of that time than the Mysteries in which St.
Joseph figures; some of his speeches ought to have a
place in the collections of Political Songs. The Emperor
Augustus has availed himself of the census to establish a
new tax: "A! lord," says the poor Joseph,

> A! lord! what doth this man now here!
> Poore mens waile is ever in weere (doubt),
> I wot by this oosters bere
> That trybute I must paye,
>
> And for greate age and no power
> I wan no good this seaven yeare;
> Nowe comes the kinges messenger,
> To get all that he maye.
>
> With this axe that I beare,
> This percer and this nawger (auger),
> Axe, hammer all in feare,
> I have wonne my meate.
>
> Castle, tower ne rich manner
> Had I never in my power,
> But as a simple carpenter
> With these what I mighte get.
>
> If I have store now any thing,
> That I must pay unto the king.[1]

Only an ox is left him; he will go and sell it. It is
easy to fancy that, in the century which saw the Statutes
of Labourers and the rising of the peasants, such words
found a ready echo in the audience.

As soon as men of the people appear on the scene,
nearly always the dialogue becomes lively; real men and
women stand and talk before us. Beside the workmen
represented by St. Joseph, peasants appear, represented by
the shepherds of Christmas night. They are true English
shepherds; if they swear, somewhat before due time, by
Christ, all surprise disappears when we hear them name
the places where they live: Lancashire, the Clyde valley,

---

[1] "Chester Plays."—Salutation and Nativity.

Boughton near Chester, Norbury near Wakefield. Of all possible ales, Ely's is the one they prefer. They talk together of the weather, the time of the day, the mean salaries they get, the stray sheep they have been seeking ; they eat their meals under the hedge, sing merry songs, exchange a few blows, in fact behave as true shepherds of real life. Quite at the end only, when the " Gloria " is heard, they will assume the sober attitude befitting Christmas Day.

In the " Towneley Mysteries," the visit to the new-born Child was preceded by a comedy worthy to be compared with the famous farce of " Pathelin," and which has nothing to do with Christmas. [1] It is night ; the shepherds talk ; the time for sleeping comes. One among them, Mak, has a bad repute, and is suspected of being a thief; they ask him to sleep in the midst of the others : " Com heder, betwene shalle thou lyg downe." But Mak rises during the night without being observed. How hard they sleep! he says, and he carries away a " fatt shepe," and takes it to his wife.

> *Wife.* It were a fowll blott to be hanged for the case.
>
> *Mak.* I have skapyd, Ielott, oft as hard as glase.
>
> *Wife.* Bot so long goys the pott to the water, men says,
> At last
> Comys it home broken.

I am aware of it, says Mak, but it is not a time for proverbs and talk ; let us do for the best. The shepherds know Mak too well not to come straight to his house ; and so they do. Moans are heard ; the cause being, they learn, that Mak's wife has just given birth to a child. As the shepherds walk in, Mak meets them with a cheerful countenance, and welcomes them heartily :

[1] " Towneley Myst."—Secunda Pastorum. *Cf.* Baugh, " Modern Philology," Ap. 1918.

> Bot ar ye in this towne to-day ?
>   Now how fare ye ?
> Ye have ryn in the myre, and ar weytt yit :
> I shalle make you a fyre, if ye wille syt.

His offers are coldly received, and the visitors explain what has happened.

> Now if you have suspowse, to Gille or to me,
> Come and rype our howse !

The woman moans more pitifully than ever :

Wife.   Outt, thefys, fro my barne ! negh hym not thore.

Mak.   Wyst ye how she had farne, youre hartys wold be sore.
Ye do wrang, I you warne, that thus commys before
To a woman that has farne, bot I say no more.

Wife.   A my medylle !
              I pray to God so mylde,
              If ever I you begyld,
              That I ete this chylde
                  That lygys in this credylle.

The shepherds, deafened by the noise, look none the less about the house, but find nothing. Their host is not yet, however, at the end of his trouble.

Tertius Pastor.   Mak, with youre leyfe, let me gyf youre barne
              Bot sex pence.

Mak.   Nay, do way, he slepys.

Pastor.   Me thynk he pepys.

Mak.   When he wakyns he wepys ;
              I pray you go hence.

Pastor.   Gyf me lefe hym to kys, and lyft up the clowtt.
          What the deville is this ? he has a long snowte !

And the fraud is discovered ; it was the sheep. From oaths they were coming to blows, when on a sudden, amid the stars, angels are seen, and their song is heard in the night : Glory to God, peace to earth ! the world is rejuvenated. . . . Anger disappears, hatreds are effaced, and the rough shepherds of England take, with penitent heart, the road to Bethlehem.

IV.

The fourteenth century saw the religious drama at its height in England; the fifteenth saw its decay; the sixteenth its death. The form under which it was best liked was the form of Mysteries, based upon the Bible. The dramatising of the lives of saints and miracles of the Virgin was much less popular in England than in France. In the latter country enormous collections of such plays have been preserved [1]; in the other the examples of this kind are comparatively few; the Bible was the main source from which the English dramatists drew their inspiration. As we have seen, however, they did not forbear from adding scenes and characters with nothing evangelical in them. These scenes contributed, with the interludes and the facetious dialogues of the jongleurs, to the formation of comedy. Little by little, comedy took shape, and it will be found existing as a separate branch of dramatic art at the time of the Renaissance.

In the same period another sort of drama was to flourish, the origin of which was as old as the fourteenth century, namely, *Moralities.* These plays consisted in pious treatises and ethical books turned into dramas, as Mysteries offered a dramatisation of Scriptures. Psychology was there carried to the extreme, a peculiar sort of psychology, elementary and excessive at the same time, and very different from the delicate art in favour to-day. Individuals disappeared; they were replaced by abstractions, and these

---

[1] See, for instance, "Miracles de Nostre Dame par personnages," ed. G. Paris and U. Robert, Société des Anciens Textes, 1876-91, 6 vols. 8vo.

abstractions represented only a single quality or defect. Sins and virtues fought together and tried to draw mankind to them, which stood doubtful, as Hercules "at the starting point of a double road ; " in this way, again, was manifested the fondness felt in the Middle Ages for allegories and symbols. The " Roman de la Rose " in France, " Piers Plowman" in England, the popularity in all Europe of the Consolation of Boethius, had already been manifestations of those same tendencies. In these works already dialogue was abundant, in the " Roman de la Rose " especially, where an immense space is occupied by conversations between Love, the Lover and Fals-Semblant.[1] The names of the speakers are inscribed in the margin, as if it were a real play. When he admitted into his collection of tales the dialogued story of Melibeus and Prudence, Chaucer came very near to Moralities, for the work he produced was neither a treatise nor a tale, nor a drama, but had something of the three ; a few changes would have been enough to make of it a Morality, which might have been called the Debate of Wisdom and Mankind.

Abstractions had been allowed a place in the Mysteries so far back as the fourteenth century. Death figures in the " Towneley " collection. In " Mary Magdalene " (fifteenth century) many abstract personages are mixed with the others : the Seven Deadly Sins, Mundus, the King of the Flesh, Sensuality, &c. ; the same thing happens in the so-called Coventry collection.

This sort of drama, for us unendurable, gradually separated from Mysteries ; it reached its greatest development under the early Tudors. The authors of Moralities strove to write plays not merely amusing as farces then also in great favour, but plays with a useful and practical aim. By means of now unreadable dramas, virtues, religion, morals, sciences were taught ; the Catholic faith was derided by

[1] In Méon's edition, 1813, ii. 327 ff. ; in Langlois' ed., iii. 180 ff.

Protestants, and the Reformation by Catholics.[1] The discovery, then quite new, of America was discoursed about, and great regret was expressed at its being not due to an Englishman :

> O what a thynge had be than,
> If they that be Englyshemen
> Myght have ben furst of all
> That there shuld have take possessyon ![2]

Death, as might be expected, is placed upon the stage with a particular zeal and care, and meditations are devoted to the dark future of man, and to the gnawing worm of the charnel house.[3]

Fearing the audience might go to sleep, or perhaps go away, the science and the austere philosophy taught in these plays were enlivened by tavern scenes, by devilry, and by the freaks of a clown or buffoon, called Vice, armed, as Harlequin, with a wooden dagger. And often, such is human frailty, the beholders went, remembering nothing but the mad pranks of Vice. It was in their eyes the most important character in the play, and the

---

[1] Plays of this kind were written (without speaking of many anonyms) by Medwall : "A goodly Enterlude of Nature," 1538, fol. ; by Skelton, "Magnyfycence," 1531 (*infra*, ii. 130) ; by Ingelend, "A pretie Enterlude called the Disobedient Child," printed about 1550 ; by John Bale, "A comedye concernynge thre Lawes," London, 1538, 8vo (against the Catholics, *infra*, ii. 195) ; all of them lived under Henry VIII. The two earliest English moralities extant are "The Pride of Life" (a fragment, in the "Account Roll of the priory of the Holy Trinity," Dublin, ed. J. Mills, Dublin, 1891, XIVth cent. ?), and the "Castle of Perseverance" about 1425, with "Mankind" about 1475, and "Wisdom" about 1460, in the "Macro Plays," ed. Furnivall and Pollard, E.E.T.S., 1904. Text of several in Farmer, "Early Engl. Drama," London, 1905 ff.

[2] "Interlude of the four Elements," London, 1510 (?), 8vo.

[3] See, *e.g.*, the mournful passages in the "Disobedient Child," the "Triall of Treasure," London, 1567, 4to, and especially in "Everyman," end of XVth cent. (?), on what may sadden or comfort the end of all men, possibly translated from the Dutch play "Elkerlijk" ; ed. Sidgwick, London, 1902.

part was accordingly entrusted to the best actor. Shakespeare had seen Vice still alive, and he commemorated his deeds in a song:

> I am gone, sir,
> And anon, sir,
> I'll be with you again,
> In a trice,
> Like to the old Vice,
> Your need to sustain,
> Who, with dagger of lath,
> In his rage and his wrath,
> Cries, ah ha ! to the devil.[1]

This character also found place on the French stage, where it was called the " Badin." Rabelais had the " Badin " in great esteem: " In this manner we see, among the jongleurs, when they arrange between them the cast of a play, the part of the Sot, or Badin, to be attributed to the cleverest and most experienced in their company." [2]

In the meanwhile, common ancestors of the various dramatic tribes, source and origin of many sorts of plays, the Mysteries, which had contributed to the formation of the tragical, romantic, allegorical, pastoral, and comic drama, were still in existence. Reformation had come, the people had adopted the new belief, but they could not give up the Mysteries. They continued to like Herod, Noah and his wife, and the tumultuous troup of devils, great and small, inhabiting hell-mouth. Prologues had been written in which excuses were offered on account of the traces of superstition to be detected in the plays, and consciences, being thus quieted, the plays were performed as before. The Protestant bishop of Chester prohibited the representation in 1572, but it took place all the same. The archbishop of York renewed the prohibition in 1575, but the mysteries were performed again for four days;

---

[1] Song of the Clown in " Twelfth Night," iv. 3.
[2] " Pantagruel," iii. 37. *Cf.* " Macro Plays," E.E.T.S., p. 17.

and some representations of them took place even later.[1]
At York the inhabitants had no less reluctance about giving
up their old drama ; they were sorry to think that religious
differences now existed between the town and its beloved
tragedies. Converted to the new faith, the citizens would
have liked to convert the plays too, and the margins of the
manuscript bear witness to their efforts. But the task was
a difficult one ; they were at their wits' end, and appealed
to men more learned than they. They decided that " the
booke shalbe carried to my Lord Archebisshop and Mr.
Deane to correcte, if that my Lord Archebisshop do well
like theron," 1579.[2] My Lord Archbishop, wise and prudent,
settled the question according to administrative precedent ;
he stored the book away somewhere, and the inhabitants
were simply informed that the prohibition was maintained.
The York plays thus died.

In France the Mysteries survived quite as late ; but, on
account of the radical effects of the Renaissance there,
they had not the same influence on the future development of the drama. They continued to be represented in
the sixteenth century, and the Parliament of Paris complained in 1542 of their too great popularity : parish
priests, and even the chanters of the Holy Chapel, sang
vespers at noon, a most unbecoming hour, and sang them
" post haste," to see the sight. Six years later the performance of Mysteries was forbidden at Paris ; but the
cross and ladder, emblems of the " Confrères de la Passion,"
continued to be seen above the gates of the " Hôtel de
Bourgogne," and the privilege of the Confrères, which
dated three centuries back, was only abolished in the
reign of Louis XIV., in December, 1676.[3] Molière had
then been dead for three years.

[1] Furnivall, " Digby Mysteries," p. xxvii. The " Chester Plays " were
still being copied as late as 1600, 1604, 1607 ; ed. Deimling, p. vii.

[2] " York Plays," p. xvi.

[3] Petit de Julleville, " Les Mystères," 1880, vol. i. pp. 423 ff.

In England, at the date when my Lord Archbishop stopped the representation at York,[1] the old religious dramas had produced all their fruit : they had kept alive the taste for stage plays, they left behind them authors, a public, and companies of players. Then was growing in years, in a little town by the side of the river Avon, the child who was to reach the highest summits of art. He followed on week-days the teaching of the grammar school ; he saw on Sundays, painted on the wall of the Holy Cross Chapel, a paradise and hell similar to those in the Mysteries, angels of gold and black devils, and that immense mouth where the damned are parboiled, "où damnés sont boulus," as the poor old mother of Villon says in a ballad of her son's.[2]

At the date of the York prohibition, William Shakespeare was fifteen.

[1] They continued later in some towns, at Newcastle, for example, where they survived till 1598. At this date " Romeo " and the " Merchant of Venice " had already appeared. There were even some performances at the beginning of the seventeenth century. The latest MS. of the Chester Plays is dated 1607 (Deimling, as above, p. ix).

[2] A drawing of this fresco, now destroyed, has been published by Sharp : " Hell-mouth and interior, from the chapel at Stratford-upon-Avon " ; " A Dissertation on the pageants . . . at Coventry," 1825, plate 6.

CHAPTER VII.

THE END OF THE MIDDLE AGES.

I.

IN the autumn of the year 1400, Geoffrey Chaucer, the son of the Thames Street vintner, universally acknowledged the greatest poet of England, had been borne to his tomb in the transept of Westminster Abbey. Not far from him sleep the Plantagenet kings, his patrons, Edward III. and Richard II. wrapped in their golden robes. With them an epoch has drawn to its close ; a new century begins, and this century is, for English thought, a century of decline, of repose, and of preparation.

So evident is the decline that even contemporaries perceive it ; for a hundred years poets unceasingly mourn the death of Chaucer. They are no longer able to discover new ways ; instead of looking forward as their master did, they turn, and stand with eyes fixed on him, and hands outstretched towards his tomb. An age seeking its ideal in the epoch that has just preceded it is an age of decline ; so had been, in past times, the age of Statius, who had professed such a deep veneration for Virgil.

For a century thus the poets of England remain with their gaze fastened on the image of the singer they last heard, and at each generation their voice becomes weaker,

like an echo that repeats another echo.   Lydgate imitates
Chaucer, and Stephen Hawes imitates Lydgate.[1]

Around and below them countless rimers persist in
following the old paths, not knowing that these paths have
ceased to lead anywhere, and that the time has come to
search for new ones.   The most skilful add to the series of
English fabliaux borrowed from France ; others put into
rime, disfiguring them as they go along, romances of
chivalry, lives of the saints, or chronicles of England and
Scotland.   Very numerous, nearly all devoid of talent,
these indefatigable would-be poets write in reality, they
too, like Monsieur Jourdain, " de la prose sans le savoir." [2]

---

[1] I try, repeatedly says Stephen Hawes,

> To followe the trace and all the perfitnes
> Of my maister Lydgate.

" The Historie of Graund Amoure and La Bell Pucle, called the Pastime
of Plesure, contayning the Knowledge of the Seven Sciences and the Course
of Man's life in this Worlde," London, 1554, 4to, curious woodcuts (reprinted
by the Percy Society, 1845, 8vo ; the quotation above, p. 2).   It is an allegory
of unendurable dulness, in which Graund Amoure (love of knowledge apparently) visits Science in the Tower of Doctrine, then Grammar, &c.   Hawes
lived under Henry VII. ; see *infra*, vol. ii. pp. 112 ff.

[2] On the fabliaux introduced into England, see above, p. 225 ; the greater
number of them are found in Hazlitt : " Remains of the early popular Poetry
of England," London, 1864, 4 vols.   One of the best, " The Wright's
Chaste Wife," written in English, about 1462, by Adam de Cobsam, has been
published by the Early English Text Society, ed. Furnivall, 1865, with a
supplement by Mr. Clouston, 1886 ; it is the old story of the honest woman,
who dismisses her would-be lovers after having made fun of them.   That story
figures in the " Gesta Romanorum," in the " Arabian Nights," in the collection
of Barbazan (story of Constant du Hamel).   It has furnished Massinger with the
subject of his play, " The Picture," and Musset with that of " la Quenouille de
Barberine."—On romances of chivalry, see above, pp. 219 ff.   A great number
of rimed versions of these romances are of the XVth century.—Ex. of pious works
in verse, of the same century : Th. Brampton, " Paraphrase on the seven
penitential psalms, 1414," Percy Society, 1842 ; Mirk, " Duties of a Parish
Priest," ed. Peacock, E.E.T.S., 1868, written about 1450; Capgrave (1394-
1464), " Life of St. Katharine," ed. Horstmann and Furnivall, E.E.T.S., 1893
(other edifying and historical works by the same, *infra*, 522) ; many similar
specimens are unpublished.—Ex. of chronicles : Andrew de Wyntoun, " Original

These poets of the decline write for a society itself on the decline, and all move along, lulled by the same melody to a common death, out of which will come a new life that they can never know. The old feudal and clerical aristocracy changes, decays and disappears; many of the great houses become extinct in the wars with France, or in the fierce battles of the Two Roses; the people gain by what the aristocracy lose. The clergy, who keep aloof from military conflicts, are also torn by internecine quarrels; they live in luxury; abuses publicly pointed out are not reformed; they are an object of envy to the prince and of scorn to the lower classes; they find themselves in the most dangerous situation, and do nothing to escape from it. Of warnings they have no lack; they receive no new endowments; they slumber; at the close of the century nothing will remain to them but an immense and frail dwelling, built on the sand, that a storm can blow down.

How innovate when versifying for a society about to end? Chaucer's successors do not innovate; they fasten their work to his works, and patch them together; they build in the shadow of his dwelling. They dream the same dreams on a May morning; they erect new Houses of Fame; they add a story to the "Canterbury Tales."[1]

Chronicle," continued to 1424, ed. Amours, Scottish Text Soc., 1903 ff., *infra.*, App. I.; Hardyng (1378-1465?), "Chronicle in Metre," 1543, ed. Ellis, 1812. Hardyng sold for a large price, to the brave Talbot, who knew little about palæography, spurious charters establishing England's sovereignty over Scotland; these charters exist at the Record Office, the fraud was proved by Palgrave. These chronicles are verily in " rym dogerel."

[1] "The Story of Thebes," by Lydgate, *infra*, p. 499; "The Tale of Beryn," anon., with a prologue, where are related in a lively manner the adventures of the pilgrims in Canterbury and their visit to the cathedral (ed. Furnivall and Stone, Chaucer Society, 1876-87, 8vo); Henryson adds a canto to "Troilus" (below p. 507). Other poems are so much in the style of Chaucer that, as we have seen, they were long attributed to him : "The Court of Love"; "The Flower and the Leaf" (on which, G. L. Marsh, Chicago, 1907); "The Isle of Ladies, or Chaucer's Dream," &c. They are found in the Morris edition of Chaucer's works and in Skeat's supplementary vol. to Chaucer's "Complete Works." All these poems are of the fifteenth century.

A gift bestowed on them by a spiteful fairy makes
the matter worse: they are incredibly prolific. All they
write is poor, and the spiteful fairy, spiteful to us, has
granted them the faculty to write thus, without any
trouble, for ever. Up to this day Lydgate's works have
baffled the attempts of the most enterprising editors. The
Early English Text Society has years ago begun to
publish them ; if it carries out the undertaking, it will
be a proof of unparalleled endurance.

Lydgate and Hoccleve are the two principal successors
of Chaucer. Lydgate, a monk of the monastery of Bury
St. Edmund's,[1] a worthy man, to be sure, if ever there
was one, and industrious, and prolific, above all prolific,
writes, according to established standards, tales, lays,[2]
fabliaux, satires,[3] romances of chivalry, poetical debates,
ballads of former times,[4] allegories, lives of the saints,
love poems, fables[5] : five thousand verses a year on an
average, and being precocious as well as prolific, leaves
behind him at his death a hundred and thirty thousand

[1] Born about 1370, at Lydgate, near Newmarket; sojourned in Paris in
1426, died in 1449 (N.Y. "Nation," March 14, 1912). Concerning the versification, the chronology and authenticity of his works, the chief of which are
being ed. by the E.E.T.S., see "Lydgate's Temple of Glas," ed. J. Schick,
E.E.T.S., 1891, Introduction; "The Minor poems . . . with . . . the
Lydgate Canon," by MacCracken, E.E.T.S., 1911 ff. His "Troy Book" is
of 1412-20 ; his "Story of Thebes," of 1420-22 ; his translation of Deguileville, of 1426-30; his "Fall of Princes," of 1431-38. The early editions, by
Caxton and Wynkyn de Worde, of several of Lydgate's works are being
reprinted by the Cambridge University Press.

[2] He gave an English version of the famous story called in French, "Le
Lai de l'Oiselet" (ed. G. Paris, 1884) : "The Chorle and the Byrde."

[3] Ex. his picturesque "London Lickpenny" (authenticity contested by
H. MacCracken).

[4] Same idea as in Villon ; refrain :

> All stant in chaunge like a mydsomer rose,

Halliwell, "Selections from Lydgate," 1840, p. 25.

[5] "Lydgate's Æsopübersetzung," ed. Sauerstein ; "Anglia," 1886, p. 1 ;
eight fables. He excuses himself :

> Have me excused, I was born in Lydegate,
> Of Tullius gardyn I entrid nat the gate. (p. 2.)

verses, merely counting his longer works. Virgil had only written fourteen thousand.

He copies Latin, French, and English models, but especially Chaucer;[1] he adds his "Story of Thebes" to the series of the "Canterbury Tales;" he has met, he says, in a charming prologue,[2] the pilgrims on their homeward journey; the host asked him who he was:

> I answerde my name was Lydgate,
> Monk of Bery, nygh fyfty yere of age.

Admitted into the little community, he contributes to the entertainment by telling a tale of war, of love, and of valorous deeds, in which the Greeks wear knightly armour, are blessed by bishops, and batter town walls with cannon. His "Temple of Glas"[3] is an imitation of the "Hous of Fame"; his "Complaint of the Black Knight" resembles the "Book of the Duchesse"; in his "Falle of Princes,"[4] of thirty-six thousand lines, he follows Boccaccio, Laurent de Premierfaict and Chaucer. The "litel hevynesse" noticed in the monk's stories is particularly well imitated; so much so that Lydgate himself stops sometimes with

> [1] O ye maysters, that cast shal yowre looke
> Upon this dyté made in wordis playne,
> Remembre sothely that I the refreyn tooke
> Of hym that was in makyng soverayne,
> My maister, Chaucier, chief poete of Bretayne.

Halliwell, "Selections from . . . Lydgate," 1840, p. 128. Similar praise in the "Serpent of Division" (in prose), ed. MacCracken, London, 1911. See L. Toulmin Smith, "Gorboduc," Heilbronn, 1883, p. xxi.

[2] He wrote nothing better than his description of himself and of the Chaucer troop. The British Museum possesses a splendid copy . . . Royal 18 D ii., with miniatures of the time of the Renaissance, see above, p. 303. Ed. Erdmann, E.E.T.S., 1911, ff.

[3] "Lydgate's Temple of Glas," ed. J. Schick, 1891, 8vo, E.E.T.S.

[4] Long popular, written for Duke Humphrey of Gloucester, over 36,000 lines; begins with Adam and Eve, ends with King John of France; ed. Bergen, E.E.T.S., 1924, 3 vols.

uplifted pen to yawn at his ease in the face of his reader.[1]
But his pen goes down again on the paper, and starts off
with fresh energy. From it proceeds a "Troy Book, or
Historie of the Warres betwixte the Grecians and the
Trojans," of thirty thousand lines, where pasteboard
warriors hew each other to pieces without suffering much
pain or causing us much sorrow[2]; a translation of that
same "Pélerinage" of Deguileville, which had inspired
Langland; a Guy of Warwick[3]; Lives of Our Lady, of St.
Margaret, St. Edmund, St. Alban; a "pageant" for the
entry of Queen Margaret into London in 1445; a version
of the "Secretum Secretorum," and a multitude of other
writings.[4] Nothing but death could stop him. He ceased
to breath and to write in 1449, enjoying a considerable
fame which he never failed modestly to declare unjustified.

The rules of his prosody were rather lax. No one will
be surprised at it; he could say like Ovid, but for other

---

[1] Myn hand gan tremble, my penne I felte quake . . .
  I stode chekmate for feare whan I gan see,
  In my way how little I had runne.

"Fall of Princes," prol. to Bk. iii. *Cf.* The final envoy, vol. iii., p. 1013.

[2] Example, fight between Ulysses and Troilus :

  He smote Ulyxes throughout his viser . . .
  But Ulyxes tho lyke a manly man,
  Of that stroke astoned not at all,
  But on his stede, stiffe as any wall,
  With his swerde so mightely gan race,
  Through the umber into Troylus face,
  That he him gave a mortal wounde,

of which, naturally, Troilus does not die. "The auncient historie . . . of the
Warres, betwixte the Grecians and the Troyans," Lond., 1555, 4to, Bk. III.,
c. xxii. First edition, 1513; modern one by H. Bergen, E.E.T.S., 1906 ff.
The work, an amplification from Guido delle Colonne, had been composed for
Prince Henry, later Henry V.

[3] Ed. Zupitza, Early English Text Society.

[4] See "The Minor Poems of John Lydgate . . . with an attempt to
establish the Lydgate Canon," by H. N. MacCracken, E.E.T.S., 1911.

reasons: " I had but to write, and it was verses." He is ready for everything ; order them, and you will have at once verses to order. These verses are slightly deformed, maybe, and halt somewhat ; he does not deny it :

> I toke none hede nouther of shorte nor longe.[1]

But let us not blame him; Chaucer, his good master, would, he assures us, have excused his faulty prosody, and what right have we to be more severe than Chaucer?[2] To this there is, of course, nothing to answer, but then if we cannot answer, at least we can leave. We can go and visit the other chief poet of the time, Thomas Hoccleve ; he does not live far off, the journey will be a short one; we have but to call at the next door.

This other poet is a public functionary; he is a clerk of the Privy Seal[3]; his duties consist in copying documents;

---

[1] " Troy Book " ; in Schick, " Lydgate's Temple of Glas," p. lvi. In his learned essay Mr. Schick pleads extenuating circumstances in favour of Lydgate.

[2] This appeal to Chaucer is in itself quite touching :

> For he that was grounde of well sayinge,
> In all his lyfe hyndred no makyng,
> My maister Chaucer y^t founde ful many spot
> Hym list not pynche nor grutche at every blot. . . .
> Sufferynge goodly of his gentilnesse,
> Full many thynge embraced with rudenesse,
> And if I shall shortly hym discrive,
> Was never none to thys daye alive,
> To reken all bothe of yonge and olde,
> That worthy was his ynkehorne for to holde.

" The Auncient Historie," London, 1554, 4to, Book v. chap. xxxviii.

[3] Thomas Hoccleve was born about 1368–9 and entered the " Privy Seal " in 1387–8 ; he died about 1450. His works are being published by the Early English Text Society : " Hoccleve's Works," 1892 ff. His great poem, " De Regimine principum," has been edited by Th. Wright, Roxburghe Club, 1860, and by Furnivall, 1897, E.E.T.S. Two or three of his tales in verse are imitated from the " Gesta Romanorum " ; another, the " Letter of Cupid," from the " Epistre au Dieu d'Amours," of Christine de Pisan. " Hoccleve's metre is poor, so long as he can count ten syllables by his fingers he is content." Furnivall, " Minor Poems," I. p. xli.

an occupation he finds at length somewhat tiresome.[1]　By
way of diversion he frequents taverns ; women wait on
him there, and he kisses them ; a wicked deed, he admits,
but he goes no further ; at least so he assures us,[2] being
doubtless held back by the thought of officialdom and
promotion.　At all events this little was even too much,
for we soon find him sick unto death, riming supplications
to the god of health and to Lord Fournivall, another kind
of god, very useful to propitiate, for he was Lord Treasurer.
He writes a good many occasional pieces in which,
thanks to his mania for talking about himself, he makes
us acquainted with the nooks and corners of old London,
thus supplying rare and curious information, treasured
by the historian.　He composes, in order to make himself
noticed by the king, an ample poem on the Government
of Princes, " De Regimine Principum," which is nothing
but a compilation taken from three or four previous
treatises ; he adds a prologue, and in it, following the example of Gower, he abuses all classes of society.　He does
not fail to begin his confession over again : from which
we gather that he is something of a drunkard, and of a
coward, that he is vain withal, and somewhat ill-natured.

He had, however, one merit, and, in spite of his defects,
all lovers of literature ought to be grateful to him.　The best
of his works is not his Government of Princes ; it is a
drawing.　He not only, like Lydgate, loved and mourned
Chaucer, but wished to keep the memory of his features,
and he caused to be painted on the margin of a manuscript

---

[1] It seems like nothing, he says, but just try and see :

> Many men, fadir, wennen that writynge
> No travaile is ; thei hold it but a game . . .
> But who-so list disport hym in that same,
> Let hym continue and he shall fynd it grame ;
> It is wel gretter labour than it seemeth.

[2] " La Male Règle de Thomas Hoccleve," in the " Minor Poems," pp. 25 ff.

the portrait mentioned above, which agrees so well with the descriptions contained in the writings of the master that there is no doubt as to the likeness.[1]

II.

Let us cross the hills, and we shall still find Chaucer. As in England, so is he mourned and imitated in Scotland. But the poets live there in a different atmosphere; the imitation is not so close; a greater proportion of Celtic blood maintains differences; more originality survives; the decline is less apparent. The best poets of English tongue, "Inglis" as they call it, "oure Inglis," Dunbar says, are, in the fifteenth century, Scots. Among the foremost are a king, a monk, a schoolmaster, a minstrel, a bishop.[2]

The king is James I., son of Robert III., of the family of those Stuarts nearly all of whom were destined to a tragic fate. This one, taken at sea by the English, when only a child, remained nineteen years confined in various castles. Like a knight of romance, and a personage in a miniature, he shortened the hours of his captivity by music, reading, and poetry; the works of Chaucer and Gower filled him with admiration. Then he found a better comfort for his sorrows; this knight of miniature and of romance saw before him one day the maiden so often painted by illuminators, the one who appears amidst the

---

[1] Al-thogh his lyfe be queynt, the résemblaunce
　　Of him hath me so fressh lyflynesse,
　That, to putte othir men in rémembraunce
　　Of his persone, I have heere his lyknesse
　　Do makë, to this ende, in sothfastnesse,
　　　That thei that have of him lest thought and mynde,
　　　By this peynturë may ageyn him fynde.
　　　　("Minor Poems," p. xxxiii.; on this portrait see above, p. 341.)

[2] Besides a priest like Rich. de Holande, author of the "Howlat" (inspired fr. Chaucer's "Parl. of Foules"), and the anon. authors of "Golagros and Gawane," of "Rauf Coilyear" (a familiar tale of Charlemagne), late XVth cent., "Scottish Alliterative Poems," ed. Amours, Scottish Text Soc., 1897.

flowers and the dew, Aucassin's Nicolette, the Emily of the Knight's Tale, the one who brings happiness. She appeared to the king, not in a dream but in reality ; her name was Jane Beaufort, she was the daughter of the Earl of Somerset, and great grand-daughter of John of Gaunt. In her family, too, there were many tragic destinies ; her brother was killed at the battle of St. Albans ; her three nephews perished in the Wars of the Roses ; her grand-nephew won the battle of Bosworth and became king Henry VII. A mutual love sprang up between the two young people, and when James was able to return to Scotland he took back with him his queen of romance, whom he had wedded before the altar of St. Mary, next to the grave of one of his literary masters, the poet Gower.

His reign lasted thirteen years, and they were thirteen years of struggle : vain endeavours to regulate and centralise a kingdom composed of independent clans, all brave and ready for foreign wars, but quite as ready, too, for civil ones. Assisted by his queen of romance, the knightly poet displayed in this task an uncommon energy, and was, with all his faults, one of the best kings of Scotland. He had many children ; one of his daughters became dauphiness of France, and another duchess of Brittany. Towards the end of 1436, he had so many enemies among the turbulent chieftains that sinister prophecies began to circulate ; one of them announced the speedy death of a king ; and as he played at chess on Christmas eve with a knight surnamed the " king of love," he said to him : " There are no other kings in Scotland save me and you ; I take heed to myself, do you likewise." But the king of love had nothing to fear. During the night of the 20th of February, 1437, an un-wonted noise was suddenly heard in the courtyard of the monastery of Perth where James lodged ; it was Robert Graham and his rebel band. Vainly did the king offer

resistance, though unarmed ; the foe were too numerous,
and they stretched him dead, pierced with sixteen sword
wounds.

The constant love of the king for Jane Beaufort had
been celebrated by himself in an allegorical poem, imitated
from Chaucer : "The Kingis Quair," a poem all aglow
with bright hues and with the freshness of youth.[1] The
prince is in bed at night, and, like Chaucer in his poem of
the Duchess, unable to sleep, he takes up a book. It is
the "Consolation" of Boethius, and the meditations of
"that noble senatoure" who had also known great reverses, occupy his thoughts while the night hours glide
on. The silence is broken by the matin bell :

> Bot now, how trowe ye? suich a fantasye
> Fell me to mynd, that ay methoght the bell
> Said to me : "Tell on, man, quhat the befell."

And the king, invoking Clio and Polymnia, like Chaucer,
and adding Tysiphone whom he takes for a Muse, because
he is less familiar with mythology than Chaucer, tells
what befell him, how he parted with his friends, when quite
a boy, was imprisoned in a foreign land, and from the
window of his tower discovered one day in the garden :

> The fairest or the freschest yonge floure
> That ever I sawe.

The maid was so beautiful that all at once his "hert became
hir thrall":

> A ! suete, are ye a warldly creature,
> Or hevinly thing in likenesse of nature ?

---

[1] "Poetical Remains of James I. of Scotland," ed. Ch. Rogers, Edinburgh,
1873. "The Kingis Quair," ed. Skeat, Scot. Text Soc., 1883. Its authenticity has been contested by J. T. T. Brown: "The Authenticity of the
Kingis Quair," Glasgow, 1896, and defended, *e.g.*, by Kaluza, "Englische
Studien," 1896, Al. Brandl, Rait, and in my "Jacques 1st fut il poète?" 1897.

To be cleared from his doubts the royal poet ventures into the kingdom of Venus, and finds her stretched on her couch, her white shoulders covered with " ane huke," a loose dress that Chaucer had not placed upon them. Then he reaches the kingdom of Minerva ; and passing through dissertations, beds of flowers, and groups of stars, he returns to earth, reassured as to his fate, with the certitude of a happiness promised him both by Venus and Minerva. A eulogy on Gower and Chaucer closes the poem, which is written in stanzas of seven lines, since called, because of James, " Rime Royal." [1]

The minstrel usually called Blind Harry sings William Wallace.[2] We are in the midst of legends. Wallace causes Edward I. to tremble in London ; he runs extraordinary dangers and has wonderful escapes ; he slays ; he is slain ; he recovers ; his body is thrown over the castle wall, and picked up by his old nurse ; the daughter of the nurse, nurse herself, revives the corpse with her milk. The language is simple, direct and plain ; the interest lies in the facts, and not in the manner in which they are told ; and this, to say the truth, is also the case with chap-books.

---

[1] Though used by others before him, and especially by Chaucer ; they rime *a b a b b c c.* Chaucer wrote in this metre " Troilus," " Parlement of Foules," &c. Here is an example, consisting in the commendation of the book to Chaucer and Gower :

> Unto [the] impnis of my maisteris dere,
>   Gowere and Chaucere, that on the steppis satt
> Of rethorike quhill thai were lyvand here,
>   Superlative as poetis laureate,
>   In moralitee and eloquence ornate,
> I recommend my buk in lynis sevin,
> And eke thair saulis un-to the blisse of hevin.

[2] " The Actis and Deidis of . . . Schir William Wallace, Knicht of Ellerslie," by Henry the Minstrel, commonly known as Blind Harry, ed. J. Moir, 1884–9, S.T.S. *Cf.* J. T. T. Brown, " The Wallace and the Bruce," Bonn, 1900 ; *Athenæum*, Feb. 9, 1901 ; Schofield, " Mythical bards," Cambridge, Mass., 1920.

Blind Harry continues Barbour rather than Chaucer, but Chaucer resumes his rights as an ancestor with Henryson and Dunbar. The former[1] sits with his feet to the fire one winter's night, takes " ane drink " to cheer him, and " Troilus " to while away the time. The little homely scene is described in charming fashion; one seems, while reading, to feel the warmth of the cosy corner, the warmth even of the " drink," for it must have been a warm one :

> I mend the fyre, and beikit (basked) me about,
> Than tuik ane drink my spreitis to comfort,
> And armit me weill fra the cold thairout ;
> To cut the winter nicht and mak it schort,
> I tuik ane quair and left all uther sport,
> Writtin be worthie Chaucer glorious
> Of fair Cresseid and worthie Troilus.

He read, but unable to understand the master's leniency towards the frail and deceitful woman, he takes pen and adds a canto to the poem : the " Testament of Cresseid," where he makes her die a dreadful death, forsaken by all.

A greater pleasure will be taken in his rustic poems, ballads, or fables. His " Robene and Makyne " is a " disputoison " between a shepherd and shepherdess. Makyne loves Robin, and tells him so ; and he accordingly cares not for her. Makyne goes off, her eyes full of tears ; but Robin is no sooner left alone than he begins to love :

> Makyne, the nicht is soft and dry,
> The weddir is warme and fair
> And the grene woid rycht neir us by
> To walk atour (over) all quhair (everywhere) ;
> Thair ma na janglour us espy
> That is to lufe contrair ;
> Thairin, Makyne, bath ye and I
> Unsene we ma repair.

---

[1] Henryson was born before 1425, and wrote under James II. and James III. of Scotland ; he was head of the grammar school at Dunfermline Abbey. " Poems," ed. D. Laing, Edinb., 1865 ; ed. Gregory Smith, S.T.S., 1908 ff.

In her turn Makyne is no longer willing; she laughs
now, and he weeps, and she leaves him in solitude under a
rock, with his sheep. This is a lamentable ending; but
let us not sorrow overmuch; on these pathless moors
people are sure to meet, and since they quarrelled and
parted for ever, in the fifteenth century, Robin and
Makyne have met many times.

Another day, Henryson has a dream, after the fashion
of the Middle Ages. In summer-time, among the flowers,
a personage appears to him,

His hude of scarlet, bordowrit weill with silk.

In spite of the dress he is a Roman: " My native land
is Rome ; "and this "Roman"turns out to be Æsop, " poet
laureate ; " there is no room for doubt: we are in the
Middle Ages. Æsop recites his fables in such a new and
graceful manner, with such a pleasing mixture of truth
and fancy, that he never told them better, not even when
he was a Greek slave, and saved his head by his wit.

Henryson takes his time; he observes animals and
nature, and departs as much as possible from the epi-
grammatic form common to most fabulists. The story
of the "uplandis Mous and the burges Mous," so often
related, has never been better told than by Henryson, and
this can be affirmed without forgetting La Fontaine.

The two mice are sisters ; the elder, a mouse of importance, established in town, well fed on flour and cheese,
remembers, one day, her little sister, and starts off at dusk
to visit her. She follows lonely paths at night, creeps
through the moss and heather of the interminable Scottish
bogs, and at last arrives. The dwelling strikes her as
strangely miserable, frail, and dark; a poor little thief
like the younger sister does not care much about burning
dips. Nevertheless, great is the joy at meeting; the
" uplandis mous " produces her choicest stores; the

"burges mous" looks on, unable to quite conceal her astonishment. Is it not nice? inquires the little sister. Excuse me, replies the other, but :

> Thir widderit (withered) peis and nuttis, or thai be bord,
> Will brek my teith and mak my wame full sklender. . . .
> Sister, this victuall and your royall feist
> May weill suffice unto ane rurall beist.

> Lat be this hole, and cum into my place,
> I sall to yow schaw be experience
> My Gude fryday is better nor your Pace (Easter).

And off they trot through the bushes, and through those heathery bogs which have by turns charmed and wearied many others besides mice.

They reach the elder sister's. There are delicious provisions, cheese, butter, malt, fish, and dishes without number.

> Ane lordis fair thus culd thay counterfeit,
> Except ane thing : thay drank the watter cleir
> In steid of wyne ; bot yit thay maid gude cheir.

The little sister admires and nibbles. But how long will this last? Always, says the other. Just at that moment a rattle of keys is heard ; it is the *spenser* coming to the pantry. A dreadful scene ! The great mouse runs to her hole, and the little one, not knowing where to hide herself, faints.

Luckily, the man was in a hurry ; he takes what he came for, and departs. The elder mouse creeps out of her hole :

> How fair ye sister ? cry peip quhair ever ye be.

The other, half dead with fright, and shaking in her four paws, is unable to answer. The great mouse warms and comforts her : 'tis all over, do not fear ;

> Cum to your meit, this perrell is overpast.

But no, it is not all over, for now comes " Gilbert " (for Tybert, the name of the cat in the " Roman de Renart "), " our jolie cat " ; another rout ensues. This time, perched on a partition where Tybert cannot reach her, the field mouse takes leave of her sister, makes her escape, goes back to the country, and finds there her poverty, her peas, her nuts, and her tranquillity.

The mouse of Scotland has been fortunate in her painters ; another, and a still better portrait was to be made of the " wee, sleekit, cowrin, tim'rous beastie," by the great poet of the nation, Robert Burns.

With Gavin Douglas, bishop of Dunkeld, of the illustrious house of the Douglas, earls of Angus, the translator of Virgil, and with William Dunbar, a mendicant friar, favourite of James IV., sent by him on missions to London and Paris, we cross the threshold of a new century ; they die in the midst of the Renaissance, but with them, nevertheless, the Chaucerian tradition is continued. Douglas writes a " Palice of Honour," imitated from Chaucer.[1] Dunbar,[2] with never flagging spirit, attempts every style ; he composes sentimental allegories and coarse tales (very coarse indeed), satires, parodies, laments.[3] His fits of

[1] "The Works of Gavin Douglas," ed. J. Small, Edinburgh, 1874, 4 vols. 8vo. Born in 1474-5, died in 1522. He finished his "Palice of Honour" in 1501, an allegorical poem resembling the ancient models : May morning, Vision of Diana, Venus and their trains, descriptions of the Palace of Honour, &c. We shall find, at the Renaissance, Douglas a translator of Virgil ; his Æneid was printed only in 1553 ; *infra*, vol. ii. p. 130.

[2] Born about 1460, studies at St. Andrews, becomes a mendicant friar and is ordained priest, sojourns in France, where the works of Villon had just been printed, then returns to the Court of James IV., where he is very popular. He died probably after 1520. "Poems," ed. Small, Mackay and Gregor, 1884, ff. Scot. Text Soc., or ed. Baildon, Cambridge, 1907 ; *infra*, vol. ii. p. 115.

[3] See, for example, his " Lament for the Makaris quhen he wes seik," a kind of "Ballade des poètes du temps jadis," a style which Lydgate and Villon had already furnished models of. In it he weeps :

> The noble Chaucer, of makaris flouir,
> The monk of Bery and Gower all thre.

melancholy do not last long; he must be ill to be sad;
however pungent his satires, they are the work of an
optimist; they end with laughter and not with tears.
He is nearer to Jean des Entommeures than to William
Langland.

His principal poems, " The Goldyn Targe," on the targe
or shield of Reason exposed to the shafts of Love,
" Thrissil and the Rois " (thistle and rose) are close imitations of the Chaucer of the " Parlement of Foules " and
of the " Hous of Fame," with the same allegories, the same
abstract personages, the same flowers, and the same perfumes. The " Thrissil and the Rois," written about 1503,
celebrates the marriage of Margaret, rose of England,
daughter of Henry VII., to James IV., thistle of Scotland,
the flower with a purple crown: that famous marriage
which was to result in a union later of both countries
under the same sceptre.

Endowed with an ever-ready mind and an unfailing
power of invention, Dunbar, following his natural tastes,
and wishing, at the same time, to imitate Chaucer, decks
his pictures with glaring colours, and "out-Chaucers
Chaucer." His flowers are too flowery, his odours too
fragrant; by moments it is no longer a delight, but almost
a pain. It is not sufficient that his birds should sing, they
must sing among perfumes, and these perfumes are coloured;
they sing

> Amang the tendir odouris reid and quhyt.[1]

---

[1] Beginning of the " Thrissil and the Rois " (to be compared with the
opening of the " Canterbury Tales ") :

> Quhen March wes with variand windis past,
>   And Appryll had, with his silver schouris,
> Tane leif at Nature with ane orient blast,
>   And lusty May, that muddir is of flouris,
>   Had maid the birdis to begyn thair houris
> Amang the tendir odouris reid and quhyt,
> Quhois armony to heir it wes delyt. . . .

These are undoubted signs of decline ; they are found,
in different degrees, among the poets of England and of
Scotland, nearly without exception.   The anonymous
poems, " The Flower and the Leaf," " The Court of Love,"
&c.,[1] imitated from Chaucer, exhibit the same symptoms.
The only ones who escape are, chiefly in the region of the
Scottish border, those unknown singers who derive their
inspiration directly from the people, who leave books
alone, and who would not be found, like Henryson, sitting
by the fireside with " Troilus " on their knees.   These
singers remodel in their turn ballads that will be remade
after them,[2] and which have come down stirring and
touching ; love-songs, doleful ditties, the ride of the Percy
and the Douglas[3] (" Chevy Chase "), that, in spite of his
classic tastes, Philip Sidney admired in the time of
Elizabeth.   Though declining in castles, poetry still thrills
with youth along the hedges and in the copses ; and the
best works of poets with a name like Dunbar or Henryson are those in which are found an echo of the songs of
the woods and moors.   This same echo lends its charm
to the music of the " Nut-brown Maid," [4] that exquisite
love-duo, a combination of popular and artistic poetry
written by a nameless author, towards the end of the
period, and the finest of the " disputoisons " in English
literature.

But apart from the songs the wayfarer hums along the
lanes, the works of the poets most appreciated at that

[1] Morris edition of Chaucer's works, vol. iv. ; Skeat's ed., vol. vii.

[2] Principal work to consult : F. J. Child, " The English and Scottish
Popular Ballads," Boston, 1882.   See above, p. 352, and further, vol. ii.
p. 405.

[3] In " Bishop Percy's Folio MS.," ed. Hales and Furnivall, London,
Ballad Society, 1867, 8vo.

[4] Text, *e.g.*, in Skeat, " Specimens of English Literature," Oxford, 4th ed.
1887, p. 96, written, under the form in which we now have it, about the end
of the fifteenth century.

time, Lydgate, Henryson, Dunbar, Stephen Hawes,[1] represent a dying art; they write as architects build, and their literature is a florid one; their poems are in Henry VII.'s style. Their roses are splendid, but too full-blown; they have expended all their strength, all their beauty, all their fragrance; no store of youth is left to them; they have given it all away; and what happens to such roses? They shed their leaves; of this past glory there will soon remain nothing save a stalk without petals.

III.

The end of the feudal world has come, its literature is dying out; but at the same time a double revival is preparing. The revival most difficult to follow, but not the least considerable, originated in the middle and lower classes of society. While great families destroy each other, humble ones thrive: only lately has this fact been sufficiently noticed. So long as the historian was only interested in battles and in royal quarrels, the fifteenth century in England was considered by every one, except by that keen observer, Commines, to be the time of the war of the Two Roses, of the murder of Edward's children, and nothing else. It seemed as though the blood of the youthful princes had stained the entire century, and as if the whole nation, stunned with horror, had remained aghast and immobile. Researches made in our days have shown this impression to be erroneous. Instead of being absorbed in the contemplation of these dreadful struggles, holding its breath at the sight of the slaughter, the nation

---

[1] The pillers of yvery garnished with golde,
With perles sette and brouded many a folde,
The flore was paved with stones precious, &c.

Stephen Hawes, "Pastime of Pleasure," Percy Soc., 1845, p. 125, *infra*, ii, 112.

paid little attention to them, regarding these doings in the light of "res inter alios acta"; it increased the number of its schools, learnt, worked, traded.

Feudalism was perishing, as human organisations often perish, from the very fact of its having attained its full development; feudal nobles had so long towered above the people that they were now almost completely severed from them; feudalism had pushed its principle so far that it was about to die, like the over-blown roses of Dunbar. While the nobles and their followers, that crowd of *bravi* that the statutes against maintenance had vainly tried to suppress, strewed the fields of Wakefield, Towton, and Tewkesbury with their corpses, the real nation, the mass of the people, stood apart and was engaged in a far different occupation. It strove to enrich itself, and was advancing by degrees towards equality between citizens. A perusal of the innumerable documents of that epoch, which have been preserved and which concern middle classes, leave a decided impression of peaceful development, of loosening of bondage, of a diffusion of comfort. The time is becoming more remote, when some sat on thrones and others on the ground; it begins to be suspected that one day perhaps there may be chairs for everybody. In the course of an examination bearing on thousands of documents, Thorold Rogers found but two allusions to the civil wars.[1] The duration of these wars must not, besides, be exaggerated; by adding one period of hostilities to another it will be found they lasted three years in all.

The boundaries between the classes are less strictly guarded; war helps to cross them; soldiers of fortune are ennobled; merchants likewise. The importance of trade goes on increasing; even a king, like Edward IV., makes

---

[1] "A History of Agriculture and Prices," vol. iv., Oxford, 1882, p. 19. See also the important chapters on Industry and Commerce in Mrs. Green's "Town Life in the XVth Century," London, 1894, 2 vols. 8vo, vol. i. chaps. ii. and iii.

attempts at trading, and does not fear thus to derogate ; English ships are now larger, more numerous, and sail farther. The house of the Canynges of Bristol has in its pay eight hundred sailors ; its trading navy counts a *Mary Canynge* and a *Mary and John*, which exceed in size all that has hitherto been seen. A duke of Bedford is degraded from the peerage because he has no money, and a nobleman without money is tempted to become a dangerous freebooter and live at the expense of others.[1] For the progress is noticeable only by comparison, and, without speaking of open wars, brigandage, which is dying out, is not yet quite extinct.

The literature of the time corroborates the testimony of documents exhumed from ancient muniment rooms. It gives an impression of a wealthier nation than formerly, counting more free men, with a more extensive trade. The number of books on courtesy, etiquette, good breeding, good cooking, politeness, with an injunction not to take "always" the "whole" of the best morsel,[2] is a sign of these improve-

---

[1] The ducal title, since conferred on the Russells, had been given to George Neville. The king, who had intended to endow the new duke in a proper manner, had changed his mind ; and on the other hand, "as it is openly knowen that the same George hath not, nor by enheritance mey have, eny lyffelode to support the seid name, estate and dignite, or eny name of estate; and oft time it is sen that when eny lord is called to high estate and have not liffelode conveniently to support the same dignite, it induces gret poverty, indigens, and causes oftymes grete extortion, embracere and mayntenaunce to be had. . . . Wherfore the kyng, by the advyse . . . [&c.] exactith that fro hensfforth the same erection and making of Duke, and all the names of dignite guyffen to the seid George, or the seid John Nevele his fader, be from hens fors voyd and of no effecte." 17 Ed. IV. year 1477, " Rotuli Parliamentorum," vol. vi. p. 173.

[2] See "Stans puer ad mensam," by Lydgate, printed by Caxton :

> T' enboce thi jowes with brede it is not due. . . .
> Thy teth also ne pike not with the knyff. . . .
> The best morsell, have this in remembraunce,
> Hole to thiself alway do not applye.

Hazlitt, " Remains," 1864, vol. iii. p. 23. Many other treatises on etiquette

ments.   The letters of the Paston family are another.[1]   In
spite of all the mentions made in these letters of violent
and barbarous deeds; though in them we see Margaret
Paston and her twelve defenders put to flight by an
enemy of the family, and Sir John Paston besieged in
his castle of Caister by the duke of Norfolk, a multitude
of details give something of a modern character to this
collection, the oldest series of private English letters we
possess.

In spite of aristocratic alliances, these people think and
write like worthy citizens, economical, practical and careful.
During her husband's absence, Margaret Paston keeps him
informed of all that goes on, she looks after his property,
renews leases, collects rents.   Reading her letters one
seems to see her home as neat and clean as a Dutch house.
If a disaster occurs, instead of wasting her time in lamentations, she repairs it to the best of her ability and takes
precautions for the future.   She loves her husband, and
may be believed when, knowing him to be ill, she writes:
" I would ye were at home, if it were your ease, and your
sore might be as well looked to here as it is where ye be,
now liefer than a gown though it were of scarlet."[2]   John
Paston, shut up in the Fleet prison, where he makes the
acquaintance of Lord Henry Percy, for prisons were then

cooking, &c.   See chiefly : " The Babes Book. . . . The Book of Norture," &c.,
ed. Furnivall, 1868, 8vo ; " Two fifteenth century Cookery Books," ed. T.
Austin, 1888, 8vo ; " The Book of quinte essence," about 1460-70, ed.
Furnivall, 1866 (medical recipes) ; " Palladius on husbondrie . . ." about
1420, ed. Lodge, 1872-9 (on orchards and gardens) ; " The Book of the
Knight of la Tour Landry . . . translated in the reign of Henry VI.," ed.
T. Wright, revised ed., 1906 (the whole published by the Early English Text
Society).

[1] " The Paston Letters," 1422-1509, ed. J. Gairdner, 1904, 6 vols.   *Cf.* the
" Cely Papers," ed. Malden, 1900, being the private correspondence of well-
to-do English merchants, 1475-88.

[2] Or in the worthy Margaret's spelling : " Yf I mythe have had my wylle, I
xulde a seyne yow er dystyme ; I wolde ye wern at hom, yf it wer your ese,

a place where the best society met, sends Margaret playful verses to amuse her :

> My lord Persy and all this house,
> Recommend them to yow, dogge, catte and mowse,
> And wysshe ye had be here stille,
> For they sey ye are a good gille. (Sept. 21, 1465.)

The old and new times are no longer so far apart; in such a prison, Fielding and Sheridan would not have felt out of place.

Books of advice to travellers, itineraries or guides to foreign parts,[1] vocabularies, dictionaries, and grammars,[2] commercial guides, the "Libelle of Englyshe Polycye,"[3] are also signs of the times. This last document is a characteristic one ; it is a sort of consular report in verse, very similar (the verses excepted) to thousands of consular reports with which "Livres Jaunes" and "Blue Books" have since been filled. The author points out for each country the goods to be imported and exported, and the guileful practices to be feared in foreign parts ; he insists on the necessity of England's having a strong navy, and exaggerates the maritime power of rival countries, so that Parliament may vote the necessary supplies. England

---

and your sor myth ben as wyl lokyth to her as it tys there ye ben, now lever dan a goune thow it wer of scarlette " (Sept. 28, 1443).

[1] *E.g.*, "The Itineraries of William Wey" (pilgrimages), London, Roxburghe Club, 1857 ; much practical information ; specimens of conversations in Greek, &c. ; "The Stacions of Rome," ed. Furnivall, E.E.T.S. 1868 (on Rome and Compostella) ; "Ye Solace of Pilgrimes," by Capgrave, *infra*, 522.

[2] See among others : "Anglo-Saxon and Old English Vocabularies," by Th. Wright, new ed. by Wülker, London, 1884, 2 vols.; "Promptorium Parvulorum [sc.] clericorum . . . *circa* A.D. 1440," ed. Albert Way, Camden Society, 1865, 4to, by Geoffrey the Grammarian, a Dominican of Norfolk ; "Catholicon Anglicum, an English Latin wordbook, dated 1483," ed. Herrtage, E.E.T.S., 1881, 8vo.

[3] In the "Political Poems," ed. Th. Wright, Rolls, vol. ii. p. 157. Probable date, 1436. *Cf.* the "Débat des hérauts de France et d'Angleterre " (written about 1456), ed. P. Meyer, Société des Anciens Textes, 1877, 8vo ; on the navy, p. 9.

should be the first on the sea, and able to impose " pease by auctorité." She should establish herself more firmly at Calais. Only the word Calais would be altered now and replaced by Gibraltar, Malta, Aden, or Singapore. The author enumerates the products of Prussia, Flanders, France, Spain, Portugal, Genoa, &c. ; he has even information on the subject of Iceland, and its great cod-fish trade. He wishes for a spirited colonial policy ; it is not yet a question of India, but only of Ireland ; at any price "the wylde Iryshe" must be conquered.

He dwells at length on the misdeeds of the wicked Malouins, who are stopped by nothing, obey no one, and are protected by the innumerable rocks of their bays, amidst which they alone know the passages. Conclusion :

> Kepte (keep) than the see about in specialle
> Whiche of England is the rounde walle ;
> As thoughe England were lykened to a cité,
> And the walle enviroun were the see ;
> Keep than the see that is the walle of Englond,
> And then is Englond kepte by Goddes sonde.

The anxious injunctions scattered in the "Libelle" must not be taken, any more than Parliamentary speeches of later date, as implying that the nation had no confidence in itself. The instinct of nationality, formerly so vague, has grown from year to year since the Conquest : the English are now proud of everything English ; they are proud of their navy, in spite of its defects ; of their army, in spite of the reverses it suffered ; of the wealth of the Commons ; they even boast of their robbers. Anything one does should be well done ; if they have thieves, these thieves will prove the best in the world. The testimony of Sir John Fortescue, knight, Lord Chief Justice, and Chancellor of England, who must have known about the thieves, is decisive on this point. He writes, in English prose, a treatise on absolute and limited monarchy[1] ; admiration for his country breaks out on every page. It is the time of the Two Roses, but it matters little with him ; like many others in his day, he does not pay while writing much attention to the Roses. England is the best governed country in the world ; it has the best laws: the king can do nothing unless his people consent. In this manner a just balance is maintained: " Our Comons be riche, and therfor they gave to their kyng, at sum tymys quinsimes and dismes, and often tymys other grete subsy-dyes. . . . This might thay not have done, if they had ben empoveryshyd by their kyng, as the Comons of Fraunce." Fortescue puts forth a theory often confirmed since then : if the Commons rebel sometimes, it is not the pride of wealth that makes them, but tyranny ; for, were they poor, revolts would be far more frequent : " If thay be not poer, thay will never aryse, but if their prince so leve Justice, that he gyve hymself al to tyrannye." It is true that the Commons of France do not rebel (Louis XI. then reigned at Plessis-lez-Tours) ; Fortescue is shocked at that, and remonstrates against their " lacke of harte."

Some people might say that there are a great many thieves in England. They are numerous, Fortescue con-fesses, there is no doubt as to that; but the country finds in them one more cause to be proud : " It hath ben often seen in Englond that three or four thefes, for povertie hath sett upon seven or eight true men and robbyd them al." The thieves of France are incapable of such admirable

---

[1] " De Dominio regali et politico," otherwise, the " Governance of England." In it he treats of (chap. i.) " the difference between Dominium regale and Dominium politicum et regale," a difference that consists principally in this, that in the second case the king " may not rule hys people by other lawys than such as they assenten unto." Fortescue was born about 1395, and d. after 1476. He wrote in Latin : " De natura Legis Naturæ," " De laudibus Legum Angliæ," &c., " Works of Sir John Fortescue, &c." ed. by Th. [Fortescue] Lord Clermont, 1869, 2 vols. 4to ; " The Governance," ed. Plummer, 1885.

boldness.   On this account "it is right seld that French men be hangyd for robberye," says Fortescue, who had never, judging by the way he talks, passed by Montfaucon, nor come across poor Villon ; "they have no hertys to do so terryble an acte.   There be therfor mo men hangyd in Englonde in a yere for robberye and manslaughter than their be hangid in Fraunce for such cause of crime in seven yers." [1]   The French should be ashamed.   As a judge, Fortescue hangs the thieves ; as an Englishman he admires their performances : the national robber is superior to all others.   A sketch in *Punch* represents a London drunkard carried off by two policemen ; the street boys make comments : " They couldn't take my father up like that," says one of them, "it takes six Policemen to run him in ! "   If this boy ever becomes Chief Justice, he will write, in the same spirit, another treatise like Fortescue's.

Thus is popularised in that century the art of prose ; the uses made of it are not unprecedented, but they are far more frequent.   This is one more sign that the nation settles and concentrates, and secures for itself a complete literature.   Previous examples are studied ; there are schools of prose writers as of poets.   Bishop Pecock employs Wyclif's irony to defend what Wyclif had attacked : pilgrimages, friars, the possessions of the clergy, the statues and paintings in churches.[2]   His forcible eloquence is embittered by sarcasms ; he continues a tradition, dear to the English race, and one which, constantly renewed, will

---

[1] Chaps. xii. and xiii., " Works," vol. i. pp. 465 ff.

[2] In his prinicipal work, the " Repressor of over much blaming of the Clergy," ed. Babington, Rolls, 1860, 2 vols.   Pecock, born about 1395, became fellow of Oriel College, Oxford, bishop of St. Asaph, then of Chichester. He wrote also, in English prose, "The Donet," ed. Miss Hitchcock, E.E.T.S., 1921, "The Folewer of the Donet," same ed. and Soc., 1924 ; " The Reule of Cristen Religioun," "The poore mennis Myrrour," "The Book of Feith." For his excessive rationalism (all beliefs must be "allowable by Reason ") the Church had his writings burnt, and relegated him to Thorney Abbey in 1459, where he died shortly after.

come down to Swift and to the humourists of the eighteenth century. Inwardly boiling with passion, he does his
best to speak coldly and without moving a finger. Wyclif
wants everything to be found in the Bible, and forbids
pilgrimages, which are not spoken of in it. But then,
says Pecock, we are greatly puzzled, for how should we
dare to wear breeches, which the Bible does not mention
either? How justify the use of clocks to know the hour?
And with great seriousness, in a calm voice, he discusses
the question : " For though in eeldist daies, and though in
Scripture, mensioun is maad of orologis, schewing the
houris of the dai bi the schadew maad bi the sunne in a
cercle, certis nevere, save in late daies, was eny clok
telling the houris of the dai and nyht bi peise and bi stroke ;
and open it is that noughwhere in holi scripture is expresse
mensioun made of eny suche." Where does the Bible
say that it should be translated into English ? [1] In
the same tone of voice Wyclif had pointed out, in the
preceding century, the abuses of the Church ; in the same
tone of voice the author of " Gulliver " will point out, three
centuries later, the happy use that might be made of Irish
children as butcher's meat.

The thing to be remembered for the moment is that
the number of prose-writers increases. They write more
abundantly than formerly ; they translate old treatises ;
they unveil the mysteries of hunting, fishing, and heraldry ;
they compose chronicles ; they rid the language of its
stiffness. In their private correspondence middle class
men take a visible pleasure in exchanging news and
compliments, in talking about themselves, their neighbours,
their horses and their hawks ; and new discoveries have
shown that the Paston case was not an isolated one. To
the same task contributes Sir Thomas Malory, with his
compilation called " Morte d'Arthur," in which he included

---

[1] " Repressor," i. ch. xix.

the whole cycle of Britain.   The work was published by Caxton, the first English printer, who was also a prose-writer.[1]

The diminished importance of the nobles and of the feudal aristocracy, the increased importance of the citizens and of the working class, bring the various elements of the nation nearer to each other, and this fact will have a considerable effect on literature: the day will come when the same author can address the whole audience and write for the whole nation.   In a hundred years it will be neces-sary to take into consideration the judgment of the English people, both "high men" and "low men," on intellectual things ; there will stand in the pit a mob whose declared tastes and exigences will cause the most stubborn of the Elizabethan poets to yield.   Ben Jonson will be less classic and more English than he would have liked to be ; he intended to introduce a chorus into his tragedy of "Se-janus" ; the fear of the pit prevented him ; he grumbles, but submits.[2]   The thrift and the toil of the English peasant and craftsman in the fifteenth century had thus

---

[1] "The Boke of St. Albans, by Dame Juliana Berners, containing treatises on hawking, hunting and cote armour, printed at St. Albans, by the Schoolmaster printer in 1486, reproduced in fac simile," by W. Blades, Lon-don, 1881, 4to (partly in verse and partly in prose ; adapted from the French).—By honest, conscientious John Capgrave, 1394-1464, "A Chronicle of Eng-land" (from the creation to 1417), ed. Hingeston, Rolls, 1858, "Ye Solace of Pilgrimes," ed. Mills and Bannister, 1911, also a Latin "Liber de illustribus Henricis," Rolls, 1858, &c. ; see above, p. 496.—Three anon. XVth cent. "Chronicles of London," ed. Kingsford, Oxford, 1905.—"A Book of the noble Historyes of Kynge Arthur and of certen of his Knyghtes," Caxton, 1485 ; reprinted with notes ("Le Morte Darthur," by Sir Thomas Malory) by O. Sommer and Andrew Lang, London, 1889, 2 vols.   Malory and Caxton will be mentioned again in connection with the Renaissance (*infra*, vol. ii. pp. 26 ff.).

[2] He has not observed, he admits, "the strict laws of time," and he has introduced no chorus ; but it is not his fault.   "Nor is it needful, or almost possible in these our times, and to such auditors as commonly things are pre-sented, to observe the old state and splendor of dramatic poems, with preserva-tion of any popular delight."—*To the readers.*

an unexpected influence on literature: they contributed
to form an audience for Shakespeare.

IV.

The new times are preparing, in still another manner;
the gods are to come down from Olympus and dwell once
more among men.

While the ancient literature is dying out, another is
growing which is to replace it in France, but which will
continue it, transformed and rejuvenated, in England.
Rome and Athens will give England a signal, not laws;
but this signal is an important one; happy the nations
who have heard it; it was the signal for awakening.

In that Italy visited by Chaucer in the fourteenth
century, the passion for antiquity goes on increasing; the
Latins no longer suffice, the Greeks must be known.
Petrarch worshipped a manuscript of Homer, but it was
for him a dumb fetish: the fetish has now become a god,
and utters oracles that all the world listens to. The
city of the Greek emperors is still standing, and there
letters shine with a last lustre. While the foe is at its
gates, it rectifies its grammars, goes back to origins, rejects
new words, and revives the ancient language of Demos-
thenes. Never had the town of Constantine been more
Greek than on the eve of its destruction.[1] The fame of its
rhetoricians has spread abroad; men come from Italy to
hear John Argyropoulos, the Chrysolorases, the famous
Chrysococcès, deacon of St. Sophia and chief Saccellary.

But the fatal hour is at hand, the era of the Crusades is
over; an irresistible ebb has set in; Christendom draws
back in its turn. No longer is it necessary to go to
Jerusalem to battle against the infidel; he is found at

---

[1] H. Vast, " Le Cardinal Bessarion," Paris, 1878, 8vo, p. 14.

Nicopolis and Kossovo. The illustrious towns of the Greek world fall one after the other, and the exiled grammarians seek shelter with the literate tyrants of Italy, bringing with them their manuscripts. Some, like Theodore Gaza, have been driven from Thessalonica, and teach at Mantua and at Sienna; others left after the fall of Trebizond.

On the throne of the Paleologues sits Constantine XII. Dragassès. Brusa is no longer the capital of the Turks; they have left far behind them the town of the green mosques, of the great platanes and tombs of the caliphs, they have crossed the Bosphorus and are established at Salonica, Sophia, Philippopolis. Adrianople is their capital for the time being; Mahomet II. commands them. Opposite the "Castle of Asia," Anatoli Hissar, he has built on the Bosphorus the "Castle of Europe," Roumel Hissar, with rose-coloured towers; he is master of both shores.

He draws nearer to the grand city, and aligns his troops under the wall facing Europe; he has a hundred and thirty cannon; he opens fire on the 11th of April, 1453. On the 28th of May, the Turks take up their positions for the onset; whilst in Byzantium a long procession of priests and monks, carrying the wood of the true cross, miraculous statues and relics of saints, wends its way for the last time. The assault begins at two o'clock in the morning; part of a wall, near the gate of St. Romanus, falls in; the "Cercoporta" gate is taken. The struggle goes on in the heart of the town; the emperor is killed; the basilica erected by Justinian to Divine Wisdom, St. Sophia, which was in the morning filled with a praying multitude, contains now only corpses. The smoke of an immense fire rises under the sky.

All that could flee exiled themselves; the Greeks flocked to Italy. Out of the plundered libraries came a number of manuscripts, with which Nicholas V. and Bessarion enriched Rome and Venice. The result of the disaster was, for intellectual Europe, a new impulse given to classic studies.

With the glare of the fire was mingled a light as of dawn ; its rays were to illuminate Italy and France, and, further towards the North, England also.

———

APPENDIX.

———◦◦◦———

I.

HUCHOUN [Above, p. 348].

THE Scottish chronicler, Andrew of Wyntoun, Prior of St. Serf in Loch Leven, a serious-minded and, for the times, conscientious historian, who died about 1422, certainly knew, loved, and held in great esteem a poet whom he mentions with high praise in Bk. v. chap. 13 of his "Original Chronicle" (ed. Amours, Scottish Text Society, 1903 ff., vol. iv. pp. 20 ff.). He calls him Huchon, Hucheon, Huchoun (a form of Hugh), adding twice his surname "of the Aule Reale," or "Auld Ryall." This poet, he says, "cunnande was in littratur," and "curyousse in his stille; fayr of facunde and subtile." Wyntoun enumerates several works written by him, viz., "A gret Gest of Arthure," the "Awntyr off Gawane," the "Pistil of Suet Susane." He speaks also incidentally of Huchoun's "Gest Historyalle," twice named, and of his "Gest of Brutis aulde story," possibly other appellations for the "Gret Gest," as he shows that under these titles the author treated also of Arthur's deeds: and we know that books about the ancient Britons and King Arthur went often by the name of Brut, from Brutus the Trojan, the supposed ancestor of Arthur. The earliest work to be called thus was Geoffrey of Monmouth's famous "Historia Regum Britanniæ,"[1] the first and foremost authority more or less freely followed during the Middle Ages by the innumerable subsequent chroniclers.

This and no more is certain. No other writer said a word or made any allusion to "Huchoun of the Aule Reale," or "Auld Ryall"; no charter, no document of any kind has been discovered containing such a name. No work has come down to us in any MS. with any attribution to him. A short anonymous poem, of real merit, written in stanzas of thirteen riming and strongly alliterated lines (*abababcdddc*) exists in five MSS., and has for its title "The Pistill of Susan," the subject being the biblical story of Susanna and the Elders (ed. Amours, "Scottish Alliterative Poems," S.T.S., 1897). This is apparently, and most probably, the one alluded to by Wyntoun. Among the anonymous mediæval poems which we possess, many of which treat of Arthur and Gawain, and are certainly the work of men, whoever they were, "cunnande in littratur," none bears exactly any of the titles given by Wyntoun to his friend's other works.

For which cause, up to a recent date, misty Huchoun had been allowed no room in many a treaty of literature, and none in the 63 original volumes of the "Dictionary of National Biography" (the volume with no Huchoun in it appeared in 1891); it had been left out in limbo with those other great shades, appropriately recalled by David Laing in his edition of Wyntoun's Chronicle, Rabirius and Valgius; Rabirius equalled to Virgil by

[1] " La fabuleuse [Historia Britonum de Geoffrey de Monmouth] ayant été connue assez généralement sous le nom de *Brutus*, les chroniques françaises en vers ou en prose qui en ont reproduit la substance, ont été fort souvent désignées par le nom de *Brut*." Paul Meyer, "Bulletin de la Société des Anciens Textes Français," 1878, i.

Seneca, and praised by Ovid; Valgius the friend of Horace and the admiration of Pliny; now nothing but "nominis umbræ."

A change has come and Huchoun has found valorous and passionate champions, Mr. G. Neilson being the foremost of them. The well-known author of "Trial by Combat" has offered the same to all comers, and in an epistolary tourney in which took part with him MM. H. Bradley, J. A. Neilson, Gollancz, J. Anderson Inman (*Athenæum*, 1900–1, 1916–7); and also in his "Huchown of the Awle Ryale," Glasgow, 1902, has tried to identify his hero (with Sir Hew of Eglintoun), and his hero's works, ascending from step to step, interpreting allusions, tying, one to the other, poem after poem, so that at length misty Huchoun could be described by his defender as one of the great luminaries of literature, whatever "overweening Philology" might allege. "Qu'est-ce que le Tiers État," Sieyès used to say; "Rien.—Que doit-il être?—Tout." The same with Huchoun: whilom so poor as to be unable to claim anything really his, he has been credited since with immense literary domains, including "Gawayne and the Green Knight," "Pearl," "Morte Arthure," the "Awntyrs off Arthur at the Terne Wathelyne," "Golagros and Gawane," "The Wars of Alexander," "Titus and Vespasian," &c., &c., between thirty and forty thousand lines; such beautiful domains, too, that Mr. Neilson could conclude: "Huchoun's range and grasp in romance place him as a unique and lofty spirit, comparable in respect of his greatness only with Walter Scott" (p. 139). No less.

This most interesting problem should be studied in Mr. Neilson's essays; a good summary of the whole discussion is to be found in Mr. Millar's "Literary History of Scotland," London, 1903, pp. 8 ff.

If I might be permitted to express an opinion on one

or two points, I would say that, with due deference to Mr. Neilson's learned researches, many, I believe, will find the greatest difficulty in agreeing to Huchoun of the Aule Reale's enjoying the honours, biography, and personality of Sir Hugh of Eglintoun. Sir Hew, as is well known, forms another problem : he is named as a poet by Dunbar and by no one else, figuring in the "Lament for the Makaris" :

> The gude Syr Hew of Eglintoun,
> Et eik Heryot, et Wyntoun
> He (Death) hes tane out of this cuntre.[1]

Sir Hew is there associated apparently with minor poetical luminaries, as honest Wyntoun is certainly no great poet, and Heryot is absolutely unknown. The more famous Chaucer, Lydgate, and Gower form a group by themselves in the preceding stanza. Several of the names in this catalogue have defeated all attempts at identification. As Dunbar wanted to draw an imposing list of poets whom Death had "tane," he not improbably included some who only as amateurs, and in a very casual fashion, could be called poets : to the extent that there is a doubt whether Scotland may glory in a poet of the name of Ettrik, or whether the name should be resolved, as above, into "Et eik," and also. Anyhow, "Gude Syr Hew" is on the list, the fact that he is there implying in no way that he was a writer of any importance. No poem bearing his name has come down to us, but we know something of his biography : he was apparently the Sir Hew, Hugh, or Hugo of Eglintoun,[2] several times sent on missions to England, a man of importance, who married a sister of

---

[1] "Poems of William Dunbar," Scottish Text Society, ii. p. 50.

[2] All the items concerning him have been collected from documentary evidence by Mr. Neilson : "Sir Hew of Eglintoun and Huchoun off the Awle Ryale : a biographical calendar and literary estimate." Proceedings of the Philosophical Society of Glasgow, 1901, vol. xxxii. pp. 111 ff.

Robert, later King Robert II. of Scotland, and who died about 1376.

Hew = Hugh, and so does Huchoun. Both men wrote poetry on the unimpeachable testimony of those trustworthy authorities, Wyntoun and Dunbar. Sir Hew was by marriage a relative of the first Stuart king, and Huchoun's surname, "of the Aule Reale," may be interpreted as meaning "Aulæ Regiæ," that is, of the Royal house or palace.

To my mind, however, one argument overweighs these and all that has been added to support them. This is the fact that the only authority who speaks of Huchoun of the Aule Reale, and who, as we have seen, certainly knew, loved, and admired him, does not connect him in any way with, but, on the contrary, represents him as a different person from, Sir Hew of Eglintoun. If Wyntoun had spoken in his Chronicle of Huchoun alone, the poet might have enjoyed the benefit of the doubt; but he mentions *both*, giving them different names, and, bent as he is on showing Huchoun at his best, he says nothing allowing any suspicion that this busy, clever writer, "cunnande in littratur," "curyousse in his stille," was also a knight, a statesman, a confidant of the king.

Each appears in only one chapter of the work. In the above-mentioned chapter 13, bk. v. of the "Chronicle," Huchoun, as will be remembered, is twice called "of the Aule Reale," or "Auld Ryall," and not otherwise. The historical knight, Sir Hew, is, on the other hand, mentioned in chapter 39, bk. viii., sub anno 1342: in that year, during a military expedition beyond the border, "fyve knychtis" from Scotland fell in the hands of the English:

> And fyve knychtis war tane,
> Stwart, Eglyntoun and Cragy,
> Boyde and Fowlartoun (l. 6006).

It seems quite clear that Wyntoun did not consider as the same person the knight whom he calls "Eglyntoun" and the literary artist whom he calls "Huchoun of the Aule Reale." If he did not, the best we can do is to imitate him, for he must have known best.

Concerning the poems which, having come down to us masterless, have been added to Huchoun's domains, one of the foremost is "Morte Arthure," a fourteenth-century alliterative poem of 4,346 unrimed lines (ed. Brock, Early English Text Society). Mr. Neilson's plea is that this poem is "recognized and accepted as definitively identified" [1] and being Huchoun's. The identification is with the work which Wyntoun sometimes calls the "Gest Historyalle," sometimes the "Gret Gest of Arthure," or the "Gest of Brutis auld story." Such a plea' seems extremely difficult to sustain. Mr. Bradley (*Athenæum*, January 12, 1901) has pointed out how unlikely it is that a Scotch writer should call his country "scathell Scotland" (mischievous, injurious Scotland), which uncomplimentary epithet she bears in the poem at the place where the author enumerates the lands subjugated by Arthur. To this may be added that not only does the author of "Morte Arthure" show himself unfriendly there to the Scotch, but that they are the *only people* towards whom he displays any spite. All the other countries on his list go with no epithet at all or enjoy admirative ones. Some are "ryche," others are "off value so noble"; others are conspicuous for "toures fulle hye." Scotland alone is singled out to go with a contemptuous epithet.[2] Was there ever such a Scotchman?

[1] *Athenæum*, June 1, 1901, p. 695.

[2] In the same way Layamon, who was *not* a Scotchman, describing at great length Arthur's conquest of Scotland, declares, by an inimical and very bad pun, that Scots are sots:—

> Tha weoren Scottes
> Ihalden for sottes.—"Brut," Madden, ii. p. 492.

According to Mr. Neilson, Wyntoun, when writing of his friend's Arthurian poems, had "Morte Arthure" in his mind, knew the work, and "certainly quoted" it (p. 40), the reference being to "Wyntoun, ll. 4271–4366 [ed. Laing]; Morte Arthure, ll. 34–47, etc." The passages alluded to contain an enumeration of the conquests and prowesses of Arthur. Resemblances in such cases, be the question of Arthur, Alexander, Charlemagne, or any one, are unavoidable and prove little enough. The lesser the proof in this case, as, far from the lists being similar, they differ on many points: Wyntoun attributes to Arthur Lombardy and Gascony, of which "Morte Arthure" says nothing, and the author of this poem mentions Germany. Brittany, Austria, Greece, Scotland, and others on which the Chronicle is silent. The most conspicuous difference consists in the fact that Wyntoun, a true and undoubted Scotchman he, allows Arthur to subdue all kinds of lands, Scotland being excepted, whatever Geoffrey of Monmouth, Wace, Layamon, and all the others might say. A Huchoun for whom Scotland was a "scathell" country would never have been a man after Wyntoun's heart.

Another proof which seems very telling at first sight is in reality no proof at all. Wyntoun takes great pains to defend his friend, who had been severely criticised for having called Lucius Iberius emperor, whereas he was only "procurator" of the Romans. The latter, indeed, is the title bestowed on him (at the same time as existence) by Geoffrey of Monmouth in his "Historia Regum Britanniæ," the main source of all the Arthurian stories.[1] And nothing better shows Wyntoun's devotion to his friend than this attempt to defend him against certain critics who, even then, could indulge into "wilful defamacionys" when they had been so lucky as to discover some-

---

[1] "Lucius reipublicæ procurator, Arturo Regi Britanniæ, quod meruit."— Beginning of Lucius [Hiberius]'s message, "Historia," bk. ix. chap. xv.

body's slip of the pen. Much has been made of the fact
that the very same "error" occurs in "Morte Arthure":

> Sir Lucius Iberius, the Emperour of Rome,
> Saluz the as sugett (l. 86).

Little enough should be made of it. In calling Lucius
"emperour" Huchoun did nothing but what was absolutely
commonplace. Lucius was called emperor not only in
"Morte Arthure," but in a number of works of different
dates in various languages, French, English, and Scottish;
in Wace, for example, who belonged to the same century
as Geoffrey; in Layamon, who wrote early in the thirteenth;
in Langtoft, in the "Chronicle of England,"[1] in Barbour, who was a contemporary of Huchoun's. In Wace's
"Roman de Brut"[2] Lucius is uniformly described as
"l'empereur de Rome." The same in Layamon:

> We sundeth of Rome
> Hider we sunden icumene
> From ure Kaisere
> Luces is ihaten (Madden ii. 639).

And throughout the work Lucius appears as the Roman
"kaisere." The same in Barbour:

> And Lucius Yber wencusyt he
> That then of Rome wes emperour (l. 554).

To which may be added that even Geoffrey of Monmouth
himself sometimes calls the "procurator" by the title of
"Imperator," giving, however, to the word its first meaning of commander, but anyhow using it: "Et Lucius
Imperator intra turmas occupatus cujusdam lancea con-
fossus interiit." Wyntoun, who knew his Geoffrey well,
does not fail to use this as the best excuse of his friend,

---

[1] Ritson, " Metrical Romances," ed. Goldsmid, ii. p. 27.
[2] ll. 10917 ff., ed. Le Roux de Lincy, Rouen, 1836, vol. ii. pp. 116 ff.

whose only mistake is that he ought to have translated "imperator" by "commawndour"; as for "procuratoure," the "cadence" prevented him:

> Hade he callyt Lucyus procuratoure . . .
> He had ma grewit the cadence
> Than had relewit the sentence.
> Ane emperoure, in propyrte
> A commawndour sulde callit be.

But there is more, and it may be affirmed with certainty that, whatever may have been the poem Wyntoun had in his mind and apparently before his eyes when he wrote his chapter on Arthur, that poem was *not* and could not be "Morte Arthure." On one characteristic of the book he refers to Wyntoun is quite positive: that book "tretyt curyously" of the events in Arthur's life down to the last battle of the king and his peers against traitorous Mordred. There it stopped, saying nothing of the last moments and death of the hero On that death Wyntoun found, he declares, not a word in his friend's work nor in "na wryt" of which he had any knowledge. Failing this he volunteers a short continuation, reproducing what possibly was not in Huchoun, but certainly was commonly known, that is, a mention of the retreat to Avalon and of the disappearance of Arthur, who was heard of no more:

> And of tressone til him done
> Be Mordrede, his systyr sone,
> Qwharfor in hast he coym agane
> And withe hym faucht in to Brettane,
> Qwhar he and his Rounde Tabil qwyte
> Was wndone and discomfyte,
> Hucheon has tretyt curyously
> In Gest of Brutus aulde story.
> Bot of his ded and his last ende
> I fande na wryt coythe mak me kende;
> Sen I fande nane that thar of wrate,
> I will say na mar than I wate,
> Bot qwhen that he had (&c).[1]

---

[1] "Original Chronicle," ed. Amours, vol. iv. p. 25.

The statement is clear enough ; it absolutely forbids our accepting as Huchoun's any poem in which the death of Arthur is related. In the best known of the king's romantic biographies (by Geoffrey, Wace, Layamon, Langtoft, &c.) it was not related, and Huchoun, usually careful, as Wyntoun says, not to waver "fra the swytht-fastnes," conformed in that to custom. But, contrary to custom, it *is* told in " Morte Arthure," and it even supplies the poem with its title ; it is told with full details, an account being given of the hero's last will and last prayers, his death, his funeral pomp, and his burial at Glastonbury.

Huchoun's work was, therefore, certainly not " Morte Arthure," but rather an adaptation and embodiment of legends such as are offered, not directly by Geoffrey of Monmouth (who ignores the Round Table), but by such free adaptations as Wace's and also Layamon's " Brut," where the Round Table figures, Lucius is emperor, and Arthur does not die.

The few lines added by Wyntoun to continue his friend's account seem to be derived direct from Wace :

> Bot qwhen that he had fouchtyn fast,
> Eftyr in til ane Ile he past,
> Sare wondit to be lechit thar,
> And eftyr he was seyn na mare.
> Bot in his tyme Schir Constantyne,
> Schir Caderis son, his awn cusyne,
> That was Duk of Cornwalle,
> He was mad kynge of Brettan haile,
> And set upon his hewide the crowne
> And gaf hym ful possessione.[1]

> En Avalon se fit porter
> Por ses plaies médiciner.
> Encor i est, Breton l'atandent,
> Si com il dient et entandent . . .
> Al fil Cador de Costentin
> De Cornuaille, un sien cosin,

---

[1] Ed. Amours, iv. p. 27.

Livra son raine, si li dist
Qu'il fust rois tant qu'il revenist.
Chil prist la terre, si la tint,
Mais ainc puis Artus ne revint.[1]

We hold, therefore, that Huchoun of the Aule Reale was not Sir Hew of Eglintoun, and that the poem or poems attributed by Wyntoun to his friend and which he calls "A Gret Gest of Arthure," the "Gest Historyalle," and the "Gest of Brutis," were not "Morte Arthure."

[1] Ed. Le Roux de Lincy, ii. pp. 230, 232.

II

GOWER'S FRENCH [Above, p. 364].

HAVING once asked Paul Meyer for his opinion as to the correctness of Gower's French, I received an answer which, coming from so competent a judge, may interest the reader.

LES MONS—NEUVILLE—DIEPPE,
18 *Août*, 1902.

CHER AMI,

Le *Miroir* français de Gower, retrouvé il y a quelques années à la Bibliothèque de l'Université de Cambridge (je suis bien aise de dire que ce volume a été acquis *après* la publication de ma notice des MSS. de cette Bibliothèque), est en assez bon français. Dans ce volumineux ouvrage, comme dans ses Ballades, l'auteur fait de louables efforts pour écrire le français de Paris et il y réussit assez bien. La versification n'est pas irréprochable ; il y a des rimes inacceptables en pur français, mais c'est, de toute façon, très supérieur à ce qu'écrivaient, au même temps, la plupart des auteurs anglais qui préféraient le français à leur langue maternelle.

Pour se faire une idée de ce qu'était alors l'anglo-french, le vrai french de Stratford-atte-Bowe, il faut voir les textes des statuts, des chartes, des lettres de ce temps : c'est déja du *law french*, un french qui est très *low* (pardonnez ce bad pun). Si vous prenez par exemple la version de l'Apocalypse en vers que j'ai publiée vers 1896 ou 97 dans la *Romania,* vous verrez qu'il n'y a plus guère de notion des genres ni des nombres, que les temps des verbes sont employés contrairement à notre syntaxe, que l'orthographe est déjà anglaise (pour les mots que l'anglais a pris du français). Et pourtant cette version de l'Apocalypse est de plus de 50 ans antérieure à Gower. Vous feriez les mêmes remarques en comparant la langue de Peter de Langtoft qui est, je crois me rappeler, du commencement du XIVe Siècle (Rolls Series, 2 vols).

Du reste il est visible qu'au commencement du XVe Siècle, peut-être plus tôt, mais je n'en ai pas la preuve, on commençait à distinguer en Angleterre, le français continental, que l'on enseignait, d'avec le français usité en Angleterre. J'imprime, en ce moment, une notice des MSS. français de Trinity College, Cambridge. Là il y a un ouvrage destiné à l'enseignement du français (déjà cité par Hickes *Thesaurus,* mais longtemps égaré—on l'a récupéré il y a peu d'anneés), où la distinction est faite très nettement dès la rubrique initiale : " Liber iste vocatur *femina,* quia, sicut femina docet infantem loqui maternam [linguam], sic docet iste liber juvenes rhetorice loqui gallicum, prout infra patebit."

Rhetorice veut dire, en français du continent. L'auteur donne l'orthographe française, ainsi *beau, enfant, bien* et il ajoute des notes pour dire qu'on doit lire (c'est-à-dire prononcer en Angleterre) *beu, enfaunt, bein,* etc." . . .

PAUL MEYER.

III

THE WYCLIFITE BIBLE [Above, p. 433].

THE weight of evidence is certainly against Abbot, now Cardinal, Gasquet's plea that the two fourteenth-century English versions of the whole Bible, usually held to be the work of Wyclifites, are, on the contrary, "only authorised catholic translations of the Bible," "semi-official" versions, "perfectly orthodox and authorised."[1]

First, that Wyclif was in favour of a translation and was strongly opposed to those who objected admits of no serious doubt: "And herfore," says he in one of his sermons, "oo greet Bishop of Engeland, as men seien, is yvel paied that Goddis lawe is writun in Englis, to lewide men ; and he pursueth a preest, for he writith to men this Englishe, and somonith him and traveilith him."[2] That he took some part in the undertaking and that his part consisted in working at the translation of the Gospel is very probable, if not even quite certain. The positive statement in Knighton's continuator, a contemporary,

[1] "The Old English Bible and other Essays," London, 1897, 8vo, pp. 137, 138, 150.

[2] Sermon lxvi., "Select English Works," Arnold, i. 209.

cannot be easily disposed of: "Hic magister Johannes Wyclif Evangelium quod Christus contulit clericis et Ecclesiæ Doctoribus, ut ipsis laicis et infirmioribus personis secundum temporis exigentiam et personarum indigentiam, cum mentis eorum esurie, dulciter ministrarent, transtulit de Latino in Anglicam linguam, non angelicam, unde per ipsum fit vulgare . . . et sic . . . gemma clericorum vertitur in ludum laicorum ut laicis sit commune æternum quod ante fuerat clericis et Ecclesiæ doctoribus talentum supernum." [1] There can be no doubt that when the chronicler says the Gospel he means the Gospel. He does not mean "Gospel in the broader signification of Christian teaching," [2] nor does he mean the spreading of that "Evangelium æternum" announced in the twelfth century by Joachim de Fiore, "de spirito profetico dotato," says Dante,[3] and supposed to have been sketched, if not actually written, by him.[4]

The chronicler is extremely indignant at a real translation of the real Gospel having been made "de Latino in anglicam linguam"; he insists at length on the event, which he deplores. He mentions with reference to it the "Evangelium æternum," but only because present circumstances remind him of former ones, "æternum" being for him in this case, and not for him alone, the equivalent of

---

[1] "Chronicon Henrici de Knighton," ed. Lumby, Rolls, vol. ii. p. 151.

[2] Gasquet, *ibid.*, p. 174.   [3] "Paradiso," end of canto xii.

[4] No such work as the "Evangelium æternum" ever existed. Joachim de Fiore (d. 1202) had announced a time when a Gospel of the Holy Ghost, an "Evangelium æternum," containing a more spiritualistic teaching, would replace Christ's Gospel; the event was supposed to be in accordance with the "Revelations," where the angel whose face is like the sun gives an open book, "librum apertum," to the Apostle (x. 1). Towards the middle of the thirteenth century appeared a work called "Introductorius in Evangelium æternum," made up of three strongly interpolated treatises of Joachim's. This compilation proved to be the work of Gerard of Borgo San Donnino; it was fraught with heresies, and was condemned by Pope Alexander IV. It created throughout Christendom an immense sensation, but is now lost, and it is only by allusions and quotations that we can form an idea of its contents.

common, vulgar, and debased. He goes back in thought to the great quarrel between the University of Paris, the friars and the Papacy in the thirteenth century ; he quotes freely from the works of the illustrious French dialectician, Guillaume de Saint Amour, who, he thinks, while defending the University and attacking the friars and the "Evangelium," seems to have foreseen and condemned in advance the Lollards and their translations. Certain men, according to Saint Amour, had been spreading a so-called "eternal Gospel," supposed to be the Gospel of the Holy Ghost, far superior to Christ's : "Well could they call it eternal," wrote he, "because vulgar and common, and in maternal language, and thus in eternal memory."[1] Wyclif's and the Lollards' works, the chronicler thereupon observes, are of the same sort; these people translate the Gospel, and their Gospel in a vulgar and common tongue can in the same way, for the same cause, be called eternal : "Quæ quidam (what Saint Amour had written) applicant ad fratres mendicantes, magis tamen congruunt istis novis populis Lollardis qui mutaverunt Evangelium Christi in Evangelium æternum, *id est*, vulgarem linguam et communem maternam et sic æternum quia laicis reputatur melior et dignior quam lingua latina." The case seems clear : the accusation is that Wyclif and the Lollards had made "Christ's Gospel" vulgar by translating it ; the fact remains and is reasserted : they *had* translated Christ's Gospel.

The main question at issue is, however, of more importance. On the one we have just mentioned Abbot Gasquet is willing to make some concessions, and writes : "I have no intention to deny that Wyclif *may* have had something to do with Biblical translations which we do not now possess" (p. 154); those we possess being held, as stated

---

[1] "Æternum congrue dici potest, quia jam vulgare et commune in materna lingua, et sic in æterna memoria." "Chronicon," *ibid.*

above, to be "the catholic versions of our pre-reformation forefathers."

Are they? They are two in number, both of the second half of the fourteenth century; one in a rougher and more literal and obscure style, to all appearances a hasty work; the other an undoubted revision of the former, which was used as groundwork by the new writer. This one took more pains and time, and, having his task made easier by the earlier attempt, improved the text throughout. That the two versions are sister versions has not been disputed. The former is connected with Wyclifism by a positive statement in one of the MSS. (Douce, 369), which stands interrupted in the midst of a sentence; thereupon follow the words: "Explic¹ translacōm Nicholay de herford" (fac-similed in Forshall and Madden: "The holy Bible . . . made . . . by John Wycliffe and his followers," vol. i. p. 1.). If this statement be not considered absolutely convincing, it must at least be acknowledged as much better than nothing; and there is no other attribution of authorship in any MS. to contradict it.

But the foremost argument in favour of these versions being the work of Wyclifites is that no attempt has been considered possible, and none has been made, to dissociate the second from the first, nor the general prologue of the second from the work itself. "In some few copies,"¹ says Abbot Gasquet, "there exists a lengthy prologue which gives an account of the method employed by the translator. Whatever the author says of these methods is borne out in the actual version; and there is no room for doubting, as Henry Wharton long ago observed, that the prologues and the translation are by the same hand" (p. 117). This being so, and the general

---

¹ Not so few. It would be found only in MSS. of the whole of the Old Testament, which are rare: yet *eleven* have come down to us with the General Prologue.

"Prolog for alle the bokis of the Bible of the oolde testament," written to preface the second version, making one with it, if it is Wyclifite, the text must be held Wyclifite too.

It *is* undoubtedly Wyclifite; and so marked are its characteristics that it is impossible to read, almost at random, any portion of it without being struck by its intense partisanship. Most of the ideas dearest to Wyclif and his followers have their echo there, including even a plea for the Lollards, mentioned by name. A few extracts will enable the reader to judge for himself:

On friars and letters of fraternity, and on preaching. "Summe cristen lordis in name not in dede, preisen and magnifien freris lettris, ful of disceit and leesingis . . . and pursuen ful cruely hem that wolden teche treuly and freely the lawe of God, and preisen, mayntenen and cherischen hem, that prechen fablis, lesingis . . . and letten (hinder) greetly the gospel to be prechid, and holy writ to be knowen and kept" (ch. x. p. 30).

Against lords appointing unworthy prelates or curates. "Specialy lordis setten idolis in Goddis hous, whanne thei maken unworthi prelatis either curatis in the chirche" (ch. x. p. 31).

A defence of Lollards. "To absteyne fro oothis nedeles and unleeveful, and to eschewe pride, and speke onour of God and of his lawe, and repreve synne bi weie of charite, is matir and cause now whi prelatis and summe lordis sclaundren men, and clepen hem lollardis, eretikis, and riseris of debate and of tresoun agens the king" (ch. x. p. 33).

Misdeeds and cruelty of the great and of prelates. The worship of images. "How myche blood lordis scheden in werris, for pride and coveitise, by counceil of false prelatis, confessouris and prechouris, it passith mannis wit to telle fully in this lijf; but of scheding of blood and sleing of pore men, bi withdrawing of almes, and in gevynge it to dede stockis, either stoonis, either to riche clerkis and feyned religiouse, were to speke now, if a man hadde the spirit of goostly strengthe.   Now men knelyn, and preien, and offren faste to dede ymagis, that han neither hungir neither coold ; and dispisen, beten, and sleen Cristen men, maad to the ymage and lycnesse of the Holy Trynite" (ch. x. p. 34).

"*Figuratif Speches*" *and the Eucharist.*   "If eny speche of Scripture sounneth propirly charite, it owith not to be gessid a figuratijf speche . . . if it seemith to comaunde cruelte, either wickidnesse, either to forbede prophit, either good doinge, it is a figuratijf speche.   Crist seith : 'If ye eten not the flesch of mannis sone and drinke not his blood ye schulen not have lijf in you.'   This speche semith to comaunde wickidnesse either cruelte, therfore it is a figuratif speche, and comaundith men to comune with Cristis passioun, and to kepe in mynde sweetly and profitably, that Cristis flesch was woundid and crucified for us" (ch. xii. p. 44).

"*Simple men*" *may by the help of God preach with better effect than clerks, religious, and men from the University.* "Worldly clerkis and feyned relygiouse don this, that symple men of wit and fynding knowe not Goddis lawe, to preche it generaly agens synnes in the reume.   But wite ye, worldly clerkis and feyned relygiouse, that God bothe can and may, if it lykith hym, speede symple men out of the universitee, as myche to kunne hooly writ, as maistris in the universite" (ch. xiii. p. 52).

Contrary to the views of wicked clerks the people at large want the Bible open; it should be translated.   "Though covetouse clerkis ben woode by simonie, eresie and manye othere synnes, and dispisen and stoppen holi writ, as myche as thei moun, yit the lewid puple crieth aftir holi writ, to kunne it, and kepe it, with greet cost and peril of here lif. For these resons and othere, with comune charite to save alle men in our rewme, whiche God wole have savid, a symple creature hath translatid the bible out of Latyn into English. First, this symple creature hadde myche travaile, with diverse felawis and helperis, to gedere manie elde biblis, and othere doctouris and comune glosis, and to make oo Latyn bible sumdel trewe. . . . The comune Latyn biblis han more nede to be correctid, as manie as I have seen in my lif, than hath the English bible late translatid "[1] (ch. xv. pp. 57, 58).

With these few quotations in mind no one, I believe, will consider it possible to maintain that the author of the general prologue, admitted to be also the author of the version, was an orthodox thinker and writer, the author of a "semi-official" work, a man with "a filial reverence for the teaching of the approved doctors of the church." He was not, for he undoubtedly was a Wyclifite.

[1] An allusion to the first version, then being remodelled, and which needed it, though, according to the "simple creature" (probably Purvey), being not a contemptible text.

INDEX.

547